Introduction to Social Problems

DATE DUE

~~JUN 05 1998~~			
~~JUN 02 2000~~			
~~APR 01 02~~			

DEMCO 38-297

ABOUT THE AUTHORS

Kenrick S. Thompson (left) earned his Ph.D. at the Ohio State University. He is Professor of Sociology at Northern Michigan University in Marquette, Michigan, specializing in the sociology of marriage and the family, deviant behavior, and work/organizations. Dr. Thompson is co-author of *Sociology: Concepts, Issues and Applications,* 2d ed. (Macmillan, 1990) and has published articles in: *Journal of Marriage and the Family, International Journal of Sociology of the Family, Sociology and Social Research, Journal of Higher Education, Journal of Psychology, Psychological Reports,* and *Instructor.*

Thomas J. Sullivan (right) earned his Ph.D. at the University of California, Santa Barbara. He is Professor of Sociology at Northern Michigan University, specializing in social psychology, medical sociology, and social research. Dr. Sullivan is co-author of *Sociology: Concepts, Issues and Applications,* 2d ed. (Macmillan, 1990) and *Applied Social Research: Tool for the Human Services,* 3d ed. (Harcourt Brace Jovanovich, 1994), and the author of *Applied Sociology: Research and Critical Thinking* (Macmillan, 1992). He has published articles in: *Humboldt Journal of Social Relations* and *Social Science and Medicine.* He serves on the editorial board of *Teaching Sociology,* the Undergraduate Committee of the Midwest Sociological Society, and the Selection Committee for the American Sociological Association Award for Distinguished Contribution to Teaching.

Authors' photos by Donald D. Pavlovski, University Photographer, Northern Michigan University, Marquette, MI 49855.

INTRODUCTION TO
Social Problems

Third Edition

Thomas J. Sullivan
Kenrick S. Thompson

NORTHERN MICHIGAN UNIVERSITY

Macmillan Publishing Company
NEW YORK

Maxwell Macmillan Canada
TORONTO

Editor: Susan Rabinowitz
Production Supervisor: Jane O'Neill
Production Manager: Jeanie Berke
Text Designer: Angela Foote
Cover Designer: Tom Mack
Cover Illustration: Julie Baker
Photo Researcher: Robert Schatz

This book was set in Galliard and Helvetica by Compset,
Inc. and was printed and bound by Arcata Graphics.
The cover was printed by Phoenix Color Corp.

Macmillan Publishing Company
866 Third Avenue, New York, New York 10022

Macmillan Publishing Company is part of the Maxwell
Communication Group of Companies.

Maxwell Macmillan Canada, Inc.
1200 Eglinton Avenue East
Suite 200
Don Mills, Ontario M3C 3N1

Library of Congress Cataloging-in-Publication Data

Sullivan, Thomas J., 1944–
    Introduction to social problems / Thomas J. Sullivan,
  Kenrick S. Thompson.—3rd ed.
        p.   cm.
    Includes bibliographical references (pp. 569–608) and
  indexes.
      ISBN 0-02-418485-3 (pbk.)
      1. Social problems.   2. United States—Social
  conditions.   3. United States—Social policy.
  I. Thompson, Kenrick S.   II. Title.
  HN28.S92   1994   92-43404
  361.1—dc20   CIP

Printing: 1 2 3 4 5 6 7   Year: 4 5 6 7 8 9 0

For Nancy, Leda, and Shelley

Preface

The study of social problems continues to be one of the most demanding, exciting, and fast-paced fields in the social sciences—in part because the world changes so fast. When we finished writing the second edition of this book, President Bush had just recently come into office and had yet to do anything that might have an impact on the problems we analyzed here. He has since had four years to provide leadership that might help reduce some of the problems discussed in this book. As this is being written, President Clinton has just been sworn in as our first Democratic president in twelve years, and he is promising new approaches and policies. In addition, a number of astonishing things have happened in the world in the past four years that have direct implications for the social problems we have chosen to analyze. For example, the Berlin Wall has crumbled, Germany is united, and the Soviet Union has collapsed, freeing the many nations that had been under its domination since World War II. These are developments we never imagined we would see during our lives. They mean that the Cold War is essentially over and world politics needs to be rewritten. Our discussions in Chapter 14 of issues of war, terrorism, national defense, arms control, and world cooperation have had to be rewritten with these developments in mind. As another example, the crack epidemic has proved to be far more destructive and resistant to intervention than had originally been thought, in part because of the powerful drug cartels that supply the drugs and in part because of the apparent failure of Bush's War on Drugs to deal effectively with the

problem. However, since the second edition of this book was published, there have been positive developments on the drug scene, especially a significant decline in drug use among some Americans. All these changes have called for consideration of new issues and programs related to drug and alcohol abuse in Chapter 10 as well as the rethinking of old approaches.

So, in the past few years, much has changed—some changes, thankfully, are for the good, but too many changes have intensified social problems. Therefore, it has been necessary to update the second edition at this time. We are quick to point out that, although the United States suffers from serious problems, there have been positive developments as well. For example, the level of affluence and material technology available to most Americans is already more substantial than most human beings ever dreamed of. However, many old nemeses continue to plague us: Poverty has been on the rise, unemployment is higher than it should be, and toxic and nuclear wastes lie like threatening clouds on society's horizon.

The optimism that many people felt in the 1960s and early 1970s regarding our ability to alleviate social problems seems to have dissipated. The old programs do not seem to have worked—or at least not as well as many hoped they would. The lingering of intransigent problems and the appearance of new ones have jarred many people into a search for new solutions. A presidential commission recently called for a "war on pornography," and the AIDS epidemic has been used by some as definitive legitimation for a renewed legal assault on homosexuality, prostitution, and drug use. New labels for some "answers" to social problems have emerged: "supply side economics," "trickle down economics," "private sector initiative," and others. As we see it, the challenge of the 1990s will be to sift through these new proposals, along with the old ones, to find the kernels, probably relatively few of them, that hold some promise of helping us solve the problems we face.

The social sciences have also changed in the past two decades: With their theoretical foundations rather solidly established, they have begun to develop in a more applied direction. Increasingly, social scientists have shaped their research tools toward evaluating solutions to social problems rather than limiting their focus to understanding the nature of those problems. Now social research often focuses on questions such as: Does it work? Who benefits? What are the negative consequences of the program? Is there a way that we can achieve the same gain for less expense? In fact, over the past few decades, the study of social problems has become, in our view, one of the most exciting and innovative wings of the social sciences because it involves the application of social science research and knowledge to the solutions of some of the most difficult, agonizing, and controversial problems that face Americans today.

FEATURES

To reflect the trends of the past few decades, we have included a number of creative elements in this book:

1. *Policy Issues inserts:* An important theme of this book is that finding solutions to social problems is a political process in which groups differ with one another over which solutions are preferred. One's choice of solutions is influenced in part by one's cultural and subcultural values. Therefore, in every chapter we include inserts titled "Policy Issues" in which we discuss contemporary debates on social policy related to that problem.

2. *Applied Research inserts:* Another theme in this book is that the application of social science research is central to solving problems and evaluating how well solutions work. Therefore, we have included inserts titled "Applied Research" in which we illustrate how and why this is the case. In this way, we emphasize the point that our choice of solutions to problems, although shaped by our personal values and the public policy debate, should be constrained by the assessment of those solutions through systematic and scientific observation. In other words, the choice of solutions to problems should involve an interplay between human values and social research.

3. *Laissez-Faire versus Interventionist Debate:* The debate over social policy and social problems in the past decade has centered in part on the role of the government in such issues. We have incorporated this debate into the text in the form of two bipolar positions. The laissez-faire stance posits that the government is, in most cases, either inefficient at finding or unable to find such solutions and should stand aside and let private enterprise and impersonal economic forces produce solutions. The interventionist position gives the government prime, although not sole, responsibility for finding and initiating solutions to problems. This debate is addressed periodically in the text where it is relevant.

4. *Myth versus Fact:* To emphasize further the role of research in understanding social problems, we point out some ways in which people's commonsense beliefs about social problems are proved incorrect by research data. This encourages the student to distinguish between beliefs that have no scientific foundation and may, in fact, be myths from facts that have been substantiated by observational testing.

5. *Theoretical Perspectives:* We have organized our discussion of social problems and their solu-

tions around the three core theoretical perspectives in sociology: functionalism, conflict theory, and interactionism. These perspectives offer tremendous insight into the sources of problems, the effectiveness of solutions, and the ramifications—both obvious and hidden—of adopting particular solutions. We use these perspectives in every chapter of the book. By doing this, we are offering the student a set of tools that can be used to analyze any social problem, including problems not directly discussed in this book.

6. *International Perspectives:* This is a new feature in the third edition. Its main intent is to provide students with a more global picture of particular social problems and their solutions. One reason this is important is the growing interdependence among the world's peoples and nations. Another reason is that we can gain insight into problems and their solutions when we observe them in societies and cultures that are different from our own. This new feature is explained in the first chapter, and an insert is included in many of the following chapters.

7. *Linkages:* To encourage the student to see the interconnections between social problems, we have included a new feature in this edition. At the end of each chapter is a brief insert that points out how a problem discussed in that chapter is linked to problems discussed in other chapters. This encourages the student to recognize that the worsening of one problem can mean that other, seemingly unconnected conditions may also deteriorate and that alleviating one problem can result in improvements in others. This new feature is explained to the student at the end of Chapter 1.

ORGANIZATION

American society confronts many serious social problems. From these, we have chosen to discuss in this book problems that are particularly serious, affect many people, and expose students to a broad array of different problems in varied sectors of American life. By studying these problems, students will gain the tools and the insight that enable them to analyze other problems and solutions not explicitly covered in this book. Thus, this book is more than a catalog of particular problems and their solutions; it is also a training manual of sorts for the study of social problems.

Chapter 1 introduces students to the sociological analysis of social problems, including a discussion of the theoretical perspectives that will be used throughout the book and of the importance of the scientific approach and applied research in the analysis of social problems and their solutions. Following this, the book is divided into four parts. Part I, consisting of Chapters 2–4, covers social problems that relate directly to some of the major social institutions in American society: government, the economy, the family, and health care systems. Part II, including Chapters 5–8, focuses on problems that are linked by the common theme of social inequality: poverty, racial and ethnic discrimination, and inequality based on sex and age. Part III, containing Chapters 9–11, analyzes problems surrounding behavior that some people consider unconventional or deviant: crime and delinquency, alcohol and drug abuse, and sexual variance. Finally, Part IV, consisting of Chapters 12–15, focuses on problems involving changes or disruptions in the physical and social world: urban problems, population growth and environmental pollution, violence and war, and new developments in science and technology.

NEW TO THE THIRD EDITION

Although the basic organization of this book has remained the same in its third edition, it has been thoroughly revised and updated so that the text reflects contemporary developments in sociology as well as new social, political, and economic developments relating to particular social problems. We have added two new features, called "International Perspectives" and "Linkages," which were described earlier under the Features heading. For the "Policy Issues" and "Applied Research" features, we have prepared two completely new inserts and substantially revised fifteen others. The remaining inserts were considered sufficiently current and useful with only minor revision. We have also added a substantial number of new and recent "For Further Readings" at the end of each chapter for students who wish to pursue topics in greater detail. In addition, we have added some new "Discussion Questions" at the end of each chapter, to be used in class as a stimulus to student involvement with the issues in the classroom.

Regarding the text material itself, we have made many revisions throughout that update discussions, present new research, or address issues that have come to prominence or have changed in some fashion since the second edition was completed. The following illustrate some of the additions and revisions that have been made, either in text material or in the special features:

- results of new field studies on arrest as the best deterrent for women batterers (Chapter 1)
- recent assessments of the savings and loan fiasco as well as recent developments in the defense fraud scandals (Chapter 2)
- recent research on the experiences of displaced workers who lost their jobs in the 1980s as well as the impact of *maquiladoras* on American workers (Chapter 2)
- discussion of new policy options that have emerged in the 1990s that deal with deindustrialization and that develop a new industrial policy (Chapter 2)
- extensive analyses of new research on the impact of day care, the problems of getting high-quality day care, and policy options for the future (Chapter 3)
- new research on gender differential in the impact of divorce (Chapter 3)

- updated research on spouse, child, and elder abuse and what to do about them (Chapter 3)
- updated information on the AIDS crisis (Chapter 4)
- new material on the impact of the corporatization of health care (Chapter 4)
- new data on the redistribution of wealth from the poorest families to the wealthiest and the increasing feminization of poverty in the 1980s (Chapter 5)
- new theoretical material on the cultural analysis of poverty, replacing the older notion of the culture of poverty (Chapter 5)
- an assessment of the Reagan/Bush policies toward the poor, such as the change in emphasis from welfare to workfare (Chapter 5)
- new research on discrimination against African and Hispanic Americans in areas such as housing (Chapter 6)
- an assessment of the advances of women in areas such as the military and politics in the 1980s (Chapter 7)
- a major new section on sexual harassment in the workplace in the post–Clarence Thomas/Anita Hill era (Chapter 7)
- new data on rates of incarceration and what programs reduce recidivism (Chapter 9)
- new data on changing patterns in the use of illegal drugs as well as current information on crack addiction and the effectiveness of the War on Drugs (Chapter 10)
- a major new section on the causes of homophobia and the extent of discrimination and violence perpetrated against lesbians and gay men (Chapter 11)
- a new analysis of declining biodiversity in the world as a result of human activity (Chapter 13)
- revised discussions of the issues of disarmament, nuclear war, and international cooperation in the light of changing world events (Chapter 14)

We feel that these additions and revisions will make the third edition of *Introduction to Social Problems* an even better vehicle for use with students in the study of social problems.

ACKNOWLEDGMENTS

We both gain immense enjoyment from teaching and writing, which is one of the forces that propelled us on the journey of writing this book. We have undoubtedly left an imprint on the students we have taught in social problems courses, but those students have also made an impression on us. They have questioned, challenged, agreed and disagreed with us, and generally forced us to be more careful, analytical, and critical in our teaching and writing than our impassioned and sometimes impulsive natures might otherwise be. All of these students over the years have helped shape this book, and we have immense gratitude for their contribution.

Many individuals at Northern Michigan University made contributions to the completion of this book. Richard D. Wright, head of the Department of Sociology and Social Work, made material contributions and created a supportive and encouraging environment that helped to sustain us in the long hours when the goal seemed so far in the distance. John Berens, head of Public Service at the Lydia Olson Library, and Roberta Henderson, Reference Librarian, provided invaluable assistance in the seemingly endless task of research on this book. We would also like to thank Jeff Fallon for his excellent efforts in doing research for the third edition.

At Macmillan Publishing Company, we have had the good fortune to work with two competent editors, Robert Miller and Susan Rabinowitz, who put up with turmoil, heavy work loads, and our persistent (and, at times, probably unwanted) phone calls in order to publish a valuable book. We also received many helpful comments and suggestions from the following reviewers: Joel Snell, Kirkwood Community College; Robert Perry, Johnson Community College; Thomas Hirschl, Cornell University; and Roland Leibert, University of Illinois–Urbana.

There are, of course, some people who made absolutely invaluable contributions but whom the readers will never see. This book is dedicated to them. They suffered our absences, tolerated our single-minded devotion to something other than them, yet remained ever available and faithful to help us maintain our perspective. They realized there would be an end to the project, at which point we would once again return them to center stage. However, they share our realization that, just as the lure of the Sirens was irresistibly tempting, a new creative endeavor will undoubtedly draw us in.

T.J.S.
K.S.T.

Brief Contents

Detailed Contents

Introduction to Social Problems

CHAPTER 1
Approaches to the Study of Social Problems

E nglish novelist Charles Dickens character-ized life in England and France in the late 1700s with these words: "It was the best of times, it was the worst of times. . . . It was the spring of hope, it was the winter of despair" (1924: 1). Dickens was expressing a deep-felt ambivalence held by many people of that era regarding life in their time. England was undergoing industriali-zation, which promised greater levels of eco-nomic productivity, wonderful inventions, and new heights of affluence. For many, however, it also meant agonizing poverty, horrid crowding in filthy cities, and virulent disease. For the entre-preneur, it was a time to dream of riches yet to be made. For the pauper, it was a time to wonder where one's next meal might be found.

Modern-day America can be viewed through an equally ambivalent lens. We, too, can find promise of a better life in emerging technologies such as computers, telecommunications, and nu-clear power. We, too, have seen remarkable inven-tions that provide a level of comfort and security thought impossible by our ancestors. Imagine, for example, how you would be limited by the ab-sence of but one amenity of modern living that you probably take for granted: electricity. Yet not much more than one hundred years ago most peo-ple lived without it.

But there is a dark side to all this promise—a "winter of despair"—that is the topic of this book. There remains poverty, violence, drug addiction, alcoholism, and a host of other social problems. Some people are alienated from their dull and de-meaning jobs, and others have no jobs at all. Lakes are polluted and dying because of acid rain, and chemical dumps make useless the water sup-plies of many Americans. In our cities, which are technological wonders in themselves, many peo-ple are frightened by crime and a few respond by turning their homes into armed camps. Perhaps nuclear power provides the best symbol for the contradictions of our time: We use it to produce our electricity, but no one wants its deadly wastes stored near them. And we stand terrified at the specter of death and destruction that would surely accompany a nuclear war.

One can understand, then, how life in today's world might be thought of as "the best of times . . . the worst of times." A principal challenge that we face is to conquer these social problems or at least to alleviate their impact on people's lives. In this book, we take a sociological approach to understanding these social problems. **Sociology** is *the scientific study of societies and human social behavior,* and it provides one of the most useful approaches for understanding social problems and a most effective tool for finding solutions to them. In fact, modern sociology might be considered an offspring of industrialization, because it emerged in Europe and America in the nineteenth century shortly after the era of which Dickens had written. A major motivation of many early sociologists was to develop a "science of society" to deal with the dislocations, disruptions, poverty, and violence that accompanied industrialization. The same purpose underlies this book: to remove, as best we can, the poverty, crime, violence, and other problems that persist as the United States moves into an advanced industrial era. Along with these early sociologists, we assume that we *can* do something to improve social conditions and to attack social problems. Furthermore, our actions regarding social problems need to be grounded in *scientific research* on the problems and in *scientific assessments* of the effectiveness of solutions. Uninformed or casual meddling in social problems can create more difficulties than it solves.

This chapter will serve as a framework for the study of specific problems in later chapters. First, we will discuss what makes a social condition a social problem and why sociology is an essential tool in understanding and solving problems. Then we will consider the three major theoretical perspectives in sociology and how they are important in the study of social problems. Finally, we will show how scientific research provides the most useful information about problems and their solutions.

WHAT IS A SOCIAL PROBLEM?

There are some issues that practically everyone today agrees are social problems, such as crime or racial discrimination. About other issues, however, there is more disagreement. There is great debate, for example, over whether water pollution, pornography, or the use of marijuana are social problems. A commonsense approach might define a condition as a social problem if it "harms people" or is "detrimental to society." But this is far too imprecise for our purposes. To develop a more rigorous definition of what is a social problem, it is helpful to distinguish problems that affect individuals from those that involve an entire society (Lopata, 1984).

Personal Troubles, Public Issues, and Social Problems

A distinction made by sociologist C. Wright Mills (1959) between personal troubles and public issues may be the best place to begin. Personal troubles are things that affect individuals and those immediately around them. When parents discover that their daughter has a serious drug problem, theirs is a personal trouble because the values and goals of only that family are threatened. The trouble is seen as being primarily that family's difficulty. Public issues, on the other hand, have an impact on large numbers of people and are matters of public debate; collective solutions, rather than individual or familial ones, are considered. When statistics reveal that our nation loses millions of dollars every year because of accidents, suicide, and worker absenteeism due to drug abuse, we are dealing with a public issue because the values and goals of a large group are threatened. The issue is debated in public forums, and collective solutions are usually proposed. So every condition that adversely affects some individuals is not necessarily an issue of great public concern toward which we should, or could, direct societal resources. Of course, public issues may translate into personal troubles in the lives of some people, but every personal trouble is not a public issue. Mills's distinction between personal troubles and public issues makes us aware that problems need to be viewed in the broad context of their impact on society.

How do we place these issues in a broader societal context? We propose the following definition: A **social problem** exists when *an influential group defines a social condition as threatening its values; when the condition affects a large number of people; and when the condition can be remedied by collective action* (Blumer, 1971; Spector and Kitsuse, 1987). Let's look briefly at each element in this definition. An influential group is one that can have a significant impact on public debate and social policy. For example, groups opposing discrimination against women in employment and other areas have been able to mount a campaign that has forced politicians and the public nationwide to listen to their demands. Groups such as People for the Ethical Treatment of Animals, on the other hand, have not been able to generate significant debate about experimentation with animals or cruelty to animals, and relatively few people consider these to be social problems. Personal troubles do not become public issues, then, unless an influential group so defines them. The mere existence of a social condition does not make it problematic, no matter how harmful it may be. For example, smoking tobacco has been a contributing factor in lung cancer for as long as humans have used the substance, but it was not defined as a social problem until biomedical research made people aware of the link between smoking and lung cancer.

Conditions are viewed as social problems when they threaten a group's values. **Values** are *people's ideas about what is good or bad, right or wrong.* We use these values as guidelines for choosing goals and judging behaviors. Because values are necessarily ranked in terms of priority in any group or society, there is disagreement over which conditions will be viewed as social problems. Some Americans, for example, place great value on work and industriousness. Because of this, they may

view people who receive welfare with considerable disdain and even consider them threatening to their own way of life. Other Americans, emphasizing religious or humanitarian values, might argue that poverty—not poor people—is the real threat and that the poor should be helped, not castigated.

Conditions do not typically become social problems unless they affect a large number of people. When they affect relatively few people, they are private issues and there is little public debate over them or search for collective solutions. The more people they affect, the more likely they are to be publicly debated and defined as a problem that society should address. When the unemployment rate is low, for example, relatively few people are adversely affected. It may be a terrible personal hardship for those few who are unemployed, but it does not threaten large or influential groups and there will likely be little societal pressure directed toward alleviating the problem.

Finally, a social condition may satisfy the previous criteria but not be regarded as a social problem because the condition does not have social causes and cannot be remedied by collective human action. Earthquakes, tornadoes, and other vagaries of nature, for example, are harmful and frightening natural disasters, but they would not be considered *social* problems because they are not produced by social conditions and cannot be prevented by collective action or changes in social policy.

The Social Context of Social Problems

Social problems differ from personal troubles because the former are public issues rather than personal ones. In addition, social problems are fundamentally social rather than personal in nature because their causes and their solutions have something to do with the workings of society. Social problems may have an impact on individuals, but their roots are found in social life. Although these ideas will be developed throughout this book, we will illustrate the social basis of social problems here by briefly describing four distinct social conditions that can play a role in the emergence of social problems: deviation from group values and norms, a decline in the effectiveness of social institutions, extensive social and cultural diversity, and the exercise of power.

Societies are generally stable and orderly, although change and disruption do occur. This social stability arises in part because societies pass on to their members values and norms that serve to guide people in their behavior. Values have already been defined; they tell most Americans, for example, that it is preferable to be materially comfortable than to be poor or that the private ownership of goods is preferred over public or communal ownership. **Norms** are much more specific and concrete than values; they are *rules of conduct that guide people's behavior.* They are expectations that people in society share about how they ought to behave. Values are general preferences, whereas norms are specific guidelines for behavior. Norms dictate, for example, that men should wear pants, not dresses, and that motor vehicles are to be driven on the right side of the road rather than the left. Note how norms, like values, can vary from one culture to another and from one group to another. In some societies, men wear dresses and in others people drive on the left side of the road.

Values and norms, then, serve as a script for how to behave, and they enable us, to an extent, to predict how others will behave and to coordinate our behavior with theirs. Thus, values and norms lend stability and orderliness to society. A basic tenet of the sociological view of society is that people live in a socially created reality in which their behavior is shaped by social objects, such as values and norms, as much as by physical objects. However, people do not always behave in conformity with accepted values and norms. *Behaviors or characteristics that violate important group norms and as a consequence are reacted to with social disapproval* are called **deviance.** Laypeople often approach deviant or unconventional behaviors in an absolute way, judging them to be good or bad,

right or wrong, by comparing them with some fixed standards, such as some religious teachings. Sociologists view deviance as relative, or based on the social definitions of some group. For sociologists, it is not behaviors or characteristics in themselves that are deviant. Rather, it is the judgments of some group whose norms have been violated that make a behavior unconventional or deviant. This makes deviance relative in the sense that a behavior is deviant only when so defined by some group. So, deviance can be understood only within the context of the norms and values of a particular culture, subculture, or group. As one sociologist put it: "Deviance, like beauty, is in the eyes of the beholder" (Simmons, 1969: 4). Deviance does not refer only to the violation of group norms; some stigma, or mark of disgrace, must also be attached to the violation that sets the deviant apart from others (Becker, 1963; Goffman, 1963). When people violate the values and norms of the influential or powerful, the reaction against the deviant can be very strong. So, some social problems—prostitution, alcoholism, and drug abuse, to name a few—arise in part because they are defined as deviant and stigmatized. Some people are unwilling or unable to conform their behavior to the dictates of influential groups.

Beyond values and norms, another important element of society is **social institutions:** *relatively stable clusters of social relationships that involve people working together to meet some basic needs of society.* The family, for example, is a social institution ensuring that children will be born and raised properly to be contributing members of society. These institutions—the family, religion, politics, education, and others—serve as further guides for people's behavior and also involve social relationships that offer people a sense of community involvement and self-worth. In fact, many behaviors and personal qualities—happiness, mental stability, morality, respect for the law, and others—arise out of such social relationships, out of a sense of community and personal involvement with others. A person who is fired from his job, for example, experiences a social loss that can result in psychological problems as well as physical ailments. Industrialization has threatened such traditional sources of support and authority as the family and religion. Unless their decline is replaced by other sources of support, crime, substance abuse, and other problems may increase. In other words, many social problems arise from the ineffectiveness of social institutions in guiding behavior and offering people a sense of community and self-worth.

Social and cultural diversity is another important element of societies. American society, for example, is extremely diverse. The norms of the inner-city slum are light-years away from those of the middle-class suburb; the values of the young have little meaning for the elderly; and many beliefs of the affluent are foreign to the poor. One result of all this diversity is that many groups in America inhabit their own social worlds, called "subcultures." A **subculture** is *a group within a culture that shares some of the beliefs, values, and norms of the larger culture but also has some that are distinctly its own.* Each of the following could be considered a subculture: teenagers, Cubans in Miami, gays in most large cities, skinheads, the drug set, prison inmates, the elderly, the disabled, even the few hippies left over from the 1960s. In fact, everyone in America belongs to a wide array of subcultures based on age, sex, social standing, religion, leisure pastimes, or other characteristics.

These people are arguing about the violence that broke out between the black and Hasidic communities in New York in the early 1990s. Subcultural diversity, as illustrated by African Americans and Hasidic Jews, is an important element in the study of social problems because differing subcultures create the potential for conflicts over values and lifestyles.

Subcultural diversity is an important element in the study of social problems because it points to the potential for conflict between groups in our society. The values of one group are likely to clash with the values of another. One group, for example, may find the widespread availability of abortion offensive to its religious tenets, whereas another views restrictions on abortion as a threat to women's reproductive choices. Such conflicts are enhanced by **ethnocentrism,** *the tendency to view one's own culture or subculture as the best and to judge other cultures or subcultures in comparison to it.* Because of ethnocentrism, people may view the practices of another subculture as a social problem because they differ from their own practices. For example, are prostitution or the use of marijuana truly problems for society, or are they just offensive to the values of some particular subcultures?

A final element of society to be mentioned here is the exercise of power. **Power** is *the ability of one group to realize its will, even in the face of resistance from other groups* (Weber, 1958, originally published 1919; Boulding, 1989). Power can arise from many sources: the strength of numbers, efficient organization, access to wealth or status, or control of the political and economic institutions that dominate society. Whatever its source, power enables its possessor to compel others to act in a particular fashion. Ultimately, societies can use force or coercion to induce conformity to values and norms or to reduce conflicts or threats to a way of life. **Authority** refers to *legitimate power that is obeyed because people believe it is right and proper that they obey.* Most Americans, for example, believe that the Congress and the president, working together, have the legitimate authority to declare war on another country and to compel military service on the part of the citizenry. Many people may prefer not to fight in a war, but they would go because they believe the government has the authority to require that of them. Most social problems are related to the exercise of power and the use of authority, either as forces that intensify problems or as crucial elements in their solution. After all, a group needs some

power in order to have a condition defined as a social problem to begin with. Then, which solutions are settled on often depends on which groups can most effectively utilize the power and authority available to them.

This brief description of four elements of society suggests the ways in which social problems are "social" in nature: They are both created and alleviated by social mechanisms. To understand and solve social problems, then, we need to know something about how society works.

The Sociological Imagination

Before going on to a more detailed analysis of the sociological perspective and social problems, it is valuable to step back and consider the implications of this perspective for your own life. The sociological perspective on human beings is a unique and remarkable one, recognizing as it does that human behavior consists of far more than individuals acting independently of one another. It emphasizes the powerful role that group membership and social forces play in shaping behavior. Sociologists focus on social interaction and social relationships rather than on individuals. The sociological perspective offers a special awareness of the world that enables people to approach their own lives with introspection and insight. Peter Berger (1963) referred to the sociological perspective as an "emancipated vista" that can free people from blind submission to social forces that they do not understand. C. Wright Mills (1959) coined the term *sociological imagination* to refer to the ability to understand the relationship between what is happening in people's personal lives and the social forces that surround them. For both Berger and Mills, the more people learn about society and social problems, the better equipped they will be to understand their own lives and the impact—both desired and intrusive—of society and social problems on them. To be emancipated, of course, is not always pleasant because we often learn that social problems hinder us from achieving sought-after goals. Poverty-stricken parents, for example, may not relish the realization that their children will be penalized by the inequities of the American school system, which has adverse effects on the poor. Nevertheless, it is precisely a better understanding of the role of such inequities that can open the door to making improvements in the educational process. So the sociological imagination involves the insight into how social forces can bring problems into our own lives and how other social forces might alleviate the problems.

THEORETICAL PERSPECTIVES ON SOCIAL PROBLEMS

Every science, including sociology, accumulates knowledge through an interplay between theory and research. In the previous section, we described the sociological perspective in very general terms. Now we need to provide a more detailed account of the theories commonly used in the sociological analysis of social problems. A **theory** is *a set of statements that explains the relationship between phenomena.* The key role of theories is to tell us why something occurred. They help us organize the data from research into a meaningful whole. In this section, we will discuss the most general and important theoretical approaches in sociology. In the next section, we will return to the importance of research.

Some sociological theories focus on specific social problems, such as the causes of juvenile delinquency or the explanations for divorce. We will discuss quite a few of these theories in this book. In addition to these highly specialized theories, however, there are a number of broader explanations of social reality that are called **theoretical perspectives.** These perspectives *provide some fundamental assumptions about the nature and operation of society and commonly serve as sources of the more specific theories* mentioned previously. Most sociologists today are guided by one or more of

the following theoretical perspectives: functionalism, conflict theory, or interactionism. The functionalist and conflict approaches are frequently referred to as *macrosociology* because they focus on large groups and social institutions and on society as a whole. The interactionist perspective falls under the category of *microsociology* because it concentrates on the intimate level of everyday interactions between people. We will first summarize the perspectives and then suggest how you should use them in analyzing social problems.

The Functionalist Perspective

The functionalist perspective grew out of the similarities early sociologists observed between society and biological organisms. The human body, for example, is composed of many different parts—the heart, the eyes, and the kidneys, to name but three—each of which performs a particular function. The heart pumps blood to the other organs of the body, the eyes transmit information about the external world to the brain, and the kidneys remove waste materials from the blood. These parts of the body do not exist in isolation, however; rather, they are interrelated and interdependent. If one of them ceases to perform its function—if the heart stops, the eyes go blind, or the kidneys fail—the effective operation of the whole body is threatened and survival itself may be in doubt.

Society, functionalists argue, operates in a way somewhat analogous to that of a biological organism. According to the **functionalist perspective,** *society is a system made up of a number of interrelated and interdependent elements, each performing a function that contributes to the operation of the whole* (Parsons, 1951; Merton, 1968; Turner and Maryanski, 1979). The elements of society include, for example, institutions such as the family, education, and the economy. The family provides for the bearing and rearing of children until they can live on their own. Educational institutions provide training in the various skills needed to fill jobs in society. The economy is responsible for producing food, clothing, and other necessities needed by families to survive, as well as for providing the books and other supplies needed for education. The family and the schools could not survive without the goods provided by the economy, and economic organizations need workers who have been socialized by the family and trained by the schools to work industriously. In addition to institutions, society is also made up of many social roles, social groups, and subcultures, and all these parts fit together into a reasonably well-integrated whole. For functionalists, then, all parts of society are interdependent and function together to provide the things that are essential to maintain society. In addition, there needs to be considerable agreement among the members of society regarding the content of important values and norms.

In a system with all the parts so tightly interdependent, a change in one element of society will probably lead to changes in other parts. For example, the establishment of compulsory education in America caused significant alterations in the economic sphere by removing children and eventually adolescents from the labor force, which made more jobs available for adults. Compulsory education also affected the family; with young people no longer working, the financial burden on parents was increased. When children could no longer help support the family financially, a gradual shift to smaller families began. Thus, changes in the educational sphere had important ramifications for family and economic structures. Small changes can usually be absorbed with relative ease, but large or sudden changes can cause major social disruption and lead to problems. Because of this, functionalists argue, social systems are characterized by stability and a tendency toward equilibrium—a state of balance in which the relationships among the various parts of the system remain the same.

A central concern of the functionalist approach is the determination of just what functions each part of society performs. This is not always easy to do because some functions are not as obvious as those in our previous example. In fact, sociologist Robert K. Merton (1968) suggests that there are two different types of functions: manifest and latent. *Manifest functions* are the intended consequences of some action or social process and refer to what most people expect to result. *Latent functions* are consequences that are unexpected or unintended. For example, one of the manifest functions of colleges and universities is to provide people with specialized training. However, institutions of higher education perform a number of latent functions. For instance, they serve as a marriage market, and they reduce unemployment by keeping some adults out of the job market. These latent functions are just as much a part of the system of higher education as its manifest purposes. In addition, some social practices may be *dysfunctional;* that is, they may disrupt social equilibrium rather than contribute to it. For example, encouraging large families, as some religious teachings do, would be dysfunctional in a society that is already overpopulated.

According to the functionalist perspective, a social problem exists when some element in society becomes dysfunctional and interferes with the efficient operation or stability of the system or the achievement of societal goals. In other words, social problems arise from social disorganization, in which the parts of society work at cross-purposes rather than together. Functionalists search for the sources of this societal breakdown. Consider how divorce might be viewed by functionalists: Marital dissolution involves the breaking up of what is perhaps society's most basic institution, the family. Divorce could be seen as a social problem if those functions that are typically served by the family were to go unperformed, such as children not being raised properly to become contributing members of society (see Chapter 3).

The functionalist perspective is a very useful one, but it does tend to overemphasize the extent of stability and order in society and to downplay the fact that social practices that are beneficial to one group in society may be dysfunctional to another. These cautions should be kept in mind when using this perspective.

The Conflict Perspective

Conflict theorists emphasize the inevitability of coercion, domination, conflict, and change in society. The **conflict perspective** is based on *the idea that society consists of different groups who struggle with one another to attain the scarce societal resources that are considered valuable, be they money, power, prestige, or cherished values.* Karl Marx provided the foundation for the conflict perspective when he viewed society as consisting of different social classes (1967, originally published 1867–1895). The two central classes of his era were the proletariat, or the workers, and the bourgeoisie, or those who owned the businesses, factories, and textile mills in which the proletariat toiled. Marx saw these classes as being in constant struggle with one another to improve their respective positions in society. The workers tried to gain more income and control over their work; the owners tried to make more profits by lowering labor costs and getting workers to work more. For Marx, this conflict was irreconcilable, because what benefits

one group necessarily works to the disadvantage of the other. Furthermore, if one group can gain an advantage in this struggle, they will use it to dominate and oppress the other group and enhance their own position. They might, for example, gain control of the government and pass legislation that limits the ways the subordinate groups could otherwise compete. A century ago in America, for example, it was illegal for workers to organize for the purposes of collective bargaining. This benefited the factory owners because workers were unable to use their strength of numbers to gain higher wages or better working conditions.

Although Marx limited his focus to class conflict, modern versions of conflict theory in sociology hold that domination, coercion, and the exercise of power occur to some degree in all groups and societies because they are the basic social mechanisms for regulating behavior and allocating resources (Coser, 1956; Dahrendorf, 1959; Duke, 1976). In addition to class conflict, groups and subcultures can engage in conflict over contrasting values. For example, some American religious groups, such as the Mormons, place great value in family life, whereas many nonreli-

The conflict perspective makes us aware that people vary substantially in terms of the social and economic resources available to them. The social programs and policies that would benefit this wealthy and well-connected New Englander are, undoubtedly, quite different from those that would benefit a homeless person or a single mother living in poverty.

gious Americans view the family as only one of a number of ways people can organize their personal lives. These two groups are likely to view social problems such as divorce and childbirth outside of marriage in quite different ways. In fact, as we have seen, whether these conditions are even viewed as social problems depends on one's values. Another source of conflict in society is the gap that can arise between values and social practices. American society, for example, professes to value equality for all. Yet at one time or another, African Americans, Italian Americans, Irish Americans, women, and Jewish Americans, to name but a few, have suffered severe discrimination.

In the conflict view, then, groups exert what power they possess over others when this serves their interests, and society consists of a wide array of such interest groups struggling to acquire a share of societal resources. An **interest group** is *a group whose members share distinct and common concerns and who benefit from similar social policies and practices*. Things that benefit one interest group may work to the disadvantage of others. Some interest groups are formally organized, such as the National Rifle Association, the Sierra Club, the National Manufacturers Association, or the American Civil Liberties Union. Other interest groups are informal, and people may not fully recognize that they are members of them. For example, college students constitute an informal interest group because all college students benefit from such things as lower tuition and increased government funding of student loans. Taxpayers without children of college age, however, might oppose such policies because their taxes would increase.

In the conflict view, social change involves redistributing scarce resources among various interest groups. A *vested interest group* is an interest group that benefits from existing policies, practices, and social arrangements, and generally resists social changes that might threaten their privileges. However, the inevitable clash of interests ensures that any existing social arrangements

eventually will be rearranged. Out of the resulting struggle, new winners will emerge and uneasy truces will be established. These truces, however, will be temporary, because new conflicts will develop that will lead to further struggle and change.

For the conflict theorist, a social problem exists when a group of people, believing that its interests are not being met or that it is not receiving a sufficient share of resources, works to overcome what it perceives as a disadvantage. Unlike functionalists, conflict theorists view a phenomenon such as divorce as normal because it represents one way of dealing with marital discord. This does not mean that the disruptive effects of divorce are ignored or that divorce is not a social problem. Rather, it means that divorce becomes a social problem when particular groups that have power regard their interests as being threatened by the extent of divorce in society.

Some caution is also called for in using the conflict perspective, especially the tendency to overemphasize the importance of conflict and inequality and to disregard the prevalence of stability and consensus in society. This can lead one to overlook factors important to social problems.

The Interactionist Perspective

Although the functionalist and conflict perspectives offer competing views of social life, the interactionist perspective is more of a supplement to the first two, showing how the social processes described in those perspectives enter into people's daily lives and shape their behavior. The **interactionist perspective** *focuses on everyday social interaction among individuals rather than on large societal structures such as politics, education, and the like* (Blumer, 1962; Hewitt, 1991). For interactionists, society consists of people interacting with one another; to understand society we must understand social interaction. It is through such interactions that groups, organizations, and society as a whole are created, maintained, and changed. The operation of educational institutions can be observed, for example, through students interacting with teachers and through school administrators making decisions. It is these day-to-day interactions that give education its shape and substance.

A central assumption of the interactionist perspective can be summarized in a paraphrase of a statement by sociologists William and Dorothy Thomas (1928): If people define situations as real, they are real in their consequences. In other words, people act on the basis of their beliefs and perceptions about situations. The term **definition of the situation** refers to *people's perceptions and interpretations of what is important in a situation and what action is appropriate*. One important element of this definition is our ability to use symbols. A *symbol* is something that stands for, represents, or takes the place of something else. Anything—any object, event, or word—can serve as a symbol. A crucifix, for example, symbolizes the beliefs of Christianity, whether it is made from wood, metal, or plastic; the Star of David likewise symbolizes Judaism. The meaning attached to a symbol is derived from social consensus. We simply agree that a particular object will represent something. During World War II, for example, Winston Churchill used two fingers extended into the air and spread apart to symbolize victory in battle, and others agreed on the meaning of this gesture. In the 1960s, the same gesture came to mean opposition to war as people used the gesture to indicate support for the peace movement.

Because of our ability to use symbols, we live in a world that we create ourselves, through the meanings we attach to phenomena. In other words, we respond to symbolic or social meanings rather than to actual physical objects or actions, and what we do is the result of how we define and interpret those meanings. For example, we attach meanings to people through the use of labels, including deviant labels that carry some stigma with them. We call people "whores," "queers," "crooks," and "crazies." These labels influence how we relate to these people. And when people have been labeled, we come to expect them to be-

have in certain ways. A central tenet of the interactionist approach is that such social expectations, or norms, tend to influence the behavior of people who have been labeled, especially when the people themselves accept the meaning of the label attached to them. The prostitute, for example, who internalizes the social meaning implied by the label "cheap whore" may not aspire toward any other way of life. Her world and behavior is shaped by the fact that she accepts the stigmatizing label, whether it is true or not.

Social life rests on the development of consensus about expected behavior. Such shared expectations guide our activities and make cooperative action possible. If this consensus breaks down, some sort of change must occur. Thus, for interactionists, social change involves developing some new consensus with different meanings and expectations.

From the interactionist perspective, a social problem exists when some social condition is defined by an influential group as stigmatizing or threatening to their values and disruptive of normal social expectations (Hilgartner and Bosk, 1988). For example, the interactionist would observe that there have been important changes in attitudes toward divorce in our society. In addition to being more common today, divorce has less stigma attached to it in modern America than it did around the turn of this century. At the same time, however, divorce is viewed by many groups as a social problem because they see marital dissolution as posing a threat to family stability. If the family is such a basic social institution, divorce may challenge shared meanings and definitions that these groups hold about this institution.

Once again caution is called for in using the perspectives. Because of the emphasis on face-to-face interaction in shaping social reality, the interactionist approach can lead one to deemphasize the part that social institutions, such as religion and politics, and large-scale social forces, such as industrialization, play in molding human behavior (Reynolds, 1987).

Table 1.1   **An Outline of the Sociological Perspectives**

	Functionalism	*Conflict Theory*	*Interactionism*
View of Society	A system of interrelated and interdependent parts.	Made up of groups struggling with one another over scarce resources.	Individuals in face-to-face interaction create social consensus.
View of the Individual	People are shaped by society to perform important functions for society.	People are shaped by the position of their groups in society.	People are symbol manipulators who create their social world through social interaction and consensus.
View of Social Change	The social system tends to resist change as disruptive.	Change is inevitable and continuous.	Change occurs when there is no shared consensus about expected behavior and a newly found consensus develops.
View of Social Problems	Caused by dysfunctional activities or disorganization in the social system.	Arise when a group believes its interests are not being served and works to overcome perceived disadvantage.	Arise when a condition is defined as stigmatizing or disruptive of normal social expectations.
Key Concepts	integration, interdependence, stability, equilibrium	interest, power, dominance, conflict, coercion	interpretation, consensus, shared expectations, socially created reality

Using the Theoretical Perspectives

The preceding discussion of the sociological perspectives is brief and simplified, and we will provide more detail in later chapters. The major elements of each perspective and its view on social problems have been outlined in Table 1.1. The three perspectives should not be viewed as either right or wrong, nor should one select a favorite and ignore the others. Instead, the perspectives should be seen as three different "tools," each of which is useful in analyzing particular social problems. The three perspectives are not equally useful for examining every social problem, nor can any single perspective explain all aspects of human behavior and society. Furthermore, to gain a full understanding of any particular problem, the use of more than one approach may be required. In a

sense, the perspectives are similar to a physician's instruments. Because of the body's complexity, a doctor needs many devices to keep tabs on people's health. Social problems are also very complex, and the theoretical perspectives are the "instruments" that sociologists have developed over the years to help them understand these problems in conjunction with human behavior and society.

RESEARCH ON SOCIAL PROBLEMS

Theories by themselves are not of great utility in understanding social problems, especially when they are untested. Until research has been done to test a theory, it is merely speculative. **Research** refers to *the systematic examination of empirical data*. Research can provide the most coherent and objective information about the causes of social problems, their extent, and the effectiveness of solutions. Without a foundation in research, our approach to problems is likely to be surrounded by speculation, misunderstanding, and bias, and we may expend resources in the pursuit of ineffective solutions. If this occurs, we have not only wasted resources but also left the real source of the problem to grow more serious. For these reasons, we must understand what good research is and how we can use its principles in our everyday assessment of social problems.

The Scientific Method

Research conducted by sociologists is based on the scientific method. **Science** is *a method of obtaining objective and systematic knowledge through observation*. The foundation of the scientific approach is the belief that claims about what is correct or incorrect must be demonstrated to be true through some observations in the world (Sullivan, 1992). Intuition, speculation, or common sense can never replace the empirical test of one's claims. Scientific theories are linked to scientific research through **hypotheses,** which are *tentative statements that can be tested regarding relationships between two or more factors*. Hypotheses are statements whose accuracy can be assessed through observation. If hypotheses are verified through observation, this provides support for the theory; if they are not, our confidence in the theory is reduced. The more empirical support there is for a theory, the more useful it is in attacking social problems.

Science is not foolproof, but it is the most effective means available for acquiring systematic, verifiable knowledge about the world and about social problems and their solution. In the Applied Research insert (see pp. 18–19), we contrast science with some other ways of gaining knowledge, and we show what makes the scientific approach

superior in this realm. Science does have its limitations, however, and it is crucial to understand which issues it cannot resolve. Science is the preferred source of knowledge on issues that can be resolved *through observation*. Some issues are not amenable to such resolution. For example, science cannot verify the existence of a supreme deity or say which religious beliefs are correct because these are not issues that can be settled through observation. They are matters of faith, choice, or revelation but not of science. Likewise, science cannot tell us which personal values are right and preferable because these are again matters of personal choice or judgment. As we have already seen, social problems and their solutions involve questions of personal and cultural values. In analyzing social problems, we need to be sensitive to the interplay between values and science, probing the extent to which values and science will play a part in the solution of problems. Science may help show us how to live up to our values, but it cannot tell us which values to live by.

Values, Interest Groups, and Objectivity

An issue that is especially important and quite controversial regarding research on social problems is that of scientific objectivity, or the attempt by scientists to prevent their personal values from affecting the outcome of their research. This does not mean that scientists are without values or passions. Many are intensely concerned about social problems such as crime, divorce, family violence, and nuclear war. At the same time, scientists realize that their personal values can, and probably will, bias their research. In the early part of this century, sociologist Max Weber laid out one position on this issue when he argued that sociology should remain as *value free* as possible because human values can distort sound scientific investigation (1958, originally published 1919). Weber felt that sociologists should suspend their personal and political values when engaging in scientific research. Contemporary advocates of Weber's position would concede that this is difficult to accomplish but that abandoning the effort would be disastrous: There would be no accurate body of knowledge about human social behavior to guide our consideration of ways of alleviating social problems (Gordon, 1988). Karl Marx (1964, originally published 1848) eloquently stated a position opposite to that of Weber's on this controversy. Marx was a strong champion of the cause of the poor and the downtrodden, and he wanted to use science to improve their plight. He felt that social scientists should bring strong moral commitments to their work and use science to change inequitable or immoral social conditions. Likewise, there are sociologists today who believe that social research should be guided by personal and political values and directed toward alleviating social ills (Harding, 1986; Fay, 1987).

Sociologist Alvin Gouldner (1976) has suggested a reasonable middle ground between these two positions. He agreed that scientists have values and that the influence of those values on research, which is often very subtle, can never be totally eliminated. But Gouldner proposed that we should deny neither our values nor the negative impact they can have on research. He urged that scientists should be explicit about what their values are. In this way, other scientists are forewarned and are thus better able to spot ways in which research findings may be influenced by personal bias.

The problem of enhancing scientific objectivity can be especially difficult for scientists who are closely associated with some interest group. Close involvement with an interest group can lead, often unknowingly, to distortions and misperceptions that throw into question the scientist's research on topics of interest to that group. For example, sociologists who are actively involved in such environmental groups as Greenpeace, Save the Whales, or the Abalone Alliance may have difficulty in recognizing ways in which the outcome of their research might be influenced by their personal position on the issues. Any research on environmental issues conducted by these people should be reviewed carefully for such sources of bias. Furthermore, scientists should cautiously review their own research plans to detect ways in which their own values might be influencing the outcome.

One final point needs to be made regarding interest groups and scientific research. In the public debate over social problems, the findings of science are often used by interest groups to further their own ends, and such groups may, wittingly or unwittingly, distort research findings to support their own position. This manipulation of scientific data can leave the public with misleading impressions. The purpose of these uses of science is to persuade people to support particular programs or policies rather than to advance our knowledge of social problems. Because science enjoys a great deal of legitimacy in the United States, such appeals to "scientific proof" can be very persuasive. Because of this, people, especially in a democracy where the citizenry participates in making public policy, need to be skilled at assessing the data and information with which they are barraged.

Assessing Data: Problems and Pitfalls

How can we detect error or bias in what we read? There are, of course, no foolproof guidelines, but we can draw some lessons from scientific research to become better informed consumers of information. The following are a few such guidelines.

Sampling Problems. A basic question to ask about any set of data is: Upon whom or what were the observations made? In scientific research, collecting data on all the people or events about whom you are interested is normally impossible. In a study of divorce, for example, interviewing all American couples who have divorced would be too expensive and time consuming, because more than a million do so every year. Instead, researchers typically study a **sample,** which consists of *elements that are taken from a group or population and that serve as a source of data.* To be useful, samples should be *representative*, or reflect the group or

APPLIED RESEARCH

Untangling Myths and Facts About Social Problems

Sociologists take the position that scientific research provides the most accurate and useful knowledge with which to cope with social problems. Science, of course, is not the only way to gain an understanding of the world. For example, people often use tradition as a source of guidance. This might take the form of religious teachings about sex and marriage or proverbs such as "Birds of a feather flock together" and "Two heads are better than one." People also turn to their own personal experience for direction. If we visit a prison and see that most inmates are nonwhite, this can lead us to believe that crime rates are much higher among nonwhites than whites. Knowledge from tradition and experience often accumulates and blends together to form what people call "common sense": practical wisdom that encourages people to make decisions that they believe are sound without having any special training or expertise.

In fact, sociology has been called "the science of common sense" by critics who assume that it merely "proves" what everybody else already knows. In fact, sociology sometimes does confirm what many people already accept. We should not be surprised that scientific research shows that some commonsense beliefs are true, because people need some accurate commonsense knowledge of human behavior to interact with others and function in society. However, research shows that other commonsense beliefs about social problems are false, or at least oversimplified. Consider these statements:

1. If welfare recipients were not so lazy and unwilling to work, there would be little need for welfare in the United States.
2. The crime rate is much higher in the lower class than it is in the middle class.
3. Reading pornography increases the likelihood that men will commit acts of sexual violence against women.
4. Because of the civil rights movement and affirmative action legislation, the gap in income between blacks and whites has narrowed in the past three decades.
5. A person who does not engage in homosexual activities or use drugs intravenously has very little risk of becoming infected with the virus for Acquired Immune Deficiency Syndrome (AIDS).

At one time or another, each of us has probably believed that at least some of these statements are true. Yet social science research has shown each one to be false, or at least to be far too simple.

1. Most people receiving public assistance are children, single mothers who cannot afford the day care that would free them for work, the aged, and the disabled. Very few adult males who could work receive welfare (see Chapter 5).
2. If we use arrest statistics as our data, then this statement is supported, but most people who commit crimes are not arrested. A growing body of evidence based on self-reports of criminal activity suggests that what distinguishes the social classes is not the amount of crime but rather the types of crimes and the likelihood of being arrested. The poor are more likely to commit highly visible crimes, such as homicide or assault, that are likely to be reported to the police and result in arrests. Middle-class people commit crimes such as embezzlement, fraud, or tax evasion that often go unreported (see Chapter 9).

3. There is no convincing evidence that pornography predisposes a person to commit sexual violence, although people who commit such crimes may also read pornography. Much pornography portrays violence against women, and it may well be the violence rather than the sexual content of pornography that encourages violence against women (see Chapter 11).

4. Unfortunately, research shows that the gap has hardly changed over the past three decades. Although many blacks have benefited from such legislation, the poverty of the black "underclass" seems to be especially impervious to change (see Chapter 6).

5. Although it is true in the United States that 85 percent of those who contract AIDS are men who have sex with other men or people who engage in intravenous drug use, heterosexual transmission of AIDS has been growing rapidly, up 500 percent between 1985 and 1990. And worldwide, 60 percent of HIV infections result from heterosexual intercourse (see Chapter 4).

What is wrong with common sense in these realms? Basically, common sense does not normally involve an empirical and systematic effort to distinguish fact from fiction. Rather, it tends to accept untested and unquestioned assumptions because "everyone knows" they are true, and to reject contradictory information. In other words, some commonsense knowledge is a "myth" in that there is little evidence of its truth, although some people still accept it as true. Commonsense knowledge is also very slow to change—even when change seems called for—because the change may threaten cherished values or social patterns. In addition, common sense often explains everything, even when those explanations contradict one another. When we see two people with similar personalities become friends, we say "Birds of a feather flock together." Yet when we see an athletic woman dating a bookish, cerebral man, we say "Opposites attract." But which assertion is true?

Scientific research does far more than merely document what we already know. Sometimes it does just that, but at other times it directly contradicts common sense. Most of the time, however, the truth is vastly more complicated than common sense suggests. Sociological research incorporates procedures that advance our knowledge by establishing facts through observation and by using procedures that reduce bias. Common sense is important and should not be ignored, but an unthinking and unverified acceptance of commonsense beliefs can blind people to social realities. This has important implications for social policy. The recognition, for example, that most people receiving welfare need it desperately just to survive is a strong argument against cutting back on public assistance programs. It is only through the development of an accurate, scientifically verified understanding of such social problems that we can hope to overcome them—even if it means relinquishing some of our most cherished commonsense preconceptions.

In each of the remaining chapters, we include two features that emphasize these points as they relate to specific social problems. At the beginning of each chapter, a Myths and Facts insert will contrast some inaccurate or misleading commonsense beliefs about some problem with the facts as they have been established through research. This will encourage the student to distinguish between beliefs that have no empirical foundation and may in fact be myths from facts that have been substantiated through observation. Elsewhere in most chapters, we include an Applied Research insert in which we illustrate the use of sociological research in solving problems or evaluating how well solutions work. This emphasizes the theme that the development of social policies about social problems should be influenced by systematic and scientific assessment of their impact as well as by our own personal values.

population that is under study in ways that are considered important.

The sampling problems that can arise when unrepresentative samples are used in the analysis of social problems—and the misleading conclusions that can result—are well illustrated by investigations of homosexuality. In the 1940s and 1950s, studies of gay men by psychologists and psychiatrists typically came to the conclusion that homosexuality is the result of a personality disturbance stemming from disordered relationships with parents during childhood. They also concluded that, as a group, gay men were unhappy and maladjusted individuals. The samples used in these studies consisted of gay men who were the patients of psychologists or psychiatrists. Virtually all the gay men in these samples were unhappy, maladjusted, and had disordered relationships with their parents—a strong association indeed. Yet the problem with the sampling in these studies should be fairly obvious: Gay men who seek psychological counseling are probably not representative of all gay men. People who seek counseling, irrespective of their sexual orientation, do so because they already have personal problems. Gay men who do not have such problems do not seek counseling, and they do not appear in samples of gays collected in this fashion. These early studies, then, contained a built-in bias, caused by poor sampling procedures, toward the conclusion that gay men are psychologically disturbed. Studies using more representative samples have concluded that sexual orientation, by itself, probably does not lead to personality disturbances or unhappiness (Ross et al., 1988; Savin-Williams, 1990).

A basic question to ask regarding any data or information, then, is whether it is based on a representative sample. Not that it is always easy to tell whether a sample is truly representative. But one should always ask: Are there people about whom conclusions are being made who are not represented in a particular sample?

Assessing Causality.   One of the major goals in the study of social problems is to find their causes. By **causality,** we mean that *one factor has an effect on or produces a change in some other factor.* Establishing causality is one way of determining why something happened. Once we have established the causes of a social problem, we are in a better position to determine what programs or policies might alleviate it. However, discovering causal relationships can be a difficult task because causality cannot be directly observed. Rather, we infer causality from the observation of *associations* or *correlations* between things in the world. If changes in one factor are regularly associated with changes in the other factor, then the first factor may be causing those changes (Hirschi and Selvin, 1967).

The early studies of gay men mentioned previously had established an association between sexual orientation and psychological maladjustment, but a little thought will show that this association alone is not sufficient to infer that psychological disturbance causes homosexuality. It is equally logical to infer that being gay, especially in a society in which homosexuality is highly stigmatized, produces psychological disturbance and unhappiness. Thus, in addition to establishing an association, a second criterion to be satisfied before inferring causality is that the *time sequence* be correct: The causal factor must occur before whatever it is presumed to cause. The psychological disturbance would have to exist before people became homosexual to infer that the former causes the latter.

A third criterion to be satisfied in assessing causality is that the association not be spurious. A *spurious relationship* is one in which the association between two factors occurs because each is independently associated with some third factor. For example, there is a strong association between rates of ice cream consumption and juvenile delinquency, but few people would argue that eating ice cream causes delinquency or vice versa. Obviously, the relationship is a spurious one in which both ice cream consumption and delinquency are related to a third factor, the summer season. School vacations and warm weather offer greater opportunity to eat ice cream and to engage in delinquent acts.

Once we have satisfied the three criteria, we can feel reasonably confident that we have discovered a causal relationship. Unfortunately, much research on social problems can satisfy only one or two of the criteria, and this leaves us less confident regarding causality. The central point here is to be cautious and critical about any claims regarding causal relationships.

Measuring Social Problems.   All scientific research involves *measurement,* which refers to making observations that are presumed to be evidence that something exists or that something has a certain value. The observations that are made are referred to as "indicators." An indicator of juvenile delinquency, for example, might be vandalism at a school gymnasium. Likewise, severe bruises on a child's forearm might be considered indicators of child abuse.

A central concern in the study of social problems is that the indicators of variables have *validity,* or that they accurately measure what they are intended to measure. A thermometer, for example, is a valid measure of temperature but not of volume. The study of child abuse provides illustrations of some of the difficulties of finding valid measures of social problems. If we define child abuse as injuring a child not by accident but in anger or with deliberate intent, then most would agree that a cigarette burn on a child's buttocks is a valid indicator of child abuse; there is no other imaginable reason why such burns should occur

"Are you questioning my methodology, Mac?"

It is essential that people assess the methods that are used in making judgments about social problems and their solutions. The consequences of uncritically accepting someone else's judgments in this realm are much more serious than an additional delay or cost in repairing a television.

(Gelles, 1987; Korbin, 1987). But what about a bruise on the arm? Some groups in our society approve of physically striking a child for disciplinary reasons, even if some bruising results. Other groups define any physical punishment as unacceptable. As another example, invalid measures of crime are often used in assessing the crime problem. The most common source of crime statistics is the reports by the Federal Bureau of Investigation, but these statistics are based on crimes for which an arrest has been made or, in some cases, crimes known to the police (see Chapter 9). Yet there are many crimes that the police do not know about or do not make an arrest for, which means that these crime statistics are not totally accurate indicators of all crime.

In assessing data relating to social problems, we must consider issues of validity because these measurement problems can drastically influence the interpretation of data. Policy based on conclusions drawn from invalid measures can be very harmful. It may lead us to think we are moving toward alleviating a problem when in fact we are not. Meanwhile, the problem may become more serious as we experiment with untested and ineffective solutions.

Assessing Claims. In many cases, we are not in a position to apply the above criteria to claims about social problems. You may not have any information, for example, about the validity of a measuring device or any basis for judging a sample. What, then, can you do to reduce the chance of deception or distortion? There are a number of additional guidelines that should be kept in mind:

1. Is the claim made by a person or group of people with a strong self-interest in a particular interpretation or conclusion? Their personal interest may be biasing their presentation or interpretation of the data.
2. Can the claim be verified by yourself or others? Even reputable newspapers and magazines sometimes report data, in good faith, that cannot later be verified. In 1977, for example,

Newsweek reported that "officials reckon" that 28 percent of the voters in San Francisco were gay. Diligent search by others failed to locate these alleged officials. Yet the *Newsweek* report became a major source of verification for data on the size of the gay population in San Francisco (Plissner, 1978).
3. Are the claims presented in a propagandistic fashion? There are a number of propaganda techniques that are used to persuade the public (Jowett and O'Donnell, 1986). For example, "glittering generalities" involve the use of highly attractive but vague and meaningless words and phrases such as "restoring law and order" or "communism." "Testimonial" is the technique of using famous and respected people to support a program or policy as a means of engendering public support.

FUTURE PROSPECTS: SOLVING SOCIAL PROBLEMS

The Interplay of Policy and Research

Our goal is not only to understand problems but also to solve them or at least to alleviate some of their more undesirable consequences. Solutions to problems, however, never magically appear. Some action must be taken if solutions are to be effected. These actions develop into what is called **social policy:** *laws, administrative procedures, and other formal and informal social practices that are intended to promote social changes focused on alleviating particular social problems* (Gil, 1990; Jencks, 1992). Social policies are inherently controversial because they are based, in part, on human values. Groups with differing values will often push for very different solutions to the same problem. Or they may, as we have seen, disagree over which social conditions are social problems. This controversy and disagreement is an inevitable feature of the debate over social problems and their solution.

Within the confines of this debate, however, sociological theory and research can be applied as tools for assessing the validity and effectiveness of particular positions and solutions. The power of scientific observation can be trained on problems and solutions to help resolve some of the controversy. Science, as we have seen, cannot tell us what values to hold, but it can help us assess whether the factors we believe underlie a problem are the actual sources of the problem. Scientific observation can also assess whether particular solutions to problems actually work. Is the problem alleviated once the solution is put into effect? Did the solution bring about the improvement, or was it something else? Does the solution have any side effects, detrimental or beneficial? The Policy Issues insert describes a successful attempt to use research as a basis for social policy. This attempt focused on a particularly disturbing problem—spouse abuse—and the effectiveness of various ways of dealing with it. Some further linkages between research and social policy are outlined in Table 1.2. In fact, there is a specialty area in the social sciences—variously called applied sociology, applied social research, or evaluation research—that is devoted precisely to this endeavor (Nathan, 1988; Sullivan, 1992). It uses modern social science research tools to assess the extent of social problems, to plan and monitor programs intended to alleviate those problems, and to determine how effectively the programs achieve their goals. The most effective approach to finding and implementing solutions to social problems, then, involves an interplay between social policy and social research. This recognizes the role of human values in the process, but it also tempers their enthusiasm and potential bias with systematic observation and assessment.

Who Provides Solutions?

Social problems, as we have seen, are conditions that can be remedied through some form of collective action. "Collective action" merely means that people work together toward a solution. In

Table 1.2 **Linkage Between Social Policy and Social Science Research**

Stages in the Policy Process	Possible Research Contribution
Problem Formulation	Assess extent of problem, who is affected, and costs of doing nothing
Policy Formulation	Assess positive or negative impact of various policy alternatives
Policy Implementation	Assess whether a program achieves policy goals in an efficient and effective manner
Evaluation	Assess whether and how a solution has an impact on a problem or on other groups in society; determine whether any new problems are created
Closure	Assess whether any further policy application would be warranted

some cases, this takes the form of interest groups working through the normal political process in the United States, at the federal, state, or local level. Politicians who are aware of a problem pass legislation to alleviate it, judges make rulings that have an impact on a problem, or private corporations and foundations develop programs to solve a problem. The solution to a problem may even be developed in good part by people who are unaffected, or at best indirectly affected, by the problem. Corporate executives, for example, may not experience poverty themselves but may feel a moral obligation to contribute some of their earnings to charity. Or they may be motivated by a fear that poverty generates an unsettled political and economic environment that adversely affects corporate profits.

Organized protest and social action outside of the normal political process represent another way that solutions to social problems can emerge. Groups affected by a problem can strike, riot, or march in the streets to force government or pri-

POLICY ISSUES

Domestic Violence: How to Intervene?

Domestic violence is a particularly tragic social problem with its jarring intrusion of injury and cruelty into the intimacy of the family. It is also a difficult problem for police officers who are often first on the scene of such violence and whose job it is to make complex and troubling decisions about how to handle the alleged perpetrator of the violence. Should the officer make an arrest? Would it be better to just order the alleged abuser out of the house to cool off? Or would mediation and counseling from the officer be more effective at preventing future abuse?

In the past, such decisions have been left to the discretion and judgment of the officer in the field. Using applied social research, criminologist Lawrence Sherman and sociologist Richard Berk have offered a basis for developing social policies regarding this issue (Sherman and Berk, 1984). Working with the Police Foundation, a research organization in Washington, D.C., Sherman and Berk designed a study to assess which actions by police officers could be shown to reduce the likelihood that a spouse abuser would be involved in future domestic violence incidents. When police officers respond to a domestic violence call, they have basically three alternatives: They can arrest the person accused of spouse abuse; they can separate the couple for a time by ordering the alleged abuser to leave the premises; or they can attempt to serve as mediators between the parties.

Sherman and Berk asked police officers in Minneapolis to randomly apply one of these three intervention strategies—arrest, separation, or mediation—to each domestic violence call of which they were a part. For ethical and practical reasons, they limited the study to simple, or misdemeanor, assault where there was no severe injury or life-threatening situation. Their measure of the effectiveness of these interventions was whether an alleged abuser was involved in another domestic violence incident in the six months following the original police intervention.

Somewhat surprisingly, their basic finding was that arrest is the most effective of the three types of police intervention. Those arrested were significantly less likely to be involved in a repeat episode of domestic violence. This was not, however, a result of the fact that being jailed left them with less opportunity than others to commit acts of domestic violence, because those arrested were released very quickly and were thus equally able to engage in such acts as were those who experienced separation or mediation.

After Sherman and Berk reached their conclusions, the Minneapolis police department established administrative policies encouraging officers to use the arrest strategy when responding to spouse abuse calls. Many other police departments developed similar policies after learning of the Sherman-Berk results, and a number of states *required* that arrests of abusers be made if there is probable cause to suspect abuse. Thus, many law enforcement agencies have begun to take a stronger stand in protecting women from domestic assault, a stand that was shown empirically by Sherman and Berk to have a better chance of reducing the problem. Because social problems are complicated, sociologists recognize that one research study is not likely to tell us all we need to know. And this is true with domestic violence. To see if the results would hold up in other places and at other times, variations on the Sherman-Berk study have been done in a number of cities, including Omaha, Nebraska, and Charlotte, North Carolina (Dunford, Huizinga, and Elliott, 1990; Hirschel, Hutchison, and Dean, 1992). Generally, the results have not been as supportive of the efficacy of arrest over other approaches in reducing repeats of spouse abuse. Why the difference in findings? It may be that Sherman and Berk, given the way they designed their study, inadvertently studied a select group of abusers on whom arrest was particularly effective. The later studies have tried to study a broader sampling of abusers. Thus, research on this topic continues in an effort to understand with which offenders and under what circumstances arrest is an effective deterrent against spouse abuse. These efforts illustrate the continuous interplay between research and policy.

These studies on domestic violence illustrate how social policy can emerge in part from scientifically supported recommendations about how to handle social problems. Although personal and cultural values will play a part in the solutions we choose, scientific research can better help us assess the consequences of particular alternatives. In the following chapters, a Policy Issues insert will analyze similar issues related to a particular social problem.

vate organizations to change their practices. In some cases, a **social movement** may emerge, *a collective, organized effort to promote or resist social change through some noninstitutionalized or unconventional means.* The civil rights movement and the environmental movement are examples of social movements that have used demonstration and protest to force recalcitrant politicians and corporations to change their practices related to social problems.

In recent years, there has been vigorous debate over the role of the government in identifying and solving social problems. Beginning with the New Deal of the 1930s and continuing through the 1960s, there was considerable support for the government to take responsibility for trying to solve social problems such as crime, poverty, and environmental pollution. In particular, the government used its ability to raise revenue through taxation—its fiscal policy—to attack social problems. For example, it raised money to support such programs as Medicare and Social Security. In addition, in times of economic downturn, the government went into debt, creating a budget deficit, to provide support for the unemployed, stimulate business activity, and create jobs to put people to work temporarily. The size of the government grew substantially, and many social programs were established. At the risk of oversimplification, we can call this approach to the role of

the government in social problems the "interventionist" approach.

With Ronald Reagan's election as president of the United States in 1980, pressure from another direction regarding social problems mounted. This pressure was based on the belief that government itself is a hindrance to the solution of many problems and should play only a limited role in attacking them. Rather, the government's primary role should be to create a climate that promotes business expansion. Then, the prosperity associated with such expansion will alleviate many, although certainly not all, social problems. Furthermore, appropriate government intervention in solving social problems should come predominantly from local and state rather than federal levels. Finally, some proponents of this approach argue for reemphasizing the importance of individualism, of people using their own efforts to improve their lot in life. These individual efforts should be sustained more by family and friends than by the federal government. Social policy, in short, should be less related to government intervention and more dependent on the actions of individuals or private groups and the working of impersonal, economic forces. Again, at the risk of oversimplification, we can label this approach the "laissez-faire" approach. The French term *laissez-faire,* meaning "to let do" or to leave people alone, refers to the belief that government should intervene as little as possible in economic affairs. George Bush's administration continued many of Reagan's laissez-faire policies into the 1990s.

Historian Arthur Schlesinger, Jr. (1986) argues that the United States experiences a cyclical shift in national involvement between these extremes, changing from an emphasis on public action to that of private interest and self-fulfillment and back again every twenty-five years or so. Whether it is cyclical or not, these contrasting views of the government's role in solving social problems certainly have been joined in debate in the 1980s and 1990s as never before. The outcome of this debate shapes which policies will be developed to attack the problems that we will address in later chapters. We will, therefore, discuss the interventionist and laissez-faire positions at greater length when they are relevant to particular social problems.

Should We Solve the Problem?

Once a social condition has been judged to be a social problem, the search for solutions begins. At this point, there may be widespread agreement, at least in the abstract, that the problem should be solved. There are still, however, some final issues that need to be weighed.

1. Can we accept the costs of a solution? Because economic resources are limited, money used to clean up the environment is not available to fight crime or build defense weapons. Any effort to solve social ills will mean that fewer resources are available to solve other problems. There are also noneconomic costs to solving problems. If televised violence has adverse effects on children, then we could ban violent programs from television. But many Americans enjoy those television shows, whereas others would see this as an unacceptable imposition of government censorship.
2. Does a solution to one problem create yet other problems? As we emphasized in discussing the sociological perspectives, a society is a complex intertwining of many parts, and changing one part may have consequences for other parts. If, for example, we could effectively eliminate prostitution and drug dealing, what would happen to the people who earn a living that way? Would they turn to other crimes to support themselves? Or might they become a further welfare burden? The point is that we need to look at all the outcomes of particular solutions in order to plan very carefully. There may be times when we decide that the "cure" is worse than the "disease."
3. Is a particular solution feasible? Given the political and social climate and the cultural values in America, are there some solutions to problems that would be impossible to accomplish because of resistance from some groups? Coping with alcoholism, for example, by banning all use of alcohol is simply not feasible, as the experiment with Prohibition in the 1920s showed. We currently use the prohibition approach to deal with drug abuse, which is equally difficult to eradicate. The point is that particular social policies may not be feasible if they go against the strongly held values and ingrained social practices of large or important groups in society.

International Perspectives: Social Problems in Other Societies

People in the United States, of course, tend to be concerned mostly about social problems in their own country. And American sociologists have tended to devote most of their attention to American social problems. However, there are two reasons why we should focus some of our attention on social problems in other societies and cultures. First of all, we can gain additional insight into problems and their solutions when we observe them in cultures different from our own. Is the nature and extent of some social problem in the United States different from other countries? If so, then we can look for the factors unique to the American experience that produce this difference.

We can also examine which solutions have worked elsewhere. This does not mean that they will automatically work here, but it does give us some insight into which solutions to consider.

A second reason for taking an international perspective is that nations today are intertwined in complex relationships where we all depend on one another to an extent. International trade agreements affect the jobs available to people in Portland, Maine, and Albuquerque, New Mexico; Bolivian farmers survive by growing coca plants, which produce illegal drugs available in the United States; political instability in Southeast Asia sends immigrants to the United States, increasing cultural diversity here and contributing to interracial conflict. We do not have the space, of course, to cover all of these international dimensions. However, we have included in our discussion of American social problems illustrations from many different societies and cultures. To highlight this, and to focus attention on this issue, we have included in a number of chapters boxed inserts that emphasize an international perspective by discussing dimensions of or solutions to a problem in other societies.

Linkages

The discussion of whether we should solve particular problems points to a final issue: Social problems do not exist in isolation from other social problems. Rather problems tend to be linked together such that the worsening of one problem can contribute to the worsening of other problems. For example, an epidemic disease such as Acquired Immune Deficiency Syndrome is a health problem discussed in Chapter 4, whereas the use of crack cocaine is related to drug abuse discussed in Chapter 10. Yet, these two problems are linked because crack addicts who use needles tend to use dirty needles and share equipment. This is fertile ground for the spread of the AIDS virus. So, as intravenous drug use becomes more prevalent, the AIDS virus has a better chance of spreading. Alleviate one problem, and we will have made some progress toward alleviating the other. Many of these linkages will be made in the following chapters, and the student will learn to draw linkages that are not explicitly mentioned in this book. To encourage this consideration of linkages, we will include a brief insert at the end of the text material in each chapter that suggests one or two of the less obvious ways in which the problem focused on in that chapter is linked to problems discussed in other chapters.

Summary

1. Sociology is the scientific study of societies and human social behavior. It offers one of the most useful approaches for understanding social problems and the most effective tool for finding solutions to them.

2. Social problems involve public issues and not merely personal troubles. A social problem exists when an influential group defines a social condition as threatening its values, when the condition affects a large number of people, and when it can be remedied by collective action.

3. Values are people's ideas about what is

good or bad, right or wrong. Norms refer to expectations that people in society share about how they ought to behave. Values and norms provide society with stability. When behavior violates important group values or norms and is reacted to with social disapproval, it is called deviance. Many social problems involve some form of deviance. Some social problems arise because social institutions have become less effective in guiding people's behavior and providing a sense of community and self-worth.

4. Modern societies also consist of many subcultures, or groups with some beliefs, values, and norms that are distinct from the larger culture. This creates the problem of ethnocentrism, the tendency to view one's own culture or subculture as the best and to judge other cultures and subcultures in comparison to it.

5. Social problems typically involve the exercise of power and the use of authority. The sociological imagination is the ability to recognize the relationship between what is happening in your own personal life and the social forces that surround you.

6. Sociological insights are formulated into theories, which are statements that explain the relationship between phenomena. Very general explanations of social reality are called theoretical perspectives, or fundamental assumptions about the nature and operation of society. The three major theoretical perspectives in sociology today are functionalism, conflict theory, and interactionism.

7. From the functionalist perspective, society is viewed as a system made up of a number of interrelated and interdependent parts, each performing a function that contributes to the operation of the whole society. Social problems arise, according to this perspective, when some element of society becomes dysfunctional and interferes with the efficient operation or stability of the system or the achievement of societal goals.

8. From the conflict perspective, society is viewed as consisting of a variety of groups who struggle with one another to attain scarce societal resources that are considered valuable. Social problems arise when a group, believing that its interests are not being met or that it is not receiving sufficient scarce resources, works to overcome what it perceives as a disadvantage.

9. The interactionist perspective shows how the social processes described by the first two perspectives enter into people's daily lives, focusing on everyday social interaction among people rather than on larger societal structures. It emphasizes the importance of definition and interpretation and the role of shared expectations in shaping behavior. Social problems arise, according to this perspective, when a condition is defined by an influential group as stigmatizing or threatening to its values and disruptive of normal social expectations.

10. Theories must be tested through research, which for sociologists is based on the scientific method. Science emphasizes objective and systematic observation as a source of knowledge. Theories are linked to research through hypotheses, which are tentative statements that can be tested about the relationship between two or more factors.

11. Although the subject is controversial, most scientists emphasize the importance of objectivity, or the attempt to prevent personal values from affecting the outcome of research. There are a number of things to watch for in assessing research data, including sampling problems, the assessment of causality, measurement problems, and assessing the claims people make.

12. The best means for finding effective solutions to social problems is through an interplay between the development of social policy and its assessment through scientific research. However, not all problems can or should be solved because the costs may be too high or there may be profound disagreement over how to solve them.

Important Terms for Review

authority	functionalist	power	social problem
causality	perspective	research	sociology
conflict perspective	hypotheses	sample	subculture
definition of the	interactionist	science	theoretical perspective
situation	perspective	social institution	theory
deviance	interest group	social movement	values
ethnocentrism	norms	social policy	

Discussion Questions

1. In deciding which social conditions were social problems, we distinguished between "personal troubles" and "public issues." List some personal troubles experienced by you or your classmates that would not be considered public issues. Why aren't they considered public issues? What would have to occur to make them public issues?

2. Make one list of subcultures at your university to which you do not belong and another list of those to which you do belong. For the first set of subcultures, describe their values and norms as best you can. How do these differ from the values and norms of the second list? How might these differences lead them into conflict over which conditions should be considered social problems?

3. List five cultural values that you believe are widely accepted in American society. Are there elements of your own behavior that reflect these values? Can you think of groups in America that do not accept the legitimacy of these values? Are there social problems that arise from people's unwillingness to accept them?

4. Consider the crimes of robbery and burglary from the functionalist perspective. You can

undoubtedly view these crimes as dysfunctional for society, but can you consider any possible manifest or latent functions that they might serve for society? What groups would be adversely affected if we could completely eliminate those two types of crime?

5. Some conflict theorists would argue that higher education is a mechanism used by some groups to protect their favored position in society against inroads by subordinate groups. Do you agree or disagree? In what ways is this position true? Is there some way that this coercive dimension of higher education could be eliminated?

6. Deviant behavior involves attaching a stigmatized meaning to a person or that person's behavior. In what ways might you or your behavior be considered deviant by some group? Which groups? Is there any member of your class that can be considered to be "without deviance"?

7. Select an article from a current newspaper or magazine that offers an assessment of some social problem. Assess the data in that article in terms of sampling problems and the other criteria discussed in this chapter. What is your conclusion regarding the article?

For Further Reading

Robert N. Bellah, Richard Madsen, William M. Sullivan, Ann Swidler, and Steven M. Tipton. *The Good Society.* New York: Knopf, 1991. This is a thought-provoking book about Americans' shaken confidence in their social institutions. It suggests some ways to revitalize and transform such institutions as the family, politics, and the economy. As you will see in this book, such transformation may well be an integral part of alleviating the many social problems that we will discuss.

Randall Collins. *Three Sociological Traditions.* New York: Oxford University Press, 1985. A short book that covers the functionalist, conflict, and "micro-interactionist" traditions in sociology. This is a complex book including considerable historical material, but it is well worth the time for the student willing to expend the energy.

Kurt Finsterbusch and George McKenna. *Taking Sides: Clashing Views on Controversial Social Issues.* 6th ed. Guilford, Conn.: Dushkin, 1990. A collection of position papers on twenty controversial issues relating to social problems. On each issue, one author takes a "pro" stance and the other takes a "con" position on such questions as whether poor people perpetuate poverty or whether the women's movement has helped women.

Howard E. Freeman, Russell R. Dynes, Peter H. Rossi, and William Foote Whyte, eds. *Applied Sociology: Roles and Activities of Sociologists in Diverse Settings.* San Francisco: Jossey-Bass, 1983. This book contains twenty-seven articles covering the complete range of applied research methods and applied settings in which sociologists can be found working on various social problems.

Willard Gaylin, Ruth Macklin, and Tabitha Powledge, eds. *Violence and the Politics of Research.* New York: Plenum, 1981. This book raises issues regarding whether researchers should be bound by moral or ethical considerations when they conduct research on social problems and whether they should be responsible for making decisions about these problems. The particular problem focused on in this volume is violence and how to control it.

William Hastings. *How to Think About Social Problems.* New York: Oxford University Press, 1979. A readable book that can help guide you through the maze of possible deceit and trickery that surrounds much debate on social policy and social problems. Hastings shows you how to assimilate and reflect on sociological information and how to analyze issues clearly and in an unbiased way.

Garvin McCain and Ervin M. Segal. *The Game of Science.* 5th ed. Pacific Grove, Calif.: Brooks/Cole, 1988. This is an easy-to-read, yet complete overview of the enterprise of science, both natural and social. In addition to covering the basic logic of science, it also gets into interesting issues such as the "culture" of the scientist.

Marvin E. Olsen and Michael Micklin, eds. *Handbook of Applied Sociology.* New York: Praeger, 1981. A compendium of articles about the efforts of sociologists to use sociological theories and research to attack social problems and improve the functioning of social institutions. As you read each chapter in this text, it might be useful to read the relevant articles in the Olsen and Micklin book for a more comprehensive view of the problem being discussed.

Howard M. Rebach and John G. Bruhn, eds. *Handbook of Clinical Sociology.* New York and London: Plenum, 1991. A detailed overview of consulting and clinical sociology, the book provides many illustrations of the specific kinds of work that applied sociologists do.

Lawrence W. Sherman. *Policing Domestic Violence: Experiments and Dilemmas.* New York: The Free Press, 1992. This book is about the research on domestic violence discussed in the Policy Issues insert in this chapter. It provides an interesting analysis of the role of social research in the development of public policy.

Sam D. Sieber. *Fatal Remedies: The Ironies of Social Intervention.* New York: Plenum, 1981. An excellent book on the many efforts at social intervention that become self-defeating when their outcomes run counter to their intentions. This book preaches a healthy dose of caution when considering social intervention.

Thomas J. Sullivan. *Applied Sociology: Research and Critical Thinking*. New York: Macmillan, 1992. This book provides a brief introduction, easily under- standable by the undergraduate, to applied social science research. It presents the many ways in which social science research can be used to shape social policy and alleviate social problems.

PART I
Problems Affecting Social Institutions

American culture places substantial value on the sanctity of the individual and the importance of democratic decision making. In fact, we go to great lengths—much further than most nations—to protect the rights of people from being intruded upon by the government or other large organizations. In the legal realm, for example, our judicial system is based on the presumption that a person is innocent until proven guilty. It is the government's burden to prove that one is guilty rather than the individual's burden to establish innocence. So we release people on bail before trial on the grounds that the government has no authority to incarcerate people until after guilt has been established. We also have a court system that makes it possible for individuals— even those with few economic or other resources—to take on large corporations or the government in the courts. For example, lawyers take some cases on a "contingency fee" basis, which means that they receive payment only if their client wins the case. This means that anyone, even poor people, can hire a lawyer with no financial risk to themselves. With such a system, powerless individuals frequently fight—and win— battles against corporations with enormous economic clout.

All too often, however, these cultural ideals are threatened by the extreme concentration of power in the hands of a few people in the political and

Myths and Facts About Business and Government

Myth: The American economy represents a pure form of capitalism.

Fact: There are no pure forms of capitalism in the world today. Even in America, the government is involved in controlling and regulating the economy in many different ways.

Myth: The people who hold stock in a corporation own the corporation and can control the policies of the corporation.

Fact: In reality, a corporate board of directors and the professional managers they hire run the daily affairs of the corporation. The vast majority of the stockholders own such a small share of the company that they have neither the time, the expertise, nor the inclination to pay much attention to how the corporation is run. In addition, stockholder meetings are held very infrequently, and thus stockholders have few opportunities for input.

Myth: Finally, in the 1980s, the growth in the size of government was halted.

Fact: The federal budget continues to grow larger each year and to constitute close to one-quarter of our gross national product. However, the number of full-time government employees has actually been dropping since 1970.

Myth: America's corporate economy works toward the common good.

Fact: The primary motivation of corporations is to turn a profit and to ensure corporate growth. For example, during the early 1970s, it was determined that the gas tanks of Ford Motor Corporation's popular Pinto automobile could rupture upon rear-end collision, causing serious injury to passengers. Ford performed an analysis of the costs of potential legal suits versus the expense of installing an eleven-dollar puncture-proof gas tank on every Pinto in America. Even though Ford owned the patent on a very safe gas tank, it elected not to exercise this alternative because it would have been more costly than paying the price of various lawsuits surrounding personal injuries.

Myth: Corporations, especially those with defense contracts, generally support increases in spending for defense because such increases enhance their profits.

Fact: Although this is often true, corporations also oppose increases in defense spending when they believe such spending will have a detrimental impact on the overall economy through such things as rising inflation or interest rates. Such opposition was found during both the Korean War and the Vietnam War.

Myth: The American economy has become uncompetitive in world markets because so many workers in the United States are members of powerful unions that force employers to pay unjustifiably high wages.

Fact: At the unions' peak in the 1950s, only one of every four American workers was a member of a union, and that number has dwindled to one out of six today. The other five workers have no organized body speaking for them and are on their own when demanding a living wage from their employers.

---

economic realms. The result is often an abuse of power that works to the detriment of many citizens. Consider the following episodes:

- The Watergate affair of the 1970s, which started when people paid by the Republican Committee to Re-elect the President broke into the headquarters of the Democratic National Committee to plant a listening device to gather information to help President Nixon defeat his Democratic rival. Investigations provoked by this scandalous abuse of power uncovered a myriad of illegal activities by people in the executive branch of government, including widespread illegal wiretapping, sabotage of the civil rights movement, interception of mail, perjury, extortion, and keeping security files on thousands of Americans whose only crime was dissent against some government policies. In the end, the Watergate scandal led to the resignation of Richard Nixon from the presidency (Kutler, 1990).

- The savings and loan fiasco of the 1980s, the most expensive financial debacle in American history, in which hundreds of savings and loan banks across the country had to be bailed out by the government in a program that will eventually cost the American public as much as $500 billion. Contributing to this debacle was the deregulation of the Reagan years, which enabled speculators and corrupt business people to engage in highly questionable business practices and investments that put their depositors' funds at great risk. The result was to gut once-sound savings and loans while regulatory agencies looked the other way. Also playing a part was a Congress that was willing to ignore all this because senators and representatives were getting hefty political contributions from the very people who were plundering the institutions (Lowy, 1991a).

- The defense fraud scandal of the late 1980s, in which corporations engaged in bribery and theft to get lucrative defense contracts from the government. In 1988, major corporations, such as Emerson Electric and Teledyne Electronics, were indicted for bribing consultants in exchange for information about U.S. defense contracts. By 1991, forty-one corporate and government officials, along with five corporations, had pled guilty to charges that included bribery and theft of information. Among these, the highest ranking government official was an assistant secretary of the navy who was accused of taking bribes from such major American corporations as Pratt & Whitney (owned by United Technologies Corporation) and Martin Marietta (Lewis, 1991). Such practices by corporations are not uncommon. One analysis of regulatory agency records found that two out of three of the largest five hundred industrial corporations in the United States had been involved in at least one illegal incident between 1975 and 1984 (Etzioni, 1985).

There is substantial concern that such abuses of power may threaten national goals. They may, for example, foster a cynicism in the average citizen that may reduce support for our political and economic institutions. To understand this problem, we need to know something about how our political and economic institutions work. **Politics** refers to *the agreements in society over who has the right to exercise control over others, who can establish laws to regulate social life, and how conflicting interests in society will be resolved*. By establishing laws and exercising control, political institutions, in effect, determine whose values will predominate and how rewards and resources will be allocated in society. **Economics** refers to *the processes through which goods and services are produced and distributed*. Although politics and economics are distinct institutions, they are closely intertwined. Both focus on a central issue in society: the exercise of power in the allocation of scarce resources. In fact, a classic description of politics could be aptly applied to *both* political and economic institutions: They determine "who gets what, when, and how" (Lasswell, 1936).

The problem associated with these institutions is not the use of power—because this is precisely their purpose in society—but rather the abuse of power: the exercise of power in ways that work against the interests of substantial numbers of less powerful Americans and results in their exploitation. Abuse of power is often linked with the size and complexity of businesses and government, along with the concentration of power in the hands of a small number of people or organizations.

As we will see, political and economic concentration of power creates many problems. In addition, political and economic institutions are often closely linked with many of the other social problems discussed in this book. Levels of poverty, for example, are clearly linked to the workings of the economy and to political decisions about whether and how to attack unemployment. Some crime, as we will see, has its foundation in economic problems. Government and corporate policies regarding such things as day care and maternity leave influence the shape of the family. So the analysis of political and economic institutions in this chapter will serve as a helpful foundation to the remaining chapters in the book.

We begin our investigation of social problems associated with government and the economy by looking at the types of economic systems that exist in modern societies.

TYPES OF ECONOMIC SYSTEMS

To survive, every society must ensure that food, clothing, shelter, and other materials are produced and distributed to the members of society who need them. The rules and social practices governing this production and distribution make up the economic institution of a society. The economies of most nations today are *market economies,* which are based on the exchange of money for goods and services in the marketplace. People sell their labor for a certain amount of money and then the money is used to purchase goods and services. Although modern economies share this market foundation, they differ from one another in significant ways. We will look at three main types of modern economic systems: capitalism, socialism, and mixed economies.

Capitalism

Capitalism contains three features that, taken together, distinguish it from other economic systems: *The means of economic production and distribution are privately held; the profit motive is the primary force guiding people's economic behavior; and there is free competition among both producers and consumers of goods* (Gottlieb, 1988). The proponents of capitalism argue that these features provide for consumer control over the quantity, quality, and price of goods. In its pure form, capitalism works like this. Seeking profits is, in a sense, merely unleashing personal greed. But this is quite appropriate, argue proponents of capitalism, because this gives capitalists the motivation to provide more and better goods and services. If there is a demand for some product, someone will come along and provide it if they can profit from doing so. Furthermore, the profit motive encourages innovation and creativity because there will be entrepreneurs looking for novel goods and services—some that the consumer has not even thought of—that they can sell for a profit. Capitalists must be constantly on the lookout for new products lest someone else beat them to the punch and corner a market. Thus, from this profit-seeking motive, consumers benefit from having more and better goods available. Open competition among capitalists also benefits consumers by enabling them to choose among a number of items, comparing price against quality. If the quality of products is too low or the price too high, people will not buy them and the capitalists will be out of business unless they change. Adam Smith referred to the conjunction of profit seeking with competition as the "invisible hand" of market forces that would ensure that the supply of goods is roughly equivalent to the demand for them and that the public has available the goods that it wants with the highest quality possible.

The role of government in this process, argue those who favor pure capitalism, should be to stand aside and let market forces operate unhindered. The government is necessary to maintain public order and protect against foreign threats, but any effort by the government to regulate the market is regarded as disastrous. Government regulation of prices or wages, for example, would interfere with both the profit motive and the competitive element and thus reduce the incentive to develop new and better products. In short, government policy under capitalism should be one of laissez-faire: The government should leave the market alone.

There are no pure forms of capitalism in the world today. Even in America, the government has always been involved to a degree in controlling and regulating the economy. Despite this, the American economy is still one of the most capitalistic in the world. There is strong resistance to government interference in the economy and little support for government ownership of utilities, railroads, or other industries that are often government owned in other capitalist societies.

Socialism

Socialism refers to *economies in which the means of production and distribution are collectively held so that the goods and services that people need are provided and equitably distributed.* In capitalism, production is based on economic demand: Goods and services are provided if people can afford to purchase them. With socialism, production is based on human need: Goods and services are produced because people need them, irrespective of whether they can afford them (Harrington, 1989; Le Grand and Estrin, 1989). Pure socialist economies reject the profit motive, recognizing that one person's profit is another's loss. In addition, socialists argue, the profit motive provides a built-in incentive for one person to exploit another, for example, by keeping wages low in order to increase profits. In other words, it is inherent in capitalism that one person is set in competition with another—either capitalist against capitalist or capitalist against consumer—and the inevitable outcome is a highly unjust and inequitable distribution of resources.

In socialist economies, the primary motivation for economic activity is to achieve collective goals, such as a higher standard of living for all citizens. To do this, the economy is highly centralized, with decisions about what to produce and how to distribute these products being made for the whole nation by national authorities. Because profit and consumer demands are not key elements in these decisions, the decisions can presumably be made with the collective interests of society as a whole in mind.

As with capitalism, pure socialism is rare. Most socialist economies do allow for the private ownership of some goods, such as personal or household items. In addition, some people are allowed to engage in capitalist activity. In China, for example, farmers are allowed to sell some of their produce in a competitive marketplace. China is also experimenting with programs in some industries in which consumer demand, rather than central authorities, determines how much is produced. In these programs, factory managers can, within limits, manipulate wages and other costs in order to break even or make a profit. Most means of economic production, however, are still collectively rather than privately owned.

At this point, a word needs to be said about *communism*, a term that is routinely misused by Americans. **Communism** is the term used by Karl Marx to describe the utopian end stage of the struggle over capitalism. In a communist society, *all goods would be communally owned; people would not work for wages but rather would give according to their abilities; and there would be no scarcity of goods and services, allowing people to receive whatever they needed. In addition, the state would become less important and its role would dwindle.* According to these criteria, there are no communist societies in the world today. Nations that are commonly referred to as communist by Americans are actually socialist.

Mixed Economies

The economies discussed thus far tend toward pure capitalism or pure socialism, although each includes some elements of the other. Another type of economy, found in England and much of Western Europe, is the **mixed economy,** *in which there are strong elements of both capitalism and socialism* (Brus and Laski, 1989). In mixed economies, most industry is privately owned and oriented toward profit making. In addition, despite considerable government regulation, there is a competitive market economy, and consumer demand determines much of what is produced. However, in mixed economies, many important industries, such as banks, railroads, the communications industry, the media, and hospitals, are state owned. Mixed economies provide for strong regulation of the private sector by the state. High taxes and an elaborate welfare system are established in hopes of achieving the national goal of a fair and equitable distribution of resources. Through such mechanisms, proponents of mixed economies hope to avoid the extensive social inequality that can accompany capitalism and the economic inefficiency that sometimes afflicts socialist economies.

Understanding these basic economic arrangements is important because the social policy debates relating to social problems often involve the question of which economic arrangements are most likely to achieve specified goals. We introduced this debate in Chapter 1, in which we discussed an interventionist approach as opposed to a more conservative, laissez-faire approach. Although we need to be careful about oversimplifying positions, many interventionists argue that we should learn from mixed economies about how government policy can help us achieve goals of fairness and equity. Laissez-faire advocates, on the other hand, argue that an approach closer to that of pure capitalism would lead to greater economic growth and affluence, which would help solve many of the problems that we face. As we will see, proposals for solving problems of corporate and government growth tend to follow one of these two approaches.

THE CONCENTRATION OF ECONOMIC AND POLITICAL POWER

The Corporate Economy

American capitalism has undergone considerable change in the past two centuries. Our economy once consisted of small, local businesses and many competitors. Consequently, power in the economic sector was decentralized, diffused, and limited to local or regional levels. It was almost impossible for businesses to accumulate substantial power at the national level. Today, our economy is very different: It is highly centralized and international in scope, and a small number of people can gain enormous control over wealth and power.

Furthermore, American capitalism is no longer based on the individual ownership of businesses. Rather, the dominant form of business today is the **corporation,** *a business enterprise that is owned by stockholders, most of whom are not involved in running the daily affairs of the business.* There are three key things that distinguish corporations from individually owned businesses. First, corporations have access to a much broader source of capital than do individuals because the former can sell stock to thousands of stockholders. Second, stockholders, who own the corporation, have only a limited liability should the corporation be sued or go bankrupt. Stockholders lose only the funds they have invested. Third, the ownership of corporations is separate from the control of its policies and daily affairs. The stockholders own a part of the corporation, but most stockholders are not involved in the actual running of the company. This is done by professional managers who are ultimately appointed by a board of directors that is elected by the stockholders. These managers typically own little or no stock in the company. Legally, the stockholders run the corporation, but for all practical purposes the board and the managers do. Most shareholders own only a small number of shares in the company, and they have neither the time, the expertise, nor the inclination to pay much attention to how the company is run. The board and the managers are in a position to make recommendations that most shareholders will accept with little thought. So the board and corporate managers control the corporation without being substantial owners of it. Unlike individually owned businesses, the ownership of corporations is easily transferable, and should a major stockholder die, the corporation continues to function as usual. Because of these characteristics, the corporate economic structure is extremely attractive to investors. Large amounts of capital can be accumulated with minimum risk to individuals.

Because of the advantages that stem from corporate organization, corporations now dominate our economy, with a relatively small number of corporations accounting for most business activity. There are over three million corporations in the United States, but most are small and have a minor impact on society. Less than 2 percent of these corporations had assets of more than $10 million. The largest two hundred corporations employ 80 percent of all people who work for corporations (U.S. Bureau of the Census, 1991). A few, however, are quite large and powerful. There are five thousand corporations in the United States, for example, with more than $250 million worth of assets. Out of all industrial corporations in 1983, the largest one hundred controlled almost half of all industrial assets such as land, buildings, and equipment in the United States (see Figure 2.1). As these large corporations have come to dominate our economy, it has become possible for some to control substantial segments of economic life to the point of restricting competition in the marketplace. One form of restrictive growth is called a *monopoly*—the control of a product or service by one company. For example, by 1990, Nintendo controlled about 80 percent of the $5 billion video-game market in the United States. Related to the monopoly is the *oligopoly*, in which a few corporations control a market. There are some sectors of the American economy that are highly oligopolistic, in some cases approach-

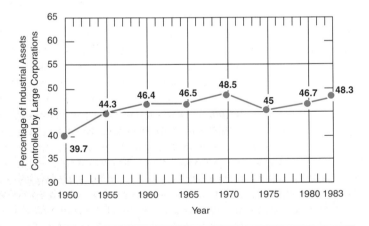

Figure 2.1   **Proportions of All Industrial Assets Controlled by the 100 Largest Manufacturing Corporations in the United States, 1950–1983**
SOURCES: U.S. Bureau of the Census, *Statistical Abstract of the United States, 1982–83* (Washington, D.C.: U.S. Government Printing Office, 1982), p. 535; U.S. Bureau of the Census, *Statistical Abstract of the United States, 1985* (Washington, D.C.: U.S. Government Printing Office, 1984), p. 522.

"MY PLAN IS THAT WE FORM A MERGER WITH AROUND 25 OF THE COUNTRY'S LARGEST CORPORATIONS, CREATE A JOINT EXECUTIVE COMMITTEE, AND TAKE OVER THE GOVERNMENT."

Courtesy Sidney Harris

ing a monopoly. In the cigarette industry, for example, the four largest corporations control close to 90 percent of production. In a recent court case, the American Telephone and Telegraph Company was forced to divest those companies that were providing local telephone service. The government has also filed suits recently against IBM for monopolizing the computer industry and against the four largest producers of breakfast cereals for monopolizing the breakfast food market.

Another form of corporate growth representing a concentration of economic power is the *conglomerate,* which is a corporation that controls other companies in fields quite different from that of the parent company. For example, in 1988 Gulf and Western, Inc., originally in the oil business, owned Paramount Pictures (maker of such hits as *Beverly Hills Cop II* and *Fatal Attraction*), Madison Square Garden, the New York Knicks basketball team, and 50 percent of the USA television network. In fact, some corporations, such as Transamerica, are in good part "holding companies" whose major purpose is to coordinate the activities and profits of all the corporations they own. Conglomerates are advantageous in that they provide stability through diversity: Losses in one industry can be counterbalanced by the parent company through profits made in an unrelated business.

As corporations have grown, the larger ones have extended their activities into a number of different countries. One consequence has been the growth in importance of *multinational corporations* as prominent forces in national and world economies. These are enormous economic enterprises with a large commitment of resources in international business that engage in manufacturing, production, and sales in a number of countries (Moran, 1985; Vernon-Wortzel and Wortzel, 1988). American corporations have gone multinational largely because this type of organization enhances profits because there are lucrative markets for their goods outside the United States. In addition, the cost of labor, land, and taxes is considerably lower in places such as Mexico, Taiwan, and Korea than in the United States. In 1988, 8 percent of all money spent by American corporations for plants and equipment was spent outside of the United States and this percentage has been growing steadily for a number of years (Uchitelle, 1989). This fact reflects the extent to which American corporations now participate in a "global economy," in which national boundaries have become less important as determinants of or restraints on economic competition. This means that American labor and capital must compete with labor and capital in many countries around the world.

Unionization

Although conglomerates and multinationals, along with capitalists and entrepreneurs, play important roles in creating and running large business concerns, they are far overshadowed in number by the masses of working people who staff these organizations. And workers have made significant efforts to concentrate economic power in their own hands. The rudiments of labor organizing can be traced to the colonial period, when impressment, or enforced labor, led to rioting among sailors and longshoremen. It was not until the late nineteenth century, however, and the emergence of business firms employing thousands of workers, that the labor movement emerged as a significant political force in the American economy. Capitalists, pursuing the profit motive, were inclined to pay workers as little as possible. The capitalists' ability to do this was made easier because large numbers of people had immigrated to America in the late 1800s, and this created a labor surplus in some industries. In response, working people organized to pursue their own interests. Capitalists staunchly opposed the labor movement, believing that higher wages would generate laziness among workers and threaten the "American way of life." The owners' resistance and the workers' determination made American labor history one of the bloodiest and most violent of any industrial nation. In Lattimer, Pennsylvania, in 1897, for example, thirteen striking coal miners were shot to death and another thirty-nine were wounded by a sheriff's posse who stopped their march. In 1913, seventy-four people, including eleven children and two women, were killed in a clash between National Guard troops and strikers in Colorado (Novak, 1978; Taft and Ross, 1969). There were hundreds of other such incidents. However, the workers eventually prevailed, and by the 1930s legislation gave them the right to organize and to bargain collectively with employers.

The number of American workers belonging to labor unions continued to grow, reaching over twenty-two million people in the 1970s. With the right to strike firmly established for most workers, unions have been in a strong position to gain even higher wages and larger fringe benefit packages for their members. Just as businesses formed conglomerates and oligopolies, labor unions from many industries have combined their forces. The American Federation of Labor and Congress of Industrial Organizations (AFL-CIO) is over fourteen million strong, for example, and almost two thirds of all American labor unions are affiliated with it. This enables unions to pool resources and information and to provide mutual support through the refusal of members of one union to cross the picket lines of another. In recent decades, public employees such as teachers and fire fighters have proved to be a significant source of recruitment to the ranks of unionization. This has occurred despite the fact that it is illegal in many states for public employees to strike. In fact, some teachers have been fired for joining illegal strikes.

Although unions have gained considerable power in American society, their future is somewhat uncertain. Union membership as a proportion of the work force has been declining since the mid-1950s and is presently at its lowest point since 1940 (see Figure 2.2). The number of people belonging to unions has declined to less than seventeen million. The primary reason for this is that occupations traditionally unionized—blue-collar industrial jobs—have been declining in numbers, whereas the number of white-collar employees, who have traditionally not unionized, is growing. In fact, America has sometimes been called a "postindustrial" society because a shrinking proportion of our work force labors in industrial occupations. Because of technology, automation, and robotization, fewer workers are needed to make the products necessary for our life-style (see Chapter 15). The largest growth in the work force has been in white-collar jobs such as sales, management, teaching, or clerical work (see Figure 2.3). A second reason for the decline in unions is that many corporations over the past four decades have relocated in states having weak union organizations. Third, unions have been facing increased hostility from the American public, especially when they demand sizable pay increases in times of high unemployment. In 1981, for example, air traffic controllers demanded what the Reagan administration considered an excessive wage hike; the controllers went on strike to push their demands, even though this action was illegal. Rather than concede, President Reagan fired the controllers for striking. There was considerable public support for his decision, even among many union members. This reflects a growing concern that unions have concentrated so much

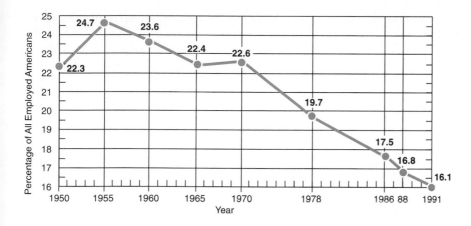

Figure 2.2 **Union Membership Among Americans as a Percentage of Total Americans Employed, 1950–1991**
SOURCES: U.S. Bureau of the Census, *Statistical Abstract of the United States, 1989* (Washington, D.C.: U.S. Government Printing Office, 1989), p. 416; U.S. Department of Labor, *Employment and Earnings,* Bureau of Labor Statistics, Vol. 36, No. 1, January 1989, p. 225; Vol. 39, No. 1, January 1992, p. 228.

power in their organizations that they can raise wages, and therefore prices, to levels having little relationship to actual worker productivity. Other episodes during the 1980s, such as the machinists' strike against Eastern Airlines in 1989, provided further evidence that the public climate in the United States had become less favorable for labor unions. Possibly in response to this, labor unions

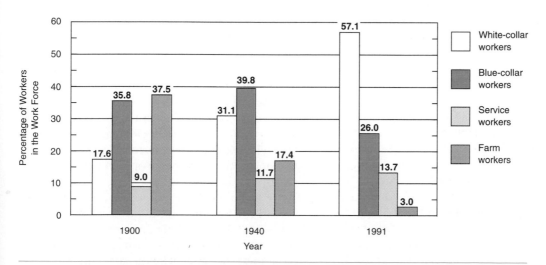

Figure 2.3 **Changing Occupational Structure in America, 1900–1991**
SOURCES: U.S. Bureau of the Census, *Historical Statistics of the United States, Colonial Times to 1970, Bicentennial Edition, Part 2* (Washington, D.C.: U.S. Government Printing Office, 1970), p. 139; U.S. Department of Labor, Bureau of Labor Statistics, *Employment and Earnings,* Vol. 39, No. 1, January 1992, p. 184.

have been noticeably less inclined to use the strike in their struggle with corporations than they were in earlier decades (see Figure 2.4).

Big Government

America's founding fathers intended for the federal government to be small and not extremely powerful. After all, the American Revolution was fueled by hatred for British tyranny over the American colonies. After winning independence, the revolutionaries wanted to avoid a domineering federal government. So the role of the central government under the new Constitution was to be limited: to raise an army, to establish a national currency, and to provide an environment in which states and individuals could pursue the common good. And the U.S. government did remain rather small throughout the nineteenth century.

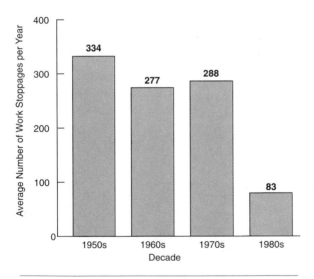

Figure 2.4   **Average Number of Work Stoppages per Year Involving 1,000 or More People, 1950s–1980s**
SOURCE: U.S. Bureau of the Census, *Statistical Abstract of the United States, 1989* (Washington, D.C.: U.S. Government Printing Office, 1989), p. 413; U.S. Bureau of the Census, *Statistical Abstract of the United States, 1991* (Washington, D.C.: U.S. Government Printing Office, 1991), p. 423.

The twentieth century, however, has been witness to a massive growth of government in the United States and other industrial nations. Since 1950, the expenditures for all levels of government—federal, state, and local—in the United States have exploded from $70 billion to over $2.2 trillion (U.S. Bureau of the Census, 1992: 279). This reflects a twentyfold increase during a period when our population did not even double in size. These expenditures have increased from $460 per person in 1950 to $7,000 today. Sixty-three percent of these expenditures involve the federal government. The federal budget has grown from 10 percent of the gross national product just prior to World War II to 25 percent today (see Figure 2.5). However, despite what many people believe, the number of people employed by the government has remained about the same since 1970 (U.S. Bureau of the Census, 1992: 330).

Several factors explain this growth in government. A major one is that industrial societies for centuries have been shifting responsibility for regulating social and economic policy to the central government. This shift has occurred because nations have grown so complex and interdependent that some central authority becomes increasingly necessary to regulate economic and social life. In the realm of social policy, for example, the government is now seen as having final responsibility for the sick, the poor, and others who are unable to take care of themselves and do not have families or other support networks to help them. Such assistance is considered essential for people to be productive members of society and have a good life-style. Most modern societies regard it as inhumane to merely leave people to fend for themselves.

Responsibility for economic policy has also been shifted to the central government, and this has become a larger and more complex task as our corporate economy has grown. The freewheeling economic environment of the last century worked reasonably well until business empires became so large that they could monopolize large parts of the economy. Then government had to step in to

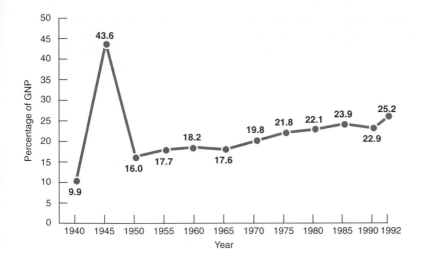

Figure 2.5 **Federal Expenditures as a Percentage of the Gross National Product, 1940–1992**
SOURCE: U.S. Bureau of the Census, *Statistical Abstract of the United States, 1992* (Washington, D.C.: U.S. Government Printing Office, 1992), p. 315.

regulate industry with the interests of the whole society in mind. Also, as technology produced increasingly complex and sometimes dangerous products, it grew beyond the ability of the average citizen to evaluate these products, and the government stepped in to offer control and regulation. Today the government shapes social and economic policy through its fiscal policy (taxation), its monetary policy (control over the money supply), and its regulatory agencies (the Environmental Protection Agency, the Federal Aviation Administration, and so on).

A second reason for the growth of government in the United States has been the emergence of the philosophy that social ills can be cured through aggressive spending policies and elaborate government-sponsored programs. This view came to dominate American politics with Franklin D. Roosevelt's New Deal during the Great Depression of the 1930s. In an effort to combat the Depression, Roosevelt used government spending policies extensively to spread money and ex-

pand the federal government into many new areas. Out of the New Deal emerged such diverse programs as Social Security, the Tennessee Valley Authority, and the Civilian Conservation Corps. Massive government spending during World War II continued this infusion of government funds into the economy. This monumental military endeavor called for highly centralized decision making and control over resources, and this further enhanced the size and impact of the federal bureaucracy. As can be seen in Figure 2.5, government expenditures increased dramatically during World War II and have never dropped to prewar levels.

A final reason why government has grown is that people demand many more services from it today than in the past. People rail against the costs of welfare, but they want the government to maintain the national park system, build monuments to Vietnam veterans, and keep our public libraries open and current. Few would want the government to stop providing insurance for individuals' deposits in banks and savings and loan institutions, and pleasure boaters whose engines die ten miles from shore are unlikely to rant about excess government expenses when a Coast Guard vessel rescues them. Americans have come to expect the government to provide many services that are not provided by private industry, and this has been a major pressure toward the growth of big government.

PERSPECTIVES ON THE CONCENTRATION OF POWER

The recent historical trend, then, has been toward the concentration of power in the hands of large political and economic organizations. Is this inevitable? Is it necessarily bad? In this section, we will analyze these issues using the sociological perspectives, and in the next section we will review some of the specific problems that this creates in the United States.

The Functionalist Perspective

According to the functionalist perspective, societies are made up of interrelated and interdependent parts, including economic and political institutions and practices as well as cultural values. These various parts should be sufficiently integrated that people can use them to work together toward common goals. As we have seen, American cultural values place emphasis on the sanctity of individuals and their right to control their destiny, the importance of democratic decision making, and the value of free enterprise and private property. Yet mammoth corporations and big government threaten these values. When corporate managers in New York make a decision to close a factory and throw thousands of people out of work in Pennsylvania, what should these displaced workers make of the value of individual autonomy and control? What control do they have over their fate? If economic power is concentrated

in the hands of a few monopolies or oligopolies, then is free enterprise and competition able to provide the most benefit for the greatest number of people? For functionalists, one of the key elements in the problem of the concentration of power is the inconsistency between cultural values and political and economic reality.

Some inconsistency between values and reality is an expected part of the social disorganization that results from rapid social change. There are good reasons why economic and political organizations have become so large: Large size is functional in order to provide large numbers of complicated goods and services to many people. For example, producing and distributing the vast array of goods that are a part of our life-style would be impossible without organizing ourselves into large nationwide business enterprises. The disorganization results because this bigness can develop in ways that conflict with cherished cultural values and threaten common goals. For functionalists, further change is needed whereby some adaptation and accommodation is made. Cultural values may have to change to recognize the reality and centrality of these mammoth structures in our lives. At the same time, new methods of exercising social control over corporations and government may need to develop to counterbalance their concentration of power.

The Conflict Perspective

From the conflict perspective, there is no necessary harmony among corporations, the government, and the various groups of citizens in society. Rather, society is made up of a variety of different interest groups who come into conflict with one another over the resources available in society. This conflict of interests is an inherent feature of American economic and political life. The accumulation of power in the hands of a few is the outcome of the struggle for advantage in society. Large corporations and big government become the mechanisms in modern society through which powerful groups maintain their control over resources. From the conflict perspective, a conflict of interests and maldistribution of resources reflect a normal state of affairs.

Concentration of power is not by itself a social problem. It becomes a social problem, from the conflict perspective, when some influential group of people believes that it is not receiving its fair share of resources and strives to do something about it. These groups sometimes combine their forces and form social movements to improve their lot. Through collective action, they can sometimes redress their grievances. Yet this does not mean that inequalities in power can be, or ever will be, eliminated. From the conflict perspective, collective action leads to a rearrangement of inequalities, not to their elimination. Furthermore, powerful economic interests are most often at a substantial advantage in this struggle. Economic advantage is routinely translated into political advantage, and control of the government can lead to the passage and enforcement of laws that benefit the powerful. The government becomes, in effect, a tool used by the powerful to protect their position.

The Iron Law of Oligarchy

Is the concentration of power inevitable? Although it may not be, there are factors that are very favorable toward its development in organizations. In 1915, Robert Michels used the term **oligarchy** to refer to *the concentration of power in the hands of a few people at the top of an organization*. From his study of political and economic organizations, he concluded that the pressures toward oligarchy were so strong that he coined the phrase "the iron law of oligarchy." Michels described the likelihood of this occurring very succinctly: "Who says organization, says oligarchy" (Michels, 1966, originally published 1915: 256). For Michels, the tendency toward oligarchy arises when groups reach a size where consensus-oriented decision making is no longer feasible, and it derives from the very nature of organizations. First, to operate effectively, any organization must develop mechanisms for coping with administrative and decision-making problems, and it is more efficient if only a few people are responsible. Spreading authority among a large number of people can create conflicting decisions and uncertainty over who has authority to do what. Second, those who emerge as leaders in organizations tend to be adept at influencing and controlling members, and they can utilize the resources of the organization to maintain their position. They can, for example, place loyal followers into strategic positions in the organizational administration. Finally, most rank-and-file members of organizations are apathetic: They do not have the time, energy, resources, or desire to contest the power of the leadership. This often leaves those at the top of organizations with considerable freedom and power to run the bureaucracy as they wish.

Given these oligarchical tendencies, it is hardly surprising that the concentration of power is a problem in our political and economic institutions. One of the major challenges we face is how to organize our political and economic life so that institutions and organizations become more responsive to a wider range of citizens.

Is There a Power Elite in America?

Researchers of both functionalist and conflict persuasions have conducted research over the past four decades to try to assess exactly how concentrated power and decision making actually are in the United States. Out of these efforts, two major models of power in America have been developed: the power elite model and the pluralist model.

The Power Elite Model. In the 1950s, sociologist C. Wright Mills (1956) proposed what has come to be called the **power elite model** to explain the exercise of power in America. Deriving his approach from the conflict perspective, Mills argued that *there exists a small group of very powerful people who make just about all of the important decisions in the United States*. This power elite consists of the people who hold top positions in the government, business, and the military. Included in this group are the president and his cabinet, the executives who run the large corporations, and the generals and admirals who run the Pentagon. According to the power elite model, the government, corporations, and the military dominate our lives today, and it is from these spheres that power is derived.

According to Mills, the power elite is a cohesive group, and the interests of its various members in the government, military, and corporate sectors tend to coincide. There are elaborate social networks that link the members of the elite to one another. For example, they attend a small number of private schools and universities, vacation in the same spots, and go to the same parties. All of this social contact helps them to maintain a consensus about what is in their interests and to develop strategies for ensuring their success. Below the elite, there is a middle level of diverse interest groups in America including most members of Congress, professional organizations, many lobbyists, and most unions. They participate in making decisions about issues of secondary importance that have little effect on the elite. At the bottom of America's political structure is the great mass of citizens who have virtually no power because they do not belong to those organizations wielding power. These people may vote, but Mills viewed this privilege as meaningless because most elected officials are in middle-level positions, while real decision-making power rests with the elite. In addition, the power elite is highly influential in determining which candidates the political parties will place before the electorate. One source of such influence is the mass media. The Applied Research insert (see pp. 52–53) analyzes how the media, especially newspapers, can help support the powerful in society.

The Pluralist Model.   Some sociologists argue that Mills's view of American society is distorted and overly conspiratorial because there is actually little concentration of power and coincidence of interests among the elite (Kornhauser, 1966; Rose, 1967). Instead, the **pluralist model** views power as *pluralistic,* or *spread over a large number of groups with divergent values, interests, and goals.* According to sociologist David Riesman (1961), there are veto groups in society with the ability to block decisions that might adversely affect their positions. For example, labor unions can exert considerable influence on issues affecting their members, such as raising unemployment benefits or minimum-wage laws. Similarly, farmers may fight to stop the lowering of price supports for farm products. To be sure, pluralists recognize that some groups have far more power and other resources than other groups, and there is considerable inequity in society. However, they argue that there is no single, cohesive, dominant elite, and power is not centralized in the hands of a few.

Below the elite, according to the pluralists, is the unorganized, but not entirely powerless, public. With the vote, the public can exercise some constraint over the behavior of those in power. In addition, there are other ways for the public to exert influence on more powerful groups. Cesar Chavez, for example, harnessed this power in the 1960s in his attempt to improve the plight of migrant farm workers. He organized a consumer boycott of the lettuce and grapes grown by those farm owners who refused to negotiate with farm workers. This boycott was effective, and the sales of lettuce and grapes dwindled. In part because of this, the farmers ultimately negotiated. The environmental movement has also used its ability to organize large numbers of people for public protest as a tool in struggling against corporate power. Especially in the areas of air and pesticide pollution, these groups have organized seemingly powerless people to successfully shape public policy (Hoberg, 1992). Given these examples, pluralists dispute the power elite view and argue that the mass of the citizenry can effectively exert an influence, even against what seem to be formidable corporate foes.

Assessment of the Models. What are we to conclude regarding who rules America? Clearly, the realities of holding power in our society are more complex than either the power elite or the pluralist models alone suggest. We can summarize some research that points to this conclusion. For example, political scientist Thomas R. Dye (1990) reviewed the corporate and governmental sectors in the United States and located approximately seven thousand positions in corporations, the government, and the military that direct most of the nation's economic and social policy. According to Dye, it is this very small group of Americans who represent Mills's power elite. Sociologist G. William Domhoff (1967, 1983) went a step further by studying the social backgrounds of the people who occupy these elite positions. He discovered that members of the upper class participate in an elaborate network of informal social contacts, just as Mills suggested. However, Domhoff did not find the cohesiveness or coincidence of interests among these people that Mills implied. Nevertheless, there are significant linkages and influence peddling among the various sectors of the power elite. Members of the corporate elite, for example, make sizable contributions to both the Republican and Democratic parties in hopes of influencing the decisions of the president, congressional representatives, and other politicians. The Bush administration, for example, had what it called "Team 100," which consisted of people who had donated at least $100,000 to help get Bush elected (Cannon, 1992). Although no explicit favors were offered these people for their donations, they in fact received many favors, job appointments, and policy decisions favorable to their corporate interests. One thing they all gained was easier access to the ear of those in the elite who make key decisions. Most Americans, who can afford to contribute at best only small amounts to either party, lack this access and its attendant influence. In fact, some would argue that, because of political contributions, corporate lobbying, and other forms of influence, the corporate elite exercises overwhelming control over politicians, government regulatory agencies, and government bureaucrats who are supposed to be controlling the corporations and protecting the rights and interests of average Americans. In this view, the average citizen has little influence and is largely at the mercy of corporate goals (Greider, 1992).

Research on the power elite has also focused on links between business and the military. In his final speech before leaving office in 1961, former President Dwight D. Eisenhower, himself a five-star general during World War II, spoke of the **military–industrial complex,** referring to *the relationship between the military that wants to purchase weapons and the corporations that produce the weapons.* Both the military and the corporations benefit from a large military budget and from policies favoring military solutions to international problems. The potential danger of a powerful military–industrial complex is that defense decisions and the development of weapons systems may be influenced by what is beneficial to the military and defense industries rather than by what is necessary for national security. One way in which the coincidence of interests among members of the military–industrial complex might occur is if there were a periodic interchange of top-level personnel between the military and defense industries. And, as Mills and others have shown, such interchanges do tend to occur. During a three-year period in the 1970s, for example, more than two thousand high-ranking defense department officials left their government jobs and accepted positions with corporate defense contractors (Edwards, 1977). A more recent study by the government found that six thousand of the thirty thousand people with the rank of army major or higher who left the Pentagon in 1983 and 1984 worked for companies doing business with the Pentagon. Many worked on the same military projects in private industry that they had worked on at the Pentagon (Cushman, 1986). This problem came before the public eye in a very dramatic way in

APPLIED RESEARCH

The Media and the Power Elite

That the media is powerful in American society is no secret. The press, in fact, is intended to be powerful and to serve a free society as an alternative source of power to the government and large corporations. Journalism showed its strength when key media sources pursued the Watergate scandal of the 1970s to its finale in the resignation of a U.S. president. In addition, the press and television routinely expose various acts of corruption, often motivating different levels of government to prosecute the offenders. Yet the media are themselves private companies and usually corporate in structure. They pursue greater profits and larger amounts of power in the same fashion as other corporations discussed in this chapter. And as has occurred in other corporate sectors, there has been concentration of power among the media:

> Sooner or later a handful of corporations [will] control most of what the average American reads, sees, and hears . . . the same few corporations will control all the important mass media not just in the United States but globally. Nevertheless, there is close to total silence in the mainstream news on the social consequences of this concentration. It is a silence that extends to the news and commentary in major newspapers, magazines, and broadcast news operations. The public learns only of the stock market transactions, the building of dazzling empires, and the personalities of the corporate leaders. (Bagdikian, 1990: x)

Historically, all American newspapers were once local affairs—small businesses whose main concerns focused on the town or county in which their readers lived. To be sure, newspaper owners, executives, and editors were often heavily involved in local issues, such as who was elected mayor or which new employers moved to town, but their influence only rarely extended beyond the local region.

Today, the press is big—and concentrated—business. Sociologist Peter Dreier (1982) found that the twenty-five largest newspaper companies accounted for 53 percent of the daily newspapers sold in the United Sates. In fact, many newspapers have achieved legal monopolies as cities both small and large have become "one-newspaper towns." In addition, the parent corporations of newspapers are often members of the power elite, with influence that stretches far beyond the local level. The newspaper companies are linked to other corporate members of the power elite through the membership of newspaper executives on the boards of business corporations, banks, and financial institutions. The Dow Jones Company, for example, which publishes the *Wall Street Journal,* had twenty-four such linkages with the thirteen hundred largest corporations listed by *Fortune* magazine; the Times Mirror Company, publisher of the *Los Angeles Times,* also had twenty-four such linkages. Newspaper executives are also involved in the "revolving door" through which members of the economic elite serve for a time in high-level government positions and then return to their corporate jobs. At the time of Dreier's research, thirty-six executives from the twenty-four largest newspaper companies had been or were then serving in one of these government positions.

So, especially if you live in an urban area, some of the men and women who own and operate your daily newspaper are, in all likelihood, members of the power elite. What is the impact of this on the role of the media in the analysis of social problems? The simple conclusion is that most newspapers become mere apologists for the power elite and corporate capitalism. Dreier found, however, that the impact was much more subtle. As newspaper companies become larger, form monopolies, and establish links with the power elite, Dreier found, they often develop a viewpoint that has been labeled "corporate liberalism," which tends to look positively on unions, social welfare programs, and government regulation. However, it is not a socialist position, as discussed in this chapter, because corporate liberalism retains the belief that a corporate economy based on private enterprise is the most efficient economic system. In this view, government programs and regulations are intended to protect people against the few weaknesses or excesses that can be found in capitalism. This corporate liberal ideology can be found most clearly expressed in the four newspapers that are most closely linked with the national power elite: the *Wall Street Journal*, the *Los Angeles Times*, the *New York Times,* and the *Washington Post.*

On the surface, these newspapers might seem to be among the strongest critics of big government and corporate capitalism. It was the *Washington Post,* after all, that pursued the Watergate affair tenaciously. Yet sociologist Herbert Gans (1979) argues that such newspaper practices are pursued not because they oppose capitalism, but because they favor responsible capitalism. In fact, the latent function of such criticism is to protect capitalism from challenges that might destabilize it in the long term. Government regulation, support of unions, and civil rights and welfare legislation in effect keep the mass of people content with existing political and economic arrangements, and this acquiescence protects the interests of the capitalist class. The newspaper directors who serve as executives of other corporations help to reinforce the corporate liberal ideology that is shared by the newspapers and the corporations.

Much has occurred since Peter Dreier published the results of his research in 1982. By 1990, over 70 percent of the daily newspapers in the United States were owned by outside corporations and fourteen of these corporations had most of the business. In the same year, three American corporations controlled practically all the publishing activities of the country's eleven thousand magazines. By the 1990s, despite the existence of over twenty-five thousand media outlets in the United States, a mere *"twenty-three corporations* control most of the business in daily newspapers, magazines, television, books, and motion pictures" (Bagdikian, 1990: 4—italics by the authors).

Christopher Shaw, an investment banker and chairman of Henry Ansbacher, Inc., likes to quote one of his clients, who has predicted that by the year 2000, all of the media in the United States will be in the hands of a half dozen conglomerates. In 1984, the now-deceased British publishing magnate Robert Maxwell went on record with this statement: "In ten years' time, there will be only ten global corporations of communication" (quoted in Bagdikian, 1990: 5–6). Communications industry moguls insist that such concentration will *improve* the media. Despite these claims, applied social researchers like Peter Dreier and Ben Bagdikian agree in their concern that concentrated power over public information is inherently antidemocratic:

> When the central interests of the controlling corporations are at stake, mainstream American news becomes heavily weighted by whatever serves the economic and political interests of the corporations that own the media. The voice of the giants become ever more loud and drown out with greater success the small media voices of dissent. Now that media owners are so large that they are part of the highest levels of the world economy, the news and other public information become heavily weighted in favor of all corporate values. (Bagdikian, 1990: x–xi)

The additionally disturbing aspect of such a trend is that, as the dissenting voices are silenced, people become less and less aware that they are being presented a distorted view because they have fewer guideposts with which to measure the accuracy or completeness of what they see, read, and hear.

1989 when President Bush recommended John Tower for Secretary of Defense. As a senator for many years, Tower had helped shape defense policy. After leaving the Senate, he served as a consultant for a number of corporations prominent in the defense industry, using his knowledge of government and public policy and his contacts in the government to assist the corporations in acquiring defense contracts. Had his appointment as Defense Secretary been approved, he would once again have been making defense policy decisions that could potentially benefit the corporations from whom he had been earning handsome consulting fees. One reason that many opposed his appointment was the belief that his personal ties to those corporations might influence his decisions as Defense Secretary. When corporations hire former government officials, they hope that their contacts and knowledge of government and the policy process will work to the benefit of the corporation.

Although there clearly are important links between the military and corporations suggesting a "military–industrial complex," the picture is considerably more complex than this. Many corporations actually oppose increases in defense spending, fearing that these will adversely affect the economy and result in higher taxes. One study, for example, found active opposition to increases in defense spending between 1948 and 1953—a period including the Korean War—among executives of some of the largest business, industrial, and financial corporations in the country, even among some firms with defense contracts (Lo, 1982). So the military–industrial complex, although important, does not exist in a vacuum. There are other powerful groups, even among the power elite, with competing interests, and there are less powerful groups that still wield considerable power, especially on domestic issues.

As the power elite model suggests, then, a relatively small group of people in America hold enormous power. They control much of foreign policy and make decisions that shape the direction of our economic development. This ruling group, although possibly not conspiratorial or completely cohesive, ranks far above most other Americans in political, economic, and social clout. Yet as the pluralist position suggests, many groups that are not a part of this elite can occasionally wield power, especially on domestic social policy and local and regional issues. This is the realm in which many of the battles over solutions to social problems discussed in this book are likely to be fought. And most Americans have an opportunity to play a part in these less powerful, but still quite important, groups.

PROBLEMS CREATED BY THE CONCENTRATION OF POWER

We have described the concentration of economic and political power in the United States and the establishment of a power elite. In what ways do these developments create problems for Americans?

Effects on Competition

One of the major problems is that corporate growth can restrict competition, which we have seen is one of the core characteristics of capitalist economies. When economic power becomes concentrated in an oligopolistic or monopolistic fashion, the individual consumer can become a relatively powerless force in the marketplace in comparison to the corporations. As we have seen, in an economy based on competition, companies that are inefficient or produce inferior merchandise are likely to be driven out of business because consumers will purchase the less expensive and higher quality products of more efficient competitors. In this kind of economy, consumers have a degree of control over businesses through their discretionary buying behavior in the marketplace. In a less competitive environment, however, the consumer is at a substantial disadvantage because corporations are able to manipulate prices, quality, and product availability in ways that benefit them and without the controlling force of competition. As these processes continue, power and wealth continue to be concentrated in the hands of a small number of gigantic business enterprises. The larger corporations can offer poorer quality merchandise to enhance their profit structure, and consumers suffer.

The growth of conglomerates can also lead to a dwindling of the competitive marketplace. For example, a particular corporation could lower the prices on videocassette recorders until they sold at well below production costs. The losses incurred could be absorbed by the profits earned in different sectors of the conglomerate. Smaller competitors in the VCR business, without the support of a conglomerate, would be unable to sell their units at less than production price. Once the competition from these less powerful companies is reduced, the corporation in control would be free to raise its prices on VCRs, and therefore profits would be not only restored but also increased because of less competition.

In the long run, this lack of competition could smother the American economy because it would mean less innovation and little technological development. Advances occur, according to the capitalist argument, because one fears being bested by one's competitor. Without competition, there is little motivation for innovation, reducing our ability to compete with foreign companies. So excessive concentration of economic power might make the American economy less competitive in world markets.

Conflict Between Societal and Corporate Goals

The concentration of economic power in corporate structures also raises the issue of whether corporations pursue goals that are broadly beneficial to society or that enhance the narrow interests of particular groups. Large corporations control such vast resources that their activities shape in very substantial ways the lives of average Ameri-

cans. With the primary goal of corporations being to make and increase profits and to ensure corporate growth, corporations may not necessarily act in the best interests of other groups or society as a whole. For example, when a corporation decides to relocate outside of a central city area to reduce its taxes, the city loses jobs and tax revenue; these losses can bring about increases in unemployment and poverty in the city. Economic decisions based solely on the criterion of corporate profit may create social problems that have negative effects on other groups in society. This issue has become especially poignant in the last few decades with the policies of some multinational corporations. In fact, a major element of the recession in the early 1980s and the weak economy of the early 1990s was the flight of American jobs overseas. This illustrates one of the major problems created by multinational corporations: Because their primary allegiance is maximizing profits, their actions can run counter to national political and economic goals. They can contribute to such problems as unemployment and poverty in the United States while pursuing policies that enhance their corporate profits. For example, the president of NCR Corporation, when asked about the competitiveness of the United States, responded "I don't think about it at all. We at NCR think of ourselves as a globally competitive company that happens to be headquartered in the United States" (quoted in Uchitelle, 1989: 13). The chairman of President Reagan's Council of Economic Advisors, reacting to comments such as these, saw a "growing tension between the global nature of American business and the goals of the territorial United States" (quoted in Uchitelle, 1989: 13). However, others argue that at least some of this drain of U.S. productive dollars is offset by foreign corporations that pump money into their American operations, which creates jobs in the United States.

Multinationals have had a variety of effects on the overseas countries in which they operate. In the first place, these corporations are sometimes wealthier than their host countries. Consequently, multinationals have enormous power and can demand that these countries adopt policies that are beneficial to the corporation. Second, governments may deliberately avoid political and economic policies inconsistent with the multinational and, sometimes, the multinational actually intervenes in the domestic affairs of the host nation. A good example of this kind of intervention occurred in Chile during the early 1970s (Sampson, 1973; Barnet and Müller, 1974). When it appeared that Marxist candidate Salvador Allende Gossens would win the election for president of Chile, executives in the International Telephone and Telegraph Company (ITT) became concerned that their substantial corporate holdings and operations in Chile would be threatened and that ITT would suffer substantial economic losses. A director of ITT, who was also a former head of the Central Intelligence Agency (CIA), offered the CIA a $1 million contribution in order to finance an operation designed to interfere with the election in Chile. After Allende won in what is regarded as a fair election, ITT drew up a plan to create economic disorder in Chile. In 1973, President Allende was killed during a military overthrow of his government. Although it is not certain that ITT's actions caused the overthrow, it is clear that this enormous multinational benefited from the outcome. Such extreme cases are apparently rare, but this one illustrates the behavior of one multinational corporation in its attempts to protect profits.

The Dwindling of Unions

Traditionally, unions have enabled employees, who have relatively little power unless they organize, to combine their efforts and counter the substantial resources available to their corporate employers. Unions remain powerful in America, but the social and economic environment in which they function is shifting. Although predicting an outcome is difficult, many people believe it unlikely that unions will play the same role in a postindustrial society that they did during the in-

dustrial period. This may mean that corporations will have a freer hand in establishing wages and working conditions. Especially if unemployment levels rise, as they did in the 1980s, workers will be competing with one another for a limited number of jobs, and union employees willing to strike over labor issues may find themselves replaced by other workers for whom a lower paying job is better than no job at all. This happened in 1989 during the Eastern Airlines labor dispute, where nonunion mechanics were hired to replace those who were on strike. It happened again in 1992 when thirteen thousand workers struck the Caterpillar Corporation. Tens of thousands of people applied for jobs to replace the strikers, showing that they would be content to work for wages and benefits the strikers were refusing. The strikers caved in and went back to work out of the fear, probably realistic, that they would be replaced if they pushed their demands. Some companies have been accused of using high unemployment rates as a tool to attack unions and diminish their strength. As this occurs, many workers, especially those with few skills, may find it more difficult to locate jobs that pay what they consider a decent wage. For some, this may mean a way of life that is little better than, and maybe worse than, that of previous generations.

As the strength of unions dwindled in the 1980s, the government's willingness to support and protect workers seems also to have declined. For example, federal enforcement of health and safety standards was substantially less vigorous than in the past, and funding for employment and training programs has dropped by one-half (Levitan and Shapiro, 1986). So the two primary protectors of individual workers against the power, neglect, or avarice of corporations—unions and the federal government—are far less substantial today than they once were.

Worker Discontent and Alienation

Industrialization has led to many changes that are regarded as positive by Americans, such as a higher standard of living and a shorter work week. At the same time, the nature of work for many Americans has changed—they work in large bureaucratic settings such as factories, schools, or corporations. Their work is often boring, repetitive, and unfulfilling. They have little control over the pace of their work, what they produce, or what happens to it once it is produced. The assembly line is the epitome of this kind of work, but increasingly office and clerical work has these characteristics. This type of work organization may be beneficial to employers in terms of efficiency and profitability, but it can result in considerable discontent among employees. Lack of control, monotony, and depersonalization often result in **alienation,** *a feeling of powerlessness in controlling one's surroundings and a sense that what one does has little meaning or purpose* (Vallas, 1988; Greenberger et al., 1989). Workers who are alienated are less productive workers; they may also express their discontent through drug or alcohol abuse or political discontent (Seeman, Seeman, and Budros, 1988).

Worker Dislocation and Unemployment

In the 1950s and 1960s, the unemployment rate rarely crept above 5 percent, and at times it was below 3 percent. In the 1970s, the unemployment rate rarely went below 5 percent and sometimes went over 8 percent. In the 1980s, the rate rarely went below 7 percent and at times rose to 10 percent. In the 1980s, the jobless rate was higher than at any time since the Great Depression of the 1930s. And there are more unemployed than these figures indicate. These official statistics do not include those people who are not seeking work but who want to work—the so-called discouraged workers. When these individuals are counted, our unemployment problem is even more grave than the official statistics suggest. In addition, some groups are especially hard hit by the unemployment problem. Figure 2.6 illustrates unemployment rates for selected groups between 1960 and 1991. These statistics show the increase

in the unemployment problem over the past few decades and how teenagers, blacks, and members of other minorities are among the most heavily affected.

One very important dimension of the unemployment problem in American society today is the dislocation of workers. Over the past two decades, many traditional American industries, such as steel and automobile manufacturing, have declined in the face of foreign competition, and in the process many people have become unemployed. Sometimes called "displaced workers," they numbered at least five million workers between 1981 and 1986 (Gainer, 1986; McKenzie, 1988). These workers are often better educated, more highly skilled, and have greater access to other sources of income in comparison to the long-term unemployed. Because these workers belong to groups with traditionally low levels of unemployment, it has often been assumed that they would easily adapt to the economic circumstances that caused them to be out of work in the first place and find a job comparable to the one they had lost. Research investigations suggest otherwise (Devins, 1986; Zippay, 1991). Some of these displaced workers never return to the labor force. Even those who do find work may, depending on their location, find themselves unemployed for one and a half years, on average, after losing their job, and almost all experienced a permanent decline in family income because of their job loss. Many were forced to accept irregular work at low-paying jobs with few fringe benefits in the service industries. In addition, black Americans were hit much harder by job displacement than were white Americans: Blacks were more likely to be displaced, were jobless for longer, and were much less likely to be reemployed (Kletzer, 1991).

The problem of unemployment in the United States has persisted and grown worse for a number of reasons. There is increasing competition from foreign workers. American employers have moved their operations overseas or contracted with manufacturers in other countries to reduce

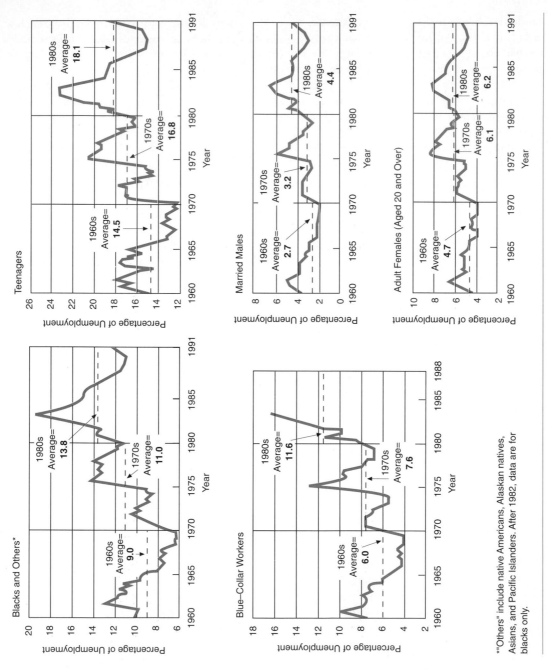

Figure 2.6 **Unemployment Rates, Selected Groups, 1960–1991**
SOURCES: U.S. Congressional Budget Office, *The Outlook for Economic Recovery, Part I* (Washington, D.C.: U.S. Government Printing Office, March 1983), p. 91; *Monthly Labor Review*, February 1985, February 1987, February 1989, February 1990, February 1992.

*"Others" include native Americans, Alaskan natives, Asians, and Pacific Islanders. After 1982, data are for blacks only.

American cultural values emphasize the sanctity of individuals and people's right to control their own destiny. Yet, decisions made by huge corporations in far-off places, such as the closing of the factory in this photo, can leave unemployed workers feeling that they have little control over their fate.

labor costs. Countries in Latin America and Asia have been especially receptive to American business. Automobile assembly workers in the United States make about $24 per hour whereas in Japan the hourly wage is $15 and in Korea as little as $2.50. Hundreds of American companies have left the United States and opened up shop in Mexico, close to the border, taking advantage of the cheap labor and lax environmental laws in Mexico. Thousands of American jobs have been lost to these *maquiladoras* who have the best of both worlds, cheap labor and easy access to American markets to sell their products. Even the so-called high-tech industries have shown themselves willing to move operations abroad. Large computer firms such as Apple, for example, have moved most of their production enterprise overseas to escape high labor costs in the United States. In addition to the problem of foreign workers, there has been considerable growth in the teenage labor market, and the number of women joining the work force has continued to grow. Still another dimension of the problem is

automation, which is discussed in more detail in Chapter 15. Some casual observers are fond of pointing to such things as laziness, too much emphasis on welfare, too high wages, and illegal aliens as explanations for our nation's unemployment ills. Data do not back up these claims, however, and changes within our nation like the ones just described may be responsible.

Unemployment, as tragic as it may be, is not the only form in which difficulties confront workers in the United States. A related problem is that the jobs available to them may not pay as well as they did in the past. In fact, by 1990, more full-time workers had low-paying jobs than was the case in earlier decades (U.S. Bureau of the Census, 1992a). In 1964, 24 percent of full-time workers had poverty-level incomes. By 1979, this had dropped to 12 percent. However, it climbed steadily through the 1980s until, by 1990, 18 percent of full-time workers had incomes that would not bring their families out of poverty. Apparently, although new jobs were created during the 1980s, the jobs tended to be at the low end of the

POLICY ISSUES

The Deindustrialization and Reindustrialization of America

As we pointed out in Chapter 1, industrialization has brought many benefits to the United States, but it has also created or exacerbated many social problems. One of the central issues in the development of social policy to deal with these problems has been the role of the economy and the government. In the 1930s, the Roosevelt administration's New Deal established the government in the role of helping those in need of assistance. This trend was reinforced in the 1960s when President Johnson's Great Society ushered in a host of government programs to attack the problems of poverty, illiteracy, hunger, and the like. The government took the initiative in establishing and pursuing social goals in a variety of realms.

In the 1980s and 1990s, a new problem has stimulated renewed debate over the roles of government and business in social policy. This new problem, often referred to as the **deindustrialization** of America, is characterized by *high rates of unemployment in the industrial sector, an aging and deterioration of our factories and other productive resources, and our alleged inability to compete with other industrial nations, especially those in Asia* (Graham, 1992). Deindustrialization has raised the specter that the American economy may have become, or will quickly become, permanently weakened. Businesses will struggle for marginal profitability, American jobs will continue to be exported overseas where land and labor are cheaper, and the life-styles of most Americans will deteriorate.

The debate over deindustrialization and what to do about it, although complex, tends to reflect the laissez-faire and interventionist positions discussed in Chapter 1. At its foundation, the controversy is over whether the government or business will play a central part in reindustrializing America.

The laissez-faire position on this issue arises from the belief that a free and competitive economic marketplace is the most efficient and effective system for allocating resources. Deindustrialization, to the extent that it exists, arises because of government interference with the free enterprise system and because our national tax and spending policies have encouraged noncompetitive elements to determine the allocation of resources (McKenzie, 1984, 1988). Government efforts to save certain companies or prevent factory closings, for example, foster the continuation of inefficient businesses, making the overall costs of products more expensive and less competitive. In addition, social programs such as school lunches for all students and loans to college students tie up societal resources that might better be used as new investment capital for developing new indsutries. As another example, laissez-faire advocates argue, the federally set minimum wage and government support of unions over the years has resulted in artificially high incomes for workers and made American industry less competitive in world markets.

According to this "hands off" policy, the solution to these problems—the way to "reindustrialize" America—is to shift power from the hands of the government to the corporate boardroom. The New Deal and the Great Society may have been valuable in their time (although some laissez-faire advocates would disagree with this), but the continued expansion of government programs funnels resources away from private enterprise and encourages the allocation of resources based on factors other than the economic marketplace. Less government spending will result in tax cuts that in turn will serve as an incentive for people to work harder, save more, and invest some of their earnings. Savings and investment will provide more capital for industry to expand, and this expansion will produce more jobs for people and reduce poverty and unemployment. For laissez-faire proponents, then, the solution to our problems is a shift toward a purer form of capitalism.

Few people in the 1990s would take a strict laissez-faire position that gives the government absolutely no role in industrial policy. Even the Bush administration supported some government programs to encourage industrial development in certain areas. However, interventionists see the government playing a much more central role in reindustrializing the United States. Interventionists begin with some very different assumptions (Harrison and Bluestone, 1988; Bowles, Gordon, and Weisskopf, 1992). Some assume, for example, that our government has always had an industrial policy of some sort, and the debate is really over how much and what kind of government intervention is called for. Others assume that national goals may differ from, and even conflict with, the goals pursued by private industry. In fact, they argue, many of the problems that we face today arise from excessive corporate greed and the search for unreasonably high profit margins. Plants are closed and people thrown out of work not because industries are unprofitable but because profit margins are judged by corporate managers to be too low. Seymour Melman (1983) argues that high labor costs are not really the culprit either. Rather, as labor costs rose, business managers took the easy way out: They sought cheaper labor overseas rather than developing more efficient means of producing goods in the United States. In addition, monopolies and defense industries have not faced a truly competitive environment, as the military has been willing to pay whatever industry asks for different defense systems. This raises prices and makes industries less competitive.

Some interventionists take a position that reflects the conflict view (Alperovitz and Faux, 1984). They argue that America is a "broker state": a society in which the public largesse is dispensed to the most vocal and best organized interest group. The corporate sector has been the best organized thus far—pouring millions of dollars into lobbying efforts—and has received the lion's share of public resources. Although we cut funds for the poor and disabled, for example, the government bails out mismanaged banks, auto companies, and defense industries. It constitutes socialism for the rich and powerful but competitive capitalism for the weak and poor.

Economist Lester Thurow (1992) argues that our unbridled emphasis on individualism, dog-eat-dog competition, and laissez-faire government places us in a very disadvantageous position in relation to our major competitors on the world scene, especially Germany and Japan, where cooperation among business, workers, and government is extensive, harmonious, and long-standing. While German and Japanese governments nurture important industries with a variety of help, we let our new industries flounder on their own, and too often we lose the competitive edge in these industries to some foreign country.

Interventionists have many and varied proposals for what the government can do to reindustrialize the United States. Thurow and many others argue for heavy government investment in the economic infrastructure, such as roads, airports, and other things that businesses need to be competitive. They also propose much more government funding for job training and education in general so that the American work force has the same skill and knowlege levels that are found among workers in other industrial countries. In their view, labor is an essential resource that needs to be nurtured rather than an expensive and balky cost of doing business. They also propose cooperation between government and industry, with the former providing funding and some leadership in promising economic arenas. This could take the form of significant public funding for some industries, as is now done in both Japan and Europe.

Other interventionists argue for legislation to restrict the ability of companies to move from one locale to another, thus dislocating workers. They also call for giving workers a larger voice in the running of the businesses in which they are employed. Overall, they want to establish a package of government programs that will enable America to reindustrialize—reduce unemployment and make America competitive once again—in a way that does not destroy some people along the way. A few interventionists even insist that we need to replace private corporate decisions with public democratic planning, possibly through community ownership of certain industries. For the interventionists, then, the solution to our problems calls for more government direction and possibly a move toward a more mixed economy.

pay scale. So, even when our economy provides work for Americans, that work is less likely to pay enough to support one's family. This does not mean, however, that these low-paid workers are living in poverty; instead, it means that someone else in the family, such as a spouse, has to work in order to bring the family's income above the poverty level. The Policy Issues installment analyzes some of the different social policy positions that have been advanced to tackle some of these problems.

Abuse of Government Authority

Is big government a problem? This depends, of course, on one's perspective, but there do seem to be a number of reasons why massive government bureaucracies can create potential problems. One reason is the opportunity for the abuse of power by government officials. When government is large and distant from its constituency, isolated bureaucrats are freer to make decisions that benefit themselves and their associates but not necessarily other groups in society. In fact, the growth of big government can become problematic through collusion between government and big business. The Department of Defense, for example, may look the other way when industries with defense contracts have enormous cost overruns. This problem goes to the very heart of freedom in a democratic society: Are people able to control the actions of elected or appointed officials? In the early 1970s, as we saw earlier, the U.S. government, through the Central Intelligence Agency, contributed to the overthrow of Chilean President Allende, who had been voted into office by the Chilean populace. The government tried to hide this from the American people. If anything, many Americans now assume that their government will keep secrets and hide misdeeds from the citizenry. Such cynical attitudes toward the government were reinforced when the Iran-Contra scandal broke in 1986. In 1989, the trial of Lieutenant Colonel Oliver North threatened to reveal embarrassing facts and threaten national security. In a free society, such secrecy is highly detrimental to the democratic process; in a democratic society, the belief that the government is deceiving the people is an insidious cancer that threatens important group values.

A second reason why big government is a problem, according to those who take a laissez-faire stance, is that big government is inherently detrimental to American society: It funnels resources away from the private sector where they could be put to better use. Because the government is not constrained by competition and demands to make a profit, it can "afford" to be highly wasteful. Government can lose money and still maintain existing programs if politicians continue to provide tax revenues. If tax money is not available, the government can borrow money and create a deficit. In fact, budget deficits played an important part in the economic and political life of the 1980s and 1990s. Many economists have argued that a major culprit in generating inflation is the budget deficits of the federal government. These deficits reflect the excess of annual government expenditures over revenues. With the exception of 1960 and 1969, the federal government has spent more than it has taken in every year since 1940. The major concern with budget deficits is that the government must borrow money to operate and thus competes with corporate and other borrowers for the finite amount of loan money available. This competition increases the cost of loan money. Thus, both government and business have to pay more for loans, and this might lead some businesses to forego business expansion or capital improvements. When businesses forego expansion and improvement, there is less economic growth and fewer jobs. Or businesses can pass the increased costs of borrowing money on to the consumer through higher prices, and this produces more inflation.

A final reason why large government can create problems involves whether individuals can play significant roles in the decisions shaping their lives. As government grows, most people find themselves further and further removed from those who actually make the decisions. As C. Wright Mills (1959) pointed out, the key decision makers are usually those people who control the large economic and government bureaucracies in modern societies. The "faceless bureaucrats" in Washington take accumulated tax revenues and then tell most Americans what they can or cannot do. You cannot dump your garbage here, you need a wheelchair accessible ramp for your store, and your school can (or cannot) allow children to pray in school. As the government grows, the values of individualism and autonomy may become increasingly remote and irrelevant. Many groups feel powerless, and there is real danger that their interests will not receive a fair hearing in the halls of political power.

FUTURE PROSPECTS

What—if anything—should be done about big business and big government is highly controversial. We will analyze the major programs and policies that have been discussed or implemented.

Reducing Government and Deficits

As we have seen, government continues to grow when measured by the money it takes in and the money it spends. Although President Reagan was an ardent advocate of smaller government, and one of our most effective presidents when pushing programs he favored, he was not able to reduce government spending even though he had eight years during which to do so. President Bush was equally unsuccessful in reducing the size of our government. This suggests that the reasons we discussed earlier for why government has grown in the past remain powerful forces in keeping government large. It is easy to shout about saving money by getting loafers off of welfare, but all of the public aid provided by the federal government amounts to about $75 billion, about one-quarter of the annual deficit and less than 7

percent of the budget. Defense spending, on the other hand, consumes more than a quarter of the budget. This does not mean that cuts cannot be made, but reducing the budget is much more difficult and complex than is often imagined and affects many more people than the poor or some other powerless group (Calleo, 1992).

Some efforts have been made to reduce the budget deficit. The Gramm-Rudman-Hollings Act was passed in 1986, with provisions that required the budget be reduced by specified amounts over a five-year period until there was no deficit. The real teeth of the act was a provision that empowered the General Accounting Office (GAO) to reduce the budgets of all government departments by the required amounts if Congress did not act. However, this part of the act was ruled unconstitutional by the Supreme Court on the grounds that budget decisions are the authority of the executive branch, not the GAO. In 1990, Gramm-Rudman-Hollings was replaced with the Budget Enforcement Act, but this legislation has no provisions for mandating budget cuts. Without such provisions, Congress and the president have not been able to develop a mutually agreeable plan to make significant cuts in the budget, and between 1985 and 1991 there was little reduction in the deficit. This whole battle over the budget deficit shows the extent to which virtually every interest group benefits from some aspects of government spending, and no one wants to see their ox gored.

Government Reorganization

Even though reducing the size of the government may be difficult, there are things that can and have been done to moderate the negative effects of big government.

Politicians and government officials can be made more responsive to the demands of the citizenry. Because of the Watergate scandal and similar political episodes during the 1970s, politicians are now required to disclose a great deal more about their personal finances, and this offers the public greater scrutiny over possible conflicts of interest. There is still, however, much more that can be done. Sociologist Herbert J. Gans (1988), concerned that most Americans will not become more politically active, has suggested some creative ways of increasing the responsiveness of elected government officials. One is to increase the staff available to them for providing constituency services. Each official would thus have more workers available to find out what their constituents want and to provide the services. A second suggestion is for more, and more diverse, public opinion polling organizations. After all, most such organizations today are very close to the political and economic elites and tend to gather information that those elites find useful. According to Gans, polls should tell elites what the public has on its mind about the issues that are important to it. Polls should tell us what should be on a politician's agenda, not what we think about a politician's already-established agenda. All of this would give citizens more input into the workings of government. Recently, consumer advocate Ralph Nader (1988: 83) has called for a "citizen-driven government" that would "enhance . . . the ability of citizens to find out what public officials are doing, to express their voice, to gain a role in the policy-making process, to challenge waste and corruption, to discipline government insensitivity."

Government agencies and officials can be regulated much more closely than at present. This, of course, might mean that we would need more agencies to do the regulating, but not in all cases. Sometimes, bureaucrats in a government agency can do the regulating themselves if they are protected against reprisals should they uncover something detrimental to those heading the agency. In many cases, such whistleblowers are fired by the agency, but when their cases come to public view, they often find considerable support among the public. Further protections for, and even rewards given to, such internal auditors could make government bureaus more sensitive to decisions that

are viewed unfavorably by the public (Glazer and Glazer, 1989).

Government programs can be made more accountable. Policy analysts David Osborne and Ted Gaebler (1992) suggest a shift in focus from government services based on civil service regulations, which try to specify in detail *how* government services should be provided, to an "entrepreneurial government" that focuses on *results*. The idea is to establish measurable performance goals or outcomes as a part of government programs, and then use competition and decentralized authority to achieve the goals. This might call for privatizing some government services if private industry can do the job better than government bureaus can. But Osborne and Gaebler recognize that government is better than private industry at doing some things, especially when issues of fairness and equity come into play. Some programs, such as Head Start (see Chapter 5), currently do focus on results, and privatizing these services has so far not shown any advantages. The problem in the past, they argue, has not been government per se but the inefficient bureaucracy that government had become.

Collective Action by Citizens

In a democracy like ours, one important way of controlling the actions of business and government is through collective, organized actions by citizens' groups to change the law or redirect social policy. In the past few decades, many such groups have emerged as watchdogs over whether government and business are acting in the public interest.

Among the most effective citizens' groups over the years have been those originated by consumer advocate Ralph Nader and his associates. Nader first came to public attention in the 1960s when he published *Unsafe at Any Speed*, a scathing critique of the auto industry. He revealed the extent to which General Motors was willing to make unsafe automobiles in order to increase profits. His campaign resulted in legislation that corrected many of the abuses in the auto industry and also pushed the government into the role of watchdog over automobile safety. Eventually, a whole variety of consumer protection groups—often referred to as "Nader's Raiders"—grew up around Nader's efforts, including the Public Safety Research Institute, the Public Interest Research Group, the Corporate Accountability Research Group, and the Center for the Study of Responsive Law. These collective efforts contributed to the passage of consumer protection legislation in many areas: to ensure quality meats, to ban cyclamates and other harmful substances, and to enhance safety procedures in mining and other occupations, to name just a few. Currently, Nader's consumer advocacy organizations are working toward restrictions in the use of chlorinated fluorocarbons, the establishment of national health insurance, and a rollback in the cost of automobile insurance (Brimelow and Spencer, 1990).

Concerns about environmental pollution and degradation have also spawned a great deal of collective action by the citizenry (see Chapter 13). Beginning in the late nineteenth century with the Audubon Society and the Sierra Club, such interest groups have lobbied for social policies to protect and preserve our natural environment. These older environmental groups have been joined by newer ones such as the National Wildlife Federation, the Abalone Alliance, and Greenpeace. In recent years, members of Greenpeace have been especially active. For example, they have sailed ships into target areas for nuclear weapons tests in order to halt the testing, and they have built an elaborate communication and information network that serves as an effective warning system when environmental problems arise. In 1984, for example, a ship containing nuclear wastes sank off the coast of Holland. At first, it was claimed that the radioactivity of the wastes was so low that they posed no threat of contaminating the ocean. However, Greenpeace organizations had been tracking nuclear waste shipments and were able to determine that this ship carried wastes of much higher and more dangerous radioactivity. These efforts led to recovery of the wastes before contamination occurred.

Some public interest groups, such as Common Cause, are not limited to any particular realm, such as environmental problems or occupational safety, but rather focus on any area where government or business appears to be ignoring public interests. Common Cause opposes waste and corruption through the legislature or the courts. Common Cause has been effective in part because it has appealed to a rather affluent constituency that has provided it with the economic resources to pursue its battles. The group has been especially active on issues of election campaign financing. Its major concern was that interest groups with substantial economic resources, such as large corporations or industries or wealthy individuals, could "bribe" public officials by making large donations to their campaigns. The average citizen does not have access to that kind of influence. Politicians, naturally looking for campaign funds, would then feel beholden to those who made large contributions. In part due to Common Cause's efforts, the Federal Election Campaign Act was amended in 1975 to require disclosure of large contributions and place limitations on the amounts that businesses and individuals can contribute to a candidate.

There are still ways to get around these limitations, however (Cannon, 1992). For example, the law limits contributions to candidates but not to political parties. People can still give unlimited amounts to the Republican or Democratic parties even if the party will spend the money to promote a particular candidate. Another way to get around the law is to have a candidate spend his or her own money, which is not restricted by the law. This is a real boon for wealthy candidates such as George Bush or Ross Perot. In addition, people can donate unlimited amounts to tax-exempt "educational" organizations that may work very hard

While pursuing what benefits them, corporations can engage in practices that hurt other groups. When this happens, citizens can attempt to rectify things through collective action, as this group did in protesting the actions of the Philip Morris Corporation.

for particular candidates or positions on issues. The only restriction is that these organizations not be used for political purposes. Acting as "think tanks," these concerns disseminate information that supports the position of particular candidates, and they analyze issues in ways that encourage people to vote for those candidates. So, although the campaign financing law helps to moderate the influence of the wealthy and powerful, these limitations in the law show that wealth still can have a powerful advantage.

Collective action of these sorts has been a valuable constraint on the excesses of big business and big government. These efforts have offered average citizens a valuable weapon in pursuing their own interests. The success of these groups has depended on

1. The ability to appeal to large numbers of people and the financial resources those people provide.

2. The strategic use of legislative and litigative tactics.

3. The effective use of the media for public relations and communication.

Many of the existing public interest groups will undoubtedly continue to function, and we will likely see the emergence of more groups in the future as issues change and new ones develop.

Economic Reorganization

Concern over alienation and loss of control in the workplace has motivated some businesses and labor specialists to search for alternative ways of organizing work, using the expertise of industrial relations experts and social scientists. One alternative to arise from this search is to dispense with the traditional assembly line and allow a group of workers to build a product, such as an automobile, from start to finish and to control the pace of their own work. Volvo and Saab in Sweden and Chrysler and General Electric in the United States have experimented with such programs (Gyllenhammar, 1977). Other companies have turned to *flextime,* a system of work scheduling that allows employees to start and stop work earlier or later than traditional working hours (Vanderkolk and Young, 1991). The goal of all these reorganizations of the traditional workplace is to offer employees more control over their working conditions and thus reduce discontent and alienation.

A more extreme and innovative approach to the problem of alienation is *worker empowerment,* involving an attempt to provide workers with management authority and responsibility. In some cases, this has involved workers gaining partial ownership in a company and having a stake in how it is run and in the consequences of their own work performance. In 1990, ten thousand U.S. firms with eleven million employees had some form of employee ownership (U.S. Bureau of the Census, 1992). In other cases, worker empowerment has involved changes in the structure of companies so that employees have more of a say in company decision making, more opportunities for advancement, and increased access to powerful people and resources in the organization (Stein and Kanter, 1980). Whatever form it takes, worker empowerment has focused on reducing the sense of powerlessness and lack of control that many workers experience. And research shows that worker participation and employee

ownership can increase a company's productivity (Blinder, 1990; Rosen and Youngs, 1991).

Whether these changes will reduce discontent and alienation among workers remains to be seen, but it is clear that American business institutions are neither perfect nor stagnant. As we become an advanced industrial economy, the problems we face are changing, and it is clear that our economic arrangements must adapt. In fact, some have suggested that these issues of concentration of power and lack of control will not be ultimately resolved without some fundamental change in our economy. Some argue that we should become more of a mixed economy, with the government taking more control of some economic realms in order to pursue collective goals. Proponents of an extreme power elite position would argue that inequality and exploitation are inherent elements of capitalism because capitalism is ultimately fueled by personal greed and acquisition. As such, capitalism can only work to benefit the powerful. Some form of a mixed economy would balance the avarice inherent in capitalism by injecting an element of the public good into economic activities. Others, including some pluralists, would argue that capitalism can benefit most citizens through the checks and balances of competing interest groups. This is not to say that capitalism can achieve equality or that everyone will benefit. But if the government encourages the development of interest groups, large numbers of citizens will be able to pursue their goals.

Linkages

Economic concentration and more low-paying jobs mean that it is harder for families to avoid poverty (Chapter 5). This situation also puts more stress on families, possibly increasing divorce (Chapter 3). It also means that more women are forced to take jobs where they earn less than men and thus increases the feminization of poverty (Chapter 7).

Summary

1. Political and economic institutions focus on a central issue in society: the exercise of power in the allocation of scarce resources. The social problem associated with these institutions is the abuse of power: the exercise of power in ways that work against the interests of substantial numbers of less powerful Americans.

2. The economies of industrialized nations are market economies, which are based on the exchange of money for goods and services in the marketplace. The three main types of modern economic systems are capitalism, socialism, and mixed economies.

3. The dominant form of business in the modern American economy is the corporation, which has many advantages over individually owned businesses. Economic resources have become highly concentrated in a small number of very large corporations. Such concentration can take the form of monopolies, oligopolies, conglomerates, and multinational corporations.

4. The number and size of unions in the United States has grown substantially over the past century, but they have declined some in the past few decades.

5. Government has also grown substantially in the past two centuries because it has taken on the responsibility for social and economic policy and because people demand so much more of it.

6. From the functionalist perspective, big government and big business are a problem because they can lead to policies and practices that are inconsistent with cultural values and political and economic reality. From the conflict perspective, concentration of power becomes a social problem when some influential group believes that it is not receiving its fair share of resources and strives to do something about it.

7. Oligarchy refers to the concentration of power in the hands of a few people at the top of an organization. Organizations have a strong tendency to become oligarchical.

8. There are two major models of power distribution in America: the power elite model and the pluralist model. The realities of holding power in America are more complex than either model suggests. A relatively small group of people do hold power, but at the same time groups that are not a part of this elite can occasionally wield power.

9. The concentration of power creates many problems for society, including a reduction in economic competition, the dominance of corporate profit-making goals over societal goals, worker discontent and alienation, worker dislocation and unemployment, and abuse of government authority.

10. Efforts to alleviate problems stemming from the concentration and abuse of power have focused on a number of policies: shrinking the size of the government and budget deficits, reorganizing government so that abuses are less likely, encouraging collective action by citizens that serves as a counterbalance to government and corporate power, and reorganizing the economy in ways that reduce worker discontent and unemployment while societal goals are pursued.

Important Terms for Review

alienation	deindustrialization	mixed economies	politics
capitalism	economics	oligarchy	power elite model
communism	military–industrial complex	pluralist model	socialism
corporation			

Discussion Questions

1. It has often been said that our capitalist economy is moving in the direction of socialism. What are some of the indications that this trend is occurring? Is this a problem for the United States? Are the many criticisms of socialist economies justified, or do they merely reflect a tone of ethnocentrism? Invite proponents of each economic system (you should be able to find them in your university's economics department) to debate these issues before your class.

2. Analyze the concentration of power in your college or university. How oligarchical is it? In what ways do the students benefit from such concentration? How does it work against their interests?

3. Over the past fifteen years, American business has been in the worst shape that we have witnessed since the Depression, yet corporations continue to expand. Unemployment remains high and many workers are alienated from their jobs, yet certain industries—computers, for example—have grown dramatically. What are the long-term implications of these trends?

4. Compare and contrast the power elite and pluralist models of government decision making. Using your college or university as an example of "government," which of these models most accurately reflects the orientation there? Describe how different people or groups on campus fit into the power structure. Do you think that this represents a problem for your university?

5. Would a conflict theorist view the power structure of American society as being a social problem? From the conflict perspective, what is required to make the public interest a more powerful force in the operation of our society? Discuss some of the future prospects mentioned in the last section of this chapter in the light of the functionalist versus the conflict perspectives.

For Further Reading

Richard J. Barnet and Ronald E. Müller. *Global Reach: The Power of the Multinational Corporations.* New York: Simon and Schuster, 1974. An excellent overview of how multinational corporations have entrenched themselves in the industrialized and developing nations of the world. This book includes a discussion of the ways in which multinationals have had an impact on America's economic problems.

Paul Brodeur. *Outrageous Misconduct: The Asbestos Industry on Trial.* New York: Pantheon Books, 1985. This is an angry book about how widespread corporate malfeasance in the asbestos industry produced much pain and suffering for its workers. It documents how corporations often pursue corporate profits even when they know their actions are hurting people.

Dan Clawson, Alan Neustadtl, and Denise Scott. *Money Talks: Corporate PACs and Political Influence.* New York: Basic Books, 1992. Political action committees (PACs) have become very influential in the American political process as a means for elites to control politicians and elections. These authors show that it is a more subtle and complex influence than merely buying politicians' votes on issues.

Peter W. Cookson and Caroline Hodges Persell. *Preparing for Power: America's Elite Boarding Schools.* New York: Basic Books, 1985. Based on in-depth interviews at elite schools, the authors document how the schools prepare the offspring of the powerful to take over positions of power in American society.

Graef S. Crystal. *In Search of Excess: The Overcompensation of American Executives.* New York: W. W. Norton, 1992. This book documents one of the small but not insignificant spinoffs of an economic system that severely concentrates power: Corporate executives at the top are compensated far in excess of what they are in other corporate economies. This means fewer resources for productive activities and less legitimacy accorded to the system by those who feel they do not receive their fair share.

William S. Dietrich. *In the Shadow of the Rising Sun: The Political Roots of American Economic Decline.* University Park, Penn.: Penn State Press, 1992. The author of this book, a corporate executive as well as a social scientist, argues strongly that our economic problems are partly political and cultural in nature. He particularly accuses our unrepentant individualism along with a lack of a strong industrial policy as contributing to our economic malaise.

G. William Domhoff. *The Power Elite and the State: How Policy Is Made in America.* New York: Aldine de Gruyter, 1990. Domhoff presents many case studies of social policy development that show how and why coalitions of the power elite get involved in various policy issues. It extends the power elite theory into the Reagan-Bush years.

Laton McCartney. *Friends in High Places: The Bechtel Story: The Most Secret Corporation and How It Engineered the World.* New York: Simon and Schuster, 1988. This is a fascinating case study of a very powerful American corporation and its influence on the United States and the world. It shows interlinkages between government and business and how, as the power elite view suggests, government can become a tool of corporate policy.

Philip M. Stern. *The Best Congress Money Can Buy.* New York: Pantheon, 1988. This book documents the extent to which politicians are in constant search of money needed to run for reelection and shows the extent to which the rich and powerful use this fact to buy influence.

David Vogel. *Lobbying the Corporation: Citizen Challenges to Business Activity.* New York: Basic Books, 1978. In this book, Vogel shows how citizen groups have worked toward making American corporations more responsible and attentive to public interest. His analysis illustrates the pluralist position in terms of how lobby groups can wield substantial power.

Michael Waldman. *Who Robbed America? A Citizen's Guide to the Savings and Loan Scandal.* New York: Random House, 1990. This is a detailed account of how the savings and loan crisis happened and who the major players were. It is a good case study of the use and abuse of power and the intertwining of corporate and government power.

S ome of the problems that we examine in this book may not seem of immediate concern to many of you because you do not believe they affect your life in a direct and personal way. Problems involving the family, however, interest virtually everyone because we all spend much of our lives in some kind of family unit. And the family, it would seem, is an institution under considerable stress these days. Most of us know someone—a parent, a close friend, possibly ourselves—who has been divorced. Stories of parents beating their children and spouses assaulting one another abound in daily newspapers. Some employers today even extend health and life insurance benefits to the unmarried domestic partners of their employees, including gay and lesbian couples. So, what had been defined as "family" benefits in the past are now sometimes extended to those in living arrangements that some would not consider "families" at all. In fact, some Americans view such developments as a virtual assault on the sanctity of the conventional family in society. What is happening to the family in America?

The family is the oldest and most fundamental of all social institutions. In fact, the family has been the center of political, economic, educational, and religious activities in most human societies throughout history. The position of the family in society today, however, has changed considerably, and there are many controversial issues and problems involved. Before addressing these concerns, we need to know what the family is and how it functions in society. The **family** is *a social institution based on kinship that functions to*

Myths and Facts About the Family

Myth: Unhappy marriages should be maintained when children are involved—"for the sake of the children."

Fact: Repeated investigations of divorce and its effects on children have failed to demonstrate the psychological benefits to children of maintaining an unhappy marriage. It may, in fact, be more damaging than divorce itself.

Myth: Divorce is a modern phenomenon and was relatively unheard of in premodern societies.

Fact: Not only did divorce exist in primitive societies, but it was sometimes easier to obtain and more common than in America today.

Myth: Love is by far more common than violence in the institution of family.

Fact: Families are filled with violence: Between 84 and 97 percent of all parents use physical punishment at some point in dealing with their children; family fights are the largest single category of police calls; a national cross section of the population revealed that one out of every four

men and one in six women approve of slapping a wife under certain conditions (Straus, Gelles, and Steinmetz, 1980).

Myth: Modern no-fault divorce laws have benefited women far more than men in terms of receiving alimony and child-support payments.

Fact: Recent research suggests that women suffer more economically after a divorce than do men. Although divorced women suffer a 73 percent decline in their standard of living after divorce, the men experience a 42 percent increase.

Myth: Teenage pregnancies are on the rise in all modern societies because of the decline in traditional values and the rise in sexual promiscuity.

Fact: The United States has many more teenage pregnancies than does any other industrial nation. In societies where effective sex education programs and contraceptives are available to teens, the rate of such pregnancies is two to three times lower than in the United States.

---

replace members of society and to nurture them. This seemingly straightforward definition hides considerable complexity and controversy, as we will see. In fact, there is a great deal of ethnocentrism associated with the family. Most people have strong feelings regarding what "the family" is and how family members should behave. This has a direct impact on social policy when people's conceptions of what the family should be like distort their analysis of family problems and restrict their consideration of ways to solve these problems.

To understand what is happening to the family and assess competing views of family-related problems, we need to evaluate the role of the family as an institution in society. We will do this before analyzing the scope and extent of these problems.

THE FAMILY IN SOCIETY

Families can take on many different forms. In some cultures, males wield most power and authority in the family, whereas in other cultures females do. In some cases, a person can have only one marriage partner at a time, whereas other societies permit and even encourage a person to have many spouses simultaneously. In American society today, cultural norms call for people to practice **monogamy,** *to have only one spouse at a time;* our culture also encourages an **egalitarian family,** in which *power and authority are shared somewhat equally by husband and wife,* although male dominance may persist in some families. But the American family of the past was different. In assessing problems in today's American family, we must recognize the changes that have taken place in the family as a consequence of industrialization. At center stage in these changes is the transition from an extended family to a nuclear family.

An **extended family** consists of *three or more generations of people who live together or in close proximity and whose lives and livelihoods are closely intertwined* (Nimkoff, 1965). Such families are often large and involve strong kinship obligations. Family members are expected to help other family members and to remain loyal to the family. In cultures where extended families are common, prevailing norms stress the importance of the family over that of the individual and his or her goals. Extended families are also often dominated by males, and tasks are divided along age and sex lines. Extended families are more common in preindustrial than in industrial societies.

A **nuclear family** consists of *a married couple and their children*. In contrast to extended families, nuclear families are small and less likely to be male dominated. Furthermore, cultures in which nuclear families predominate emphasize values of individualism to a greater extent. Nuclear families are the most common family type in industrial societies. Actually, many families found in modern societies are, strictly speaking, neither extended nor nuclear. Rather, they are **modified extended families,** in which *elaborate networks of visitation and support are found even though each nuclear unit lives separately* (Reiss, 1962; Shulman, 1975).

Why does such variation in family types occur from one culture to another or from one time period to another? The answer to this is provided by the three sociological perspectives.

The Functionalist Perspective

Functionalists argue that some form of the family exists in all societies because the family performs certain basic functions that are essential to human survival and the maintenance of society (Ogburn, 1938; Eshleman, 1991). Six major contributions that the family makes to society have been identified.

1. *Regulation of sexual behavior and reproduction.* All societies have rules governing who can engage in sexual activities with whom and under what conditions children should be conceived and born. In most societies, both sexual behavior and childbearing are limited to marriage and family contexts, which provide a stable setting for having and nurturing children. In this way, the family contributes to the process of replacing people from one generation to the next.

2. *Socialization and education.* All human beings must learn the values, norms, and language of their culture and develop the skills that are necessary to be useful in society. Parents and other family members usually have primary responsibility for ensuring that children are properly socialized. Thus, the family is the major agency of socialization.

3. *Status conferral.* Families confer upon their children a place in society—a position or status relative to other people. By virtue of being born into a particular family, we have certain resources or opportunities available to us. Our racial or ethnic heritage, religion, and social class are determined by the family into which we are born, although some of these characteristics may change later in life. At a minimum, our family confers upon us some initial status in society.

4. *Economic activity.* The family often serves as the basic unit for economic production, with kinship ties defining who is obliged to work together in order to catch game, grow food, or build shelters. Family members work together to accomplish the economic tasks necessary for survival. Kinship ties also determine the distribution and consumption of economic goods by establishing who has a right to a share of the goods produced by a family.

5. *Protection.* Families in all societies provide various forms of care and protection to their

members, helping them when they are too young, weak, sick, or old to help themselves.

6. *Affection and companionship.* All human beings need love, affection, and psychological support, and for many people these needs are fulfilled by family members. Such support enables us to develop a positive self-concept and sense of self-worth and to dispel loneliness.

All these functions taken together contribute to the continuity of society by ensuring that new members are born and properly socialized.

Although these six functions are often performed by the family, they can be accomplished in other ways. In fact, the family has been undergoing a major transformation over the past few centuries as a consequence of industrialization, and alternative ways of fulfilling many of these functions are emerging. For example, although most childbearing still occurs in marriages, a growing number of women are having children without marrying. By the 1990s, one million births to unmarried women were recorded by the Census Bureau each year, in comparison to about 400,000 in 1970 (U.S. Bureau of the Census, 1991: 67). This is happening in part because women in industrial societies are better able to work and support their children without the assistance of a husband or other relatives. With regard to socialization and education, day-care centers, schools, and colleges are becoming increasingly important in transmitting culture and passing on skills and knowledge. Furthermore, people's positions in industrial societies are determined less by family position and more by their achievements than in the past, although family position does give a person a start in life. In terms of economic activity, most people work outside of the home, and the family no longer serves as the center of economic production. Finally, we have hospitals, nursing homes, retirement villages, and many other ways to offer the care and protection that people need.

In other words, the role of the family in performing these functions for society has become less central as other institutional means of accomplishing them have arisen through industrialization. As a consequence, the traditional roles of family and kinship in society have changed, because they are simply not as important as they once were. As this has occurred, the extended family that performed most of these functions in preindustrial societies has become less common. At the same time, the nuclear family has become more prominent because it is better suited to an urbanized industrial society (Goode, 1963). Industrialism calls for geographic mobility so that workers can go where the jobs are, and nuclear families with weaker kinship ties make this possible. Industrial societies also emphasize achievement rather than ascription, and these modified kinship relations make it easier for people to be upwardly mobile. Furthermore, large extended families are dysfunctional in urban settings where children are not economic assets. In preindustrial societies, children could work in agricultural settings and therefore contribute economically to the family. Small families are better suited to industrial societies; in fact, the size of the average American family has declined substantially throughout this century, and people are more likely to be living alone or in nonfamily households (see Figure 3.1). So extended family ties are sometimes called the "traditional" family because they were considered the most appropriate form of the family throughout much of our history and some still believe that they are most acceptable; today, the nuclear or modified extended family is the "conventional" family in that many people now view it as the most appropriate family form.

The part that families play in society, then, has changed with industrialization, and this has contributed to such things as a rising divorce rate and the emergence of a number of alternatives to traditional family life-styles. These social developments become a social problem when the changes in the family threaten society with disorganization or instability. One of the key debates regarding family problems centers on whether the traditional family functions can be adequately performed by other institutions. Can day care, for

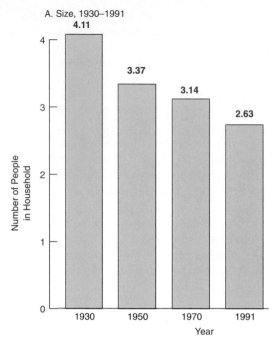

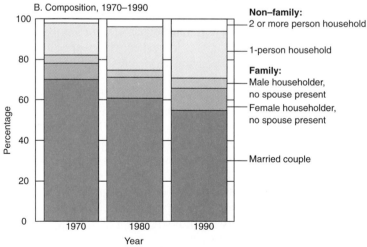

Figure 3.1   **The Average Size and Composition of American Households**
SOURCES: U.S. Bureau of the Census, *Statistical Abstract of the United States, 1982–83* (Washington, D.C.: U.S. Government Printing Office, 1982), p. 43; U.S. Bureau of the Census, *Statistical Abstract of the United States, 1991* (Washington, D.C.: U.S. Government Printing Office, 1991, p. 6, 45; U.S. Bureau of the Census, Current Population Reports, Series P-20, No. 458, *Household and Family Characteristics, 1991* (Washington, D.C.: U.S. Government Printing Office, 1992), p. 5.

example, provide the same kind of socialization to cultural values and development of personality that occurs in the traditional family? This issue is analyzed in the Applied Research insert. Do divorce and one-parent families result in less effective socialization and consequent behavior problems for youth when compared with two-parent families? We will analyze this question later in the chapter. The function of the family that has probably changed least during this process is the provision of affection and companionship, and nuclear families can probably perform this function as well as extended families did. But even this function might be fulfilled in other ways than by the traditional family.

The Conflict Perspective

According to the conflict perspective, the family, along with other social institutions, serves the interests of the dominant groups in society, and there is no reason to assume that a single form of the family would benefit everyone. Rather, the version of the family that is most prominent in society is likely to be the one that is consistent with the values and benefits of the dominant groups. For example, **patriarchy** refers to *a family in which males dominate in the regulation of political and economic decision making, whereas women and children are subordinate*. This is the most common type of authority structure in families, and it serves the interests of men by enabling them to be dominant. In some societies, in fact, women have been so powerless in the family that they were virtual slaves (Chagnon, 1968). In industrial societies, male domination is not this extreme, and fewer women today are willing to accept such a subordinate position and are demanding more egalitarian family roles. However, this change is occurring because women have been accumulating resources that enable them to resist coercion by males. For example, male dominance can be expressed in the form of spouse abuse, which usually involves husbands assaulting their wives. However, research indicates that married women

with greater economic, social, and educational resources are less likely to be abused and more likely to leave physically abusive husbands (Gelles and Cornell, 1990; Straus, 1991; Stets, 1991).

The dominant form of the family in society also benefits particular economic interests. For example, the nuclear family serves the interests of capitalist economic institutions because it maximizes the number of consumption-oriented units in society. Each nuclear family buys many consumer items even though some are used only infrequently. Most families, for example, own their own television, stove, food processor, and automobile. A washing machine is used for only a few hours a week, yet most families purchase their own rather than share one with others. In extended or communal families, fewer such consumer goods would be needed because they would be shared, and thus the market for these goods would be smaller, which would hurt the interests of capitalists. Communal families, which are based on the belief in common ownership of at least some material goods, also threaten the basic value of private property on which a capitalist economy rests. Conflict theorists would also argue that family systems can contribute to the perpetuation of social and economic inequality because inheritance in many societies, especially capitalist ones, is based on kinship. This makes it possible for a family to accumulate and perpetuate its wealth over generations. Such American families as the Carnegies, the Rockefellers, the Astors, the Kennedys, and the Gettys have amassed enormous fortunes. Anyone who can inherit wealth—of whatever amount—clearly has an advantage over those who come from modest or poor backgrounds. Thus, the family in such societies becomes a vehicle for perpetuating patterns of dominance and subordination.

Conflict theorists argue that the dominant groups protect against threats to their position by teaching people through the schools, the media, and other means that monogamy, nuclear families, family inheritance, and private property are best. Through socialization and education, people

APPLIED RESEARCH

Day Care: Problem or Solution?

Two decades ago, one-quarter of women with children under six years of age were working; by the 1990s, this figure had grown to 58 percent (Veum and Gleason, 1991). In some cases, both parents work in order to pursue a career or provide adequate income for their families; in other cases, a single mother must work in order to support her family. In either case, someone must care for these children while the parents work. When relatives or friends are not available to provide these child-rearing services, increasing numbers of parents turn to day care. Day care has been controversial because it seems to violate the traditional notion that children should be raised by their parents, and for some, this is a symptom of the erosion of the modern family. Yet, growing numbers of parents use day-care services: Less than 1 percent of young children of working mothers were in day-care centers in the mid-1970s compared with over 10 percent by the 1990s (Veum and Gleason, 1991). One issue surrounding day care, which will be addressed in the future prospects discussion, is what kind of assistance society should provide to parents in raising their children. A second issue, which has been the target of much social science research, is whether day care can do as good a job of raising children as parents can.

Critics of day care, such as psychoanalyst Selma Fraiberg (1977), argue that children need much love and understanding in their early years if they are to become emotionally healthy adults. Day-care workers, she argues, are often overburdened—with high children-to-staff ratios and substantial turnover among employees—and cannot provide the intimate involvement and sense of attachment that children need. Another critic, director of Boston's Center for Parent Education, Dr. Burton White, comments: "A child needs large doses of custom-made love, [and] you can't expect hired help to provide that. I see the trend to-

ward increasing use of day care as a disaster" ("What Price Day Care?" 1984: 16).

Child rearing is a sensitive topic because our attitudes about it are so strongly influenced by traditional values relating to the family. In the United States, we see the family as very important and also value the privacy of the family unit. Tradition places the family, and especially maternal care, as the primary and essential element of good child rearing. Given these strong values, opinions about child rearing may be subject to considerable ethnocentrism, in which traditional ways of raising children are seen as the only proper ways of doing so. In just such situations, social science research can help to alleviate the danger that one's values will lead to biased and inaccurate conclusions about which child-rearing approaches will be effective. Two decades of such research have now accumulated, comparing children in various types of day-care centers with children raised in the home by parents, relatives, or others. Virtually all this research shows that children exposed to day care do at least as well, and often better than, children raised exclusively in the home by their parents (Clarke-Stewart, 1991). Day-care children do as well in verbal and cognitive abilities, creativity, cooperation, and social competence as do home-raised children. Children placed in day care do at least as well as children raised at home in intelligence and psychosocial development; they do at least as well in sociability and academic achievement; and economically disadvantaged children in day care show less decline in IQ scores than is typically found among such children (Belsky and Steinberg, 1978; Belsky, 1984; Ispa, Thornburg, and Gray, 1990; Wasik et al., 1990). Day-care children are also as attached to their parents as are children cared for in the home (Kagan, Kearsley, and Zelazo, 1978). Some researchers have cautioned that infants under one year of age may be detrimentally affected by day care, but other research concludes that its effect is no different from home care (Kahn and Kamerman, 1987; Mott, 1991).

Research does suggest a few situations in which day care may not be the best for children. For example, children enrolled in day care for extended periods may become more aggressive and less cooperative, and economically disadvantaged children are often sent to poor quality day-care centers, which may adversely affect their emotional development (Belsky and Steinberg, 1978). But this mass of research leaves us fairly confident that good day care can do at least as good a job raising children as the parents can. Actually, this should not be surprising because day-care centers have the resources to offer children much more—in terms of people to interact with, adults trained in child development and education, and such physical resources as games and educational materials—than does the average home. The typical nuclear family offers a child a much more limited range of social contacts and educational experiences.

Recent research has shifted focus from the issue of whether day care can do a good job to that of the quality of day care in the United States. And that quality is disturbingly low. One national survey of day-care centers found that most day-care classrooms were "barely adequate" in terms of developmentally appropriate activities for the children, with only 12 percent being rated as "good" (Zaslow, 1991). And quality of day care is related to children's development: Children in better quality day care exhibit more cognitive and social development compared with children in lower quality day care. This is a problem especially for less affluent families because research shows that the day care available to them tends to be of lower quality.

One of the reasons that the quality of day care is often lower than it should be is that we do not pay much for day care. Day-care workers are overwhelmingly female, young, and disproportionately minority. They are a well-educated, dedicated, and committed group of people. They are also paid, on average, poverty-level wages, receive few benefits such as health insurance or retirement, and do a very taxing and difficult job (Hofferth and Phillips, 1991; Phillips, Howes, and Whitebook, 1991). The picture one gets is that Americans are willing to pay autoworkers large salaries, but they scrimp when it comes to paying those who care for their children.

Higher quality day care is found where workers have higher wages, more extensive benefits, and better working conditions. Better quality day care is also found when there are low child-to-staff ratios (or more staff for a given number of children), and stability of care, with low turnover among the staff. The average annual turnover among staff in day-care centers is 41 percent—almost one out of every two workers leaves each year! (Phillips, Howes, and Whitebook, 1991). The main reasons workers leave, of course, are low wages, poor benefits, and unsatisfactory working conditions.

What it comes down to is that good day care costs money. This creates a problem, however, because higher costs will price some parents out of the day-care market—they will not be able to afford it. In a sense, day-care workers have been subsidizing inexpensive day care for parents over the years by accepting poverty-level wages. So there is a tension between spending more money to improve the quality of the day-care services available to our children and keeping day care affordable to parents, especially single parents or those with low incomes. This tension becomes especially noticeable when day-care centers are private, profit-making organizations, which is often the case in the United States. The pressure to increase profit margins can lead to cost-cutting measures that reduce the quality of care. Research shows that for-profit day-care centers, when compared with nonprofit centers, tend to pay lower salaries, have fewer staff per child, provide a lower quality of service, and have more staff turnover (Culkin, Morris, and Helburn, 1991; Kagan, 1991).

Social science research of the sort described in this insert has dispelled the traditional notion that family and maternal care for children is inherently superior to care provided in day-care centers. This research is now serving as a foundation for developing social policy on the future of day care in the United States.

internalize these beliefs and they are unlikely, therefore, to even consider other forms of the family, such as communal arrangements. In addition, strong normative pressures motivate people to live in socially acceptable forms of the family. From the conflict perspective, family forms change when new groups acquire the power necessary to gain acceptance for a new form of family. The organization of family life becomes a social problem when groups with the power to make their concerns heard believe that the existing family structure is not serving their interests and they act to change it. The dispute over the proper family form, however, is not couched in the language of personal interests but rather in conflicting values.

The Interactionist Perspective

Given the many forms of the family, which one is "right"? That, according to the interactionist perspective, is a matter of social definition. Every society has rules and norms that shape family and kin relationships. Once the norms are established, people are socialized to accept their society's form of the family as "natural." The rules become embodied in central cultural values that are internalized, and their violation becomes unthinkable for the majority. In most societies, there is substantial social consensus regarding the proper form of the family and the appropriate way for family members to relate to one another. Most Americans, for example, probably consider monogamy to be the most "civilized" type of marriage. Few Americans could accept for themselves the Tibetan practice in which a woman who marries a particular man is considered to be the wife of all of that man's brothers—even brothers yet to be born at the time of the marriage (Goldstein, 1971). Yet strict monogamy is one of the less common forms of the family, being practiced by only about one-quarter of all human societies.

What behavior is acceptable is interpreted in the light of cultural values and societal develop-ment. As society and its values change, the interpretations of behavior also change. In an earlier era, for example, when the traditional family was essential to accomplish such things as child rearing, family life was given a sacred or religious meaning, and divorce was highly stigmatized. By expressing shock or disgust at those who divorce, people in their daily lives helped to foster the "reality" that "marriage for life" was the right way to live. In a male-dominated society, the ritual by which women take on their husband's last name symbolized the distribution of power in the family and in society. Family violence was viewed as a "family affair" because it also reflected power relations in society, either the dominance of males over females or parents over children.

Today, the consensus regarding family and family-related behavior is much less widespread than it once was. People today are faced with issues that in the past were settled by strong social pressures: Should I get married? Should I stay married? Should I have sex, or even children, outside of marriage? Should I take my husband's name or keep my own? There is a growing inconsistency regarding acceptable behavior in these realms. This creates tension for individuals who must make choices without the clear-cut guidance and support of society. According to the interactionist perspective, when people are not provided with clear expectations for how they should behave, the stability of society is threatened because people may make choices that are defined by others as detrimental to society. Whether such practices are in fact detrimental is, of course, another matter. What *is* essential is that some groups define these practices as threatening to their values and as a social problem.

The interactionist perspective, then, points to the fact that what is considered the family is a matter of social definition, becoming a part of the social reality that people create and live by. Variations in the family may come to be seen as deviant and may be highly stigmatized because they violate the shared expectations of some groups about how to lead one's life. If this occurs, these groups may view changes in the form of the family as a social problem.

ATTITUDES TOWARD MARRIAGE AND THE FAMILY

Given the changes that have occurred in the role of the family in industrial society, are marriage and family living still popular today? It would seem so: More Americans marry than ever before, well over 90 percent. In 1991, almost 65 percent of all adult men were married, as were 60 percent of all adult women. These figures are higher than they were in 1940 but somewhat lower than at any time since 1950 (see Figure 3.2). Surveys in the 1980s revealed that both young people and their parents have quite positive attitudes toward marriage and family ("Marriage vs. Single Life,"

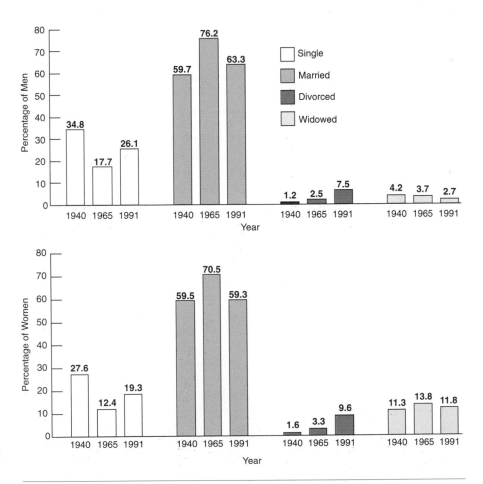

Figure 3.2 Marital Status of Adults in America, 1940–1991
SOURCES: U.S. Bureau of the Census, *Statistical Abstract of the United States, 1982–83* (Washington, D.C.: U.S. Government Printing Office, 1982), p. 38; U.S. Bureau of the Census, *Statistical Abstract of the United States, 1992* (Washington, D.C.: U.S. Government Printing Office, 1992), p. 44.

1982; Martin and Martin, 1984; Moore and Stief, 1991). In a national sample of high school seniors, three-quarters reported that marriage and family life were "extremely important" to them, and a survey of young adults aged eighteen to twenty-two found that most of them plan to marry before the age of thirty. The vast majority of them also believed that when people marry, it should be "for life." The surveys detected some important changes, however: These young men and women, when compared with their parents, have fewer negative attitudes toward staying single and see fewer advantages in getting married over remaining single. In fact, the people interviewed seemed reluctant to choose either marriage or singlehood as the preferred alternative. In short, marriage is viewed quite positively by many Americans today, but alternatives to marriage are also becoming more popular.

These attitudes may reflect the culmination of a long transition from "arranged marriages" to "participant-run" romances. In preindustrial societies, in which the extended family and kinship were core social institutions, parents played a key role in deciding when and who their children would marry. Because the family in these societies was the major institution performing the important functions described in the previous section, it is not surprising that marital decisions were not left to whim or fancy. In many of these societies, *arranged marriages* occurred in which parents would select marriage partners for their children, sometimes shortly after their birth. The selection was based on what was considered best for the family, and the prospective marriage partners had little other choice. Such arranged marriages are still common in India and some other societies, and their members generally accept this practice as the wisest way to make marital choices.

A modified form of arranged marriage existed in preindustrial America, with young people having some choice in selecting a marriage partner but with parents still retaining substantial control over the ultimate decision. Courtship was common, but it occurred under the ever-watchful eyes of parents and other elders in the community. It was a *parent-run* courtship process: Young men and women were allowed to choose from among a pool of partners who were considered acceptable by their parents but were strongly discouraged from going outside of that pool (Gordon, 1978a).

In modern industrial societies, the selection of a marital partner is based primarily on the individual desires of the prospective mates. Parents can and do play a role in this process, but their influence is typically secondary and often no more important than the suggestions of a close friend. This courtship process, then, is more *participant run*, with romantic love as a primary factor drawing couples toward marriage. One reason for this declining role of parents over the years is that kinship is less important in modern societies, and one's kin, including one's parents, have considerably less stake in who marries whom. A second reason is that children have a greater degree of economic independence from their parents in industrial societies, and parents therefore have less leverage with which to demand a say in the choice of a marriage partner. In the past, parents could withhold economic support from a couple, which usually made it very difficult for them to establish a household. Today, young people are better able to get jobs independently of their families and to support themselves. As the position of the family in society has changed, then, people have gained more freedom of choice regarding a marriage partner. Today, it seems, people are also gaining more freedom of choice regarding whether to marry at all. Although most people will continue to marry, there is no longer as strong a stigma attached to remaining single.

Just as attitudes toward marriage are evolving, so are attitudes about having children. Traditionally, a family was viewed as consisting of parents and their children. Today, however, many people question whether children are an essential ingredient in the family equation. People still face strong social pressures in our society to have children, and childless couples are often stereotyped as having less fulfilling and lonelier lives (Thompson, 1980). Despite this, the number of childless couples is not inconsiderable, although it does fluctuate over time. From 1950 to 1965, childlessness declined, but it has since increased. In 1950, 20 percent of all women in their forties who had ever been married were childless; this dropped to 7 percent in 1975 and then rose to over 10 percent by the 1990s (U.S. Bureau of the Census, 1978: 64; 1992: 71). It seems that many couples forego parenthood because they weigh the costs of having children as greater than the benefits children afford. In particular, it appears that having children is viewed as a threat to the wife's ability to maintain her place in the labor force and pursue a career (Ory, 1978; Houseknecht, 1987).

So, just as people feel less pressure today to marry, they also feel reduced pressure to have children, and these changes in norms document the extent to which the family, at least in its more traditional and conventional forms, is less central in modern society. For many, these changes in the family—seeming to signal its collapse—are a serious problem of our times. We will look at three major problem areas: the high divorce rate, lifestyle alternatives to the traditional family, and violence in the family.

DIVORCE

The Divorce Rate

People usually view the widespread incidence and easy availability of divorce as having arisen only recently. In fact, the option for a married couple to dissolve a marriage has existed in many premodern societies. In some hunting and gathering bands, for example, a marriage could be easily ended when a couple decided to stop living together (O'Kelly and Carney, 1986). Nevertheless, to those who believe that marriage should be a lifelong commitment involving a deep emotional sharing between the married couple, today's high divorce rate is viewed as a threat to the family as a social institution.

In calculating the incidence of divorce, most sociologists use a statistic called the **refined divorce rate,** *which is determined by dividing the number of divorces each year by the total number of existing marriages in that year.* This method provides a valid way of comparing the stability of marriages from one year to the next. As Table 3.1 illustrates, the divorce rate has more than doubled since 1940, going from 8.8 to 20.7. As a point of comparison, it has been estimated that there were

Table 3.1 **The Rate of Marriage and Divorce in the United States, 1940–1988**

	1940	*1945*	*1950*	*1955*	*1960*	*1965*	*1970*	*1975*	*1980*	*1985*	*1988*
Marriage Rate[a]	82.8	83.6	90.2	80.9	73.5	75	76.5	66.9	61.4	57.5	54.6
Divorce Rate[b]	8.8	14.4	10.3	9.3	9.2	10.6	14.9	20.3	22.6	21.7	20.7
Remarriage Rate[c]						127.8	123.3	117.2	91.3	81.8	78.6

[a]marriages per 1,000 unmarried women over 15
[b]divorce and annulments per 1,000 married women over 15
[c]marriages per 1,000 divorced women over 14

SOURCES: U.S. Bureau of the Census, *Statistical Abstract of the United States, 1985* (Washington, D.C.: U.S. Government Printing Office, 1984), p. 80; National Center for Health Statistics: Advance Report of Final Divorce Statistics, 1988. *Monthly Vital Statistics Report*, Vol. 39, No. 12, DHHS Pub. No. (PHS) 91–1120. Public Health Service, Hyattsville, Md. May 21, 1991, p. 7; National Center for Health Statistics: Advance Report of Final Marriage Statistics, 1988, *Monthly Vital Statistics Report*, Vol. 40, No. 4, DHHS Pub. No. (PHS) 91–1120. Public Health Service, Hyattsville, Md. August 26, 1991, pp. 9, 12.

only 1.2 divorces for every 1,000 marriages in 1869—reflecting a seventeenfold increase during the past century (Saxton, 1980: 380). Although the trend in divorce rates over the past fifty years has been up, the rate has fluctuated considerably. It rose to 17.9 in 1946, one year after the end of World War II, a rate that is close the rates found in the past fifteen years. Since 1975, the divorce rate has pretty much leveled off.

If we want to know the probability that a given marriage will end in divorce, we need a different statistic. As Figure 3.3 illustrates, the likelihood that a marriage would end in divorce in 1870 was 8 percent. By the 1980s, this figure had risen to over 50 percent. So though it may be disturbing to many, the statistical likelihood of marriages beginning today ending in divorce is about fifty-fifty. However, those people who divorce are apparently not totally disillusioned with marriage because 75 to 80 percent of them will eventually remarry. But a slightly greater number of these second marriages will end in divorce in comparison to first marriages (Collins and Coltrane, 1991). However, this percentage is a little deceiving because it includes a small number of people who divorce and remarry many times. When this group is removed, second marriages are reasonably successful, and many couples in their second marriage report that they are happy.

The divorce rate, however, is but one measure of marital dissolution. Approximately 3 percent of all marriages end in legal separation, where the

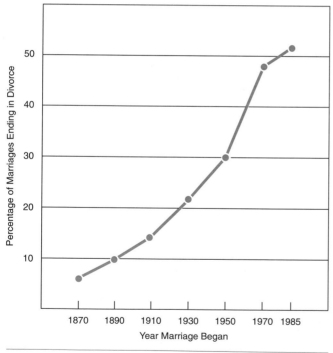

Figure 3.3   **The Rising Percentage of Marriages Ending in Divorce**
SOURCES: Andrew J. Cherlin, *Marriage, Divorce, Remarriage* (Cambridge, Mass.: Harvard University Press, 1981); Arthur J. Norton and Jeanne E. Moorman, "Current Trends in Marriage and Divorce Among American Women," *Journal of Marriage and the Family*, 49 (February), 1987: 3–14.

"The work being done on your marriage—are you having it done, or are you doing it yourselves?"

In modern societies with fairly high divorce rates, marriage is often no longer considered "for keeps," and people expect they will have to "work on" their marriage in order to avoid divorce.

partners decide to end their relationship but prefer, perhaps for religious reasons, not to divorce. Desertion is another way in which marriages are dissolved, although it is difficult to know the extent of these. In any event, we need to be aware that only a portion of all marital dissolutions is reflected in the divorce rate. In fact, given these marital practices, we might refer to our marriage system as one involving serial monogamy rather than monogamy. **Polygamy** refers to *having more than one spouse at the same time*. **Serial monogamy** means that *we are allowed to have more than one spouse, just not at the same time*.

People get divorces for many personal reasons—their spouse has become insensitive, they feel trapped by limited career opportunities, or their sex lives are no longer exciting. However, sociologists prefer to focus on the societal conditions that result in a high divorce rate rather than personal reasons for divorce. At least four such conditions account for the rising divorce rate over the past century.

First, we have seen that the family performs fewer functions today than in the past, and this means there are fewer pressures on couples to stay together if they are unhappy. In the past, the same unhappy couple might have remained married because neither spouse felt they could raise the children alone or they needed the family for support in old age. Today, single parents are better prepared to raise a child, and most people are supported by retirement plans in their old age. In fact, the high levels of affluence afforded by industrialization have made people less dependent on kinship ties for support, with consequent changes in the family as an institution. Second, the increasing equality between men and women has created both opportunities and tensions that contribute to the divorce rate (Brehm, 1985). In terms of opportunities, many women today are part of the labor force and thus have the economic ability to support themselves and their children without a husband. This reduces the likelihood of women being willing to remain in unsatisfying relationships. In terms of tensions, sexual equality has led to a redefining of the roles in the family, which can cause disagreements and stress that may precipitate divorce. A husband, for example, may feel that his wife should do most of the household chores, whereas she feels these tasks should be divided equally. This is especially a problem for women who, after marrying, decide to pursue a career. This life change disrupts an established marital pattern and requires a renegotiation of male and female roles in the family, which is sometimes unsuccessful (Houseknecht, Vaughan, and Macke, 1984). A third reason for the rising divorce rate is that there is considerably less stigma attached to divorce today than in the past (Thornton, 1985). Divorce in the past was often viewed as a serious failing in a person's life, with divorced people frequently labeled as morally inferior. Females in particular bore the sigma of the divorcee as a "fallen" woman. In precommunist China, for example, the divorce rate was extremely low, but the suicide rate for wives was very high. Wives were guided by a disturbing adage: "Good women should hang themselves; only bad women seek divorce" (Yang, 1965: 81). Today, with fifteen million divorced people in the United States, divorce is viewed by many as merely another life-style choice rather than a reflection of one's allegedly weak character. Finally, as negative attitudes toward divorce have eased over the past three decades, pressures have surfaced to simplify the legal process for obtaining a divorce. These developments have encouraged more people to seek dissolution when they encounter marital difficulties.

Taking all of these factors together, we can make an important overriding observation about the reasons for divorce: Americans expect a great deal from the marriage relationship. We allow people to form families largely on the basis of romantic love, which can be fickle and unpredictable. Then we expect those relationships to afford a lifetime of emotional fulfillment, sexual gratification, companionship, and commitment. Is it so surprising, then, that many marriages fail to achieve these ideals? In the past, there were other, more pragmatic pressures for couples to stay together, such as economic constraints, reputation, religious ideals, and maintaining the marriage "for the sake of the children." Today, if the romantic ideal fails, other "barrier strengths" maintaining the marriage are less likely to prevent marital dissolution (Levinger and Moles, 1979).

Who Gets Divorced?

Some couples are at considerably greater risk of getting a divorce than are others (Bahr, 1989). Couples with an increased likelihood of divorcing have the following characteristics:

1. *Social differences between the couple, such as differences in religion, race, social class background, or values.* These differences can place substantial stress on a marriage.
2. *Low socioeconomic standing, such as low income or education.* Unemployment and other stresses that often accompany low social standing probably make it more difficult to achieve a successful marriage.
3. *Young age at marriage.* Very young couples seem especially ill equipped to make a go of marriage.
4. *Whirlwind romances.* People who have known one another for only a brief period are more likely to choose a partner with whom they will later prove to be incompatible.

The Effects of Divorce

As we have said, some fear that a high divorce rate will result in the collapse of the family as an institution. This implies that the family would fail to perform its functions, such as socializing children and providing emotional support. If this occurred on a widespread scale, the consequences could threaten society with severe stress and disorganization. Let us see what some of the effects of divorce are.

Widespread divorce has complicated kinship relationships and brought about what has been called a **blended family:** *a family based on kinship ties that accumulate as a consequence of divorces and remarriages* (Chilman, 1988). These families involve relationships that are more complex than the standard nuclear family. For example, a child may live in a family with a full-blood sibling, a half-blood sibling, and a sibling with no blood and only marital ties. The same child may have a "real" mother and father as well as a stepfather or stepmother, and three sets of grandparents. Such arrangements, with their attendant complex kinship and legal linkages, can create complications and tensions that are less likely in traditional nuclear or extended family arrangements (Ambert, 1986; Johnson and Barer, 1987; Johnson, Klee, and Schmidt, 1988). In fact, sociologists now speak of "remarried couple households," defined as married couple households in which one or both spouses have been divorced. In 1988, 46 percent of all marriages involved a remarriage by at least one of the partners (National Center for Health Statistics, 1991).

Divorce can be a disruptive and troubling experience, as those who have experienced it will attest. Marital dissolution often precipitates feelings of failure, loneliness, and rejection, along with intense anger and frustration. For many, it represents an assault on their sense of self-worth. Even when divorce is preferred by a person, an intimate bond is dashed nevertheless, and there is often nothing to immediately take its place. Symptoms of psychological distress, sometimes quite severe, are common among the newly divorced. This is also sometimes associated with increased problems of physical health, with divorced people having more serious illnesses and more chronic disabling conditions (Verbrugge, 1979; Kiecolt-Glaser et al., 1987). As further documentation of the distress of divorce, suicide is far more prevalent among the divorced than it is among single or married people. Men and women are affected by different elements of the divorce situation: Women's distress is more likely to arise from the fact that divorce leaves them with a lower standard of living and increased parental responsibilities; men's distress tends to arise from their difficulty in maintaining a close and supportive network of personal ties (Gerstel, Riessman, and Rosenfield, 1985).

There has been considerable debate over the years regarding whether the husband or the wife is treated more unfairly in divorce proceedings. Husbands complain about being gouged for alimony or child-support payments, whereas wives protest over allegedly meager or missing payments from husbands. Social scientists have done considerable research on this issue, comparing the experiences of divorced women with those of divorced men and also looking at people's circumstances before and after divorce. The conclusions are remarkably consistent: Women are much more likely than men to suffer economic decline after divorce, and even when men suffer, their economic slide is much less severe and much more short-lived than is that of women (Holden and Smock, 1991). Sociologist Lenore Weitzman (1985), for example, has concluded that divorced women and their children are rapidly becoming an underclass in America. The women she studied and their dependent children suffered a 73 percent decline in their standard of living after divorce. By comparison, the men in her sample experienced an increase of 42 percent. One reason women end up worse off is that courts typically only divide up tangible property, such as a home, automobile, or belongings. Less tangible but often far more valuable property, such as a professional license that can translate into considerable income through-out a career, is usually not considered a part of the property settlement. It is the man who is far more likely to possess these less tangible forms of property. There are other reasons for the postdivorce economic decline of women: It is typically the woman who takes custody of children after divorce, and child support awarded by courts is usually meager compared to the father's income; only a minority of fathers comply fully with child-support awards; women earn substantially less than men (see Chapter 7); and women, having child-rearing responsibilities, suffer barriers in looking for jobs and finding child care. All this means that most women suffer an economic decline after a divorce. Women who are especially likely to suffer are the homemakers who devoted themselves to the housewife and mother roles. After divorce, with few marketable skills, these women suffer the most severe deprivation (Devillier and Forsyth, 1988).

Court rulings could create some change in these realms. For example, some courts have ruled that a spouse divorced after helping support a mate through medical or professional school might be entitled to a share of his or her mate's future earnings. Although these rulings have typically been overturned by a higher court, many experts are predicting that such rulings in the future may result in an expansion of the definition of "property" in divorce cases: Anything that might produce future income, such as a medical or law degree, could be considered property to be shared as a part of a financial settlement (Holden and Smock, 1991).

As far as the children of divorce are concerned, the jury is still out regarding whether they would be better off staying in a conflict-ridden, unhappy home rather than experiencing the divorce of their parents. Divorce is without question difficult for children, and living in a loving home is certainly preferable to experiencing an unhappy home or divorce. We simply lack the research to know all the effects if an unhappy family remains intact. There are some things that we do know, however

(Wallerstein and Blakeslee, 1989; Furstenburg and Cherlin, 1991). First, the impact on children depends on their age. Children between five and ten, for example, often feel some responsibility for their parents' divorce, and this may lead to feelings of guilt and failure. Preteens often express tremendous anger at their parents. Teenagers, on the other hand, are often confronted with the matter of "parental loyalty," feelings that they must take sides in the conflict and form a coalition with one or the other parent. Furthermore, although adolescents are better able to understand the reasons for divorce, they are often very worried about the effects of separation on their future. In fact, one investigation determined that eighteen months after separation, the vast majority of all the children continued to oppose the divorce, with only 10 percent preferring their postdivorce situation to the one they had had before. A full five years after separation, 28 percent of the children approved of their parents' divorce, 30 percent disapproved, and 42 percent took an intermediate position on the issue (Wallerstein and Kelly, 1980). A second thing we know about the impact of divorce is that children in divorced homes seem more prone to delinquency (Rankin, 1983; Wells and Rankin, 1991). Third, a common consequence of divorce for both boys and girls is a decline in school performance. One study involving the effects of marital disruption on children's behavior determined that disruption is exacerbated by multiple marital transitions: a pattern that is becoming more common today. Negative effects appear to be lower if the child lives with the same-sex parent following divorce or maintains a good relationship with one or both parents (Peterson and Zill, 1986). Despite these negative consequences, there is evidence that children in one-parent families sometimes benefit in some ways because their parent gives them greater responsibilities and more participation in family decision making. Some of these children become more independent and resourceful, and the parent turns to them for some of the support previously sought from a spouse (Amato, 1987).

So divorce does have some substantial negative consequences for society, and later in this chapter we will discuss ways of alleviating their impact. First, however, we will look at some life-style alternatives to the conventional nuclear family.

EMERGING FAMILY LIFE-STYLES

People who divorce and those who never marry develop some type of life-style, including personal relationships and living arrangements, to replace the conventional family. These life-styles are considered by many to be another dimension of the problems surrounding the family today. Figure 3.4 illustrates some of these changes in family structure over the past two decades. These alternative life-styles did not emerge arbitrarily; they are a reflection of the diversified and to a degree fragmented society in which we live. Some of these life-styles arise as people adapt to the void left by divorce, but some are chosen because elements of modern society make them more attractive options than in the past (Davidson and Moore, 1992). Following are three such elements of today's society:

1. There is an *increasing atmosphere of tolerance* about sexual and personal behavior that has reduced the stigma that is attached to divorce, as well as enabled people to find sexual gratification without getting married.
2. There is *greater individualism and egalitarianism,* including increased geographic mobility

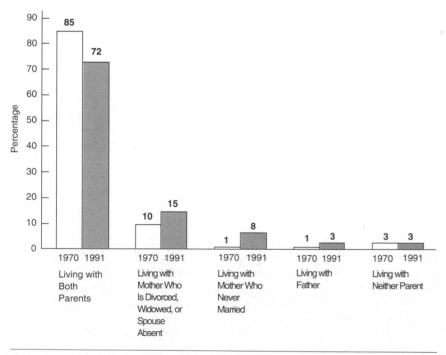

Figure 3.4   **Living Arrangements of People Under 18 Years of Age, 1970–1991**
SOURCE: U.S. Bureau of the Census, *Statistical Abstract of the United States, 1992* (Washington, D.C.: U.S. Government Printing Office, 1992), p. 55.

and an emphasis on individual careers, that has produced an atmosphere of separation from the group, including the nuclear family. It also reduces barriers to sexual involvement during courtship and other expressions of sexuality.

3. There has been a *marketing of life-styles and sexuality* in the mass media, providing role models for young people and making non-traditional life-styles newsworthy and often presented by the media as "trendy" and "fashionable." This helps to spread their popularity.

We now review some of the major alternatives to the conventional family with an eye on what future developments are likely.

Dual-Career Families

In the conventional nuclear family in America, women either did not work outside the home or their jobs were considered secondary to their husbands'. Today, in just over one-half of all two-spouse families, the wife works (see Figure 3.5). In addition, there is an increasing number of

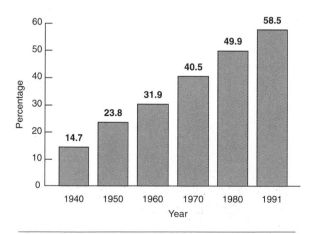

Figure 3.5 Percentage of Married Women with Spouse Present Who Are Employed, 1940–1991
SOURCES: U.S. Bureau of the Census, *Statistical Abstract of the United States, 1978* (Washington, D.C.: U.S. Government Printing Office, 1978), p. 404; U.S. Bureau of the Census, *Statistical Abstract of the United States, 1992* (Washington, D.C.: U.S. Government Printing Office, 1992), p. 387.

dual-career families *in which both wives and husbands are committed to career-oriented occupations that offer them fulfillment and opportunities for advancement.* Although it is difficult to estimate the number of dual-career families, census statistics suggest that the number of dual-career couples has grown from 900,000 in 1960 to 3.3 million by the mid-1980s (Sekaran, 1986).

One of the major tensions that people in dual-career families face is how to resolve disputes over whose career will take precedence. Such disputes can arise, for example, if either husband or wife wants to move to another city or state in order to advance a career, especially if such a transition would be detrimental to his or her spouse's career. On a routine basis, there may be disagreement over whose career must suffer in order to raise children or to accomplish household chores. Although these tensions suggest that dual-career marriages are more susceptible to divorce, there is little convincing evidence on this issue so far. Evidence does suggest that women who work out of choice are more satisfied with their marriages than women who work out of a sense of financial obligation, and the men in dual-career families seem to be happy with their marriages (Gilbert, 1985; Piotrkowski et al., 1987; Vannoy-Hiller and Philliber, 1989). In addition, dual-career couples are more likely to remain childless and childless couples tend to have higher levels of perceived marital satisfaction than do couples with children (Houseknecht, 1987). A recent investigation of dual-career couples working in senior management positions described such marriages as "more equal than others" in that the couples share a more equal partnership, with a more egalitarian decision-making structure, than do couples in more traditional marriages. Furthermore, women in such marriages have greater opportunity to continue to pursue careers, as well as raise their children, in comparison to women in traditional families (Hertz, 1986).

Careers are attractive to both men and women because their work offers financial rewards, status, and excitement. However, the time and commitment devoted to careers competes with the energy people devote to family life, and this can create tensions in the family. Higher rates of childlessness among dual-career families may be an effort to avoid such competing demands. This might create other problems, however (Hunt and Hunt, 1982). If more people choose careers in the future, it is possible that many will resolve competing demands by choosing not to have children, possibly even choosing not to get married. This may well create a substantial difference in the standard of living between those who devote their energies to careers and those who feel family is important: Careerists will have a substantially more affluent life-style, and this may make the decision to remain childless appealing to even more people. The outcome, potentially, might be the birth of even fewer children in society. This in turn could lead to a number of problems. For example, it would lead to an increasingly aged and dependent population that would be difficult and expensive to support (see Chapter 8).

Singlehood

Today, forty million adults in the United States have never been married. This figure includes slightly more males than females. Many of these people, of course, will eventually marry, but some will choose singlehood over marriage as a lifelong life-style. In addition, although the proportion of our population that is single declined between 1940 and 1965, it has increased considerably since then (see Figure 3.2). Added to these never-married people are the many widowed and divorced who, at least temporarily, are living their lives as single men and women. In 1989, for example, there were ten million widowed people over sixty-five years of age in the United States, 80 percent of whom were living alone (U.S. Bureau of the Census, 1989: 42).

Many people who elect to remain single do so because they believe this life-style affords them distinct advantages: freedom from unnecessary commitments, economic independence, opportu-

nities to meet new people and develop new relationships, room for personal growth, and the ability to have a more varied sex life that is free of guilt (Cargan and Melko, 1982; Macklin, 1987). This does not mean of course that there is necessarily a lack of emotional involvement with a partner who is at least semipermanent. Many singles develop intimate relationships, but they refuse to allow these to become permanent bonds based on marital exclusivity. However, as with childlessness among dual-career couples, singlehood—especially if chosen permanently and in large numbers—may have a long-term impact on the birthrate.

Cohabitation

Cohabitation, or what is commonly called "living together," refers to *relationships in which two people live in the same household and share sexual, emotional, and often economic ties without being legally married.* In 1988, a survey showed that 5 percent of women between the ages of fifteen and forty-four were in a cohabitation relationship, and fully one-third of all those women had cohabited at some point in their lives (London, 1990). Most of the couples involved are young, with over 65 percent involving partners under thirty-five years of age. But a substantial number of the couples, as much as 7 percent, involve one partner over sixty-five, and 40 percent of the cohabiting men and 43 percent of the women were previously married (U.S. Bureau of the Census, 1991: 44).

People cohabit for many reasons. For some, it is a "trial marriage," a time for the couple to get to know one another and determine whether they are compatible before establishing the legal bond (Gwartney-Gibbs, 1986). For others, who may or may not intend eventually to marry, cohabitation is the preferred way of carrying on a sexual relationship, rather than the more secretive sexual relations of a few decades ago. For still other people, cohabitation is a replacement for marriage, which, as an institution, may be viewed as an unnecessary legal tie that cannot help and could possibly hurt an intimate relationship. Finally, for some elderly couples, for whom marriage means a reduction in Social Security income, cohabitation may be a matter of economic convenience or necessity (Jacques and Chason, 1978; Blumstein and Schwartz, 1983).

As the number of cohabiting couples has grown, the stigma associated with this life-style has declined. It is now widely accepted in cities and college communities, and it will probably become even more popular, especially among young people:

> *The number of people involved may be small [around 4 percent of couples], but . . . if we look at households where the man is under twenty-five, the picture becomes more impressive. The percentage of cohabitors more than doubles . . . [This] may mean that the future will contain more cohabiting couples than the present statistical pattern would indicate. (Blumstein and Schwartz, 1983: 38)*

As cohabitation has become more common over the past few decades, controversy has arisen about the legal status of the partners in the relationship. As was mentioned in the beginning of the chapter, some employers, including some city and county governments, have established "domestic partner" provisions that accord cohabitants much the same benefits and rights as married couples. Although this is still not widespread, it may well become more common in the future as employers adapt to the kinds of personal arrangements their employees seem to prefer for their lives. As a significant number of employees choose not to marry, employers are taking this into consideration in their policies. In addition, a number of courts have ruled that the relationship between cohabitants is not unlike that of married couples. For example, cohabitants can make legal arrangements to share their property, and one partner can sue the other for a share of the property and for support payments, or "palimony," should the relationship dissolve. So, although some people continue to see marriage as the pref-

erable route for organizing one's life, a growing number of people are choosing cohabitation, and the courts are establishing a legal framework that sees cohabitation as being very much like marriage.

Single Parenthood

A rapidly growing alternative to the conventional two-parent nuclear family is one in which there is only one parent. Today, almost 25 percent of all families with children under eighteen years of age are headed by only one parent, mostly by women (U.S. Bureau of the Census, 1992: 52). Furthermore, one out of every four children lives in a family in which one or both parents are absent (see Figure 3.4), and half of all children may spend at least part of their childhood in a single-parent home. Although some families have only one parent due to the death of a spouse, most are the result of divorce. Increasingly, however, children live with parents, usually mothers, who choose not to marry at all. In 1991, more than three million families were headed by a parent who had never been married. The number of children living with a mother who had never married increased over eight times to over 8 percent between 1970 and 1991. In 1988, 25 percent of all births were to unmarried women, in comparison with 4 percent in 1950 (U.S. Bureau of the Census, 1991: 53, 67).

Given these trends in divorce and single motherhood, the proportion of single-parent families is likely to grow considerably in the future. In fact, a small but growing number of women are beginning to view childbirth outside of marriage as an acceptable life-style alternative (Kamerman and Kahn, 1988). Some urban professional women, for example, find that, for one reason or another, they have not married but still want to have a child. So they go ahead and do so. In 1981, a group of such women organized Single Mothers by Choice in New York to provide support and information for women making this choice (Klemesrud, 1983). Needless to say, people who view

In many cultures, people live in extended families, with close kinship ties with parents, grandparents, uncles, and other relatives. In today's society, divorce is more common and families are smaller, which means that this single father must take on responsibilities for his daughter and son that used to be spread over a number of adults in the family.

marriage as the only acceptable context for raising children find such developments highly threatening to their values.

Single parents face many serious problems, but the most difficult one of all for some single parents is poverty. When the decision to have a child is well considered by a woman with the social and economic resources to raise the child adequately, the outcome does not raise serious problems for society, although it might clash with the personal or religious values of some groups. However, single parenthood is especially widespread among groups who are more likely to lack the financial resources to support the child, such as minorities and teenagers. For example, over half of all births to African American and Puerto Rican American women are to unmarried women, and both of these groups have some of the highest rates of poverty in the United States (U.S. Bureau of the Census, 1992: 69). Teenagers represent only 25 percent of all women of childbearing age, but they

account for 32 percent of all births outside of marriage. For teenagers in particular, becoming a mother is a difficult burden: they are less likely than adults to have the maturity and economic resources for good child rearing, and the burden often curtails or severely limits their educational and employment opportunities. This is especially true for teens from poor families and from families with a history of welfare use (Chase-Lansdale, Brooks-Gunn, and Paikoff, 1991). Although the rate of teenage pregnancy is steady or falling in other industrial nations, it has risen over the last two decades in the United States. Teen pregnancy rates are now two to three times higher in the United States than in most industrial nations, and they are higher in the United States than *any* other industrial nation (Moore and Stief, 1991). Because of the declining stigma associated with unmarried motherhood, relatively few of such children are given up by mothers for adoption today in comparison with several decades ago.

These statistics reveal one of the principal social problems associated with single parenthood: Many of the children have mothers who are young or poor and thus likely to be socially and economically unprepared to assume the enormous responsibilities of parenthood. Consequently, these young women and their dependent children become one-parent families that are incapable of sustaining themselves financially, and society often ends up assuming some welfare responsibility for their care and keeping. This exacerbates the problem of poverty in American society and contributes to other family-related difficulties such as child abuse and delinquency.

Another problem confronting single parents is that they are compelled to perform all the economic, social, and psychological functions that are assumed by two parents in conventional nuclear families and by many people in extended family units (Kamerman and Kahn, 1988). The single parent must serve as breadwinner, disciplinarian, coordinator, and counselor. For the single parent who works outside of the home, there is often the additional economic burden of child-care costs. For poor women, single parenthood can act as a barrier to obtaining the educational or vocational training that could prepare them for a good job. In addition, single parents feel considerable pressure to marry or remarry, even though it is more difficult for a man or woman with children to compete for marriage partners, in comparison to younger people without children. For the children, however, there is little evidence that living in a single-parent family has serious detrimental consequences as long as there are adequate financial and emotional resources available (Klein, 1973; Greif, 1985). (See the earlier discussion of the impact of divorce on children.)

VIOLENCE IN THE FAMILY

The family is usually viewed as a place where love and affection abound, but one research team concluded that there is a darker side to family life: "Violence between family members is probably as common as love" (Straus, Gelles, and Steinmetz, 1980: 13). In fact, these experts comment that "the family is the most physically violent group or institution that a typical citizen is likely to encounter." Part of the reason for the contrast between people's views of the family and the reality of violence relates to the social construction of reality. People are naturally reluctant to admit that such violence occurs in their own families for fear of being stigmatized. As a consequence, especially in the past, we would hear few if any reports of such violence, and the silence would lead us to assume that such behavior was in fact rare. Its occurrence in our own families, we would conclude, was isolated, odd, and best kept a secret. Thus, the social reality of the loving affectionate family was maintained despite the fact that family violence was common.

Given the widespread nature of family violence, let us examine the three major types: marital violence, child abuse, and abuse of the elderly.

Marital Violence

Family "violence" can be defined in a number of ways. For example, Murray Straus and Richard Gelles (Gelles and Cornell, 1990) employed an extremely general definition of violence, including everything from pushes and shoves to "throwing something" to "beating up their spouse" to "using a knife or a gun." On the basis of their national survey involving more than six thousand households, they determined that one-sixth of married people have engaged in at least one act of violence against their spouses each year, although these figures probably underestimate the total amount of violence between husbands and wives because people are often reluctant to admit such goings on in their family. They estimate that more than 50 percent of married couples have had violent exchanges with each other at some point during their marriages. Using these broad criteria, of course, a good deal of the "violence" reported lies in a category where no serious physical harm comes to victims. Even so, it is obvious that a serious problem exists. It is estimated that, of the fifty-one million married couples in America in 1985 at least 6 percent experienced conjugal violence involving kicking, biting, punching, or even more severe forms of violent behavior (Straus, 1991). Violence of this sort also occurs among dating couples and cohabitants. A review of studies among college couples, for example, found that one out of every five couples experiences kicking, biting, slapping, or more serious violence while courting (Murphy, 1988). Although spouse abuse has declined in the past decade, there is still far too much of it.

How are we to explain this high incidence of marital violence? On a general level, keep in mind that the use of violence to settle conflicts is widely accepted in American society, especially among males. Serious violence within families is disproportionately a problem of the poor and the economically disadvantaged. Families with low educational and occupational attainment are especially at risk of spouse abuse. However, Table 3.2 summarizes some other significant factors associated with spouse abuse. An important thing to note is the role of sexual inequality (Kalmuss and Straus, 1982; Crossman, Stith, and Bender, 1990; Straus, 1991). Traditional norms in many American subcultures support male domination in marriage. Considering that more and more women today are working and earning money, some husbands may feel threatened that their power in decision making is being questioned and lash out in physical violence in response to their fear of change. In fact, men with traditional, or nonegalitarian, views toward sex-role relationships are more likely to approve of using violence against a spouse and are more likely to have actually used severe violence against their spouse. Straus and his colleagues found that wife beating is much more likely to occur in families where power over decision making is concentrated in the husband's hands—approximately twenty times the rate in families where egalitarian decision

Table 3.2 Facts About Spouse Abuse in Relationship to Educational and Occupational Achievements[a]

1. More than two thirds of the couples reported at least one incident of abuse in the twelve months preceding the interview with researchers.
2. Sixteen percent of the women reported at least one act of physical aggression.
3. Many of the violent couples are those in which the women occupy the two highest occupational strata and the men are in lower status occupations.
4. Men whose job status is inconsistently low for their amount of education are more likely to engage in violence.
5. Especially high risks of violence are observed when the woman's occupation is incompatible with the partner's job.
6. Increased risk of spouse abuse occurs when either the woman's job is low in comparison to her partner's job or when the man's job is low in relationship to his partner's job.
7. When the woman's job is high relative to her partner's, life-threatening acts occur more than six times more often than when their jobs are compatible. In the same fashion, when the man's occupational position is lower than expected in view of the woman's occupation, life-threatening violence also occurs about six times more frequently than when the couple is compatible in occupational attainment.

[a]These data were drawn from a random sample of 1,553 women living in the state of Kentucky.
SOURCE: Carlton A. Hornung, B. Claire McCullough, and Taichi Sugimoto, "Status Relationships in Marriage: Risk Factors in Spouse Abuse," *Journal of Marriage and the Family*, 43 (August 1981): 675–692. Copyrighted 1981 by the National Council on Family Relations, 3989 Central Avenue N.E., Suite #550, Minneapolis, Minnesota 55421. Reprinted by permission.

making is accepted (Straus, Gelles, and Steinmetz, 1980). We mentioned earlier that women with more social and economic resources are less likely to be abused and more likely to leave abusive husbands. Spouse abuse is also more likely when the victim is socially isolated from people other than their spouse. This makes it more difficult for him or her to define the abuse as unjustified and to seek assistance (Stets, 1991). It has also been documented that alcohol consumption is often associated with marital violence (Leonard and Blane, 1992). Finally, previous experience of spouse abuse on the part of one or both of the partners (seeing it in a previous marriage or between their parents) increases the probability that abuse will occur (Kalmuss and Seltzer, 1986).

Child Abuse

Equally, if not more disturbing than the conclusions about marital violence are the findings concerning violence by parents against children, with more than 60 percent of the couples sampled acknowledging at least one violent act against a child. One investigation reported that more than 10 out of every 1,000 children under the age of eighteen are the victims of serious abuse or neglect every year (Straus and Gelles, 1986). More specifically, this same report showed that more than 200,000 children per year are the victims of serious physical assault; more than 100,000 are victimized by severe neglect so that injury, death, or impairment results; nearly 45,000 children suf-

fer some form of sexual abuse by a parent; 1,000 children die every year as the result of abuse; and another 137,000 suffer serious injury. Researchers in this field regard these figures as conservative. Some research suggests that the rates of child abuse are increasing in the United States, but this conclusion is controversial and depends on how child abuse is measured. If we look at child abuse reported to police and health care workers, abuse appears up; but if we ask parents if they have shoved, hit, or in other ways hurt their children, rates appear down. A definitive conclusion on whether abuse is increasing is just not possible at this time (Gelles and Conte, 1990; Egley, 1991).

As with marital violence, there are economic and occupational correlates of child abuse. Investigations have shown that the maltreatment of children is concentrated not only among low-income families but also among the extremely poor. This is especially true for severe violence (Pelton, 1978; Gelles, 1992). Figure 3.6 provides a graphic illustration of the relationship between poverty and child abuse.

Critics have proposed that these class differences may be due more to disproportionate report-

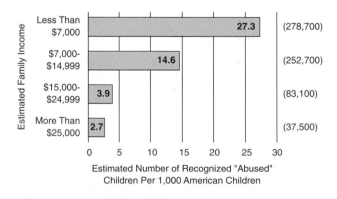

Figure 3.6   Poverty and Child Abuse in America Based on Estimated Annual Family Income of Maltreated Children
SOURCE: U.S. Department of Health and Human Services, *National Study of the Incidence and Severity of Child Abuse and Neglect* (Washington, D.C.: National Center on Child Abuse and Neglect, 1982), p. 10.

ing of child maltreatment involving lower-class families, but other statistics that avoid the differential reporting problem still suggest a higher involvement of economically disadvantaged families. For example, the death of children through physical abuse is difficult to conceal, even for the affluent, and one study of child deaths in New York City determined that 70 percent of the families of children who died as a consequence of abuse were poverty stricken (Garbarino, 1981). These economic hardships interact with immediate situational stressors—disputes between parents, a burdensome number of children, a child who creates problems for parents—to bring about incidents of child abuse. Especially at risk of using the most abusive forms of violence against their children are poor and young parents, poor parents with young children, and poor single mothers (Gelles, 1992).

Irrespective of social class considerations, it appears that child abuse is a behavior pattern that is passed on from generation to generation in some families. For example, a review of studies on child abuse found that although between 2 percent and 4 percent of parents abuse their children, that rate is as high as 30 percent or more among parents who were themselves abused as children (Gelles and Conte, 1990).

Abuse of the Elderly

One form of violence in the family that has not received as much attention is abuse of the elderly by their spouses, offspring, or guardians. In 1985, the House Subcommittee on Health and Long-term Care uncovered episodes of abuse such as these: a seventy-five-year-old man was attacked with a hatchet by his son; a seventy-four-year-old woman was beaten and raped by her son-in-law and then threatened by her daughter not to squeal to anyone about it; a sixty-eight-year-old woman was neglected by the son with whom she lived and starved to death in a feces-fouled house while her son was well fed (Bruno, 1985).

The elderly can suffer the same kinds of abuses as do children and spouses: physical violence, psychological abuse such as insults and threats, and neglect of one's important and basic needs of daily living. Current estimates are that 32 of every 1,000 older people suffer some type of abuse, with well over half of that being physical violence (Pillemer and Finkelhor, 1988). This means that somewhere between 700,000 and 1.1 million older Americans have suffered abuse. Surprising to some, men are more likely to be victims of elder abuse than are women, and women are more likely to abuse their elder husbands than men are to abuse their elder wives. However, women suffer more injuries and emotional distress when they are abused than do men. In addition, and despite the examples given by the House Subcommittee report, the elderly are more likely to be abused by a spouse than by a son, daughter, or other nonspousal caregiver. Finally, those who live alone or who are not married are less likely to suffer abuse than those who are married or live with others, and those who live with a spouse and an offspring are especially at risk of suffering abuse.

One conclusion these findings lead to is that elder abuse is in part a matter of opportunity; as one set of experts put it: "An elder is most likely to be abused by the person with whom he or she lives" (Pillemer and Finkelhor, 1988: 55). Those who live alone or with fewer people are less likely to be abused. This is probably part of the reason why men suffer more abuse than women: Because women live longer than men, older women are more likely to be living alone than are older men. A second conclusion that these findings lead to is that much elder abuse is probably more like spouse abuse than child abuse. It is shaped by some of the same factors that fuel spouse abuse rather than involving a powerful caregiver and a dependent recipient of care. However, some abuse of the elderly may arise from the stress of taking care of a dependent older parent or grandparent who is physically or mentally impaired (King, 1984; Steinmetz, 1987).

To some extent, abuse of the elderly reflects one of the weaknesses of the modern nuclear family: It lacks the extensive support network and additional helping hands that are available in the extended family or even the modified extended family. As we have seen, we often expect each person in the nuclear family to be a breadwinner, a companion, and so on. When society burdens one person with a wide range of difficult tasks, including taking care of a child or an impaired older parent, the stresses will sometimes accumulate to the point where abuse is likely. Recent research, however, points to a different relationship between dependency and abuse: Abuse is more likely to occur when the caregiver is dependent on the elderly person under his or her care. This is especially true when the caregiver is financially dependent on the elderly person under his or her charge, is personally or emotionally troubled, or abuses alcohol or drugs (Pillemer and Finkelhor, 1989; Greenberg, McKibben, and Raymond, 1990). In these situations, caregivers may be responding to their feelings of powerlessness in the relationship and resorting to one of the few power resources they have available: force and violence.

So, research on abuse of the elderly provides further evidence for the part that inequitable distributions of power and resources play in family violence. Those who are dependent—whether they be children or frail elderly—are at risk of suffering violence at the hands of others. Those with access to economic and social resources, such as wives with careers or the elderly who can live on their own, are better equipped to avoid violence. And those who feel helpless and powerless—such as poor, single mothers or caregivers who are dependent on their elderly charges—may lash out in violence as a reaction to their circumstances.

FUTURE PROSPECTS

Most sociologists are confident that the family as a social institution will survive. The family is based on kinship that can derive from common ancestry, marriage, or social agreement. The family functions to replace members of society and to nurture them, and a family of some type will undoubtedly continue to perform these functions in the future. In fact, such arrangements as cohabitation and single parenthood may be considered "families" because they can and do perform these functions for some people. The real issue is not whether the family will survive but what form it will take. Observing current trends, it would seem that modern industrial societies are developing a **pluralistic family,** one in which *a number of different types of family exist side by side, each having an attraction for some segment of the populace.* Thus, neither the extended family nor the traditional nuclear family predominates, although each can be found. Singlehood, one-parent families, cohabitation, and other alternative life-styles better fill the needs of some Americans. Given the extreme diversity of our culture and the changing role of the family, such pluralistic family arrangements are probably more adaptive. They permit people of many religions, occupations, ethnic groups, and life-styles to find a form of the family that fits their values and circumstances. And Americans as a whole will probably remain tolerant of this increasing diversity in family life-styles, although some will continue to find particular alternatives offensive.

We have seen, however, that these diverse forms of the family can create problems for society, problems that need to be addressed.

The Future of Divorce

Despite the rapid rise in divorce in recent decades, the divorce rate will not necessarily continue to rise substantially in the future (Norton and Moorman, 1987). In fact, since 1975, the increase in the divorce rate has been rather small in comparison to previous decades. In part, this is due to a considerable decline in the marriage rate, which has dropped by about one-third over the past thirty years (see Table 3.1). However, it may also be that the divorce rate has risen as high as it is likely to go in response to changing social conditions resulting from industrialization. On the other hand, there is no reason to believe that the divorce rate will decline significantly in the future. The current divorce rate may well be one that is commensurate with social conditions and the position of the family in a mature industrial society.

In the past, religious teachings, social norms, and practical considerations inhibited people from dissolving their marriages. Today, as we have seen, these factors are less prominent. Yet these traditional controls may be replaced with others. For example, our schools and colleges could offer more and better courses in marriage and family training so that young people would be prepared to make sounder marital choices and work more effectively at maintaining relationships. Such courses could help people identify the factors associated with successful and unsuccessful marriages so that they could use this information in making important life choices. In fact, the state of California, recognizing that people who marry at a young age are especially likely to divorce, requires people under eighteen to obtain a court order to marry and to submit to premarital counseling if directed. We might consider requiring all prospective marriage partners to take a course in premarital counseling. After all, we require people to pass a test of knowledge and skills related to driving laws before permitting them to drive an automobile. We might also encourage couples to seek periodically the advice of trained marriage counselors so that trouble spots in a relationship could be identified. By the time many couples seek such advice today, their difficulties are often beyond help. Steps such as these would not eliminate divorce, but they may help to reduce the divorce rate—and the agony of such dissolutions—to a degree, although probably not to pre-industrial levels. It might also be possible to give people some training in divorce and how to survive it. At a minimum, we need to avoid the more painful ways in which children can be treated during and after a divorce, such as the

growing number of cases of child stealing, in which a parent without custody kidnaps the child from the parent with legal custody. The Policy Issues insert in this chapter presents some interesting alternatives to traditional divorce and also points to changes that could reduce some of the problems in divorce situations.

Reducing Family Violence

One of the most positive steps toward reducing family violence has been bringing the issue into the open. This has enabled us to concentrate resources on solving this problem. In the mid-1970s, the Child Abuse Prevention and Treatment Act was passed to help states and communities develop programs for abusive or neglectful parents. The government has also funded research to find the causes of child abuse and the most effective ways of dealing with it. Programs have been established to train parents in "parenting skills" as a way of preventing future episodes of abuse. Prevention can also be enhanced when parents are connected to organizations and services in the community because this increases the chances of getting help before abuse recurs. Substance abuse treatment programs are made available to parents who might be at risk of abusing their children because of the known role of alcohol in child abuse. Self-help groups such as Parents Anonymous, in which a supportive personal relationship is used to help parents stop mistreating their children, have also emerged. Finally, programs such as day care that ease the pressure and burden on parents may reduce the precipitating factors that can initiate episodes of violence.

Spouse abuse has also received much attention recently, and this has resulted in accelerated efforts toward pinning down its sources. As we mentioned earlier, the improving economic and social position of women in society will likely make them less vulnerable targets of abuse in the future. Furthermore, spouse abuse centers can now be found in most communities, and these offer sanctuary and support to women who seek to change

POLICY ISSUES

Family Mediation as an Alternative to Traditional Divorce

Traditionally, if a marriage were to be dissolved, the divorce took place in a court before a magistrate or judge, and these court proceedings were uniformly *adversarial*. Although laws surrounding divorce varied from state to state, one of the partners was always required to act as a plaintiff and blame the other partner, the defendant, for being "at fault" and, persumably, for causing the failure of the marriage. This approach to marital dissolution prompted an atmosphere wherein people who decided to terminate their marriages felt that they had "failed"; some people, on the other hand, elected to maintain unhappy marriages to avoid the social label of "failure."

A critical turning point in divorce law was reached in California in 1970 when the California Family Law Act abolished the requirement to establish *fault* in divorce proceedings. In a short period of time, a version of this California statute was adopted by nearly every other state in the country. As *no-fault divorce* became the norm, it was no longer necessary for a married man or woman to claim some form of "marital misconduct." The term *marital dissolution* became a substitute for divorce, and *irreconcilable differences* replaced such commonplace "grounds for divorce" as infidelity, mental cruelty, and alienation of affection. Although no-fault divorce made "blameless" divorces possible, it did not *require* such an approach. In fact, in many cases, one of the partners still "files" for divorce, and in the legal record, this party becomes the plaintiff, whereas the partner who receives the "complaint of divorce" becomes the defendant by default. Even though the process is technically guided by the no-fault concept, a clear majority of divorces still retain a distinctly adversarial flavor, complete with the predictable argumentation and contention that characterize other courtroom struggles.

In recent years, another effort has been made to create the opportunity for less contentious marital dissolutions. This has been accomplished through the development of a new kind of professional who serves as an alternative to the court system in family-related issues (Vroom, Fassett, and Wakefield, 1981; Davidson and Moore, 1992). These *family mediators* do not function as attorneys or counselor-therapists. Rather, they act as

or leave an abusive relationship. Continuing controversy surrounds the cases of women who respond to abusive husbands with violence of their own, sometimes to the point of killing their spouses. Feminists have argued, and a few court cases have agreed, that some of these killings are justifiable homicides on the grounds that some women have been socialized into submission to men, and thus other options—such as calling the police—are not realistic alternatives for them (Johann and Osanka, 1989). In addition, police often do not detain abusive husbands for long, and the women involved are then vulnerable to subsequent and perhaps even more serious incidents of abuse.

Efforts to control abuse of the elderly have not been as extensive as those focusing on other forms of family violence, but some progress has been made (Ross, 1991; Olinger, 1991). For example, many states have adopted laws that require reporting of abuse of the elderly to the police. They have also established many protective services for

facilitators and trainers who help people learn how to negotiate problems and resolve conflicts. Mediation can be used with family-related problems such as teenage pregnancy, runaways, unmarried cohabitants, domestic violence, wills, and estate planning, as well as in cases of separation and divorce. In the state of California, where family mediation is commonly used, all child custody disputes must involve a mediator.

Mediation is becoming an increasingly popular method for partners to arrive at agreeable terms for divorce, and to work out arrangements *after* the divorce, particularly with respect to children who may be involved. The parties in conflict meet with an impartial mediator who is trained to help them work out their disagreements. Ultimately, the agreements reached in mediation become legally binding in the final divorce decree, but such arrangements are *mutually decided,* rather than *ordered by a judge.* The divorce mediation process does not preclude the partners from being represented by attorneys. In some divorce cases in which mediation is used, the partners are able to work out acceptable terms on some arrangements, such as child custody and visitation, but then appear in court with their attorneys to negotiate complex financial arrangements.

Just as no-fault statutes have helped to remove some of the adversarial qualities of divorce, divorce mediation encourages spouses to attempt resolution of their differences through negotiation and compromise with the assistance of a trained mediator. Some licensed divorce mediators are attorneys who also handle divorce cases in court (although they are prohibited from acting *simultaneously* as mediator and legal counsel in the same case). Other qualified mediators are family specialists with backgrounds in psychology, sociology, and social work.

The most important element in family or divorce mediation is that these strategies strive to foster "constructive disconnection," to minimize the pain and suffering that accompany any legal dispute, and to preserve positive relationships between the spouses and their children (Elkin, 1982; Ahrons and Rodgers, 1987). Even in cases in which the parties negotiate some of their disagreements in court, if they have settled other disputes, such as child custody arrangements, through mediation, these divorced couples are less likely to return to court at a later time to settle still-unresolved issues and the children are less likely to suffer as a consequence (Pearson and Thoennes, 1982).

In earlier societies, kin and community served as the backdrop for the establishment and negotiation of family-related agreements such as marriage and divorce. As we approach the twenty-first century, these domains of our lives seem to be moving beyond the kinship context. Family and divorce mediators will likely become more important elements in terms of family support. With this in mind, it appears even more crucial that social issues like the one we have discussed here be given serious consideration by our society's policymakers.

---

the elderly, increased penalties for abuse or neglect of the elderly, and created provisions for confidentiality in the reporting of cases of elder abuse. Yet there remain substantial restraints on what the authorities can do. Most states have no penalties for many forms of abuse or neglect of a parent. In the case of the sixty-eight-year-old woman who starved to death, criminal charges against her son were dropped because of a loophole in the law. According to a police sergeant working on the case: "You can't let your children, your wife, or your dog starve to death, but there's nothing in the penal code that says you've got to feed your mother" (Bruno, 1985). Even mandatory reporting has its weaknesses. Because the abused elderly are often dependent on their caregivers for support, they may choose not to seek needed medical care if they believe signs of abuse will be reported to the authorities by their doctor. What needs to be done is to establish a range of services that could defuse tensions in the family or help the elderly escape abusive settings. These ser-

INTERNATIONAL PERSPECTIVES

Families and Children in Other Societies

Regarding families and children, American social policy has historically been very laissez-faire, leaving people to get by on their own with little assistance from the government. This contrasts sharply with virtually all other advanced industrial nations, where social policies are based on a consensus that everyone benefits when families and their children are supported (Kamerman, 1991; Kamerman and Kahn, 1991). These nations take responsibility for protecting children, providing good early childhood education, serving children with special needs, supporting mothers' desires to continue working, maintaining family income during and after the birth of a child, and encouraging a birth rate that at least maintains current population size.

To achieve these goals, most industrial nations make publicly funded preschools universally available to children beginning at age three and continuing until the child enters school, irrespective of parents' income or work status. In France and Belgium, for example, the preschools are publicly financed and operated as an integral part of the educational system. All children are eligible, beginning some time after their second birthday, and the schools are free, with parents paying only for things like lunch or certain after-school programs. Similar programs are found in many other countries, including Israel and Hungary. In Sweden and Finland, preschools are separate from the school system and are heavily subsidized by the government, although parents do pay some fees if they can afford them. All children are eligible for these programs until compulsory school attendence begins at age 7, and the government enforces strict standards regarding such things as staff–child ratios and teacher qualifications. Such preschool education is coming to be

vices could take the form of shelters for abused elderly, counseling services, legal and nutritional services, and day-care programs for the elderly. Thus far, few funds have been directed toward these ends.

As family violence has commanded more attention in recent years, government agencies have started to "get tough." In the first chapter, we discussed a research project in Minneapolis that eventually led to more strict policies toward spouse abuse on the part of many police departments (Sherman and Berk, 1984). In the mid-1980s, a Justice Department Task Force on Family Violence called for toughening the actions that could be taken to arrest, bring to trial, and imprison offenders (Brozan, 1984). Noting that domestic violence has often been ignored in the past, the Task Force made some powerful recommendations, including:

1. Adopting the attitude that family violence in all forms should be regarded as criminal.
2. Establishing arrest as the preferred method of immediately dealing with such crimes.
3. Processing all complaints of family violence as reported criminal offenses.
4. Giving the victim and the suspect a statement of victim's rights.
5. Organizing special units to process family violence cases.
6. Eliminating the requirement that a victim sign a formal complaint before charges can be filed by the prosecutor, unless mandated by state law.

viewed, by many of these European nations, as a "right" of citizenship, just like one has a right to a basic education.

Almost all advanced industrial nations also provide some level of maternity or parenting leave that enables one or both parents to stay home with their infant for a period after birth. These programs permit the parent to receive some level of their previous income while on leave and protect their job until they return to work. In France, for example, women are given a six-week leave before delivery and ten weeks after delivery, all with pay, and business leaders seem unconcerned about its effects on worker productivity or corporate profits. French parents can also take two years off after having a child without worrying about whether their job will be there.

Given that maternity/parenting leaves enable parents to stay home with their infants and preschool takes care of children aged three and older, the only children in need of child care in these industrial nations are those one and two years of age. While child-care programs are much more limited in these countries than are the infant and preschool programs, child care is increasingly being seen as a public responsibility and an entitlement for children. In addition to these pro-grams, most industrial nations also provide publicly funded health care and housing allowances to families, paid leave to parents to care for sick children, and sometimes even direct subsidization of family incomes to reduce the economic disparity between those who choose to have children and those who choose to remain childless.

Despite the fact that United States policy leaves families very much on their own, the need for support seems greater in the United States than in these other countries (U.S. Bureau of the Census, 1991: 837–838). In the United States, 8 percent of all households have a single parent, compared to 5 percent in France and 3 percent in Sweden. In fact, just about all industrial nations have fewer single-parent households and a lower divorce rate than does the United States. So, the regulated capitalism of France and Sweden has produced family policies that protect and nurture children because children are seen as key resources to the future. The United States, on the other hand, leaves children to the largely unregulated free market which has so far meant that many children living in less affluent families go without while others suffer low quality, inadequate, and possibly damaging preschool experiences.

7. In the case of child abuse, relaxing the regulations governing the introduction of evidence into trials.

Although some may debate over the judiciousness of some of these steps, society clearly is taking a strong stand against family violence, and this posture will help to reduce the extent of such violence in the future.

Children and the Family

The changes that the modern family is undergoing create a number of problems beyond those of children in divorced families. There is concern, for example, that children born into single-parent families sometimes do not receive the best parenting. Social policies designed to deal with this problem, especially teenage pregnancies, have been highly controversial because they intrude into some very sensitive areas of family life. One way of reducing teen pregnancies is to make birth control information available to teens, and many family planning agencies have done so without informing the parents of the teens. In fact, one study found that countries with low rates of teen pregnancies also had liberal attitudes toward sex, made contraceptives easily available to teenagers, and provided effective sex education programs (Brozan, 1985). Research in this country shows that teen pregnancy can be reduced by providing access to contraceptives, along with school counseling and job training (Miller and Moore, 1990). However, such programs are controversial because they rest in part on the assumption that many teenagers will continue to be sexually active. By contrast, recent social policies have emphasized sexual abstinence and parental involvement in their children's decision making. For example, the Adolescent Family Life Act of 1981, which is currently the only federal program designed to address teenage pregnancy, focuses on reducing teen pregnancies by preventing or postponing adolescent sexual activity and encouraging adolescents to seek the guidance of their parents or other family members (White and White, 1991). Yet, research clearly shows that the most effective way to control teen pregnancies is through education in how to prevent conception and the provision of birth control devices.

We have discussed how some modern developments, such as dual-career families or singlehood, might lower the birth rate or lead to a two-tiered society in which those who have children will be substantially less well off than those who do not. In fact, some fear that our nation's children could become a permanent "underclass" (Weitzman, 1985). To ensure an adequate birthrate and sufficient resources for families to raise children, some have argued for a more explicit social policy on family issues (Ferber and O'Farrell, 1991). The International Perspectives insert describes the family policies currently being used in some other societies. As that insert points out, social policies in the United States tend to be laissez-faire, with comparatively little government direction regarding families and children. This situation changed somewhat in 1993 when President Clinton signed into law a family leave bill that requires large employers to give their employees unpaid leave to care for newly born children or ill family members. This protection, however, is still considerably more limited than that described in the insert in other industrial countries.

Another area where support for a coherent family policy in the United States has been emerging is day care. In fact, our nation's employers have been developing day-care programs over the past decade (Hayghe, 1988). About 2 percent of the nation's employers sponsor day-care centers for their employees' children, and another 9 percent offer at least some employees financial assistance for day care or information and referral services to guide parents in finding day care for their children. Furthermore, 61 percent of employers provide indirect day-care assistance in the form of flexible work schedules, flexible leaves, and part-time work for parents of young children. Not surprisingly, employers with large numbers of women of childbearing age in their work force are most likely to have some day-care policy, and it is the better-paid and more powerful employees who are most likely to be offered these services by employers. The motivation for employers to sponsor these programs is in good part pragmatic: Research has shown that the problems employees face in arranging care for their children tend to result in absenteeism, tardiness, low morale, and productivity problems. Also recruiting new employees is easier when an employer can offer child-care services to prospective employees, especially in heavily female segments of the labor market such as nursing. As one authority on workplace issues put it:

> *The organizations that provide a child-care benefit recognize that family and work life are no longer separable, that tensions between them affect the work performance of employees, and that it may be in the organization's best interest to do what it can to alleviate those tensions. (Auerbach, 1990: 391)*

This may be increasingly true in the future because young women will likely make up a large proportion of new entrants into the labor pool. Laissez-faire advocates would argue that this largely private-sector initiative is the most appropriate way to handle day-care policy: Let employers respond to the needs of their employees. Child care should become another fringe benefit—like health-care insurance and vacation time—that is negotiated between employer and employee.

With more single-parent families and families in which both parents work, society must create settings other than the traditional family to take care of young children. One such alternative, about which policies are now emerging, is preschool day-care programs.

Both the state and the federal governments provide funding for child care, but often as a part of programs with goals separate from child care itself. For example, the federal government currently provides at least $6 billion per year for child-care programs. To illustrate, the Head Start program, which is basically a poverty program, serves a child-care function for some poor families (see Chapter 5). Community Development Block Grants, which focus on the economic development of communities (see Chapter 12), can be used in part to construct nonprofit child-care facilities. The Family Support Act of 1989, which reformed the welfare system with work requirements, provides child-care services for welfare parents who are in job training programs. The Child Care and Dependent Tax Credit allows working parents to make a partial deduction of their day-care expenses on their federal tax return, but the deduction allowable declines as income rises. Half of the states also provide some support for day care through their tax codes. In addition, all state governments provide some funds for the training of child-care workers or the provision of child-care services, although state funding sometimes goes to only a limited number of people, such as the very poor.

There are other state and federal supports for child care, but the point is that there is not one coherent policy on the issue as is found commonly in other advanced industrial nations. Instead, the United States has scattered and piecemeal day-care programs that are parts of other programs. There is as yet no consensus that day-care services should be available to all American families, irrespective of their economic circumstances.

Another controversy in current child-care policy is over *privatization:* Should policies encourage the private sector to develop and provide the services people want, or should the government directly provide the services? Privatization policies provide parents with vouchers to purchase child care or tax credits for money spent on child care, and then parents seek the services where they wish, often from private, profit, or nonprofit centers. Needless to say, laissez-faire advocates support this approach. Interventionists argue that programs such as Head Start, where the government runs the child-care centers, are preferred because their mission is focused exclusively on providing the best services available without interference from the desire to make a profit. As we saw earlier, there is some evidence that nonprofit and government-run centers do provide better services than for-profit centers. Nevertheless, this controversy has still not been resolved in the United States.

Linkages

Changes in the family, especially increases in divorce and single parenthood, have made more women the sole breadwinner for their family, which makes them more vulnerable to discrimination and inequality based on gender (Chapter 7). Family problems are exacerbated by drug and alcohol addiction (Chapter 10) because poor parents are more likely to become addicted, and domestic violence is associated with drug and alcohol addiction.

Summary

1. The family is a social institution based on kinship that functions to replace members of society and to nurture them.

2. In American society today, people practice monogamy and egalitarianism is encouraged. Families vary in configuration but usually fall into one of three categories: extended, nuclear, or modified extended.

3. The functionalist perspective views some form of family existing in all societies because the family performs certain basic functions that are essential to human survival and the maintenance of society.

4. The conflict perspective views the family as serving the interests of the dominant groups in society, and the version of family most prominent in society is very likely the one that is consistent with the values and benefits of the dominant groups. The dominant form of family also benefits particular economic interests.

5. The interactionist perspective points to the fact that what is considered the family is a matter of social definition, becoming a part of the social reality that people create and live by.

6. Marriage and family relationships are popular in American society today, but these kinds of intimate associations are more likely to be participant controlled rather than parent run, the latter being more common prior to the industrial revolution.

7. The divorce rate has been steadily rising in American society, which may be attributed to the fact that Americans expect a great deal from the marriage relationship. Some couples are at

considerably greater risk of getting a divorce than are others. Widespread divorce has complicated kinship relations and brought about the blended family, referring to the kinship ties that accumulate as a consequence of divorces and remarriages.

8. There are many different family life-styles that have emerged over the past few decades in American society. These life-styles are considered by many to be another dimension of the problems surrounding the family today. Among them are dual-career families, singlehood, cohabitation, and single parenthood.

9. Violence among family members is common in American society, usually occurring between married couples or directed at dependent children or the elderly.

10. Most sociologists are confident that the family will survive as a social institution, but that family relationships will be pluralistic in the future, with different forms of family existing side by side, each having an attraction for some segment of the populace. The face of the family is changing. The divorce rate may actually decrease in the future. Steps are being taken in American society to lower the rate of family violence. A continuing concern regarding the configuration of families in the future relates to children: locating suitable environments for children to grow up in.

Important Terms for Review

blended family	extended family	nuclear family	refined divorce rate
cohabitation	family	patriarchy	serial monogamy
dual-career family	modified extended family	pluralistic family	
egalitarian family	monogamy	polygamy	

Discussion Questions

1. Make a list of some of your relatives who are living (for example, grandparents, siblings, uncles, aunts, cousins, and so on). Describe how involved you are with each person, emotionally speaking, and how frequently you deal with them on a face-to-face basis. What support or assistance do you offer each other? What activities do you engage in together? Use this analysis to assess how important kinship is in your own life.

2. Marriage is viewed quite positively by many Americans today, but alternatives to marriage are also popular. If you are married or divorced, why did you decide to marry in the first place? If you are unmarried, do you want to become married? Why or why not?

3. Using the functionalist perspective, how might we lower the divorce rate? Should it be lowered? What impact might steps to lower the divorce rate have on other social institutions such as the economy, our legal system, or education? What problems would be encountered if steps were taken in this direction?

4. Should any of the alternatives to the traditional form of the family be discouraged or encouraged? Do any of the alternatives that we have discussed pose greater social problems than,

say, monogamy? Are emerging family life-styles brand-new problems or adaptations to social change?

5. Use the interactionist perspective to evaluate violence in the family as a social problem. Consider that marital violence and child abuse have existed for a long time; although they may not be more widespread today, as a society, we are much more aware of their prevalence. Discuss how we have come to define domestic violence as more problematic today than in the past.

6. The functionalist perspective can help us to understand why illegitimacy is viewed as a social problem. Using what you know about how functionalists approach family-related issues, discuss the problematic implications of each issue.

7. Some observers of the family in American society have commented that as an institution, the family is "searching for a future." Others insist that the future is already here and that the family has a bright tomorrow. In the light of the text's discussion, consider what the future of family may be like. What are the plans of your friends and acquaintances about marriage and family issues? Do they plan to marry? What other alternatives do they consider?

For Further Reading

Brigitte Berger and Peter L. Berger. *The War Over the Family: Capturing the Middle Ground.* New York: Anchor Press/Doubleday, 1983. A controversial book in which two well-known sociologists argue that the traditional nuclear family should be embraced as a repository of important personal values and social virtues. It is a spirited defense of the embattled nuclear family.

Jessie Bernard. *Self-Portrait of a Family.* Boston: Beacon Press, 1978. An interesting collection of letters between a well-known family sociologist and her children. It suggests some of the difficulties she encountered as a parent with a career and offers some personal insights into the problem.

Philip Blumstein and Pepper Schwartz. *American Couples: Money/Work/Sex.* New York: William Morrow, 1983. This is a report on a large survey of American couples. It offers some interesting insights on the differences between couples who are reasonably happy and those who are not.

John Crewdson. *By Silence Betrayed: Sexual Abuse of Children in America.* Boston: Little, Brown, 1987. This book is based on interviews with abused children, the people who abuse them, and those who prosecute and defend the abusers. Crewdson is a Pulitzer-Prize-winning journalist who has written a disturbing account of the problem.

Leon Dash. *When Children Want Children: The Urban Crisis of Teenage Childbearing.* New York: William Morrow, 1989. This is an interesting book on the extent of teenage parenting and the difficulties that teen mothers face, as well as the problems created for society.

Andrew M. Greeley. *Faithful Attraction.* New York: Tor Books, 1991. This sociologist marshals survey data to present a positive image of the family: most people getting married, being satisfied with their spouses, and not having extramarital affairs. This is a good antidote to the "family in crisis" view that is often presented.

Christopher Lasch. *Haven in a Heartless World: The Family Besieged.* New York: Basic Books, 1977. A dismal look at the modern family as a social institution with little to do. Lasch argues that even the family's role as an emotional buffer, a "haven in a heartless world," may be disappearing.

Marcia Millman. *Warm Hearts and Cold Cash: The Intimate Dynamics of Families and Money.* New York: The Free Press, 1991. This author recognizes that, in addition to love and affection, families also harbor rivalry, uncertainty, dependence, and guilt. She produces an intriguing account of how the positive emotions as well as the negative get intertwined in family relations.

Phyllis Moen. *Working Parents: Transformations in Gender Roles and Public Policies in Sweden.* Madison: University of Wisconsin Press, 1989. This book explores some innovative social policies in Sweden that are focused on encouraging women to have children and continue working. Some of the policies might be useful to consider for the United States.

Daniel Patrick Moynihan. *Family and Nation: The Godkin Lectures, Harvard University.* San Diego: Harcourt Brace Jovanovich, 1985. A very important statement by a sociologist-politician wherein the author claims that poverty among children is exacerbated by the disintegration of the traditional family structure and the growth of single-parent families. Moynihan's social policy recommendations are certain to be controversial.

Maureen A. Pirog-Good and Jan E. Stets (eds.). *Violence in Dating Relationships.* New York: Praeger, 1989. Because dating typically precedes family formation and because violence while dating may presage violence after marriage, violence between dating partners is a useful topic to understand in the analysis of family problems. This book presents research on the correlates and consequences of both physical and sexual abuse.

Arlene Skolnick. *Embattled Paradise: The American Family in an Age of Uncertainty.* New York: Basic Books, 1991. This thought-provoking book includes some history of the American family in the twentieth century. It takes a generally positive view of the changes that have occurred and criticizes the "decline of the family" moralizers for not seeing the benefits of the new changes.

Judith Stacey. *Brave New Families: Stories of Domestic Upheaval in Late Twentieth Century America.* New York: Basic Books, 1990. This is a fascinating account of the changing American family as seen through a narrative of the experiences of two families in particular. It shows the incongruous, unpredictable, and contested nature of some of today's families.

CHAPTER 4
Health and Illness

W hat problems do we confront in the area of health and illness? Joseph Califano, Jr., Secretary of Health, Education, and Welfare under President Carter, summarizes them as "colossal costs, inefficiency, waste, and abuse" (Califano, 1986: 36). The costs of health care have truly skyrocketed. In 1960, our health-care expenditures amounted to $142 for each Ameri-

can; thirty years later, that amount had exploded to $2,566—a sixteenfold increase! Americans spend an estimated $6 billion each year on coronary bypass surgery alone. People demand the surgery in hopes that it will prolong their lives, and surgeons are more than willing to perform such a lucrative procedure. Does it work? Based on a review of major studies on the effectiveness

Myths and Facts About Health and Health Care

Myth: The poor receive shoddy health care, finding it difficult to see a doctor or gain admission to a hospital.

Fact: Some poor people are quite a bit more likely than the affluent to see a doctor or be hospitalized. Government health insurance for the poor has given some of them far more access to health care than ever before, although it may be of lower quality than the care available to more affluent Americans.

Myth: Women are healthier than men (or vice versa).

Fact: Reality is complicated on this issue. Men have higher mortality rates, but women are more likely to have acute, non-life-threatening illnesses. Men, on the other hand, tend to have higher rates of serious, chronic illnesses. So the facts on sexual status and health depend on how you measure "health."

Myth: Controlling physicians' fees would stop the rise in medical costs.

Fact: Although it would help, physicians' services account for less than one of every five dollars spent on health care. And the proportion of the health-care dollar spent on physicians' fees has declined considerably over the past forty years.

Myth: Thanks to modern science, people today have a healthy diet and can look forward to a long life.

Fact: People in most hunting and gathering societies probably had healthier diets than most Americans have today. They ate a wide range of fruits, nuts, grains, and other plant foods and relied on meat relatively little. Hunters and gatherers could, if they survived infancy and childhood, look forward to a relatively long life.

---

of coronary bypass surgery, Califano concludes that

> *At least 60 percent, and possibly 80 percent of the 200,000 Americans who submitted to . . . coronary bypass surgery in 1984 gained no increase in life span beyond what they would have achieved through [the considerably less expensive, invasive, and dangerous] medical management of their condition with beta blockers and other modern drugs. (Califano, 1986: 83–84)*

Other, more conservative, estimates suggest that "only" one-third of bypass surgeries are unnecessary (Barron, 1989).

As Americans spend all this money on health care, what they actually receive is not clear: French males live as long as American males, yet Americans pay almost twice as much for their per capita health bill as the French do. The high costs and profit making that are a part of our health-care system, then, point to some dimensions of the very controversial problems surrounding health and illness. Other dimensions of the problem include our unhealthy life-style. Americans smoke and drink to excess and gorge themselves on foods that have little nutritional value but do contribute to health problems through obesity and high blood pressure. Thirty-eight percent of our populace has high blood pressure and 26 percent is overweight (National Center for Health Statistics, 1992). Although we spend billions on bypass surgery, infant mortality rates, especially among nonwhites, are distressingly high. A physician reported to a congressional hearing in 1986 that infant mortality rates in parts of Detroit are "as high or greater than post–World War II Europe, where conditions of starvation and malnutrition existed" (Daugherty, 1986). This is the case even though there are relatively inexpensive ways to reduce these rates: provide pregnant women with pre-natal care, offer nutrition programs to increase the birth weight of infants, and make available sex ed-ucation and contraceptives to teenagers who are more likely than adult women to experience infant mortalities.

In this chapter, we address these and other problems related to health and illness in the United States. Califano (1986: 10) believes that after we have grappled with these problems, "the health-care industry of tomorrow is going to be unrecognizably different from today's world of medicine. Whether it will be better depends on how we shape the revolution." We will begin our analysis of the problems by developing an under-standing of the role of health-care institutions in society.

PERSPECTIVES ON HEALTH CARE

People tend to view health and illness as biologi-cal phenomena. However, health and illness also have a very important social dimension, and this is what we need to focus on as we approach prob-lems surrounding health and health-care delivery. Social factors, for example, influence what dis-eases people contract, who receives health care, and who benefits from the type of health-care or-ganization that is dominant in society. The soci-ological perspectives can help us analyze how social factors shape social problems in this area.

The Functionalist Perspective

Disease is a threat to the social order because those who are ill may be unable to make useful contributions to society. People who are ill may not be able to raise food, build houses, drive trucks, or rear children as they are expected to. This makes them burdensome and nonproductive.

In extreme cases, ill health can threaten the very survival of society. Many native American groups, for example, were decimated by infectious dis-eases, such as venereal disease, during their early contact with European explorers to the New World. Some people today feel that a nuclear war would cause so much injury and disease that the survival of some societies would be threatened. So disease can be viewed as a social problem when it threatens the ability of a group to survive and prosper.

Given these consequences of disease, sociolo-gist Talcott Parsons (1951) pointed out that being healthy is the preferred or most functional human condition. When people are ill, they can no longer fulfill their expected role obligations. Society responds to this, Parsons argued, by cast-ing them into a "deviant," or socially disvalued, role. Society must help these deviants to become "normal" again. Ostracizing or imprisoning sick people, which is a common response to many de-viant behaviors, is ineffective. Instead, sick people are given a special social role, the sick role, which is intended to facilitate their return to health. The **sick role** refers to *a set of expectations intended to guide the behavior of people who are ill* (Parsons, 1951; Gordon, 1966). People who occupy the sick role are excused from their normal role obli-gations (to the extent that the illness calls for), and they can claim assistance and sympathy from others. However, they are also expected to seek competent care and to cooperate with those who are trying to cure them.

The role of the health-care system, then, is to return people to normal social functioning. The system becomes a social problem when it fails to perform this function effectively. Ideally, people who need health-care services would receive ex-actly what they need, no more and no less. To the extent that this ideal is not reached, social disor-ganization exists. In this chapter, we will review the extent to which the American health-care sys-tem deviates from this ideal. We will also look for the sources of the disorganization. One source is the lack of integration between different parts of the social system. For example, health care in the United States is operated largely as a profit-making institution, as is the rest of our economy (see Chapter 2). Because large sums of money can be made from medical services and products, there is considerable abuse in these areas, such as unnecessary surgeries and the overutilization of pharmaceuticals. In addition, people who are unable to pay for services often do not receive adequate medical care. The point is that the profit-making dimension of the health-care system is not well integrated with, and may work against, the goal of achieving the highest possible level of health.

The Conflict Perspective

Health and health care are highly valued in all societies, and they are also scarce resources. Interest groups compete with one another to gain what they feel is their fair share of those resources, as they do with other scarce resources. Staying healthy depends on having access to adequate food, satisfactory employment conditions, clean water, and good health care. Generally, as we shall see, people with higher social and economic standing in our society have greater access to these resources, and they are generally healthier than the less affluent. For example, high infant mortality among the poor is not surprising, from the conflict perspective, because the poor are less able to afford nutritious food, sanitary living conditions, access to prenatal care, and the other things that reduce infant mortality.

In addition to the issue of whether groups receive services is the problem of how much those services will cost—in both monetary and non-monetary terms—and who benefits most from health-care treatment. In this context, the health-care system is an arena for competition among a variety of groups: health-care consumers, doctors, nurses, hospital administrators, medical technicians, pharmaceutical companies, and a host of others. People must pay, in some fashion, for health-care goods and services, and many people

make a living through providing those goods and services. Naturally, what benefits one group, such as low health-care costs for the consumer, may work to the disadvantage of other groups, such as doctors and nurses. Beyond money, prestige and power are also involved in the health-care delivery process.

The inequitable distribution of money, prestige, and power in the health-care system, then, is viewed as a social problem by those groups who feel they are receiving less than their fair share of resources. There is no state of the system that is "preferred" or necessarily beneficial to all. If some group gains additional benefits, other groups must lose something. What determines who gains and who loses is the exercise of power. Groups have various power strategies available to them. Nurses and doctors, for example, can go on strike or in other ways withhold their services in order to force concessions from competing groups. Recently, many doctors began refusing to provide obstetrical services because of the substantial increase in malpractice insurance for that specialty. Another power strategy that can be used is to influence Congress and state legislatures to approve legislation that benefits particular groups. In fact, many interest groups in the health field have formed political action committees to collect contributions and press their interests. The American Medical Association and other physicians' groups have been very effective at lobbying over the years, partly because of the substantial economic resources of their constituents. For example, the AMA has successfully fought all efforts to establish a national health insurance program.

The Interactionist Perspective

The interactionist perspective emphasizes the fact that sick people are cast into a social role, part of which has been described as the sick role. This role may include socially devalued and stigmatized elements. A person with venereal disease, for example, may be viewed as immoral, whereas the mentally ill are seen as dangerous. In other words,

POLICY ISSUES

Stigma and the AIDS Epidemic

In 1987, then Secretary of Health and Human Services Otis Bowen predicted that AIDS would make the Black Death look "pale by comparison" (Langone, 1989). Bowen's comment stands out for two reasons. First, it appears fortunately to have been somewhat of an overreaction because AIDS, although a very serious epidemic, is unlike the Bubonic Plague. The Plague was easily transmitted, whereas AIDS is not. AIDS is transmitted through intimate contact with blood or semen, particularly through the transfusion of contaminated blood or through unprotected sexual intercourse. To date, there are no documented cases of transmission through saliva, human tears, shaking hands, or other casual contact. The second reason Bowen's comment stands out is that it reflects a serious societal interest in AIDS that was lacking for a number of years prior to his comment—with devastating consequences.

Diseases such as the Bubonic Plague and AIDS involve a complex intertwining of biology with political, social, and cultural considerations. As the interactionist perspective suggests, health, illness, and disease are given meaning by people in a particular social and cultural environment, and how we treat those who are ill is a function of these meanings. The impact of social and cultural forces on the treatment of the ill is especially evident in seriously threatening diseases (Sigerist, 1977). Among the Kubu people of Sumatra, for example, serious diseases that produced high fevers were viewed as highly threatening. In fact, they so frightened the Kubu that the sick person was shunned—isolated completely—as if he or she were dead. The ancient Babylonians had a different view of disease: It was punishment for sin and wickedness—it was believed that people who suffered pain and discomfort were paying for their sins. Because of the spiritually unclean nature of sick people, they were marked by the Babylonians with a stigma. They were not physically shunned, but they were socially isolated until some atonement for their sins had occurred. More recently, and continuing into this century, a disease like leprosy has provoked reactions of both stigmatization and shunning or isolation.

We might be tempted to think that by the last half of the twentieth century, our reactions to disease have become more "rational" and "scientific" than those of the Kubu or the ancient Babylonians. Yet social life is complex, and our reactions to disease are no exception. In the case of AIDS, many social and cultural factors came together to produce a significant delay in our attack on the disease. When AIDS cases first began to appear in the United States around 1980, the first thing that sociologists, epidemiologists, and other medical researchers from the Centers for Disease Control (CDC) noticed was that healthy gay men and intravenous drug users were dying of unusual infectious diseases rarely seen in humans before (Shilts, 1987). What became clear very quickly from looking at these early victims and their life-styles was that AIDS might be transmitted through sexual contact. As one sociologist at the CDC put it, after looking at the life-styles of the early victims and the spread of the disease: "It looks more like a sexually transmitted disease than syphilis" (Shilts, 1987: 87).

Despite the growing scientific evidence in the early 1980s about the mode of transmission of AIDS and the ominous realization about the potentially monstrous dimensions of this epidemic, tragedy was heaped upon tragedy when research and policy development were delayed as the disease spread. The reasons for this delay were complicated, but some of them are strikingly similar to the reactions to disease among the Kubu and ancient Babylonians. First of all, stigmatization of the supposedly unclean or morally suspect clearly played a role: The disease was linked with homosexuality and illegal drug use. Many people

Political attention to the AIDS epidemic developed slowly. Without question, demonstrations and protests by AIDS activists demanding increased funding for AIDS research and treatment have been critical in focusing societal resources on attacking this serious health problem.

in positions of political and economic power either felt that these were powerless groups whose problems need not be seriously attended to or that they were disreputable groups whose lifestyle ought to be discouraged if not eradicated. In fact, some fundamentalist religious leaders declared that AIDS was punishment for the sins of homosexuals—not a far cry from the ancient Babylonian belief about disease. One conservative columnist wrote: "The poor homosexuals—they have declared war upon nature, and now nature is exacting an awful retribution" (quoted in Shilts, 1987: 311). The feeling on the part of some seemed to be that these groups were sufficiently unrespectable that they were getting what they deserved, and the government need not respond too quickly to the growing epidemic.

A second reason for the delayed response to AIDS was the Reagan administration policy of smaller government and austerity in social and health programs. The first AIDS victim in the United States appeared in 1980, and the Reagan administration entered office in 1981. The competition for government funds in the early 1980s was fierce, and AIDS researchers typically lost out in the battle. A third reason for the delay had to do with urban politics. New York City had the largest number of AIDS cases in the country, yet New York Mayor Edward Koch refused to do anything about it for a number of years, apparently because of the belief that support for gay causes would link him with the gay rights movement and hurt his chances for reelection. Fourth, the politics of gay communities figured into the delay. There were intense conflicts among gays over how, or whether, to respond to the AIDS epidemic. Some gays proposed closing gay bathhouses on the grounds that these places, where unprotected sex and multiple sexual partners were common, helped spread the disease. The owners of the baths objected strenuously, as did many gays who felt that this was an attack on their sexual freedom and an attempt to restrict the open expression of their sexual orientation. As a consequence, the gay community found itself divided and unable to launch a united campaign for more research and programs on AIDS.

The overall consequence of these political and social factors was that AIDS research and programs were delayed significantly and the disease gained a substantial foothold. Had the government acted as quickly and aggressively as it has with other diseases (such as Legionnaire's Disease in the 1970s), the spread of AIDS would have been much less substantial. Once the cause of the disease and the mode of transmission were established, steps were taken to control it. The gay community, in particular, has emphasized health education, the practice of safe sex, and a change in sexual life-styles as ways of preventing the spread of the disease. And this has resulted in dramatic declines in risky sexual behavior among some gay men, although there is evidence of a "relapse" to unsafe practices when public

concern over AIDS is less prominent (Lifson, 1992). Among intravenous drug users, their sexual partners, and their babies, however, incidence of the disease continues to grow.

Even if the disease were to stop spreading entirely, it is still a huge health problem. Over 200,000 Americans have AIDS and close to two million are infected with the HIV virus. This will translate into massive health-care costs as these people develop full-blown AIDS. In the United States, about 85 percent of adolescents and adults contracting AIDS, including new cases in the last few years, are either men who have sex with other men or people who engage in intravenous drug use (Centers for Disease Control, 1992). Half of the women who contract AIDS are IV drug users, and most of the rest are women who have sex with IV drug users or HIV-infected men. In addition, heterosexual transmission of AIDS has been growing rapidly, from less than one hundred new cases in 1985 to over six hundred new cases per year by 1989 (Centers for Disease Control, 1990). Worldwide, 60 percent of HIV infection results from heterosexual intercourse. Of those diagnosed with AIDS, 80 to 90 percent are dead five years after diagnosis. The drugs we have available today can only prolong the lives of those with AIDS, not cure the disease. AIDS is a huge epidemic by any standards, and its magnitude has been exacerbated by the complex social and political forces that influenced society's response to the disease.

The reaction to AIDS brings home to us how much we are like the Kubu, the Babylonians, and all other human groups. Our response to disease is shaped by the biomedical nature of disease as well as by the social meanings we impart to disease and its victims. By understanding this, we are better able to shape a more rational health policy that can effectively attack disease and protect heatlh.

---

we attach social meanings—sometimes very negative ones—to various illnesses, and we expect people to behave in conformity to those meanings. For example, some health-care institutions

treat people in a dehumanizing and impersonal fashion, which can lead to low self-esteem and a negative self-concept and may drive people away from seeking the health care they really need.

HEALTH, ILLNESS, AND SOCIETY

One of the central problems related to health and health care is that there are a variety of social factors—things that we have some control over—that can lead to illness. In this section, we will look at how the diseases that are a threat to us have changed over time and how social and life-style factors can put us at greater risk of illness.

Health and Societal Development

Most diseases can be classified as acute diseases or as chronic ones. **Acute diseases** are *those with fairly quick, and sometimes dramatic and incapacitating, onset and from which a person either dies or recovers.* They are often caused by an organism or parasite that infects or invades the body and disrupts its functioning, such as with influenza, tuberculosis, and gastroenteritis. **Chronic diseases,** such as heart disease and cancer, *progress over a long period of time and often exist long before they are detected.* Early symptoms of these diseases are often absent or easily ignored. They are usually caused by a mixture of biological, social, and environmental factors.

In preindustrial societies, infectious and parasitic diseases posed some of the more serious health threats (Dunn, 1978; Black, 1978). Diseases such as influenza, diphtheria, and typhoid could strike quickly and were highly contagious and often fatal, especially among infants, the weak, and the elderly. Accidents such as drowning or burns could also take their toll, as did mortality due to cannibalism, infanticide, and human sacrifice. All of these threats added up to a life expectancy in preindustrial societies that was rather short by today's standards, probably around twenty-five to thirty-five years. However, this short life expectancy was due in good part to high rates of infant and childhood mortality; if one survived the illnesses of infancy and childhood, one had a reasonable chance to live much longer (Antonovsky, 1972).

People with certain illnesses and disabilities can be stigmatized and discriminated against by others in society. This attitude can limit the opportunities of the handicapped and the contributions they can make to society.

Likewise, the staff in a mental hospital expects their patients to be dependent and confused, and the patients often conform to those expectations.

So from the interactionist perspective, the health-care system is considered a social problem when it produces stigmatized and devalued behavior or self-concepts among either the providers or consumers of health care. This perspective is particularly useful in understanding the societal reaction to some diseases, such as acquired immune deficiency syndrome (AIDS; see Policy Issues insert), and to mental illness, discussed later in this chapter.

With the emergence of industrial societies, there has been a dramatic increase in life expectancy, to around seventy-five in the United States today (U.S. Bureau of the Census, 1991). The death rate has also changed appreciably, dropping from 17 deaths per 1,000 people in the United States in 1900 to 8.5 deaths today (see Figure 4.1). The declining death rate and increasing life expectancy can be attributed in good part to two related factors: declines in infant and childhood mortality and changes in life-style.

Infant mortality today is less than one-sixth of what it was a century ago. So a newborn infant today has a far better chance of surviving than did infants in earlier times, and this means that someone born today has a better chance of living into old age. For those who survive through childhood, however, industrialization has led to considerably smaller increases in longevity over that of their preindustrial counterparts. A study in Massachusetts, for example, revealed that the life

expectancy of fifteen-year-olds in 1869 was only five years less than that of fifteen-year-olds a century later (Vinovskis, 1978). Furthermore, there was virtually no increase in the life expectancy of thirty-year-olds between 1869 and 1969. Another study showed that Americans born in 1980 can expect to live twenty-four years longer than those born in 1900. Someone who was twenty years old in 1980, however, could expect to live only about twelve years longer than a twenty-year-old could in 1900 (National Center for Health Statistics, 1984). This illustrates that a major benefit of industrialization in terms of health and longevity is that we have a much greater chance of living through infancy and childhood. Industrialization provides less benefit in terms of longevity once we reach adulthood.

The second key factor in increasing longevity has been changes in people's life-styles. In fact, this has probably been more important than modern treatments offered by contemporary med-

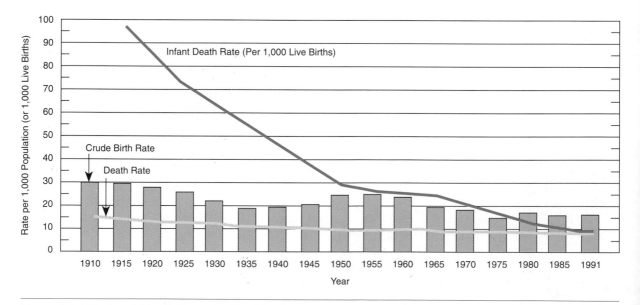

Figure 4.1 **Birth and Death Rates in the United States, 1910–1991**
SOURCES: U.S. Bureau of the Census, *Statistical Abstract of the United States, 1982–83* (Washington, D.C.: U.S. Government Printing Office, 1982), p. 60; National Center for Health Statistics: Births, Marriages, Divorces, and Deaths for March 1992, *Monthly Vital Statistics Report*, Vol. 41, No. 3, DHHS Pub. No. (PHS) 92–1120, Public Health Service, Hyattsville, Md., July 31, 1992.

icine (McKeown, Brown, and Record, 1972; McKeown, Brown, and Turner, 1975). Industrialization has made available better diets, improved sanitation, better sewage disposal, and cleaner water. Consequently, people are exposed to fewer infectious and parasitic diseases and are better able to resist those to which they are exposed. The death rate for scarlet fever, for example, had dropped to practically zero by the 1940s, when effective medical treatment for this disease first became available (McKinlay and McKinlay, 1977).

Despite declining mortality rates and increasing longevity, we must all die someday, and the diseases we die of today are different from those of the past. In 1900 in the United States, the top three killers were acute infectious diseases, and they accounted for well over twice the number of deaths than did heart disease and cerebrovascular disease (see Figure 4.2.) Today, four of the five leading causes of death are chronic diseases, the fifth being accidents. So acute infectious diseases have become relatively unimportant in terms of mortality, and chronic diseases confront society with a different set of problems than did the acute ones in an earlier era (Mumford, 1983). Chronic diseases develop over a long period of time, may

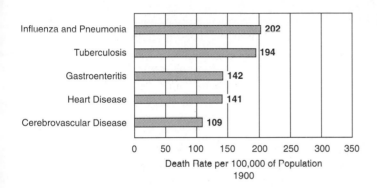

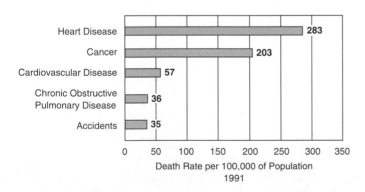

Figure 4.2 **Leading Causes of Death in the United States, 1900 and 1991**
SOURCES: U.S. Bureau of the Census, *Vital Statistics Rates in the United States, 1900–1940* (Washington, D.C.: U.S. Government Printing Office, 1943), pp. 210–215; National Center for Health Statistics: Births, Marriages, Divorces, and Deaths for March 1992, *Monthly Vital Statistics Report*, Vol. 41, No. 3, DHHS Pub. No. (PHS) 92–1120, Public Health Service, Hyattsville, Md., July 31, 1992.

go unnoticed until extensive damage has occurred, and are often associated with people's lifestyles. Effective treatment of such diseases calls for continual rather than intermittent health care and may require that people change their life-styles. Furthermore, the most effective and least expensive way of dealing with most chronic diseases is probably **preventive medicine,** *changes in life-style or other steps that help avoid the occurrence of disease* (Epstein, 1979; McKinlay, 1986). Yet modern medicine is not organized around prevention but rather toward **curative** or **crisis medicine:** *treating people's illness after they become ill.* Modern medicine arose early in this century when acute infectious diseases were the major health problems, and medical education trained doctors with a "crisis" orientation. This is an effective approach with such infectious diseases as influenza, pneumonia, or diphtheria, in which medical measures introduced after a person becomes ill can often return the person to complete health. With chronic diseases, however, much damage has already been done—and often cannot be reversed—by the time symptoms manifest themselves and medical intervention occurs. A person who suffers a heart attack, for example, may already have severe blockage of coronary arteries, and the damage typically cannot be completely undone with such modern medical measures as angioplasty or coronary artery bypass surgery. To date in the United States, preventive medicine has had a considerably lower priority—in terms of research and program funding, the construction of medical facilities, and the allocation of health-care personnel—than has crisis-oriented medicine. (Mumford, 1983). In fact, Joseph Califano argues that our crisis orientation has led to a "sick" care system rather than a "health" care system:

> We have been paying for a sick care system. Fundamentally, we've provided too many financial incentives for doctors to treat us when we are sick rather than teach us how to stay well, to send us to the hospital rather than keep us out of it. (Califano, 1986: 186)

So we have come to depend on medical practitioners intervening after we have become sick and returning us to health. Some have argued that this has become a pathological dependence because it blinds people to the part that they can play in maintaining and protecting their own health (Illich, 1976). Believing that "miracle" medicine can save them under virtually any circumstances, people may continue to smoke, overeat, and eat foods high in cholesterol. Too late they find out that medicine may be able to help them but it often cannot "save" them. People suffering with emphysema from smoking all their lives can gain some extra years of life from oxygen tanks and respirators, but there is no way that the damage to their lungs can be undone. People want to believe in the myth of miracle medicine, and medicine itself often helps to perpetuate it.

So one of the major problem areas in the health-care system today is that our health-care organization has not adapted to the changing nature of the diseases we face. Another problem is that, although death rates are down and life expectancy is up, we are not so well off when compared with some other countries. For example, the life expectancy of women in seventeen other nations exceeds that of American women, whereas American men have shorter life spans than their counterparts in twenty-one other nations (see Figure 4.3). Men in Cuba and Costa Rica and women in Puerto Rico and Greece live longer than American men and women. Likewise, the United States had a higher infant mortality rate than twenty-two other nations. (see Figure 4.4). In fact, infant mortality rates in the United States are almost *twice* as high as in Japan and Sweden. Part of the reason the health status of Americans is this low is that certain social and cultural factors have a detrimental impact on the health of many Americans.

Social Factors in Health and Illness

Who suffers from higher rates of illness and death? We will look at the four major sociocul-

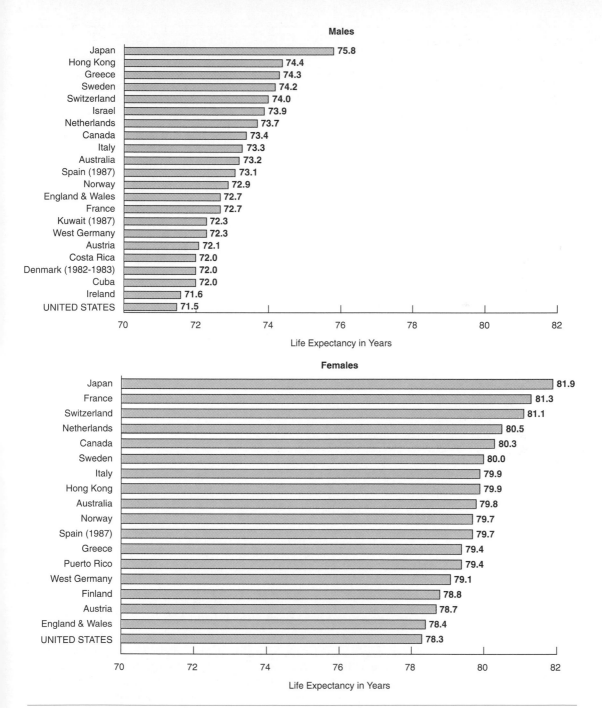

Figure 4.3 **Life Expectancy at Birth in the Countries with the Highest Life Expectancies, by Sex (for 1988 unless other year mentioned)**

SOURCE: National Center for Health Statistics, *Health, United States, 1991*, DHHS Pub. No. (PHS) 91–1232 (Hyattsville, Md.: Public Health Service, 1992), pp. 150–151.

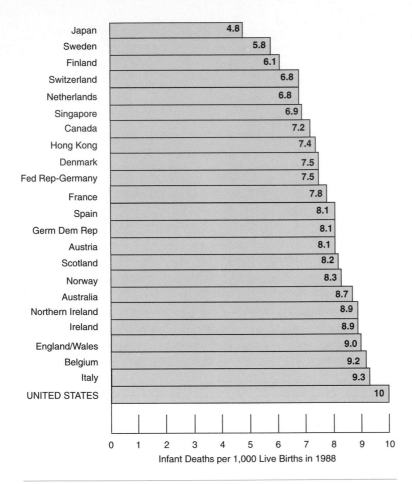

Figure 4.4   **Infant Mortality Rates: Selected Countries, 1988**
SOURCE: National Center for Health Statistics, *Health, United States, 1991,*
DHHS Pub. No. (PHS) 91–1232 (Hyattsville, Md.: Public Health Service,
1992), p. 149.

tural factors that have the greatest impact on health and illness.

Socioeconomic Status.   *Socioeconomic status* (SES) refers to people's position in society as measured by their income, educational attainment, and occupational status. The effect of SES on health is very clear: Those who are lower on such things as income, educational achievement, and occupational status have substantially higher disease rates and death rates than do their more affluent coun-

terparts (Freund and McGuire, 1991). With very few exceptions, the incidence of diseases such as cancer, heart disease, diabetes, high blood pressure, arthritis, and many others is higher among those in the lower SES ranges. Infant mortality is also substantially greater among children born into low SES families. One of the major reasons for the substandard health status of the poor is that they live under conditions that substantially increase their general susceptibility to disease (Syme and Berkman, 1979). They live under less sanitary conditions, have less nutritious diets, and are less likely to take preventive health actions such as obtaining routine physical examinations. Regarding infant mortality, poor women are less likely to have prenatal checkups and more likely to have poor diets that result in infants with low birth weights. These things contribute to infant mortality. Furthermore, despite the considerable advances brought about by Medicare and Medicaid, many poor people are not covered by these programs, and some health care still depends on out-of-pocket costs, which the poor usually cannot afford. Finally, the medical care that the poor do receive is likely to be of lower quality. They are more likely to be treated in a hospital outpatient clinic or emergency room where continuity of care, follow-up treatment, and patient education are less common than in a physician's office.

Sex.　Women appear to be healthier than men, especially if we consider longevity as the key measure of health. The life expectancy of women today is seven years greater than that of men, compared with only three years more at the turn of the century (Figure 4.3; National Center for Health Statistics, 1984). Women also have lower rates of most serious chronic illnesses. What accounts for these differences? First, it may well be that women are biologically more capable of survival than are men (Waldron, 1986). Males have higher death rates than females at every age, including deaths of fetuses. This suggests that women may have some sort of biological advantage in comparison with men, but the explanation is more complex than this. Higher mortality among males is probably also due to traditional sex-role definitions that encourage males to be aggressive and to seek more stressful and dangerous occupations where they might, for example, come in contact with industrial carcinogens. In addition, the life-styles of American men have traditionally been less healthy than those of women. For example, men drink more alcohol and smoke more tobacco. One health researcher concluded that "Cigarette smoking is the primary cause of

men's excess lung cancer and emphysema mortality. . . . The total pathological effect of smoking . . . makes a major contribution to the sex differential in total death rates" (Waldron, 1986). Although the gap between men and women in smoking and drinking has narrowed, it is still there. Finally, cultural definitions of women as the "weaker sex" may lead women to respond more quickly to symptoms and to seek medical care earlier in an illness episode. If so, this treatment may enhance the likelihood of effective medical intervention for women.

In the realm of mental illness, women also have higher rates of psychological disorders, especially for neuroses, anxiety disturbances, and depression. Part of the reason for this is that sex-role socialization seems to lead men to turn to drugs or alcohol in stressful situations. Women, on the other hand, are more stigmatized for doing this and are more likely to cope with stress through symptoms of depression or other mental disorders. Many of the symptoms of these mental disorders—dependence, withdrawal, self-devaluation, indecisiveness—are characteristics that have traditionally been a part of the stereotype of women. So women have been socialized to behave in ways that, when used as means of coping with situations, are seen as symptomatic of mental illness (Franks and Rothblum, 1983).

Race.　Most studies of the relationship between health status and race have involved comparisons between African Americans and Anglo Americans. All these studies reach distressingly similar conclusions: Blacks in America are at a serious disadvantage when it comes to health, having considerably higher death rates, shorter life expectancies, and more serious life-threatening health conditions such as hypertension and diabetes than do whites (Manton, Patrick, and Johnson, 1987). One major reason for this, of course, is that race is associated with socioeconomic status, with blacks being considerably lower in SES on the average than whites (Keil et al., 1992). Yet even when researchers control for SES, some racial differences persist. This is probably accounted for by the unique social position of blacks in America: The combination of years of racial oppression, poverty, and physically demanding occupations probably works to generate more stress in the lives of blacks than in other racial groups at the same SES level. This stress, in turn, produces greater susceptibility to disease. Minorities other than blacks also suffer substantial health problems. Native Americans, especially those on reservations, have disproportionately high mortality rates from such things as accidents, alcoholism, and suicide, and this occurs because of longstanding problems of poverty and unemployment (Bachman, 1992).

Life-style Factors.   Industrialization has unquestionably improved our lives, but it has also created health hazards largely unknown in preindustrial societies and that contribute to death and misery. For example, it is estimated that between 70 and 90 percent of all human cancers are caused in part by environmental conditions, such as air pollution or chemicals in the water and soil (Epstein, 1979). (Solutions to problems of environmental pollution are discussed in Chapter 13.) Occupational stress is linked to heart disease and hypertension (House, 1974; Schnall and Kern, 1986). Unemployment, or even the threat of it, is associated with many physical and mental disorders (Kessler, House, and Turner, 1987). The use of alcohol, tobacco, and other drugs can also cause serious health problems. There even appears to be an association between health and the quality of a person's family life: People who are married and have children are healthier than people who are single or have no children (Verbrugge, 1983). Finally, as Figure 4.2 illustrates, accidents have become one of the leading causes of mortality in modern society.

We could go on at length on this topic, but the point should be clear: There are many elements of our life-style that adversely affect our health. Any overall solution to health problems must take into account the ways in which people's lives and social circumstances can be changed to improve their health.

MENTAL ILLNESS

During the past three decades, there has been a dramatic rise in the numbers of people seeking help for psychological problems. In 1986, for example, 6 million people received inpatient or outpatient treatment at mental health facilities. This compares with only 1.6 million in 1955 (U.S. Bureau of the Census, 1982; Manderscheid and Sonnenschein, 1990). During the same period, the rate of use of such facilities has increased from 1 person per every 100,000 people to 2.5 per 100,000. These figures do not include the millions of people who received psychological services in settings other than a mental health facility: patients in hospitals for physical disorders who also seek psychiatric services, people who visit psychiatrists' or psychologists' offices, or people who seek the services of counselors and other therapists. Furthermore, there are many who need mental health services but never receive them.

This increase in mental health service utilization does not necessarily mean that there is more mental illness today; rather it reflects in part the greater availability of such services today than in the past. In addition, attitudes toward mental illness have changed, and there is less stigma attached to seeking mental health care. Irrespective of the reasons for the increase, mental illness is a very costly problem for American society. We spend upwards of $23 billion each year just to operate mental health facilities (U.S. Bureau of the Census, 1991: 114).

The Nature of Mental Illness

There is substantial agreement about the basic nature of most physical disorders: Some malfunction of pathology has occurred. For example, organic malfunction includes such things as a broken leg or an injury to the eye that impairs sight. The cure of such ailments involves, at least in part, some repair work on the person's body, such as setting the leg or operating on the eye. With mental disorders, however, there is no such agreement about their basic nature. In fact, there are at least three positions on this issue (Cockerham, 1992).

The Medical Model. The most popular approach to understanding mental disorders is to view them as having the same basic nature as physical disorders: People's normal personality and psychological processes have malfunctioned and produced pathological behavior. Their behavior is a symptom of the underlying disturbance in their psyche. The mental "disease," it is thought, can be cured by treating the individual's mental disturbances. If left untreated, the condition will become progressively worse.

This position is very popular among psychiatrists, psychologists, nurses, and many other mental health professionals. They may disagree on the precise causes of the mental disturbance. Some believe, for example, that all mental disorders are biochemical or genetic in nature; others believe that they grow out of disturbed parent–child relationships. Most of these clinicians agree, however, that the basic nature of mental disorders is directly analogous to physical ailments. Despite its popularity, this medical model of mental disorders has its limitations. In particular, its emphasis on the individual as the location of the disorder tends to restrict our focus and may result in a disregard of the many factors in the social environment that contribute to the problem. Treatment may ignore the broad social conditions that caused or contributed to the difficulty.

Mental Illness as Deviance. The symptoms of mental disorders show up in people's behavior, and human behavior, as the interactionist perspective suggests, is based in part on shared social expectations. This insight has led some sociologists to suggest that some disordered behavior of the mentally ill reflects not the inner workings of a twisted psyche but people's efforts to conform to social expectations. Sociologist Thomas Scheff (1984), for example, based his view of mental illness on the interactionist perspective. He argued that the behavior of the mentally disturbed violates normal social conventions, so his view is that of mental illness as "deviance." For example, the person who shouts obscenities on a crowded street violates norms about appropriate behavior in that setting. When we notice these transgressions, we try to understand the behavior, especially if it is threatening, by labeling the person. In this case, we might label the person as drunk. If this individual is not under the influence of alcohol and we cannot come up with another reasonable explanation for his behavior, we might then conclude that the person is mentally disturbed. Why else would he shout obscenities in public? The label of "mental illness" offers us some comfort that we understand the person's behavior and that the world is a predictable and comprehensible place.

Scheff argues that at times everybody engages in behavior that could be labeled as mental illness. In many cases, these behaviors are not noticed by others and are called **primary deviance:** *the violation of social norms in which the violator is not labeled as a deviant.* In other cases, such behavior might be attributed to something other than mental illness, such as overwork, drunkenness, or some physiological ailment. However, in a few cases, people are given the label of "mentally ill," and to be so labeled is to be cast into a social role with certain expectations associated with it. Depending on the circumstances, we may expect those labeled as mentally ill to be dependent, helpless, or even dangerous; we may even make it difficult for them to behave otherwise. For example, we might deprive them of some household or occupational duties. Then, a *self-fulfilling prophecy* may occur as the person begins to live up to our expectations. Scheff calls this **secondary deviance:** *behavior that a person adopts in reaction to being labeled as mentally ill.* This self-fulfilling

Labeling and Depersonalization in Mental Hospitals

To understand a social problem, it is sometimes helpful to view it from the perspective of its victims, whether they be AIDS sufferers, crime victims, or mental patients. D.L. Rosenhan and his associates (1973) did this with a careful observational study of mental institutions. They used a type of research called "participant observation," in which the researchers take part in the daily activities and routines of the people being studied. To do this, Rosenhan's researchers sought entrance into mental hospitals as patients. Their goal was to see first if they would be admitted and then how they were treated after admission. The people who sought admission were, as far as could be determined, sane. In fact, three were psychiatrists and one was a psychologist. The results were quite disturbing and sent howls of protest through the psychiatric community.

Each researcher, called a "pseudopatient" by Rosenhan, approached a hospital seeking voluntary admission. During their intake interviews, they described having vague symptoms, such as hearing unclear voices that said words sounding like "empty" and "hollow." All except one of the pseudopatients were admitted with a diagnosis of schizophrenia and remained hospitalized for an average of nineteen days. Once admitted, the pseudopatients acted normally, making no special effort to convince the staff that they were mentally ill. A review of the records gave no indication that any staff members developed any suspicions that the pseudopatients might be sane. The pseudopatients were eventually discharged with a diagnosis of schizophrenia "in remission."

Rosenhan's research makes us painfully aware of some disturbing dimensions of our mental health system. First of all, our ability to detect mental illness and to diagnose it reliably is distressingly weak. In other words, it is sometimes difficult for mental health professionals to detect the sane from the insane. To be sure, we might be able to diagnose extreme cases, such as a suicidal person or someone in a catatonic stupor. With less extreme symptoms, however, we find it difficult to separate the actions of normal people from those of the "insane." We also find it difficult to say reliably which mental disorder is involved in a particular case. (Although all of Rosenhan's pseudopatients presented the same symptoms, eleven were diagnosed as schizophrenic and one as manic-depressive psychotic.) Does this mean that perfectly sane people might be thought to be insane, to be institutionalized, and have rights taken away from them? It undoubtedly has hap-

prophecy is most likely to result when people are experiencing some personal crisis and they are especially sensitive to the reactions of others and vulnerable to any signs of disapproval.

Scheff readily admits that some behavioral disturbances have organic, biological, or psychological causes. His point is that sporadic violations of norms are organized into a stable pattern of be-

havior when people conform to the expectations of the social role of the mentally ill. Furthermore, he argues that mental disorders with such internal causes can be perpetuated and extended through the emergence of secondary deviance. When mental health professionals label someone as mentally ill, they may be contributing to the emergence of secondary deviance. So Scheff shifts our focus

pened and could happen again. In addition, Rosenhan's findings raise the concern that people with serious mental disorders might not be receiving treatment or, more likely, be treated for the wrong disorder.

The second dimension of Rosenhan's research is that it documents the power of labeling in mental health settings. Once the pseudopatients were given the label of "insane," no one questioned that label. Because the institution had officially labeled the people, apparently no one believed the diagnoses incorrect. Furthermore, all of the pseudopatients' behavior was interpreted in the context of assuming that they were, in fact, insane. "Normal" behavior was either overlooked or interpreted as further symptoms of the mental disorder. For example, the pseudopatients openly took notes to record their observations for the research project. Rather than questioning this unusual behavior, the staff accepted it as the bizarre actions of the insane. Because the people were already judged to be "crazy," the staff did not think it possible that there was a sane reason for their note taking. As the interactionist perspective suggests, the label, once successfully applied, becomes the social reality to which people respond. What shapes behavior is what people believe to be true.

Rosenhan's pseudopatients made another disturbing observation during their research: These mental institutions contained powerful sources of depersonalization for their patients. The interactionist perspective points out that people gain a sense of positive self-regard when others treat them in a loving, respectful way. We get feedback about ourselves from the way others interact with us. **Depersonalization** refers to *feelings of detachment from people and social groups that give life meaning and provide a sense of importance and self-worth*. The pseudopatients found themselves and other patients being dealt with in a condescending, insulting, and thoroughly negative manner. They saw patients being ignored or treated like children. They saw patients being undressed in semipublic rooms in total disregard of their privacy or their desire to control what happened to them. The impact of all this was a virtual assault on the patients' self-concept: The patients showed few signs of independence and autonomy and few feelings of self-worth. For most patients, some degree of depersonalization had set in. In fact, a self-fulfilling prophecy had occurred: The patients became the kind of people that the staff treated them as. Such characteristics as autonomy, confidence, and self-control—things we associate with mentally healthy people—declined among those in the institutions. This depersonalization does not always occur, and it does not have to occur (Weinstein, 1990b). However, the features of many institutional settings increase the likelihood that it will occur. For example, the low status of aides and orderlies both inside and outside the institution can lead some of them to bolster their own image by treating patients in a degrading fashion. In addition, lack of staff and resources can make it difficult to provide a less depersonalizing environment.

Participant observation research such as Rosenhan's is extremely valuable in understanding social problems because it offers a perspective that is often neglected—the perspective of the victim. There is real truth to the saying that you cannot truly understand a person until you have walked in his or her shoes.

away from the individual in understanding mental disorders and toward social relationships. The Applied Research insert provides a case study of the impact of some of these processes.

Mental Illness as Problems of Living. Psychiatrist Thomas Szasz's (1970; 1987) view of mental disorders is very different from those previously discussed. He believes that mental disorders should not be viewed as "illnesses" at all but rather as problems of living: expressions of the fact that human life is a continual struggle of deciding how to live and relate to others. Human existence means making choices about what makes life meaningful and valuable. Life is not, says Szasz, without considerable stress, anxiety, and conflict—nor should it be.

Szasz feels that the medical model of mental disorders is not only incorrect but also a potentially dangerous myth that can lead us to seek medical solutions to personal and ethical problems. If a psychiatrist classifies your behavior as a mental disorder, this is a value judgment regarding how you should lead your life. It limits your own exercise of judgment and freedom of choice. Furthermore, defining behaviors as symptoms of a mental disorder can lead to the dangerous step of absolving people of responsibility for their behavior. If you are not responsible for the nausea and fever that accompanies influenza, then should a father be held responsible for the rage and child beating that accompanies the "illnesses" of personality disorders? Szasz believes that people should be held accountable for the social and ethical choices they make in their lives.

There is as yet no real consensus regarding which of these views of mental disorders is most accurate or useful. However, each makes us aware of different things about the problem of mental illness. The medical model suggests that we can clearly define what mental illness is and unambiguously state that certain behaviors are pathological. Scheff and Szasz claim that social reality is much more complex than this. What is considered pathological in one context is viewed as normal in another. Furthermore, there is a danger, they argue, that we will abdicate in making moral choices in our own lives by turning the decision over to mental health "professionals" who are more than ready to tell us the "healthiest" way to live our lives. So it is important to recognize that this controversy exists when assessing problems related to mental health.

The Treatment of Mental Disorders

Problems with Diagnosis.   Mental health professionals use many concepts to describe the mental disorders that they believe exist: schizophrenia, depression, paranoia, and the like. They assess the existence of these disorders by observing people's behavior. Psychiatric diagnosis basically involves linking the behavioral display of a particular person with one or more diagnostic categories. If this diagnostic process is to be useful, it must be reliable, which means that the same diagnosis is made of the same patient by different professionals.

Unfortunately, psychiatric diagnoses are not nearly as reliable as we would hope. Recent reviews of studies spanning many decades found only a few studies in which reliability of the diagnoses was above the minimum level acceptable for good scientific research (Kirk and Kutchins, 1992). In some cases, psychiatrists reached the same diagnosis in only one of every three cases. In the American Psychiatric Association's most recent version of its *Diagnostic and Statistical Manual of Mental Disorders-Revised* (called the DSM-III-R), studies of reliability with more positive results are reported, but even here there were few findings with more than 80 percent agreement; a few had agreement as low as 30 percent. In addition, these studies were limited in scope and not well controlled (American Psychiatric Association, 1987).

The unreliability of psychiatric diagnoses is a serious problem because it throws into question whether mental health professionals can accurately detect mental disorders. If they cannot accurately detect them, can they possibly treat them effectively? Furthermore, with such unreliability, it well may be that some people are being treated for the wrong disorder while others are being treated who have no disorder at all. In addition, this unreliability may reflect the fact that the medical model of mental illness, on which these diagnostic categories rest, is not a very useful vehicle for understanding some mental disorders.

Community Treatment.   In the past thirty years, something called the "community mental health movement" has arisen and has come to play a key role in the delivery of mental health services (Mechanic, 1989). Growing in part from the kinds of concerns expressed by people such as

Szasz and Scheff, its basic thrust can be summarized in a few statements:

1. Mental health services should be delivered to a total community rather than just to individuals.
2. Services should be delivered in the community where people live rather than in state hospitals or other institutional settings removed from the community.
3. Sources of stress or other problems in the community that have implications for mental health should be detected and attacked.
4. Preventive services should be delivered as well as crisis-oriented ones.

In other words, the community treatment approach assumes that the whole community is its clientele. In addition to traditional therapies such as psychotherapy, community mental health centers should offer vocational placement, compensatory education, or other programs that would alleviate stress and help people lead more fulfilling lives. This should result in improved mental status for individuals. So the community approach tends to promote social change as well as individual adjustment.

Some of the goals of the community mental health movement appear to have been at least partially achieved. There are about as many mental hospitals today as thirty years ago, but they are much smaller. Furthermore, although the rate of admission to psychiatric hospitals has not declined, the length of stay has dropped dramatically. Most striking of all, a substantial shift has occurred in where mental health services are delivered. Today, only about 11 percent of psychiatric services are delivered in mental hospitals, compared with 56 percent thirty years ago. Today, people are usually treated in the psychiatric wards of general hospitals or as outpatients in hospitals or community mental health centers. In fact, this shift has been so dramatic that it has been called the "deinstitutionalization" of the mentally ill. In addition, the community mental health movement has provided psychiatric services to the aged, the poor, the underprivileged, and other groups that had in the past been underserved in this realm.

Not everyone has been enamored with the community approach (Brown, 1985). Some critics have charged that the process of deinstitutionalization did not commence when community mental health centers were established in the 1960s; rather, it began a decade earlier when drugs that control violence and depression became available. These drugs controlled the most disruptive symptoms of mental disorders, and they made it possible for some people to live in the community. The community mental health approach has also been criticized on the grounds that it does not accomplish many of its innovative goals, such as reducing community stressors or promoting social change, but rather ends up providing the traditional types of therapies to individuals. Yet another criticism of the community mental health approach is that it releases mental patients into the community without regard to the therapeutic value of the setting in which they will live. Living in the community may not always be the most desirable alternative for those who are mentally ill. As one study of newly released mental patients living in the community found: "For those without supportive homes to which to return or without sufficient competencies with which to sustain themselves independently in the community, community life is often difficult and dissatisfying" (Sommers, 1988: 225). All too often, critics charge, there are few coordinated follow-up services available in the community. As a result, the mentally ill in the community find themselves without the personal resources to cope with their problems and also often face financial exploitation and physical assault. Finally, the basic philosophy of keeping the mentally ill in the community has been questioned on the grounds that, if the community environment contributes to the mental disorder, then we may be simply compounding the problem by leaving people in the community. This is especially true when the mentally disturbed in the community have no family ties and few follow-up services available.

PROBLEMS IN HEALTH CARE

We have seen how a variety of social and cultural factors can contribute to the health problems of Americans. We have also discussed some special problems associated with mental illness in the United States. There are some other major problems associated with health and illness: rising costs, a lack of access to health care for some Americans, poor quality services, and sexual inequality in the health field.

Rising Health-Care Costs

For most of this century, the rise in the cost of health care has been remarkably rapid and consistent. In 1970, it cost about $74 to stay in a major hospital for one day. By 1990, the average cost of a one-day hospital stay had risen to an astounding $687 (U.S. Bureau of the Census, 1992: 114). Per capita expenditures for health care have increased over thirtyfold since 1950 (see Table 4.1). We now pay $2,566 each year for health-care goods and services for each man, woman, and child in the United States—over $10,000 a year for a family of four. Inflation accounts for some of this increase, but inflation during the same period increased overall prices only about four times. What accounts for the skyrocketing growth in health-care costs? There are a number of factors involved (McCue, 1989).

First and probably most important is the fact that there has been a growing demand for health-care services, and a basic economic principle is that increasing demand for something tends to push up prices. Our population is larger, more affluent, and older, and these factors tend to increase the demand for a finite amount of health-care goods and services. Affluent people can afford more and better health care, and they are

more knowledgeable about what services are available. Older people have more health problems and require more health-care services. These services are also more widely available today because there are more physicians and more hospital services available in suburbs and small towns.

Second, and probably equally important, is the availability of diagnostic and treatment procedures that were unheard of five, ten, or twenty years ago, and these procedures can be very costly ("High Tech Health Care . . . ," 1989). Premature babies who would have died two decades ago are now saved in expensive neonatal intensive care units (but at a high cost: from $200,000 to $1 million for an infant who weighs only one pound at birth). Laser surgery, CAT scanners, cobalt treatment, ultrasound, coronary bypass operations, angioplasty procedures, magnetic resonance imaging—these and many other procedures did not exist a few years ago. Some feel that heart transplants will be routine in the not too distant future, and they now can cost upwards of $300,000 apiece. The Health Care Financing Administration estimates that the increasing demand for services and the development of new medical procedures together account for 37 percent of the rise in health-care costs (Mumford, 1983).

Third, health care is a labor-intensive industry—it requires many people to provide health care—and the cost of health care rises quickly when health-care providers lobby for higher salaries. Nurses, nurses' aids, medical technologists, and many others feel they have been underpaid in the past and are demanding salaries they believe to be commensurate with their training and responsibilities. In addition, physicians' incomes have been rising at a much faster rate than the incomes of most Americans: Surgeons' and radiologists' incomes nearly doubled during the 1980s, whereas full-time workers' incomes went up by 40 percent and full-time female workers' by only 12 percent (Anstett, 1992). Also, savings through automation are not as easy to achieve in the health field as in other industries. Advances in

Table 4.1   **National Health Expenditures in the United States, 1940–1990, Expressed in Percentages**

	1940	*1950*	*1960*	*1970*	*1980*	*1990*
Percentage of GNP	4.0%	4.6%	5.2%	7.2%	9.1%	12.2%
Per capita expenditures	$29	$78	$142	$334	$1,054	$2,566
Percentage spent for						
Hospital care	25.0	30.7	32.9	37.4	41	38.9
Physicians' services	24.4	22.4	21.6	19.4	18.9	18.9
Dentists' services	10.4	7.8	7.5	6.5	6.2	5.1
Other professional services	4.5	3.2	3.3	2.0	2.3	4.7
Drugs and sundries	16.0	13.7	13.9	10.3	7.6	8.2
Eyeglasses and appliances	4.6	3.9	2.9	2.6	2.0	1.8
Nursing home care	.7	1.5	1.9	5.5	8.2	8.0
Other health services	2.4	3.3	4.0	3.2	2.4	1.7
Expense for prepayment and administration	4.1	3.6	3.9	3.6	3.7	5.8
Government public health activities	4.0	2.9	1.6	2.1	2.9	2.9
Research and medical facilities construction	3.5	7.0	6.6	7.4	4.8	3.4

SOURCES: Robert M. Gibson and Charles R. Fisher, "National Health Expenditures, Fiscal Year 1977," *Social Security Bulletin,* 41 (July 1978), p. 15; Katharine R. Levit, Helen C. Lazenby, Cathy A. Cowan, and Suzanne W. Letsch, "National Health Expenditures, 1990." *Health Care Financing Review,* 13 (Fall 1991), pp. 29–47.

health technology often involve completely new procedures, which call for new technicians, rather than replacing something that had been done less efficiently by older technology. So, improvements in health technology often result in the need for more, not fewer workers.

Fourth, economic competition and the check on costs that this can afford are weaker in the health field than in other economic areas. This means that physicians and hospitals can raise costs with less concern about market considerations. Recall from Chapter 2 that free competition is a key element in a capitalist economy, ensuring the lowest prices and the highest quality goods and services. The ways in which the health field diverges from the ideal of free competition are discussed in the Policy Issues insert.

Fifth, there is a tendency toward overutilization of health-care services and even to perform completely unnecessary diagnostic and treatment procedures. One reason for this involves the way we pay for health care, which leaves both the physician and the patient with little reason to show constraint in the use of services. The most common mode of payment is through **third-party medicine,** in which *the patient pays premiums into a fund and the doctor or hospital is paid from this fund for each treatment provided the patient.* The first two parties in the transaction, of course, are the patient and the doctor or hospital. The third party might be a private health insurance company or a government program such as Medicare or Medicaid. The basic flaw in such payment schemes is that the party paying the bill—the third-party source of funds—does not participate in the decision about how much or what kinds of services to provide. Patients have already paid their premiums and do not have to pay more as additional services are rendered, and physicians and hospitals benefit financially when more services are provided. The result is too many and sometimes completely unnecessary medical procedures being done. In 1992, for example, *Consumer Reports* published a study concluding that as much as 20 percent of all surgeries and medical services provided in the United States are unnecessary, costing health-care consumers $130 billion each year (Anstett, 1992). This is especially a problem with very profitable procedures, such as coronary artery bypass surgery, of which 30 percent may be unnecessary, and cesarean births, of which 50 percent may be unnecessary (Barron, 1989). In 1978, Chrysler Corporation paid $3.5 million to podiatrists for their work on the feet, toes, and toenails of Chrysler employees and their dependents. Because these costs had increased enormously, Chrysler decided to bring some control to bear by requiring that the medical necessity of foot surgery be established before it is performed. This ruling resulted in a 60 percent reduction in such surgeries and a $1 million savings for Chrysler (Califano, 1986). (Interestingly, not one Chrysler employee complained about this, but the podiatrists sued Chrysler over their loss of business.) The experience at Chrysler has been repeated innumerable times: When someone with no financial benefit in doing certain procedures oversees their necessity, the number of procedures found to be necessary drops considerably.

Finally, there are a number of other factors contributing to increasing costs. The number of malpractice suits and the size of the financial judgments against physicians in these litigations have increased. Consequently, malpractice premiums for physicians rose by 18 percent per year in the 1980s, with some specialties seeing much greater increases (Brostoff, 1992). This rise in costs is then passed on to the health-care consumer. In addition, as we mentioned above, crisis medicine tends to be more expensive in the long run than preventive medicine, but our health-care system still tends to emphasize the former. Finally, there are many powerful interest groups benefiting from rising costs: physicians, hospital administrators, the pharmaceutical industry, and so on. Health-care consumers benefit most from controlling costs, but they have yet to organize into a powerful lobby group.

For some critics of our health-care system, the problem of rising costs is only a symptom of deeper, structural problems that must be attended to. The Policy Issues insert analyzes the role that the corporatization of health care and the profit-making nature of the system may play in exacerbating the problem.

Access to Medical Services

Many Americans do not have easy access to medical care when they need it. Because health care is a commodity sold in the marketplace in America, those who can afford to pay get medical services, whereas those who cannot afford it are left to fend for themselves. We have seen how expensive health care is today, which means that only the wealthiest can afford to pay out of their own pockets for medical services. Most Americans rely on health insurance, either purchased by themselves or provided by an employer. The poor and less well-to-do Americans, who cannot find a job that provides it, are out in the cold. This situation has been eased somewhat with the introduction of programs of publicly financed health insurance such as Medicaid. Since these programs became available in the 1960s, the health-care utilization rates among the poor have increased considerably. When looking at people with equivalent health status, however, the poor still have considerably less access to health care than do the nonpoor. Being eligible for Medicaid certainly improves the access of the poor to health-care services. However, considerably less than one-half of the poor are eligible for Medicaid (Howell, 1988; Newacheck, 1988). As a consequence, fully one-third of the poorest Americans under the age of sixty-five have no health insurance coverage at all; for them, access to medical care is quite limited. In addition to the poor, there are others who find themselves without health insurance: laid-off employees; people who retire before they are eligible for Medicare; young people who are too old for coverage under their parents' health insurance plan; and widows, widowers, and divorced people who had depended on their spouses' health insurance. Altogether thirty-seven million Americans, or 15 percent of our populace, are without health insurance (Lindorff, 1992).

One critic of the health-care delivery system argues that we have a four-tier health-care system (Steinberg, 1985). The top tier consists of people with full health insurance coverage or some other means to pay for necessary care. They have complete access to excellent health care. Below them resides those with limited health insurance coverage, who do not have complete access but do have their essential health needs taken care of. The third tier consists of those on Medicaid, who have access to the health-care system if they can find someone to offer treatment or nursing homes that will admit them (Hochbaum and Galkin, 1987). Some Medicaid recipients find it difficult to locate physicians who will treat them. At the bottom of the system are the uninsured for whom access to health care is practically nonexistent.

Another dimension of access to health care is the availability of services. In this regard, it has been residents of the inner city and rural areas who are underserved. Physicians prefer to practice in locales where they would like to live and can find a profitable clientele, and neither the inner city nor rural areas can satisfy this preference. Native American youth in rural areas have been heavily affected by this; they are isolated from services and the services available tend to focus more on the health needs of children and adults (Davis, Hunt, and Kitzes, 1989). Access to health care is also affected by the availability of "primary care" physicians who serve as a person's first contact (hence, primary) with the health-care system.

They handle people's simple and routine health care and coordinate the care of specialists when these are necessary. This was a task performed by general practitioners in the past, but GPs are now on the decline, with only about 12 percent of physicians now acting as GPs (U.S. Bureau of the Census, 1991: 103). Whether for the money, the prestige, or the desire to learn well a small part of an increasingly complex body of medical knowledge, physicians of the past few decades have opted for specialty training.

Quality of Medical Services

The American health-care system is a highly centralized, specialized, and bureaucratized organization. Most physicians specialize; nursing requires extensive training, often at the baccalaureate or postbaccalaureate level; and no hospital can survive without an army of licensed practical nurses, respiratory therapists, dietitians, and other specialized personnel. The actions of all these people are coordinated with a bureaucratic form of organization. The outcome, at times, is that the patient may be treated in a standardized, impersonal, and possibly dehumanizing fashion. The person may be treated as merely a symptom vehicle—"the hernia repair in 704"—rather than a person with feelings, dreams, and fears. Such routinization of patient care may benefit health-care providers, whose jobs are easier if they do not have to deal with angry, complaining, or crying patients. For the patient, however, treatment may become a lonely, frightening, and perhaps demoralizing experience.

Yet if people receive expert medical treatment, does it matter if they are emotionally dissatisfied by the experience? Much evidence indicates that it does. Studies of the "placebo effect" document that what people think and feel about their treatment—their faith that they will be cured—plays a part in the cure. In addition, research shows that patients who receive group or emotional support from friends or health-care providers recover more quickly from heart attacks or surgery

POLICY ISSUES

Health Care: Profits and Privileges

Much of the American health-care system is profit oriented, and health-care providers sometimes closely watch the profit margin when they make medical decisions. Consider these examples:

1. A young woman is admitted to a for-profit hospital in Tennessee with a life-threatening irregular heartbeat. When the hospital learns that her health insurance only covers 80 percent of her hospitalization and that, being of modest means, she would be hard pressed to pay the remaining 20 percent, they recommend she be transferred to a nearby university hospital. When that hospital has no room for her, the for-profit hospital discharges her with medications to take at home—a move that independent medical experts called "totally inappropriate" for "a patient who is a candidate for sudden death" (Lindorff, 1992: 16).

2. Some for-profit hospitals offer physicians financial support, such as free or discounted rent on office space and equipment or a guaranteed first-year income for those newly out of medical school. The *quid pro quo* is that the physicians will admit patients—and in large numbers—to the hospitals offering them such largess. If the physicians do not come through, their deal with the hospital is off.

3. One health maintenance organization that employs its own physicians withholds 20 percent of their income until the end of the year when it reviews their "profitability." "Profitable" physicians—the ones who do not order too many expensive diagnostic tests or consultations with specialists—receive the withheld income whereas the unprofitable ones go without.

4. One hospital sent some of its physicians a memo informing them that their position at the hospital would be terminated if they did not admit more patients. It also kept a physician profile showing how many patients each one admits, how long the patients stay, and whether they pay their bill. Physicians who admit the "wrong" kind of patient—the really sick, the elderly, the expensive, and the ones whose bill is not paid fully by someone—find they lose their privileges at the hospital.

5. Some hospitals refuse to treat ailments that are expensive and unprofitable. Many have closed their emergency rooms because these attract people of modest means who do not have health insurance and cannot pay their bills. One entrepreneur explained why his chain of community hospitals dropped all obstetric and orthopedic procedures: "Because these two are the biggest areas for malpractice [lawsuits], and also obstetrics are where you get most of your Medicaid patients" and Medicaid pays less for medical procedures than does private insurance (Lindorff, 1992: 78).

The hospitals involved in these practices are privately owned and intended to make a profit for their investors, just like a car dealership, a bakery, or a tavern. In other words, health-care institutions are a part of the American capitalist economic system described in Chapter 2. Now this is not new. After all, physicians have been business entrepreneurs in this country since its founding, pharmaceutical companies have always tried to make a profit selling people drugs, and there have always been privately owned hospitals. What is different today is the size and scope of the privatization and corporatization of health care in the United States. In the past, nonprofit hospitals were run by communities or by religious or service organizations. Their primary goal was to provide for all of the health needs of a community. Although such hospitals can still be found today, the hospital industry is slowly being taken over by national corporations that own chains of hospitals and manage local hospitals from a centralized business office (one in four acute care hospitals is now investor owned). In these corporate settings, control and authority over medical decisions and issues is gradually shifting from the hands of patients, physicians, and community leaders to corporate headquarters and medical industry entrepreneurs, and the primary motivation of these corporations is to increase corporate profits. The public sector of community and nonprofit hospitals is being forced to adopt some of the same strategies or be run out of business.

The corporate takeover of hospitals began with the emergence of Medicare and Medicaid, which meant that there were huge profits to be made treating the recipients of these programs. The elderly now account for 60 percent of hospital admissions, and the Medicare payments along with tax advantages available meant that a hospital was a very good investment in the 1960s and 1970s. By the 1980s, in the Wall Street world of medicine, patients were known as "revenue bodies," hospitals were "profit centers," and the goal was to "maximize the return on each admission." What has emerged is a rather chilling trend: "Charging every penny that can be charged for patient care, and avoiding as much as possible the treatment of patients unable to pay. It also means marketing, or offering paying patients what they *think* they need, while eliminating services a community might *really* need but which aren't profitable" (Lindorff, 1992: 18). So young professionals with good health insurance get valet parking and luxurious birthing rooms, but poor pregnant women, even when they have Medicaid, find that they are not welcome. And the professionals have to travel further to find a community hospital that offers emergency services when they have an accident.

There are, of course, benefits to this privatization. Especially for those with good health insurance or the wealthy who can afford to pay on their own, American medicine provides some excellent services. As we saw in Chapter 2, capitalism is based on the assumption that competition and profit seeking will work in the interests of the consumer by providing the widest range of goods and services at the lowest price. These incentives should, in theory, encourage private health-care businesses to provide high-quality, inexpensive health care.

However, it does not seem to work out that way (Lindorff, 1992). In areas where many hospitals compete with one another for patients, both for-profit and nonprofit hospitals charge about the same for various procedures; when there is no competition, for-profits actually charge more for services than do the nonprofits. It seems that, in a noncompetitive environment, the temptation to raise charges, and thus increase profits, is too great to resist. The overall lower costs of nonprofit hospitals is especially surprising because they do not dump expensive services such as obstetrics in the way that the for-profits have.

The privatization and corporatization of health care also means that those who cannot afford health care—the poor who do not qualify for Medicaid and those who do not have health insurance on the job—do not have access to the health services they need. Even those with Medicaid find that they have limited access to the system because corporate hospitals and doctors prefer to serve those whose insurance will pay larger bills than will Medicaid. In addition, expensive medicine, such as obstetrics and emergency medicine, gets dumped onto publicly owned hospitals, which further taxes their ability to provide quality care to their patients. And some question whether profit seeking by doctors and hospitals always works in the best interests of the patient. As one health economist put it: "The real threat to health care is when the doctors' and the hospitals' interests become aligned against the interests of the patient. It's possible that the corporations could usurp the physicians' power" to act as an advocate for the patients (quoted in Lindorff, 1992: 86).

Dr. Arnold S. Relman (1980), editor of the prestigious *New England Journal of Medicine*, calls this a **medical–industrial complex**: *a coincidence of interests between physicians and other health-care providers and the industries producing health-care goods and services, with both parties profiting from the increased use of these commodities while the health-care consumer pays enormous costs for inadequate care.* This is analogous to the military–industrial complex discussed in Chapter 2. It can lead to a conflict of interest because many of the businesses are owned by doctors or employ doctors. Like other enterprises, these businesses stand to increase their profits by "selling" as much of their commod-

"I'M AFRAID YOU'RE IN BAD SHAPE, MR. CAUSEY — YOUR MEDICAL HISTORY SHOWS THAT YOU'VE SUED FOUR DOCTORS!"

The physician-patient relationship is in part an economic relationship, and economic considerations can interfere with the provision of care that is in the best interests of the patient.

ity as they can, just as a person who sells cars profits by increasing sales. This raises the question of whether health-care decisions are motivated by the health needs of the consumer or by the profit needs of the medical–industrial complex.

Looking at these problems with our privatized health-care system, some critics have argued that they arise, in part, because health care is different from other segments of the economy: It has elements that make it less subject to the laws of competition and the marketplace.

1. Ninety percent of our populace is covered by some form of third-party insurance, which means that they do not have to pay for many health-care goods and services out of their pockets. Because they do not pay directly, they have less incentive to shop around for the best buy.

2. In most economic situations, consumers decide how many goods or what kinds of services they will purchase. Health-care consumers, however, are heavily dependent on their doctors—the very ones who benefit economically from the provision of services—for expert advice on what they need. It is the physician who recommends that we have surgery, for example, and few health-care consumers have the expertise to ignore that advice.

3. Many practices common in other realms are not available in medicine. Consumers cannot, for example, test a health-care service before purchasing nor can they obtain a money-back guarantee to protect against faulty procedures.

Despite these differences between health care and other economic spheres, health care is still largely a private-enterprise, profit-making activity in the United States. This has been cited by many critics as a major factor leading Americans to pay more for lower quality health care than they should (Mumford, 1983).

There is contentious debate about what, if anything, to do about all these problems (Wohl, 1989). Relman has urged the American Medical Association to discourage physicians from commercially exploiting health care by being financially involved in health-care businesses. Other critics, such as Ronald Kotelchuck (1976) and Ivan Illich (1976), believe that the capitalist nature of our health-care system is the fundamental problem. For these radical critics, only a complete restructuring of the system, possibly through nationalization by the government, can prevent widespread abuses and exploitation. Current social policy tends to support the profit-oriented nature of the system, but changes are possible in the future.

(Mumford, Schlesinger, and Glass, 1982). In comparison, lonely people who have been dehumanized by the system may have far less faith that the actions of the medical personnel will be beneficial. There is another way in which the emotional state of health-care consumers is important. Evidence indicates that the demeanor of health-care providers and their relationships with patients can influence whether the patient continues to take medications, follows medical advice, and returns to the physician for a follow-up appointment (DiMatteo and DiNicola, 1982). Although the relationships are complex, basically if people are satisfied with their relationships with their doctor, they are more likely to follow his or her medical recommendations. And patients are more satisfied when they receive personal treatment, clear explanations of their condition and instructions about carrying out their treatment, and generally feel that the health-care providers know and care about their needs as a patient. Such feelings of satisfaction are less likely if the health-care system is impersonal and bureaucratized (Like and Zyzanski, 1987). In fact, the public's distrust of physicians has grown substantially over the past thirty years, probably because the doctor–patient relationship has become a more impersonal, specialized, and short-lived encounter (Betz and O'Connell, 1983).

Sexual Inequality in Health Care

Sexual inequality pervades our health-care system, with widespread ramifications. First, the health-care industry in the United States is male dominated, with men holding most of the prestigious, well-paying, and powerful positions (see Figure 4.5). Men make up 80 percent of today's physicians, for example, whereas 95 percent of the registered nurses are women. Almost all dentists are men, whereas practically all dental assistants and dental hygienists are women. Clearly, the health-care system involves men in positions of authority telling women what to do. This was not always the case. In the last century, women, working as midwives or other types of healers, provided much of the medical care for families. As more medical schools developed in the late 1800s, women were excluded from most of them. By the turn of the century, legislation banned the "practice of medicine" by anyone not trained in a state-approved medical school. The result: Women were effectively banned from the practice of medicine. During the first half of this century, medical schools admitted few, if any, women. Even through the 1960s, medical and dental education were male preserves: Although a few women were admitted, they were often met with hostility or demeaning jokes, making the difficult drive through school an even tougher road. It has not really been until the last fifteen years that medical and dental education have opened up to women. Today about one-third of both medical and dental students nationwide are women (see Figure 4.6). There has been little change, however, in the sparse numbers of men in nursing schools.

One reason for concern about male dominance in the health field is that it has severely restricted women's access to lucrative and prestigious occupations. These issues of economic discrimination are discussed in more detail in Chapter 7. Another reason for concern is that male dominance may have had a detrimental effect on the health and health care of American women. Male physicians over the years held the same stereotypes about women that other American men did, and this influenced what physicians defined as illness and what treatments they made available. For example, one stereotype viewed menstruation as "unclean" or "abnormal," and physicians fed into this by "medicalizing" menstruation or defining it as a medical condition or weakness calling for some intervention. In the nineteenth century and well into this one, menstruation has been viewed as a pathological condition sometimes having serious consequences and influencing women's ability to think and make decisions. In fact, the reputed ill effects of women's reproductive biology have been an important staple in a sexist ideology jus-

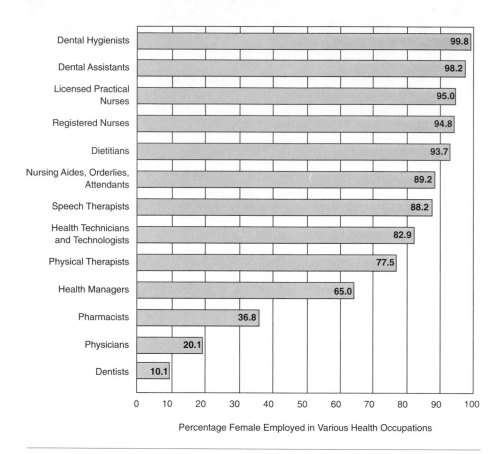

Figure 4.5   **Men and Women in Health Occupations, 1991**
SOURCE: U.S. Department of Labor, Bureau of Labor Statistics, *Employment and Earnings*, Vol. 39, No. 1, January 1992, pp. 185–190.

tifying the inequitable treatment of women. From the late 1800s until recently, the very process of childbirth itself has been viewed as a medical procedure rather than the profoundly natural and personal event that it really is. Women were routinely given powerful anesthetics that prevented them from experiencing the birth of their children. Then they might not even be permitted to see their infants for a few days after birth, interfering with the bonding that occurs between mother and child soon after birth. More recently, the number of cesarean births has grown from 5 percent to almost 25 percent of all births, giving the United States the highest rate of such births (Taffel et al., 1991). Some cesareans, of course, are medically justified, but there is much suspicion that some are performed for the convenience of medical personnel, to protect against malpractice suits, or because doctors and hospitals are reimbursed more for surgical births. In any event, the mother loses control of the birth process when it becomes overly medicalized. Over the years, then, male dominance in medicine has meant that men have been the "authorities" telling women about their own bodies, and what the men told the women often did more to bolster inaccurate

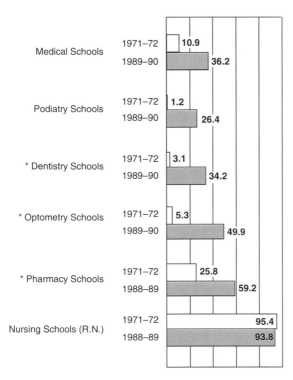

Medical Schools	1971–72	10.9
	1989–90	36.2
Podiatry Schools	1971–72	1.2
	1989–90	26.4
* Dentistry Schools	1971–72	3.1
	1989–90	34.2
* Optometry Schools	1971–72	5.3
	1989–90	49.9
* Pharmacy Schools	1971–72	25.8
	1988–89	59.2
Nursing Schools (R.N.)	1971–72	95.4
	1988–89	93.8

* First-year enrollment only.   Percentage of Female Students

Figure 4.6 **Enrollment of Women in Schools for Health Occupations, United States, Academic Years 1971–1990**
SOURCES: National Center for Health Statistics, *Health, United States, 1990*, DHHS Pub. No. (PHS) 91–1232, Public Health Service (Washington, D.C.: U.S. Government Printing Office, 1991), p. 172; National Center for Health Statistics, *Health, United States 1991*, DHHS Pub. No. (PHS) 92–1232, Public Health Service (Washington, D.C.: U.S. Government Printing Office, 1992), p. 254.

stereotypes or line the pockets of physicians than to benefit the health of women.

The medical procedure that is among those most likely to be performed unnecessarily—the hysterectomy—affects only women. Conservatively, one-third of all hysterectomies over the years were probably medically unjustified (Stroman, 1979). Some observers have questioned whether a medical profession dominated by women would have so routinely performed such surgeries. In addi-

tion, feminists argue that medical research has been dominated by the sexist assumption that it is the woman's responsibility to orchestrate birth-control efforts. The impact has been that most birth-control research has been on female contraceptive devices with few resources devoted to finding effective procedures for male contraception.

BIOETHICS: TECHNOLOGY AND HEALTH

Modern technology has opened up some wonderful opportunities, but it also confronts us with some difficult and potentially frightening issues. A fictional description of one such possibility is found in the medical thriller *Coma* by novelist Robin Cook (1977). In this account, hordes of people who have lapsed into comas are kept alive artificially as a source of organs for transplantation—the veritable farming of people for their valuable organs. Although the technology involved is a bit futuristic, the theme of harnessing medical technology to exploit people in ghastly ways struck a responsive chord in many readers. The final chapter of this book deals with the impact of science and technology on our lives, but here we want to address a few special concerns that relate to health issues. **Bioethics** refers to *the study of ethical questions that relate to the life and biological well-being of people* (Brody and Engelhardt, 1987). It involves an intertwining of ethical, medical, and biological considerations. We will discuss three major issues in this realm: the prolongation of life, the distribution of limited medical resources, and genetic screening. Keep in mind that these ethical issues have come to the fore, in part, because of the very success of science and medicine in attacking illness and injury.

The Prolongation of Life

When people die, their respiratory, circulatory, and nervous systems—the major life-sustaining body systems—normally fail at about the same time. With modern technology, however, respiration and circulation can be machine assisted far beyond the point at which the body itself could sustain them. These machines do not provide medical treatment but merely assist the body to stay "alive." Thus, severely injured, critically ill, or very old people can be kept alive for long periods of time. A particularly disturbing case gained prominence in California in 1984 (Malcolm, 1984). A seventy-year-old man was hospitalized with five normally fatal diseases, including inoperable lung cancer. He could not breathe on his own, so a machine breathed for him through a passage in his neck. Other tubes fed him and drained his wastes. Electronic monitors warned nurses of any change in his condition. Everyone involved agreed that the man would never leave his hospital bed alive. Both the man himself and his wife requested that the breathing machine be turned off so that he could die naturally. His physicians refused the request on the grounds that the man would die if removed from the machine. They even tied his arms down so that he would not be able to remove the tubes himself. The man's wife sued the hospital to have the machines turned off, but the man died before the case was resolved. His medical and legal bills were estimated to be over $500,000. A similar dilemma is faced by relatives and medical personnel who must decide whether to withhold life-prolonging medical treatment from loved ones.

The expense of such life-support systems can devastate a family's finances. Even with health insurance, there are deductibles to be paid, and society as a whole must still bear these costs. There is also a tremendous psychological burden for the family who has to watch a loved one go through a prolonged period of debilitation before death. Finally, from the individual's perspective, there is the loss of dignity that comes from helplessness. Even if comatose, many would prefer not to end their lives with tubes inserted in their bodies and machines powering their hearts—almost as if the body must fight against modern technology in order to die.

Technology has made the line between life and death more vague. It has become a difficult practical matter to say exactly when death occurs in many cases. The same technology can maintain the lives of terminally ill or comatose people, even when there is little or no hope of recovery. This situation creates a dilemma regarding who should decide whether to discontinue life support. Parents or relatives would seem to be the natural ones to make such decisions, but they could be swayed by such considerations as the psychological or economic costs of maintaining a critically ill relative over time. Medical personnel also play a role in such decisions. But their mission is to save lives, and they may be rightly concerned about civil or even criminal suits resulting from their decisions in such cases. As a consequence, their choices may not be in the patients' best interests.

A number of developments have had an impact on this problem of the artificial prolongation of life. One has been the emergence of social movements whose major theme is "death with dignity." Those involved have lobbied for the acceptance of "living wills," in which people state, while they are still healthy, the conditions under which medical efforts to save their lives should be stopped. A few states have accepted these living wills as legal documents, but their ultimate legality is likely to be debated in the courts. Another development has been the acceptance of a revised definition of death, which used to be defined as the cessation of breathing and heartbeat. The newer approach defines death as the prolonged absence of brain waves, or "brain death." This gives physicians some legal standing in withholding life-sustaining efforts from those who show virtually no possibility of recovery. Some have lobbied for an even more controversial position that death be declared when "higher brain functions"—those controlling conscious thought and emotion—have ceased, but there has been no legislative support for this position so far. A final development has been the establishment of panels in hospitals to make recommendations about decisions of whether to withhold treatment or turn off life-support equipment. The panels are made up of doctors, nurses, social workers, psychologists, and even laypeople. These panels relieve physicians of the difficult burden of making such decisions alone, and, by including many different opinions, they reduce the likelihood that personal bias will result in judgments at variance with the patient's interests.

Whom Shall We Treat?

As we have seen, health care is expensive and is becoming more costly all the time. A part of the problem is the growing number of technologically complex and costly procedures that are available. This raises the question of whether we can afford to provide these treatments to everyone with a medical need for them (Merrill and Cohen, 1989). After all, the money we spend on health care is money we cannot spend on defense, social services, automobiles, and recreation. In 1989, for example, $700 of the cost of each automobile Chrysler produced went to pay health-care premiums for Chrysler workers, retirees, and their families (Iacocca, 1989). This plan provides excellent health-care coverage for Chrysler workers, but it means more expensive cars and less money for auto consumers to spend on other items. One option, of course, is to limit the availability of some medical procedures, possibly the more expensive ones. But how do we decide to whom these procedures will be made available? Such decisions rest on some "principle of social justice." There are a number of these principles that can serve as the basis of medical allocation decisions (Veatch and Branson, 1976; Hingson et al., 1981).

1. *Ability to pay:* offer services to those who can afford to pay part or all of the costs.
2. *Merit:* offer services on the basis of people's merits, such as their achievements or societal contributions.
3. *Utilitarian:* offer services to those who would provide the greatest benefit—in economic, personal, or social terms—to the greatest number of people should they live.
4. *Compensatory justice:* offer services to those who have already suffered some social wrongs or have been deprived of resources.
5. *Egalitarian:* offer everyone who needs services an equal opportunity to receive them.

Which of these principles, or combinations of principles, would you use to allocate health-care resources? The egalitarian concept is probably the most popular one in the United States. In fact, some physicians in the 1960s chose kidney dialysis patients on the basis of a random lottery. The point, of course, is that, as medical technology becomes more expensive, we may have to decide how to limit its use by adopting some principles of social justice on which to rest the allocation process.

Genetic Screening

Medical technology has advanced to the point where we can determine many things about the health status of a fetus through intrauterine testing (Henifin, Hubbard, and Norsigian, 1989; Hubbard, 1990). Amniocentesis, for example, is a procedure in which amniotic fluid is withdrawn from around the fetus and analyzed for abnormal cells and genetic content. Such procedures can determine the sex of the child and whether the child suffers from a number of serious defects or disorders such as Down's syndrome or cystic fibrosis. When the fetus is found to have some serious problem, especially one for which there is no known treatment, the parents are confronted with a potential dilemma: Should they continue the pregnancy? For people strongly opposed to abortion, of course, the answer is yes. For others, however, the prospect of raising a retarded or severely ill child may be sufficiently difficult or disturbing that abortion is considered a viable option. So genetic screening, made possible by ad-

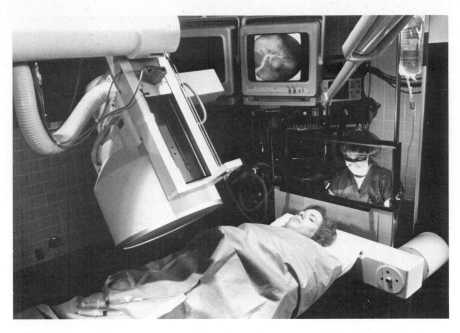

The problem of rising health care costs is linked to the problem of access to good quality health care. Higher costs and more limited access raise the bioethical question of whether we can afford to provide all the health care that people need with the level of quality they expect.

vances in medical technology, confronts people with ethical dilemmas that were much less common in the past.

Amniocentesis also raises a future problem that could be disturbing. Because we can learn the sex of a fetus, might this information be used in deciding whether to continue a pregnancy? Would a couple desperately wanting a boy abort a female fetus? In a society placing more value on males than females, would people continue having abortions until the woman was pregnant with a male fetus? Would cultural values or fashions determine whether people continue pregnancies with a fetus of a given sex? These are not, of course, problems at the moment in the United States, but the technology is very new. And it does raise some disturbing possibilities. As we will see in Chapter 15, genetic engineering on a substantial scale may be possible in the near future, with disturbing social implications.

FUTURE PROSPECTS

In attacking the problems of the cost of, access to, and quality of health care, there is an overriding issue to be resolved: Is health care in the United States a right or a privilege? One view is that access to high-quality health care should be a fundamental right of all Americans. We have reviewed the functionalist argument that the health status of citizens is central to the maintenance of society. Society needs to ensure that people are healthy so that they can make contributions to the maintenance of society. The opposing view is that access to health care should be a privilege of those with resources to obtain it. Like the conflict perspective, this position holds that health care is a valued commodity to be distributed to those who can afford it. This reflects the capitalist and market foundations of our economy: Health care is merely another economic service, and it can be most efficiently produced and distributed through competition in the marketplace.

Although most industrial nations today view health care as a citizen's right, there is still some controversy regarding this in the United States. The lack of resolution of this issue is reflected in the programs proposed to solve problems in the health area.

Publicly Funded Health Insurance

One approach to increasing people's access to health care is through publicly funded health insurance.

Medicare and Medicaid.   Two government programs that have probably had the most profound effects on health-care delivery in the United States are Medicare and Medicaid, both established in 1965. These programs are based on the assumption that all Americans have a right to medical treatment irrespective of their financial circumstances. **Medicare** is *government health insurance for those over sixty-five years of age*. This program pays some of the costs for hospitalization, nursing-home care, and some home-health care. For a monthly fee, the elderly can also purchase medical insurance from Medicare that will cover other services such as doctors' fees and outpatient services. **Medicaid** is *a joint federal-state program to provide medical care for low-income people of any age*.

These two programs have gone a long way toward reducing the differences in utilization rates between the affluent and the poor. Unlike the past, the poor today visit doctors and enter hospitals more frequently than the well-to-do. To that extent, these two programs have achieved one of their major goals, which was to make health care available to all citizens regardless of financial circumstances. But these plans are not without their problems. First they are very expensive and growing more expensive. Medicare expenses rose from $7 billion in 1971 to over $100 billion today—a fourteenfold increase in a little over two decades.

Medicaid payments are about half as large (U.S. Bureau of the Census, 1992: 102). Both payment schemes are third-party arrangements and suffer from the same cost problems of all such fee schemes. In the early 1980s, the government cut some of the benefits in both programs in an effort to hold down costs. A second problem, especially with Medicaid, has been fraud, committed by both recipients and providers of health care. Some physicians have provided unneeded treatments, and some medical laboratories have routinely charged for tests never performed. Some abuse is inevitable in such large programs, but it has been extensive and expensive. A third problem is that some providers have refused to treat Medicaid and Medicare patients because of delays in receiving payments or because the payments were inadequate. Medicaid has been criticized over the years for paying physicians too little for services. Medicare began a new fee schedule in 1992 that sometimes reimburses physicians less than half what they charge their private paying patients. Physicians claim they cannot even cover their overhead with what the programs pay (Freudenheim, 1992). This problem may be creating a two-tiered health-care system in which Medicare and Medicaid patients receive lower-quality care by lower-paid physicians in crowded settings, whereas Americans with private health insurance have good quality services available to them. Finally, as we have seen, the eligibility level for Medicaid in most states is so low that people who truly need it do not have access to it. Raising the eligibility ceilings would provide health insurance to many who currently have no insurance whatsoever.

A number of efforts have been made to control the skyrocketing costs of Medicaid and Medicare. Some states have developed "preferred provider" programs for Medicaid in which a hospital or a group of doctors agrees to provide all health-care services to Medicaid recipients in a particular geographic area, receiving, in return, one annual, lump-sum payment. This encourages the providers to prevent costs from exceeding the annual amount that they are paid because they will not receive any additional payments and are contractually required to provide services. For Medicare, the federal government instituted a new payment mechanism in the early 1980s called diagnostically related groupings, or DRGs. This strategy involves placing each hospitalization episode into one of about 450 diagnostic groupings. Then all treatments in a single diagnostic grouping receive the same reimbursement, whether any particular case actually costs more or less. If a case costs more to treat, the hospital must make up the difference; if it costs less, the hospital keeps the surplus. The purpose is to offer doctors and hospitals a financial incentive for keeping an eye on lowering costs. Opponents of the DRG approach argue that people's illness episodes are too individualized to be treated in this assembly-line fashion: Some people bleed more, others take longer to recuperate, whereas others are fast healers. Furthermore, doctors would have to consider DRGs when they make diagnoses rather than being guided solely by the condition of their patients. Although the program is new and thus difficult to assess conclusively, it seems to have produced a few changes: Hospital stays for the elderly are shorter than they used to be, hospitals are trying to draw in more patients to take up the slack, and hospitals have aggressively developed outpatient services (Freund and McGuire, 1991).

National Health Insurance.   Medicare and Medicaid amount to government health insurance for the poor and the elderly. Some have proposed that these benefits be extended as a right to all citizens through national health insurance. Great Britain had such a program as early as 1911. In fact, the United States and South Africa are alone among the industrial nations in not providing some form of national health insurance or health service (Lindorff, 1992). National health insurance would alleviate a number of problems. It would ensure health insurance coverage to the many people who do not currently have any, such as low-income people ineligible for Medicaid and people who are between jobs. It would also give

the government a more direct means of controlling health-care costs. Finally, it would reduce the likelihood of a two-tiered health-care system. However, national health insurance would still be a third-party payment system that could be costly if it did not include some cost containment mechanisms, such as DRGs.

There was much debate about national health insurance in the 1970s, and some were predicting the quick adoption of such a program. During the 1980s, such discussion dwindled as government social programs were more likely to be cut or eliminated than established or expanded. However, the 1990s will see continued debate over the rising cost of health care and health insurance. Some workers are already being squeezed as employers, struggling to deal with the cost of employee health plans, are trying to get employees to pay more of those costs. These issues have been central factors in a number of labor strikes. Such concerns may lead many Americans to take another look at national health insurance as a mechanism for spreading out the costs of health care. The relatively low level of enthusiasm for extending publicly financed health insurance to all Americans, however, suggests that some ambivalence remains regarding whether health care is a right or should be a privilege. As the International Perspectives insert points out, this contrasts sharply with the approach taken in many other societies.

Compulsory, Employer-Financed Health Insurance.   Some would prefer that the government not get involved in the actual provision of health insurance but rather just ensure that all Americans have access to some health insurance. Because many of the currently uninsured have jobs with no health insurance benefits, one proposal is to have the government require that all employers provide comprehensive health insurance for their employees. As this textbook is being written in early 1993, the Clinton administration is considering a variation of comprehensive health insurance for employees called "managed competition"; in this plan, employers would have to provide health insurance for their employees, and the government would pay the insurance premiums of those who don't work or work for employers who are too small to afford health insurance. Such a program would be expensive, of course, and it would put a burden on small businesses. In addition, the American consumer would pay for it through higher prices for goods and services. Yet it would provide many more Americans with access to health care. It is also more acceptable than programs such as national health insurance to many laissez-faire advocates because it accomplishes the goal with minimal government involvement. In fact, something similar could be done with Medicare and Medicaid: Instead of the government providing the insurance, the government could pay the private health insurance premiums for those who are eligible for the programs.

Access to Health Services for Special Groups

Providing more extensive health insurance coverage is a major way to increase access to services. However, we saw that there are other barriers that reduce access, such as the isolation of native Americans on reservations. These problems need to be approached by developing very focused programs for delivering services to particular groups. One program, for example, focused on the health needs of native American teenagers, by providing substance abuse counseling, suicide prevention services, and pregnancy testing—thereby addressing problems that many young native Americans in rural areas are likely to confront (Davis, Hunt, and Kitzes, 1989). Services were provided in the local school to make them readily available in an isolated community with few health resources. Access to health services can also be limited if health providers and institutions behave in an arrogant or insensitive manner to people of particular groups. Native American utilization of health services has been limited by the feeling that Anglo providers are insensitive or judgmental. Community involvement in the development and operation of health services can go a long way toward reducing this problem.

In most cases, these focused health-delivery programs will be financed at least in part by government funds, which have been scarce in the past decade. The private health-care economy has not been effective in dealing with the problems of these special groups because they do not have the economic resources to attract providers and services.

Health Maintenance Organizations

Although most people pay for their health care through health insurance, there is another way that this can be accomplished: by joining a prepaid group plan or health maintenance organization (HMO). A **health maintenance organization** is *an organization that agrees to provide for all of a person's health-care needs for a fixed periodic premium* (Luft, 1987). Unlike third-party medicine, there are only two parties involved here: the HMO providing the services and the patient. Therefore, the HMO assumes some of the financial risk in the provision of services and this creates an incentive for cost containment. The larger HMOs own their own health-care facilities and employ all of the personnel, including doctors, who provide the care. Currently, somewhere between 3 percent and 6 percent of the populace is covered by HMOs.

HMOs seem to provide some benefits in contrast to third-party health insurance. They are quite a bit less expensive for enrollees; they have lower rates of hospitalization and perform fewer surgical procedures—especially those that are most likely to be unnecessary, such as tonsillectomies and hysterectomies; and they have lower mortality rates and fewer premature births. These benefits may result from the HMOs' unique mode of financing, in which the health-care provider has an economic incentive to economize. This may make HMOs less likely to overutilize services or perform unnecessary procedures or surgeries. It

INTERNATIONAL PERSPECTIVES

Paying for Health Care in Other Societies

Earlier in this chapter, we ran across two rather disturbing facts. One is that the United States doesn't come off very well in international comparisons of health status. For example, in comparison to most other industrial nations, we live shorter lives and lose more of our infants to death. The second disturbing fact is that we pay more for our health care than do these other nations. Why do these other nations pay less and get more than we do? Some critics attribute this to the largely unregulated, laissez-faire nature of our health care system which leaves many people with limited or no access to the health care system.

In Sweden, France, Australia, Germany, Canada, and many other nations, health services are paid for with money collected by the government (Cockerham, 1989). This is similar to Medicare and Medicaid in the United States. Employers and employees pay taxes that are placed in a fund from which medical bills are paid. Canada, for example, provided hospital insurance for its citizens beginning in 1961 and physician's care

insurance in 1971. The entire population is covered and 95 percent of hospital and physician costs are paid by federal or provincial taxes. There are some amenities, such as private hospital rooms and cosmetic surgery, that the system won't pay for. Everything else is paid for, and Canadians hardly ever even see a hospital bill. Patients can choose their own physicians, and physicians are private, self-employed practitioners, not government employees. Hospitals also operate on a budget that is set largely by provincial governments. So, Canada has an essentially private health care system that is paid for almost entirely by public money.

One way in which this universal coverage can be paid for is by keeping costs down. For example, in Canada, the government sets all doctor and hospital fees, and physicians can't charge more for services than the insurance will pay. Canadian physicians do not earn the lucrative incomes that American physicians do, although physicians are still among the highest paid professional groups in Canada. However, Canadian

---

may also be, however, that healthier people join HMOs. In addition, HMOs provide extensive preventive health care, and this may account for their ability to operate at lower costs. In any event, if HMOs become more popular in the future, they may help to lower health-care costs.

Social Control of Health Care

The American health-care system is capable of delivering very high quality health care. However, as the increase in malpractice suits and other evidence suggests, incompetence and poor quality services do exist. Efforts to deal with this problem

have focused on detecting such poor quality when it does occur and preventing incompetent practitioners from continuing to practice medicine. One major approach toward this has been peer review, in which physicians are watched by their peers and incompetence or poor clinical judgment brought to people's attention. This approach can work, especially in group medical practices where there are a number of partners in practice together who have an interest in seeing that good quality medical care is provided. However, research shows that, although physicians are willing to criticize one another in informal discussion groups, they are much more reluctant to do so as

doctors don't have to worry about billing patients, preparing insurance forms, or writing off bad debts. Another way Canada pays for its system is through progressive taxes, or tax rates that increase with income. This makes for a larger kitty from which to pay for health care. In the United States, health insurance premiums tend to be the same, irrespective of people's income.

Of course, you can't spend less on health care and cover more people, as the Canadians do, without some costs. One cost is that there are sometimes waits for hospital beds and some types of surgical procedures, especially non-emergency surgeries. In addition, some state-of-the-art technology, such as magnetic resonance imaging (MRI) machines, is not as widely available as in the United States. Yet another cost is the higher taxes to pay for the universal government-provided coverage.

These costs, however, don't seem to hurt too badly because Canadians still live longer and have less infant mortality than do citizens in the United States. In addition, we should look at health care financing programs in terms of *who* bears the costs. Currently, in the United States, those who benefit the most are the affluent, those fortunate enough to have good, employer-provided health insurance, and the elderly with Medicare. A shift to a Canadian-style system would mean redirecting some of the benefits from those groups to the poor, the unemployed, the under-employed, and other marginal groups. So, it comes down to *how* health care will be rationed, not whether it will be rationed. Will some poor and unemployed be denied basic health care, such as prenatal care or frequent doctor visits for sick people? Or will some of the affluent be denied rapid access to elective surgeries or exotic technologies, such as coronary bypass surgery for elderly patients?

Sweden has a truly socialized health care system, with the government nationalizing most health care facilities and employing health care workers. Health services are free to anyone who needs them, and little money changes hands between patient and health care providers. Taxes support the health care system, and Sweden does have high taxes. However, the Swedes are also among the healthiest people in the world. They live three years longer than Americans and have half the infant mortality. Sweden is an interesting contrast with both Canada and the United States in that it runs a generally effective, socialized system of health care in a capitalist country.

Canada and Sweden suggest some of the ways in which health care can be made more available to all citizens, recognizing that there are advantages and disadvantages to each approach.

part of formal proceedings where a physician might be sanctioned for poor procedure (Millman, 1977).

Another approach to the social control of health care is to create an oversight structure that is independent of physicians themselves. This was done in 1970 when the government established Professional Standards Review Organizations that were to evaluate the care given to patients of Medicare and Medicaid. Today, many insurance companies have their own quality review organizations to assess the care given to patients they insure. A major motivation for some of this review is cost control, but it also focuses on the quality issue. Another step toward creating more independent oversight structures was taken in 1990 when the National Practitioner Data Bank began full operation (Harty, 1991). This data bank lists all medical malpractice awards or settlements against health-care professionals and any disciplinary proceedings, including denial of hospital privileges to physicians. Health-care facilities are required by law to consult the data bank when making decisions about medical privileges. The goal is to make it more difficult for health-care professionals to get privileges in another hospital or other health facility after getting into trouble somewhere else. However, access to the list is limited to doctors and hospitals; the general public cannot consult it when making decisions about choosing health-care providers.

New Health-Care Practitioners

Another approach to lowering costs and increasing accessibility to health care is to expand the types of providers giving primary care and reduce our dependence on highly trained and expensive specialists. For example, a new specialty called "family practice" began in the 1960s and was intended to increase the ranks of primary-care physicians. After medical school and a year of internship, family practice physicians go through a residency program in which they receive advanced training in a broad range of medical specialties. This enables them to treat many health problems themselves and to refer more complex cases to the appropriate specialist. In fact, the government encouraged the development of this specialty by requiring medical schools that receive federal funds (meaning all medical schools) to allot a certain percentage of their first-year residency positions to primary-care specialties.

Until recently, there has been a shortage of physicians in the United States, especially in rural and inner-city areas. To alleviate this problem, the government has supported the development of physician extenders, practitioners trained to perform some of the simple and routine health-care tasks traditionally accomplished by physicians. Nurse practitioners (NPs), for example, are registered nurses with advanced training that in some cases includes the master's degree in nursing. Physicians' assistants (PAs) have some medical training and can work only under the supervision of a physician. NPs and PAs do such things as conduct routine physical examinations, provide simple emergency and prenatal care, and the like. They normally work under the guidance of a physician and may serve as the initial contact that patients have with the health-care system. In these ways, nurse practitioners and physicians' assistants provide medical doctors with more time to make complex diagnostic and treatment decisions. Studies show that NPs and PAs can do the things they are trained for as well as physicians can, and they can do it at substantially less cost (Robyn and Hadley, 1980).

Many alternatives exist to highly trained, specialized, and expensive physicians in the delivery of health-care services. Midwives, for example, deliver babies in many rural areas, and they do so as safely as do physicians delivering in hospitals, especially when life-saving technology is not immediately needed during the delivery (Durand, 1992). In fact, physicians tend to make more life-saving interventions that are not necessary, and this actually increases the risk to the mother and infant. Health policymakers had hoped that these alternative healers would produce less reliance on traditionally trained physicians and thus make health care more accessible and less expensive. This may not be happening, however, to the extent that it could. One reason is that some doctors are reluctant to accept these personnel, believing that only physicians are competent to provide key medical services. In addition, a surplus of physicians is now emerging, at least in some specialties. As this occurs, physicians may come to see these other providers as competition for a shrinking health-care dollar. So the situation remains unsettled.

Self-Care and Changing Life-styles

Social commentators such as Ivan Illich (1976) and Joseph Califano (1986) have severely criticized our health-care system for creating as much illness as it cures. It creates illness, for example, when a hospital patient gets an infection or suffers complications in surgery. This is called *iatrogenic illness:* illness or injury that arises while receiving treatment. However, a more subtle form of iatrogenesis can occur when our health-care system and cultural values convince us that we must rely on medical professionals to remain healthy or to overcome illness. We see ourselves as virtually helpless without medical support. When these beliefs predominate, we tend not to do things that might enhance our health status. To overcome this problem, Illich and Califano argue, people should rely more on self-care and life-style change as a way to improved health.

We have seen that one of the major causes of many chronic illnesses is the life-style of modern Americans: We eat, drink, and smoke too much; we suffer periodic stresses of divorce or unemployment; and we pollute our environment. We can improve our health status if we attack these problems. In fact, this whole text relates to health problems to the extent that improvements in our physical and social environment have beneficial health consequences.

Linkages

Society's health problems are exacerbated by increases in drug abuse (Chapter 10), because intravenous drug users are at a high risk of contracting the AIDS virus and spreading the epidemic by sharing dirty needles. The amount of illness and injury we have to cope with is also increased considerably by environmental pollution (Chapter 13), violent crime (Chapter 9), and violence, war, and terrorism (Chapter 14).

Summary

1. From the functionalist perspective, illness threatens the survival of society because sick people cannot accomplish essential tasks. The health-care system becomes a problem when it fails to return sick people to normal social functioning.

2. From the conflict perspective, health and health care are scarce resources that interest groups compete over. The inequitable distribution of these resources will reflect the overall inequitable distribution of resources in society. This becomes a problem when some group feels that it is not receiving its fair share of these resources.

3. The interactionist perspective recognizes that illnesses involve a network of social meanings and social expectations. Health care can be considered a social problem when it produces stigmatized or devalued self-concepts among consumers of health care.

4. Diseases can be classified as acute or chronic, with the former contributing more to the death rate in preindustrial societies. In industrial societies, the death rate drops substantially and life expectancy increases. This is due largely to declines in infant and childhood mortality and changes in life-style.

5. The four major sociocultural factors that affect health and illness are socioeconomic status, sex, race, and life-style.

6. There are three positions regarding the nature of mental illness: The medical model views mental disorders as having the same basic nature as physical disorders; interactionists view mental illness as people's response to the expectations associated with being in the role of mentally ill; Szasz views mental illness as a problem people face making choices about their lives.

7. Given the unreliability of psychiatric diagnoses, there is some debate over whether mental health professionals can accurately detect mental disorders. There has been a trend over the past twenty years toward a treatment approach known as community mental health, which involves delivering services to a whole community and providing treatment in the community.

8. There are a number of problems associated with health and illness in the United States: Health-care costs have been rising rapidly; some Americans do not have access to the health services that they need; some of the health services that people receive are impersonal, dehumanizing, and unpleasant; there is substantial sexual inequality in the health-care field.

9. Bioethics refers to the study of ethical questions that relate to the life and biological well-being of people. Three major issues in this realm are whether to prolong the life of someone who is terminally ill; how to distribute limited medical resources; and how extensively to engage in genetic screening.

10. A central issue in deciding how to attack problems in the health-care field is whether access to health care should be every citizen's right or whether it is a privilege of those who can afford to pay for it. Problems in this field have been attacked through publicly funded health insurance, the emergence of health maintenance organizations, the elaboration of societal control over health-care providers, the development of new health-care practitioner roles, and changes in the life-styles of Americans.

Important Terms for Review

acute disease	curative medicine	Medicaid	primary deviance
bioethics	depersonalization	medical–industrial complex	secondary deviance
chronic disease	health maintenance	Medicare	sick role
crisis medicine	organization	preventive medicine	third-party medicine

Discussion Questions

1. List some illnesses that often lead to a negative stigma being attached to the person who has the illness. Do you think that this influences the likelihood that a person will seek medical care? Will it influence his or her chances for recovery? How could this stigmatization be changed?

2. Make a list of the ways in which modern industrial society makes us healthier people. Now make a list of the ways that industrial societies make us less healthy when compared with preindustrial societies. On the whole, do you think we are better off now? Or were people better off in preindustrial societies?

3. Recall that the existence of mental illness can be detected only through the occurrence of some social behaviors that people define as symptomatic of mental illness. Have you or your friends ever behaved in such a way that someone might have called you mentally ill? How did you escape this labeling (assuming that you did)? How can you be certain that someone else is mentally ill?

4. One way to control rising health-care costs is to encourage more competitive practices in the health field. In what ways might this be done? Are there disadvantages to these programs?

5. Find a case in the news in which the decision about whether to continue or withhold treatment from a person is being debated. Describe the case. If you were a member of an ethics committee that had to make a recommendation regarding this case, what would you recommend? Why?

6. In this chapter, we briefly discussed five principles of social justice that could be used as a basis for allocating scarce health resources. For each of these principles, find a case in which someone would receive care under each principle and someone would not. Use these examples as a basis for a discussion of how fair and useful each principle is and which principles would be preferred when allocating resources.

For Further Reading

Gena Corea. *The Invisible Epidemic: The Story of Women and AIDS.* New York: HarperCollins, 1992. This disturbing book documents how gender influences the provision of health care and the medical paternalism that pervades our health care system. It reports how medicine underreports and misdiagnoses AIDS in women, with tragic results.

M. Robin DiMatteo and Howard S. Friedman. *Social Psychology and Medicine.* Cambridge, Mass.: Oelgeschlager, Gunn, and Hain Publishers, 1982. An excellent summary of the role of social forces in health care. It covers such topics as factors affecting people's decisions to seek health care, why people do not cooperate with their doctors, and communication between doctors and patients.

Elizabeth Fee and Daniel M. Fox (eds.). *AIDS: The Making of a Chronic Disease.* Berkeley: University of California Press, 1992. The readings in this book analyze many social and political aspects of AIDS, including how it is represented to the public, how policy on it is made, and how it affects different groups.

Peter E. S. Freund and Meredith B. McGuire. *Health, Illness, and the Social Body: A Critical Sociology.* Englewood Cliffs, N.J.: Prentice Hall, 1991. This book offers a general introduction to the topics covered in this chapter and offers a good overview of the issues and problems that sociologists study in the field of health and medicine.

Ivan Illich. *Medical Nemesis: The Expropriation of Health.* New York: Bantam Books, 1976. A scathing and rather iconoclastic critique of our health-care system on the grounds that it is as detrimental to our health as it is beneficial. Illich's argument is an extreme one that may prompt protest but will also stimulate thought.

Theodore H. Koff. *Hospice: A Caring Community.* Cambridge, Mass.: Winthrop Publishers, 1980. A very useful summary of hospices as a way of allowing people to die with dignity. This book discusses what hospices are, how they operate and are managed, and how they can be evaluated.

John Mirowsky and Catherine E. Ross. *Social Causes of Psychological Distress.* New York: Aldine de Gruyter, 1989. These authors present convincing evidence to show that mental illness, especially depression and anxiety, are profoundly influenced by some very important social conditions.

Vicente Navarro. *Crisis, Health, and Medicine: A Social Critique.* New York: Tavistock, 1986. This is a sophisticated and fundamental criticism of our health-care system that sees the profit orientation as one of its key problems.

Sheryl Burt Ruzek. *The Women's Health Movement: Alternatives to Medical Control.* New York: Praeger, 1978. Discusses issues, groups, schisms, and major events in the women's health movement. Ruzek shows how feminist health activities are challenging institutionalized medical authority and may prompt some changes in our health-care delivery system.

Victor W. Sidel and Ruth Sidel. *A Healthy State: An International Perspective on the Crisis in United States Medical Care.* Rev. and Updated ed. New York: Pantheon Books, 1983. A very readable comparative perspective on our own health-care system. By looking at other countries and our own health-care system through history, the Sidels offer a unique view on problems we face today.

Paul Starr. *The Social Transformation of American Medicine.* New York: Basic Books, 1982. A very insightful analysis of the changes in the power and authority of the medical profession over the past two centuries. This is not an easy book, but it is one well worth spending time with.

Duane F. Stroman. *The Quick Knife: Unnecessary Surgery U.S.A.* Port Washington, N.Y.: Kennikat Press, 1979. An analysis of the extent of one of the major problems in the health-care field and what can be done about it.

E. Fuller Torrey. *Nowhere to Go: The Tragic Odyssey of the Homeless Mentally Ill.* New York: Harper and Row, 1988. This is a serious criticism of the "deinstitutionalization" of the mentally ill, focusing mostly on the homeless mentally ill. The book also provides a good history and analysis of the development of social policy relating to the mentally ill in the United States.

Elliot S. Valenstein. *Great and Desperate Cures: The Rise and Decline of Psychosurgery and Other Radical Treatments for Mental Illness.* New York: Basic Books, 1986. This book provides a history of various somatic treatments for mental illness that have become popular at some time, especially psychosurgery. It is a cautionary tale, suggesting that the forces that make "desperate" cures popular tend to recur in new forms.

PART II
Problems of
Social Inequality

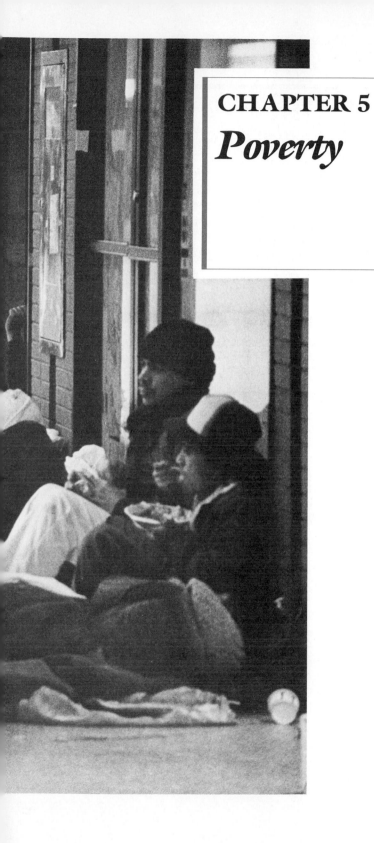

CHAPTER 5
Poverty

W hen it comes to economic resources, the United States is truly a nation of contrasts. We are, few would dispute, among the wealthiest nations in the world. We produce more goods and services for each man, woman, and child than do most other nations. The signs of this opulence are not difficult to find. There are palatial mansions and fine automobiles. Expensive restaurants and clothing stores cater to the whims of those with large sums of money to spend. There are those who ski in the Alps, the Andes, and the Rockies—all in one season, if not one month. Most Americans, of course, do not share in such unbelievable wealth, but most are nevertheless quite comfortable materially, with spacious homes, more than adequate diets, and audiovisual entertainment centers in their homes.

Amidst this wealth, however, one in seven people lives below the officially defined poverty level. This includes one of every three black Americans, one of each four Hispanic Americans, and one of every four Mississippians (U.S. Bureau of the Census, 1991: 462). Despite the material opulence in the United States, the Children's Defense Fund released a disturbing report in 1992 exposing the fact that almost one out of every two chil-

Myths and Facts About the Poor

Myth: The poor are a drain on the public treasury that affluent Americans have to support out of their hard-earned dollars.

Fact: Both poor and affluent Americans are a drain on the public treasury, and both pay to support it. Critics of the American approach to welfare have argued that we have a "dual" welfare system, one for the poor that is highly stigmatized and one for the affluent that many people pretend does not exist. What "government handouts" do the affluent receive? Consider the following:

- Government-subsidized loans for college students.

- Government payments to medical schools to support medical education.

- Government payments to farmers ($11 billion in 1989 for price supports, disaster relief, and other assistance).

- Tax deductions for home mortgage interest and property taxes (if we consider such tax deductions to be housing subsidies comparable to the housing vouchers given to low-income families, then families earning more than $50,000 per year receive 52 percent of all federal housing subsidies, whereas families earning less than $10,000 per year receive only 19 percent of these subsidies.)

- Tax deductions for business meals and entertainment (poor people are looked down upon for taking food stamps).

The similarity is that both the affluent and the poor receive public assistance. The difference is that the poor are labeled disreputable for their use of the public dole.

Who pays more? Certainly, the nonpoor pay the bulk of the tax bill, but the poor pay income taxes if they have sufficient income. And the poor and near-poor do not have access to the many tax loopholes that the more affluent benefit from. For example, a physician who makes house calls can deduct the cost of an expensive car from his taxes, but the Aid to Families with Dependent Children mother cannot deduct the subway fare she pays to shop for her family. In addition, some very wealthy people can use tax loopholes to avoid paying any taxes at all, and this is completely legal. The tax laws are written in ways that benefit the affluent. Finally, some state income taxes and all sales taxes are flat rate taxes, which means that people pay the same percentage of taxes no matter how wealthy or poor they may be. Thus, the sales tax on food and other goods takes the same bite from the poor as from the rich.

---

dren in New Orleans, Detroit, and Laredo, Texas, were growing up in poverty (Chargot, 1992). Despite the promises of virtually all politicians to ease the problem of poverty, the poverty rate has increased over the past twenty years. In fact, some Americans are so impoverished that they do not even have homes, living instead on sidewalks, in train stations, in steam tunnels, or in parks. In addition, our nation has, possibly, one of the most callous and unfeeling attitudes toward those less fortunate members of our society who do not share in the wealth. We do less for the poor than most other modern nations, and we often do so grudgingly—as if the mere existence of poor people is an affront to our belief in America as the land of opportunity.

Why should we be concerned with the problem of poverty? Why not relegate the poor to the dustbin of underachievers who are reaping the just rewards of people who are unwilling to work or have little to offer society? There are a number of reasons why all Americans should pay attention to this problem. Some people are poor, as we will see, not through any fault of their own but because societal barriers make it difficult if not impossible for them to improve their circumstances. In short, there is a discrepancy between our ideal culture, which calls for equal opportunity for all, and our real culture, in which social forces prohibit some people from improving their lot. Beyond this, there are a number of practical concerns about the widespread existence of poverty: Unemployment, welfare, and other social costs of the poor are a substantial burden on all Americans; crime, illness, and other costly social conditions are linked with poverty; and poverty is a potential seedbed for social unrest and even outright rebellion that could threaten the political and social order.

In this chapter, we first discuss what constitutes poverty in the United States and how extensive it is. Then we examine the social characteristics and circumstances of those who are poor. This examination is followed by an analysis of the causes of poverty using the sociological perspectives. We conclude the chapter with a look at current and future policies that might alleviate the problem of poverty.

THE EXTENT OF POVERTY

Defining Poverty

People often think of poverty in terms of deprivation—being short of food, for example, or not having enough money to buy adequate clothing. This is somewhat misleading, however. There have been many societies in which people, by our standards today, were severely deprived, yet poverty did not really exist. The reason is that virtually everyone was so deprived. In societies in which there was little accumulation of food or material resources, everyone had pretty much the same access to the resources available. When a surplus of resources exists, however, it is possible for some people to accumulate more than others. There then emerges a system of **social stratifica-**

tion, *the ranking of people into a hierarchy in which the resources considered valuable by society are unequally distributed.* With this development, people could be differentiated from one another based on how much of those valuable resources they possessed. Those with the least could be defined as "poor": so deficient in resources that they could not maintain a life-style considered minimally acceptable in that society. Thus, **poverty** *does not refer to a deprivation of resources alone but to an uneven distribution of the resources available.*

Defining poverty becomes even more complex, however, when we try to specify what a "minimally acceptable life-style" is. In fact, there is probably no completely satisfactory definition of poverty. Three such definitions are widely used today (Ruggles, 1990).

Absolute Deprivation.   Some definitions of poverty attempt to establish an economic level below which people are unable to achieve the basic necessities of life. But what are the "necessities" of life? A reliable automobile? A juicy steak? A summer vacation at the beach? While recognizing that "necessities" is a somewhat relative term, we can nonetheless define it in terms of a diet, clothing, housing, medical care, and the like that will enable people to remain healthy and productive. Nutritionists, for example, can tell us what is a minimally adequate diet. You do not need a steak to maintain health, but the human body does need a certain amount of protein, vitamins, and minerals from some food sources. Likewise, a house without indoor plumbing might be viewed as unacceptable in modern times because of the health hazard it creates. The point of this **absolute definition of poverty** is that *it establishes a fixed economic level below which people are considered poor, and this level does not necessarily change as society on the whole becomes more or less affluent.*

Government programs for the poor in America are based on this absolute definition of poverty. For such programs, a fixed annual income cutoff point is established below which people will be unable to purchase what are considered the necessities of life. In the 1960s, Mollie Orshansky, then a social research analyst with the Social Security Administration, developed an ingenious and somewhat objective technique for establishing the poverty level, a technique still in use today (Ruggles, 1990). It is based on how much it costs to buy a nutritionally adequate diet. Once the amount of money necessary for this has been established, it is multiplied by three to arrive at the poverty income, based on the fact that the average American family spends one-third of its income on food. Thus, three times the cost of food is assumed to provide adequate income for food, housing, medical care, and the other necessities of life. Actually, the poverty level is a series of income cutoffs based on factors that can increase a family's cost of living, such as the size of the family, the number of children present, and the cost of living in the community where the family resides.

Relative Deprivation.　We pointed out earlier that poverty is not just the absence of resources; it also involves the inequitable distribution of resources. According to the **relative definition of poverty,** *people are poor relative to some standard, and that standard is partially shaped by the life-styles of other citizens.* A lack of indoor plumbing is considered a sign of poverty today, whereas a century ago that was the norm for many people. But people usually compare themselves with their contemporaries, not their predecessors. People look around and see what most others have and assess their own lives based on that comparison. To take this relative nature of poverty into account, some have suggested defining the poor as those people who are on the lowest end of the income scale, say the lowest 5 percent or the lowest 7 percent. In the 1950s, one commentator on poverty suggested that the poor be defined as those living in families with incomes that are less than one-half of the median family income in the United States (Fuchs, 1956). Such a definition would mean that poverty would always exist, irrespective of how affluent society became. The poor would be those who share least in such affluence. In fact, using the relative definition, poverty could be eliminated only if the inequitable distribution of resources was eliminated.

Cultural Definitions.　Absolute and relative approaches to poverty define it as the economic resources necessary to achieve a certain life-style. However, some have argued that poverty is a cultural as well as an economic condition (Hayes, 1970). The **cultural definition of poverty** *views poverty not only in terms of how many resources people have, but also in terms of why they have failed to achieve a higher economic level.* For example, some people are poor because they have no skills that would enable them to get a job. Others are poor because they have young children at home and cannot afford day care while they work. Still others are poor because they have chosen to go to college and endure temporary low income in order to enhance their earning power in the future.

Using this cultural definition of poverty, we can identify the poor as those who are permanently and unwillingly poor. These are people who are likely to remain poor for a long time, possibly generations, and it is toward them that poverty programs should be directed. This would probably include most of the people who are defined as poor when using purely economic criteria, but it would exclude people such as college students who temporarily and willingly choose poverty. The rationale for this is that the real problem of poverty lies with the chronic long-term poor. College students who are poor, although suffering some personal troubles, are not really a societal problem because they will likely improve their circumstances in a relatively brief period. This cultural definition of poverty avoids the rigidities of strict economic definitions and enables us to direct resources toward the entrenched problem of poverty.

Which one of the above definitions of poverty is used, of course, depends on *values* (Beeghley, 1984). The absolute definition is used in many social policy decisions today, and it reflects widespread American values regarding the role of the government in poverty problems. It especially reflects many Americans' belief that the government should provide equal opportunities for people to achieve resources rather than ensure an equitable distribution of those resources. In this view, the government's role is to provide people with the minimum necessary resources that will enable them to achieve on their own. Whether people then realize such achievement is regarded by many as a personal matter.

The Extent of Poverty

The official poverty level in the United States, then, is based on the absolute definition of poverty. In 1991, a nonfarm family of four people with an annual income of less than $13,924 was considered by the government to be poor (see Table 5.1). This meant that more than thirty-five million Americans—approximately one out of every seven of our citizens—were living in poverty. Throughout the 1980s, the poverty rate re-

Table 5.1   **Persons Below Poverty Level: 1960–1991**

| Year | *Persons Below Poverty Level* | | *Average Poverty Income Cutoffs for Nonfarm Family of Four* | *Median Family Income of all Families* |
	Number (Millions)	*Percentage of Total Population*		
1960	39.9	22.2	$ 3,022	$ 5,620
1966	28.2	17.3	3,223	6,957
1970	25.4	12.6	3,968	9,867
1975	25.9	12.3	5,500	13,719
1976	25.0	11.8	5,815	14,958
1977	24.7	11.6	6,191	16,009
1978	24.5	11.4	6,662	17,640
1979	25.3	11.6	7,412	19,661
1980	29.3	13.0	8,414	21,023
1981	31.8	14.0	9,287	22,388
1982	34.4	15.0	9,862	23,433
1983	35.5	15.3	10,178	24,549
1984	33.7	14.4	10,609	26,433
1985	33.1	14.0	10,989	27,735
1986	32.4	13.6	11,203	29,458
1987	32.5	13.5	11,611	30,853
1988	31.7	13.0	12,092	32,191
1989	31.5	12.8	12,675	34,213
1990	33.6	13.5	13,359	35,353
1991	35.7	14.2	13,924	

SOURCES: U.S. Bureau of the Census, *Statistical Abstract of the United States, 1992* (Washington, D.C.: U.S. Government Printing Office, 1992), pp. 449, 456; U.S. Bureau of the Census, *Current Population Reports*, P-60, No. 175, *Poverty in the United States, 1990* (Washington, D.C.: U.S. Government Printing Office, 1991), pp. 4, 194; Tim Bovee, "Ranks of Poor Swell, Again," *Detroit Free Press*, September 4, 1992, p. 3.

mained higher than it was at any point in the 1970s; in 1991, the poverty rate was higher than it has been since the mid-1960s, and more people are poor than in any year since 1964. Furthermore, the gap between the resources of the non-poor and of the poor has been growing larger as the median family income has increased at a faster rate than the poverty cutoff. The poverty line was 54 percent of median family income in 1960, whereas it was 35 percent in 1990. So, using the relative definition of poverty, the poor are worse off today than thirty years ago (see Figure 5.1). Another way to assess the status of the poor relative to an earlier time period is to look at what percentage of the total income in the United States goes to poor families. Once again, the poor seem worse off today than in the past. As Figure 5.2 shows, the percentage of income going to the poorest families declined during the 1980s; in fact, the only groups who saw their share of total

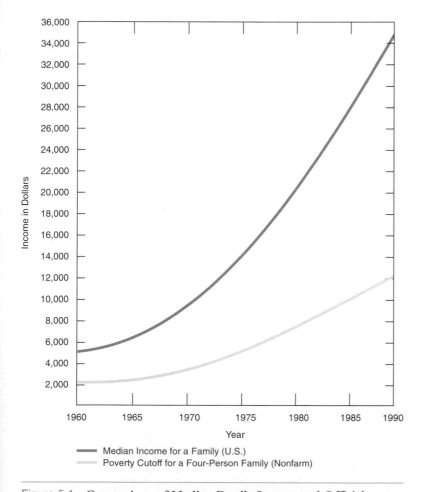

Figure 5.1 **Comparison of Median Family Income and Official Poverty Cutoff for a Family of Four, 1960–1990**
SOURCE: U.S. Bureau of the Census, *Statistical Abstract of the United States, 1992* (Washington, D.C.: U.S. Government Printing Office, 1992), pp. 452–462.

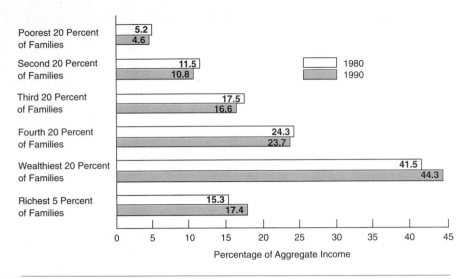

Figure 5.2   **Percent Distribution of Aggregate Income to Families from the Poorest 20 Percent to the Richest 5 Percent, 1980–1990**
SOURCE: U.S. Bureau of the Census, *Statistical Abstract of the United States, 1992* (Washington, D.C.: U.S. Government Printing Office, 1992), p. 450.

income increase were the wealthiest 20 percent of families. This topic has been hotly debated, but most assessments agree with what Figure 5.2 suggests: In the last twenty years, the rich in the United States have gotten richer and the poor have gotten poorer (Nasar, 1992b). There are a number of reasons for this: a declining number of low-skill but adequately paying jobs for low-income workers, changes in the tax laws that place a heavier tax burden on lower income families, and a decline in government programs that assist low-income families.

The absolute approach to defining poverty provided by the Orshansky poverty cutoffs is used by the government for making social policy decisions, such as who is eligible for various government social programs. These cutoffs, however, do have flaws as an accurate measure of people's economic circumstances. One such flaw is that the assumptions for establishing the poverty thresholds were defined in the 1950s and 1960s based

on family consumption patterns and basic needs of that era, and things have changed since then. For example, the poverty index relies on the purchase of food in determining the poverty level. However, for some poor people, especially in urban areas, other expenses such as housing can consume a larger share of the family income than they do for the average American family. In earlier decades, American families spent 34 percent of their income on housing, whereas today it is more like 42 percent. Despite changes such as these, the poverty cutoffs are still based on the old assumptions. One expert estimates that today's poverty line would have to be 50 percent higher to be comparable, in terms of the ability to buy food and other basic needs, to the standard established in 1963 (Ruggles, 1990). This means that a family of four in 1991 would really need $20,886 to purchase the same standard of living as a poverty-level family in the 1960s. If this were the poverty cutoff in 1991, the poverty rate would be between

"*The poor are getting poorer, but with the rich getting richer it all averages out in the long run.*"

In a slightly wry way, this cartoon points to an important element of the problem of poverty in the United States: Many well-to-do Americans do not see poverty as the serious problem that it is to the poor or near poor.

20 percent and 25 percent instead of 14 percent.

WHO ARE THE POOR?

A few years ago, a popular bumper sticker read: "I fight poverty . . . I work!" Implied in this is a characterization of the poor as lazy and somewhat disreputable people who are poor because of their own unwillingness to work for a living. This highly stigmatizing view of the poor is quite popular in the United States, where a majority believes that a willingness to work is the primary ingredient necessary to achieve at least a modest degree of success (Smith and Stone, 1989). Assessing the veracity of these beliefs is central to developing a social policy regarding poverty in

America. A first step in this direction is understanding who the poor people are in this country.

Social Characteristics

Racial and Ethnic Minorities.   Contrary to what many Americans believe, most of the poor in America—66 percent—are white (see Figure 5.3). Looking at each racial group separately, however, nonwhites are more likely to be poor than are whites. Although 31.9 percent of blacks and 28.1 percent of Hispanic Americans are below the poverty cutoff, only 10.7 percent of whites are at that income level (see Figure 5.4). About 23 percent of American Indians and 35 percent of Vietnamese have incomes below the official poverty level. This is reflected in the median income of different groups: $36,915 for white families in 1990 compared to $23,431 for Hispanic families and $21,423 for black families (U.S. Bureau of the Census, 1992: 449). So although nonwhite families constitute a relatively small proportion of our populace, they contribute disproportionately to the ranks of the poor.

The reasons for these racial and ethnic differences are complex and will be dealt with in more detail in the next section of this chapter and in Chapter 6. However, a key factor in all cases has been oppression and discrimination. Blacks have felt the brunt of slavery and, after the abolition of slavery, decades of severe oppression during which it was difficult for black families to advance from poverty. Hispanics, especially those of Mexican and Puerto Rican ancestry, have also experienced a great deal of discrimination in their efforts to establish a niche in American society. American Indians have confronted some unique problems in the form of the reservation system and the Bureau of Indian Affairs (BIA), which were intended to work for the benefit of Indians but seem instead to have worked to their disadvantage.

Children.   Over one-third of the poor are children under the age of fifteen, and more than half

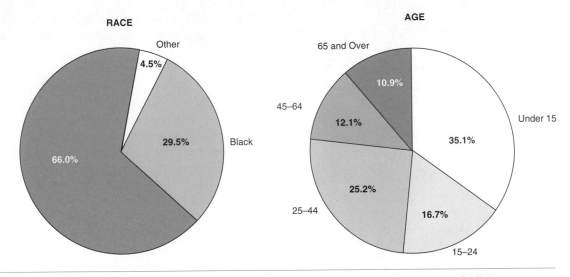

Figure 5.3   **People Living Below the Poverty Level by Race and Age, as a Percentage of All Poor People, 1990**
SOURCE: U.S. Bureau of the Census, Current Population Reports, Series P-60, No. 175, *Poverty in the United States, 1990* (Washington, D.C.: U.S. Government Printing Office, 1991), p. 15.

of these children live in single-parent families headed by women. Almost one-half of all black children and more than one-third of all Hispanic children live in poverty, which will make it more difficult for the next generation of racial and ethnic minorities to lift themselves out of poverty (see Figures 5.3, 5.4, and 5.5). Children living in large families are especially likely to live in poverty. This is so because economic resources must be spread more thinly in a large family and because the mother is less able to work outside the home when she has many children. The large number of children among the poor serves to deflate the belief that poverty derives from a lack of initiative because we presume that children are not responsible for supporting themselves. This tendency toward poverty shows no sign of ceasing for the youngest Americans. Poverty rates among children have remained unchanged or increased slightly since the late 1960s (Duncan and Rodgers, 1991). A major reason for the persistently high poverty among children is changes in the

American family structure—higher divorce rates, more children born to unmarried women, and more female-headed families (Eggebeen and Lichter, 1991). All this means that children today are more likely to live in a single-parent household headed by a woman. In 1990, 53 percent of children living in such families were poor—more than five times the rate for children in two-parent households (see Figure 5.5). In addition, the parents of poor children today are younger—our teenage pregnancy rate is far higher than that in most other industrial nations (see Chapter 3). Finally, young workers today earn relatively less than did young workers in the past. The consequence of all this is that poor children today have fewer resources available to them and live in worse circumstances than did poor children thirty years ago.

The Elderly.   Although poverty among the elderly is relatively low, it is higher than among non-elderly adult Americans, and the figure is

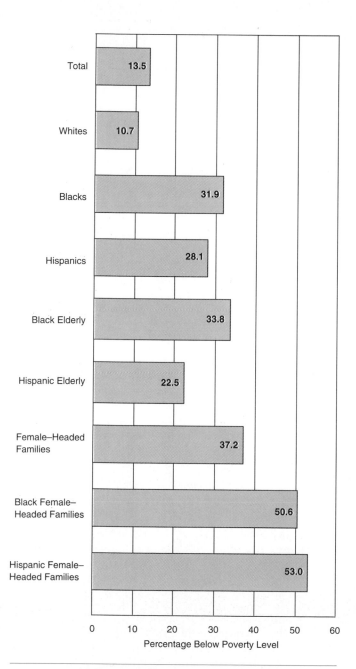

Figure 5.4 **Percentage of People in Various Groups Below the Poverty Level, 1990**
SOURCE: U.S. Bureau of the Census, Current Population Reports, Series P-60, No. 175, *Poverty in the United States: 1990* (Washington, D.C.: U.S. Government Printing Office, 1991), pp. 24–28.

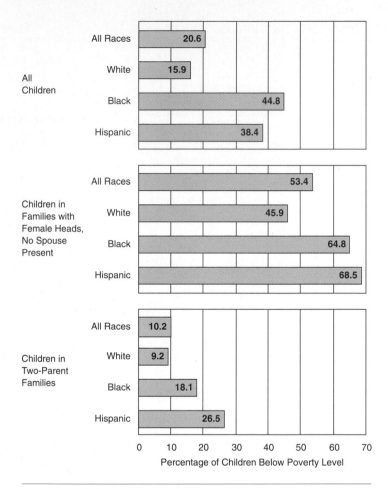

All Children

Children in Families with Female Heads, No Spouse Present

Children in Two-Parent Families

Percentage of Children Below Poverty Level

Figure 5.5 **Percentage of Children Under 18 Living Below the Poverty Level, 1990**
SOURCE: U.S. Bureau of the Census, Current Population Reports, Series P-60, No. 175, *Poverty in the United States: 1990* (Washington, D.C.: U.S. Government Printing Office, 1991), pp. 24–28.

much higher for black, Hispanic, and female elderly. The special problems of the elderly are dealt with in more detail in Chapter 8.

Women. A development that has been viewed with some alarm in recent years is what has been labeled the "feminization of poverty," referring to the growing number of women among the poor. Despite the increasing emphasis on equality be-

tween the sexes in recent years, women, especially those who head their own households, have made little progress. In 1990, for example, 13.5 percent of all people lived below the poverty level, whereas in single-parent families headed by a woman it was 37.2 percent. Things may actually be getting worse in some respects: In 1959, 23 percent of all families in poverty were headed by women; by 1990, this figure had grown to 53 percent. However, the poverty rate in single-parent female-headed families is now lower than it was in 1959 but a little higher than it was in the late 1970s (see Figure 5.6). As we will see in Chapter 7, which discusses the problems of women in more detail, the incomes of women still lag far behind those of men. There is evidence that growing up in a female-headed family increases the risk that children will still be poor as adults. This is probably caused by the greater economic deprivation in such families rather than by the absence of a father figure (McLanahan, 1985; McLanahan and Bumpass, 1988).

Central-City and Rural Dwellers. Poverty tends to be concentrated in certain places in our country, particularly in the centers of our cities and in rural areas. Almost 40 percent of the poor live in central-city areas, places with high unemployment and few places to find work (U.S. Bureau of the Census, 1991a: 54). As we will see in Chapter 12, businesses and industries have left the cities for the suburbs in large numbers, leaving fewer jobs behind. The jobs that remain tend to be white-collar occupations requiring some college education, which the poor are unlikely to have. This is particularly true of the older cities of the Northeast and Midwest.

One-quarter of the poor live outside metropolitan areas (Duncan, 1992). Pockets of poverty can be found in rural parts of the South, Southwest, the Ozarks, Appalachia, and the Upper Great Lakes region. Blacks living in farming communities are especially hard hit by poverty. Small plots of land and poor soil make for a meager existence for these farmers. In nonfarming rural areas, people do a variety of things to survive, such as mining and lumbering. The rural poor face problems similar to but more intense than their central-city counterparts. Employment opportunities are scarce and transportation is often a costly hindrance. Unemployment is high and the jobs that can be found are likely to be low paying.

The Disabled. Poverty is often associated with physical disability. Twenty percent of the poor are too physically disabled to work and another 8 percent have partial disabilities that prohibit them

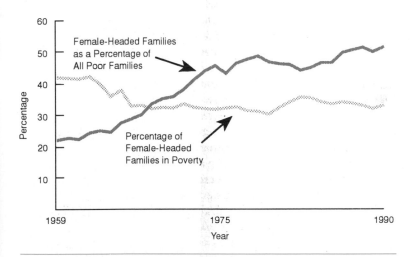

Figure 5.6 **Poverty Rate of Single-Parent Families Headed by a Woman, 1959–1990**
SOURCE: U.S. Bureau of the Census, Current Population Reports, Series P-60, No. 175, *Poverty in the United States, 1990* (Washington, D.C.: U.S. Government Printing Office, 1991), p. 7.

Many of the poor in the United States are disabled, making it difficult, if not impossible, for them to support themselves through work.

from doing the work that they did before becoming disabled. Blacks, Hispanics, and people over the age of forty-five are most likely to have such disabilities (U.S. Bureau of the Census, 1989: 363). Approximately 3.3 million people receive medical assistance from Medicaid because they are blind or totally disabled. These figures lead us once again to recognize that poverty is often not a problem of failed ambition or motivation but rather one of people being victimized by social or personal tragedy.

Social Circumstances

There is considerable mythology surrounding the circumstances under which poor people live. Because most poor are "invisible" or conveniently out of sight to most Americans, it is easy to believe that the poor lead a leisurely, if spartan,

life-style while feeding at the public trough (Harrington, 1984). Reality is actually quite different from this.

The Working Poor.   Despite common misconceptions, many adults below the official poverty level actually work for a living. Approximately 60 percent of poor families earn wages from work, with about 20 percent having at least one member working year-round full-time (U.S. Bureau of the Census, 1991a: 127). Only one-third of the poor families receive cash public assistance income, although others receive such government assistance as unemployment benefits, Social Security payments, disability assistance, government pensions, and the like. Fully one-third of the poor families receive no government transfer income at all (U.S. Bureau of the Census, 1991: 359). The people who were removed from the welfare roles by the Reagan budget cutting of the 1980s responded by working more, but they still did not earn enough to make up for the lost welfare payments, and life generally became more difficult for them (Pear, 1984b; Liebschutz and Taddiken, 1986).

So the poor are, in general, not a bunch of loafing parasites. Many are unable to work because of disability, age, or retirement. Others struggle with low-paying or part-time work that, despite their efforts, fails to bring them above the poverty level. The number of poor males who are able to work, but do not, is low: probably about 8 percent of all poor males. In most cases, they cannot work because of high unemployment and a lack of the job skills that are in demand. The incidence of unemployment among able-bodied poor women is higher. Fifty-seven percent of the female heads of poor households do not work at all. In many cases, these women have been left with the task of supporting their families. More than 50 percent of the children receiving Aid to Families with Dependent Children (AFDC) are eligible because their fathers have died, divorced, or deserted their mothers (U.S. Bureau of the Census, 1991a: 127). And poor women who head their own households are the least likely to be working full time because of the chore of child rearing along with a lack of job skills (Gronbjerg, Street, and Suttles, 1978).

The Illiterate.   In 1985, education critic Jonathan Kozol published a book titled *Illiterate America,* wherein he reports that sixty million Americans—more than one-third of the entire adult population of the United States—are illiterate. Kozol calculates that

> *Twenty-five million American adults cannot read the poison warnings on a can of pesticide, a letter from their child's teacher, or the front page of a daily paper. An additional 35 million read only at a level which is less than equal to the full survival needs of our society. (Kozol, 1985: 12)*

According to Kozol, 16 percent of white adults, 44 percent of blacks, and 56 percent of Hispanic citizens are functional or marginal illiterates. One-half of the heads of households classified below the poverty level cannot read an eighth-grade book, and more than one-third of mothers who receive support from welfare are functionally illiterate.

In 1982, the executive director of the National Advisory Council on Adult Education estimated that the U.S. government would have to spend $5 billion to eradicate or seriously reduce the illiteracy problem. There can be no question that the problems of illiteracy and poverty are inextricably linked. In the 1970s, Kozol estimates, $6 billion yearly went to child welfare costs and unemployment compensation, because illiterate adults were unable to perform at standards necessary for available employment.

The Unemployed.   About 48 percent of the householders in poverty-level families do not work; 57 percent of householders in female-headed households do not work (U.S. Bureau of the Census, 1991a: 103, 127). Fifty percent of the poor who do not work are either ill, disabled, or retired or have looked but could not find work;

another 32 percent were prevented from working by child-rearing or other family obligations. Others have given up on trying to find work after years with no success. The official unemployment rate in 1991 was 6.6 percent, which translates into 8.4 million people who are looking for work but cannot find it. Many of these people are among the poor.

An unemployment rate of 7 percent or more means that people who are poor will find it exceedingly difficult to improve their lot by finding well-paying jobs. The unemployed receive unemployment benefits for a time, but these are exhausted eventually. When they do end, the unemployed person may still have payments to make on a home mortgage or an automobile loan. Some of the unemployed become eligible for welfare assistance when unemployment benefits end, but not all unemployed are eligible for welfare. To be eligible, people may have to sell their homes and use up most of their savings. Temporary unemployment, then, could devastate a family that had worked and accumulated resources over the years. This happened to many longtime workers in the recession of the early 1980s.

As we move further into a postindustrial social organization, there will be larger numbers of industrial workers who are "displaced" by the movement from an industrial to an information-based society. In addition, technological innovations such as computerization and robotization are responsible for the displacement of previously employed workers, and many American jobs have been exported overseas where labor and other costs are lower (see Chapter 2). As a consequence, employment in some industries declined substantially in the 1980s: Employment in the steel industry dropped from almost six hundred thousand in the late 1970s to three hundred thousand by the mid-1980s; during the same period, the textile industry experienced a decline from nine hundred thousand workers to seven hundred thousand (McKenzie, 1988). Although there has been job growth in other segments of the economy, it has tended to be in service occupations,

This shelter for homeless families is one response to the disturbing fact that 40 percent of the homeless in the United States are parents and children who cannot afford a permanent roof over their head at night.

which pay considerably less and have fewer employee benefits, such as retirement plans.

The Homeless.   Some of the poor are homeless, with no permanent residence. The National Academy of Sciences estimates that as many as seven hundred thousand Americans may be homeless on any given night, with one hundred thousand of them being children (Blau, 1992). Other estimates are higher, but it is a difficult thing to measure with any precision. A more disturbing fact is that 40 percent of the homeless are families—parents and children out on the street—double the percentage of a decade ago. It is a disturbing problem whose causes can be found in recent social trends, especially the decline in the number of industrial jobs that pay a living wage (see Chapter

2), the flight of jobs from the cities where poor people live, the contraction of social welfare, and the decline in the amount of low-income housing available (Hoch and Slayton, 1989; Schutt, 1990). These factors coming together mean that more people are wandering the countryside, searching for a job and living out of their car or truck. Some sleep on park benches, in subway stations, or in steam tunnels. Some eventually land a job and find housing, but others live on the streets for years. Homelessness is also linked with the trends in our health-care institutions discussed in Chapter 4: At least one-third of the homeless are mentally ill people who were released from mental hospitals because of the process known as "deinstitutionalization," the emphasis on treatment in the community rather than in institutions

(Torrey, 1988). As we saw, many of these former mental patients receive little in the way of psychological or financial assistance.

THE CAUSES OF POVERTY

Programs intended to alleviate poverty must rest on a clear understanding of its causes, and those causes are complex. People often focus on the weaknesses or failures of individuals as the causes of poverty. He is poor, people say, because he is unwilling to work, or she is poor because she had too many children and did not pursue her education. Although there may be some truth to these statements in particular cases, they ignore the part that societal factors play in generating widespread poverty. The three sociological perspectives remedy this by focusing on various elements of the structure of our society that contribute to producing poverty. It is these structures that social policy makes an effort to change in order to alleviate poverty.

The Functionalist Perspective

The Stratification System.   Functionalists argue that stratification exists because it makes some useful contribution to the ongoing maintenance of society. According to sociologists Kingsley Davis and Wilbert Moore (1945), for instance, all societies must ensure that people will fill essential positions and perform important tasks. Somebody must produce food, build shelter, heal the sick, and raise the young. If these tasks are not accomplished, society cannot survive. However, some positions and tasks are more important or more difficult than others. For example, physicians are more crucial than janitors, and it takes more skill to be a judge than an assembly line worker. Some positions call for scarce natural talents or qualities, whereas others require extensive and difficult training. The stratification system

serves to motivate people to occupy and work hard at all of these essential positions. People who fill the more difficult or more essential tasks are given greater rewards—both economic and social—as a consequence.

Thus, the stratification system in society is an essential mechanism for differentially allocating rewards in order to motivate people to perform socially useful tasks. Furthermore, according to the functionalist view, people who do not perform useful tasks should receive fewer rewards. Poverty, then, is society's mechanism to discourage people from neglecting their social duties. If those who do not work were to receive the same rewards as those who do, then many people would choose not to work and society might be threatened.

There has been an ongoing debate over Davis and Moore's functionalist approach to poverty: Are rewards really related to the importance of a position or to the scarcity of qualified personnel to fill it? There does appear to be a relationship between the contributions that people make to society and the rewards they receive (Cullen and Novick, 1979). However, some studies have found that the importance of positions is unrelated to the rewards people receive (Wanner and Lewis, 1978). In addition, a study of public school teachers over a forty-year span showed little support for the functionalist prediction that incomes of teachers would be higher when the supply of teachers was scarce (Betz, Davis, and Miller, 1978). Thus, although these functionalist factors may play a part in causing poverty, there are clearly many exceptions in which people receive low rewards for some other reason. Even when the functionalist argument is true, it cannot account for the vast disparities between the well-to-do and the poor. Clearly, some people earn far more than would seem warranted by their contribution to society and others make far less. When the link between what a person does and what he or she receives becomes vague or broken entirely, then social disorganization can result. People no longer believe that work will be rewarded, and the stratification system no longer serves as the motivation that it is intended to be. In addition, if people are prevented from making a contribution—because of discrimination in the job market, for example—then a similar sense of disorganization can occur.

The Economy.   According to the functionalist perspective, society is made up of many interrelated and interdependent parts, and a change in one part can have implications for the other parts. In the realm of poverty, normal and sometimes desirable changes in the economy can affect the level of poverty. One of these changes has to do with inflation. Many economists believe that unemployment is related to inflation. As unemployment drops, more people are working and have money to buy things. This demand for goods causes prices to rise, producing inflation. To reduce inflation, then, it may be necessary at times to let unemployment increase. This was the policy followed by the Reagan administration in the early 1980s. Inflation dropped, but unemployment and poverty increased (see Table 5.1). In this view, then, a certain amount of poverty is an unfortunate side effect of maintaining other elements of the economy.

Another important source of economic change has been technological innovation, which has brought such improvements as automation. But automation can throw people out of work and reduce the number of jobs in the economy, contributing to the problem of poverty. The automobile industry, for example, is rapidly automating in response to foreign competition. As a consequence, many of the auto workers laid off during the recessions of the 1980s and 1990s will never be called back to work in the auto plants. Many of these workers will find work elsewhere, but in the interim their lives have been dramatically dislocated. Unemployment in cities such as Detroit and Flint, Michigan, has remained very high even though the automobile business has experi-

enced an upswing. Because such automation is constantly replacing workers somewhere in the economy, it always contributes to the level of unemployment and poverty.

In addition to automation, another type of economic change is the rise and decline of various economic sectors. The ghost towns in California attest to the once-booming and now largely dead gold mining in that state. For a good part of this century, heavy industries such as steel and automobile manufacturing were booming. In the past few decades, these industries have been on the decline. Other industries, especially service industries and computers, have surged to prominence. These changes also result in dislocations as some communities experience high levels of unemployment as their industries decline. People in these communities, too, will likely find work elsewhere, but before they do, they will also contribute to unemployment and poverty.

These kinds of changes, some economists argue, are necessary for a healthy economy, but their cumulative impact is to increase rates of unemployment and poverty. This is sometimes called **structural unemployment** because *it is a part of the very structure of our economy.*

The Functions of Poverty.   According to some functionalists, one of the reasons that poverty persists is that it performs some positive functions for society or at least for some groups in society. Although it is difficult to think of poverty in this light, this view illustrates a point that we have made elsewhere: Social conditions or practices that some find undesirable or even repugnant, such as poverty or crime, may nonetheless make a positive contribution to society. How can poverty be functional? Herbert J. Gans (1971) suggests that among the benefits to society from poverty are

1. The existence of poverty ensures that society's "dirty work" will be done. There are many boring, underpaid, or undignified occupations

that most Americans would prefer not to do, even though they need to be done. Jobs such as washing dishes, scrubbing floors, or picking farm produce would probably go undone unless people either received high wages to do them or had no other choice. The poor have little choice and are essentially coerced into taking these "dirty" jobs.

2. Poverty subsidizes many of the activities of the more affluent because the poor are willing to work for low wages. For example, the poor do domestic work and housecleaning for the affluent, which frees the affluent to engage in professional, cultural, or leisure activities.

3. Poverty creates jobs for all those people who serve the poor, such as social workers, or who protect society from them, such as police and corrections officers.

4. Poverty creates a market for inferior goods and services that others will not buy. The poor buy day-old bread, run-down automobiles, and secondhand clothes. They also rent deteriorating apartments in run-down neighborhoods that would otherwise go vacant. Needless to say, the people who sell these goods and services benefit from the poor.

5. The poor help to support and symbolize the status of the nonpoor by serving as the official "losers" or "underdogs" in the societal race for success. In a hierarchical society such as ours, someone has to be on the bottom, and this lets everyone else know where they stand. Relative to the poor, the nonpoor can feel that they have "made it."

We could list other functions of poverty, but our point should be clear: Poverty exists in part because it performs positive functions for many groups in society. Not that these groups consciously wish poverty to continue or actively campaign for its persistence. They may not even be aware of the extent to which they benefit from poverty. But it does mean that these groups feel little pressure to alleviate poverty. In fact, although we have discussed this issue under the functionalist perspective, it has elements of the conflict view of poverty, to which we now turn our attention.

The Conflict Perspective

Most conflict views of poverty derive at least in part from the view of Karl Marx, and his position contrasts sharply with that of the functionalists. Marx viewed society as involving a constant struggle between social classes over scarce resources, with some groups managing to capture more of these resources than others. This results in the inequitable distribution of resources that makes up the stratification systems of modern societies. Yet this unequal distribution, said Marx, has little to do with rewarding talent or filling important positions. Instead, people gain desirable positions in the stratification system through coercion, exploitation, and possibly inheritance. Once their position is acquired, they work to protect it against inroads by less fortunate groups. This can be done in many ways. For example, employers seek the cheapest labor possible because this increases their profits. The tax system is used to benefit the more affluent who can use tax loopholes, unavailable to the less affluent, to avoid paying their share of income tax. Even the legal system tends to benefit the affluent. The crimes they commit, such as business fraud, are less likely to be detected and punished than are the crimes of the poor, such as assault and armed robbery.

It should not be surprising that the affluent benefit in these ways, because it is the affluent who write the tax laws, design the legal system, and pay the police to enforce the law. For Marx, the affluent are merely using the resources available to them to protect their own position. There is an even more subtle way in which dominant groups can protect their position: They can convince subordinate groups that the existing distribution of resources is "natural" or preferable to any other. This is done in part by persuading the poor that they, too, can become affluent. Through schools and the media, for example, people can be taught to believe that everyone will be successful if they apply themselves. The implication of this belief, of course, is that poverty is caused by one's not having worked hard enough. Being poor, then, is one's own fault. This belief deflects people's attention from the societal structures and barriers that contribute to maintaining some groups in power. Poverty is viewed as a personal problem rather than a societal one, and the poor are less inclined to demand changes in the system.

Once people have become successful, they tend to pass on their success to their children, and this makes it more difficult for people on the bottom to move up. **Social mobility** refers to *the movement of people from one social position to another in the stratification hierarchy*. Although upward social mobility is fairly widespread in American society, our stratification system is also characterized by considerable stability with a high degree of occupational inheritance. Most of the mobility that occurs is short range, such as the child of a blue-collar worker who advances to a somewhat better-paying blue-collar job. For the most part, children tend to take jobs that are not too different in socioeconomic status from those of their parents (Featherman and Hauser, 1978; Hout, 1988). Furthermore, children of the affluent have much greater access to a good education, which has become a key requirement for success. In fact, a national tragedy is the fact that our society spends considerably less on the education of poor children, who are more desperately in need of these resources, than it does on the education of affluent children. And relatively little is being done to rectify this (Kozol, 1991). All of this means that the poor do not have the same chances for mobility as the more affluent. By virtue of being born poor, they are already at a serious disadvantage. Even the intelligent and capable among the poor suffer such disadvantages, for the stratification system tends to perpetuate itself. In fact, the first Applied Research insert in this chapter focuses on the growth of an "underclass" of poor who do not have the education and skills that are essential to

landing a good job today. For some in this group, poverty has become a permanent, intergenerational problem.

The Interactionist Perspective and Cultural Analysis

The functionalist and conflict perspectives focus on the role of social and economic structures in creating poverty. By contrast, the interactionist perspective focuses on the importance of the subjective element of social reality—how people define themselves and their opportunities through day-to-day social interaction with others around them. This has led to a **cultural analysis of poverty** that focuses on *the values, attitudes, and psychological orientations that may emerge among groups of people who live under conditions of poverty* (Marks, 1991). The basic idea is that people who live in poverty develop a cultural orientation that helps them adapt to their life circumstances in a way that enables them to still feel good about themselves. However, elements of this cultural orientation can make it more difficult for poor people to improve their circumstances. Anthropologist Oscar Lewis (1966) was one of the first to speak of a "culture of poverty"—the beliefs, values, and norms that emerge among the long-term poor and help them adapt to their circumstances. The poor tend to be isolated from centers of power and decision making in society and from influential groups and organizations. As a result, their cultural orientation tends to emphasize fatalism and powerlessness, feeling that they have little control over what happens to them. In addition, the experiences of the poor have shown them that, despite their own efforts, the future is unlikely to get a lot better for them. So, their cultural orientation tends to be present-oriented—seeking enjoyment now—because they see little point in sacrificing for a future that looks bleak.

More recently, William Julius Wilson (1991) has suggested that prolonged joblessness contributes to this cultural orientation by leaving people with a general sense that they are unable to achieve goals that they might set for themselves, that there is little point in making efforts or taking on challenges. Another element of this cultural context applies to African Americans, whose ancestors were brought to this country against their will, suffered slavery, poverty, and racial oppression over the centuries, and were forcibly kept out of the mainstream of American life. Among some of these poor people there has developed a conflictual subculture that defines their circumstances as due to the racial oppression and dominance exercised by more powerful groups. As they see it, it is racism and discrimination that controls and limits their lives (Peterson, 1991b).

With such a cultural orientation, poor people may despair of ever improving their lot. They may see little point in making efforts to change their circumstances because their fate, they believe, is out of their control. They may not sacrifice for the future because they see no link between present effort and future gain. If racial discrimination, over which they have no control, severely limits any opportunities they might have, then they may see little point in continuing with school or applying for a job that they probably will not get. In fact, if things are that hopeless, they may find that it may make more sense to rip the system off through crime or other means and enjoy what they can. When such a cultural orientation develops, argue proponents of cultural analysis, poverty may become, to a degree, self-perpetuating. The values and norms that make up this orientation may get passed on unwittingly from one generation to the next. When this happens, poverty can become a vicious, difficult-to-break cycle.

Cultural analysis has been controversial because it seems to "blame the victim": Poor people are blamed for their own difficulties by arguing that poverty is due to the character flaws of, or lack of effort by, those affected (Ryan, 1976). However, that is not the point of cultural analysis. Rather, it argues that certain social conditions—discrimination, lack of opportunity, social isolation—can produce a culture of poverty, and this culture in turn perpetuates the victimization of the poor. It is flaws in the social system that are at the root of the problem and that must be changed to combat poverty.

A second reason the culture of poverty thesis has been controversial is that research suggests that it applies only to a limited number of poor people. In fact, the traits that characterize the culture of poverty are probably found among less than half of all poor people and are more common among some poor, such as Hispanics, than among other poor people (Irelan, Moles, and O'Shea, 1969; Coward, Feagin, and Williams, 1974; Kutner and Kutner, 1987). Research also shows that some poor people do improve their lives, despite the culture of poverty. So, although the culture of poverty may inhibit some poor people from making things better for themselves, its impact on perpetuating poverty in general is probably limited, although not unimportant. Many things other than this cultural orientation make life difficult for the poor and account for their limited capacity to improve their lot.

Although the functionalist and conflict perspectives focus on the structural causes of poverty, cultural analysis suggests how poverty, once it exists, may be perpetuated in the lives of some people through the subjective orientations it creates.

FUTURE PROSPECTS

We have discussed many social conditions that cause poverty and others that contribute to its persistence. Given the large number of such conditions, it should not be surprising that many solutions to the problem of poverty have been proposed. We will review the major programs that hold promise today.

Full Employment

Because poverty is related in part to unemployment, it is sensible to promote policies that encourage **full employment:** *a situation in which*

The Underclass in American Society

Although we can establish a poverty level using dollars and cents, as we did earlier in this chapter, people's actual experiences with poverty vary considerably. For some people, poverty is a temporary status out of which they will ultimately move. For other people, poverty is more permanent, sometimes persisting from one generation to the next. This latter group has presented researchers and policymakers with the greatest challenge in terms of relieving poverty. In fact, some researchers have labeled this group an "underclass," implying that they inhabit a quasi-permanent, underprivileged nether region from which escape is, at best, difficult.

Most sociologists consider the underclass to be not only people who are poor, or those who have been poor for a long time; in addition, the underclass is a group whose members are severely disadvantaged, isolated from mainstream America, and living in communities with limited access to the resources that might enable them to improve their lot. For this underclass, chronic unemployment is the norm, crime is taken for granted, and welfare is a fact of life (Marks, 1991). Only about 3 percent of the poor would be considered members of the underclass, and they account for a disproportionate share of problems such as teen pregnancies, crime, and drug abuse (Ricketts and Sawhill, 1988).

What accounts for the emergence of the underclass in the United States? Sociologist William Julius Wilson (1978; 1987) attributes it to some fundamental structural changes in the American economy that have been in progress for a number of decades. One such change is the transition from a product-based economy to an information-based service economy. People in the underclass are without the skills or work experience useful in the latter type of economy, which is more likely to emphasize verbal talent rather than physical brawn, and educational qualifications rather than manual labor. Another basic change in our economy has been the relocation of industries away from the communities where poor people live.

This has occurred because of a number of factors, such as government policies providing funds to build new housing in the suburbs and freeways to get there (see Chapter 12). The outcome has been that factories, businesses, and jobs have fled poor neighborhoods and relocated in non-poor areas. This has been especially disastrous for African Americans who, because of discrimination in housing, have been forced to live in segregated neighborhoods where there are few good jobs (Massey, 1990).

The labor market in modern industrial economies has also changed in such a way that people with no work skills or little education are hard pressed to compete successfully for most jobs. At one time, there were ample jobs for people with strong backs and a willingness to work. By contrast, in today's economy, in which a high school degree (and, increasingly, post–high school training) is the entry-level requirement for most jobs, people who lack these credentials are relegated to the lowest-paying jobs or, increasingly, to no jobs at all. So, given these structural changes in our economy, the underclass consists of those marginally skilled people who have little opportunity to gain the education or skills necessary to succeed in modern industrial economies.

Furthermore, changes in the communities in which poor people live have contributed to the perpetuation and expansion of the underclass. In particular, as employers have abandoned the inner city, so too have the working- and middle-class people who held those jobs, leaving behind the poorer residents. When the working people and nonpoor leave, so do many of the small businesses and merchants, who prefer to locate elsewhere. The consequence is that poor neighborhoods eventually contain mostly the poor and the unemployed. Not only do factories relocate, but so do the small businesses that might employ neighborhood residents. In addition, without working people living in the community, there are fewer respectable role models for the young to look up to. The role models remaining are more commonly those who do not work, who commit crimes, or who take drugs. When the youth in poor communities look around, they see little reason to have high aspirations because none of the people they see in their community seems to have achieved any success. When urban neighborhoods included working-class as well as poor residents, the former provided a kind of buffer to negativism and deviant behavior, with their example providing an incentive for others to work hard and avoid crime. Without that example, a strong sense of resignation can permeate poor urban residents. Negative behavior becomes the norm and spreads to other communities as well (Wilson, 1991).

Sociologist Christopher Jencks (1992) points to some additional things that help perpetuate the underclass: Because of stereotyping and racism, employers are reluctant to hire blacks, especially young black males. After all, even though jobs have left a community, ghetto residents can seek jobs outside their neighborhood, even in the suburbs. But Jencks can point to research showing that employers direct hiring efforts toward white neighborhoods and prefer not to recruit inner-city blacks, especially males (Neckerman and Kirschenman, 1991). Employers may perceive young black males as less skilled, educated, or trustworthy than white workers. In addition, cultural conflict and racism may also be involved. In the 1980s and 1990s, ghetto culture has emerged as a distinct cultural phenomenon in the United States, in part because blacks have not been permitted to assimilate into the mainstream Anglo culture as many ethnic minorities have. This ghetto culture involves a distinctive manner of speaking (such as black English), new modes of cultural expression (such as rap music), a different type of interpersonal demeanor (which Anglos often interpret as hostile and aggressive, especially when exhibited by young males), and an acute awareness that blacks in the United States today still suffer serious discrimination if not outright oppression. According to Jencks, this has an impact on employers:

> Employers' distaste for ghetto culture does not seem to me to have declined. Indeed, it may have increased. A generation ago, most employers expected young ghetto blacks to "know their place." Today employers anticipate that ghetto blacks will be far more assertive. Few employers want unskilled workers who are assertive, regardless of their race. Even fewer want assertive workers from an alien culture they don't understand. (Jencks, 1992: 128–129)

Jencks sees this as symptomatic of a basic cultural conflict. Whites perceive white culture as superior and black culture as alien and threatening; blacks are hesitant to adopt elements of the Anglo culture, even when they are allowed to, because it is a culture they perceive as having oppressed and humiliated them for centuries. One consequence of all this is the profound difficulty blacks, especially young males, have in finding and keeping jobs that will enable them to support a family. So, this cultural conflict contributes to the perpetuation of the underclass.

Using their research as a foundation, Wilson, Jencks, and other sociologists have made recommendations to Congress and other government agencies about what to do about the underclass. Their recommendations basically suggest ways in which the negative impact of the economic structural changes on people's lives can be alleviated. In particular, they have focused on programs to provide people with the education and skills necessary to find good jobs in postindustrial society. They point out that programs that expand job opportunities for those with good job qualifications, such as college graduates, will not have an impact on the underclass. Wilson even criticizes affirmative-action programs on the grounds that they benefit affluent minorities rather than the underclass. What is needed are programs to provide people with the basic literacy skills, a high school diploma, or other qualifications needed to gain entry into our modern service-based economy. For, despite all the crime, single parenthood, and other behaviors among the poor that mainstream American culture frowns on, research clearly shows that poor people cling to conventional behaviors when they see a chance of succeeding. As sociologist Herbert Gans puts it: "only when the poor lose the struggle to escape poverty do they give up mainstream behavior" (Gans, 1992: A56). Research shows that people in the underclass, especially the youth, want to work and are willing to work (Freeman and Holzer, 1986). It is not desire or ambition that they lack, but rather the opportunity to find jobs that pay enough to enable them to support their families in a respectable fashion.

everyone or nearly everyone who wants to work can find a job. Although most politicians would probably support such a concept, the controversy is over how to do it. The Reagan and Bush administrations promoted an essentially laissez-faire approach to full employment. At the foundation of this approach is the idea that the government should play only a limited part in matters of unemployment and poverty. According to this view, the poor benefit from a free and growing economy because the wealth such an economy produces "trickles down" to the poor in the form of more jobs created by economic expansion. Government spending and regulations increase the cost of doing business, make products and services more costly, and thus reduce the level of economic activity. Another element of this laissez-faire approach is to support lower taxes as a way of encouraging economic activity. Lower taxes mean that people earn more for their work and will thus work harder. It also means that people have more money to spend for goods and services or to invest. President Bush's Secretary of Housing and Urban Development, for example, promoted the establishment of "enterprise zones" in poor communities where businesses would be charged lower taxes and subject to fewer government regulations; he also proposed no income taxes on the wages of the poor and the near poor (Kemp, 1990). These policies, it is believed, would encourage entrepreneurs to start new businesses, which would create jobs for poor people and thus reduce unemployment and poverty. (Enterprise zones are discussed in more detail in Chapter 12.)

Certainly, any program that proves effective at creating more jobs would probably receive widespread support, but some cautions about such programs are in order. First, most of the poor, as we have seen, are not able-bodied nonworkers. Rather, they are people who would be largely unaffected by the creation of more jobs: children, the elderly, the disabled, and women raising their children alone. Second, many of the jobs created are likely to be low-paying, unskilled, or part-time jobs that will not pull people out of poverty (Serrin, 1989). In fact, people with such jobs may have fewer economic resources than those on welfare because the former may not receive Medicaid, food stamps, or other in-kind income. Third, as we will see in Chapter 12, there is heated controversy over whether laissez-faire policies such as enterprise zones actually create *new* jobs or whether they just shift jobs from one locale to another. These cautions show that full employment is no panacea for the problem of poverty.

Education, Training, and Jobs

Some social policies aimed at reducing poverty focus on preparing the poor to compete effectively in the job market. The idea is that, for some poor people, the major factor holding them in poverty is that they lack the education, skills, or motivation to find and keep good-paying jobs. A number of programs have been created over the years to focus on these issues.

Head Start.   The Head Start program was established by the Economic Opportunity Act of 1964. This program is based on the belief that people fail in life because their access to conventional channels to success—especially education—is blocked. The presumption is that poor children live in an environment, especially at home, that discourages educational achievement, initiative, and a positive self-concept. By intervening on behalf of these poor children, it is argued, the intergenerational cycle of poverty might be broken. Head Start provides preschool children with enrichment and early learning experiences that middle-class children presumably receive at home.

Although early reports on the impact of Head Start were not favorable, research over the past two decades has shown that the program does achieve many of its goals. Children enrolled in Head Start, when compared with other poor children who do not have such preschool experience, show clear benefits (Parker, Piotrkowski, and Peay, 1987; Lee et al., 1990; Besharov, 1992).

Head Start children are less likely to be assigned to special education classes or to be kept back a grade in school. They also do better on mathematics achievement tests and show more improvement in IQ scores, and they are less likely to repeat a grade, get in trouble with the law, or become teenage mothers. Head Start children also have a better family life and a more positive self-concept. Finally, as young adults, the Head Start children may be more likely to go to college or to hold a steady, skilled job. With benefits such as these, it seems that children who are exposed to such preschool educational experiences will be better equipped to avoid poverty as adults. The extensive evaluation of Head Start is important in assessing solutions to social problems such as poverty. The contribution of social research to this process is analyzed in the second Applied Research insert in this chapter.

Jobs Programs.   Whereas Head Start is an indirect, long-term approach to the problem of poverty, other programs have involved more direct and immediate efforts to train people and to find them jobs. Two of the largest such programs over the past few decades were WIN (Work Incentive Program) and CETA (Comprehensive Employment and Training Act).

The WIN program was established in 1967 to provide job training for adult welfare recipients, especially women with dependent children, and to assist them in finding jobs and getting off welfare (Segalman and Basu, 1981). The CETA program was established in 1973 with the intent of providing the unemployed with job training and work experience. It provided testing and placement services, on-the-job training, and temporary public-service jobs. It also established special programs for the chronically unemployed, such as youth, criminal offenders, and people with limited English language abilities. The assumption was that with this support and experience people would be better prepared to land permanent jobs. Although both programs did help some people, they were not great successes. Relatively few who partici-

pated in the programs eventually got off welfare and held permanent jobs, and in many cases, the jobs that the participants could find paid less than they would have received by staying on welfare. In addition, the programs did not create new jobs, and CETA and WIN monies were often used to pay regular municipal employees when communities faced budget cuts, thus providing little assistance to the poor. Eventually, both CETA and WIN were eliminated.

In 1982, the Reagan administration established its own program, the Job Training Partnership Act or JTPA (Kellam, 1992). One key feature of this approach was that some of the training was provided by programs run by private industry with federal funds. The belief was that this private-sector involvement would result in better training and the creation of more jobs. The JTPA also included a Dislocated Worker Program to provide retraining for the displaced workers (discussed in Chapter 2) who were laid off from industries that face substantial foreign competition, such as the steel and automobile industries. However, the JTPA also seems to have fallen far short of its goals. Many of the trainees were people with high school degrees who probably would have gotten jobs on their own, and most would have been hired and trained by their employers even if JTPA funds had not been available. In addition, the JTPA did not create many new high-paying jobs, and most trainees ended up in minimum-wage jobs.

In 1988, a major piece of welfare legislation with significant provisions for training and jobs programs became law. The Family Support Act represented a considerable shift from past policy on welfare and poverty ("Congress Clears . . . ," 1988). Basically, it involved a transformation of the welfare system from an emphasis on income maintenance to an emphasis on education and training in order to help people find jobs. The new law requires states to operate a Job Opportunities and Basic Skills (JOBS) program. These programs require single parents on welfare whose children are older than three to either find a reg-

APPLIED RESEARCH

Evaluating Poverty Programs: Head Start

One of the challenging tasks for social researchers is assessing whether social policies intended to alleviate social problems really achieve their goals. Answering the question "Do the programs work?" is difficult but essential. Assessments of the Head Start program illustrate both how these evaluations can be made and what the benefits of good evaluation research are.

A central element of all social programs is a statement of what the program intends to achieve. For Head Start, the goal was to provide poor children with the preschool experiences that would enable them to do better in school and in life. To evaluate the program effectively, however, these general goals need to be translated into observable and measurable goals. In other words, we need some "indicators" that the program achieves its goals. In research, an *indicator* is an observation that we assume to be evidence that something has occurred or that something has a certain value (Monette, Sullivan, and DeJong, 1990). What would be possible indicators of the success of Head Start? Some fairly immediate ones are such things as better grades in school, reduced need for remedial education, and lesser likelihood of being held back a grade in school. There might also be long-term indicators of program success, such as rates of graduation from high school or entrance into college. All these indicators can be readily quantified and measured. Youngsters who have been through Head Start can be compared with youngsters who have not to see which group has higher grades in school, requires less remedial education, and so on.

As we have seen in the text, research suggests that Head Start children perform better in terms of these indicators than do other youngsters. This illustrates how objective, observable, and measurable data can be used to evaluate social policy programs. An evaluation such as this provides a much more solid foundation for public policy debate than does common sense, anecdotes, or unsubstantiated speculations. In fact, Head Start

has gained considerable support over the years in part because its benefits to poor children and their families could be clearly demonstrated by such research. During the budget-cutting years of the Reagan administration, Head Start received considerable protection. In 1989, Head Start received a healthy endorsement from the Bush administration, which proposed a 40 percent boost in the program's funding by 1993. President Bush justified this in terms of equality of opportunity: "Give any American kid an equal place at the starting line and just watch what that kid can do. Head Start helps kids get that equal place" ("Everybody Likes Head Start," 1989: 49).

Even though the evaluation of Head Start has shown its effectiveness and has increased its supporters in the government, debate over the program is likely to continue. One reason for this is that people are reluctant—and understandably so—to base policy solely on the outcomes of social research. As we saw in Chapter 1, personal and cultural values also play a part in this policy-making process. Another reason the debate continues is that some question whether the costs of Head Start are worth the gains it offers. This gets into a type of evaluation research known as cost-benefit analysis. A youngster who graduates from high school will usually earn more money in his or her lifetime, pay more taxes, and be less of a welfare burden on society than would a youngster who does not graduate. Likewise, a teenage pregnancy usually means another client on the welfare caseload and an additional cost to society. A cost-benefit analysis involves the calculation of all the costs of a program such as Head Start (particularly the government appropriations to run the program) and all the benefits (such as a reduced welfare burden and higher taxes paid). Then an assessment can be made about whether the benefits outweigh the costs. This enables policy planners to assess whether the benefits of Head Start are "worth" the costs.

ular job or to enroll in educational and job-training courses that are provided by federal and state governments. Earlier job training and welfare programs did not have this coercive element. In some cases, welfare recipients will be required to participate in community work activities or other unpaid work in order to continue receiving welfare payments. States must provide child care for parents who work or attend courses, provide continuing eligibility for Medicaid health-care coverage for families, and offer transportation and other support to the participants. The overall design of the law is to discourage long-term dependency on welfare and to foster a transition to job-holding independence.

This federal "workfare" policy is still too new for us to determine its impact. However, many states have established similar compulsory training programs and work requirements as a part of their welfare systems, and assessments of these programs do not give cause for great optimism over workfare. The assessments show that these state programs do not save much welfare money, they do not move many people off welfare, and those who do get off welfare experience only a very modest increase in their earnings over their welfare payments (Burtless, 1989). One reason for these meager outcomes is simple: Many people go on welfare because they cannot find jobs that pay more than their welfare payments. Giving them job training does not help if the jobs are not there. Another reason the state-level workfare programs do not have more positive outcomes is that states are reluctant to spend much money on them; as a consequence, the job training tends to be brief and part-time. Full-time, extensive training might have a better outcome, but Americans seem reluctant to pay for that.

However, irrespective of whether the new workfare policy gets people off welfare or gets them jobs, it clearly represents a shift in sentiment in the United States regarding welfare: Rather than viewing welfare as a right of those Americans who have fallen on hard times, it is now organized as a privilege for those who can demonstrate that they are making an effort to help themselves.

Income-Maintenance Programs

Modern governments have taken on the responsibility of assisting those in need through a variety of programs that provide them with some minimal level of resources. In the United States, these programs can be divided into two general categories: social insurance and public assistance. **Social insurance** refers to *programs offering benefits to broad categories of people, such as the elderly or injured workers, who presumably were working and paying for the insurance before becoming eligible for it.* There is no "means" test to receive social insurance; that is, there is no income minimum necessary to be eligible. Also, one can receive outside income while insured, and there is little stigma associated with it. In fact, 80 percent of the social welfare dollar is spent on the nonpoor. **Public assistance,** which is what most people mean when they use the term *welfare*, refers to *programs in which a person must pass a "means" test to be eligible.* Those whose assets are above a certain level are not eligible.

There are various social insurance programs in the United States. At both the federal and state levels, over $430 billion were spent on such programs in 1988 (U.S. Bureau of the Census, 1991: 356–358). Among the best known and most expensive are

1. *Social Security.* Old Age, Survivors, and Disability Insurance (OASDI), commonly referred to as "Social Security," is intended to provide income for retired or disabled workers and their survivors. It also provides unemployment compensation and benefits to workers for on-the-job injuries. Benefits also go to dependent spouses over age sixty-two and dependent children under age eighteen. In 1988, the OASDI expenditure was about $300 billion. Social Security benefits lift as many as fifteen million people a year out of poverty,

making it one of the government's most effective weapons against poverty (Pear, 1988). Without Social Security, the poverty rate would probably be over 20 percent. Because Social Security is primarily focused on the elderly, we discuss it in more detail in Chapter 8.

2. *Medicare.* Medicare is a health insurance program for the elderly and for some others who are receiving Social Security. It also provides supplementary medical insurance in return for a monthly premium. The expenditure on Medicare in 1988 was over $83 billion. We consider Medicare further in Chapters 4 and 8.

There are also a variety of public-assistance programs, costing at least $125 billion in 1988.

1. *Supplementary Security Income.* Supplementary Security Income (SSI) is given to certain categories of poor people with little income and few assets. To be eligible, one must be over sixty-five, blind, or disabled. SSI provides these people with a guaranteed minimum income. At state and federal levels, this program cost over $12 billion in 1988.

2. *Aid to Families with Dependent Children.* Aid to Families with Dependent Children (AFDC) is a combined federal-state program to provide assistance to parents or guardians who do not have the financial resources to support their children. It also covers families in which the father is disabled and thus unable to support his children. Most families receiving AFDC are headed by women who are widowed, divorced, deserted, or unmarried. AFDC cash payments exceeded $18 billion in 1988.

3. *General Assistance.* When a person falls into poverty, there is usually a period of time before SSI or AFDC funds are available. In addition, some poor people are not eligible for these programs. For example, a childless couple that is not old, blind, or disabled could not receive funds from either program. Such is also the case for partially handicapped people. General Assistance (GA) is for people ineligible for SSI or AFDC. GA is funded by state or local governments, but only about half the states have GA, and the amount of assistance and the eligibility requirements are highly variable from one locale to another. In some areas, local officials have considerable discretion over who receives GA funds. Because able-bodied adults sometimes find it necessary to seek temporary GA funds, they are often viewed as the "undeserving" poor. GA expenditures in 1988 reached almost $3.9 billion.

4. *Medicaid.* Medicaid is a program providing medical and hospital services to people who cannot pay for them themselves. Generally, Medicaid goes to people who meet the means test for other public-assistance programs, but it can also go to people who can provide for their own economic support except for necessary medical care. Medicaid payments reached over $54 billion in 1988.

5. *Noncash Benefits.* A number of public-assistance programs provide poor people with resources that are not direct cash payments. For example, food stamps are given to people on public assistance with the idea that, because the stamps can only be redeemed for food, children and poor people will be assured of a nutritionally adequate diet. There is also housing assistance for the poor, either in the form of public housing with low rents or government assistance in paying rent for housing in the private sector. There is also a school lunch program to assist poor children in receiving a good diet.

The history of income-maintenance programs and people's attitudes toward them in the United States show one thing clearly: Americans are willing to give government assistance to "deserving" people, those who have worked to support themselves and now find themselves, because of age, disability, or other conditions, in difficult times; on the other hand, Americans show reluctance to support the "undeserving" poor, such as single mothers or marginally employable men, who are perceived as being partially responsible for their plight or at least capable of improving their circumstances on their own (Jencks, 1992). Going back as far as the New Deal programs of the 1930s when Social Security was established, the intent clearly was to assist nonpoor, reputable people from falling into poverty. Even Aid to Dependent Children, as AFDC was then called, was originally intended for widowed mothers, not for single or divorced mothers. Most people then were opposed to both single motherhood and divorce and figured that it was within the control of these women to avoid both. The Great Society programs of the 1960s, on the other hand, focused more on helping the poor to rise out of poverty. They were based on the assumption that providing equal opportunities to all would enable people to rise out of poverty, and they tended to direct resources toward the "undeserving" poor.

The last twenty years have produced some disillusionment among Americans regarding income-maintenance programs, especially considering that poverty has not been eliminated. Social Security and Medicare still willingly go to those who have worked and now find their incomes limited by retirement, and these programs tend to be fairly impervious to budget cutting; on the other hand, states and the federal government have felt much freer to slash the AFDC and GA rolls and to find ways to deny or restrict benefits to people. In the 1980s, President Reagan and many others believed that welfare went to many who ought to be able to make it without government assistance. Welfare programs were viewed as wasteful and subject to fraud. Reagan's view was to provide a government "safety net" to help the "truly needy." As a consequence, many welfare programs had their budgets reduced substantially. Many people were dropped from the welfare roles and fell further into poverty. Probably one-half of the increase in poverty in the 1980s was due to the Reagan budget cuts (Rosenbaum, 1984). This reluctance to support the poor continues today. For example, only 50 percent of the children living in poverty receive any welfare, down from

80 percent in the early 1970s (DeParle, 1992). Today, some states reduce benefits unless teenage parents stay in school, others deny payments to women who have additional children, and still others drop teen mothers from the welfare rolls unless they live with a parent or guardian (Dumas, 1992). Although some of these policies may have beneficial outcomes, they clearly arise from frustration over the continuing growth in welfare costs and in reaction to continuing recessionary conditions in the American economy. Given the reluctance of Americans to support the "undeserving" poor, these policies do reflect a degree of "welfare bashing" rather than policy alternatives that have been shown to produce a positive outcome.

One outgrowth of all this is the Family Support Act of 1988, which is an attempt to transform welfare from an income-maintenance system to one that stresses education, training, and assistance in job searching. As mentioned, this "workfare" approach represents a shift in public sentiment from viewing welfare as a "right" of those who have fallen on bad times to a "privilege" that can be revoked. The legislation also attacks welfare dependency through the work-incentive elements previously described and by requiring states to spend 55 percent of their welfare budget on those showing long-term dependency on welfare. This is an effort to tackle the most intractable cases of welfare dependence; it assumes that those who are only dependent for short periods will have a good chance of getting off welfare despite what the government does. The law provides for extending welfare benefits to families in which both parents are unemployed, so that fathers will not leave their families in order to make them eligible for benefits. The law also contains stiff measures to enforce child-support payments in the hope that some families could be kept from going on welfare to begin with.

Welfare has always been a controversial topic in the United States, and some sharply contrasting views of welfare are presented in the Policy Issues insert. The International Perspectives insert

POLICY ISSUES

Does Welfare Work?

There are probably very few people who are satisfied with our current system of public welfare. Some are inclined to view those on welfare as cheats, chiselers, and lazy loafers who have found a free meal at the public trough. Others see welfare recipients as victims: people who, by virtue of disability, discrimination, or some other reason, cannot find and keep a job that will provide them with a minimally decent life-style. Which of these views is most accurate is a topic of considerable debate. In fact, reality is probably more complex than either of these stereotypes. But social policy is often based on such stereotypes. Two more sophisticated, yet opposing views of our welfare system are presented by writer Charles Murray (1984) and Professor Christopher Jencks (1992).

Although there may be some lazy people collecting welfare, Charles Murray does not believe that laziness need really be considered in understanding why people choose welfare over work. Rather, he argues, the welfare regulations are such that, for some people, going on welfare may be the most rational economic choice to make. First, AFDC payments, along with such in-kind income as food stamps and Medicaid, often amount to more each month than a person can make at the low-paying jobs that are available to people with little education and few skills. Because those low-paying jobs are often boring and unpleasant, why should a young man or woman work if he or she can stay home and collect more income from public assistance? In addition, people can supplement their welfare income by working, and for each dollar they earn, they lose considerably less than a dollar in AFDC. And if a woman on AFDC lives with a man without being married, what he earns is not deducted from her public assistance. As a final critique of the welfare system, Murray argues that when people go on welfare, they become dependent on it and lose

the values of hard work and self-sufficiency that would enable them to support themselves. In fact, the more welfare we provide, the more dependent people become and the more poverty we create. Slash welfare and poverty would actually decline as people are forced to support themselves.

Murray's solution to this problem is extreme, but he believes it is defensible. It is very consistent with the laissez-faire approach to social problems: Dismantle the entire federal welfare system and income-support structure for working-age people! These people would have to find a job, locate family or friends who can assist them, or get assistance from local public or private social service agencies. He proposes this not out of callous disregard or anger at "welfare loafers" but from the recognition that the current welfare regulations make it preferable, in the short term, for some people to choose welfare over work. Murray thinks that it is in society's long-term interest to get these people working. Welfare is a dead end; it can lead to permanent dependence on the public dole. If federal welfare payments were removed, some recipients would face only inconvenience because their payments were only for a short period or constituted only a small portion of the income available to them. Other recipients will have to scramble around to find a job or a relative to support them. This will definitely involve great disruption for some of them, but it will also have the long-term benefit of changing their behavior in positive ways. Parents, not wanting to support their adult children or grandchildren, will apply greater pressure to avoid pregnancies or to get a job. A single adult woman will probably want to avoid such dependence on her parents. To be sure, some will have to work for lower wages at dissatisfying jobs for a time. However, many of these people—not all, Murray recognizes, but many—will find that they have acquired some skills after a time and can move on to better jobs.

They will also have acquired a sense of independence and pride in supporting themselves.

The billions of dollars saved on welfare each year will be spent by some Americans and saved by others. The spending will create more jobs and the savings will be available to business for capital investments and improvements, which will also create more jobs. Some of the savings on welfare will undoubtedly be shifted into local public and private social service agencies that will support those—and there will be some—who cannot find a job or other source of support. Murray does recommend retaining unemployment insurance, but this is a temporary support between jobs, not a permanent dole. Once unemployment payments run out, there would be no sources of continuing support from the federal government.

Christopher Jencks defends the record of achievements by the federal welfare system. First, he argues that it has substantially improved the circumstances of many of the truly needy among the elderly, the disabled, and children. At the same time, the so-called undeserving poor—single mothers and able-bodied males—have fared much worse. The latter receive no federal assistance and little local assistance, whereas the former have found the purchasing power of their AFDC payments actually declining in the past two decades. Furthermore, Jencks and other researchers present evidence that disputes many of Murray's points. For example, there is little evidence that the availability of AFDC leads women to go out and have children out of wedlock. Over the past thirty years, rates of single parenthood have increased steadily, whereas welfare benefits have gone up and down. If Murray is right that more welfare produces more out-of-wedlock children, then declining welfare rates should lead to fewer such children. It has not. The reality, says Jencks, is that the increase in single-parent families has been a broad cultural trend that shows up in both welfare and nonwelfare women. It reflects a more tolerant approach toward sex and reproduction, a growing cultural individualism, and a greater commitment to personal freedom, and these trends have affected the decisions of all American women. Welfare payments do enable poor women to get out of undesirable marriages and avoid rushing into a second marriage to

support themselves and their children. However, Jencks sees these outcomes as benefits because getting out of, or staying out of, a bad marriage probably reduces the levels of child abuse and child abandonment by poor parents. As for the argument that welfare breeds dependency and increases poverty, political scientist Sanford Schram (1991) presents data showing the opposite: when welfare spending *declines,* the poverty rate tends to go up.

Jencks also does not believe that economic growth will do much to reduce welfare loads because most of the poor—the elderly, the disabled, and women heading their own households—are precisely the groups that benefit least when economic conditions improve. The reality is, says Jencks, that welfare mothers cannot support their families on their AFDC payments. The truth is that many welfare mothers work! They do not usually tell the welfare office about their work because they lose welfare payments if they do. But despite Murray's and others' image of welfare mothers choosing leisure and indolence over hard work, reality is more complex. Most welfare recipients would quickly choose work over welfare if they could find jobs that paid enough to support their families. Many welfare mothers supplement AFDC payments with wages from low-paying jobs; many get support from parents or boyfriends; a few turn to selling drugs or prostitution to narrow the gap between what AFDC pays and what they need to support their children. In short, they work—and show considerable initiative in coming up with supplemental income in a difficult situation.

Given these realities, Jencks says, dumping welfare altogether would be destructive and mean spirited. However, "any successful social policy must strike a balance between collective compassion and individual responsibility" (Jencks, 1992: 87). Based on the assumption that it is better to work and help yourself, Jencks' basic premise is that people who work should always be better off than those who do not work and receive welfare. This might mean providing such assistance to low-income workers as health insurance, child-care assistance, housing subsidies, and the like. One reason women choose welfare over work is that they lose Medicaid and some of their AFDC payments when they work. This means that, for these women, working typically means being less well off, or at least not much better off, than when only taking welfare. So, says Jencks, take this out of the equation by offering health insurance and other assistance to working mothers. In other words, if the woman works, her overall financial package should always be greater than if she only receives welfare. Once again, the reality is that many welfare mothers do work; this policy would provide even more encouragement for these habits of work and self-sufficiency. As income from work grows, the amount of welfare and other support would decline. However, given that these women have few job skills and are likely to find only low-paying jobs, some level of welfare support is likely to be needed in the future. This is a recognition that our economy, at least as currently organized, does not provide enough jobs with adequate pay to support all the families that need them.

---

explores how such issues are dealt with in other societies.

Collective Action

Many of the programs intended to alleviate poverty have been designed by politicians, economists, sociologists, and other experts who are not themselves poor. This raises the question of whether these experts have different interests from the poor or whether they have an accurate and sincere understanding of poverty and its related problems. Leslie Dunbar (1988), who has interviewed many poverty-stricken people at length, believes that policymakers and the general public hold inaccurate stereotypes of the poor as unthinking, unambitious, irresponsible, and possibly even dangerous social misfits. In reality, after listening to poor people speak, Dunbar found that the poor value many of the same things that other Americans do, such as ambition, self-reliance, and family life. Most want to work and support themselves, but because of bad luck or circumstances, they find themselves destitute. If policymakers

---

INTERNATIONAL PERSPECTIVES

Wealth, Poverty, and Welfare in Other Societies

Figure 5.2 shows a very lopsided distribution of wealth in the United States, with close to half of all income going to the wealthiest 20 percent of the families. Are we out of line in this ratio compared to other societies? It depends on who we look at (The World Bank, 1989). In many less developed countries around the world—such as Kenya, Peru, Brazil, and Panama—the wealthiest 20 percent of the families nab 60 percent or more of family income. In Brazil and Panama, the poorest 20 percent of the families receive only 2 percent of annual income—a very small share indeed! So, we have a more equitable distribution of wealth than do these nations. In comparison to the wealthier nations in the world, however, the U.S. income distribution is somewhat lopsided. In only three of the twenty wealthiest nations do the top 20 percent of the families receive as large a share of income as in the United States; in none of those twenty nations does the bottom fifth receive as small a share as in the United States. For comparison, the Netherlands probably has the most equitable distribution, with the top 20 percent of families receiving 36 percent of the income and the poorest 20 percent receiving 8 percent of the income. Compare those numbers with the comparable ones in the United States from Figure 5.2. So, economic development and increasing wealth seem to produce a more equitable distribution of wealth in society, although the United States remains among the least equitable of these societies.

Poverty rates also tend to be higher in the United States than in many other industrial countries, especially Germany, Switzerland, the Netherlands, and the Scandanivian countries (Rodgers, 1990). Practically all of these societies also provide more comprehensive assistance to the low income, the poor, and single parents. And they take a very different approach to issues of welfare and public assistance than does the United States. For one thing, these industrial nations focus on preventing social problems, including poverty and crime, by assisting people to avoid poverty. For example, they have housing programs and child or family allowances that go to the nonpoor as well as the poor. In this way, people can avoid tumbling into self-perpetuating poverty if they come on hard times. A second difference is that many of the assistance programs in these nations are universal rather than "means tested" as in the United States. In many countries, for example, all families receive some child or family allowance, although the amount varies by income level. Such universal programs are more effective at preventing social problems; they receive more widespread public support because everyone gains from them, and those who receive "welfare" are less likely to be stigmatized.

A third difference in the approach of these countries, especially Japan and the Scandanavian countries, is to use public resources and government intervention to keep unemployment as low as possible. In 1989, Japan's unemployment rate was 2.3 percent while Sweden's was an unbelievable 1.3 percent! (Compare those figures with the United States in Chapter 2.) Low unemployment can be a significant factor in keeping poverty down. A final difference with the U.S. approach is that all of these other industrial countries make health care services available to both the poor and the nonpoor. In the United States, many people stay on welfare rather than work because they lose Medicaid eligibility if they work. The jobs available to the poor are not likely to have health insurance as a benefit and pay too little to enable them to purchase health insurance, which is quite expensive. So, the choice for the poor in the United States is often either to work but forego health insurance or to get health insurance by not working and remaining eligible for welfare.

Countries that spend more on public assistance don't necessarily have lower rates of poverty (Lawson and George, 1980). This is probably because there are powerful structural and economic determinants of poverty that are unaffected by increasing levels of welfare expenditure. One such structural factor is the number of single-parent families, which is linked with higher poverty levels. In the United States, 8 percent of all households are single parent as compared to 3.2 percent in Sweden, 4 percent in the United Kingdom, and 2.5 percent in Japan (U.S. Bureau of the Census, 1991: 837). Another reason why welfare expenditures don't clearly reduce poverty is that, in many of these industrial countries, a good portion of social welfare dollars is not directed at the poor but at assisting people who work to keep working and achieve a satisfactory lifestyle. For example, we saw in the International Perspectives insert in Chapter 3 that many European societies provide family benefits, such as day care and maternity leave, to everyone, even those who could afford to get them on their own. So, some nations have high public assistance expenditures and low poverty rates because some of the public assistance is directed at the nonpoor.

So the experiences of these other industrial nations suggest that it is not necessarily the amount of public assistance that reduces poverty but rather the approach taken: universal programs that focus on reducing social problems and unemployment and that make health care available to all.

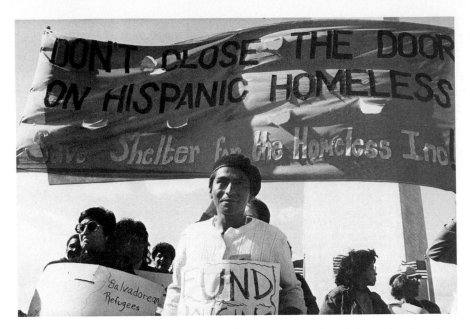

There are times when the poor may be better off taking matters into their own hands and using collective action to ensure that poverty policies, such as those relating to availability of shelter and affordable housing, truly work in the interests of the poor.

and the public misunderstand the poor and have different interests than they do, then the programs these officials develop may not necessarily further the interests of the poor. As one illustration of this, our welfare system tends to emphasize getting people off welfare rather than making sure that all people eligible for government funds actually receive them. As a consequence, possibly as few as one-half of the people eligible for welfare actually receive it (Cloward and Piven, 1974). Such a system is oriented more toward keeping costs down than ensuring that all the needs of the poor are properly taken care of.

Given these problems, the poor may need to take matters into their own hands through some collective action that would further their interests. In fact, the poor have done this periodically. The original war on poverty of the 1960s was in part a reaction to the focus of the civil rights movement aimed at the problems of poor blacks in America. Since then, groups such as the United Farm Workers Union and the National Welfare Rights Organization have lobbied and protested in support of policies that are in the interests of the poor. Richard Cloward and Frances Fox Piven (1974) suggest that a coalition of poor groups and civil rights organizations could be an effective weapon to bring about change. A strategy such as this has its dangers, of course. It could create a backlash against the poor and result in substantial reductions in public assistance. However, it does illustrate the point that disadvantaged groups in American society have traditionally used collective action as one avenue to pursue their interests. The poor have not utilized this strategy as much as they might.

Linkages

Poor people become more deeply entrenched in poverty when segregation into urban ghettos (Chapter 12) makes it more difficult for them to find jobs and when corporate concentration of power (Chapter 2) makes it easy to close factories and move them away from where the poor live.

Summary

1. Poverty arises not from a deprivation of resources alone but from an uneven distribution of the resources available in a society. The system of social stratification in society refers to the ranking of people into a hierarchy in which the resources considered valuable by society are unequally distributed.

2. There are three widely used definitions of poverty: One is based on absolute deprivation, the second on relative deprivation, and the third on cultural elements. Most social policy on poverty in the United States uses the absolute definition.

3. Poverty is more common among blacks and some other racial and ethnic minorities than among whites; among children than among adults; among female-headed households than among male-headed households; and among central-city and rural dwellers. Among the poor can also be found the working poor, the illiterate, the unemployed, and the homeless.

4. The sociological perspectives focus on how the workings of society and certain social processes contribute to the existence of poverty. From the functionalist perspective, poverty exists to discourage people from neglecting their social duties. If people do not contribute to society, they are "punished" by receiving little in terms of wealth, status, or other rewards. In addition, poverty exists because it performs some positive functions for society, such as ensuring that society's dirty work will be done.

5. From the conflict perspective, poverty exists because some groups are deprived of the opportunity to accumulate the resources that would make possible a minimally acceptable lifestyle. The affluent gain their positions through coercion, exploitation, or possibly inheritance, and then they use their position to protect what they have from inroads by the less fortunate. The poor are those with little power and few resources.

6. According to the interactionist perspective, living in poverty can lead the poor to define situations or interpret reality in ways that make it more difficult for them to improve their circumstances. A part of this is called the culture of poverty, or values and norms that help the poor adapt to their life circumstances. This should not be interpreted, however, as a "blame the victim" argument.

7. One approach to reducing poverty is to strive for full employment, a situation in which nearly everyone who wants to work can find a job. How to achieve this, or whether it can be achieved, remains controversial.

8. Another approach is to provide the education and training that will prepare the poor to find and keep jobs. Head Start seems to have been fairly successful at this. Other jobs programs, however, have had mixed success.

9. To assist the poor, a variety of income-maintenance programs has been made available. The two general types are social insurance and public assistance. To keep able-bodied people from living off welfare, some states require that people do some publicly useful work in order to receive welfare. There is considerable debate over whether welfare is beneficial or detrimental to people and society.

10. Some have argued that the only effective way for the poor to get programs that truly benefit them is through collective action.

Important Terms for Review

absolute definition of poverty	cultural analysis of poverty	relative definition of poverty	social stratification
cultural definition of poverty	full employment	social insurance	structural unemployment
	poverty	social mobility	
	public assistance		

Discussion Questions

1. Reviewing the various ways that poverty can be defined, which do you think is the most preferable? Why? If we did change the way our government defines poverty, what would be the social policy implications?

2. Take the functionalist view to an extreme by describing what society would be like if people received rewards based only on their own accomplishments. Inheritance or any other advantage that you did not create yourself would be eliminated. What would society look like? What would happen to such institutions as the family and education?

3. Visit a state Department of Social Services office in your community. Ask the people working there to describe their clients and their clients' problems. If possible, talk to some of the clients yourself. From these experiences, describe who the poor are and what their lives are like.

4. To get some insight into life for the poor, locate a welfare mother who would be willing to come to class and discuss her problems and difficulties. This is a good way to find out how far meager AFDC payments will really stretch and how demeaning the bureaucratic shuffle in social service systems can be. Another interesting exercise is to identify how much a family can receive in AFDC payments in your community and then prepare a budget for the family. You might even want to go to the store and see how much food can be purchased with what is left after you have paid for rent, clothing, transportation, and so forth.

For Further Reading

Ken Auletta. *The Underclass*. New York: Random House, 1982. An intriguing book by a journalist who lived with people at the bottom of the stratification system: welfare recipients, street criminals, addicts, and drifters. Auletta's commentary provides a stark, realistic view of how such people live out their troubled lives.

Janet M. Fitchen. *Poverty in Rural America: A Case Study*. Boulder, Colo.: Westview Press, 1981. The author reports her findings from an investigation of poverty in a rural community in New York State. Fitchen's analysis shows how socioeconomic factors such as education, income, and occupation interact to perpetuate poverty.

Stephanie Golden. *The Women Outside: Meanings and Myths of Homelessness*. Berkeley: University of California Press, 1992. This is an interesting report on women who are homeless, written by a woman with experience working in shelters for the homeless. It shows how the intersection of two statuses—gender and low socioeconomic standing—affect these women.

Michael Harrington. *The New American Poverty*. New York: Holt, Rinehart and Winston, 1984. The author of the well-known *The Other America* reviews the war on poverty, arguing that this movement never really got off the ground because of the Vietnam War. In this book, Harrington tells the story of poverty in America using revealing anecdotes, combined with an analysis of the roots of the new poverty that he finds all too visible.

Alex Kotlowitz. *There Are No Children Here: The Story of Two Boys Growing Up in the Other America*. New York: Doubleday, 1991. This is a very realistic and wrenching description of what it is like to grow up poor and black in Chicago. It helps you see what it is like to be poor through the eyes of the poor.

Jonathan Kozol. *Rachel and Her Children: Homeless Families in America*. New York: Crown, 1988. This is a bird's-eye view of what it is like to be homeless for one woman and her family. It shows the difficulties and the degradations of such a life.

Lawrence M. Mead. *The New Politics of Poverty: The Nonworking Poor in America*. New York: Basic Books, 1992. Mead disputes some of the arguments of Jencks, Wilson, Murray, and the culture of poverty theorists discussed in this chapter. He provides another interesting perspective on what to do about those on welfare.

Richard H. Ropers. *Persistent Poverty: The American Dream Turned Nightmare*. New York: Plenum, 1992. This is a good analysis of how poverty results from long-term economic, social, and political policies and trends rather than from the inadequacies or shortcomings of the poor themselves. It documents the inconsistencies in government policies that contribute to the problem.

Loretta Schwartz-Nobel. *Starving in the Shadow of Plenty*. New York: McGraw-Hill, 1981. A journalist and policy analyst shows that poverty and hunger are widespread in America and that government policies have made many Americans worse off than ever before. She makes numerous suggestions about what can be done to alleviate the problem of poverty.

CHAPTER 6
Race and Ethnic Relations

A central value in American culture is equality—the belief that people should be treated with dignity and respect and have access to social opportunities regardless of their particular racial, ethnic, religious, or sexual group membership. In addition, Americans take pride in boasting of how a "little person on the bottom can make it" in their country. For example, Ronald Reagan was born in a small town in Illinois and lived in a small apartment above a store as a child. He went on to gain considerable wealth as an actor and as a spokesman for corporations and, of course, was elected to the highest public office in America. His life, along with the lives of such people as Abraham Lincoln, John D. Rockefeller, Andrew Carnegie, and H. L. Hunt, supports the contention that opportunity awaits those who want to work hard. Yet how true is this?

One of the most fascinating and enriching aspects of life in America is the great physical and cultural diversity of the peoples who have settled here. This diversity has provided America with a large range of life-styles. At the same time, however, it has been a major source of divisiveness and conflict for our society. Despite our cultural emphasis on equality, groups with different traditions, values, and languages have struggled with one another over power, privileges, and prestige. In fact, American history has been a chronicle of unequal treatment of racial minorities, stretching from the enslavement of black Africans for the benefit of white Europeans settling the New

Myths and Facts About Race and Ethnicity

Myth: The Civil Rights Act and related social policies (such as equal employment opportunity, affirmative action, and so on) have eliminated racism in American society.

Fact: Despite such legislation, discrimination persists. For example, the U.S. Supreme Court ruled recently that any policy having damaging effects on a particular racial group is not unconstitutional unless it can be demonstrated that the intent of that policy was discrimination. Thus, certain policies exist that involve discrimination and can be utilized to foster racism.

Myth: Native Americans have got it made because they receive all kinds of benefits from the government for being Indian.

Fact: Of all American minorities, Indians are among the poorest. As a group, they suffer very high unemployment rates, ranging from 50 to 80 percent at any given time. The median income of

native Americans is less than half the national average, and more than one-third of all Indian families live below the official poverty level. Although it is presumed that reservation housing is opulent because of federal funding, the average home on a reservation has but two rooms, housing nearly six occupants.

Myth: Nonwhites in the United States continue to lag behind whites in education, income, and occupational status in the 1990s.

Fact: There is much variation in the circumstances of racial and ethnic groups in the United States. Although blacks, native Americans, and some Hispanics do lag behind, Cuban Americans do rather well in terms of socioeconomic status, and Chinese Americans and Japanese Americans are among the best-educated groups in our country. This documents the complexity of the racial and ethnic experience in the United States.

World to the persisting barriers to advancement that confront some black, Hispanic, and Asian Americans today. More often than not, one group has tried to impose its own way of life on other groups. The hostility that has characterized American race and ethnic relations is epitomized by derogatory epithets such as *coon, wetback, honky, beaner, wop, mick, hymie,* and innumerable others. Events such as the civil rights movement during the 1950s and 1960s, the violent race riots of the 1960s and early 1970s, the race riots of Miami and a few other American cities in the 1980s, and finally the highly destructive riot in south central Los Angeles in 1992, all document why race and ethnic relations persist in being regarded as a social problem in the United States.

Characteristics such as race and ethnicity are called *ascribed statuses* because they are assigned to

people and represent social positions over which people have little or no say about occupying. Whether the people occupying these statuses like it or not, such positions can and do serve as the basis for unequal treatment of groups, functioning as criteria for allocating resources and determining life chances and life-styles. Such groups are referred to by sociologists as minority groups, and a discussion of what constitutes a minority group is our first topic in this chapter.

MINORITY GROUPS

A **minority group** is *a group whose members are viewed by dominant groups as inferior, who have less access to power and resources than do other groups,* *and who are accorded fewer rights, privileges, and opportunities* (Marden, Meyer, and Engel, 1992). Black, Hispanic, Vietnamese, and some white ethnic groups such as rural Appalachians are considered minority groups because each has lower levels of educational and occupational attainment than other groups, and each has borne the brunt of considerable hostility. In Chapter 7, we will see that despite their numerical majority in our population, women are also considered a minority group because they have been denied equal access to education, jobs, and important positions that men have controlled for some time. Then, in Chapter 8, we will consider the plight of the young and the old in our society, who can also be considered minorities because they are sometimes exploited and deprived of rights and privileges because of their age. In this chapter, however, we focus only on minorities whose disadvantaged status arises from their racial or ethnic group membership. The key to understanding racial conflict is the differential power that exists between groups, and that power must be viewed in terms of economic, social, and political resources (Stone, 1985).

The term *minority group,* then, refers not to numerical size but to one's position in the stratification system of society. A rather extreme case of a numerically large group of people being dominated by a much smaller group can be found in South Africa's traditional system of *apartheid* (Adam and Moodley, 1986). About 85 percent of South Africa's population is made up of black Africans. Under *apartheid,* these people had virtually no power, and a system of legal segregation maintained a rigid separation between the social worlds of blacks and whites. Blacks could not vote, they received extremely limited educations, they were restricted to certain occupations, their travel in their own country was rigidly controlled, and they could live only in certain designated areas. The dominant group in South Africa has been the white Afrikaners, a small group of descendants of early Dutch or Huguenot immigrants, who possessed virtual control over the political, economic, and social life of South Africa. Although change has been occurring in South Africa in the 1990s, as recently as the late 1980s black South Africans could not vote for central government candidates, residential and school segregation still existed, and legislation placed 87 percent of South African land in white hands. These arrangements made South Africa one of the most rigidly stratified societies in the world. As we saw in Chapter 5, social stratification refers to the ranking of people into a hierarchy in which the resources considered valuable by society are unequally distributed. Ascribed characteristics such as race and ethnicity often determine a person's position in the stratification system. But the terms *race* and *ethnicity* can be easily misunderstood.

Race and Ethnicity

People use the term *race* quite freely and often with only a vague understanding of its precise meaning. Although we think of races as biologically distinct groups of people, it is sometimes difficult to say which biological characteristics distinguish one race from another because there has been so much interbreeding among the races throughout human history. Indeed, if we were to take a representative group of people from two different races in the United States, it would be difficult to determine, based on visible physical characteristics, where one race left off and the other began. However, although the biological reality of race may be hazy, its social reality is not. In fact, sociologists' definition of race is based on people's belief in racial differences: A **race** is *a group of people who are believed to be a biological group sharing genetically transmitted traits that are defined as important.* Thus, race is a social category because in our society, as in others, people make important distinctions between people on the basis of such presumed biological differences, even when these variations are actually vague or nonexistent.

An **ethnic group** is *a people who share a common historical and cultural heritage and sense of group identity and belongingness.* Groups that share distinctive cultural traits such as a common language, national origin, religion, or a sense of historical heritage have been a major source of diversity that has enriched all of our lives. Hispanic Americans, Polish Americans, gypsies, the Amish, and the Jews are but a few of the many ethnic groups in the United States that have made significant contributions to our way of life. On the other hand, much of the tension, conflict, and violence that have been part and parcel of America's history and still characterize social life today have focused on ethnic differences.

Racism

The subordination and oppression of minority groups is commonly supported by an ideology that assumes that members of the minority are innately inferior and thus deserving of their subordinate status. **Racism** is *the view that certain racial or ethnic groups are biologically inferior and that practices involving their domination and exploitation are therefore justified.* Racist ideologies in Nazi Germany justified genocidal attacks on the Jews, just as racism in America has been at the core of discrimination against blacks, Asians, and other racial groups. For example, in 1979, five social activists, mostly black, were killed in Greensboro, North Carolina, by a group of Nazis and Ku Klux Klan members, motivated in part by racist beliefs, who were later acquitted of murder charges in the slayings (Wheaton, 1987). In 1989, a black teenager was killed by a group of whites in New York because they thought that he was dating a white girl from their neighborhood.

Despite our highest hopes about equality, racism still persists in some parts of the United States. At this point in our discussion, we need to understand how this kind of ideology arises and, in particular, how prejudice and discrimination develop and affect minority groups.

In the 1980s and 1990s, white supremacist groups, such as the Ku Klux Klan, neo-nazis, and skinheads, have continued to find support among some Americans. This illustrates the extent to which racism still persists in the United States.

SOURCES OF PREJUDICE AND DISCRIMINATION

Prejudice and discrimination are closely intertwined, so much so that people are likely to view them as the same thing. In reality, they are quite distinct. A **prejudice** is *a negative attitude toward certain people based solely on their membership in a particular group* (Levin and Levin, 1982). Individuals are "prejudged" on the basis of whatever undesirable characteristics the whole group is presumed to possess. **Discrimination,** on the other hand, refers to *behavior, particularly unequal treatment of people because they are members of a particular group.* The type of discrimination we are most concerned with is the denial of equal access to resources, privileges, or opportunities, practices that are often based on illogical and irrational grounds.

The relationship between prejudice and discrimination is complex. Although they are likely to go together, Robert K. Merton (1949) has demonstrated that sometimes they do not. In fact, people may combine prejudice and discrimination in four different ways. The most desirable combination, from the point of view of American political and social values, is the *unprejudiced nondiscriminator* who accepts other racial or ethnic groups in both belief and practice. The *prejudiced discriminator,* on the other hand, has negative feelings toward a particular group and translates these sentiments into unequal treatment of people in that group. Members of the Ku Klux Klan, for example, have a strong prejudice against blacks and members of other racial groups; they advocate segregated schools and neighborhoods. These first two possibilities involve a consistency between belief and practice, but there are other possibilities. The *prejudiced nondiscriminator* is a kind of "closet bigot" who is prejudiced against members of some groups but does not translate these attitudes into discriminatory practices. A landlord, for example, may be prejudiced against Asian Americans, yet still rents apartments to them because of laws forbidding housing discrimination. Because there are now many laws against discrimination that are strictly enforced, the incidence of this kind of relationship between prejudice and discrimination is likely to increase. The *unprejudiced discriminator* treats the members of some groups unequally because it is convenient or advantageous to do so rather than out of personal antipathy toward them. Salespeople in a real estate agency, for example, may have no personal prejudices but still decline to show houses in certain neighborhoods to blacks because of the prejudices of people who already live in those neighborhoods.

Next we will review the major sources of prejudice and discrimination and then look at some of their consequences—the factors that lead them to be viewed as social problems.

Social Sources

Problems of poverty and discrimination are closely linked because the result of discrimination is often that minorities are poor, with little access to valued resources. Because of this, prejudice and discrimination can be understood in part through the theoretical explanations of wealth and poverty presented in Chapter 5: the functionalist, conflict, and interactionist perspectives. We will not repeat that discussion here. Instead, we will discuss some additional elements of the perspectives that apply especially well to problems of prejudice and discrimination.

Ethnocentrism. **Ethnocentrism** is *the tendency to view one's own group or culture as an in-group that follows the best and the only proper way to live.* An **in-group** is *a group that we feel positively toward and identify with, and that produces a "we feeling."* Feeling positively about one's own group, of course, is good because it gives one a sense of belonging and self-worth. For functionalists, ethnocentrism is functional because it produces loyalty, cohesiveness, and strong group ties. All this helps groups stick together and achieve their goals. It can, however, lead one to believe that other groups—especially those that are very different—have unfavorable characteristics. If one's own way of life is the only proper way to live, it seems that other life-styles are improper. This can be used to justify unfair, hostile, and even genocidal attacks on other groups. Under Adolf Hitler, for example, the Nazis were so thoroughly convinced of the superiority of the alleged Aryan "race" that the Jews became a despised out-group. Likewise, many American colonists believed that their European heritage contained all that was wise and desirable, and these racist beliefs fueled their treatment of native Americans in the New World. So if ethnocentrism gets out of hand, it can become dysfunctional and create social disorganization in the form of hostility, conflict, and discrimination, which can threaten the social order. Although ethnocentrism can have these negative consequences, according to functionalists, such outcomes are not inevitable if people are aware of and guard against them.

Competition.   According to the conflict perspective, prejudice and discrimination arise when groups find themselves in competition with each other. This competition is often economic, for jobs or land, but it can also be based on noneconomic valued resources, such as access to attractive marriage partners or the right to practice a preferred religion. The more intensely groups compete, the more threatening each group becomes to the other and the more likely negative and hostile views are to emerge. When there are obvious differences between the groups, such as in skin color or religious practices, these can become the focus of prejudice. Discriminatory practices may emerge, sanctioned by law or custom, as a way to limit the access of the less powerful group to the scarce resources. Prejudice and discrimination can arise from competitive situations in a number of specific ways.

One type of competitive situation has been called a split labor market by sociologist Edna Bonacich (Bonacich, 1972). A **split labor market** is *one in which there are two groups of workers willing to do the same work, but for different wages.* In a split labor market, lower-priced laborers have a competitive advantage because employers prefer to hire them. Higher-priced workers find their position threatened by those willing to work more cheaply. In such a situation, the higher-priced workers will be inclined to discriminate against the inexpensive laborers in an effort to exclude them from certain occupations. Bonacich argues that this is a key factor in much racial, ethnic, and sexual antagonism because the presumed biological differences between the two groups can serve as the focus of discrimination and can be justified on racist grounds. If people believe that members of a particular racial group are lazy or untrust-

worthy, then this is a rationale for excluding them from jobs that demand hard work and trustworthiness. Likewise, if people believe that women are best suited for clerical and secretarial positions, then this belief can be used to discriminate against them when they try to get more lucrative jobs in construction or the professions (Cheng and Bonacich, 1984; Boswell, 1986).

Another type of economic competition is one in which a powerful group exploits a weaker one for its own gain. A clear case of this would be the relationship between the slaveholder and the slave in which the former gains substantially from the relationship, to the detriment of the latter. Slavery in the United States was clearly a form of economic exploitation supported by racist beliefs about the inferiority of blacks. Many of the poor today suffer a similar kind of exploitation because their work at low-paying and demeaning jobs benefits the more affluent in society (see Chapter 5). A variant of this type of exploitation is **internal colonialism,** in which *a subordinate group provides cheap labor that benefits the dominant group and is then further exploited by having to purchase expensive goods and services from the dominant group* (Doob, 1993). For example, the poor in the United States not only provide cheap labor but also purchase expensive health care, televisions, food, and other products that provide substantial profit to dominant groups.

Socialization.   Once patterns of prejudice and discrimination arise, they become incorporated into the values and norms of the group. Prejudice and discrimination toward particular groups then become legitimated, transmitted to new members through the socialization process, and frequently internalized (Blalock, 1982). A study of regional differences in prejudice toward blacks during the 1960s, for example, found, not surprisingly, that there was greater prejudice in the South, especially within the states of the old Confederacy (Middleton, 1976). It also found, however, that people who lived in the South as children and then moved to other regions were less prejudiced than those who remained in the South. In the same way, people who grew up outside the South and then moved there were more prejudiced than those who remained outside the South. In other words, people tend to adopt the prejudiced beliefs, values, and norms that are considered appropriate in the groups they belong to.

Institutionalized Discrimination.   Prejudice and discrimination sometimes become incorporated into social policies and practices, and this can result in the perpetuation of prejudice and discrimination through **institutionalized discrimination:** *the inequitable treatment of a group resulting from practices or policies that are incorporated into social, political, or economic institutions and that operate independently from the prejudices of individuals.* One form of institutionalized discrimination is the use of physical size requirements as qualifications for certain jobs. Many police departments, for example, set minimum height requirements for police officers. Asian Americans have protested against this because Asians are, on the average, shorter than whites and many therefore cannot qualify for police work. Discrimination in this form is not direct; people are not excluded from jobs because of their race. Rather, it is the minimum entrance requirements that effectively bar most members of a particular minority group from the jobs while serving as a barrier to only a few people in the dominant group. Through institutionalized discrimination, social inequality can persist long after prejudicial attitudes may have changed. In fact, much of the civil rights effort in the United States over the past thirty years has been concentrated on eliminating this kind of discrimination.

Psychological Sources

A number of psychological factors can play a part in the emergence of prejudice and discrimination.

Stereotyping.   One psychological factor involves the human tendency to categorize. The physical and social world is sufficiently complex

that we need to simplify it by thinking in terms of general categories or by lumping together the elements that have something in common. Categories, however, can become *stereotypes*—rigid and oversimplified images in which each element or person in a category is assumed to possess all the characteristics associated with that category (Lippman, 1922). Because some Jews work in banking, for example, some people might assume that all Jews are proficient in financial matters. Thus, stereotyping can contribute to prejudice and discrimination.

Frustration and Aggression.   Prejudice and discrimination can arise when people become frustrated by their inability to achieve sought-after goals. Psychologists have shown that frustration can lead to aggression in both overt and covert forms (Dollard et al., 1939; Berkowitz, 1971). Aggression can be expressed by direct physical assaults or through prejudice or discrimination. One form this aggression can take is *scapegoating,* or placing the blame for one's troubles on an individual or group incapable of offering effective resistance. This happened, for example, in the American South between 1880 and 1930 when thousands of blacks were lynched by angry mobs of whites, many of whom were suffering from unemployment or other economic difficulties. Such racial hatred and discrimination can serve as a form of release for frustrated people, offering the hope, however false, that they are attacking the true source of their difficulties.

The Authoritarian Personality.   Another psychological approach has been to search for personality types that are more prone toward prejudice and discrimination. For example, motivated by the dread that the events of Hitler's Germany in the 1930s might occur again, a group of social scientists initiated a research project that ultimately found a series of personality characteristics, now called the authoritarian personality, that tend to be associated with prejudice (Adorno et al., 1950). The **authoritarian personality** is characterized by *a rigid adherence to conventional life-*

styles and values, admiration of power and toughness in interpersonal relationships, submission to authority, cynicism, and emphasis on obedience, and a fear of things that are different. Authoritarians tend to be suspicious, anti-intellectual, and insecure about their own self-worth. They are also likely to be conformists and upset by ambiguities, preferring a world characterized by absolutes with few gray areas. Numerous studies over the years have documented the link between authoritarianism and prejudice. Furthermore, this relationship has been discovered in many cultural contexts, such as white prejudice against blacks, Arab prejudice against Jews, and Israeli prejudice against Arabs (Hanson, 1975; Heaven and Furnham, 1987; Dekker and Ester, 1991; Kluegel and Bobo, 1991).

The sources of prejudice and discrimination are complex, resulting from the intertwining of numerous sociological and psychological factors. Most sociologists hold that social factors such as ethnocentrism, competition, socialization, and institutionalized discrimination play the most important roles in that these "set the stage" for the operation of psychological mechanisms. Without this social underpinning, prejudice and discrimination resulting from the psychological mechanisms alone would likely be sporadic and unorganized. Unfortunately, the social sources of prejudice and discrimination are all too often present, and the consequences can be devastating to both society and individuals.

Consequences of Discrimination

Prejudice by itself can be relatively harmless, but it can become destructive when it fuels discrimination. Discrimination marks the spot where the social problems surrounding race and ethnic relations begin. In modern societies, discrimination against minorities has had a detrimental impact, although some groups benefit in the short run. First and most important, discrimination forces some groups into a disadvantageous position in the stratification system and adversely affects their life chances. We saw in Chapter 4 that discrimi-

nation results in higher rates of illness, injury, and death for minorities. In this chapter, we will see that most minorities in American society enjoy fewer socioeconomic resources and opportunities than do members of dominant white groups. Because our society's ideology holds out the promise that all can share in the American dream, being deprived of these opportunities can produce simmering resentments that periodically erupt in destructive violence.

A second consequence of discrimination is its effects on people's views of themselves. Those who feel the brunt of discrimination may come to accept the devalued and stigmatized view of themselves that is implied by their being powerless and on the bottom of society. Minority youth, for example, often have more negative self-concepts and a poorer sense of self-worth than do nonminority youth. This does not always occur, and the negative consequences can be overcome by supportive families, high-quality schools, and a minority culture that insulates people from the negativism implied by low social standing. Yet the research is clear that racism can and does result in lower self-esteem among minorities in some contexts (Pallas et al., 1990; Martinez and Dukes, 1991). And people with negative views of themselves and their worth may contribute less to American society, and may well detract from social order and contribute to existing social problems through criminal behavior, long-term poverty, domestic violence, child neglect, and the like.

A third consequence of discrimination is that it creates tense and hostile encounters between dominant and minority group members, thus inhibiting trust, communication, and cooperation (Poskocil, 1977). In settings such as school or the workplace where members of different groups interact, discrimination makes it difficult for people to work together. For example, racial clashes have plagued the American military, and these clashes make it more difficult to develop a cohesive, coordinated, and effective military organization. In a relevant investigation, sociologist Albert Szymanski (1976) reported that white workers in

America actually lose economically rather than gain from discrimination against nonwhite workers. The reason for this is that discrimination increases hostility and reduces the possibility of cooperation between lower-paid whites and nonwhites, making it more difficult for either group to work toward better economic conditions for themselves. Collective action on the part of whites and nonwhites, such as unionization, becomes less feasible when the two groups are split from one another by hostility.

A final consequence of discrimination is that it can undermine our social and political values and institutions. Because America professes to value equality and human dignity, the violation of these values because of racism and discrimination can generate cynicism regarding our political and economic institutions. It can also threaten the legitimacy of those institutions if people see them merely as tools to benefit those fortunate enough to have acquired some power in society. From the functionalist perspective, this may represent the most serious of trends to combat—when people begin to lose faith in the system's core values and foundation, that system's survival may be in jeopardy.

With this understanding of prejudice and discrimination and their consequences, it is time to look at how these factors affect different minority groups in our society. The situation is not a pretty one nor one of which we can be very proud. Keep in mind that there are racial and ethnic groups that do not receive treatment here, as we will focus on those that are the largest numerically or have encountered some of the most severe problems.

RACIAL AND ETHNIC MINORITIES IN AMERICA

The United States is, of course, a land of immigrants. The only difference between groups in this regard is the time of their arrival. Even the group with the deepest roots in American soil, who claim the title "native" Americans, are descendants of immigrants who traversed the Bering Straits land bridge from Asia to the Americas tens of thousands of years ago. Beyond immigrant status, however, there is considerable variation in the positions of racial and ethnic groups in the United States today. Their treatment today and in the past illustrates how prejudice and discrimination have functioned in our own history and helps to illuminate how race and ethnic relations represent a social problem.

African Americans

African Americans comprise the largest nonwhite minority group in the United States, numbering approximately thirty million, or about 12.4 percent of our total population in 1990 (U.S. Bureau of the Census, 1992). They are also one of the oldest minority groups, with the first blacks arriving from Africa in 1619, not long after the first permanent European settlers in the New World. They are also the only minority group to have been enslaved in the United States. When the British colonized the New World, they followed the practices of the Spanish and Portuguese before them in bringing black African slaves to the New World (Westermann, 1955; Phillips, 1963). Black Africans were particularly vulnerable to slavery because many of them lived in small, isolated tribes and were unable to protect themselves against more formidable foes. In fact, some of the larger African tribes, such as the Ashanti, actually sold other Africans into slavery (Sowell, 1981).

Technically, all blacks in America gained their freedom with the end of the Civil War. However, after a short period during which African Americans exercised a degree of freedom and political control, white southerners began to reassert their dominance when federal troops left the South in 1877. In 1896, the Supreme Court ruled in *Plessy v. Ferguson* that it was constitutional to provide "separate but equal" public facilities for members of different races, and the era of widespread legal segregation began. For six decades, the *Plessy* case served as the foundation for discrimination against African Americans in schools, housing, and other areas. During this sixty-year period of time, a split labor market in black–white relations prevailed in America (Marks, 1981). Because of deteriorating race relations after the *Plessy* decision and economic distress in the South, a massive migration of young southern blacks to eastern and midwestern cities began. This was the beginning of large black ghettos in cities such as New York, Detroit, Boston, and Chicago. These concentrations of blacks in cities would later serve as an important mobilizing element in the efforts of blacks to gain equality.

The 1950s and 1960s were a period of considerable change in the lives of African Americans. In the *Brown v. The Board of Education* decision of 1954, the U.S. Supreme Court ruled that the separate but equal doctrine was unconstitutional. The southern states were ordered to integrate their schools "with all deliberate speed," but this process turned out to be rather slow. However, the civil rights movement emerged and, along with more militant black groups, initiated a drive for more economic and social opportunities for blacks. Out of the demonstrations, protests, and rioting came the Civil Rights Act of 1964 and the Voting Rights Act of 1965. Later, affirmative-action programs and school busing would be used to provide greater opportunities for blacks in America.

The position of blacks in America has improved substantially over the past three decades. For example, the number of blacks enrolled in college has increased six times since 1960, whereas enrollment of whites has only tripled (U.S. Bureau of the Census, 1991: 157, 256). The number of blacks in professional occupations also increased at a much faster rate than among whites. The percentage of blacks registered to vote has doubled, and the number of blacks holding elected political office has increased by five times.

The current picture, however, is by no means one of unblemished progress because blacks still lag behind many other groups in terms of access to education, power, and economically rewarding jobs (see Tables 6.1 and 6.2). For example, al-

Table 6.1   **Educational Attainment, by Race or Ethnicity, Among People Twenty-Five Years Old and Older, 1960–1991**

Educational Level	Group	1960	1970	1991
Percentage completing less than five years of school	Whites	6.7	4.5	2.0
	Blacks	23.8	14.6	4.7
	Hispanics	NA*	19.5	12.5
Percentage completing four years of high school or more	Whites	43.2	54.6	79.9
	Blacks	20.1	31.5	66.7
	Hispanics	NA*	32.1	51.3
Median school years completed	Whites	10.9	12.1	12.8
	Blacks	8.0	9.8	12.4
	Hispanics	NA*	9.1	12.0

*Data not available

SOURCES: U.S. Bureau of the Census, *Statistical Abstract of the United States, 1989* (Washington, D.C.: U.S. Government Printing Office, 1989), p. 131; U.S. Bureau of the Census, *Statistical Abstract of the United States, 1992* (Washington, D.C.: U.S. Government Printing Office, 1992), p. 144.

Table 6.2   **Income of White, Black, and Hispanic Families, 1960–1990**

Year	Median Income			Ratio of Black to White Income	Ratio of Hispanic to White Income
	White	Black	Hispanic		
1960	$ 5,835	$ 3,230	NA*	.55	
1965	7,251	3,993	NA*	.55	
1970	10,236	6,279	NA*	.61	
1975	14,268	8,779	$ 9,551	.61	.67
1980	21,904	12,674	14,716	.58	.67
1985	29,152	16,786	19,027	.58	.65
1990	36,915	21,423	23,431	.58	.63

*Data not available

SOURCE: U.S. Bureau of the Census, *Statistical Abstract of the United States, 1992* (Washington, D.C.: U.S. Government Printing Office, 1992), p. 451.

though the average income of blacks has climbed in the past thirty years, so has the income of white people, and the position of blacks relative to that of whites has changed very little. The ratio of black income to white income is virtually the same as it was thirty years ago. Although channels of mobility are open to some blacks, others are trapped in poverty or in occupations that offer little prestige or hope for advancement (see Chapter 5). In 1990, for example, the number of blacks in poverty was actually higher than it had been in 1965, with the poverty rate being three times as high for blacks as for whites (U.S. Bureau of the Census, 1992). In addition, although blacks now constitute a larger proportion of suburban populations than ever before, this appears to be the result of "spill-over," in which housing in the central city is torn down, forcing blacks to move to the inner ring of the suburbs that are adjacent to the city. Relatively few blacks move into previously all-white, suburban neighborhoods (Clark, 1988).

Improvement for blacks has been difficult for a number of reasons, and these are analyzed in the Policy Issues insert in this chapter. However, a clearly overriding factor is the fact that prejudice and discrimination against African Americans have been deeply embedded in American history since the period of slavery and, although improvements have occurred, racism is still a powerful force in the United States (Harvey, 1991; Hacker, 1992). As just one recent illustration of this, a report published in 1991 documented persisting discrimination against black Americans attempting to rent or purchase a home ("Study Finds . . . , 1991). Researchers sent a black person and a white person, with the same income and educational levels, to inquire about the same housing. In over half of the cases, the black person experienced discrimination by being told the housing was no longer available when it actually was available, being charged more rent, being shown fewer housing units, or being steered to housing in predominantly minority neighborhoods. Clearly, as this and other research shows, African Americans are still not treated equally, nor are their opportunities the same as those for white Americans.

Hispanic Americans

Hispanic Americans, or Latinos, are Americans whose ancestral home is Central America, South America, or the Caribbean. They include Mexican Americans (Chicanos), Cubans, and Puerto Ricans. In 1990 there were twenty-two million Hispanic Americans in the United States, or about 9 percent of our population. There are also an estimated three to six million Hispanics in the United States illegally.

The largest Hispanic group in the United States, 62.5 percent of the total, is the Mexican Americans (see Figure 6.1). This group has a long history of settlement in the United States (Moore, 1976; Acuna, 1987). In fact, there have been Spanish communities located throughout what is now the American Southwest since before Mexican independence from Spain in 1821. However, as the white population in the Southwest grew during the 1800s, the economic prospects for these early settlers declined. Light-skinned, pure Spanish settlers who had adopted the white lifestyle were accepted into the white world, but the darker-skinned settlers who maintained their heritage, especially those with some Indian heritage, were viewed as inferiors and bore the brunt of prejudice and discrimination (Vigil, 1980). Following the Mexican Revolution in 1909, hundreds of thousands of Mexican peasants migrated to the Southwest, where there was much demand for inexpensive labor because of expanding agriculture and railroads. The status of these more recent migrants to the United States, how-ever, was low, although perhaps slightly higher than it had been in Mexico. The Depression of the 1930s resulted in a decline in farm work, driving many Mexican Americans into the cities to seek employment or public relief. The first urban barrios, or Spanish-speaking neighborhoods, began to spring up in such cities as Denver, Phoenix, and Los Angeles.

Since World War II, the position of Mexican Americans has changed substantially. First, their numbers have grown steadily because of a continuing stream of migrants from Mexico and a high birthrate among Mexican Americans. By 1980, this group made up almost 20 percent of the California population and had larger concentrations in many urban areas in the Southwest: 62 percent of El Paso residents, for example, were of Spanish heritage. Second, in part as an outgrowth of the civil rights movement, the Chicano movement gained support in the 1960s in championing the rights of all Hispanics. Cesar Chavez organized the United Farm Workers to fight for better pay and working conditions for Chicano farm workers, and Reyes Lopez Tijerina started *La Alianza Federal de Mercedes* to demand the return to Chicanos of land in the Southwest deeded to their ancestors in the Treaty of Guadalupe Hidalgo in 1848.

In the past two decades, Mexican American efforts have focused more on conventional politics and consciousness raising than on confrontation. A number of Chicano organizations, such as the Mexican American Political Alliance (MAPA) in California, were founded in the 1960s and continue to be powerful forces on the political scene, pursuing the interests of Mexican Americans as a group. Consciousness raising and ethnic awareness have been encouraged by Chicano student organizations in high schools and colleges and by pressures for bilingual education in communities with large concentrations of Mexican Americans (Lucas, 1981). What has emerged is a more complex form of Chicano identity sometimes called Chicanozaje or Chicanismo, a historical awareness that Chicanos have a multiple heritage

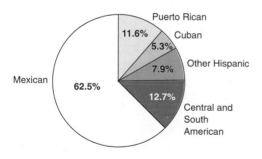

Figure 6.1 **Percentage Distribution of Hispanic Americans by Type of Spanish Origin, 1991**
SOURCE: U.S. Bureau of the Census, *Statistical Abstract of United States, 1992* (Washington, D.C.: U.S. Government Printing office, 1992), p. 41.

As this parade in Chicago illustrates, Hispanic Americans are one of the more prominent ethnic minorities in the United States.

containing native American, Spanish, Mexican, and Anglo elements (Bacalski-Martinez, 1979; Schaefer, 1993). There is a growing recognition that their present-day culture has been shaped by their heritage as well as by their experiences as an oppressed minority in America.

Puerto Rican Americans are the second largest Hispanic group in the United States, comprising 11.6 percent of all Hispanics. Puerto Ricans were granted American citizenship, as a group, in 1917. A small number of Puerto Ricans immigrated to the mainland United States before World War II, mostly attracted by farm labor jobs but a few by factory work in the East. Following World War II, this immigration increased dramatically, in large part because of the chronically depressed economy of Puerto Rico. Puerto Ricans have tended to settle in New York City and Chicago (Fitzpatrick, 1987).

Mexican Americans and Puerto Rican Americans today face much the same problems as African Americans: poverty, low educational levels, and poor health in comparison to Anglos (see Ta-

ble 6.1 and 6.2 and Figure 6.2). In 1989, for example, 43.2 percent of the Puerto Rican families in the United States were living in poverty, and just 51 percent of Americans of Spanish origin had completed four years of high school or more, whereas 79 percent of whites had done so. As with African Americans, the incomes of Hispanic families have persistently lagged behind those of white families, remaining at less than 70 percent of white incomes for the past twenty years.

Latinos in the United States today are a diverse group. In addition to the variation among groups already mentioned, for example, Cuban Americans have generally been different from other Latinos in that they come from more middle-class and affluent origins. Despite their diversity, some Latino groups may be moving toward a more common Latino ethnic identity and consciousness (Totti, 1987). Being of a different color, having a common origin in the "south," speaking a common tongue, many sharing the experience of discrimination and outsider status—all this may be forging an ethnic awareness that spans across the

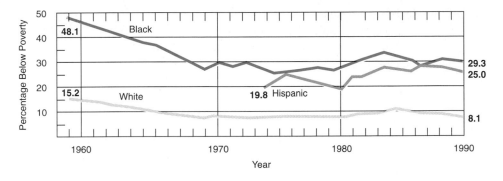

Figure 6.2   Percentage of American Families with Incomes Below the Poverty Level, by Race, 1959–1990
SOURCE: U.S. Bureau of the Census, *Statistical Abstract of the United States, 1992* (Washington, D.C.: U.S. Government Printing Office, 1992), p. 459.

diversity found in such Hispanic groups as Mexican Americans and Puerto Rican Americans. In addition, groups such as the League of United Latin American Citizens and the Latino Urban Political Association have recognized that Latinos—who may soon be the largest ethnic minority in the United States—can become an effective force for political and social change if they can get beyond their differences and combine their forces.

Native Americans

During the fifteenth and sixteenth centuries, there were probably between one million and ten million native Americans living in North America (Snipp, 1989). By the late 1800s, there were only about 250,000. After the founding of America, the federal government was required by the U.S. Constitution to negotiate treaties with native American groups, but this did not prevent whites from robbing Indians of their land. In 1824, the Bureau of Indian Affairs (BIA) was created by Congress as a division of the War Department to seek a military solution to what many Congressmen referred to as the "Indian problem." By 1830, Congress succumbed to pressures for opening up more Indian lands to white settlement and

ordered the BIA to relocate all Indians west of the Mississippi River. It was not until 1924 that Congress passed the Indian Citizenship Act, granting U.S. citizenship to all native Americans. In 1968, Congress enacted the Indian Civil Rights Act, which extended the basic human rights guaranteed by the Bill of Rights to persons living on tribal lands. Although this undoubtedly had many positive benefits, it may have had the negative effect of undermining tribal control and unity among native American groups who possessed their own judicial systems based on tribal customs (Schaefer, 1993).

By 1990, there were 2.1 million native Americans in the United States (U.S. Bureau of the Census, 1992: 16). In 1983, 2.3 percent of American land, fifty-three million acres, was still being managed by the Bureau of Indian Affairs "on behalf of" native Americans. In 1980, there were 350,000 American Indians, Eskimos, and Aleuts living on reservations in the United States (Thornton, 1987). The BIA, now part of the Department of the Interior, has conservation as its prime directive rather than economic development. This deemphasis on economic matters has contributed to the problems of native Americans by making it more difficult for them to improve their economic position (Guillemin, 1980).

Native Americans suffer significant social, economic, and health disadvantages in comparison to other ethnic and racial groups (Sandefur and Sakamoto, 1988; Snipp, 1989). Nonreservation Indians are somewhat better off than their reservation counterparts, but half of all Indians live on reservations that are in rural areas. They suffer high levels of unemployment, low levels of income, and poverty rates disproportionate to their numbers in the population. They are also less likely to graduate from high school than people in most other groups. A comprehensive survey in the 1990s of adolescents attending school in reservation communities serviced by the Indian Health Service documented the extensiveness of these problems (Blum et al., 1992). When compared with rural white adolescents, the native American youth were much more likely to be in poor health, suffer sexual abuse, attempt suicide, commit suicide, eat a poor diet, and suffer severe emotional distress.

We have seen that the 1960s were years when many minority groups began to resist oppression, and native Americans were among them. In 1969, a group of Indians seized Alcatraz Island to call attention to their exploitation. In 1973, members of the American Indian Movement (AIM) staged an armed takeover of Wounded Knee, South Dakota, where thousands of native Americans had been killed by whites in the late nineteenth century. These protests may be in part responsible for some recent court decisions ruling that Indian tribes should receive payment for land taken from their ancestors during the nineteenth century. Still, there is a lingering feeling among many native Americans that exploitation continues, albeit in more subtle ways than before (Prucha, 1985).

Asian Americans

Between 1820 and 1970, more than one million legal immigrants from China, Japan, the Philippines, Hong Kong, Korea, and India came to America—a mere 3.7 percent of all immigration taking place during that period (Daniels, 1988).

The heaviest migration of Chinese to the United States occurred between 1849 and 1882. Although racial prejudices existed toward the Chinese prior to 1849, once their immigration began in large numbers, these sentiments intensified. There was a feeling among many Americans that the Chinese would deprive whites of jobs in mining and railroading, another illustration of the split labor market discussed earlier. These feelings culminated in the Chinese Exclusion Act of 1882, which prohibited the entrance of Chinese laborers into the United States for ten years.

Between 1882 and World War II, racist attitudes in America characterized the Chinese as a "yellow peril." Many Chinese returned to their own country because of this hostility. Those who remained were forced to move to ghettos called Chinatowns, where many people of Chinese descent still live today. Chinese people were often referred to with the pejorative term *coolies,* and the racism toward Chinese often implied biological differences between Chinese and Anglos. An anthropological study in 1877, for example, concluded, "It is true that ethnologists declare that a brain capacity of less than 85 cubic inches is unfit for free government, which is considerably above that of the coolie as it is below that of the Caucasian" (quoted in Miller, 1969: 145).

These anti-Chinese attitudes persisted in the United States until the 1940s. Following Japan's attack on Pearl Harbor, hostilities shifted to Japan, and the Chinese came to be regarded in a more positive way. In 1943, the Chinese remaining in the United States were granted citizenship. Between 1950 and 1970, Chinese Americans became upwardly mobile, with children of the original immigrants attending colleges and universities and moving into professional and technical positions. Today, the socioeconomic status of Chinese Americans is considerably above the average for Americans as a whole (Hirschman and Wong, 1981, 1986).

The peak period of Japanese immigration to the United States began after the Chinese Exclusion Act between 1880 and 1924. Unlike the

Chinese, Japanese immigrants were permitted to bring their wives with them, which aided in the formation of stable Japanese families, and early relations between Americans and the Japanese were positive. After Pearl Harbor, Japanese Americans were the object of considerable discrimination, being forced to sell their property and interned in concentration camps (Kitano, 1976; Hohri, 1987). Along with the enslavement of blacks and the genocidal attacks on native Americans, the imprisonment of Japanese Americans—none of whom had been proven disloyal to America—stands as one of the darkest examples of racism in America.

After release from the concentration camps, Japanese Americans led successful lives, exceeding many whites in occupational achievements, and most Americans appear to have a high regard for Japanese Americans today (Petersen, 1966; Ima, 1982). Still, there are occasional flare-ups of the racism that was so prevalent during World War II.

Significant immigration from Asia to the United States has continued in recent decades. For example, in the 1970s and 1980s, tens of thousands of refugees entered the United States from Vietnam, Laos, and Cambodia as well as Japan, China, the Philippines, and other parts of Asia (Daniels, 1990). These recent immigrants have largely followed the route of their predecessors as far as integrating themselves into the United States, taking undesirable jobs that most American workers tend to reject or opening small businesses to make a living. Although there is little widespread discrimination against Asian immigrants, violence does occur. In the 1992 riot in south central Los Angeles, for example, Korean-American businesses were apparently targeted for looting and burning by black and Hispanic rioters who were angry over what they perceived as mistreatment of blacks by Korean store owners. This reflects the economic sources of racial discrimination and conflict discussed earlier. Blacks and Hispanics find themselves in a position of economic subordination to Korean store owners. This has led to stereotyping on both sides, with Koreans accusing blacks and Hispanics of stealing and blacks and Hispanics accusing Koreans of selling poor products at high prices and refusing to hire black or Hispanic employees. Exacerbating this situation is the fact that Koreans have little contact with blacks and Hispanics outside of this economic (merchant–customer) context. The importance of this situation is explored in more detail in the Applied Research insert (see pp. 218–219).

So the experiences of the various racial and ethnic groups in the United States have been quite variable. Some of the implications of this variation are discussed in the Policy Issues insert in this chapter.

Today's Immigrants

In 1965, a totally revamped immigration act removed all racial and ethnic quotas for immigrants to the United States. As a consequence of this and other trends, today's immigrants are quite unlike those of the past (see Figure 6.3). For most of our history, over three quarters of the immigrants have been from Europe, with very small proportions coming from Asia or Central and South America. Today, only 10 percent come from Europe, 42 percent come from Asia, and another 42 percent from Central and South America.

The data in Figure 6.3 include only people who are legal immigrants to the United States. They do not include tourists, those visiting relatives, and those here on business. Also excluded from those figures are those people who enter the United States illegally. It is difficult to know for sure how many illegal aliens there are in the United States, but most considered estimates place the number somewhere between four and eight million (Daniels, 1990). Most are from Central and South America, with about one-half crossing into the United States from Mexico. Most of these illegal immigrants are economic refugees, fleeing the squalor and poverty in their homelands. Some are hoping to remain permanently in the United States, although most plan

POLICY ISSUES

Economic Success Among Immigrants

The experiences of the various racial and ethnic groups in this country have been quite different. All have suffered from severe racism and discrimination. But some, such as Japanese and Chinese Americans, have become quite successful, whereas others, such as African Americans and Puerto Rican Americans, still lag behind on most indicators of socioeconomic status. Why the different outcomes? The answer to this lies, in part, in the cultural experiences of different groups.

The oppression of Japanese Americans has certainly been severe: incarceration in relocation camps during World War II without benefit of formal charges or a trial. They were considered a security threat, even though none of them was actually proven to be such a threat. Nonetheless, they were sent thousands of miles to bleak camps; many lost all their possessions, including home and property; some families were separated. This was clearly a racist operation because no Italians or Germans—including those who were aliens—were treated similarly. Yet despite such ill treatment, four decades later Japanese Americans are one of the best-educated groups in our country and have one of the highest median incomes of all groups. As a group they are solidly middle class.

What accounts for the rise of Japanese Americans since World War II? A good part of it has to do with the cultural context and heritage of Japanese Americans (Kitano, 1976, Shibutani, 1978). First, there is a work ethic in Japanese culture that is quite congruent with the values regarding work found in dominant groups in America. Thus, Japanese culture imbued Japanese Americans with

orientations that made it possible for them to gain an education or make money in America. Second, the Japanese family is highly valued, and family reputation and goals are regarded as more important than individual ones. Individuals gain a sense of self-worth from family membership, and they work hard to avoid bringing shame or disrepute to their family by their own failings. Individual success reflects positively on the family. Third, the Japanese who came to America never identified with the lower classes, even when living in poverty. They perceived themselves as successful and respectable, and they passed on middle-class expectations and aspirations to their children. They never developed the cultural orientation described in Chapter 5 that makes achievement more difficult. With a cultural heritage like this, young Japanese Americans were fairly well equipped to compete in various economic arenas if given the opportunity to do so.

So, the Japanese experience suggests that "cultural legacy" is the key factor: The values, skills, and traditions that people bring with them play a big part in their success. This has certainly also played a part in the experiences of some recent immigrant groups, such as Koreans, Vietnamese, Arabs, and Cubans. These immigrants often were part of the business and professional classes in their native lands, and this background endowed them with an entrepreneurial spirit, an educational background, or some business experience that made it easier for them to do well in this country. Yet cultural legacy does not always carry the day. For example, in Ireland and other European countries in earlier centuries, Protestants were generally more prosperous than Catholics. Yet Irish Catholic immigrants to the United States have done better than Irish Protestant immigrants (Jencks, 1992).

So, although cultural legacy can play an important part, we need to look at other factors, some of which may be unique to particular groups. One is the mutual aid organizations that spring up to provide support for immigrants. This played a role in the success of Irish Catholics as well as some recent immigrants. Koreans and some other recent immigrants, for instance, have been able to raise venture capital among friends and family within the ethnic community and sometimes from relatives in their native lands. In some cases, organized "investment clubs" emerge among an ethnic group to provide loans to start businesses. In other cases, immigrants have ties to the business community in their native lands, which provide them with information and support in starting a new business (Katz and Ryan, 1992).

Some differences between the experience of African Americans and that of other immigrant groups help explain why their struggle for success has been so difficult (Jencks, 1992). One is that, unlike most other immigrants, they came involuntarily. European immigrants saw migration as a new opportunity to be seized and planned to adapt and make it their home. Those who did not like it or did not do well could return home. Not so for African Americans. Many Africans were forcibly torn from their native lands with little regard for their culture or their heritage and were given no freedom to achieve or develop in the land to which they were brought. Slaves from many different cultural backgrounds were forced together. Slaves were strongly sanctioned for showing initiative or independence, and there was often little regard for the integrity of the black family. Whatever entrepreneurial spirit existed in their native cultures was largely destroyed during the slave experience.

A second difference is that African immigrants

had, at best, an ambivalence toward the legitimacy of the social and legal institutions that enslaved them. For many it was outright hostility and resentment. As a consequence, the African American culture that emerged incorporated this resentment and tolerated if not admired resistance to what some perceived as illegitimate social institutions. A third difference is that European immigrant groups, if they shed their ethnic heritage, could become "just plain Americans" and participate in the American success story. Because of visible differences, blacks were never allowed to do this and so there was less incentive to adopt mainstream culture. Fourth, the social and economic discrimination against blacks in the United States has been persistent and universal. In comparison, European immigrant groups could always find some niche where they could avoid discrimination and be rewarded based on their achievements. Finally, the mutual supports that some ethnic groups could offer their members have been almost nonexistent among African Americans. Living in poverty in the United States with no link to their native lands meant that there was nowhere to turn for investment loans or other supports.

So, the factors that lead to success among immigrant groups in the United States are complicated. We cannot assume that, because one group has made it, all have the same opportunities. Their historical experiences and current opportunities are so varied that the outcomes for each group must be considered separately. For African Americans, it has only been in the past few decades that the structures of racial discrimination and oppression have begun to be dismantled, and as we have seen, discrimination still persists in many forms. As these structures are further dismantled and a supportive cultural environment is allowed to emerge, the achievements of African Americans will likely improve. It takes time to overcome the ghastly legacy of our treatment of African Americans.

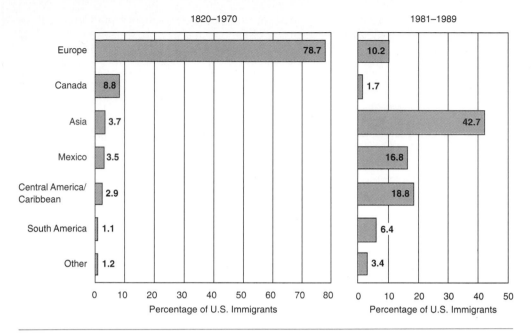

Figure 6.3   Immigrants to the United States, by Country of Last Permanent Residence, 1820–1989
SOURCES: U.S. Department of Justice, *1984 Statistical Yearbook of the Immigration and Naturalization Service* (Washington, D.C.: U.S. Government Printing Office, 1984), pp. 4–5; U.S. Bureau of the Census, *Statistical Abstract of the United States, 1991* (Washington, D.C.: U.S. Government Printing Office, 1991), p. 10.

to stay only for a short period and then return to their homelands. The United States currently has no policy to allow economic refugees to remain here. In 1986, Congress approved the Immigration Reform and Control Act, which made it possible for illegal aliens who entered the United States prior to January 1, 1982 to become legal residents, and, after two years of lawful temporary residence, to apply for American citizenship. Any other illegal entrants, however, if caught, are still deported. The reason for this is not so much a lack of sympathy as it is a fear that a policy of allowing illegal entrants to stay would open the floodgates to millions of people around the globe who are trying to improve their lives.

The impact of these economic refugees on our country is complex. On the one hand, they accept jobs that many Americans seem disinclined to do:

low-paying, back-breaking farm work, for example. In other words, they perform many of the functions, discussed in Chapter 5, that poor people have traditionally served. On the other hand, there is some concern that illegal aliens also take some jobs that Americans may be willing to hold. To protect against this, the 1986 legislation declared that hiring illegal aliens is against the law and subjected employers who did so to economic penalties and even imprisonment (Schaefer, 1993). It was hoped that this measure would help keep illegal aliens out of jobs that citizens would like to have.

Another concern with illegal entrants is the high cost of trying to contain illegal immigration: It is expensive to maintain a border patrol and the investigation section of the Immigration and Naturalization Service. There are also more subtle costs, such as the harassment experienced by some Hispanic Americans who might be questioned or detained in the search for illegal immigrants.

In recent years, there have also been smaller and less publicized episodes of immigration that have created problems of prejudice and discrimination. For example, it is estimated that ten thousand immigrants from Arab countries arrive in Detroit and southeast Michigan each year (Franklin and Hundley, 1983). Some are fleeing the war in Lebanon; the Chaldeans from northern Iraq are Christians fleeing religious persecution by Muslim Arabs; others are joining relatives who migrated to the United States in earlier decades. Most Arab immigrants have headed for the Detroit area because earlier Arab immigrants settled there, and thus a supportive network exists for the new immigrant. There has been sporadic but serious conflict between Arab American store owners and black American patrons in the Detroit area that mirrors the black–Korean conflict mentioned earlier in Los Angeles. Once again, there is economic competition in a superior–subordinate relationship. The result has been isolation, stereotyping, and occasional violence. Because the role of social contact and social isolation is so important in intergroup relations, we will explore it in more detail in the Applied Research insert in this chapter.

FUTURE PROSPECTS

Assimilation or Pluralism?

A review of the history of racial and ethnic minorities in the United States shows that relations between minority and dominant groups have taken a number of different forms (Simpson and Yinger, 1985). For blacks, for example, *segregation* from whites in schools, housing, and transportation has been common and still lingers in some realms today. For many minorities, *subjugation*, in the form of subordination and exploi-

tation, has been a major problem. The grisly experiences of native Americans came close to *genocide*, or the annihilation of an entire group. Estimates are that at least two-thirds of the native American population was annihilated by the direct and indirect actions of white Europeans, with some tribes being completely eliminated. Today, however, the most common relationships between racial and ethnic groups in America involve assimilation and pluralism. **Assimilation** is *the process by which a racial or ethnic minority loses its distinctive identity and way of life and becomes absorbed into the dominant group*. Despite the considerable amount of assimilation that has occurred in America, there are still many racial and ethnic minorities that preserve their heritage. This pattern of intergroup relations is called **pluralism,** *which exists when a number of racial and ethnic groups live side by side, each retaining a distinct identity and life-style while still participating in some aspects of the larger culture.*

What pattern of minority–majority relations is most desirable in America—assimilation, pluralism, or some other? People's response to this question is often colored by a misconception about what has happened historically. America is often referred to as a *melting pot* in which the beliefs, values, and life-styles of many different racial and ethnic groups have been blended together into a unique mix that is called "American." If this had occurred, it would be a form of assimilation in which all groups change to some degree in creating an American identity. Actually, the experience of most immigrants to the United States has come closer to what Milton Gordon has called *Anglo conformity:* To fully share in the American dream, immigrants have been required to renounce their ancestral culture in favor of the beliefs, values, and life-style of the dominant WASPs, the white Anglo-Saxon Protestants (Gordon, 1964; 1978b). These WASPs were among the earliest European immigrants to North America. They came from the British Isles and Germany, and they dominated political, economic, and social life in the United States from the six-

APPLIED RESEARCH

Combating Prejudice and Discrimination

The horror of the genocidal attack on Jews and other ethnic groups during World War II dramatically portrayed the extremes to which prejudice and racism might go. Although it is hard to fathom now, these attacks were perpetrated in the name of protecting the presumably superior "Aryan" race. One positive spinoff from these atrocities was that they pushed many European and American social scientists to conduct research on the sources of prejudice and discrimination, and many of the results of that research have been summarized in this chapter. The findings of this body of research can also be applied to seeking ways of combating racism.

How do we reduce racist attitudes and encourage people to view members of another racial or ethnic group more positively? We will describe one program at a summer camp for children where this was done (Clore et al., 1978). The camp included equal numbers of black and white children, and they came from all levels of the socioeconomic hierarchy. In the camp, all children had the same rights and the same work duties. There was also an equal mix of blacks and whites among the administrators and counselors in the camp, so that the authority structure of the camp was not racially biased. In other words, blacks were as likely to exercise power over the children as were whites. During their one-week stay at the camp, children were required to work on cooperative tasks involving group, rather than individual, goals.

What did this camp accomplish? Basically, children who entered the camp with negative attitudes toward members of the other race showed positive improvements in their views by the end of their stay. Why did this change occur? The answer to this question is complex. The results of past research and the outcomes of current programs, such as the one described above, are very clear in showing that intergroup contact can reduce prejudice if the conditions of the contact are right (Miller and Brewer, 1984; Brewer and Miller, 1988). Contact should have these characteristics if it is to reduce prejudice:

1. The contact should have high "acquaintance potential," which means that people have the time and opportunity to get to know one another and to have some personal and intimate associations.

teenth through the nineteenth centuries. The WASPs were sufficiently fearful of people who immigrated after them—from places such as Ireland, Italy, and Eastern Europe—that they attempted to "Americanize" them rather than let them build their own social institutions and way of life. Many people today still insist on a version of Anglo conformity by arguing that groups such as Hispanics and Asians should learn English and not be given a bilingual education.

Although Anglo conformity worked for quite a while, it has not persisted. Over time, the original WASP group became such a small minority that it became more difficult for it to force its lifestyle onto others. The outcome, at least to this point, is that America remains a highly pluralistic society with many distinct racial and ethnic subcultures. Furthermore, some minorities, especially groups such as blacks and Hispanics, who were never allowed to assimilate by the dominant white

2. The contact should be between people of equal status, rather than a low-status minority interacting with a higher-status member of the dominant group.

3. The behavior of the minority-group person in the contact should contradict the stereotype held of members of that group.

4. As a part of the contact, the people should work toward cooperative and interdependent goals rather than competitive ones; that is, no one in the group can achieve their individual goals unless everyone works together and achieves their goals.

5. The contact situation should have the support of legitimate authorities, such as a school or church, and should involve social norms dictating friendliness and respect between people.

One can readily see that many of these features were built into the children's summer camp described above. One can also recognize that many everyday interpersonal contacts between members of different races violate these principles. Black and white prison inmates, for example, live together in intimate contact, but it is a very tension-filled contact with little inducement for cooperation or interdependence. Many races intermingle in schools, but school is often highly competitive. And how often is the equal status element violated when a black or Hispanic person deals with a white teacher, a white social worker, or a white prison guard?

We cannot, of course, change all these settings. On a smaller scale, however, we can structure social situations over which we do have control with the above principles of intergroup contact in mind. This was done very well in the children's summer camp. A similar approach has been used successfully many times with adults in the form of small-group interaction and sensitivity training. The goal of these efforts is to bring members of different races together for lectures, discussions, and group activities over a period of days or weeks. Through the use of role playing and other group techniques, participants are encouraged to explore stereotypes, diagnose interracial problems, and cooperatively develop strategies for alleviating those problems. This was done, for example, in Houston in the late 1960s when police–community relations became very tense and hostile following a violent clash between black college students and police in which one police officer was killed. Hundreds of police and community residents participated in the program, and it had a positive effect on people's attitudes and reduced the number of citizen complaints against the police (Bell et al., 1969).

Given what we have learned about the impact of intergroup contact on prejudice and discrimination, we can use this knowledge to bring about other structural changes in society. School integration, for example, brings students of different races together. We now have a pretty good idea how to do this so that the positive impact is maximized.

---

groups, prefer it that way. Whether this is desirable, however, is a matter of considerable controversy (Pettigrew, 1988; Triandis, 1988). Many Americans argue that extensive pluralism will promote tensions that could flare into conflict in the future. They point to the efforts of French Canadians in Quebec to secede from Canada as the kind of problem that pluralism can generate. In fact, concern over this has become so strong in some groups that, by 1988, seventeen states had passed laws making English the official language. Proponents of pluralism, on the other hand, contend that racial and ethnic diversity contributes to the richness of American culture and symbolizes America's roots as a nation open to the oppressed of all lands. Furthermore, ethnic identity can be a source of pride and positive self-regard for individuals, and speaking in one's native tongue can play an important part in this. Among Latinos, for example, speaking Spanish and having a large

In many cities in the United States, the signs in stores and shops are printed in many languages, attesting to the extent of racial, ethnic, and cultural pluralism that exists today.

and powerful Spanish-language media in the United States are sources of cultural pride and ethnic identity (Totti, 1987).

The past few decades have generally been a time of improvement in the relationship between minorities and dominant groups in America. Many of the more explicit forms of discrimination have been reduced, and these changes have lessened the inequalities that exist in the stratification system. In addition, racial and ethnic minorities in America today are more organized, confident, and optimistic than they were in the past.

The New Racism

Have we entered a new era of race relations in the United States where we can say that racism is mostly a thing of the past? To answer this question, we must clarify the meaning of the term *racism* (Lowy, 1991b). Many whites interpret this to mean support for white superiority or white supremacy, or a devaluing of or hostility toward people because of their race. This idea of racism focuses on individual attitudes and beliefs, and whites believe that this kind of racism has declined or largely disappeared. One thing that does seem clear is that blatant expressions of racism—blanket, negative castigations of all members of a particular racial or ethnic group—are limited mostly to a few, relatively marginal groups, such as skinheads or the remaining remnants of the Ku Klux Klan.

Many blacks, on the other hand, define racism as institutional racism or discrimination that is built into the systems of power and social institutions of a society. In one interview, for example, black college students clearly saw the white-dominated power structure on their campus as racism, even though particular white college administrators or faculty might not have expressed racist attitudes themselves (Bunzel, 1991). With this view of racism, many blacks believe that racism is still pervasive in the United States because whites still retain thorough control over political and economic institutional structures.

So, has racism declined or not? Or, has the social climate merely made overt expressions of racism socially unacceptable? Some social scientists argue that blatant racism has merely been replaced by a new form of racism, sometimes called *symbolic racism*, in which hostility toward particular groups is expressed not directly but through opposition to policies or practices that benefit those groups (Sears, 1988). With symbolic racism, antiblack sentiments become more general and diffuse. One could express prejudice toward African Americans, for example, by opposing affirmative-action or school-busing policies that are intended to provide major benefits to African Americans. Furthermore, this symbolic racism is rationalized on the basis of support for mainstream American values, such as self-reliance, hard work, obedience, and discipline. The idea is that if blacks worked hard, were obedient, and engaged in disciplined behavior, they would not need affirmative action to get ahead. They want affirmative action because they are unwilling or unable to emulate these values in their own lives. As another example of symbolic racism, antiblack sentiment could be expressed and reinforced by presenting a preponderance of blacks on television news when showing crime suspects—what might be called the Willie Horton effect, after the infamous political ad used in the 1988 presidential campaign. In this way, television news shows can stimulate and reinforce whites' animosity toward blacks without expressly stating such. However, the symbolic racism thesis argues that the real source of people's feelings toward blacks and affirmative action is still today racism against blacks.

The symbolic racism thesis is difficult to assess, in part because the weaknesses of surveys on racism make it hard to tell whether opposition to a policy is genuine or a symptom of deeply felt prejudice. Recent surveys attempting to do so have produced equivocal results—some evidence supports the idea, other evidence does not (Sniderman et al., 1991). Is there evidence other than survey data that indicates the persistence of racism? The separation and tension between white and nonwhite students on some college campuses, the antagonism toward welfare and other policies that are perceived by many as benefiting mostly minorities, the vicious police beating of black motorist Rodney King in 1991, the violence surrounding the riot in south central Los Angeles in 1992, and the lyrics of some rap music popular among some young African Americans, all could indicate that prejudice and racism are still very much with us. Certainly some symbolic racism exists in the United States today, and many blacks believe that racism, at least by their definition of it, is still pervasive. What we cannot say with certainty is how much levels of racism have declined overall in the past few decades. It may be that some (or much) of that decline has merely represented a shift from overt racism to a more covert form.

Race Relations Today: Race or Class?

As we discussed earlier, some minority groups, such as blacks, still lag significantly behind other groups on various indicators of socioeconomic status. There is considerable debate over whether this is because of racial discrimination or because of the class position held by many blacks, which places them in a weak situation from which to compete for jobs and income.

Sociologist William Julius Wilson argues that class, rather than race, is the most important factor in determining the social positions of blacks today (Wilson, 1978; 1987). Wilson certainly does not deny that racial antagonism is still with us, or that substantial discrimination against and oppression of blacks not only has clouded American history but also may still linger today. But he points out that the real problem today lies in the continuing existence of an "underclass" of poor, marginally skilled blacks who have little opportunity to obtain the education and skills necessary to succeed in a modern industrial society (see the Applied Research insert in Chapter 5). Such an underclass can also be found among Puerto Ricans and some other Hispanic groups (Tienda, 1989). Wilson attributes the persistence of this underclass to basic changes in the structure of the American economy, including the relocation of industries away from the communities where many minorities live and a labor market in which people with few job skills or little education are limited to low-paying work with little opportunity for advancement. The primary barrier that this underclass faces, argues Wilson, is the lack of appropriate job-related skills, not racial discrimination. Blacks or Hispanics with job skills or a college education, he argues, will enjoy opportunities and privileges similar to those of their white counterparts in the class hierarchy and will probably not face significant discrimination even if economic conditions deteriorate.

On the other side of this argument are sociologists Charles Willie (1980) and Richard Lowy (1991b) who argue that racial oppression is still a key factor influencing race relations in the United States. They argue that blacks are still oppressed and discriminated against because of their race, although the forms and mechanisms of racial oppression may have changed since the 1950s and 1960s. One difference today is that the overt individual racism of the past has declined considerably, but there is still widespread, institutionalized racism in which such things as residential and school segregation place barriers before the advancement of many blacks but few whites. Another difference today is that more blacks have made it into the middle class, and this can justify the belief that we have eliminated discrimination and achieved equality. If this is true, then the many blacks who do not make it can be blamed for their own failures: Their poor work attitudes, lack of job skills, or dependency on government help, it is argued, renders them unable to help themselves. This is the cultural analysis explanation of poverty that was discussed in Chapter 5. So, although a few superior blacks have the wherewithal to make it, the reasoning goes, most are doomed to failure. Contributing to this view that most blacks do not have the qualities that enable whites and a few blacks to succeed, according to Christopher Jencks (1992), is a cultural conflict that also involves elements of individual racism: Many whites find the black urban culture of the 1990s alien and threatening (see Chapter 5). Because of this they are less likely to hire blacks, particularly young males. In addition, says Jencks, employers have other motivations for discriminating against blacks in hiring. For example, an employer might believe that a black employee will drive away white customers. This was done in professional sports for many years when owners and managers believed that white fans would not pay to see black players. This still occurs today when companies refuse to hire blacks for highly visible positions, such as receptionist or salesperson, when customers are white. For all these reasons, sociologists such as Willie and Lowy argue that "race" still very much determines the position of African Americans as a group in the United States.

So, controversy continues over whether the continuing chasm between the achievements of blacks and whites is due predominately to "class" or mostly to "race." Although it may be difficult to resolve the proportionate role of each, it is certain that each plays some part. The issues involved are important, because the contrasting positions on this controversy point to very different policy recommendations for their solution. So let us turn to some of the policies put forth in the past few decades to improve the quality of race relations in the United States.

Collective Protest

The civil rights movement of the 1950s and 1960s marked the beginning of some significant developments in racial and ethnic discrimination in the United States (Morris, 1984). In its early days, the civil rights movement relied on protest, nonviolent demonstrations, and alliances with powerful—mostly white—politicians to pursue the goal of greater racial equality and improved economic opportunities for minorities. In the 1960s, some of the protest took a decidedly more violent form as many civil rights advocates began to despair of ever achieving significant gains with nonviolence. Eventually, riots broke out, and many cities found neighborhoods engulfed in flames and communities becoming armed camps. Although the conflict and riots of the 1960s were certainly costly and destructive, they played a part in improving race relations in America. This collective action generated sufficient political pressure that major pieces of civil rights legislation were passed, beginning with the Civil Rights Acts of 1964 and 1965.

Civil Rights Legislation

By the end of the 1960s, laws had been established that made it illegal to discriminate against people in jobs, housing, schools, or public facilities on the basis of race or ethnicity. Voting rights legislation was also passed to ensure that adult Americans did not confront barriers to the voting booth. These laws have become the tools for bringing about impressive improvements in the problem of discrimination. Educational, employment, and housing opportunities are now available to minorities who, three decades ago, would have had those doors to opportunity completely closed. Despite advances, however, discrimination still persists. Although it is illegal, some employers and landlords still turn away blacks, Asians, or others because of their race. This discrimination is difficult to eliminate because it is often hard to prove that denial of a job, for example, was motivated by an applicant's minority-group membership rather than by the superior qualifications of another applicant. So civil rights legislation has been a good foundation, but additional efforts have been made to eliminate the lingering effects of discrimination in the form of affirmative action.

Affirmative Action

Affirmative-action legislation requires schools and employers to take active efforts to seek qualified minority applicants for openings and even to establish hiring and admissions practices that give a preference to minorities. In some cases, this may call for establishing quotas whereby a certain proportion of openings will go to minority applicants, even if that necessitates hiring a less qualified minority applicant over a more qualified white applicant. The rationale underlying affirmative action is the belief that a school or business with few minority students or employees is itself evidence that discrimination has occurred. The burden is then on the school or the employer to prove that they have not discriminated by actively seeking out minorities.

Affirmative action has created a great deal of controversy over what is referred to as *reverse discrimination,* in which established quotas of affirmative-action programs result in qualified majority-group members being excluded from a job or school because of their race. The best-known reverse discrimination case to date is that of Allan Bakke, a white male who was initially denied admission to the medical school at the University of California at Davis. He alleged reverse discrimination, because several minority students with lower grades and lower scores on the Medical College Admissions Test were accepted ahead of him under the university's minorities quota policy. In the *Bakke* decision in 1978 and later rulings, the Supreme Court ruled that strict racial quotas are unconstitutional but that race can be used as one among many criteria in admissions decisions. During the 1980s, the Reagan and Bush administrations scaled back significantly programs to encourage hiring preferences based on race. The Supreme Court, dominated by Reagan-Bush appointees, further weakened the legal basis for bringing successful affirmative-action lawsuits against employers. For example, the Court rejected strict racial quotas, required much stricter judicial scrutiny to establish affirmative-action programs, and made it harder to prove that hiring practices resulting in a racially imbalanced work force are discriminatory. The Civil Rights Act of 1991 reversed some of this by making it easier for workers to win lawsuits against employers, but the overall trend of the past twenty years has been a weakened affirmative-action policy.

Because affirmative action applies only to job vacancies, it has had a limited impact in situations in which seniority systems are in effect. In fact, a 1984 Supreme Court decision ruled that the use of strict racial quotas in deciding who should be terminated in job cutbacks was unconstitutional if it violated contractually agreed upon seniority systems. In 1986, the Supreme Court ruled that the layoff of white workers to preserve racial balance in the workplace was unconstitutional, but it continued to endorse racial hiring goals as a constitutional tool to remedy past discrimination.

Despite this controversy, affirmative-action programs have eliminated the more flagrant forms of discrimination, and minority job applicants have been provided with a better chance of being seriously considered. It also alleviates another problem that results because minorities have been kept out of many jobs in the past. We all know that people are sometimes hired because they know someone who already works for a company or agency. Through a father, sister, or friend, you learn quickly that a job is open, and your early application increases your chances of landing it. However, because minorities have been kept out of many jobs—especially the better ones—in the past, a young minority person today is less likely to have that father, sister, or friend already working for a particular employer. Affirmative action gives the minority person some help by forcing the company to seek out minorities in hiring.

Affirmative action has produced considerable resentment among whites, especially males, over what they see as unfairness to them and opportunities lost because minorities have been treated preferentially. Whites generally favor affirmative-action programs that provide training and education for minorities to help them compete for jobs; what they do not like is preferential hiring where less qualified minorities are hired before more qualified whites. Many whites also feel that they have personally suffered because of this reverse discrimination (Lynch and Beer, 1990; Bunzel, 1991). This has produced feelings of frustration, resentment, anger, and cynicism among many whites toward social and political institutions and policies. At the same time, the perception arises that minorities can only succeed if they have help—that they are not capable of doing it on their own. This tends to reflect on minorities who do succeed because people assume that they are less capable than a white with similar levels of success. Christopher Jencks (1992) argues that the way affirmative action has evolved—particularly toward reverse discrimination and quotas—has produced a situation where both whites and minorities feel that they are being hurt by the system. In addition, the resentment felt by whites probably increases feelings of hostility toward minorities, which is not surprising because this is precisely the kind of competitive situation that produces feelings of prejudice. So affirmative action, at least as it has developed over the past twenty years, has had its costs.

Some economists, such as Thomas Sowell (1981), argue that minorities would be best served by a laissez-faire economic system in which people compete for jobs on the basis of their own abilities and wits. This has certainly been true for some immigrant groups, such as Irish and Jewish Americans, both of whom ended up at least as well off as those who discriminated against them when they were still new immigrants to this country. But these groups suffered only sporadic discrimination, not the nearly universal and persistent discrimination that African Americans have faced. In addition, as we have seen, employers sometimes see it as in their interests to discriminate against particular groups. Under these conditions, says Christopher Jencks, laissez-faire policies will not achieve equal opportunity, and some form of affirmative action through government intervention is called for. However, he also agrees that reverse discrimination or separate standards for particular groups is counterproductive in the long run. He argues for affirmative-action "targets": soft quotas that employers make a good-faith effort to meet. As long as the effort is made, failure to meet the precise numerical goal is not seen as failure. This policy keeps government pressure on employers to seek out minority employees without forcing employers to make unfair or irrational decisions.

School Programs and Busing

In 1966, sociologist James Coleman and his colleagues published a report on school segregation that quickly became known as the "Coleman Report." In it, they presented data that showed extensive segregation in American schools and that showed African Americans performing more poorly than other racial or ethnic groups. These black students, Coleman and his coauthors argued, suffer from poor facilities and teachers and from school and home environments that provide little motivation to the students to excel. They also showed that black students who attend desegregated schools with a better "motivational atmosphere" showed improved academic performance. The motivational atmosphere in the school basically had to do with the proportion of lower-class to middle-class pupils in the school. Blacks attending schools with a "middle-class" atmosphere did better than blacks attending schools with a "lower-class" atmosphere. In part because of the Coleman Report, a number of programs were developed to assist minority and white students in improving their academic performance and possibly their career opportunities. Some programs focused on compensatory education to make up for the deficiencies students might experience because of a poor school or home environment. Other programs focused on school integration, sometimes by busing students from one school to another. The employment of busing to achieve school integration has since become a highly controversial issue in American education. Such integration, it was believed, would not only improve the performance of minority students, but also reduce prejudice and discrimination in the long run.

In the late 1960s, court-ordered school busing was instituted in southern states. In the beginning, blacks as well as whites went along with busing in the South. Then a series of protests began, including opposition to busing by the Nixon administration, and Nixon's successor, Gerald Ford, took steps to test the busing issue through the Supreme Court. A subsequent decision limited busing to solitary school districts and prevented busing between predominantly black urban areas and primarily white suburbs.

A controversy that was aroused by busing in the 1970s and 1980s was that of "white flight"— the extent to which white students have left certain school districts for suburban or private schools to avoid either busing or integration. Research clearly shows that whites do tend to avoid schools in which the majority of students is black or Hispanic (Rossell, 1990; Smock and Wilson, 1991). The controversy enters in trying to determine how much of this white flight is due to busing. From reviewing the research it seems reasonable to conclude that, although busing is not the sole culprit, it has made a significant contribution to the flight of whites from many public school districts (Carr and Zeigler, 1990; Armor, 1991). In any event, some courts have interpreted the research to mean that busing produces white flight and thus helps to resegregate the schools. Based on this, by the 1990s, some courts have allowed school districts to dismantle busing programs in order to stop white flight and avoid further resegregation of their schools.

Has school integration achieved its goals? In terms of school achievement, some studies have found improvements with integration and others have not (Rist, 1979; Crain and Mahard, 1983; Longshore and Prager, 1985; Armor, 1989). Overall, integration has probably made modest improvements in school achievement by blacks, especially when students are integrated in the early grades. The reason that the impact has not been more uniformly positive is because so many other factors—socioeconomic status, family background, racial tensions in the schools, and the manner in which integration is accomplished—also influence achievement. However, there are signs that school integration may be producing benefits beyond its impact on school achievement. Research in the early 1980s suggested that school integration has helped to reduce racial isolation in the United States, and that this will reduce racial tensions and stereotyping in the future (Hawley et al., 1983). Furthermore, recent research suggests that the experience in desegregated schools has an impact on blacks later in life: They are more likely to attend predominantly white colleges, socialize with whites outside of school, and live in integrated neighborhoods as adults (Braddock, Crain, and McPartland, 1984;

Braddock, 1985). In addition, concerns about integration and busing have led to creative developments in schools designed to attract both white and minority students. For example, some school districts have established "magnet" schools that focus on specific skills such as computer applications or the performing arts. Students are free to choose among these magnet schools. So it may be that the impact of school integration will be more subtle and will surface only after integration has been a reality for a long period, possibly decades. Rather than a dramatic increase in school performance, we may see a gradual easing of racial tensions as young people of different races mingle in the schools, or an improvement in our schools as they strive to attract an acceptable racial mix among their students.

In the final analysis, busing remains a hotly contested issue, and there are many emotional feelings about this process on the part of blacks and whites alike. Still, despite all these conflicts, court-ordered busing persists into the 1990s and has become an established device for achieving school integration.

Improving the Economy

Those who view contemporary racial problems as a "class" problem and those who take the laissez-faire approach to solving social problems argue that improvements in the economic environment in America will narrow many of the disparities between dominant groups and minorities. Differences in family income, for example, or education or life expectancy can be narrowed if people have access to better jobs and can improve their lifestyles. This does not deny the occurrence of discrimination or exploitation in the past, but it does say that the future calls for different emphases. The government's role in the future, they argue, should be focused on improvements in the economy. Some of the specific proposals have been reviewed in Chapter 5 and need not be repeated here.

There have been many improvements in race relations in the United States in the past two decades. Although there is much in our history to be lamented, we can be proud of the recent advances. Yet there are reasons for uncertainty about the future. Whereas racial violence has been limited of late, periodic outbursts document that such violence is just below the surface. The riot in south central Los Angeles in 1992 was the most recent manifestation of the anger and resentment that can trigger such violence. (The reasons for this outburst are analyzed in detail in the Applied Research insert in Chapter 14.) The same thing happened in Miami in 1989 when a police officer shot and killed a black man on a motorcycle. These violent riots express the anger that many minority youths feel about their position and opportunities in the 1990s. They illustrate the potential for racial conflict that simmers below the surface despite the improvements that we have made. This suggests that the potential for prejudice, discrimination, and racial violence is still very strong and can be rekindled if the proper social conditions arise.

Linkages

The current pattern of racial segregation in housing between our cities and suburbs was underwritten by the urban policies of the federal government going back to the 1930s (Chapter 12). By building freeways to the suburbs and providing mortgage loans to whites (but not blacks) to buy houses in the suburbs, the government helped create the racial isolation we are living with today. This racial segregation in turn has made poverty more extensive and entrenched for African Americans (Chapter 5) because it magnifies the difficulties they confront in finding jobs.

Summary

1. A minority group is a group whose members are viewed by dominant groups as inferior because of certain characteristics. They have less access to power and resources than do other groups, and they are accorded fewer rights, privileges, and opportunities. The term *minority,* as used by sociologists, relates to a group's position in the stratification system rather than to numerical size.

2. A race is a group of people who are believed to be a biological group sharing genetically transmitted traits that are defined as important. An ethnic group comprises people who share a common historical and cultural heritage and sense of group identity and belongingness. Racism is the view that certain racial or ethnic groups are biologically inferior and that practices involving their domination and exploitation are therefore justified.

3. A prejudice is a negative attitude toward certain people based solely on their membership in a particular group. Discrimination is behavior—the unequal treatment of people because they are members of a particular group.

4. Prejudice and discrimination result from different social and psychological sources. Among the social sources are ethnocentrism, competition, socialization, and institutionalized discrimination. Psychological sources include stereotyping, frustration and aggression, and the authoritarian personality.

5. Discrimination has a number of consequences, including an adverse effect on people's life chances and an increase in tension and hostility in society.

6. Among racial and ethnic groups, blacks and Hispanics are the largest nonwhite minorities, and they lag considerably behind other groups in access to education, power, and economically rewarding jobs. One of the most important reasons for this is the long history of discrimination and oppression suffered by both groups, making it difficult for them to improve their position in American society.

7. Native Americans experience some of the worst conditions of all minority groups in American society. Some Asian Americans, on the other hand, have been able to attain a degree of affluence despite the substantial prejudice and discrimination they have experienced.

8. Today, the most common types of relationship between dominant and minority groups in America are assimilation and pluralism. Although most minority groups have experienced some degree of assimilation, there is considerable emphasis today on the pluralistic nature of American society. There is considerable debate over whether racism in the United States has declined, or just changed to a more subtle and symbolic form. There is also controversy over whether ongoing socioeconomic differences between the members of dominant and minority groups is a result of racial discrimination or class position.

9. Civil rights legislation, affirmative-action programs, school programs and busing, and efforts to improve the economy are techniques that have been used in trying to improve race and ethnic relations in the United States.

Important Terms for Review

assimilation	ethnocentrism	internal colonialism	race
authoritarian personality	in-group	minority group	racism
discrimination	institutionalized	pluralism	split labor market
ethnic group	discrimination	prejudice	

Discussion Questions

1. Have you or has someone you know well ever been discriminated against because of your race, ethnicity, or some other characteristic that accorded you minority status? What did the discrimination involve? Did you feel that you or the group you belonged to was being economically exploited by another group or were there other sources of the discrimination?

2. Even though people have become more sensitive to prejudicial feelings and discriminatory practices, most of us still have prejudices. Consider your own prejudices. Have any of them been translated into discrimination? Which of Merton's four categories of prejudice and discrimination would you place yourself in?

3. Minority groups such as Hispanics, African Americans, native Americans, and Asian Americans all display a history of discrimination. What do these groups have in common with respect to discrimination from dominant groups? What, if any, are some of the differences between them in terms of experience?

4. In the United States today, there are immigrants from dozens of countries, most recently from Vietnam, Haiti, and Cuba. What are the social implications of having so many different racial and ethnic minorities with heterogeneous lifestyles living in close proximity? Does the fact that we have a racially and ethnically mixed population pose problems for our society? In what way?

5. The debate continues over whether the problems facing blacks and other racial groups are attributable to race, as Richard Lowy and Charles Willie argue, or to class, as William Julius Wilson sees it. Consider where you stand on this issue and why.

6. Government legislation such as affirmative action and programs such as school busing are designed to help minority groups of all kinds, yet each such effort has its staunch critics for one reason or another. Locate people in your class or in your college who have benefited from one of these programs. How did they benefit? Can you find someone who has been hurt by the same programs? Overall, do you think that these programs are helping or hurting race and ethnic relations in the United States?

For Further Reading

Bob Blauner. *Black Lives, White Lives: Three Decades of Race Relations in America.* Berkeley: University of California Press, 1989. This book is based on interviews with the same group of people in 1968, 1979, and 1986. It shows how race relations and racial change affect people's lives.

Robert C. Christopher. *Crashing the Gates: The DeWASPing of America's Power Elite.* New York: Simon and Schuster, 1989. This interesting book points to the advances that have been made in this century toward spreading power to many racial and ethnic groups in the United States. It is sometimes good to remember that we have made significant progress.

Harry Edwards. *The Struggle That Must Be: An Autobiography.* New York: Macmillan, 1980. An autobiography of a sociologist who grew up black and poor in the 1950s. Although sports played a role in Edwards's chance to go to college, he strongly opposes enticing blacks into sports on the very small chance that they will be successful.

Bil Gilbert. *God Gave Us This Country: Tekamthi and the First American Civil War.* New York: Atheneum, 1989. This is a fascinating book about the relationship between the European settlers in the New World and the indigenous Indians, particularly the Shawnee and Iroquois in what was the original western frontier: Ohio, Indiana, Illinois, and Michigan. It contains a vivid history of the Indian tribes.

William B. Helmreich. *The Things They Say Behind Your Back: Stereotypes and the Myths Behind Them.* New York: Doubleday, 1982. A very readable study of popular stereotypes about ethnic groups in America. Helmreich also tries to show that there is little truth to most stereotypes.

Alvin M. Josephy, Jr. *Now That the Buffalo's Gone: A Study of Today's American Indians.* New York: Alfred A. Knopf, 1982. An excellent overview of American Indians, including the history of native American efforts to gain freedom amidst the frequent tyranny of the white majority.

Jonathan Kozol. *Savage Inequalities: Children in America's Schools.* New York: Crown, 1991. This book explains why, if you are born poor and minority in the United States, the schools will not be of great assistance in climbing out of poverty. The schools Kozol describes, whose students are mostly poor and mostly black, are in horrendous shape. The students who need societal help the most get the least in terms of good quality education.

J. Anthony Lukas. *Common Ground: A Turbulent Decade in the Lives of Three American Families.* New York: Alfred A. Knopf, 1985. This book is a very sensitive account of the impact of school busing on the lives of three families, one black and two white.

David Milner. *Children and Race.* Beverly Hills, Calif.: Sage Publications, 1983. A very readable book summarizing the research on how children develop racial attitudes as they grow up. The author also discusses the impact of racism on the psychological development of black children and some educational programs to promote positive race relations.

Earl Shorris. *Latinos: A Biography of the People.* New York: W. W. Norton, 1992. This excellent book explores the lives and history of the fastest growing minority group in the United States, the descendants of the Spanish conquest of the native American peoples. Through wonderfully insightful biographical sketches, the author communicates the complex diversity today in the group that is given the single designation of "Latino."

Thomas Sowell. *Civil Rights: Rhetoric or Reality?* New York: William Morrow and Co., 1985. An excellent history of the civil rights movement in America, with Mr. Sowell's personal evaluation of what effects various legislation has had on minorities in this country.

David E. Stannard. *American Holocaust: Columbus and the Conquest of the New World.* New York: Oxford University Press, 1992. This book catalogues an "unbroken string of genocidal campaigns" by the Europeans against the native peoples of the Americas after Columbus's voyages. The author attempts to explain the brutality and devastation that occurred in terms of European attitudes toward race, religion, war, and conversion.

Ronald Takaki. *Strangers from a Different Shore: A History of Asian Americans.* Boston: Little Brown, 1989. This is an acclaimed history of Asian immigrants to the United States. The author argues compellingly that all Asian immigrants have had to confront the reality that the dominant groups in the United States have always viewed this country as a fundamentally white society.

Studs Terkel. *Race: How Blacks and Whites Think and Feel About the American Obsession.* New York: New Press, 1992. In this volume you can hear Americans expressing in their own words what their opinions are about race relations in the United States. There is a range of opinion expressed here that people are often not exposed to.

Gary A. Tobin. *Jewish Perceptions of Antisemitism.* New York and London: Plenum, 1988. This book summarizes research on how much antisemitism exists in the United States and on Jews' perceptions of their status. It is an excellent analysis of the problems of prejudice and discrimination affecting one of the more successful ethnic groups in the United States.

Melvin I. Urofsky. *A Conflict of Rights: The Supreme Court and Affirmative Action.* New York: Charles Scribner's Sons, 1991. This book focuses on one particular affirmative-action case that went to the Supreme Court and presents perspectives on the case from both sides. It shows that the issues in affirmative-action policy are complicated and not easily analyzed in terms of one side's being right and the other wrong.

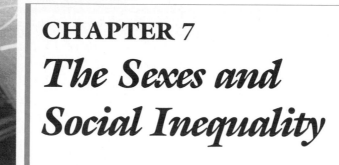

CHAPTER 7
The Sexes and Social Inequality

I t is difficult, maybe impossible, for those who have not experienced discrimination and oppression to truly comprehend what they are like. This may account for why many men tend to take sexual harassment and assault less seriously than do women: Most men have not experienced these things. Recent highly publicized cases have brought these issues into the forefront: the Mike Tyson and William Kennedy Smith rape cases, the raucous Clarence Thomas–Anita Hill sexual harassment hearings, and the accusations in 1991 that naval officers sexually assaulted twenty-six women—including some of their fellow naval of-

ficers—at a wild party. Men's and women's reactions to such episodes are sometimes divided by chasms of misunderstanding. Many men tend not to see such episodes as so earthshaking; women are outraged that men do not understand how important the issues are (Johnson, Stockdale, and Saal, 1991).

In some ways, sexual harassment and assault may be an appropriate microcosm in which to view inequalities between the genders, partly because men and women tend to perceive them so very differently. But also because they can function as weapons of oppression, tools that discour-

Myths and Facts About Sexual Inequality

Many efforts have been made over the past few decades to reduce the disadvantages suffered by women, and one can get the overall impression of significant progress being made. And many gains have been made. However, as with so many social problems, reality is more complex than first impressions might suggest, and many statements of fact, if not qualified, are so misleading as to almost constitute myths.

Myth: Women have taken their place in the work force with men, holding more varied jobs and getting higher pay relative to men than ever before.

Fact: More women work, but their pay still lags significantly behind that of men for doing the same work. In addition, relatively few companies make accommodations for child care for their employees, and most men still consider child care and housekeeping to be primarily the woman's job, even when she works full time. Also, many low-paying, low-prestige jobs are still female ghettos, with 99 percent of secretaries, 97 percent of receptionists, and 98 percent of dental hygienists being women in the 1990s.

Myth: More women are seeking political office than ever before.

Fact: Women, who make up 51 percent of our populace, held 6 percent of the seats in the United States Senate in 1993 and a paltry 10 percent of the seats in the House of Representatives. Women also make up only 18 percent of state leg-islators and 17 percent of mayors. The United States is still a country ruled by men.

Myth: Modernized divorce laws enable women to get out of bad marriages and get alimony and child support from their ex-husbands.

Fact: Women with children who divorce suffer a serious decline in their standard of living, whereas men who divorce actually experience an improvement in their standard of living. One study found that, on average, women's standard of living dropped by 73 percent after divorce and men's increased by 42 percent.

Myth: By the 1990s, our nation is now solidly supportive of equal rights for women.

Fact: The Equal Rights Amendment to the Constitution, which would prohibit discrimination on the basis of gender, has yet to be approved.

Myth: The courts have ruled that barring women from service and community organizations such as Rotary and the Kiwanis violates antidiscrimination laws. Thus, women now have the same access as men to community and business arenas.

Fact: This is true in communities that have antidiscrimination laws. In the thousands of communities where there are no such laws, however, women can be and are excluded from such organizations. In fact, former Presidents Reagan and Bush belong to a very influential social club, the Bohemian Club, at which many very powerful businessmen and politicians gather and to which women are completely excluded.

age women from taking jobs or entering other arenas that had been the exclusive domains of men. The evidence is clear that sexual harassment on the job is pervasive: In one survey, 88 percent of working women said that they had experienced sexual harassment (Thorkelson, 1985). Ninety percent of the companies on the Fortune 500 have received complaints of sexual harassment from employees, and more than one-third of these companies have been sued over harassment (Sandroff, 1988). A report on sexual harassment in the military, released in 1991, stated that "the majority of women (64%) and 17 percent of men reported experiencing some form of sexual harassment ranging from jokes to actual assault while on duty" (Martindale, 1991: 201). Five percent of the women in the military reported that someone raped them or attempted to rape them during the preceding year. In 1991, a California commission held hearings on the issue of why so few women take jobs in the construction trades. What they heard from the women who testified was of a systematic, unrelating campaign of sexual harassment, sometimes bordering on terror, perpetrated by their male coworkers to drive women out of these jobs (French, 1992b). The men were verbally hostile and pinched and fondled the women as they tried to do their job. Male workers urinated next to the women and hung lewd pictures in the women's toilet. The women were constantly confronted in the workplace with pinup calenders and close-up pictures of female genitals. The nasty comments and teasing were constant. One electrician was doused with water as she worked on live electrical wires, putting her life in danger. All this treatment seemed to reflect a campaign by the male workers to drive women out in order to preserve a bastion of "maleness" in which women did not intrude. And this testimony, remember, was being given in 1991, not 1961! Practically all women who have worked for any length of time can recall their own experiences with sexual harassment.

Sexual harassment and job discrimination are two elements of the problem of social inequality based on sexual status, but such inequality takes many more subtle forms. For example, a suit was filed during the early 1980s against the state of Kentucky alleging that female prisoners in the state prison system were not given the same privileges as male prisoners. New female inmates could not wear street clothes or makeup, display pictures of their families, or make telephone calls. New male inmates were subject to none of these restrictions. Female inmates also received little vocational training, and the training provided to them was for jobs, such as seamstress, that are low paying and would be considered sex stereotyped outside of prison. Male inmates, on the other

Prominent events of the past few years have led to heightened awareness of the negative impact of sexual harassment on women and to greater efforts by both women and men to fight against it.

hand, received training in welding, plumbing, television repair, and printing—all potentially high-paying occupations (Rawls, 1982).

Although many strides have been made in the past few decades to provide women with the same opportunities as men, the examples just discussed illustrate that the problem still lingers. In this chapter, we will review the reasons why such inequality occurs, its dimensions in the United States, and what can be done to alleviate it.

MEN AND WOMEN IN SOCIETY

Sex is an *ascribed status:* It is a position in society that is assigned to a person; people have virtually no control over their ascribed statuses. Unlike achieved statuses, such as one's educational level or occupation, there is little if anything, that people can do to alter their sexual status. Sex is also a *master status* because it has considerable social significance in all societies. It is a central determinant of how people view themselves and how others respond to them, and it frequently serves as a basis for social differentiation. In fact, sexual inequality is an important element of the stratification system in society. In some societies discrimination based on sexual status is so irrevocable that women have virtually no chance to improve their status. To understand how sexual status shapes the structure of modern American society, it is helpful to understand why sex is an element of social differentiation in societies at all. We will examine four different views on this issue.

The Biological Perspective

One perspective on the role of sexual status in determining one's position in society is that innate biological differences between men and women shape the contributions each can make to society. One question this raises, of course, is: What precisely are the biological differences between the sexes. Modern research has documented some differences and shown that allegations of other differences are not supported by the available evidence. These findings are summarized in Table 7.1. Are these differences caused by biology? In only a few realms is there any evidence that they are (Parsons, 1980; McCoy, 1985). Higher levels of aggressiveness in males, for example, are very common in other species, such as rhesus monkeys, and it is almost universal in human cultures. It has also been reported that levels of aggressiveness can be affected by changes in sex hormones. Thus, there is the suggestion, but by no means conclusive proof, that higher levels of aggressiveness in males are in part biological. In terms of the differences in verbal and spatial-visual ability, there is some evidence that the brains of males and females are organized differently in this regard. In men, verbal skills are focused on one side of the brain and the spatial-visual skills on the other. In

women, each skill can be found on both sides of the brain. This difference in the organization of the brain may account for why women tend to have more verbal skills and men are more adept at spatial-visual tasks. With regard to greater upper-body strength, this is probably attributable to the higher levels of the hormone testosterone among males.

So there undoubtedly are some biological differences between men and women that have implications for social behavior. However, the differences are far fewer and much smaller than were once thought to be the case. Furthermore, the differences appear to relate to general tendencies, such as aggressiveness, rather than to specific social behaviors, such as fighting or playing football. In addition, despite any biological differences, men and women are highly flexible and extremely malleable in terms of what they are capable of doing. Most of our behavior is learned rather than biologically programmed, which means that men can learn to behave in a stereotypically female fashion, and women can learn to behave in ways that we would expect men to behave (Tavris, 1992). A final point is that the differences between men and women refer to average levels of performance, which ignores the significant overlap between the sexes. Many women, for example, are more aggressive than some men, and some men are less aggressive than many women. Because of this, sexual status alone is a rather poor basis for establishing social policy or allocating social tasks and rewards.

The Functionalist Perspective

Functionalists argue that some tasks were allocated to men and others to women in preindustrial societies because such arrangements were more convenient and practical (Ford, 1970; Giele, 1978). On the whole, males are physically stronger than women and free of the responsibility of having and nursing children. Women, on the other hand, were expected to have many children during their lives and to spend much of their adult lives either

Table 7.1 **Sex Differences and Similarities**

Physical Attributes

Strength	Males taller, heavier, more muscular.
Health	Females less vulnerable to illness and disease, live longer.
Activity level	Some evidence that preschool boys more active during play in same-sex groups; sex differences for school-age children are qualitative, not quantitative.
Manual dexterity	Women excel when speed is important; findings hard to interpret.

Abilities

General intelligence	No difference on most tests.
Verbal ability	Some evidence that females acquire language slightly earlier; males more often diagnosed as having reading problems; females excel on various verbal tests after age ten or eleven.[a]
Quantitative ability	Males excel on tests of mathematical reasoning from the start of adolescence.[a]
Spatial-visual ability	Males excel starting in tenth grade, but not on all tests or in all studies.[a]
Creativity	Females excel on verbal creativity tests, but otherwise no difference.
Cognitive style	Males excel on spatial-visual disembedding tests starting at adolescence, but no general differences in cognitive style.

Personality Characteristics

Sociability	No consistent findings on infants' responsiveness to social cues; school-age boys play in larger groups; women fantasize more about affiliation themes, but there is no evidence that one sex wants or needs friends more.
Empathy	Conflicting evidence; probably depends on situation and sex of participants in an interaction.
Emotionality	Self-reports and observations conflict; no convincing evidence that females feel more emotional, but they may express certain emotions more freely.
Dependence	Conflicting findings; dependence appears not to be a unitary concept or stable trait.
Susceptibility to influence	Preschool girls more obedient to parents; boys may be more susceptible to peer pressure; no overall difference in adult susceptibility to persuasion across different settings in laboratory studies.
Self-esteem and confidence	No self-reported differences in self-esteem, but males more confident about task performance; males more likely to take credit for success, less likely to blame selves for failure.
Nurturance	No overall differences in altruism; girls more helpful and responsive to infants, small children; some evidence that fathers are as responsive to newborns as mothers are, but issue of maternal versus paternal behavior remains open.
Aggressiveness	Males more aggressive from preschool age on; men more violent, more likely to be aggressive in public, more likely to be physically aggressive in situations not involving anger.

Values and Moral Perceptions

	Some controversial evidence that males and females approach choice and conflict somewhat differently. Males seem more likely to emphasize abstract standards of justice, fairness, balancing of individual rights. Females seem more likely to emphasize the ethics of care, human attachments, balancing of conflicting responsibilities.

[a]Differences statistically reliable but quite small.

SOURCE: From *The Longest War: Sex Differences in Perspective,* Second Edition, by Carol Tavris and Carole Wade, copyright © 1984 by Harcourt Brace Jovanovich, Inc., pp. 42–43. Reprinted by permission of the publisher.

pregnant or rearing their children. In addition, women were a more valuable reproductive resource in that the loss of a woman, as in war, would reduce the reproductive potential of society. The loss of a man, on the other hand, could easily be made up for through increased sexual activity on the part of other men. There would be no loss in the overall reproductive potential of society. Given these considerations, functionalists argue, it was more practical in preindustrial societies to assign to men tasks, such as hunting or felling trees, that are physically demanding and might draw one away from home for long periods of time. Men were also assigned the dangerous tasks, such as protecting the group against attack from enemies. Women, on the other hand, who were limited by pregnancy and nursing their young, were considered better suited to such tasks as gathering roots or berries, cooking food, and making pottery. Once these sex-role distinctions had become firmly established as a part of a group's tradition, they were then supported by strong group norms that made these differences independent of their origins. They came to be seen as the "natural" ways for men and women to behave rather than as practical means of accomplishing societal tasks (Brown, 1970; O'Kelly and Carney, 1986).

Industrialization ushered in a number of significant social changes: the separation of work from family life, smaller families, and a longer life expectancy. As a consequence, women tended to be isolated in the family and given prime responsibility for homemaking and child-rearing duties, whereas men went out and worked. Sex roles became divided along the lines of instrumental and expressive tasks (Parsons and Bales, 1950). **Instrumental tasks** refer to *the goal-oriented activities of the group, such as hunting, building something, or managing a work team.* Males were seen as having responsibility for most of these tasks. **Expressive tasks** refer to *activities focused on the relationships between people—maintaining happiness, harmony, and emotional stability.* These tasks were seen as primarily a woman's responsibility. In fact, for men, it became a status symbol to have a wife who did not work. A nonworking wife was taken as an indication of how capable the man was at producing economically and supporting his family. To justify this, sexist beliefs emerged that a woman's place was in the home and that women were not biologically equipped for most forms of male work. However, in most preindustrial societies, women were not removed from economically productive roles. Much of what they did, such as gathering roots, tending crops, or herding flocks, contributed significantly to the economic support of the group. They were by no means limited to child rearing or expressive tasks. Likewise, men were by no means limited to instrumental tasks in preindustrial societies (Murdock, 1934).

From the functionalist perspective, then, a social problem exists when the sex-role division of labor is no longer consistent with the needs of a particular society. To confine women to child rearing or expressive activities would waste a valuable resource. Families have few children today, and they have many supports, such as day care, to help in raising them. So it is no longer necessary for adults—either male or female—to devote their lives to such tasks. It would be better if they used their intellectual, creative, and productive abilities to make additional contributions to society. Because our birthrate is low and most jobs in industrial societies are not dangerous, there is no need to protect women as a reproductive resource, as was the case in the past. In addition, great physical strength is no longer necessary for most jobs in our highly automated, technological society. For all of these reasons, functionalists argue, it is not particularly useful to use sex as a criterion for allocating jobs today. It would be more functional to assign tasks based on individual abilities.

The Conflict Perspective

Many sociologists have questioned whether the fact of a woman having children is the central element in shaping sex roles in society and especially whether it explains the continued existence of sex stratification. For example, sociologist Randall Collins (1971) has argued that there is an inherent conflict of interest between men and women and that sex roles can serve as a mechanism by which one group dominates the other. In part, this domination results because males in general are physically stronger than women, which better equips them to use power to their own advantage and gain dominance. But the situation is more complex than this. Through the socialization process, a subtler form of power is exerted and control achieved: People learn to want those things that are in the interests of the dominant group in society. In most societies, women have learned to accept the dominance of males and their own subordinate positions as appropriate and even desirable.

The economic competition discussed in Chapter 6 also contributes to sexual inequality. In simple hunting and gathering societies, there is a division of labor based on sex, as we have seen, but there is also considerable equality between men and women. The reason for this is that women produce as much as and sometimes more than men. Gathering nuts, roots, and berries produces a steady and dependable food supply, whereas the results of hunting can be very sporadic. It might be days or weeks before men can fell some game. In the interim, women provide food for the group. In agricultural societies, men tend to dominate economic productivity, in good part because their physical strength and freedom from child-bearing duties enable them to engage in extensive, heavy agriculture that might take them away from home for hours or days at a time. This leaves women economically subordinate and unequal. As functionalists point out, this inequality continues into early industrial societies as men work and women stay home. This arrangement benefits men, of course, because they have a corner on the prestigious and powerful positions in society, and most men wish to continue those social practices.

These social practices have continued well into the twentieth century in the United States. During World War II, for example, large numbers of women joined the work force, replacing men serving in the military and showing they were capable of performing many traditionally male jobs (Van Horn, 1988). Most people assumed that these women were housewives who had no financial need to work, but who were doing their part for the war effort, and who wanted to return to their traditional roles after the war. In fact, government and industry, through such groups as the Office of War Information and the War Advertising Council, mounted a propaganda effort to encourage the public to believe this. Reality for many of these working women, dubbed "Rosie the Riveters," was quite different: Many of them were married and needed these well-paying, previously all-male jobs to support their families; some were single parents or single women for whom these jobs were their sole source of economic support; and many of these women wanted to continue in these jobs after the war. Despite the fact that these women had shown themselves to be capable of performing well in many traditionally male jobs, there was a backlash against them when the war ended and returning servicemen competed with the women for jobs. Many people felt that the women had done their duty and now should return to their homes and families ("where they belonged") and make jobs available for returning servicemen. Public pressure and job discrimination resulted in most of these women leaving the traditionally male jobs (Honey, 1984). From the conflict perspective, then, sexual differentiation becomes the "battleground" for a struggle over scarce resources—in this case, for jobs and prestige. However, this economic competition for jobs—a form of the split labor market discussed in Chapter 6 because women are typically paid less than men—was translated into the sexist ideology that women were incapable of performing the jobs as well as the men.

From the conflict view, sexual inequality becomes a social problem when some group—in this case, women—realizes it is being exploited and that something can be done about it. In the past thirty years, women have come to realize that their inferior status has been caused by male domination, not biological inheritance. Once this realization emerged, sexual inequality came to be viewed as a social problem and entered the arena of public debate.

The Interactionist Perspective

According to the interactionist perspective, human beings relate to one another on the basis of symbols that have social meaning within a given culture or society. Those social meanings are created, communicated, and reinforced as people interact with one another on a daily basis. So we can understand a lot about the creation and maintenance of sexual inequality if we watch how men and women interact in various settings. It is through those interactions that the place of men and women in society is defined. Probably the most important symbol system for human beings is language. Interactionists point out that many values, beliefs, and social meanings find expression in different language forms, and an analysis of some of these forms suggests a continuing sex bias in our language usage. For example, the sex-specific pronouns *he* and *his* can be used when referring to both men and women, and this may be a veiled way of maintaining male dominance. Recent investigations suggest that such sexist language is still very much with us and show conclusively that use of the generic *he* does create predominantly male images in people's minds, especially for men (Gastil, 1990; Switzer, 1990). When people read or hear *he,* instead of *she* or *they,* they think of men, and this can be a symbolic reinforcement of the exclusion of women from many aspects of society. This linguistic usage, then, may reinforce and help perpetuate sexist thought and action, especially among men, by encouraging a predominantly male imagery when thinking about activities or realms of which both men and women might be a part.

The interaction styles of men and women can have direct implications for gaining and keeping positions of leadership and a place in decision making in groups. One investigation focused on the order in which people speak in mixed sex groups (Aries, 1985). In general, men initiate more conversation and receive more interaction than women. People who initiate the most interaction in groups take up the most time and are considered by others in the group to be leaders. So if women are taught to be submissive or timid around men, they may be less likely or less able to assume leadership in groups.

Conversational styles also reflect and reinforce these patterns of dominance and subordination. For example, although it is widely believed in our culture that women talk more than men (the stereotype has it that women "chatter on" about frivolous subjects), many investigations of conversational behavior in mixed groups show that men talk more than women and interrupt while others are talking more than women do (Richardson, 1988). Men also answer questions not addressed to them and continue talking when there is an overlap in conversation. The impact of these different patterns of conversation on sexual inequality is quite direct:

> The beliefs that women talk too much and talk about insignificant subjects function to keep women quieter than they might be and to allow men to monopolize social conversations and work groups. The expectation that whatever a woman says is trivial and unimportant creates insecurity, timidity in presenting ideas, and lower feelings of self esteem. . . . The lack of authority attached to female speech patterns lowers a woman's chances for success in many fields and can reinforce the belief that women should stick to the traditional careers of mother and homemaker. (Kirsh, 1983: 74–75)

So it is through interaction patterns such as these that beliefs and practices regarding sexual inequality are maintained and reinforced. In preindustrial America, the roles of men and women were relatively clear-cut and accepted by most people, even though those roles reflected substantial inequality. In modern industrial society, however, the social structure is changing at a rapid pace, and forms of sexual differentiation formerly accepted are now challenged by many people. So sexual inequality becomes a social problem when there is a lack of consensus and a lack of shared expectations about the roles of men and women in society. As expectations change, so too do people's self-concepts in relationship to their sexual status—these are more likely to be uncertain and ambiguous.

THE SOCIALIZATION OF MEN AND WOMEN

There is a compelling tendency to believe that being born male or female automatically implies specific behavioral differences between people. Yet scientific research has demonstrated that most of our behavior as males and females is not a function of biology but rather of learning. This leads to the distinction that sociologists make between *sex* and *gender*. *Male* and *female* are used as sex-related terms—the innate, biological feature of sexual identity. **Sex** refers to *the biological role that each of us plays, such as in reproduction. Masculine* and *feminine,* on the other hand, are used as gender-specific terms. **Gender** refers to *learned behavior involving how we are expected to act as males and females in society.* One of the key issues in analyzing sexual inequality is how we learn to be masculine and feminine and how this contributes to sexual differentiation and inequality. This learning occurs in good part through the socialization process, with three major agencies of socialization being primarily responsible: the family, the schools, and the media.

The Family

Infancy represents the most crucial period for human development because patterns of personality and behavior are established during these years. These early years are also extremely important in the establishment of beliefs about appropriate masculine and feminine behavior. There is a growing body of literature that clearly demonstrates how parents are likely to treat male and female infants and young children in ways consistent with how they view masculinity and femininity. For example, fathers are typically "rougher" with boys and more gentle with girls, and both mothers and fathers tend to speak more softly to girls than to boys (Rossi, 1984; MacDonald and Parke, 1986).

By the age of three, children have acquired a sexual identity, which means that they can correctly label themselves as male or female. But at this point, their identity is oversimplified and highly stereotyped. It is also based more on such things as hairstyle or dress than on an accurate awareness of genital differences between the sexes. Once the child's gender identity has been established, he or she then attempts to master the behaviors that are associated with that gender. Behaving "like a boy" or "like a girl" becomes rewarding because it brings approval from adults and peers. Parents still today tend to encourage boys to engage in instrumental play, such as building something, whereas girls are encouraged toward expressive play, such as making themselves look attractive.

Even in childhood, it appears that male activities are valued more than female ones (Martin, 1990). For example, girls often display a fondness for the higher prestige of the masculine role by becoming "tomboys." "Tomboyism" is acceptable to a much greater extent than a little boy's being a "sissy." In fact, girls are more prominent in boys' games than boys are in girls' games—testament to the less negative reactions to "tomboys" than to "sissys." Other investigators have discovered that boys play more competitive games than girls and that girls typically do not learn how to deal with direct competition (Best, 1983; Berliner, 1988). Children learn from their family experiences what it means to be male and female, and these are extremely strong influences.

The Schools

A very significant part of the socialization process occurs in the schools. School systems are characteristically staffed in such a way that children's perceptions of masculinity and femininity are reinforced. Although most elementary schoolteachers are female, most elementary school principals are male. Thus, from the beginning of school, children see men in positions of authority and dominance over women (Richmond-Abbott, 1992). In addition, children are significantly affected by the expectations of their teachers. Investigations have shown that female teachers are more likely to encourage independence and assertion in boys than in girls (Best, 1983). Teachers also tend to view girls as less creative than boys, to provide less attention to girls, and to reward female students for conforming and male students for being aggressive (Tavris and Wade, 1984; Berliner, 1988). The way teachers do this is quite subtle. Dependence in girls, for example, is encouraged by not sending them off to work on their own, although boys often work alone. As for aggressiveness, boys often have to misbehave to gain their teacher's attention, whereas girls who are quiet and demure are more likely to receive attention from the teacher. So teachers, most often without realizing it, reward their students for behaving in a fashion consistent with their own sex-role stereotypes.

During the 1970s, a survey by the Michigan Women's Commission revealed that in grade school textbooks used in that state, male characters were pictured more frequently than female characters. In fact, female gender specific pronouns such as *her* were totally absent from books used in the first grade of Michigan schools (Michigan Women's Commission, 1974). Adult men's and women's roles were also portrayed in stereotypical fashion in many elementary schoolbooks of the time, as another investigation showed: Men appeared in 213 different occupations whereas women were pictured in only 39, and women were typically shown as working only if they were not married (Fisher, 1974). But have there not been changes in all this in the past twenty years? Not as much as one might think. Things have improved, especially when efforts are made to produce materials that are nonsexist in their presentation. However, stereotyping still persists. Recent studies of children's picture books, for example, find that more women are portrayed than in the past but still less than men (only one-third of the illustrations are of women), almost no women are portrayed as working outside the home, women are still shown in fewer occupations than men, and women are portrayed as less brave and adventurous and more helpless (Williams, Jr. et al., 1987; Peterson and Lach, 1990; Purcell and Stewart, 1990). Furthermore, although men are sometimes portrayed as expressing their emotions, denying one's feelings is still characterized in these books as a normal aspect of maleness. Even college textbooks are not immune to these influences. Recent studies of the pictorial content of texts for college-level psychology and sociology courses found that women are shown less than men and are portrayed more passively and negatively than men (Ferree and Hall, 1990; Peterson and Kroner, 1992). For example, the psychology texts portray women as the victims of mental disorders and the clients in therapy, whereas men are pictured as the therapists. All these portrayals help to perpetuate the cultural stereotype that men tend to be stronger, more active, and working in the world to solve problems, whereas women are more likely to be weaker, more passive, and focusing their interests around home and family.

Because young schoolchildren are at a very formative and impressionable stage in life, the impact that these school experiences have on them is substantial and long-lasting. Evidence shows that sexism in the schools does result in lower self-esteem for female grade school and high school students (Martinez and Dukes, 1991). Even at the college level, as the first Policy Issues insert in this chapter suggests, the interaction between faculty and female students can involve strong doses of sexism, with potentially detrimental influences on female students' performance. At the same time,

POLICY ISSUES

Sexism and Discrimination in Higher Education

The most blatant forms of discrimination are probably the easiest to eradicate. Fifty years ago, a woman could be rejected for admission to medical school on the basis of her gender alone. Today, such overt inequality of opportunity is illegal, and any school practicing it would be inviting a lawsuit. But discrimination in colleges and universities can take subtler forms as well. Sexism of this sort cannot be so easily controlled through legislation; the patterns of behavior it reflects are too deeply embedded in our culture. Often, neither faculty nor students are aware of these patterns or their effects. According to the report of the Association of American Colleges' Project on the Status and Education of Women (1982), these subtler forms of sexism can do much harm.

Some offensive behaviors are fairly obvious. Professors may disparage women's intellectual abilities or academic commitments. Sexist humor may be used in class to "spice up" dull lectures, and discussions of female students' work may be diverted toward a discussion of their physical attributes or appearance. Inadvertent or not, such comments can have a powerful negative influence on the educational atmosphere of a classroom. Fortunately, most professors are sufficiently sensitive to the issue of sexism that they avoid making blatantly offensive remarks. Without being aware of it, however, even those educators with the best intentions may inadvertently favor male students over females. The report listed the following behaviors, among others, as having a "chilling effect" on the classroom environment for women:

- calling directly on men students but not on women students. Male faculty may be especially likely to address male students more often than females.
- "coaching" men but not women students to work toward a fuller answer by probing for additional elaboration or explanation.

- waiting longer for men than for women to answer a question before going on to another student.
- interrupting women students or allowing them to be disproportionately interrupted by peers.
- responding more extensively to men's comments than to women's.
- using classroom examples that reflect stereotyped ideas about men's and women's social and professional roles, as when the scientist, doctor, or accountant is always "he" and the lab assistant, patient, or secretary is always "she."
- using the generic "he" or "man" to represent both men and women, as in "When a writer is truly innovative, what criteria can we use to measure his achievement?"

The report by the Association of American Colleges provoked considerable debate and numerous research efforts to assess the extent and exact forms that such "chilly" behaviors might take (Constantinople, Cornelius, and Gray, 1988; Crawford and MacLeod, 1990). The research consistently shows that male students do dominate college classroom discussions more than female students do. However, there is less evidence that it is the "chilly" behavior of male college professors that elicits greater participation from the male students. Some colleges may have a classroom atmosphere that is generally friendlier to male students, but in most colleges the sex of the professor does not seem to be a big factor in producing the dominance of males—it occurs in the classrooms of both male and female professors. It may be that males come to college more prepared to actively and aggressively project themselves into classroom discussions, and the professors in turn may respond more positively to those students, irrespective of sex, who show such initiative and speak up in the classroom.

So, although colleges and professors still need to make sure that such "chilly" behaviors do not creep into the classroom, they also need to look at things they can do to encourage more participation from the female students in their classes. In addition, educational institutions need to look at why male students dominate classroom discussions. It may be due to the general socialization experiences discussed elsewhere in this chapter, or it might be due to experiences in grade school or high school classrooms. Another intriguing finding in some of this research is that female professors create an atmosphere in the classroom in which students feel more comfortable interacting, and they elicit more student participation than do male professors. Female professors seem to be more aware of the interpersonal dynamics in the classroom that might discourage participation. Their male counterparts might be able to learn something from them.

If the climate in the classroom is "chilly" for women in general, it is "freezing" for minority women (Richardson, 1988: 64). Despite the fact that black female high school seniors have higher educational aspirations than white females or black males, once these black women reach college, they are often subject to harassment, devaluation, and invisibility (Benokraitis and Feagin, 1986: 127). In 1988, for example, a black female cheerleader at The Ohio State University claimed that she was regularly jeered and harassed by crowds at basketball games due to her race. Subsequently, she brought suit against the university administration, alleging that the university tolerated this behavior rather than taking a public stand against it. Black college students—both male and female—routinely report feeling socially and culturally isolated on campuses that they perceive as largely white institutions, totally insensitive to the needs and concerns of blacks (Bunzel, 1991).

The college climate is chilly for women faculty as well as for women students. Even for women who receive their doctoral degree and manage to land a position teaching in a university, their experiences finding and securing a job tend to be different from those of their male counterparts (Gallagher et al., 1992). The women are more likely to choose a college teaching job on the basis of where their husband can find work, whereas men are freer to choose jobs that will provide the most benefit to their careers. This means that the first job these women get after completing their training is at a lower status university than the men get, and it means that women who change jobs experience more downward mobility in their subsequent jobs than do men. This illustrates how the interlinkage of the institutions of education, the economy, and the family have different effects on men and women. Even after receiving high educational degrees that make them eligible for good jobs at prestigious universities, women are more constrained in their choices by demands of childbearing and rearing than men are. Women are still expected to accommodate their career aspirations to family needs more than men are, and if a conflict arises, wives are more often expected to adapt their careers to their husbands' advancement than vice versa.

Despite laws that prohibit any preferences concerning hiring, promotions, and salary, women are still underrepresented in jobs in higher education. Fewer than 10 percent of the presidents of colleges and universities, including those that are all female, are women. Figures regarding academic rank are particularly revealing: Ninety percent of academics holding the rank of full professor are male, as well as 80 percent of the associate professors and nearly 70 percent of the assistant professors (Sadker et al., 1986). Furthermore, according to the American Association of University Professors, it is only in the least well-paid and least secure jobs—instructors and lecturers, who are often forced to accept part-time appointments—that the proportions of female faculty begin to equal those of the male faculty (Richardson, 1988: 65).

So, although advances have been made in the struggle with prejudice and discrimination in the United States, they are still widespread, although in much more subtle forms than in the past. It appears that a statement once made about racism can also be applied to issues of equality for women: Sexism won't disappear by itself—it has to be dealt with. It cannot even be attacked, however, until we learn to recognize it in the subtle forms in which it pervades our daily lives.

APPLIED RESEARCH

How Would Your Life Be Different?

Have you ever thought about what it would be like to be a member of the opposite sex? How would your life be different? A professor at Colorado Women's College, who at one time was affiliated with the Institute for Equality in Education at the University of Colorado, investigated this issue in some depth. Dr. Alice I. Baumgartner surveyed nearly two thousand children in grades three through twelve across the state of Colorado (Baumgartner, 1983). Dr. Baumgartner and her colleagues asked these youngsters how their lives would be different if they woke up tomorrow and discovered that they were a member of the sex opposite from their own.

Many of the answers that she received are disturbing because they exemplify the subtlety and pervasiveness of the problem of sexual inequality and sex-role stereotyping. The belief is widespread today, especially among the young, that problems of sexism have been solved; that equality and egalitarianism are now the norm; that modern American males and females are happy with their sexual status and would not have reason to change a thing. Dr. Baumgartner's investigation did not find that boys and girls think there are benefits and disadvantages to being either sex. On the contrary, she found a fundamental contempt for females by both boys and girls.

For example, the elementary school boys whom she surveyed often titled their answers with catchy phrases such as "The Disaster" or "Doomsday." One sixth-grade boy commented, "If I were a girl, I'd be stupid and weak as a string." Another remarked, "If I woke up and I was a girl, I would hope it was a bad dream and go back to sleep." One even said, "If I were a girl, I'd kill myself." The girls, on the other hand, wrote repeatedly about how much better off they would be if they were boys. One said, "If I were a boy, I would be treated better." Another observed: "People would take my decisions and my beliefs more seriously." One extremely poignant response from a third-grade girl cuts right to the quick: "If I were a boy, my daddy might have loved me."

Generally speaking, there was a sense of envy on the part of the girls to the effect that, if they were boys, they would not have to be so concerned about their appearance. Boys, on the other hand, talked about the hassles involved with being female: "I'd have to curl my hair and put on makeup." "I'd have to shave my whole body!" Boys had a critical or hostile reaction to female activities, but not a single girl in Baumgartner's sample expressed a negative reaction to male activities. The general views are summed up in the words of one boy, who said, "Girls can't do anything that's fun" and of one girl, who remarked that her expectation as a female was "to be nothing." We could go on, but the point should be clear.

What about young adults? We decided to experiment with a slightly different version of Dr. Baumgartner's exercise. We asked students in many of our sociology classes to imagine what it would be like to be a member of the opposite sex for a day. What would they want to do during that period of time? While qualitatively different from the responses of Baumgartner's elementary and secondary school-aged youngsters, the

it has been shown that college experiences have a liberalizing effect on men's and women's gender-role attitudes, especially for those who go on to graduate (Funk and Willits, 1987).

The Media

The media is an extremely important influence on gender role socialization through its portrayals of men and women. Despite the fact that *Cosmopoli-*

comments of our college students still reflect some of the same kinds of feelings about sexual status.

A clear majority of the males expressed curiosity about the sex lives of females—"what it would be like to have an orgasm as a women," "how it would feel to be propositioned in a bar," "what it would be like to sell sex for money." Interestingly enough, some males had very little to say at all about imagining what it would be like to be female. Some actually sat in their chairs for fifteen minutes and wrote nothing. Several had written but a sentence or two, expressing a version of the following actual statement: "If I were female for twenty-four hours, I would find a closet to lock myself in, and wouldn't come out until I changed back to being male." Admittedly, there were some male students who expressed sensitivity to the social liabilities of being male, such as having to limit emotion in certain situations. For example, one male wrote: "It would be comforting to know that I could cry when I felt like it, rather than having to hold it all in." Another remarked: "I would be able to tell other people [females] about how I really felt; I'd be able to tell them what I can't tell the guys."

Many of the females' responses hark back to the same kinds of sentiments found in Baumgartner's sample of younger people. A clear majority of females expressed feelings of being dominated by males and feelings that many attractive activities are monopolized by males: "I would be able to be more dominant in conversations with other men"; "I could talk to professors and not note any difference in treatment"; "I could go into a bar *alone*"; "I could play sports with other men and be treated equally"; "I would get more respect in my work." Some college-aged women expressed similar curiosity about physiological issues as their male counterparts: "I would be able to urinate standing up"; "I would be able to relieve myself in the woods without all the hassle"; "I would like to have sexual intercourse as a male and see what it feels like." Other responses reflect different elements of envy related to our social attitudes toward male versus female behavior: "I would like to get up in the morning, decide not to take a shower, not to shave, to put on some grody clothes, and go out to places without feeling like I'll get looked down on for it"; "I would eat all I wanted to and not worry about getting fat"; "I would go to the gym and work out, sweat a lot, and not worry about what other people are saying"; "I would stay out until all hours without worrying about the consequences."

Some married women, and often parents, expressed a slightly different kind of reaction to being "male for a day": "I would come home in the evening, take off my shoes, grab a beer from the fridge, turn on the TV, and wait until my dinner was ready"; "I would enjoy coming home and telling my wife that I had to go back to work after dinner—so 'I can't take the kids to hockey practice; you will have to take them'"; "I'd be able to make the *final* decision about what color the new car will be."

There were many women who indicated that they would not change a thing; that they enjoyed being female and appreciated the challenge of confronting the changes occurring in gender roles. However, the upshot of both Baumgartner's and our own research is that we are far from having eliminated all the controversy about sexual stratification in American society. The blatant sexism of past decades may be largely gone, but it has been replaced for many people by more subtle feelings about being men and women. Although things have certainly improved, men still receive more of society's tangible rewards. This occurs even though virtually all young people today believe that men and women should be treated equally.

---

tan magazine is allegedly a publication for "modern women," for example, the cover photographs generally focus on very seductive women wearing clothing that is sexually suggestive. In popular romance novels, women are typically portrayed as the victims of male aggression, and this victimization is usually attributed to the nature of their relationship to the aggressors (which is an excel-

Advertising still routinely uses female sexuality to sell products, and this can help perpetuate the belief that sexuality and physical beauty are the primary standards for assessing women's worth.

lent example of "blaming the victim," as discussed in Chapter 6). The impact of these books is significant, because millions of Americans read them every year. In a recent investigation that examined the roles played by men and women in newspaper photographs, it was determined that men appear far more often than women. Furthermore, men are typically portrayed in professional roles, whereas women are cast in domestic roles (Luebke, 1989).

Perhaps the most significant media influence on young people is television. It has been estimated that between kindergarten and sixth grade, children watch from ten to twenty-five hours of television every week. In fact, "children spend more time watching television than they do reading books, listening to the radio, or going to the movies" (Richmond-Abbott, 1992: 98). Despite the fact that television has "cleaned up its act" to some extent, this powerful medium still overwhelmingly portrays stereotyped gender roles. Investigations of television programs reveal that many of them present a grossly distorted view of family life, with 75 percent of male roles por-

trayed in prime time reflecting the images of unmarried men who are "tough" and "cool." Even on public television, there have been strong indicators of sexual differentiation—the female puppets on *Sesame Street* have been observed to portray predominantly strident, loudmouthed types. Over the last three decades, only 20 percent of the characters on prime time television shows were female, and most of the women shown were young, unemployed, family-bound, and in comic roles (Richmond-Abbott, 1992).

There have, of course, been improvements in the portrayal of women in the movies and on television over the past decade. Women have been portrayed as skilled physicians (*St. Elsewhere*), competent attorneys (*L.A. Law*), realistic police officers (*Cagney and Lacey*), and working single parents (*Kate and Allie*). Some of the old stereotypes linger, however, and there is evidence that they affect youngsters' attitudes about these matters. A longitudinal study of sex-role attitudes of teenagers was completed in the 1970s (Morgan, 1972). It found that watching a lot of television did not seem to make boys more sexist. However, the teenagers who had the least sexist attitudes to begin with—fairly intelligent girls—were most affected by television: Those who watched it a lot developed more sexist attitudes. This again illustrates the subtle ways in which people can develop views of the world that help maintain patterns of dominance and subordination.

There is a tendency, especially for young people today, to claim that the issue of differences between the sexes is passé. The Applied Research insert in this chapter (see pp. 244–245) suggests, through a creative form of research, that the issue is far from settled.

THE EXTENT OF SEXUAL INEQUALITY

Although women are a numerical majority in our society, they comprise a minority group, and there are a number of important similarities between women and other minorities (see Chapter 6). Like blacks, they still have unequal access to valued resources and suffer discrimination on many fronts. Although we will focus primarily on the way in which women suffer from sexual inequality, we will also look at some ways in which men have been discriminated against by unreasonable differentiation based on sex.

Economic Discrimination

Women occupy a subordinate position in comparison to men on virtually every dimension of socioeconomic status (SES). The three main dimensions of SES are education, occupation, and income.

Education.   Education has long been a key channel of social mobility in the United States, particularly for members of minority groups or others who were disadvantaged. Today, a college education is especially important in gaining prestigious and powerful positions in society, but higher education has never been equally available to all. Until about 1850, women were almost completely excluded from colleges. It was assumed that women needed less education because their careers would be as homemakers and mothers. In fact, in 1873, the U.S. Supreme Court ruled that an Illinois woman could be denied a license to practice law on the grounds that she was female. One Supreme Court justice of the era defended this stance by saying, "the paramount mission and destiny of women are to fill the noble and benign offices of wife and mother. This is the law of the Creator" ("The Brethren's First Sister," 1981: 17).

Since 1950, the number of Americans twenty-five years of age and older with some college training has quadrupled, and there have been dramatic increases in the proportion of women who pursue some form of advanced education in the United States. The percentage of doctoral degrees going to women has grown from 14 percent in 1971 to 35 percent today, and 40 percent of law degrees go to women today, compared with only 5 percent in 1970 (U.S. Bureau of the Census, 1991: 168–169). Still, many more men attain these degrees than do women, and as Figure 7.1 illustrates, the percentage of men who complete college still considerably exceeds that of women. Although women have gained slightly on men in college graduation rates in the past thirty years, the gap has been narrowed only slightly. The problems that women face in getting an education, especially in a professional school, can often be subtle and difficult to detect. For example, one study of admission to medical school found that the personal interview part of the admissions process counted more heavily for female than for male applicants (Clayton, Baird, and Levinson, 1984). Furthermore, the women were rated lower on the average on these interviews than were men. This suggests that these interviews, which are very subjective assessments by those doing the interviewing, serve as a mechanism to limit women's opportunities to enter medical school. An interesting side issue is that among blacks, men are

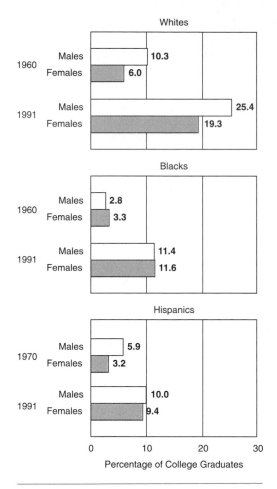

Whites

1960
Males   10.3
Females   6.0

1991
Males   25.4
Females   19.3

Blacks

1960
Males   2.8
Females   3.3

1991
Males   11.4
Females   11.6

Hispanics

1970
Males   5.9
Females   3.2

1991
Males   10.0
Females   9.4

Percentage of College Graduates

Figure 7.1   **Percentage of People, 25 Years Old or Older, Completing Four Years or More of College, by Sex and Race, 1960 and 1991**
SOURCES: U.S. Bureau of the Census, *Statistical Abstract of the United States, 1988* (Washington, D.C.: U.S. Government Printing Office, 1987), p. 131; U.S. Bureau of the Census, Current Population Reports, Series P-20, No. 462, *Educational Attainment in the United States: March 1991 and 1990* (Washington, D.C.: U.S. Government Printing Office, 1992), p. 96.

slightly worse off in terms of educational achievement than women, suggesting that decades of oppression and racial discrimination have made it especially difficult for black males to be upwardly mobile (see Chapter 6).

Work and the Workplace.   In the occupational realm, women are concentrated at the lower end of the status hierarchy. Table 7.2 illustrates that women tend to hold jobs such as secretary or receptionist, which provide relatively low income and prestige. The better occupations, such as physician or lawyer, are held primarily by men. Evidence suggests that some of this difference, even in the 1990s, is the result of discrimination in hiring practices. Some employers still prefer to hire men for jobs requiring technical or managerial skills based on the gender-role stereotype that men are more competent at such tasks. This is especially true when there is no evidence to suggest superior job performance on the part of either the male or female applicant for a job (Gerdes and Garber, 1983; Zebrowitz, Tenenbaum, and Goldstein, 1991). Table 7.2 illustrates that the job opportunities for women have improved in the 1970s and 1980s, with considerably more women moving into such lucrative jobs as lawyer, physician, or engineer. But the dark side of the issue is that the low-paying and low-prestige jobs are still almost exclusively filled by women. In addition, research shows women who take traditionally male, blue-collar jobs encounter a very hostile climate in terms of how they are treated by their male coworkers and supervisors. These women, as a result, are less satisfied with their jobs and experience more stress at work than do women in traditionally female jobs (Mansfield et al., 1991).

Even when educational opportunities are available to women, their chances for success in an occupation are often blocked by obstacles that men usually do not face, such as subtle forms of discrimination in hiring practices. In the legal profession, for instance, access to jobs in large law firms is one of the major routes to success, but for many years such law firms closed their doors to women (Epstein, 1981). In 1968, one woman lawyer (now a federal district judge) was told by a law firm that "we don't hire women; the secretaries might resent it" ("The Brethren's First Sister," 1981: 17). There has been an upsurge in the number of women lawyers in recent years—from 2.8

Table 7.2 **Employment Positions Held by Women, 1976–1991**

Some Jobs Show Changes			*Some Jobs Show Little Change*		
Employment Positions	*Percentage of Jobs Held by Women*		*Employment Positions*	*Percentage of Jobs Held by Women*	
	1976	*1991*		*1976*	*1991*
Cashiers	87.7%	80.9%	Secretaries	99.0%	99.0%
Food counter clerks	85.5	71.0	Receptionists	96.2	97.1
Food service workers	68.7	59.3	Child-care workers	98.2	96.7
Real estate sales	41.2	51.5	Typists	96.7	95.1
Accountants and auditors	26.9	51.5	Bank tellers	91.9	90.3
Cleaning service workers	33.5	43.1	Bookkeepers	90.0	91.5
Financial managers	24.7	44.7	Health-service workers	86.2	88.6
College and university teachers	31.3	40.8	Hairdressers, cosmetologists	88.0	90.2
Lawyers and judges	9.2	18.9	Librarians	82.4	83.0
Physicians	12.8	20.1	File clerks	85.5	80.9
Police and detectives	3.7	14.0	Schoolteachers (except college and university)	70.9	74.3
Engineers	1.8	8.2	Social workers	61.0	68.0
Fire fighters	0.0	2.3	Construction trades	1.6	1.8

SOURCE: U.S. Department of Labor, Bureau of Labor Statistics, *Employment and Earnings*, Vol. 24, No. 1, January 1977, pp. 8–9; Vol. 39, No. 1, January 1992, pp. 185–190.

percent of the profession in 1970 to about 19 percent today. Yet women still make up only about 2 percent of the partners in the largest law firms, and research documents that, through the 1980s, women lawyers still were discriminated against in promotions in major U.S. law firms (Spurr, 1990).

Another obstacle that women face in the occupational realm is that they tend to be saddled, more so than men, with familial obligations (Ferree, 1991; Spade and Reese, 1991). Even when both spouses work, and even though men have taken on more responsibilities for these tasks in recent decades, women are still expected to take on more responsibility for raising the children,

keeping up the home, and taking care of sick relatives. In fact, research shows that the cost of child care is an important reason why women sometimes quit the jobs they do get (Maume, 1991). Even among college-educated people, it is the rare couple who has a truly symmetrical relationship in which both partners share equally in household and work responsibilities.

Even women who start their own business are at a disadvantage in comparison to men (Loscocco et al., 1991). They have more difficulty securing capital from banks and contracts from the government, in part because of the belief that female-owned businesses are more likely to fail. Women are more often excluded from social networks where contacts are made and business deals can be discussed. Women also tend to start small businesses, which are more likely to fail than large businesses, and they go into business sectors where profits tend to be lower and failure rates higher, such as services or retail trade. Finally, women have less experience in the business world than do men. All these factors combined result in women's businesses being less profitable and more subject to failure.

Income. Classical economic theory claims that wages are determined by the competitive forces of supply and demand. Employers are rational and pay workers what they are worth in terms of the employer's ability to produce goods and services for a price that consumers are willing to pay. In this view, discrimination in pay based on gender or other characteristics is irrational and thus will not persist in the long run. Many economists and much sociological research suggest that this is a very simplistic view of the factors that influence the setting of wages (Jacobs and Steinberg, 1990; Peterson, 1990). In addition to market forces, income levels are also influenced by how much power different groups of workers possess and by cultural stereotypes of what different workers are worth as well as by the traditional levels of pay for different jobs. The effect of these "irrational" factors on women has been to be paid considerably less than men.

In 1990, the median income for American males working year round and full time was $29,172; for females, it was only $20,586 (U.S. Bureau of the Census, 1992). Women's income is about 70 percent of men's income, and this has changed only slightly since 1970 (see Table 7.3). Such gender inequality is found in virtually all industrial nations, with women in Australia doing best by earning 79 percent of what men make and in Japan doing worst with 46 percent of men's incomes (Rosenfeld and Kalleberg, 1991). This is a substantial difference. Even if we look at income levels of male and female workers in the same occupational categories who work year round and

Table 7.3 **Ratio of Female/Male Median Income, by Age, 1970 and 1990, Among Year-round, Full-time Civilian Workers**

Age	1970	1990
All ages	0.59	0.70
15 to 19 years	0.96	}0.89
20 to 24 years	0.74	
25 to 34 years	0.65	0.79
35 to 44 years	0.54	0.69
45 to 54 years	0.56	0.61
55 to 64 years	0.60	0.63
65 years and over	0.72	0.64

SOURCES: U.S. Bureau of the Census, *Statistical Abstract of the United States, 1989* (Washington, D.C.: U.S. Government Printing Office, 1989), p. 448; U.S. Bureau of the Census, *Statistical Abstract of the United States, 1992* (Washington, D.C.: U.S. Government Printing Office, 1992), p. 452.

full time, women earn substantially less than men in every job category (see Table 7.4). Some of these differences in income result from the fact that most men have been working longer than women and thus have gained seniority and salary increases that have boosted their income. However, studies that have taken this into account still conclude that women have tended to earn less than men for doing the same job (Frieze, Olson, and Good, 1990). A recent study by the U.S. Department of Education looked at the experiences of men and women who graduated from high school in 1972 and thus would be in the middle of their careers at the time of the study (Adelman, 1991). What they found was that women on the whole did better in high school and college than men did, they finished college faster, and they had more positive attitudes toward their educational experience. However, by the midpoint in their careers, women earned less than the men and were more likely to be unemployed. The study looked at comparable men and women, such as those who had no children and had been working equal lengths of times, but still found pay inequities: In

Table 7.4   **Median Annual Income for Year-round Full-time Workers, by Sex and Occupational Category, 1990**

Occupational Group	Male Income	Female Income	Ratio Women/Men
Professional specialty	$41,100	$29,181	.71
Executive, administrators, and managerial	40,541	25,858	.64
Sales	29,652	16,986	.57
Precision production, craft and repair	26,506	18,739	.71
Service workers	18,550	12,139	.65
Technical and related support	30,897	23,992	.78
Administrative support	26,192	18,475	.71
Machine operators, assemblers, and inspectors	22,345	14,652	.66
Transportation and material moving	24,556	16,003	.65

SOURCE: U.S. Bureau of the Census, *Statistical Abstract of the United States, 1992* (Washington, D.C.: U.S. Government Printing Office, 1992), p. 414.

only seven of the thirty-three occupations studied did pay equity between men and women occur. The other twenty-six occupations showed men making significantly more than women. No occupation showed women making more than men. Even among men and women in the same age brackets, income differences persist (see Table 7.3). Although there is little sex-based difference in income between teenagers, differences emerge among young adults and grow larger among older adults. In addition, although the 1970s and 1980s were a time of much concern about sexual inequality, some research suggests that income inequality between the sexes actually increased during that period (Smith, 1991). It is safe to say that not a lot of improvement has occurred, and the prospects for income equality in the near future are not great.

In Chapter 6, we discussed social inequality based on race and ethnicity. People in whom a subordinate racial or ethnic status is combined with a subordinate sexual status are even worse off than women in general (see Figure 7.2). Among

full-time workers in 1991, white males earned a median weekly income of $509 and white females $374. Black males earned the same as white females, and Hispanic males earned $46 less. Black women, on the other hand, earned $323 and Hispanic women $293. Clearly, minority women in the United States are in a very weak and vulnerable position when it comes to competing for economic resources. Even when they have full-time jobs, they tend to be concentrated in those jobs with the lowest income or prestige (Higginbotham, 1987; Blea, 1991).

Discrimination in the Military

Even women who choose the military as a career do not have the same opportunities as men. Even though they constitute 11 percent of the armed services, they are currently barred from serving in many combat positions (Spitzer, 1992). In 1993 the Clinton Administration opened some, but not all, combat positions to women. This is important because serving in combat positions is one of the

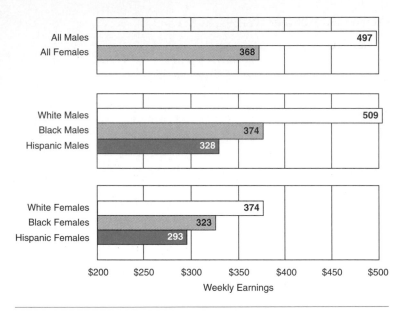

Figure 7.2   **Median Weekly Earnings of Full-time Workers, by Sex and Race, 1991**
SOURCE: U.S. Department of Labor, Bureau of Labor Statistics, *Employment and Earnings*, Vol. 39, No. 1, January 1992, p. 221.

best ways to advance one's career in the military. The partial ban on women in combat units continues to exist despite the fact that, during the Gulf War of 1991, female soldiers found themselves in combat, performed well by all standards, and were killed in action and taken prisoner by enemy troops. In fact, a poll taken during the Gulf War indicated that half the American public feels that women should have combat assignments if they want them (Fuentes, 1991). The major arguments against women in combat positions, especially ground infantry units, is that they do not have the physical strength or aggressive nature needed for the job, that they would disrupt the cohesiveness and "bonding" that occurs among men in combat and is important to combat success, and that it violates deep-seated cultural values regarding manhood and womanhood in Western civilization. Supporters of equal opportunities for women argue that women can be trained for the strength and aggressiveness and

that they proved themselves in the Gulf War. Furthermore, there is no reason to believe that women could not "bond" in a military unit as well as men. The major stumbling block, according to this view, is that fighting and military combat are one of the last bastions where men can maintain a separate "male" world into which women are not allowed. Of course, a major factor fueling the movement of women into the military over the past thirty years has been the needs of the military itself, which is ultimately concerned with finding a sufficient number of educated and motivated recruits. Along these lines, three factors are propelling the greater utilization of women: the all-volunteer military; the increasingly high-tech workplace, which calls for brains and dexterity more than brawn; and the increasing feminization of the work force. Given these trends, the military may see that it is in its own interests to expand opportunities for women, maybe by opening up more combat positions to them in the future.

Other Types of Discrimination

Discrimination on the basis of sex is not confined to education, occupation, and income. There are various other ways in which women are placed at a disadvantage in American society. For example, our legal system has built into it a great deal of discrimination against women. In 1990, most states still provided husbands with some loopholes to avoid prosecution for raping their wives (Russell, 1990). In eight states, men cannot be charged with raping their wives as long as they are living together and the wife has not filed for divorce or protection. Twenty-six other states allow charges of marital rape but with exemptions. Depending on the state, for example, a man cannot be charged with raping his wife unless he has kidnapped her or threatened her with a weapon; some of these states do not permit rape charges if the wife is unable to consent to having sex because she is drugged or unconscious. Only sixteen states accord wives the same protection as other women by treating marital rape like any other rape. In some states, wives are required to accept their husband's choice of domicile, and men can be granted divorces based on their wives' "gross neglect of duty," including refusal to clean the house, care for the children, or have sexual intercourse (Richardson, 1988: 105). The Equal Credit Opportunity Act (ECOA) of 1974 outlawed discrimination on the basis of sex or marital status in credit transactions, so single or married women can now establish their own credit record and obtain loans. Yet some women are still the objects of credit discrimination. For example, creditors are required to record the credit histories of both spouses only if requested. Thus, some women may unwittingly find that their credit records have not been established even though no violation of the ECOA has occurred.

Women have also experienced discrimination in the realm of retirement income. Retirement plans have traditionally paid women a smaller monthly income than they pay to men with the same accumulated retirement assets. This inequity has been based on the fact that women live longer, on the average, than men. The rationale has been that women will draw the same total assets from their retirement plan as men, but they will draw it out in smaller amounts over a longer period. Women, of course, have complained that this penalizes them for being healthy. They have also argued that there are many other criteria than sex that could be used to determine retirement income, such as genetic susceptibility to disease such as heart disease or behavioral factors such as smoking.

The International Perspectives insert highlights the issue of gender inequalities in some other societies and suggests what it is about societies that tends to increase gender inequality.

Sexual Inequality Involving Males

Most discussions of sexual inequality focus on women, but men also suffer from unreasonable sexual differentiation. Some have even spoken of a "masculine mystique" and the "myth of masculinity": a set of stereotypes about men, such as their being strong, dominant, tough, unemotional, and so forth (Pleck, 1981; Kimmel and Messner, 1992). Socially imposed expectations concerning male behavior can be as limiting for men in our society as the stereotypes involving females have been for women. In terms of professional careers, for example, male secretaries were often regarded as social oddities not that long ago. Men who entered such unconventional male roles had to be prepared for incredulous and sometimes even abusive reactions from others. At that time, most men probably did not even consider a profession such as nurse or secretary, even in the late 1970s, when jobs for college graduates in nursing were plentiful and other jobs were scarce. Still, today, very few men go into nursing.

The stereotypical male role also limits the opportunities open to men in terms of domestic activities, emotional expression, and relationships with children. Not that many years ago, if a male executive were to ask his employer for paternity leave, his boss would probably have laughed. To-

INTERNATIONAL PERSPECTIVES

The Treatment of Women in Other Societies

When we look at cultures other than our own, it is not hard to find women being treated, even today, in ways that Americans would find abhorrent. In Bangladesh, for example, mothers with limited resources give their sons the first pick of the food available whereas daughters have to be satisfied with what is left over. Since Bangladeshi culture discourages women from doing paid work outside the home, males are seen as the more important breadwinners in the family and are thus fed and cared for with more zeal. As a consequence, Bangladeshi girls are often underfed and suffer stunted growth. In Saudi Arabia, religious police, or Mutawin, patrol in jeeps looking for women who are not properly attired, according to the Islamic code. Unacceptable attire, which might mean having an ankle visible beneath the mandatory long black robes, is met with harassment and in some cases arrest (Hijab, 1988; Sadik, 1989). Such cultural beliefs and practices are reflected in women's and men's opportunities in the workplace. In Bangladesh, less than 10 percent of adult women work, compared to well over half of women in the United States. In Saudi Arabia, women and men are segregated in many workplaces and schools.

A close look at these and other examples of gender inequalities in many cultures makes one thing clear: While gender inequality is pervasive, and often more extensive than in the United States, it is also complicated and influenced by many factors. One such factor is religion. Both Bangladesh and Saudi Arabia are Islamic countries, and Islamic societies have tended to keep women subordinate and out of the labor force. At the same time, there are many modern and well-educated women in such Islamic countries and many Muslim men who support greater education of and opportunities for women (Hourani, 1991). In fact, many Muslims interpret parts of the Koran (the Islamic holy book) as giving religious affirmation to gender equality. So, the picture is one of a tension between an admittedly very strong and pervasive social custom of male dominance on the one hand, and the desire of some women and men to open up a broader range of opportunities for both genders on the other hand. Which of these tendencies predominates shifts over

day, leaves of absence for new fathers are becoming more common in some companies. At the same time, there is still a form of institutionalized discrimination involved, because the man who takes such a leave often loses ground in the competition for advancement and seniority. Although there are very few males who identify themselves occupationally as "house husbands," it is more common than it once was for men to accept equal responsibility with their partners for domestic tasks (Lewis, 1984; McCall, 1988). In fact, despite the cultural assumption that work is the chief activity for men, a recent investigation found that 90 percent of the male respondents to a survey expressed strong attachments to their roles as husbands and fathers and defined their marital and parental roles as the most important (Cohen, 1987).

The legal system also discriminates against men in several different ways. For example, many states have laws that make it a punishable offense for men (and presumably other women) to use obtime. But this fluctuation in attitude is also true in the United States. We have documented in this chapter a move toward greater gender equality in the United States. On the other hand, we also read Susan Faludi's argument about a recent backlash against equality that seems to have brought considerable resistance to further advances for women—a tension like that in Islamic countries, although at a different level.

Another factor that influences gender equality is wealth and modernization, with the wealthier and more industrialized nations according more equal opportunities to women. Yet, Saudi Arabia, one of the wealthiest nations in the world, is also one of the more patriarchal. Even among the industrialized nations, levels of gender equality vary. In countries like the United States, Canada, and Sweden, for example, over half of all women work. However, in Belgium and the Netherlands—both modern, industrial nations—the figures are 28 percent and 37 percent, respectively (U.S. Bureau of the Census, 1991: 847). In these two societies, special cultural traditions have produced less support for women working outside the home, especially after they have children. Religion also influences practices in industrial nations, with heavily Catholic countries like Italy, Ireland, and Spain having only about one-third of all women in the work force.

Although opportunities for women seem to increase with industrialization, in some traditional societies women end up worse off, at least in the short run, as the economy shifts from agricultural to industrial production. "As agriculture becomes more mechanized and less labor intensive, men tend to take over the mechanized farming jobs. Women may be displaced or relegated to routine tasks associated with agriculture, such as the sorting of coffee beans. As women lose jobs in the agricultural sector, there are generally few employment opportunities for them in the industrial sector, as men are preferred" (Stockard and Johnson, 1992: 78). This trend may reverse, as it did in the United States as the expansion of industrial and service sectors of the economy provided a new source of jobs for women. However, this same pattern may not prevail in all societies. In addition, as we have seen in this chapter, the jobs that become available to women as industrialization proceeds tend to be at the low end of the pay and prestige scale. The fact that more women work does not mean that gender equality has been achieved.

So, patterns of gender inequality are complex and influenced by many elements of a culture, such as religious beliefs, wealth, level of industrialization, and other factors. How much gender inequality exists in a particular society depends on that society's unique blend of all those elements at a given time. This cross-cultural and international viewpoint serves as a warning not to oversimplify the reasons for gender inequality or the patterns that it can take in our own society.

scene language in the presence of females. In some states, only men must secure a test for venereal disease prior to obtaining a marriage license. Some statutory rape legislation makes it a criminal offense for an adult male to engage in sexual relations with a minor female, but no similar law applies to adult females and minor males (Deckhard, 1979). Many insurance companies charge higher automobile insurance premiums to young males because of the higher rate of automobile accidents among that group. Thus, a young man who is a careful driver is penalized by virtue of his sexual status. Finally, men but not women are required to register for the military draft, and only men could be inducted into the military should the draft itself be reinstated. Women are not required to make any equivalent contribution to national public service. This is true despite the fact that a public opinion poll during the Gulf War in 1991 showed that half of Americans believe that any future draft should include women (Fuentes, 1991).

In recent decades, more men have moved into positions that were traditionally held by women. Yet, sex-role stereotyping still severely constrains the choices of men as well as women. Men still avoid jobs like secretary, nurse, and child-care worker while few women become fire fighters or construction workers.

THE FUTURE OF SEXUAL INEQUALITY

Sexual inequality is more widely recognized as a social problem today than in the past, and it is also more likely to be considered an unacceptable kind of inequality. A major reason for this is that more women today work outside the home and view discrimination as an important hindrance to their futures. In addition, the number of single-parent families headed by women continues to rise, and these women find discrimination based on sex to be an unacceptable barrier to their ability to provide for their families. We now examine the future of sexual inequality, recognizing as we did in the beginning of the chapter that social reality is complex in terms of how much progress has occurred.

Collective Action and the Feminist Movement

The feminist movement probably has its earliest roots in the growing sensitivity to individual rights and democracy that characterized Western life during the seventeenth century. Much later, in the late 1800s, American women such as Susan B. Anthony and Elizabeth Cady Stanton campaigned for women's right to vote. Finally, in 1920, the Nineteenth Amendment to the Constitution—the Women's Suffrage Amendment—was passed. In the first half of this century, the nation became involved in two world wars, and these events took most of the attention away from women's rights for decades. In the late 1940s, fueled by women's work experience during World War II, women renewed the campaign for equal rights, but were beaten back by the conservative champions of another movement: the "return to normalcy" (Deckhard, 1979). Women were pressured to quit jobs that they held while American men had been at war and to return to the home so that the country could resume "normal" operation again.

In 1963, a well-known advocate of women's rights, Betty Friedan, wrote a book titled *The Feminine Mystique*. She took issue with the assumption that women "belong in the home," and her argument became the classic indictment of women being presumed to function best as mothers and homemakers. In 1966, Friedan and other feminists organized the National Organization for Women (NOW). At the time, this body of activist women was regarded as radical in mission, but many modern observers feel that "its style was actually somewhat conservative, and it stressed working through established legislative channels to achieve rights for women" (Richmond-Abbott, 1992: 354).

NOW concentrated much of its efforts toward passage of the Equal Rights Amendment, a constitutional amendment that would have banned discrimination based on sex. In 1982, the deadline for ratification passed on the ERA because an insufficient number of states were willing to endorse it. The ERA was viewed by many as the Emancipation Proclamation for women. Proponents of the ERA viewed its defeat as a significant setback for the women's rights movement, and it certainly suggests that sentiment still lingers in American society against complete equality for women. But again, reality is probably more complex than this. Some people opposed the ERA because they believed that existing legislation protected women adequately and that the amendment was redundant, whereas others thought it would produce unisex bathrooms and sanction homosexual marriages. Some women opposed it because they did not want to give up special privileges that they do receive, such as preference in child custody and divorce award cases. So, people opposed the ERA for many reasons, some of them having little to do with resistance to equality for women (Richmond-Abbott, 1992).

Seen from another perspective, the ERA issue is one of *status politics:* Opposition to or support for the amendment is in part a controversy over who has the power to enforce their definition of appropriate sex-role behavior on American society. Beyond any practical effect it might have, passage of the ERA would symbolically demonstrate the power of NOW and other feminist groups. Likewise, the defeat of the ERA shows that people supporting more traditional definitions of the sexes have the power to draw the line somewhere. According to the status politics point of view, the passage of legislation is as important as a symbolic demonstration of the exercise of power as it is for its practical outcome (Scott, 1985).

The feminist movement persists, but there is dissension among different camps within the movement and disagreement about what represents the next best steps to take. In fact, through the 1980s, there has been a reaction against feminism. Many young people, including women, have come to view feminism in an unfavorable light, and politicians, journalists, and the media have attacked feminism and the campaign for women's equality for being responsible for making women more miserable than they were in the past. In fact, journalist Susan Faludi (1991) sees a backlash in all this, a reaction against the advances that women have made. If one believes what one sees and hears on television, in the newspapers, or from the mouths of many politicians, says Faludi, feminism has produced women who cannot find a man to marry, who burnout in fast-track careers, who are infertile over thirty, and who suffer depression and unhappiness because they deny their "true" nature as women. If these are the products of equality, these images seem to say, then who needs it? Faludi argues that these false images emerge and are perpetuated because they support the belief, still held by many men and some women, that women should not seek complete equality with men—that things may have gone too far as it is. Although Faludi could find no evidence that any of these things were happening or that women's quest for equal treatment had a negative impact on women or men, this imagery is presented so commonly and so broadly that some people have accepted it as reality. Even though, as we have seen, women still suffer from serious inequalities, this backlash tends to deflate support for further efforts toward equality. When many people believe that women have achieved equality and that they are miserable because of it, the women's movement faces some substantial challenges in making further advances.

Despite all this, some promising changes are occurring in a number of realms.

Changes in the Law

Over the past twenty years in American society, a significant amount of legislation has been approved that contributes to the reduction of sexual inequality. The Credit Bill we alluded to earlier prohibits discrimination in loan eligibility based on sex or marital status. Title VII of the 1964 Civil Rights Act makes illegal any sex discrimination in employment practices. Title IX of the Educational Amendments Act specifies that any educational institution discriminating on the basis of sex will be denied federal aid. Other examples of legislation that helps women are the Displaced Homemaker Act (which assists women who have divorced but have few skills with which to support themselves) and legal provisions for wives who have been abused by their husbands.

In the past few years, a new idea for reducing the economic inequities suffered by women has emerged, called "comparable worth." The basic idea is that people whose jobs make equivalent demands on them and that call for similar skills, education, or responsibility should receive roughly similar pay; in other words, "equal pay for comparable worth" (Hill and Killingsworth, 1989; Blum, 1991). For example, a judge in Seattle ruled in 1983 that the state government was in violation of Title VII of the 1964 Civil Rights Act because it routinely paid jobs performed mostly by women less than those performed mostly by men. His ruling was based in part on a comparison of state jobs in terms of "worth points," with points given for such things as knowledge and skills required, mental demands, accountability, and working conditions. Since then, twenty-two states have begun to reassess their pay schedules with these ideas in mind. In fact, in Ontario, which is one of Canada's largest provinces, the Ontario Pay Equity Act, covering 1.7 million workers in public and private settings, now demands adherence to the principle of comparable worth (Freudenheim, 1989).

It has been a highly controversial development with opponents arguing that it is impossible to really compare the "worth" of different jobs and that the free market should determine what people are paid. These opponents argue that if women are dissatisfied with the low pay in some jobs, they should compete for the higher-paying jobs. Some even suggest that such interference with market mechanisms would disrupt our whole economic system. Supporters argue that women face more barriers in the competition for jobs and that comparable worth would help overcome generations of discrimination in the way salaries are set. So far, comparable worth has not substantially altered the position of women in society, but it is likely to become a central issue over the next decade (Aldrich and Buchele, 1986; Peterson, 1990).

Despite these changes, an observation we made in Chapter 6 is in order here. It is one thing to prohibit discrimination, but it is quite another to enforce these prohibitions and to protect them against inroads that could weaken their effect. After all, women's access to abortion is under attack and more limited than a decade ago, and the Reagan and Bush administrations have shown at best weak support for challenges to sex discrimination. So, the quest for equal and fair treatment is a constant and never-ending one.

Changes in the Workplace

Women's participation in the work force in the United States continues to enlarge, and as we have seen, many of the old inequalities persist, such as discrimination in pay and segregation into low-status and low-paying jobs. These are issues that can be attacked through changes in laws, such as comparable worth, or changes in the way we socialize children. However, as the number of women in the work force has increased and as they have moved into more traditionally male occupations, some new issues have risen to prominence, especially some more subtle and unexpected barriers to advancement that affect women in the 1990s. One study of male and female managers in large business concerns, for example, found that the women promoted to middle-management positions by male supervisors were the less aggressive, less threatening women who did not rock the boat or "make waves" (Harlan and Weiss, 1981). However, these middle-management positions were dead ends for these women because supervisors wanted more aggressive and dynamic people for top positions. This same research also disputed the belief that sexism in the workplace would decline as more women were employed. They found that resistance to women declines at first, but as the proportion of women passes 15 percent, renewed resistance emerges because men feel their opportunities are being reduced due to competition with women. Research has also found that when many women are employed in the same job, that job comes to be defined as a woman's job. Once this happens, the job tends to be devalued, with less pay and a smaller budget than when more men held that position (Baron and Newman, 1990; Reskin and Roos, 1990).

Another emerging reality concerning women in executive management positions is that many who occupy these positions are "bailing out" of the managerial work force because trying to combine full-time, demanding careers with being wives and mothers has proved to be "too much of a hassle." A recent study showed that the rate of turnover in management positions is nearly three times higher among women than among men, and many women who take maternity leave do not return to work (Schwartz, 1989). In addition, young women appear to be less drawn to high-powered business careers in the 1990s than they were in the 1970s. For example, women today make up a smaller proportion of applications to graduate programs in business than six years ago (Cowan, 1992). It seems that women today are less willing to make as many compromises in the family area as some young women did twenty years ago. To alleviate this tension between work and child rearing, it has been suggested that corporations could offer women two career tracks. One, called career-primary, would involve the

conventional expectations placed on male employees: career comes first, no time out for personal reasons, and work on nights and weekends if corporate needs demand it. The second track, called career-and-family or the "mommy track," would allow women to pursue careers while also devoting themselves to their families. For example, maternity leave would not be frowned on and excessive demands would not be placed on the women's free time. Critics of such proposals argue that those in the career-and-family track would be discriminated against in any event through smaller pay increases or reduced opportunity for promotion. In fact, research shows that women who interrupt their careers for family reasons, such as raising children, never catch up, in terms of income or promotions, to their female counterparts who stay on the job (Jacobsen and Levin, 1992). Apparently, their employers think they are not as serious about or as committed to their jobs. So, the career-and-family track would likely produce the same old outcome: Women who choose to have children would be discriminated against because they did not follow the male model of career development.

Despite this, we can predict that women will continue to join the work force in even larger numbers. Substantial improvement is already observable. Nearly one-third of the small businesses in the United States today belong to women, up from 23 percent in the early 1980s. Some labor experts project that this may hit 40 percent by the year 2000 (O'Hare and Larson, 1991). Keep in mind that these numbers do not include large corporations, where it is difficult to determine ownership, and that most women's businesses are small. Nonetheless, the growth has been impressive, and credit and capital are now more available to women who wish to start or expand a business. In addition, research shows that college-educated women are becoming much more like their male counterparts in terms of the emphasis they place on work as being essential to a person's life and happiness (Fiorentine, 1988). As these changes occur, mechanisms are developing to overcome some of the barriers that women have faced in the

POLICY ISSUES

Fighting Sexual Harassment in the Workplace

Since the Anita Hill–Clarence Thomas episode, the climate in the workplace certainly seems to have changed in relation to how people of different sexes treat one another. Both men and women seem more willing to report episodes of sexual harassment and assault. In fact, in 1992, it came out that a number of women serving in the military in Saudi Arabia and Iraq during the Gulf War were subjected to sexual assault—not by the enemy but rather by their fellow soldiers. Such behavior is now more likely to come under the harsh glare of publicity, and lawsuits have made sexual harassment expensive for employers to ignore. In 1980, the Equal Employment Opportunity Commission placed sexual harassment under the Civil Rights Act of 1964 as a form of civil rights violation. The Civil Rights Act of 1991 provided beefed-up protection and additional legal weapons in the fight against sexual harassment in the workplace. Some states also have strong antidis-crimination statutes that include sexual harassment. However, because of stringent standards set by the courts, winning a sexual harassment case is not easy. In particular, many courts require that harassment be so severe that a "reasonable employee" would find her or his psychological well-being and work performance seriously affected because of it, but some of the behaviors that women find demeaning and disturbing are not perceived by judges and juries to be that serious ("Sexual Harassment . . ." 1991).

Part of the problem with sexual harassment is that men and women tend to perceive behaviors quite differently. Most men and women agree that demanding sexual favors as a condition of employment or promotion is wrong. However, the Equal Employment Opportunity Commission also defines as harassment behaviors that create a "hostile" environment that makes it more difficult for people to do their job. So, repeated sexual

past. For example, women are excluded from fewer of the social and business networks that can assist one in a career or business. Because of court challenges based on antidiscrimination legislation, women have gained access to some chapters of such organizations as Rotary, the Lions Club, and the Kiwanis where businesspeople often gather. And it makes a big difference to success in business. As one businesswoman put it after she joined Rotary, "Suddenly I was having lunch every week with all the movers and shakers in town. Now they think of me when business opportunities come up" (quoted in Zane, 1991: 35). In addition, new networks have emerged to help women. For example, WomenVenture is a nationwide organization that offers seminars and workshops to women on how to start or expand a business, as well as financial backing to twenty-five hundred businesswomen each year. The Women's Media Group in New York sponsors lunches and other events where people can make contacts, learn whom to call about a job, or be introduced to an employer with a position open (Quindlen, 1981). Such organizations and contacts can make the difference between advancement and stagnation in one's business or career. The opportunities for advancement for women in the 1990s will undoubtedly improve with the further availability of such supports for women. However, thousands of clubs and organizations still do not admit women because there are no state or local antidiscrimination laws to force

advances by a coworker, even if not linked to employment or promotion, could constitute harassment because they are disturbing to the woman and create an environment in which it is difficult for her to work. And this is where men's and women's perceptions tend to differ. Many men see such behaviors as relatively harmless and claim they would even be flattered if they were the recipients of such actions by coworkers. Most women, on the other hand, find such behaviors disturbing, insulting, and offensive, and such behaviors do create a "hostile" atmosphere in many women's minds. This is why, during the Anita Hill–Clarence Thomas confrontation, we repeatedly heard women exclaim about men: They just don't get it. In other words, men just fail to understand why women find such behaviors offensive, demeaning, and maybe even frightening.

To give both men and women a better perspective on women's views of these issues, attorneys William Petrocelli and Barbara Kate Repa (1992), experts on the legal issues of sexual harassment, suggest the following simple test to help decide whether a remark or a behavior is appropriate:

1. Would you say or do the same thing in front of your spouse?

2. How would you feel if the same remarks or behavior were directed at your mother, sister, wife, or daughter?

3. How would you feel if a man made the same remarks or took the same actions toward you?

If your reaction to any one of these questions is negative, then the remark or behavior might well be seen as inappropriate harassment by a female coworker.

Many employers have been taking steps that experts recognize will reduce the likelihood of sexual harassment or assault occurring in the workplace: have a written and publicized policy against such actions, vigorously enforce the policy, educate employees about what constitutes harassment and how to file a complaint about it, and provide sincere and significant top-management support for the policy (Webb, 1991). Such steps should make the workplace of the 1990s a much more hospitable one for women. However, as we saw in Chapter 6, discrimination, as well as harassment, tends to rear its ugly head when competition between groups grows fierce. As more women enter the work force and take jobs traditionally held by men, harassment may emerge as a response to threatened losses. So additional vigilance may be necessary to alleviate this problem.

---

them to do so. In fact, former Presidents Ronald Reagan and George Bush belong to an elite businessmen's social club, the Bohemian Club, which refuses to admit women.

As we discussed in the beginning of the chapter, sexual harassment and assault are serious problems that women face in the workplace, making work for them more difficult and demeaning and in extreme cases impossible. As the second Policy Issues insert in this chapter shows, some important strides have been made in overcoming this problem.

The Changing Face of Politics

One image from the Anita Hill–Clarence Thomas confrontation in 1991 was unforgettable: a black woman confronting a panel of the all-white, all-male faces of the members of the Senate Judiciary Committee. It brought into stark reality the truth that, although women make up 51 percent of our populace, very few of them are among our elected representatives at the national level. Of the one hundred senators, the number of women among them fluctuated from a low of none to a high of two between 1970 and 1992, rising to six in the 1992 election (U.S. Bureau of the Census, 1991). However, this hides some very dramatic gains that women have made in politics over the past few decades. In 1970, only twenty-five women ran for seats in the U.S. House of Representatives; by 1992 this had increased six times, to 150 women. Although only 10 percent of the representatives in 1993 were women, that is almost four times greater than the 2.7 percent of twenty years earlier. Gains have been especially impressive at the state and local levels. Twenty years ago, women made up less than 5 percent of all state legislators, compared with 18 percent today. Twenty years ago, a paltry 1 percent of the mayors of American cities of more than thirty thousand people were women; today it is 17 percent. Although women are still far underrepresented in politics, they are beginning to move into more powerful and nationwide political positions. It takes time to get significant numbers of women entrenched in the political system to the point where they can make a run for a Senate seat. We will likely see more of this in the future.

Masculine, Feminine, or Human?

Some of the problems surrounding sexual inequality may arise in part because of the oversimplified view that people tend to have of gender, seeing things as either male or female, but not both. In reality, each individual can be seen as a combination of both feminine and masculine characteristics. In fact, masculinity and femininity may not be polar opposites but rather two independent sets of characteristics. So, for example, some very feminine women may have few masculine characteristics, whereas other very feminine women might have many masculine traits. In fact, the word **androgyny** (from the Greek *andro,* "male," and *gyn,* "female") has been coined to describe *a condition where male and female characteristics are not rigidly assigned and there is a blending of the traits, attitudes, and roles of both sexes.* From this perspective, people explore a broad range of gender-role possibilities and choose emotions and behaviors without regard to gender stereotypes. This does not mean that gender distinctions disappear but that one's biological sex becomes a less rigid determinant of which masculine and feminine traits a particular individual will exhibit. This means that people can be more flexible in their role playing and express themselves in a variety of ways other than the traditionally masculine or feminine ways. People can choose roles or tasks at

which they are most competent and express emotions or attitudes with which they feel most comfortable—all without regard to whether they will be ridiculed for choosing the "wrong" roles or emotions for their sex. In fact, some evidence suggests that sex-role traditionalism, where males exhibit a largely masculine/instrumental orientation and women a mostly feminine/expressive orientation, is less common today. Some research shows that women are more inclined than in the past to take on traditionally male orientations, and other research suggests that men today are more likely to express androgynous or feminine orientations (McBroom, 1984; Hyde, Krajnik, and Skuldt-Niederberger, 1991). However, it is probably too soon to say how extensive or enduring these trends will be. What is certain is that different sex-role orientations do have an impact on people's behavior (Shichman and Cooper, 1984; Gunter and Gunter, 1990). People (whether men or women) with a masculine orientation tend toward the more instrumental aspects of life, such as preparing the family income taxes or mowing the lawn; those with a feminine sex-role orientation tend toward the more expressive activities, such as taking care of children or keeping in touch with relatives. Androgynous individuals, on the other hand, tend to choose and enjoy both instrumental and expressive activities.

Using the interactionist perspective, the social problem of sexual inequality will be alleviated only when there is shared consensus about expectations for men and women in American society. This could be achieved by reestablishing traditional sex roles or by changing to something closer to androgyny—as long as there was consensus about these expectations. On the other hand, there must be consistency between gender roles and the other roles that people perform. We could not, for example, expect women to exhibit a certain kind of self-concept as women—passive, dependent, less intelligent—and then be required to have a contradictory self-concept in some other role that they play, such as business executive or soldier. As women and men move into nontraditional roles in society, their self-concepts and identities will be changed by their experiences in these new roles. As this occurs, our values about existing sources of sexual inequality will also be likely to change. But only the future will reveal the extent to which these changes will alter the present fabric of sexual differentiation.

Linkages

Gender inequality and fewer opportunities for women can lead some poor women (Chapter 5) toward prostitution and pornography (Chapter 11) as ways to support themselves and their families. This is especially tempting for poor single mothers whose opportunities are severely limited. Prostitution and pornography are in great demand by men, but the women who satisfy that demand are considered morally tainted by those same men.

Summary

1. Sex is an ascribed and a master status. The text examines four different views of sex as an element of social differentiation: the biological perspective, which assumes that innate biological differences between men and women shape the contributions that each can make to society; the functionalist perspective, which argues that a problem exists when the sex-role division of labor is no longer consistent with the needs of a particular society; the conflict perspective, which views sexual inequality as a problem when some group (women) realizes they are being exploited and strives to do something to change the situation; and the interactionist perspective, which emphasizes social definitions and symbolic representations of appropriate behavior for males and females in trying to understand sexual inequality.

2. Male and female are sex-related terms; gender refers to learned behavior involving how we are expected to act as males and females in society. One of the key issues in analyzing sexual inequality is how we learn to be masculine and feminine and how this contributes to sexual differentiation and inequality. This learning occurs through the socialization process, with three major agencies of socialization being primarily responsible: the family, the schools, and the media.

3. Sexual inequality is widespread in American society. Women occupy a subordinate position in comparison to men on virtually every dimension of socioeconomic status (SES). Discrimination on the basis of sex is not confined to education, occupation, and income. Women also experience unequal treatment in the military, before the courts, and in matters of credit. Sexual inequality also affects men when they are discouraged from pursuing certain kinds of jobs and can be drafted into the military when no equivalent service is asked of women.

4. The future of sexual inequality will depend on the progression of the feminist movement and how much collective action is mobilized to deal with the various forms of discrimination. Changes in the law and new legislation affecting women, such as comparable worth, will also be important. The workplace is changing, with increasing numbers of women joining the labor force. Any meaningful changes in the situation surrounding sexual inequality will involve a redefinition of both masculinity and femininity.

Important Terms for Review

androgyny   gender   instrumental tasks   sex
expressive tasks

Discussion Questions

1. Evaluate the extent to which men and women are represented on the faculty at your college or university. (You could do this with a current issue of the school bulletin or by contacting the office of institutional research.) Which disciplines have larger proportions of women? Interview people in those fields to find out why. Is there any evidence that your school discriminates against either women or men in hiring practices?

2. Use the comparable worth method to evaluate different employment categories at your college or university. Are there some jobs, held mostly by men, that involve the same training and responsibility but higher pay than other jobs, held most by women? Should this situation be rectified? If so, how? Ask someone from each of these jobs to come to your class to discuss the issues.

3. We have discussed a number of forms of discrimination that are experienced by men and women in American society today. Can you locate other types of discrimination—either explicit or subtle—that we have not mentioned? Have you experienced any types of discrimination yourself? What should be done to rectify these problems?

4. The Equal Rights Amendment (ERA) has been debated in Congress for many years. Organize a debate on the pros and cons of attaching an equal rights amendment to our Constitution, especially considering the social circumstances in the 1990s.

5. One bastion of malehood still remains in the United States: military combat. Although women can serve in the military in many capacities, they are still exempt from the draft and from combat duty. Is this equitable? Create a panel to argue the pros and cons of having a truly nonsexist military establishment. Invite someone from the military science department at your school to take part.

For Further Reading

Joan Acker. *Doing Comparable Work: Gender, Class, and Pay Equity.* Philadelphia: Temple University Press, 1989. This is an insider's view of a pay equity study done by the state of Oregon by a woman who was on the legislative task force that did the study. It is a fascinating view of the political and technical problems of doing the job classification and evaluation that is required for comparable worth.

Susan Brownmiller. *Femininity.* New York: Linden Press/Simon and Schuster, 1984. Best known for her writings on the crime of rape, journalist Susan Brownmiller explores the topic of femininity in this informative volume. Although not really a sociological treatment of gender, this book helps the reader to appreciate the differences between biological sex (female) and gender identity (femininity).

Marilyn French. *The War Against Women.* New York: Summit Books, 1992. This is a very angry book that documents, across cultures and centuries, the many ways in which women have suffered at the hands of men. As the title implies, the author sees this as an organized, concerted campaign on the part of men to keep women subordinate.

Arlie Hochschild with Anne Machung. *The Second Shift: Working Parents and the Revolution at Home.* New York: Viking, 1989. This book is about who cares for children, who does the housework, and whose career suffers as it becomes increasingly normal for both men and women to work outside the home. Hochschild has been in this domestic bind herself, so she can speak forcefully on the basis of her research and her personal experience.

Alice Kessler-Harris. *Out of Work: A History of Wage-Earning Women in the United States.* New York: Oxford University Press, 1982. This book shows how women from colonial times to the present have served as a low-paid reserve labor force but were kept from gaining any positions of dominance in the occupational sphere.

Ethel Klein. *Gender Politics: From Consciousness to Mass Politics.* Cambridge, Mass.: Harvard University Press, 1984. An excellent overview of the use of the political process to achieve more equality for women. This is a good historical overview of the women's rights movement.

Mirra Komarovsky. *Women in College: Shaping New Feminine Identities.* New York: Basic Books, 1985. An intriguing book about the lives of college women in the 1980s based on interviews with one class of students. Among other things, the book illustrates the problems men and women have in developing relationships today.

John Nicholson. *Men and Women: How Different Are They?* New York: Oxford University Press, 1984. In this book, a British psychologist explores the origins of male dominance in different societies, focusing on the question of whether this phenomenon is an inevitable consequence or the result of aspirational differences between men and women.

Michele A. Paludi, ed. *Ivory Power: Sexual Harassment on Campus.* Albany: State University of New York Press, 1990. This book documents the extent of sexual harassment of college students and college faculty and discusses why it occurs. It also provides a blueprint for what to do about it.

Peggy Reeve Sanday. *Fraternity Gang Rape: Sex, Brotherhood, and Privilege on Campus.* New York: New York University Press, 1990. Rape may be the ultimate form of control that men exercise over women. This book documents how college women are controlled by it and some of the social and cultural dynamics that encourage gang rapes on campus.

Jean Stockard and Miriam M. Johnson. *Sex and Gender in Society,* 2d ed. Englewood Cliffs, N.J.: Prentice Hall, 1992. This is one of the better texts on the sociology of gender. It covers the sociological and social policy issues in this field in much greater depth than was possible in this chapter.

Christine L. Williams. *Gender Differences at Work: Women and Men in Nontraditional Occupations.* Berkeley: University of California Press, 1989. This study focuses on men in nursing and women in the Marine Corps—people in jobs that are usually done by the opposite sex. It offers a valuable look at our gender stereotypes and our accepted definitions of masculinity and femininity.

Naomi Wolf. *The Beauty Myth: How Images of Beauty Are Used Against Women.* New York: Morrow, 1991. This is an intriguing book about how our culture encourages a conception of beauty that tends to coerce women into doing things that are not in their best interests. It is a thoughtful illustration of how cultures can exercise social control in very subtle and often unrecognized ways.

CHAPTER 8
Age and Social Inequality

Most cultures contain positive images of both the young and the old. In the United States, for example, we call youth the "tender years" or the "springtime of life," implying that the young are more innocent and less troubled than older people and possess as yet unrealized potential and promise. The later years in life are referred to as the "golden years," and old people are presumed to have gained more wisdom and patience than the young. But beyond these positive images, the young and the old share something considerably less valued: They bear the brunt of inequitable treatment in society. They are more likely than other age groups to be unemployed; they experience discrimination in the job market and other realms; because of their powerless position, they are subject to victimization and exploitation by others in degrading ways; and they are more likely than others to be excluded from the adult world of work, contribution, and responsibility.

All these things afflict the young and the old by virtue of their age. In this chapter, we will document the extent of these problems and what can and is being done about them. First, however, we need to understand the way in which age—an ascribed status like race and sex—influences a person's position in society.

Myths and Facts About Age and Social Inequality

Myth: Teenagers are too young to have achieved maturity, and this is why they are required to stay in school rather than work for a living or begin raising a family.

Fact: In preindustrial societies, most people have joined the adult world of work by their teenage years and may have even begun raising a family. Industrial societies have created a new social category called adolescence, consisting of people who are biologically mature but still considered dependent and emotionally immature. The purpose of this category is to allow for an extended period of education and to reduce competition with adults for existing jobs.

Myth: In the past, people respected their elders because this was the right thing to do.

Fact: Respect for elders flowed in part from the fact that older people in the past controlled many political, social, and economic resources and thus could demand respect from younger people.

Myth: The exploitation of child labor in the United States is largely a thing of the past.

Fact: Although child-labor problems have been reduced, there are currently few restrictions on youngsters working in some jobs, such as farm laborer. It is estimated that one quarter of the farm laborers in the United States may be under age sixteen.

Myth: The elderly consider their low financial status to be their most serious problem.

Fact: In one survey, only 17 percent of people over sixty-five thought money was a serious problem for them. However, a majority of younger people think money is a problem for the elderly.

Myth: Because most Americans today have retirement plans where they work, retirement income for the elderly in the future will not be a problem.

Fact: Less than half of working Americans today have retirement plans. In addition, many Americans do not work for one company long enough to have retirement funds vested (or become their own personal property), so they end up with no personal pension plan.

AGE, LIFE COURSE, AND SOCIAL STRUCTURE

Gerontology is the *scientific study of aging*. It began as the study of why some people are especially long lived, but it now focuses on all the biological, psychological, and social aspects of growing old (Atchley, 1991). It studies people of all ages because the process of aging begins the day we are born. As people age, societies tend to carve out their lives into a series of stages, with different things being expected of them at each stage. The content of these stages depends on a person's biological age and the social needs of a particular society. All these stages taken together constitute the life span or life course, which is *a succession of statuses and roles that people in a particular society experience in a fairly predictable pattern as they grow older* (Neugarten and Datan, 1973). Biology plays an important role in the life course, especially at the beginning and the end. As infants and young children, each of us is highly dependent on others for our survival, and thus the statuses that are open to us are limited. In very old age, physical deterioration may limit our capabilities and again make us dependent on others. Society cannot rely on us during these periods to the extent that it can during other stages of the life span. Between infancy and very old age, however, the social structure is more important than biology in shaping the life span. Thus, although biology does play a role, we should be cautious about viewing life-span stages as biologically created. Rather, they make up a socially approved sequence of stages, adjusted for certain biological limitations, that guides people's behavior as they live their lives. The sociological perspectives provide insight into how society shapes the life course.

The Functionalist Perspective

Functionalists argue that the stages of the life span are intimately related to the social needs of particular societies. For this reason, the stages that occur may differ substantially from society to society (Aries, 1962; Flacks, 1971). In preindustrial societies, for example, people usually learn how to fill adult positions fairly early in life. The technology is relatively simple, so little training or education is required. People do not need to know how to read or write in order to make contributions to society. So the transition from childhood to adulthood generally occurs early, somewhere between age eight and the mid-teens. People continue to work as they grow old, being limited only by physical infirmity. Only among small groups within society, such as a ruling group or a priesthood, is inactivity or nonproductivity common among older adults.

Industrial societies, on the other hand, with a complex technology and an elaborate division of labor, need a highly educated and well-trained work force. Thus, training and education must be more extensive than in preindustrial societies. Furthermore, the sophisticated technology of industrial societies makes it possible for a small number of people to provide all of the goods and services that are needed. As a consequence, it is not necessary for all adults to participate in the work force. These factors contribute to two major differences in the life course of industrial societies in contrast to preindustrial ones. First, the age at which people are allowed to enter the adult world is postponed in industrial societies (Kett, 1977). Childhood continues into the early teens and is

followed by a new stage in the life span, adolescence, which runs roughly from thirteen to eighteen years of age. Adolescence is viewed as a time of preparation for adulthood, in terms of both education and psychological maturation. Adolescents are not considered adults and are not expected to assume adult responsibilities, such as supporting a family. They are also not accorded many adult privileges, such as being able to vote or join the adult work force on a full-time basis. The second difference between the life cycle of industrial and preindustrial societies involves old age. In industrial societies, most men and women are encouraged to leave the work force, or forced from it, long before they die, often when they are still healthy and capable of working. Presumably, younger workers are more healthy and vigorous and make a better contribution to the work world. But irrespective of the capabilities of older workers, retirement serves as a way of reducing the number of workers who are competing for a limited number of jobs.

From the functionalist perspective, the treatment of the young and the old becomes a social problem when it is inconsistent with their capabilities and development, both biological and social. When age is used as an arbitrary criterion for inequitable treatment, it is dysfunctional and can lead to social disorganization. If young people, for example, are prevented from gaining prestige by joining the work world, they may turn to drugs or crime as a way of gaining a sense of self-importance. Likewise, forced retirement among the elderly can lead to depression and alcoholism. So societies need to provide socially acceptable statuses for their members at every stage of life. People need to feel that they are making an important contribution to society. With the transition from a preindustrial to an industrial social order, however, something has been lost. A degree of social disorganization has arisen as there are more and more young and old people with fewer and fewer contributions that they are allowed to make to society. They do not work, head families, or rear children. As we mentioned when discussing both race and sex, it is probably most functional in modern societies to allocate tasks and roles on the basis of abilities rather than ascribed statuses.

In addition, each stage in a person's life should be integrated with other stages. One stage might be a preparation for later stages, whereas another stage is viewed as a reward for earlier contributions. This continuity in life motivates people to perform well by making their tasks at one stage in the life span understandable and meaningful in terms of their place in the whole cycle. Thus, a comfortable old age might be seen as a reward for earlier contributions. For some, however, old age is not viewed as an outgrowth of earlier life stages, and this lack of continuity can be a social problem.

The Conflict Perspective

The position of the young and the old in modern societies is not unlike that of other minority groups (see Chapters 6 and 7). They have less access to social, political, and economic power, and they are dominated by groups with more resources. This has not always been the case. In most preindustrial societies, the elderly held considerably more power because they owned and controlled many economic resources, especially property. In addition, kinship ties were much more important then than today, and people often needed the support of their parents to get a start in life. It was from their parents that young adults learned a trade or acquired some land to farm. This meant that sons and daughters were economically dependent on their parents. In such a situation, social customs and laws tended to support and reinforce the dominant position of the elderly in society. In other words, respect for the elderly in preindustrial societies flowed from their control over political, social, and economic resources. Such respect may have been functional for the times, but it was enforced through custom and law.

In industrial societies, people are not as heavily dependent on their parents to make a living.

Trades can be learned in school, and most people will be salaried employees of a corporation or government agency. So entry-level positions in the economy can be gained with little if any parental support. In addition, family ties in general have become less important. As a consequence, kinship ties are not a source of power and prestige for many elderly. The outcome of all this is that the status of the elderly has declined because they no longer hold positions of economic power, and their children are no longer dependent on them for their economic livelihood.

From the conflict perspective, then, the position of any age group in society is determined by the social, political, and economic resources that group has access to. The access of the young and old to jobs and other sources of social and economic reward has been restricted because this exclusion benefits the large group of people in early to middle adulthood. In an economic system with a scarcity of jobs, this helps to reduce competition. Fewer young workers enter the labor market, and older workers are forced out by retirement in order to open positions for younger adults.

Society, of course, does not couch these social practices in such contentious terms. Rather, cultural norms hold that the restrictions placed on the young and old are for their own benefit. The young, it is said, need time to grow and mature because people in their teens do not have sufficient biological development to take on adult responsibilities. Likewise, the old suffer some physical deterioration, such as failing eyesight or loss of hearing, that makes them less able or willing to work. An ideology emerges to legitimize these social practices, just as sexism justifies discrimination against women and racism justifies the domination of particular racial groups. **Ageism** refers to *an ideology, or set of beliefs, holding that people in a particular age group are inferior, have negative attributes, and can be dominated and exploited because of their age.* The term was originally coined to describe reactions to the elderly, but it applies to any age group that experiences such prejudice and discrimination. In addition, like sexism and racism, ageism is often defended on biological grounds. In fact, one of the travesties of our treatment of the elderly is the all-too-quick assumption that any failing or memory loss is due to irreversible biological senility. With such beliefs, age becomes an important factor in differentiating among people in society.

Furthermore, the young and old are taught to expect these restrictions for themselves. The young, it is alleged, deserve a carefree adolescence. For the old, retirement is claimed to be a reward for a long life of productive work. In short, the victims are taught to desire precisely those things that work to the benefit of other groups.

The Age Structure of American Society

Demography is *the study of the size, composition, and distribution of human populations and how these factors change over time*. Demographers have found that societies vary in the proportions of their populations that are at different stages in the life cycle. They refer to this as the **age structure** of society, *the distribution of people into various age categories*. In preindustrial societies, such as the United States of more than a century ago, the age structure is "bottom heavy" with young people representing a large proportion of the population (see Figure 8.1). In such societies, as much as 40 to 50 percent of the populace might be fifteen years of age or under with less than 6 percent being over age sixty-five. The reason for this, which will be discussed in more detail in Chapter 13, is that preindustrial societies have high birthrates and high death rates. Many people are born, but a smaller proportion of them live into old age than

in industrial societies. Industrial societies, with lower birthrates and a longer life expectancy, tend to "age," making their populations "top heavy." Older people make up a growing proportion of the populace. Today, a little over 26 percent of the American population is under age eighteen, compared with about 12 percent sixty-five or older (see Figure 8.2). This is quite a dramatic shift from preindustrial America, and this trend will intensify. By the year 2050, when the younger students reading this book will be among our senior citizens, the young and the old will come very close to constituting equal proportions of our populace: possibly over 23 percent and 18 percent, respectively. In that year, there will be sixty-eight million Americans over age sixty-five, compared with only three million in 1900 and thirty-one million today.

From their analysis of the age structure of society, demographers can develop a very important statistic called the **dependency ratio,** which *shows the relative size of the group in our society that is economically dependent for support on others who are working*. The dependency ratio is often calculated by comparing the number of people over sixty-five with the number between eighteen and sixty-four. Of course, not all people over sixty-five are unemployed and dependent and not all between eighteen and sixty-four are working. But this comparison gives us an approximation of the trends occurring (see Figure 8.3). In 1900, the dependency ratio in the United States was 7, meaning that there were seven older people for each one hundred people between eighteen and sixty-five. Today the ratio is about 20. By the year 2050, projections suggest that it will be 40, or four older persons for every ten adults of working

Figure 8.1   **(A) (B) (C) Age–Sex Population Pyramids for the United States: 1900, 1940, 1989**
SOURCES: United States Bureau of the Census, *Census of Population: Characteristics of the Population* (Washington, D.C.: U.S. Government Printing Office, 1940, 1970); U.S. Bureau of the Census, *Statistical Abstract of the United States, 1991* (Washington, D.C.: U.S. Government Printing Office, 1991), p. 13.

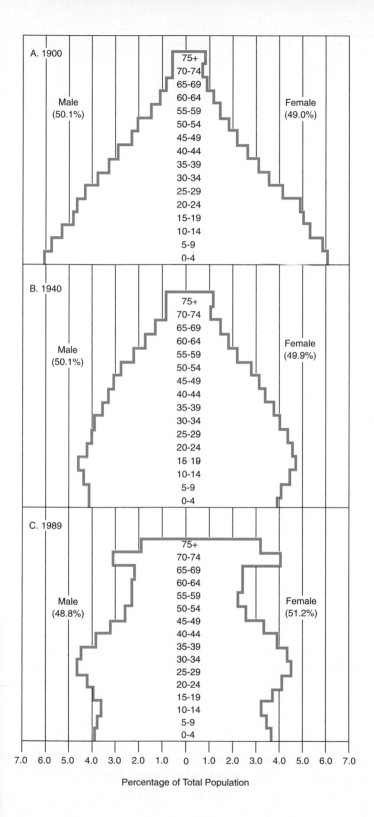

Percentage of Total Population

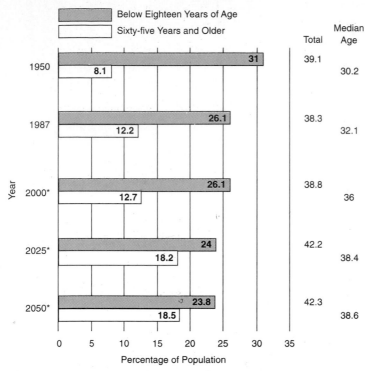

Below Eighteen Years of Age
Sixty-five Years and Older

Year		Total	Median Age
1950	31 / 8.1	39.1	30.2
1987	26.1 / 12.2	38.3	32.1
2000*	26.1 / 12.7	38.8	36
2025*	24 / 18.2	42.2	38.4
2050*	23.8 / 18.5	42.3	38.6

Percentage of Population

* Estimates based on the assumption that the population reaches
zero growth around the middle of the twenty-first century.

Figure 8.2   **The Distribution of Young and Old in the United States, 1950–2050**
SOURCES: U.S. Bureau of the Census, *Statistical Abstract of the United States, 1978* (Washington, D.C.: U.S. Government Printing Office, 1978), pp. 8–9; U.S. Bureau of the Census, *Statistical Abstract of the United States, 1989* (Washington, D.C.: U.S. Government Printing Office, 1989), p. 13.

age. However, the traditional dependency ratio may underestimate the proportions of dependents to workers because there is a tendency today for a growing number of people to enter the labor force at an older age than eighteen and retire younger than sixty-five. If we assume that people begin work at age twenty and retire at sixty, then the dependency ratio gets even larger. So, as society ages, those who are dependent become a significantly larger proportion of the populace.

The major concern about this issue, of course, is whether or at what level society can or will support such a large dependent population. It also raises the question of whether working people will be willing to continue supporting a growing number of elderly at a high standard of living. Potentially, it sets one interest group against another. Later in this chapter, we will address some possible solutions to the problems created by shifts in the age structure of the United States.

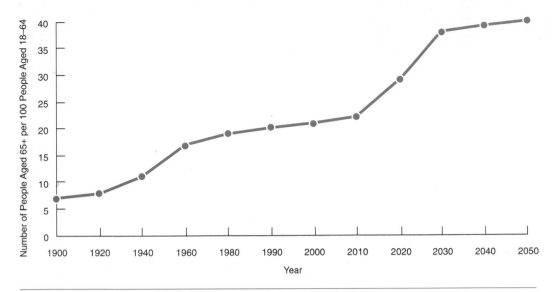

Figure 8.3 Dependency Ratio in the United States, 1900–2050
SOURCE: U.S. Department of Health and Human Services, *Aging America: Trends and Projections*, DHHS Pub. No. (FCoA) 91-28001 (Washington, D.C.: Department of Health and Human Services, 1991), pp. 18–19.

DISCRIMINATION BASED ON AGE

The Young

Human beings remain dependent on others after birth for much longer than is the case with most species. Infants are completely defenseless and must rely totally on others for their survival. Through most of childhood, human beings are immature and their development would be seriously threatened were they not supported by others. In modern societies, as we have seen, this dependence is extended into adolescence, during which physically mature human beings are denied complete access to the adult world. This extended period of dependence is beneficial in many ways, as we have seen, but it also makes the young easy targets for discrimination, exploitation, and violence.

There have been ageist ideologies throughout history that have justified the unequal treatment of the young (Gillis, 1974; Takanishi, 1978; Purdy, 1992). For example, children—and in modern societies adolescents—are typically viewed as immature, irresponsible, and in need of protection. Parents or other guardians are given the duty of watching over and caring for the children. In many cultures, this translates into the belief that children are the property of their parents or guardians. As such, it is claimed, children should be totally subordinate to their parents and do their parents' bidding. Parents, of course, have the obligation of supporting their children, but mothers and fathers also have the right to expect their complete obedience and acquiescence. The parents are presumed to act in the best interests of their children, but it is often the parents alone who decide what those interests are. Even in the United States today, society is reluctant to intervene in that parent–child relationship, leaving the parents with considerable freedom to do with their children as they please.

Economic Exploitation.   Children in most societies participate in some form of economic productivity, but it is usually by joining with family members in hunting or farming. In some cases, however, children work in nonfamily settings as wage laborers (Bequele and Boyden, 1988). They work in mines, factories, and as self-employed workers engaging in street trades. Many of these children confront terrible economic exploitation: working long hours in potentially harmful environments for relatively little pay. In nineteenth-century England and America, for example, children worked in factories for eleven or more hours per day. Toddlers barely three years old worked in cotton mills, crawling on the floor and retrieving cotton waste. Young boys were hired as chimney sweeps because their small bodies enabled them to climb up chimneys, sweeping away soot with their clothes. In the early part of this century, children as young as four years of age were hired to shuck oysters and peel shrimp in Gulf Coast canneries (Paradise, 1922). They worked from 3 A.M. until evening in damp, drafty, cold sheds. They stood all day, with cuts and abrasions on their hands, and some contracted serious infections from the shrimp. Many did not attend school, and they were discriminated against in pay, receiving substantially less than adults for the same work.

Legislation has been adopted in most countries in the past fifty years to control the labor exploitation of the young (Taylor, 1973; Kotin and Aikman, 1980; Bequele and Boyden, 1988). In the United States, the Fair Labor Standards Act of 1938 outlawed the employment of people under sixteen years of age in some industrial settings, and it has since been amended numerous times to prohibit child labor in many other circumstances, especially hazardous occupations. However, child labor is by no means a thing of the past. In fact, families sometimes have to put everyone to work—including the children—to keep out of poverty. In 1990, a congressional committee investigating child labor heard of a fifteen-year-old boy working in a bakery who died when pulled into a dough-mixing machine, a thirteen-year-old boy whose leg was torn off by a blowing machine while working in a car wash, a fifteen-year-old girl whose finger was cut off in a slicing machine at a fast-food restaurant, and a fourteen-year-old boy who worked thirteen hours a day picking strawberries, inhaling pesticides, and earning "at best" $2.80 per hour (Lantos, 1992). The number of violations of federal child-labor laws more than doubled during the 1980s, mostly for working youngsters too many hours per day, too late at night, or in hazardous jobs with dangerous equipment. However, current legislation places few restrictions on youngsters working in some jobs, including that of farm laborer. It is estimated that one-quarter of the farm laborers in the United States may be under age sixteen. These children work in hot, unpleasant conditions for low wages and receive few, if any, benefits such as retirement or health insurance. Many agricultural states have no minimum age for farm laborers, and state laws often do not apply to the children of migratory farm laborers.

Child laborers around the world work in jobs that pay the minimum wage or less and offer few benefits. In the United States, fast-food restaurants, self-serve gas stations, and grocery stores employ youngsters of high school age or younger as a means of reducing costs and maintaining flexibility in their work force. Adolescents are much less likely than adults to demand pay increases or to view such fringe benefits as retirement pensions to be important. They are also less concerned about unionization and long-term job security. The young are more likely to go quietly if released from a job. In 1989, Congress passed a bill, which President Bush signed, establishing a "subminimum" wage that would allow employers to pay teenagers a wage below the legal minimum wage. Although it has been touted as a tool for reducing teenage unemployment, it would have the effect of creating a two-tiered labor market, with teenagers being paid considerably less than adults for the same work.

Child-labor laws are intended to protect young people from exploitation, and compulsory school attendance laws are meant to offer them important opportunities in life. Some young people, however, feel that these legal statutes are themselves discriminatory because they prohibit them from working. The notion that people should not begin full-time, adult work until after they are eighteen years of age is a product of the last half century. There are many people under eighteen today who would prefer to work than attend school. Through legislation or social pressure, however, most youths feel compelled to remain in school and work at part-time, low-paying jobs. In recent decades, child-labor legislation has been amended to reduce the minimum legal age for employment in some occupations and to broaden the opportunities to work while attending school. The result has been to make it a little easier for adolescents to work (Kotin and Aikman, 1980).

Poverty.   We analyzed the statistics on poverty among children in Chapter 5. The poverty rate among children is higher today than it was twenty years ago: 14 percent in 1969 compared with 20 percent today. And it is twice as high as the poverty rate among the elderly. More than one-third of our nation's poor people are under the age of sixteen, and the children of the United States are worse off than children in most other industrial nations. What accounts for these appalling circumstances among our nation's young? Although some teens earn income, the economic circumstances of children are determined almost entirely by that of their parents—another manifestation of their dependency. And some critical trends of the past few decades, already reviewed in Chapter 5, have contributed to the growing poverty among children. Unemployment has increased and family incomes have not grown and in many cases have declined. More children today live in single-parent families, which have much higher poverty rates than two-parent families. All these conditions have had a very heavy impact on nonwhite children. These economic circumstances that children confront are especially troubling because children, for the most part, cannot walk away from them or work to improve their lives as some adults can. They are heavily dependent on adults. Poverty is simply something they must live with until they become adults, and often they face further poverty in adulthood because their poverty-stricken childhood failed to provide them with the resources and the motivation to achieve as an adult.

Sexual Exploitation.   Children and adolescents are highly susceptible to sexual exploitation in a variety of forms. This came to light in an especially grisly fashion in the 1980s when people working in day-care centers in New York and southern California were arrested for criminal sexual assault on children under their care. Children are especially susceptible to such abuse for two reasons. First, parents often find it very difficult to admit that their children might be exposed to such treatment at schools to which they themselves have sent them. Second, assailants can easily manipulate children with threats if the children reveal what has happened.

The more common form of sexual exploitation of the young is sexual assault by a parent, adult relative, or guardian. Sexual assault can involve sexual intercourse, fondling, or indecent exposure. Once again, the young are at a disadvantage, especially when assaulted by a family member or relative, because the attack is often couched as an expression of love or affection. This often inhibits the child from reporting the assault. Such attacks can continue for years because children are often afraid of hurting the adult by reporting the incidents.

Adolescents are susceptible to yet another version of sexual exploitation: prostitution and pornography. Teenage runaways, for example, find it difficult to support themselves through legitimate jobs, which are likely to be either unavailable or low paying. Such teenagers are sought after by pimps and pornographers because they are defenseless and exploitable. The teenagers are afraid to go to the police and have no other adults to protect them. In large cities such as New York, Chicago, and Los Angeles, prostitutes as young

APPLIED RESEARCH

How Well Off Are Our Children and Youth?

Are America's children and youth better off in the 1990s than they were in earlier decades? Many have computers, VCRs, and compact discs, along with many other luxuries and technological wonders of the age, but overall, has life for our young gotten better or worse? Economists Victor R. Fuchs and Diane M. Reklis (1992: 41) give a gloomy answer: "American children are in trouble. . . . Many observers consider today's children to be worse off than their parents' generation in several important dimensions of physical, mental, and emotional well-being." They reach this conclusion by looking at statistics that can give us a glimpse of prevailing social trends. These are among the trends that contributed to their depressing assessment:

- Since 1960, the performance of American children and youth on standardized aptitude tests has declined steadily.

- Since 1960, the teen suicide rate has tripled.

- Since 1960, the teen homicide rate has almost tripled.

- Since 1960, obesity is up sharply, especially among children.

- The percentage of children living in poverty dropped until 1970 and has increased steadily since then.

- Since the mid-1970s, reports of child abuse have tripled.

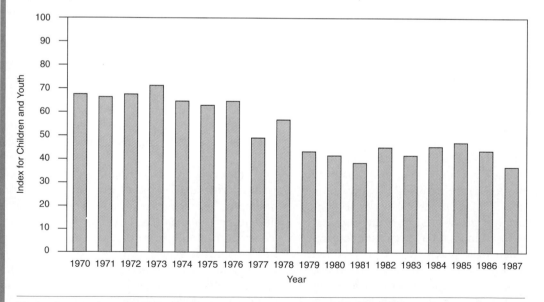

Figure 8.4   **Index of Social Health for Children and Youth, 1970–1987**
SOURCE: Marc L. Miringoff, *The Index of Social Health, 1989: Measuring the Social Well-Being of the Nation* (Tarrytown, N.Y.: Fordham Institute for Innovation in Social Policy, 1989), p. 6.

- Since 1960, the proportion of children who live in a household without an adult male present has tripled.

The Fordham Institute for Innovation in Social Policy has combined data on these kinds of trends with data on drug abuse and high school dropout rates among teens and developed an Index of Social Health for Children and Youth, a composite score on how well our children are doing (Miringoff, 1989). The Index documents that the social health of our youth has declined dramatically in the last twenty years. In fact, 1987, the last year for which data are available, was the worst year since 1970. In 1970, the Index stood at 68, with a higher score indicating greater social health; by 1987, it had plummeted to 37 (see Figure 8.4). On the whole, and despite the substantial affluence in the United States, life for our children and teenagers appears to have gotten demonstrably worse over the years. Some positive trends have occurred over the past thirty years, such as declines in infant and child mortality, but the number of negative trends is disturbing, especially in what is one of the wealthiest and most powerful nations in the world. Also, some of these indicators, such as teen suicide and homicide, clearly point to the significant failure of our society to provide for its young.

Many factors contribute to this situation and are discussed in this chapter and in Chapter 5. Fuchs, Reklis, and other social scientists point to another factor: In the struggle for a share of society's resources, children and youth have not done nearly as well as some other interest groups. Although we spend more on government programs for children now than thirty years ago, government programs that benefit adults have grown at a much faster pace. In addition, Americans over age sixty-five have gained the largest increase in government support. The government spends more on the health-care needs of the elderly during the last year of their life than it spends on *all* the health care of *all* American children. Overall, the government spends eleven times as much on each American over sixty-five as on each under eighteen (Hewlett, 1991). As we discuss the circumstances of the young and the old in this chapter, we will return to this issue of whether the current allocation of resources to different age groups is the most effective.

as twelve years old—both male and female—can be found. There are even organized rings nationwide to provide the services of young prostitutes to those who desire them (Campagna and Poffenberger, 1988). Such youngsters typically lack the economic and social resources necessary to extricate themselves from these situations and are likely to continue being exploited until arrested.

Child Abuse. Because of their dependent status, it is often children who experience the brunt of their parents' frustrations or failures. Too often, this reaction takes the form of child abuse. As with sexual exploitation, children are usually too weak and defenseless to protect themselves against such abuse. In addition, their fear of their parents is often mixed with love, making it especially difficult for them to seek assistance. The problem of child abuse is discussed in more detail in Chapter 3.

The Applied Research insert in this chapter discusses some of the evidence that social scientists use to document the condition of our youth and assess whether things are getting better or worse.

The Elderly

Work and Retirement. In all societies, what people do to make a living is important to them. Our work status is how we support ourselves, and it is a major source of self-esteem and sense of personal self-worth. For many, the work world is a source of intrinsic satisfaction, whereas for others it is a place to meet and be with friends. Yet many Americans have been, and some still are, forced to retire from work at an age when they are still quite capable of working, and this has been one of the major forms of discrimination against the elderly.

In some cases, older Americans are forced out of work, or "terminated," before retirement age as a way of reducing company costs or saving on retirement benefits. After all, younger workers are cheaper than older workers because they make less income and place less strain on company resources such as health costs. Thousands of complaints of such age discrimination are made to the Equal Employment Opportunity Commission each year (Cooper, 1987). When companies restructure to cut costs, they may feel especially tempted to lay off workers over fifty-five because the savings are so much greater when compared with younger workers. These older workers will also find it difficult to locate new jobs, in part because of their age.

Workers are also forced out of work by their age when they are pressured to, or required to, retire at an age when they are still quite capable of working. Prior to this century, retirement was a privilege that only the rich could afford. Most others had to continue working throughout their lives to support themselves. Not until 1891 were there any laws that forced people to retire. It was then that German Chancellor Otto von Bismarck established seventy as the official retirement age for German workers (McConnell, 1983). The United States followed suit in 1935 when the Social Security Act set sixty-five as the mandatory retirement age. The Age Discrimination in Employment Act (ADEA), originally enacted in 1967, was amended in 1978 to raise the mandatory retirement age for most workers to seventy. The ADEA was further amended in 1986 to bar mandatory retirement for people in most occupations. In fact, few people continue working after age sixty-five, about 16 percent of all men and 8 percent of all women (U.S. Department of Labor, 1992). In contrast, 60 percent of the men over sixty-five continued working in 1900. Indeed, a majority of Americans believe that people ought to be able to continue working at any age if they wish to and are able to do so. In addition, roughly half of all Americans, both working and retired, claim that they want to continue working after retirement age ("Work Over Retirement . . . ," 1979).

A major concern about retirement is whether it has a beneficial or detrimental impact on people's lives. One view is that occupational roles and identities are so important and pervasive that their loss invades all parts of a retiree's life and being in very negative ways. In their place, the retiree is left with an ambiguous status that gives life little direction and whose social prestige is difficult to determine. In fact, gerontologist Ethel Shanas (1972) has called retirement a "roleless" role to emphasize the point that what society expects of a retiree is much less well defined than are most social roles. Despite this, however, retirement for many is a positive experience (Atchley, 1991). According to a recent summary of research, people are likely to enjoy retirement if

> *(1) retirement is voluntary rather than forced; (2) one's income and health are good enough to live comfortably in retirement; (3) work is not the most important thing in one's life; and (4) some preparation and planning for retirement have occurred. (McConnell, 1983: 340)*

There have been a number of suggestions for changing our nation's retirement practices to make the transition to retired status easier and more gradual. One such proposal has been to shift to a system of gradual retirement in which people continue to work as long as they are able but for a decreasing period of time each year. This would allow for a steady adjustment to the status of retiree but would still open up jobs for younger workers. Although some employees can arrange such gradual retirements, there are no serious proposals to make them a widespread part of our economy.

Abuse of the Elderly.   In Chapter 3, we discussed the problem of the physical and psychological abuse of older people by their caretakers. Just as the dependence of the young makes them vulnerable to abuse, the elderly face the same problem. Some abuse of the elderly results from the stress or frustration of taking care of an older parent or grandparent who is physically or mentally impaired. The burden at times becomes too much, and the nuclear family does not provide the extensive support network that would help spread these stresses over many people. Abuse of the elderly also occurs when it is the caretakers who are dependent on those they care for, possibly for financial support. This dependence of a younger adult on an older adult can lead to pent-up frustration that may find release in violence, especially when the caretaker has personal or financial problems or abuses drugs or alcohol.

PROBLEMS OF THE ELDERLY

The problems confronting the elderly in American society have received increasing attention in the past few decades. Keeping in mind that these problems derive in good part from the place of the elderly in the life cycle, we will review their major dimensions.

Poverty

The poverty rate among Americans over sixty-five years of age was 12.2 percent in 1990, only slightly above that of Americans between the ages of eighteen and sixty-four, which was about 10.7 percent. As Figure 8.5 shows, this represents astonishing progress over thirty years ago when 28 percent of the elderly were poor—almost three times higher than nonelderly adult Americans. So the elderly have come a long way. However, as Figure 8.6 illustrates, the annual income of a family headed by a person sixty-five years of age or older is considerably less than that of other fami-

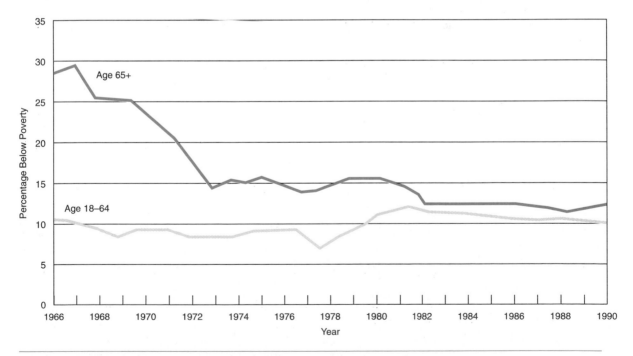

Figure 8.5 **Poverty Rates of Elderly and Non-elderly Adults, 1966–1990**
SOURCE: U.S. Bureau of the Census, Current Population Reports, Series P-60, No. 175, *Poverty in the United States, 1990* (Washington, D.C.: U.S. Government Printing Office, 1991), p. 18.

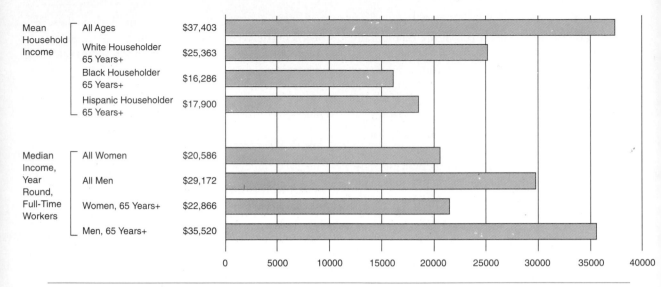

Figure 8.6   **Income and Age, 1990**
SOURCE: U.S. Bureau of the Census, *Statistical Abstract of the United States, 1992* (Washington, D.C.: U.S. Government Printing Office, 1992), pp. 447, 452.

lies. In addition, Figure 8.7 demonstrates that some groups among the elderly are not doing so well. Poverty rates are still unacceptably high among older women living alone, older African Americans, and older Hispanics. Three-quarters of the poor among the elderly are women (Meyer, 1990). This reiterates the points we made in Chapters 6 and 7 about the impact of sexism and racism on the position of minority-group members and shows that a considerable number of older Americans are at a financial disadvantage.

There are a number of reasons to be cautious, however, in comparing the economic circumstances of older and younger Americans. One reason is that, when we look at total wealth or total net worth, the elderly are in some ways better off than younger adults (Peterson, 1991a). During the 1980s, for example, the net worth of families headed by someone over sixty-five increased, whereas the net worth of families headed by someone fifty-five or younger decreased. In addition, the share of the total wealth going to the elderly went from 26 percent in the 1960s to 33 percent today, whereas adults aged thirty-five or

younger got only 6 percent of that wealth then and today. So the elderly seem to have cornered a substantial, and growing, portion of society's wealth over the last three decades. A big reason for this is that the elderly have accumulated resources over their years of living, especially equity in a home. A second reason for caution in assessing poverty rates among the elderly is that the elderly tend to have fewer expenses than do younger adults. Older people are more likely to have paid off their home mortgage and to have fewer, if any, child-rearing expenses. A third reason for caution is that many elderly do not consider finances as among their most serious problems. A survey conducted for the National Council on Aging, for example, found that only 17 percent of the people over sixty-five claimed that money was a very serious problem for them. In contrast, 68 percent of those under sixty-five thought that a lack of money was a serious problem for the elderly (Weaver, 1981).

The economic status of the elderly results in large part from three factors. First, the elderly are more likely than other adults to be outside the

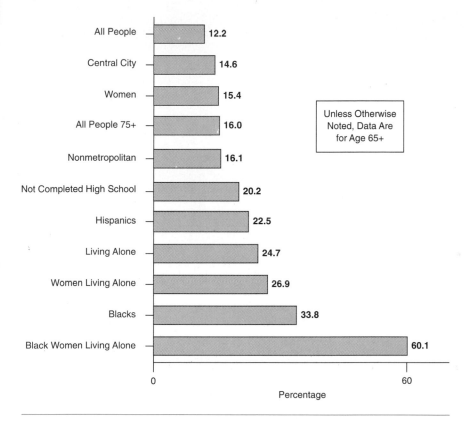

Figure 8.7 **Percentage of Elderly Below the Poverty Level, by Selected Characteristics, 1990**
SOURCE: U.S. Bureau of the Census, *Current Population Reports*, Series P-60, No. 175, *Poverty in the United States, 1990* (Washington, D.C.: U.S. Government Printing Office, 1991).

work force and thus prevented from earning a high income. Only 17 percent of the income of people sixty-five years old or older comes from earnings (see Figure 8.8). The rest of their income is from Social Security, retirement benefits, assets, or public assistance. The elderly who do work full time earn as much as, if not more than, younger workers (see Figure 8.6). However, the elderly are discouraged from working because they lose some of their Social Security benefits if they earn more than about $8,000 a year (Gustman and Steinmeier, 1991). Second, people retiring today began their work careers thirty to fifty years ago when the level of affluence in America was much

lower and inflation had not so seriously eroded the value of the dollar. This made it difficult for these workers to accumulate personal assets— such as equity in a home, real estate, or stocks and bonds—that would enable them to maintain their life-style after retirement. One-third of the elderly have no equity in a home, and the other assets of many older people are too meager to provide any real economic security (Walther, 1983). Third, many workers toiled for years with either no private retirement plan where they worked or one that offered few benefits. As recently as 1960, for example, only 37 percent of all nongovernmental employees had retirement programs where they

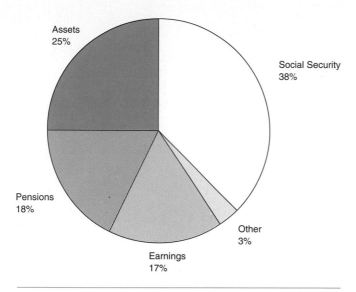

Figure 8.8　**Income Sources of People Age 65 + , 1988**
SOURCE: Susan Grad, *Income of the Population 65 or Over, 1988*, Pub. No. 13-11871 (Washington, D.C.: U.S. Social Security Administration, June 1990).

worked; by 1990, this had increased to only 40 percent (U.S. Bureau of the Census, 1978: 344; U.S. Bureau of the Census, 1992: 363). Only one-sixth of all income available to the elderly comes from pensions (see Figure 8.8). As a consequence, some elderly find themselves dependent solely on Social Security or other transfer income from the government. The ironic thing about this situation is that, from its inception in 1935, Social Security has not been intended to serve as a person's sole retirement income, but rather as a supplement to other sources of financial support. Because of this, Social Security payments are low, and those solely dependent on them are in difficult financial straits. Women, especially, are likely to have inadequate retirement incomes because most retirement plans, including Social Security, are tied to the extent of paid labor a person has done during his or her life. Women, when compared with men, tend to work less, get paid less when they work, and change jobs before gaining ownership of their pension resources. As a result,

women have smaller pension resources available to them than men do (Meyer, 1990).

Social Isolation

In preindustrial societies, older people normally remained with their family because there were few other alternatives. Today, however, an aging person is much more likely to be cast adrift without family ties. In fact, a major concern of younger people today is the threat of isolation and loneliness when they are old: In a survey for the National Council on Aging, 65 percent of those under age sixty-five reported loneliness as a very serious problem for the elderly (Weaver, 1981). The prospects of separation from their families is a real one for the elderly: Thirty-one percent of the elderly lived alone in 1990 compared with 18 percent in 1960 (see Figure 8.9), and this was especially true for women and the very old. In contrast to the fears of younger adults, however, only 13 percent of the older people surveyed by the

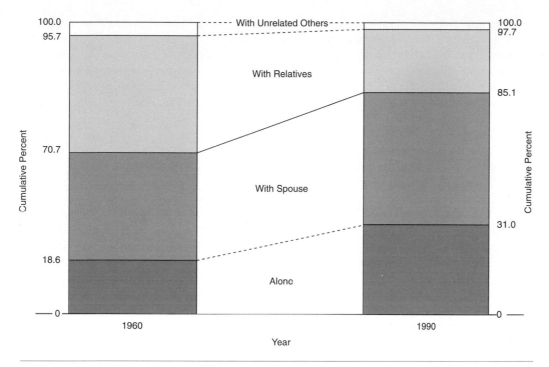

Figure 8.9 **Distribution of the Elderly by Living Arrangements, 1960 and 1990**
SOURCES: Congressional Budget Office, *Changes in the Living Arrangements of the Elderly: 1960–2030* (Washington, D.C.: U.S. Government Printing Office, March 1988), p. 3; U.S. Bureau of the Census, Current Population Reports, Series P-20, No. 450, *Marital Status and Living Arrangements, March 1990* (Washington, D.C.: U.S. Government Printing Office, 1991), p. 12.

National Council on Aging viewed loneliness as a serious problem. Older people maintain relatively extensive contacts and involvements with friends and acquaintances, albeit fewer than do younger people. People in advanced old age (more than seventy-five years of age) and those with serious physical ailments are most likely to suffer from severe social isolation. It is these elderly who are least likely to visit friends, go to the library, or attend social events. In addition, socioeconomic status plays an important part in this. Middle-class elderly have more friends, are more likely to develop new friendships, and visit their friends more often than do their working- and lower-class counterparts (National Council on Aging, 1975; Atchley, 1991). These differences are not a result of financial status but rather are attributable to the social skills acquired by middle-class people that enable them to develop and maintain friendships more easily.

Health Problems

Health is one of the major problems faced by the elderly. Paying for the health care of the elderly poses considerable difficulty for society as a whole, as we saw in the discussion of Medicare in Chapter 4. Medicare currently costs $102 billion each year, which translates into over $400 for every man, woman, and child in the United States. Forty percent of all hospital beds occupied each day are filled by people over sixty-five. Almost one-half of Americans over sixty-five years of age experience some limitation in their activities because of chronic illnesses, many of those limitations being major ones. Overall, the health-care expenditures of the elderly are three and one-half times greater than those of people under sixty-five. Medicare and other government health insurance pays for 63 percent of these costs, but 28 percent of the health expenditures of the elderly are paid out of their own pockets (U.S. Department of Health and Human Services, 1991). These costs are likely to increase in the future as the number of very old people, those over eighty years of age, increases.

Because the elderly face such severe health problems and also because our culture places such value on youthfulness and physical fitness, the elderly are especially susceptible to quackery that promises to alleviate their pain and improve their functioning. The elderly are the victims of 60 percent of all health-care frauds and are cheated out of an estimated $10 billion each year (Pear, 1984a). Some of these practitioners promise magical remedies for serious conditions, such as arthritis, that medical science cannot currently cure. Other frauds focus on diseases that medicine can treat, and they tempt people to use fraudulent cures in place of those known by medicine to be effective. A few years ago, for example, something called Dr. Kaadt's Diabetic Remedy was sold as a cure for diabetes, for which medical science has yet to find a cure (Schaller and Carroll, 1976). This fraudulent potion contained vinegar, saltpeter, resorcinol, and a number of other ingredients that were to be consumed with digestive and laxative tablets. This was a treatment especially appealing to diabetes sufferers because, supposedly, dietary restrictions and insulin injections—the standard treatment for diabetes—could be ignored. The perpetrators of this fraud made millions of dollars before they were put out of business. People who took Dr. Kaadt's Remedy and went off the diet and insulin regimen suffered from such things as coma, gangrene, and damaged vision.

The reason that the elderly are especially susceptible to such fraud is that they suffer from many more painful and chronic diseases than do younger people. Loneliness and social isolation can also make them an easy mark for a friendly and glib salesperson who is willing to show them some sympathy and understanding. Mental deterioration and social isolation may also cloud the judgment of some older people, leading them to make decisions that they might not otherwise make.

Fear of Crime

Older people commit relatively few crimes. Their arrest rate is less than one-tenth that of people in their twenties, and the median age of people in jail is twenty-five years. As we will see in Chapter 9, crime tends to be a problem of the young. Instead, the elderly tend to be the victims of crime, or at least many elderly fear that they will be (Ward, LaGory, and Sherman, 1986; Webb and Marshall, 1989). Actually, the rate of crime perpetration against the elderly has dropped about 25 percent over the past two decades (U.S. Bureau of the Census, 1991: 181). Despite this, one poll found that crime was considered by older people to be one of the most serious problems that they face, more severe than health, poverty, or loneliness (Schack and Frank, 1978). Street assault, such as purse snatching, is one of the more common crimes perpetrated against older people, and it is one that they particularly fear. The problem of crime victimization among the elderly arises in part because some older people find themselves living in neighborhoods that, although once middle class and respectable, have deteriorated over the years.

When they are victimized by criminals, the elderly tend to suffer more than others. They are less able physically to defend themselves, and injuries such as a broken bone take longer to heal. In addition, many elderly live on fixed incomes, which means that a loss of money due to robbery or fraud cannot be easily recouped. Finally, although all victims of crime feel a psychological sense of helplessness and violation, the elderly are much more likely to feel intimidated and vulnerable in the face of younger and far more powerful criminals.

Institutions and Nursing Homes

There are more than 25,000 nursing homes in the United States with 1.5 million residents (U.S. Bureau of the Census, 1991: 112). Yet most older people do not live in nursing homes or other extended-care facilities. In fact, only about 5 percent do. However, between 40 percent and 60 percent of the elderly will live in a nursing home for at least some time before they die (Kemper and Murtaugh, 1991). So the reality for most elderly in America is that they will likely spend their final days, if not their last years, in such institutions. This is especially true for women, those with fewer financial resources, and people with fewer social ties in the community.

Being institutionalized in a nursing home is sometimes a last option because an elderly person is too ill to remain in the community (Mutchler and Burr, 1991). Often this occurs when the social supports necessary to remain in the community disappear. A woman, for example, who had been taking care of her elderly husband dies, and there is no one else willing or able to take care of the man in his home. Or the stress on caregivers of caring for a frail, elderly person may become too great, especially if the caregiver is also elderly.

The overriding concern with nursing homes is whether they offer the elderly a pleasant and healthy environment. Many residents are sick and vulnerable, making them easy targets for exploitation by the unscrupulous. Some homes suffer from unappetizing and poorly prepared food, dark corridors and stairwells, and severe boredom and apathy. Sometimes basic physical care, such as prompt assistance to the bathroom, is slow or lacking. Residents are sometimes tied to their bed or wheelchair or given powerful tranquilizing drugs in circumstances that are more for the benefit of the staff than the safety of the residents (Kolata, 1991). Elderly nursing-home residents also sometimes suffer from physical and psychological abuse at the hands of nursing home personnel (Pillemer and Moore, 1990). Medical care can be poor and dental care scarce.

Such conditions exist for a number of reasons. First, in profit-making, or proprietary, institutions, there is a tension between the necessity of making a profit and the desire to provide services to the residents. Medicaid and private insurance carriers pay for people's nursing-home care on a flat-fee basis, meaning a set per diem charge for each resident. If the facility actually spends less to care for a resident, it keeps the difference. This means that the less care provided, the greater the institution's profits. And over 80 percent of the nursing homes in the United States are proprietary institutions (U.S. Bureau of the Census, 1991: 113). So there is a built-in incentive to watch carefully the extent of services provided. There are also, of course, incentives to provide good care because many groups, including the government and relatives of the residents, are watching over the institution. Whenever those oversights are lacking, however, the potential for exploitation is there, and a majority of the proprietary homes probably fall short of providing the service and comfort that the elderly deserve.

A second reason for poor conditions in nursing homes is that they have difficulty hiring and keeping qualified staff. People with little or no training in health care or gerontology are often hired because they will accept low salaries and cannot find other work. Such people are not likely to have the empathy that can lead to good care or the professionalism that will result in innovative programs in the home. Because of low pay and poor working conditions in nursing homes, there is often a high turnover rate among the skilled nursing staff. This makes it extremely difficult to maintain the continuity of care and the leadership that would help sustain adequate and innovative services.

A particularly pernicious problem that can occur in nursing homes is *depersonalization*, which was discussed in the context of mental institutions

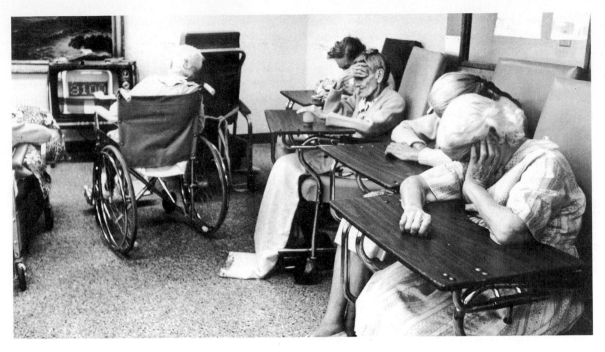

Most elderly spend some part of their lives in a nursing home, which challenges American society to make sure that such homes provide a decent and stimulating environment for the elderly.

in Chapter 4. It refers to the feeling of detachment from the people or social groups that give life meaning and provide people with a sense of importance and self-worth (Coe, 1978). Institutions can take control over people's lives, regulating what and when they eat and when various activities will occur. The residents can be treated as dependent and helpless individuals. When this happens, a self-fulfilling prophecy can occur: The residents become products of the institutional treatment and view themselves as dependent and powerless. This is especially true in all-encompassing institutions such as nursing homes, particularly those with a highly authoritarian and impersonal organization. The residents respond by withdrawal or extreme depersonalization. For example, they may stop thinking of themselves in terms of social statuses such as mother or hus-

band. In extreme cases of depersonalization, a person can drift into a psychotic world of delusions that represents a complete break with reality.

The behavior that is symptomatic of depersonalization is often attributed to senility in an ageist attempt to claim that physiological deterioration accounts for such behavior in nursing homes. In many cases, however, this is incorrect. Instead, the people affected are responding to their social surroundings, with depersonalization being their reaction to their treatment by the institution. Such depersonalization can be avoided, but it is costly. To do so calls for skilled nursing care and other changes in the institutional environment. One such change, for example, is to develop programs that involve residents in interesting or important group activities. Some nursing homes have done this by including the residents in making the decisions about how to run the institution. This offers the sense of social involvement that is so important to people's sense of self-worth.

FUTURE PROSPECTS

There have been numerous developments in social policy related to problems of age in the past few decades, and more will follow. We will review the major developments and prospects for the future.

Economic Resources

Social policy regarding retirement in the United States rests on the assumption that the elderly's economic support will consist of three elements: personal pensions, Social Security, and accumulated savings and assets. Unfortunately, one or more of these elements is either absent or inadequate for many retired people.

Retirement Pensions.   As we have seen, many elderly have little or no income from personal retirement pensions. In the 1970s, the government tried to alleviate this problem by passing legislation that requires employers with more than ten employees to offer their workers a pension plan. This legislation also regulated the "vesting" of pensions. A "vested" pension is one that is the property of the employee rather than the company, so that the employee keeps the accumulated funds in the plan even if he or she no longer works for that company. In the past, some pension plans were never vested so that people had to keep working for a particular company until they retired in order to receive retirement benefits. All too often, people would work for a company for many years, only to be laid off in their fifties and lose all their retirement income. In fact, some companies had been accused of purposely laying off older workers to save the pension money. Federal legislation now requires that pensions be vested in the employee after five years of employment.

Recent legislation has also been enacted to protect some older women, especially those who were homemakers throughout their life and never established a pension plan of their own (Rankin, 1985). Such women are dependent on their husbands' retirement, but some husbands chose—without consulting their wives—to have retirement benefits end at their death. These women, who often outlive their husbands, find themselves with no pension after their husbands die. The Retirement Equity Act of 1984 requires employees to take their retirement in a form that provides the spouse with a pension after the worker's death, unless the spouse agrees in writing to another arrangement. The legislation also provides for the spouse to receive a death benefit from vested retirement funds if the working spouse dies before reaching retirement age.

Current legislation involving retirement plans is a vast improvement over the far less regulated environment of the past. Still, however, many people find themselves with few accumulated pension funds when they retire. Some people jump from one job to another every few years and never achieve a vested pension plan. This problem could be considerably alleviated by shortening the vesting period to two to four years of employment. This would provide many more workers with retirement income, but it would also cost employers more and possibly increase prices.

Social Security.   We discussed the Old-Age, Survivors, Disability, and Health Insurance Program (OASDI) briefly in Chapter 5. OASDI, popularly known as Social Security, is one of the most important income-maintenance programs in the United States. First established by Congress in 1935, Social Security is a compulsory retirement insurance program, meaning that all qualified employees and their employers must contribute. Currently, income up to $55,500 is taxed for Social Security at a rate of 15 percent.

For the elderly who can retain their health and live independently, life can be fulfilling and rewarding.

(If you pay Social Security taxes, the amount is shown in the box labeled "FICA" on your pay stub.) The employer and the employee each pay half of the tax, with self-employed persons paying the full tax at a lower rate. When people retire, they receive monthly benefits based mainly on total contributions they made to Social Security over the years.

Social Security income constitutes 38 percent of all the income available to the elderly. Although Social Security was never intended to be a person's sole retirement income, it is for some people, and Social Security payments are barely sufficient to live on. For example, in 1990, the average monthly benefit for a retired worker and spouse was $1,027, for an annual income of $12,324—poverty-level income (U.S. Bureau of the Census, 1992: 361). Many elderly receive much less than this average. So retirees who must rely exclusively on Social Security are in desperate straits.

In the late 1970s and early 1980s, Social Security got into trouble as the number of people receiving benefits from the program grew faster than the number contributing to it. In some years, the system paid out more than it collected. In 1983, a rescue package was assembled that trimmed some benefits, increased payroll taxes, provided for partial taxation of Social Security benefits, lowered benefits to those who retire early, and delayed full benefits until recipients reach sixty-seven years of age. The goal was to encourage people to keep working and be less reliant on Social Security in their old age. In addition, money was transferred from the general tax fund to the Social Security fund. These policies worked, and Social Security is now running large surpluses, which will probably continue for the next few decades unless the policies are changed or economic conditions deteriorate (Axinn and Stern, 1990). The basic problem remains, however: With an aging population, the elderly are still growing in proportion to those still working. Unless we reduce the benefits to the recipients or raise the taxes on working people, the system will eventually be jeopardized once more.

Savings and Assets.   Savings and accumulated assets, such as stocks and bonds, are a third source of economic support in retirement, but many elderly do not have any significant amount of such assets (U.S. Department of Health and Human Services, 1991). This is especially true for minority elderly, among whom probably less than 20 percent have such assets. If people who are able could be encouraged to save and accumulate assets while working—beyond money put into a pension or Social Security—this would help alleviate the financial problems of some older people. In the past two decades, the government has moved to encourage this. It allowed Individual Retirement Accounts, or IRAs, which are tax-deferred savings or investment plans that have some tax benefits that make them attractive. The money cannot be withdrawn without penalty until the person is fifty-nine and one-half years old. An IRA is not a particular type of investment but rather a designation of an investment as a retirement plan. Many types of investments can be designated as IRAs, such as savings accounts, stocks, bonds, or certificates of deposit. Funds can be shifted from one investment to another, as long as they are not withdrawn as cash to spend. IRAs are intended for employees; there are equivalent plans for self-employed people. In 1989, one-fifth of all households had IRAs, with a total value of $465 billion (U.S. Bureau of the Census, 1991: 366).

Tax-deferred savings and investments have become very popular and will be important ingredients in the economic picture of many retired people in the future. Although legislation recently restricted access to IRAs among high income earners, some have suggested that the policies should be liberalized. For example, the maximum allowable contribution to IRAs could be raised or even eliminated altogether. Although there will probably always be a limit to how much one can invest, such opportunities may be expanded in the future. The Policy Issues insert in this chapter contains a discussion of what should be at the foundation of our provision of economic support to the elderly.

Health Care

The availability of health care to the elderly has been vastly improved through the Medicare and Medicaid programs. Recall from Chapter 4 that Medicare is a program of health insurance for people over sixty-five, whereas Medicaid is health insurance for the indigent. These programs have gone a long way toward relieving the financial burden of health care for the elderly, and they have made the decision of whether to seek health services an easier one for older people to make.

These programs, however, are not without their problems. First, they do not cover all services. The elderly still pay substantial out-of-pocket health-care costs. Supplemental health insurance can be purchased through Medicare, but the recipient must pay a monthly premium for this coverage. A second problem is that Medicare is very costly for society. It currently costs nearly $102 billion, as compared with $7 billion in 1970 (U.S. Bureau of the Census, 1991). That represents a fourteenfold increase in twenty years. However, despite the budget cutting that hit social programs in the early 1980s, Medicare emerged relatively unscathed. This suggests that the benefits provided are not likely to be significantly reduced in the future, although expenditures for additional benefits will probably be scrutinized very closely. In any event, Medicare makes it possible for people to worry less about whether they will have access to needed health care in their old age.

POLICY ISSUES

Age or Need? Policies for the Elderly and Youth

In the past fifteen years, we have seen many social programs cut or eliminated in an effort to reduce budgets and institute laissez-faire policies regarding government support for those in need. During the period, Social Security and Medicare have probably been affected less than other government programs. In fact, over the past few decades, Social Security and Medicare have become increasingly generous to the elderly. As Figure 8.10 shows, these two programs have been consuming a larger and larger proportion of the federal budget—30 percent by 1990. By the end of this century, more than one out of every three federal budget dollars will probably go to these two programs that support primarily the elderly. This sacrosanct status of programs for the elderly can probably be attributed to two things. First, there was a time, not too many decades ago, when the elderly were much worse off than today and undoubtedly deserved a large share of societal largess. Second, as we have seen, the elderly have become a powerful interest group nationally, and politicians are hestitant to oppose them.

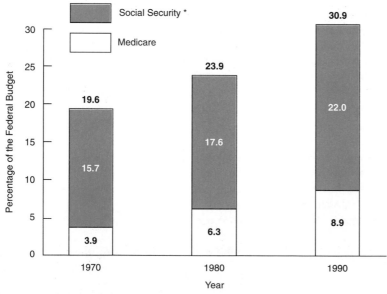

* Includes only old age and survivors insurance.

Figure 8.10   **Medicare and Social Security as a Percentage of the Total Federal Budget, 1970–1990**
SOURCE: U.S. Bureau of the Census, *Statistical Abstract of the United States, 1992* (Washington, D.C.: U.S. Government Printing Office, 1992), pp. 97, 315, 359.

However, the circumstances of the elderly have changed over the past thirty years, and this is leading some policymakers and gerontologists to rethink our approach to programs for the elderly (Crystal, 1986; Longman, 1987). Many elderly today are quite comfortable, with retirement plans that offer them a life-style that they enjoy. In fact, as we have seen, most elderly people do not view financial problems as being among their more serious concerns. This has led gerontologist Bernice Neugarten to comment that "age itself is becoming a poor indicator of an older person's circumstances and needs" (Neugarten, 1982: 25). Yet the vast array of social programs that has been established since the Great Depression to help the elderly—in income maintenance, housing, health services, social services, and the like—has utilized chronological age as an easy criterion for eligibility. This may be a convenient way for legislators or administrators to develop and run programs, but we need to assess whether it is the most equitable and efficient utilization of societal resources.

There are, as we have seen, groups of elderly who are still very much in need; but age-based services may actually draw resources away from those elderly who are in most desperate need of help. It also draws resources away from other groups whose needs may be greater than the needs of some elderly. We saw earlier in this chapter that the social health of our youth seems to have deteriorated over the past few decades, whereas the circumstances of the elderly have gotten better. If Neugarten's policy of focusing on need rather than age is adopted, then resources now flowing to the elderly might be rechanneled toward needy youth. Resources must be spread more thinly if they have to cover a whole age category, such as all elderly, rather than being directed toward those with identifiable needs irrespective of age.

Neugarten makes the point that advocates of age-based legislation may be perpetuating ageism and age discrimination at the same time that they claim to be advocates for the elderly. This can occur because age-based policies can help to perpetuate the misperception of "the old" as a homogeneous group with numerous problems not experienced by other age groups in society. This

can reinforce the notion that "being old" is a highly stigmatized status. People identify "old age" itself as a social problem rather than focusing on those conditions, such as poverty or physical infirmity, that can be found among all age groups, although possibly more often among the old. Thus, Neugarten argues, we should focus on poverty, not old age, as the key social problem in devising social policy. Neugarten summarizes her view by saying that income, health care, housing, and other goods and services should be provided, not according to age, but according to need (Neugarten, 1982).

Neugarten's position could translate into social policy in a number of possible ways:

1. Medicare could be made available to all people over sixty-five, but the financially independent elderly might pay a higher deductible, a larger percentage of their charges, or possibly monthly premiums for the coverage.

2. Social Security could be based on need, with the poor elderly receiving larger payments and the well-to-do-elderly receiving little or no Social Security. If Social Security were redefined as a poverty program rather than a general retirement program, it might be preferable to incorporate it into the public-assistance programs discussed in Chapter 5.

These are merely some suggestions for social policy to stimulate thought about Neugarten's ideas. Certainly, some policies would be difficult to establish, especially because current workers have already contributed to Social Security in anticipation of receiving support from it in their old age. They might be understandably reluctant to drop Social Security and forego that source of retirement income. However, these are technical problems that can be solved. The more difficult hurdle is to decide whether our policies will be based on age or need.

Neugarten's position is a controversial one because there are many groups whose interests would be threatened if policies and programs were to become based on need rather than age. Her position is also a complex one because it causes us to assess the many other ways in which age is used as a legal and administrative criterion. Is it equitable, for example, to allow sixteen-year-olds to drive a car but prohibit fifteen-year-olds from doing so? Teens, of course, are required to attend school until a certain age, usually sixteen; labor legislation discourages them from competing with adults for jobs by limiting the types of jobs they can hold and the number of hours they can work; and a high school diploma is a minimum qualification for many jobs. Because they are relegated to a marginal part of the labor force, it is difficult for teens to do the things adults do, such as support themselves or marry and have children. There are, of course, good reasons for teenagers to stay in school, but the point here is that society does place these people in a dependent position, which encourages them to view themselves as dependent and less mature than adults.

Until now, age sixteen was the point after which society would no longer force youngsters into a dependent status. Now, however, some states are beginning to stretch that point: A few states have passed laws that withdraw the driver's licenses of teens who drop out of high school before graduating. Without being able to drive, many jobs would be out of their reach and their social life would be severely curtailed. It seems that society has created another club to use on those youngsters who try to achieve independence before they have reached the level of training mandated as appropriate by society. These practices raise critical questions of equity: Is it fair to treat members of a group in this fashion merely because of their age? It also makes one wonder what the future holds: Will the line be stretched even further? Might society eventually revoke the driver's licenses of students who drop out of college?

Once we begin to view age as an ascribed status that may be an inappropriate criterion for allocating most resources and privileges, we may find that many of our social practices need scrutiny.

Living Arrangements

Because old people are increasingly unlikely to live with and be cared for by their children, where do they live? A number of alternative living arrangements have arisen.

Retirement Communities.   The elderly who are healthy and financially secure most commonly live in their own home or apartment. Over the past few decades, planned retirement communities have evolved for those who can afford them. These communities are often owned by private development corporations and include many easily accessible amenities such as golf, tennis, and community centers. There is also sometimes restricted access in order to ease the residents' fears of victimization. Also, children and adolescents are not allowed to live in some of these communities. These communities appeal to elderly people because they can associate with others in their age group in a safe and relaxed atmosphere.

Despite their appeal, there has been some controversy over how beneficial these planned communities actually are. One criticism of them is that they isolate the elderly into a segregated subculture in American society. We know from considerable research that stereotypes, often quite negative ones, develop between groups that have little communication and social contact. We saw in Chapter 6 that this was an element in creating and maintaining patterns of prejudice and discrimination against racial and ethnic minorities. If such stereotyping occurs, taking the form of ageism discussed earlier, it can lead to prejudice and discrimination against the elderly. So planned retirement communities, which create geographical and social isolation, may contribute to misunderstanding and possibly even hostility between the elderly and younger people.

Age-Integrated Housing.   In 1970, Maggie Kuhn, founder of the Gray Panthers, began developing what she called "shared housing" arrangements for herself and other old people. Shared housing involves a number of people, both young and old, sharing a home and the various chores and responsibilities of home ownership. This is not necessarily communal living, because each person may pay rent or a share of the mortgage and keep his or her finances and belongings separate from those of the others. Proponents of such arrangements believe they offer many advantages to the elderly, including social ties to replace the family. In a shared housing setting, there are young people to make difficult repairs and do hard labor; there are people present to alleviate feelings of isolation; and there is help for the elderly if they develop some activity limitations. These arrangements also reduce the segregation and stereotyping that may result from age-segregated housing (Danigelis and Fengler, 1990).

Age-integrated housing arrangements can take forms other than shared housing. They might involve a community with separate houses or apartments that are available to people of all ages. Proponents of such living arrangements have argued that they offer the elderly stimulation, novelty, and the delight of relating to people of all age groups. However, the evidence is not clear on whether age-integrated settings or age-segregated settings are more beneficial to the elderly (Burby and Rohe, 1990). Elderly in age-segregated housing seem more satisfied with how their living arrangements are managed and are more active and involved with people around them. But the impact is not great, and there are some negatives, such as a greater fear of crime in age-segregated settings. So it seems that integration or segregation by age is only one of many factors that affects the satisfaction of the elderly. Also influencing this is whether adequate services are provided and protections against crime are available.

Government-Subsidized Housing.   The housing priority of the many elderly with low or moderate incomes is very basic: to find a place to live that is safe, clean, and affordable. The government has offered assistance in this area for many years, beginning with the Housing Act of 1937. Since then, much legislation has been passed relating to the housing needs of the poor and the elderly. They include such things as building low-income housing, offering rent supplements for private apartments, and providing mortgage insurance for elderly with low or moderate incomes (Kerschner and Hirschfield, 1983).

While these government programs have gone a long way toward helping the elderly acquire decent housing, problems remain that need to be addressed. For example, the problem of crime is still sizable in the deteriorating neighborhoods and public housing projects in which many elderly people live. In addition, much of the public housing already constructed is beginning to deteriorate and is badly in need of repairs. Finally, elderly homeowners on fixed incomes are especially hard hit by rising property values. Particularly in cities where property values have been increasing at rapid rates in the 1970s and 1980s, some elderly can no longer afford houses that they have lived in for many years because the taxes are so high.

Supported-Living Environments.   One of the difficult problems elderly people face is coping with the physical infirmities that can accompany aging. These infirmities have a particular impact on the ability of people to live independently. Family members, especially adult daughters, provide most of the care for aging parents in the United States (Abel, 1991). This places a considerable burden on those family members, and some supports for them have developed, such as in-home physical therapy or other assistance. But often the infirmities become too much for family members to handle, and they must turn to some kind of institutional setting for the elderly person.

In the past few decades, a variety of such institutional settings has emerged to help the elderly cope with infirmity (Struyk et al., 1989). Taken together, they are called *supported-living environments* because all provide some level of support

INTERNATIONAL PERSPECTIVES

Public and Familial Assistance for the Elderly in Other Societies

Around the world and throughout history, families have provided much of the support people need in their old age, and we often hear calls in the United States for a return to family values. However, today's families may not be able to play such a central role because family structures have weakened in virtually all societies in the modern world (Kosberg, 1992). Even in more traditional and highly religious societies such as China or Mexico the family is changing as these societies industrialize and modernize: Families have become smaller, the elderly are less revered and more likely to live alone, and marital disruption is more common. All these factors suggest that modernization has caused pervasive changes in the family that make it a less than complete or perfect support for the elderly. In addition, in all societies, some elderly do not have families, while some families are too poor to offer much assistance. In other cases, the elderly do not get along with younger members of the family and may even suffer abuse at their hand. Finally, in societies as different as Argentina, Sweden, and the United States, surveys show that many elderly do not *want* to be dependent on their adult children or other family members. For all these reasons, a shift of responsibility for caring for the elderly has been occurring in all societies, with the government becoming increasingly active in providing this assistance.

One form of government assistance to the elderly is public pensions. The United States has one of the lowest mandatory contribution rates to a public pension plan (Social Security) of all the industrialized countries. Furthermore, our public pension policy leaves some elderly with little or no pension income because the amount of income a person receives from Social Security depends on their lifetime work and earnings. Such a policy discriminates against those, often women, who never worked or who worked part-time or intermittently. In practically all societies, women are given primary responsibility for taking care of home and family. In the majority of cases, this can be done only by cutting back on paid employment. Societies such as Israel, the United Kingdom, and the Scandinavian countries try to alleviate this problem by also providing a universal pension that is payable to all citizens who reach a certain age, irrespective of whether or how much they have worked (Nusberg, 1984; Cnaan, Olsson, and Wetle, 1990). In Israel, for example, this universal pension provides all individuals with 16 percent of the median income of employed persons, while couples receive 24 percent. Swedish policy provides for three sources of income: a flat-rate pension for all citizens, an earnings-related pension for those who have worked, and mandatory worker pensions provided by employers and trade union organizations. With

for people who cannot or do not want to live independently. Some of these homes are nonprofit institutions run by religious groups, business organizations, or labor unions for the benefit of their members. Others are commercial or proprietary institutions that are run to make a profit for

their owners. The range of support they provide is quite varied. At one extreme are homes for the aged that care for reasonably healthy people who no longer want responsibility for running a home and caring for themselves. At the other extreme are nursing homes that take people who have se-this system, destitution among Swedish elderly is practically nonexistent.

Since public pensions are rarely large enough to provide for all the needs of the elderly, many industrial nations, like France and Sweden, require almost universal private pension coverage for employees through nationally negotiated agreements. While less than one-half of American workers have private pension coverage, 90 percent of workers in Sweden and 80 percent in the Netherlands have that coverage. Switzerland actually has an amendment in their constitution that mandates that all workers will have pension coverage.

To provide protection for women and men with meager work histories, Germany, New Zealand, and Canada split pension credits accumulated during a marriage at the time of a divorce. This is sometimes done for both public and private pensions, and it means that a nonworking spouse shares in the pension accumulation of the working spouse. For earnings-related public pensions, Switzerland and the United Kingdom permit people to use a deceased or former spouse's earnings record at the time the marriage ended to calculate retirement benefits. In some cases, if a wife's earnings record does not qualify her for a pension, she can combine it with her husband's earnings record. Programs of this sort have been considered in the United States but not yet implemented.

In order to assist retirees in maintaining something close to their preretirement lifestyle, some societies set goals for how much of a worker's preretirement income should be replaced by the combination of public and private benefits. In the Netherlands, for example, the goal is that retirement pay be 70 percent of a retiring worker's final pay, while in Switzerland it is 60 percent. In addi-

tion, to ensure that all work contributes to a worker's retirement pay, many societies have much more liberal vesting policies. In Sweden and Switzerland, for example, for workers who have reached their late twenties, full vesting occurs as soon as one begins to work or within a few years of employment. This means that people who switch jobs after a few years still accumulate some retirement funds that are permanently their own. This especially benefits women, who are more likely to work for short periods and to switch jobs.

All industrialized countries recognize the value of maintaining the elderly in their own homes because it is more humane and less expensive than caring for them in a nursing home or other institutional setting. Denmark, Norway, and Sweden, for example, provide such things as chore and escort services, meals-on-wheels, laundry services, counseling, transportation, friendly visiting services, and other practical but essential supports that allow older people to continue living in their homes as they become more frail and limited. In some cases, these services are universal rather than age-based or income-based—anyone with functional impairments is eligible for them. This increases political support for them and encourages people to view them as a right of citizenship rather than a welfare handout. While these services are free to those with low incomes, others pay according to their abilities which helps defray the costs of the programs and reduces demand. Some of these services are available to the elderly in the United States, but these other societies have a much more elaborate infrastructure of such services. This infrastructure ensures that these services are more universally available and that the goal of maintaining the elderly in their own home is more achievable.

vere physical limitations and require extensive support. In some homes, people purchase or rent an apartment with cooking facilities and can either cook for themselves or eat in a dining area with the other residents. All repairs and maintenance for the apartments are provided by the

home. There are homes that will accept people with greater physical limitations, such as those confined to a wheelchair or who use a walker. These homes are designed to be barrier free and may still offer separate, fully equipped apartments for their residents. Some homes provide the whole range of support. People can enter when they are reasonably healthy and be assured of support by the community if their physical status deteriorates. There are even homes that provide day-care centers where older people who live at home can come during the day for meals, medical and social services, and leisure pursuits.

The care and programs available in these living environments are quite variable. Generally, the nonprofit homes run by religious groups or labor unions have the financial resources and the motivation to provide excellent care and a wide range of services. Other homes charge high fees and still find it difficult to provide high-quality care. This is especially true of proprietary institutions that cater to low- and moderate-income groups. To alleviate these problems, the government has developed an elaborate set of regulations to be followed in order for a home to be licensed. It has also developed programs to train nursing-home personnel and nursing-home inspectors. The government has also encouraged the development of programs that enable the elderly to remain independent and avoid institutionalization. The Meals on Wheels program, for example, provides hot meals for homebound elderly people, certainly a less expensive and more desirable alternative than nursing homes.

The International Perspectives insert (see pp. 296–297) provides a comparison of financial and other services available to elderly in the United States with those in some other societies.

Collective Action

There is little doubt that it has been older people themselves who have been the most vocal about the treatment of the elderly in the United States. The elderly have shown, and continue to show, signs of increasing political activism, and even radical militancy, focused on changing traditional conceptions of old age and advocating social policies that might alleviate the problems of the elderly (Wallace et al., 1991). Two popular organizations promoting the interests of the elderly are

Elderly people constitute an interest group that has organized very effectively to pursue policies beneficial to themselves. Groups such as the Gray Panthers have been increasingly reluctant to allow conditions detrimental to the well being of the elderly to continue without challenge.

the American Association of Retired Persons (AARP) and the National Retired Teachers Association (NRTA). These groups offer many programs and services for the elderly, such as courses in income tax preparation and public speaking. They have also been very active at the local, state, and national levels in lobbying for programs that are beneficial to the elderly.

The Gray Panthers is a group that is considerably more extreme than AARP or NRTA. The group, whose official name is Consultation of Older and Younger Adults, believes that the problems of the aged in America stem from some basic defects in the social structure. The most fundamental defect, they argue, is our emphasis on materialism and the consumption of goods and services, rather than on the quality of life and personal relationships. In a materialist society, the elderly are viewed as useless because they are less economically productive. Because of this, they are abandoned, like worn-out automobiles. The Gray Panthers hope to liberate people from what they perceive as outmoded ways of thinking about the elderly and to encourage independence and self-determination among the elderly.

These various groups and social movements have been quite successful in protecting and advancing the interests of the elderly. In the early 1980s, for example, when many social programs were being severely trimmed by the government, Medicare, Social Security, and other programs providing benefits for the elderly suffered the least. A primary reason for this was that politicians were concerned about the strong reaction they could expect from the very well organized groups backing the elderly. Such successes are likely to enhance support for groups such as AARP, NRTA, the Gray Panthers, and other groups working for the elderly. In addition, the elderly have more financial and economic resources available today than they did decades ago, and this will be even more true in the future. They also have more time to pursue their interests than do younger people who must work. Finally, older people take their duty to vote much more seriously than do younger people. In the 1990 election, only 22 percent of the people in their early twenties bothered to vote, whereas 60 percent of the people over sixty-five did so (U.S. Bureau of the Census, 1992: 269). This affords the elderly considerably more political clout. People between fifty and sixty-five also vote in large numbers. Because these people are also concerned about issues related to the elderly because they will soon be in that group, they comprise a substantial voting bloc.

So collective action on the part of the elderly is likely to continue as one of the most powerful forces working against ageist attitudes and social policies in the United States.

Linkages

Providing support and assistance to the elderly has contributed to skyrocketing health-care costs because Medicare has become so expensive and increased demand considerably for health-care services (Chapter 4). At the same time, the elderly are more likely to be battered and injured by a caretaker who abuses drugs or alcohol (Chapter 10).

Summary

1. Gerontology is the scientific study of aging. All societies carve out people's lives into a series of social stages, and this is called the life course. The life course is determined in part by biology and in part by the needs of a particular society.

2. Functionalists argue that the stages of the life cycle are intimately related to the social needs of a particular society. The life cycle in preindustrial societies differs significantly from that in industrial societies.

3. From the conflict perspective, the position of the young and old in society is related to their access to social, political, and economic power. The elderly have less power today than in the past because they control fewer resources and the young are less dependent on them.

4. Ageism refers to the ideology holding that people in a particular age group are inferior, have negative attributes, and can be dominated and exploited because of their age. The age structure of industrial societies is becoming more "top heavy" as our society ages and the dependency ratio grows larger.

5. Throughout history, there have been ideologies that justified the inequitable treatment of the young. The primary forms of discrimination against the young are economic exploitation, sexual exploitation, and child abuse.

6. A major form of discrimination against the elderly is mandatory retirement. The major concern about mandatory retirement is whether it has a detrimental effect on people's economic position and their sense of self-worth. The elderly also suffer from physical and psychological abuse.

7. The elderly face a number of serious problems: they are poorer than other adult Americans; they suffer from social isolation, especially when they are very old; they have more health problems than others and are more susceptible to fraud and quackery; they fear being the victims of crime; and they are in danger of being exploited in poorly run nursing homes when they need some type of supportive living environment.

8. Efforts to improve the economic status of the elderly have focused on ensuring that more people have personal pension plans and that the plans provide more adequate support. It has also been suggested that Social Security could be improved and put on a more sound financial basis. Policies have also been established to encourage people to increase their assets for retirement through tax-deferred savings and investments.

9. The health care available to the elderly has been increased substantially with the establishment of Medicare and Medicaid. Also, numerous new approaches to the living arrangements of the elderly have alleviated the problems of isolation and infirmity in old age.

10. Much of the attention focused on problems of the elderly has arisen because the elderly have been very vocal about things that work against their interests. Through moderate and radical political activity, the elderly have gained much and protected what they have fairly effectively.

Important Terms for Review

ageism	demography	gerontology	life span
age structure	dependency ratio	life course	

Discussion Questions

1. What will happen if demographic trends continue as projected, with the young making up a smaller proportion of our population and the old a larger proportion? How will this trend change social institutions, such as the schools, religion, and the media?

2. Can you recall any times that you were discriminated against or exploited because of your age when you were young? Do you think it was justified? In what ways could we ensure that the unjustified exploitation of the young did not occur?

3. Organize a debate on the issue of mandatory retirement. Have three teams: one arguing for no mandatory retirement at all, a second arguing for raising the mandatory retirement age, and the third arguing for lowering the mandatory retirement age. On the blackboard, list all the arguments made for and against each position.

When the debate is over, take a class vote on the issue.

4. Send small groups of students to nursing homes or other facilities for the aged in your community. Have each team report their observations to the class: the positive as well as the negative elements of the setting. For each facility, develop a set of feasible recommendations for improvement and communicate them to the director of the facility.

5. Invite a social worker from the child protective services division of your department of social services or an officer in the juvenile division of your police department to come to class and discuss his or her experiences with the exploitation of youth. Particularly ask about the problems of child abuse and neglect and teenage prostitution and pornography in your community. You will likely be surprised at what you hear.

For Further Reading

Advisory Council on Social Security. *Social Security and the Future Financial Security of Women.* Washington, D.C.: Advisory Council on Social Security, 1991. This is an excellent report that documents the financial difficulties that older women will confront well into the next century and what can be done about it.

Phillippe Aries. *Centuries of Childhood: A Social History of Childhood.* New York: Random House, 1962. An excellent history of how childhood has been viewed in many different cultures.

Joel Best. *Threatened Children: Rhetoric and Concern About Child-Victims.* Chicago: University of Chicago Press, 1990. This is a very good book on the "constructionist" approach to social problems, emphasizing the point we made in Chapter 1 that conditions do not become social problems until an influential group defines them as such. The author focuses particularly on the various threats and dangers, such as abuse and kidnapping, that confront children in our society.

William F. Clark, Anabel O. Pelham, and Marleen L. Clark. *Old and Poor: A Critical Assessment of the Low-Income Elderly.* Lexington, Mass.: Lexington Books, 1988. This book is about what it is like to be old and poor in the United States today. The elderly suffer some significant disadvantages that other people do not face.

J. Kevin Eckert. *The Unseen Elderly: A Study of Marginally Subsistent Hotel Dwellers.* San Diego: Campanile Press, 1980. A penetrating look at the lives of elderly people who live in SROs, or "single-room occupancy" hotels. Most of these people are poor or near-poor, and they lead a rather marginal existence.

Victor W. Marshall. *Last Chapters: A Sociology of Aging and Death.* Monterey, Calif.: Brooks/Cole, 1980. A view of death in the context of its social meanings and how the elderly view their impending death and experience it.

Matilda White Riley, Beth B. Hess, and Kathleen Bond. *Aging in Society: Selected Reviews of Recent Research.* Hillsdale, N.J.: Lawrence Erlbaum Associates, 1983. For students interested in current research on social gerontology, this book is an excellent summary of recent research on a wide range of topics. These papers were originally prepared for the White House Conference on Aging in 1981.

Susan Sheehan. *Kate Quinton's Days.* Boston: Houghton Mifflin, 1984. This is an absorbing look at what it is like for one person to be very old. It is often not pleasant reading, but it forcefully makes us confront the realities of how we treat some old people.

Thomas T. H. Wan, Barbara Gill Odell, and David T. Lewis. *Promoting the Well-Being of the Elderly: A Community Diagnosis.* New York: Haworth Press, 1982. This book provides a good illustration of how the tools of applied social research can be focused on a particular community to assess the needs of older citizens and propose programs to meet those needs.

PART III
Problems of Unconventional and Deviant Behavior

When novelist Chip Elliott and his wife, a psychiatrist, moved to Los Angeles in the late 1970s, they were hoping to lead pleasant, quiet lives. They were young and embarking on promising careers. Both would certainly have regarded themselves as peaceful people. The world of assaults, street crime, juvenile gangs, and handguns all seemed far away. In a short time, however, the Elliotts found out otherwise. Their neighborhood turned out to be a battleground for two juvenile gangs: "When they shot at each other—as they did less than one week after we had moved in—they shouted to us . . . to get out of the way. We did" (Elliott, 1981: 33).

The Elliotts' home was broken into and some of their friends were robbed. Going against their previous values, they purchased handguns and even obtained permits to carry them. Walking

Myths and Facts About Crime

Myth: There is a clear line between the "criminal element" in society and the law-abiding and respectable people. If we could put that criminal element behind bars, the crime problem would be solved.

Fact: Once again, social reality is far more complex than many commonsense beliefs would have it. It turns out that many crimes are committed by people who would be considered quite respectable by most people. For example, who commits vandalism? Teenage punks? Hostile and alienated losers? Social psychologist Philip Zimbardo conducted an intriguing study of people who vandalize automobiles in New York (Zimbardo, 1973). After seeing many stripped and battered automobiles on his way to work, he decided to observe who the vandals were. He bought an old car, left it on a street near New York University, and watched from a hidden location. Within ten minutes, the first vandals appeared: a father, mother, and their eight-year-old son! The mother served as lookout while the father and son removed the battery and radiator. Later, another vandal was pushing an infant in a baby carriage. There followed a virtual parade of people who removed everything of value from the car and then began battering what was left. These vandals

were often well dressed and chatted amiably with passersby as they toiled. Zimbardo's research leads to the ineluctable conclusion that many criminals not only appear quite respectable but also probably consider themselves quite law abiding.

Myth: Crimes are committed by the less educated members of society, whereas those fortunate enough to attend college understand the importance of obeying the law.

Fact: We asked college students in the state of Michigan to indicate which criminal activities they had engaged in (see Table 9.1). Their responses showed that every student who responded could have been jailed for at least one year for offenses they had committed. Michigan is probably no different in this regard than any other state.

Some groups may commit more crimes than others, or more of certain types of crime, but the crime problem is by no means limited to one or a few groups. The social factors that lead people to commit crimes are very complex and affect all of us to a degree. If all the criminals were behind bars, would anyone be left on the outside? Probably not many.

home one night, Elliott was confronted by five young men. Elliott was carrying a 9mm automatic pistol.

We were directly under a streetlight and less than fifty feet from an intersection thick with traffic. Their leader pulled a kitchen knife, smiled at me, and said: "Just the wallet, man. Won't be no trouble." That was a very long moment for me—it was supposed to be one of those moments that are charged with electricity. It wasn't. It was hollow, silent, and chilly. I pulled the automatic, lev-

eled it at them, and said very clearly, "You must be dreaming." The leader smiled again, muttered an obscenity, and began to move toward me with the knife. His buddies laughed. I aimed the automatic at the outer edge of his left thigh and shot him. I backed off and walked away with the gun still in my hand. I remember thinking, shouldn't I call a doctor? And then I thought, would he have called a doctor for me? And I kept on walking. I am not proud of this. I did not swallow it easily either. More than a year passed before I talked about it with anybody, even my wife. But

Table 9.1 **Criminal Activities Under the State of Michigan Penal Code**

1. You attempt to physically strike another person, but do not succeed. (Sec. 750-81/750.92: Attempted Assault and Battery)
2. During a fight, you break your opponent's nose. (Sec. 750.81a: Assault and Battery with Bodily Harm)
3. You set a fire in a wastebasket located in a public restroom. (Sec. 750.73-.81: Arson)
4. You intentionally damage somebody else's property. (Sec. 750.377a: Malicious Destruction of Property)
5. You knowingly trespass on another person's property. (Sec. 750.552: Trespass)
6. You write a check, knowing that it exceeds the amount you have in your account. (Sec. 750.218: False Pretenses)
7. You shoplift minor articles (candy bar, cigarettes, magazines). (Sec. 750.356: Larceny)
8. You purchase a compact disc player that you know or believe is stolen. (Sec. 750.535: Receiving Stolen Property)
9. You hide in the trunk of a friend's car in order to gain entrance to a drive-in movie without paying the admission fee. (Sec. 750.292-93: Failure to Pay)
10. You participate in sexual activity with an animal. (Sec. 750.158: Crime Against Nature)
11. You are married, and you have voluntary sexual intercourse with a person other than your spouse. (Sec. 750.29: Felonious Adultery)
12. You engage in an act of sexual intercourse for money. (Sec. 750.44: Soliciting and Accosting)
13. You participate in procuring a prostitute for another person or direct that person to a place of prostitution. (Sec. 750.450: Aiders and Abettors)
14. You engage in sexual intercourse with any female under the age of 16 years. (Sec. 750.13: Enticing Away Female Under Age 16)
15. You are involved in a fight involving two or more persons in a public establishment. (Sec. 750.167: Disorderly Conduct)
16. You use obscene, profane language in the presence of women and children. (Sec. 750.337: Improper Language)
17. You throw an empty can of soda out the window of your car. (Sec. 752.901: Littering)
18. You play poker for money at a friend's home. (Sec. 750.301: Accepting Money or Valuable Thing Contingent on an Uncertain Event)
19. You hide a firearm or knife with a blade exceeding three inches on your person while outside of your home. (Sec. 750.227: Concealed Weapons, Carrying)

SOURCE: *Michigan Compiled Laws, Vols. 38–39* (St. Paul, Minn.: West Publishing Company, 1987).

I did it. And I could do it again if I had to.
(Elliott, 1981: 33–36)

Elliott's experience graphically illustrates the problems of crime and delinquency and their impact on people. When Elliott moved to Los Angeles he did not own a gun. A growing fear of crime, however, drastically changed both his attitudes and his behavior. He adapted by buying a pistol, and having to use that pistol was the price he paid for living in a dangerous society.

Elliott's experience also highlights an element of the sociological view of deviant behavior that was discussed in Chapter 1. Elliott shot a person and then walked away. Does that make him a deviant? Some people would argue that under the circumstances it does not, just as most would say that the young men who attempted to rob him at knifepoint were deviant. In other words, it is not the act itself that is deviant; rather, it is our interpretation of it or judgment about it that makes it deviant. Deviance exists in the social context of an event rather than in the act itself.

In this chapter we will try to understand and find solutions to various types of crime. Not all crime is as graphic, violent, or public as the ones Elliott experienced. We need to remember that crimes are committed by people in business suits and corporate board rooms, and they can be just as harmful to society as violent street crime. We begin our discussion of crime and delinquency by examining different explanations of these behaviors.

EXPLANATIONS OF CRIME

Like all behavior, crime and delinquency are complex, and many people find them hard to understand. In fact, because crime and delinquency are often so frightening, it is tempting to settle for overly simple explanations of them. Over the years, many people have sought *biological explanations* of crime, which view criminal behavior as arising, at least in part, from a person's physical constitution or genetic makeup. Some people, it is argued, are simply biologically less capable of conforming their behavior to conventional norms (Wilson and Herrnstein, 1985). Mounds of research results, however, have shown that biology makes, if anything, only a small contribution to the crime problem. Criminologists today agree that criminal behavior is for the most part due to psychological and social forces (Gottfredson and Hirschi, 1990; Chambliss, 1991).

Unlike their biological counterparts, *psychological approaches* to crime still receive considerable support. From this perspective, criminality is linked to personality disorder or maladjustment, often developing during childhood. Evidence in support of such connections comes from research on personality defects and disorders among delinquents, mental disease in prisoners, and studies of psychopathic and sociopathic personalities (Mednick, Moffitt, and Stack, 1987; Eysenck and Gudjonsson, 1989). Although sociologists recognize the importance of personality and psychological processes in our lives, such explanations offer only a partial understanding of crime and delinquency. In many cases, people who commit crimes are free from the psychological disorders that are presumed to cause crime, and people with those disorders often do not commit crimes. In other cases, it can be the criminal life-style, along with the stigma and fear of imprisonment, that leads people to develop unique personality characteristics rather than the other way around (Jeffrey, 1967). In addition, many of the psychological maladjustments that lead to crime are the products of social circumstances, and social conditions also contribute to the cause of crime in many cases where psychological factors do not come into play. So, social conditions contribute substantially to the level of crime in society. Therefore, policy designed to reduce crime needs to focus on the social conditions that produce it, and the sociological approaches to crime provide the basis for doing this. These perspectives emphasize the role of culture, social structure, and social interaction in bringing about criminal and delinquent behavior.

The Functionalist Perspective

An early functionalist, Emile Durkheim, provided one of the explanations for high levels of crime in industrial societies. One of the key features of industrial societies, he argued, is the weakening of many of the social bonds important in preindustrial societies. Ties to family, community, and church become less important in industrial societies as families become smaller and workers more mobile and independent of their families (see

Chapter 3). People are more free to pursue their own needs and fulfill their own desires; they are less constrained by the need to please relatives or account to a priest or minister. But this freedom has its costs. The reduction in social constraints also results in a degree of social disorganization as people pursue needs and goals that may be detrimental to the overall good of society. After all, bonds to family and church were one of the key mechanisms constraining people from committing crimes or engaging in other socially disapproved activities. When those bonds are weakened or removed, a certain amount of crime and social disorder will result. For Durkheim, then, crime is one of the costs that we must pay to live in the type of society that we do. More recently, Durkheim's views have been applied to juvenile delinquency in the form of a "social control" theory of delinquency. The basic idea is that the chances of delinquency occurring can be reduced if youngsters maintain attachments and commitments to the conventional world of their parents, schools, and peers (Hirschi, 1969; Agnew, 1991).

Another influential functionalist approach to crime and delinquency is sociologist Robert K. Merton's **anomie theory** (1968). Merton observed that *people in our society are taught to strive for certain goals but are not always provided with the culturally approved means necessary to attain these goals.* Merton referred to *such inconsistencies and the confusion they can cause in people* as **anomie.** In American society, for example, an important cultural goal is success, which is defined largely in material terms. One culturally approved way to become successful is to get an education and work in some legitimate occupation. Some people, however, are prevented from succeeding in this fashion because of poverty, discrimination, or some other social condition. When people are thus hindered from achieving desired goals, deviance in one of its many forms may result. Deviance is the person's "mode of adaptation" to the anomie, although the person may not think of it this way.

The most common mode of adaptation to anomie Merton called *innovation,* in which people pursue the cultural goals through illegal or other socially disapproved means. This is likely to occur when people feel that legitimate routes to success are closed and that their only option is to turn to illegitimate ones. People who are unemployed or underemployed, for example, can provide for their families and themselves through robbery or burglary. Likewise, a person running a marginal business concern can survive by cheating on taxes or using deceptive advertising practices. Recent research on crime supports anomie theory. For example, crime rates, especially for property crimes, are higher in communities with greater economic inequality or with a larger disparity between incomes among groups. In such cities, the less fortunate can readily see the affluence around them, and some turn to crime to improve their own circumstances (Simons and Gray, 1989). Crime also goes up somewhat when there is an economic recession (Devine, Sheley, and Smith, 1988). Crime rates are high among the unemployed and low among the employed (Allan and Steffensmeier, 1989; Lafree, Drass, and O'Day, 1992).

The importance of anomie theory for understanding crime should be clear: Much criminal activity derives from the social and economic conditions of American society. With high unemployment, high inflation, and reduced government spending on social services, economic disparities are exacerbated. In fact, criminologist Eliot Currie has argued that the low crime rate in industrial societies such as Japan results in part from their programs promoting high employment and the fact that income disparities are much smaller than in America (Currie, 1985).

The functionalist perspective also emphasizes the interrelatedness of the various parts of the social system. Changes in one part bring about changes in other seemingly unrelated parts. Certain social trends and changes in our life-style over the past few decades have increased the opportunities for committing certain kinds of crime, particularly burglary, larceny, and theft (Cohen and

Felson, 1979; Cohen, Felson, and Land, 1980; Miller and Ohlin, 1985). For example, the number of women working has increased dramatically in the past three decades; there has been an increase in the number of households with only one adult member; and Americans take more vacations now than in the past. The result of these three trends is that homes are much more likely to be left unattended for a part of the day and therefore become tempting targets for burglars. There has also been tremendous growth in consumer spending for items such as televisions and automobiles that are likely objects for theft. In short, the rise in crime results in part from increasing opportunities made available by trends that many Americans view as desirable. Unless alternative means of controlling such crimes are found, we may have to settle for the realization that some crimes represent an unfortunate by-product of our affluent and leisured life-style.

The Conflict Perspective

In reviewing the functionalist argument, conflict theorists observe that the analysis of the "crime and delinquency problem" tends to focus heavily on criminal behavior that is more likely to occur among the less powerful groups in society: the young, the poor, and the nonwhite. In fact, the Federal Bureau of Investigation's Crime Index, the most widely publicized statistic on the amount of crime, emphasizes crimes such as assault, which the less well-to-do are more likely to commit, rather than embezzlement, gambling, or tax evasion, which appeal more to middle-class and respectable people. The so-called crime and delinquency problem, then, as it is defined by the police, the courts, and the public, results from the activities of the less fortunate in society.

From the conflict perspective, the legal and criminal justice systems are geared to benefit the dominant groups in society (Quinney, 1974; Kennedy, 1990). Laws, after all, are mechanisms whereby some groups exercise control over the activities of other groups. Generally, it is the powerful who establish legislation defining what activities will be considered criminal and who decide what the penalties will be for those crimes. Thus, removing a television from a store is regarded as criminal, whereas polluting a stream may not be. Armed robbery can bring a fifteen-year prison sentence, whereas price fixing that costs the public millions of dollars in excess expenditures may be punished with a light prison sentence or a fine.

It is also the powerful who can get the police to enforce the laws against some crimes while ignoring other infractions of the law. The powerful also determine the extent of resources that will be devoted to controlling particular types of crime. For example, the U.S. attorney general appointed by President Reagan in 1981 publicly declared that street crime was the most serious criminal threat in America and would be given maximum attention by the government. In 1989, the Bush administration declared "war" on illegal drugs, proclaiming that this problem is America's number one crime issue. From the conflict perspective, then, the social problem of crime is not simply a matter of social disorganization; it is also influenced by the preferences, predilections, and interests of various groups in society (Caringella-Macdonald, 1990).

Conflict theorists who have been influenced by the writings of Karl Marx view the causes of crime very differently from the functionalists. These conflict theorists blame certain characteristics of capitalism as an economic system (Headley, 1991). Capitalism is characterized by a constant search for greater profits, or at least a struggle against falling profits. This process can be especially fierce in a worldwide economy such as we have today where countries at many different levels of development compete with one another. In the process, capitalists search for ways to enhance profits by reducing costs through mechanization or automation of work or through relocation to areas where resources and labor are cheaper. Both mechanization and relocation put people out of work or force people into competition for lower-wage jobs. Because this process is a continual one, capitalism inevitably contains recurring cycles in which people are thrown out of work and communities are decimated by the loss of jobs. These inherent features of capitalism, then, mean that certain levels of poverty and the crime associated with it will always be with us, although which groups or communities are affected may shift over time.

In addition, capitalists need to sell their goods to make a profit, so capitalists must instill in people a desire for the many products that capitalism can produce. At the same time, capitalists attempt to keep wages low to reduce the costs of production. A mass of unemployed people also benefits a capitalist economy by serving as a cheap labor force when new workers are needed. The unemployed also serve as a lesson to employed workers: Do not demand too high a salary or you, too, may be among the unemployed. The result, according to sociologist William Chambliss (1975: 151), is a contradiction: "capitalism creates both the desire to consume and—for a large mass of people—an inability to earn the money necessary to purchase the items they have been taught to want." For these people, crime is one way of resolving this dilemma. Unlike anomie theory, however, Marxian conflict theory does not assume that the problem can be alleviated through full employment; rather, it sees these contradictions as inherent in a capitalist economy.

The Interactionist Perspective

Interactionist approaches do not dispute the sources of crime pointed to by the functionalist and conflict views. But interactionists see these views as incomplete because they do not explain how a person becomes criminal or why one poor person responds to anomie through crime and another does not. To understand this, we need to look at the socialization and interaction processes that influence people's daily lives.

Cultural transmission theories posit that *crime and delinquency are learned and culturally transmitted through socialization*. The most influential of these theories is the **differential association theory,** developed by criminologist Edwin Sutherland in the 1920s and 1930s. According to Sutherland, *crime and delinquency are learned in interaction with other people, for the most part within intimate primary groups such as families and peer groups* (Sutherland and Cressey, 1978). There are two elements of this learning process. First, people learn the specific techniques for engaging in criminal behavior. For example, by becoming a member of a delinquent gang, a person might learn how to buy drugs or where to obtain weapons. Learning these things makes it more possible and likely that a person will engage in some criminal or delinquent acts. Second, people learn to value criminality more highly than conventional behavior. By associating with other people who engage in criminal behavior, people are more likely to learn to view these activities as desirable and learn a rationale for why they are preferable to a more conventional way of life. Delinquent gangs or prison inmates, for example, are likely to value a life-style in which a person makes money the "easy way"—through crime—and to denigrate the "chumps" who work every day for a small wage. Someone who falls in with groups such as these may well be influenced by their values. Whether people become criminals or delinquents depends on the extent and intensity of contacts with groups that value a particular form of criminality and on the age at which the contacts occur. It also depends on whether a person identifies with these criminals. Association with such people without identification is not likely to result in valuing criminal behavior.

According to cultural transmission theories, then, learning to be criminal or delinquent involves mechanisms of socialization similar to those associated with learning any social status. If people have close group ties with others who conform to established group values, they are likely to learn to conform to that life-style. Those who associate with criminal or delinquent groups are more likely to adopt criminal or delinquent values.

Another interactionist approach to understanding crime and delinquency is labeling theory, which shifts our attention away from the individual transgressor and toward the ways that others react to the deviant (Cavender, 1991). **Labeling theory** suggests that *whether other people define or label a person as deviant is a critical determinant in the development of a pattern of deviant behavior.* According to this theory, many of us engage in activities that are defined as criminal, at least occasionally. In all likelihood, you have engaged in actions that have been so defined (recall the criminal activities listed in Table 9.1). Few of us, however, are caught and labeled—either by our friends or by official agencies—as criminals or delinquents. Labeling theorists refer to this *violation of social norms in which a person is not caught and labeled as a deviant* as **primary deviance** (Lemert, 1951). But the theory does not attempt to explain this type of behavior. Labeling theory concentrates on **secondary** or **career deviance**—*the deviant behavior that a person adopts in response to the reaction of others to their primary deviance.* Consider how this could happen. We know that shoplifting among teenagers, at least of small items, is not uncommon. Imagine that a teenager, possibly out of curiosity or on a dare from peers, engages in a single act of shoplifting. This would constitute primary deviance, because there has been no labeling and no change in the teenager's or the community's image of him or her. If, however, the young person's shoplifting is brought to the attention of the police, they may begin the labeling process by notifying the young person's parents. If this label becomes "public," it is quite likely that some stigma will attach to this teenager's reputation—perhaps a criminal record.

One key consequence of this labeling process is its effect on a person's self-concept: Because the teenage years are formative ones in terms of personal identity, the person may respond to others' reactions, at least in part, by accepting their judgment. After all, the stigma associated with deviant labels such as "criminal" and "delinquent" implies something very negative about people who behave in that fashion. The terms *murderer, thug,*

robber, and *thief* suggest the strong emotions that underlie these deviant labels, and such labels can affect the way people view themselves. A second key consequence of labeling involves the effect that labeling has on people's social relationships. If the criminal activity becomes publicly known, some of the person's conventional friends may shun him or her out of fear for their own reputations. The person may also find it difficult to develop new friends, at least among conventional peers, finding acceptance, instead, among youngsters who are already engaging in delinquent or criminal actions on a widespread scale.

As a result of these changes in self-concept and social contacts, labeling theorists argue, the likelihood of a deviant career developing is increased. Thus, labeling can perpetuate crime and delinquency because, once people have been labeled, they have fewer alternatives, and the deviance becomes a part of their social identity (Paternoster and Iovanni, 1989). This represents secondary deviance because it results from a person's efforts to cope with the responses of others to their primary deviation. It also represents, in a sense, a *self-fulfilling prophecy* in that the deviant label helps to bring about the pattern of career deviance that people thought they were merely identifying when they first attached the label.

These major sociological theories of crime and delinquency should help us to better understand why sociologists take the position that criminal behavior is *relative*. According to anomie theory, what is defined as criminal or delinquent depends on what are considered socially approved means and goals in a particular society. For cultural transmission theory, criminality is a result of socialization, and people are capable of learning a wide variety of things. Conflict theorists see crime and delinquency within a framework of definitions and judgments that are formulated and enforced by those people in powerful positions in society. As we review the different types of crime, keep in mind that the line between criminality and acceptable behavior, between delinquency and nondelinquency, is shifting and vague rather than clear and obvious.

TYPES OF CRIME

A **crime** is *an act that violates a criminal code enacted by an officially constituted political authority.* The Federal Bureau of Investigation (FBI) publishes an annual document called the Uniform Crime Reports (UCR) that summarizes crime statistics collected by the FBI each month from law enforcement authorities in more than sixteen thousand cities and towns. In the UCR, the FBI distinguishes between what are called Part I, or more serious criminal offenses, and Part II, or less serious offenses (see Table 9.2). Part I offenses are considered more serious because many believe they pose the greatest and most direct threat to personal safety and property. The FBI also publishes the Crime Index, which is the official crime rate typically reported in the media. The Crime Index comprises the number of Part I offenses known to the police for every one hundred thousand Americans.

Violent and Property Crime

Violent crimes such as murder, assault, robbery, and rape are clear violations of group norms and

Table 9.2   **Classification of Criminal Offenses by the Federal Bureau of Investigation**

Part I Offenses		Part II Offenses
Murder and nonnegligent manslaughter	} violent crimes	Other assaults
Forcible rape		Forgery and counterfeiting
Robbery		Fraud
Aggravated assault		Embezzlement
		Stolen property; buying, receiving, possessing
		Vandalism
Burglary	} property crimes	Weapons; carrying, possessing, and so on
Larceny-theft		Prostitution and commercialized vice
Motor vehicle theft		Sex offenses (except forcible rape and prostitution)
Arson		Drug abuse violations
		Gambling
		Offenses against family and children
		Driving under the influence
		Liquor laws
		Drunkenness
		Disorderly conduct
		Vagrancy
		All other offenses (except traffic)
		Suspicion
		Curfew and loitering law violations
		Runaways

the law. There were over twenty-three thousand murders committed in 1991, along with over one million aggravated assaults (Federal Bureau of Investigation, 1992). Murders tend to be situational, in that they often occur as a result of some dispute, frequently trivial, over money or some element of personal demeanor; they are only rarely planned in advance. The victim is usually a relative, friend, or acquaintance of the assailant. In 1991, one-third of all homicides arose from an argument, whereas only 20 percent occurred during the commission of a felony (Federal Bureau of Investigation, 1992: 21). Assaults are much more likely to involve strangers than are murders. In addition to these offenses, there are more than a half million robberies every year, some of which involve personal injury to the victims.

Forcible rape, another violent criminal offense, occurs when an assailant sexually assaults another person. In 1991, there were more than one hundred thousand rapes known to the police in the United States, but many estimates place the actual number much higher because victims may be reluctant to report the crime. According to survey results, rape is the crime that women, especially those under thirty-five years of age, fear the most. Especially in urban areas, this fear affects their daily lives as they avoid going out alone, refuse to enter certain neighborhoods, and install deadbolt locks in their homes (Gordon and Riger, 1989). In addition to the physical danger and degradation experienced by rape victims, the act also has a political element in that it symbolizes and reinforces the power and domination of the assailant over the victim. As one social scientist put it regarding female rape victims: "Rape is to women as lynching was to blacks: the ultimate physical threat" (Brownmiller, 1975: 254). Only in recent decades, because of pressure from women's groups, have states begun to make raping one's wife a crime (Russell, 1990). Yet, not all states have done so. In eight states in 1990, men could not be charged with raping their wives as long as they were living together and the wife had not filed for divorce or protection. Twenty-six other states allowed charges of marital rape but with exemptions. Depending on the state, for example, a man could not be charged with raping his wife unless he had kidnapped her or threatened her with a weapon; some of these states did not permit rape charges if the wife was unable to consent to sex because she was drugged or unconscious. Only sixteen states accorded wives the same protection as other women by treating marital rape like any other rape. So some states still seem to believe that a wife is, to a degree, the "property" of her husband, at least for sexual access, which outrages many women and men.

Although people are most alarmed about violent crime, they are much more likely to be victims of property crimes in which the costs are usually economic rather than physical. Three million burglaries, eight million thefts, and one and one-half million auto thefts are reported to the police each year. There are hidden costs of property crime that are frequently underestimated, such as the enormous amount of money that citizens pay in insurance premiums to protect property from burglary, theft, and arson.

Organized Crime

Much of the crime so far described is sporadic and individualized in nature, such as the lone mugger or the small group of juveniles who rob homes. There are, however, forms of criminal activity that benefit from large-scale organization. For example, gambling and prostitution can be highly profitable to those who organize them. Other crimes, such as drug smuggling, involve large overhead costs (front money to purchase the drugs, for instance) that are difficult to fund without some organization. This leads to organized crime or *syndicates:* criminal operations in which several criminal groups coordinate their illegal activities. Although a great deal of criminal activity in our society is organized to some degree, there is considerable debate about the structure and extent of this kind of crime in America. One view is illustrated by the image of the Mafia, consisting of a nationwide alliance of families, based on kinship and ethnic solidarity, that coordinate their criminal actions and control large areas of criminal activity. Whether the Mafia or La Cosa Nostra was ever as powerful and consolidated as its portrayal in the media suggests is subject to debate, but it is probably not nearly that large, cohesive, or controlling today (Albanese, 1989). Organized crime today also includes many other racially or ethnically based criminal gangs, including Asian organized crime, Colombian drug trafficking organizations, and Hispanic street gangs. Many of these gangs operate in local or regional criminal markets, although some do gain a national reach (Delattre, 1990). In addition to illegal activities, organized crime also develops interests in legitimate business, such as real estate, trucking, and food processing, at least in part as mechanisms to launder the vast sums earned through their illegal activities (Santino, 1988). The amount of money that flows into the coffers of organized crime is difficult to determine because of its hidden nature, but one government estimate placed it at between $26 billion and $67 billion annually (Zawitz et al., 1988). This is probably a conservative estimate.

The social context of organized crime must be kept in perspective. Organized crime does perform functions for society. After all, if there were no demand for the services it provides, it would perish. In addition, organized criminals may well have alliances with government and law enforcement groups in order to operate as freely as they do. What is perhaps even more unsettling is that the benefits of organized crime stretch far beyond the core criminal elements. Some legitimate business interests, political figures, labor leaders, and other respectable citizens undoubtedly share in the profits of organized crime, sometimes unknowingly, thus contributing to its ongoing activities (Fijnaut, 1990).

White-Collar Crime

White-collar crimes are offenses committed by people in positions of respect and responsibility

during the ordinary course of their business (Sutherland, 1949; Coleman, 1989). One such offense is antitrust violations, or attempts by businesses to monopolize a segment of the economy. White-collar crime can also take the form of price fixing, in which competitors agree to sell their products for a price higher than they would be able to in a truly competitive market. In the mid-1970s, for example, a price-fixing scheme involving the four major breakfast cereal makers in the United States is estimated to have cost the public some $128 million. Another type of white-collar crime is the fraudulent use of funds. In 1985, E. F. Hutton, one of the nation's largest investment firms, was convicted of an elaborate fraud in which it shuffled millions of dollars among numerous banks and bank accounts, making the funds appear to be in more than one bank account at a time. Hutton collected $8 million in interest on the same money from more than one bank. Finally, white-collar crime can take the form of fraudulent insurance claims, which amount to an $11 billion loss each year.

As these illustrations should make clear, white-collar crime can be very costly to society. Despite this, the FBI classifies most white-collar crimes as less serious offenses. The public in both the United States and Canada also seems to view most white-collar crimes as less serious than other crimes (Cullen, Link, and Polanzi, 1982; Goff and Nason-Clark, 1989). Occasionally, corporate criminals go to jail: During the past decade, a chairman of LTV Corporation was sentenced to four years for insider stock trading and a Tennessee financier was given twenty years for financial irregularities. Between 1987 and 1990, Michael Milken, Ivan Boesky, and a number of other influential and wealthy stock traders were sent to prison for securities fraud, illegal insider trading in stocks, and various other violations of the securities laws (Stewart, 1991). We saw in the beginning of Chapter 2 that a number of business people and government officials were recently convicted in defense fraud cases. But critics argue that these tend to be the exception rather than the rule and that the law is very lenient on white-collar criminals, especially the influential ones. Some of this leniency may come from the fact that white-collar criminals often cooperate with prosecutors in exposing other participants in illegal activities. In fact, both Boesky and Milken cooperated, and they spent relatively little time behind bars and left prison as fairly wealthy men.

Victimless Crime

Victimless crimes are offenses such as gambling, drug violations, and prostitution, in which the "victims" are willing participants in the crime (Schur, 1965; Stitt, 1988). In 1991, more than one million arrests were made for these crimes (Federal Bureau of Investigation, 1992). There are obviously far more victimless crimes than these statistics suggest because many offenses are never reported to the police. Although no accurate estimates of the total number of victimless crimes are available, it is safe to say that most Americans have participated in such offenses, if only by betting in a football pool or purchasing small quantities of marijuana. When highly desired goods and services are made illegal, a black market is likely to develop to provide them. One of the controversies about having victimless crimes on the books is whether the government ought to be controlling what some people feel are personal or moral issues, such as gambling, drug use, or prostitution. A second controversy is that, because victimless crimes are illegal, people sometimes commit additional crimes, called "secondary crimes," while doing the victimless crime. Thus, an addict may rob to buy drugs, which are very expensive in part because they are illegal. If the victimless crimes were legal, less secondary crime might occur. Finally, victimless crimes are related to public corruption in that bribes are sometimes given to police or other public officials to ignore the illegal flow of drugs, sex, or gambling.

Juvenile Delinquency

A juvenile delinquent is a young person who has committed a crime or has violated a juvenile code.

Youthful offenders are young people, in most states between the ages of seven and seventeen, who commit offenses for which, if they were adults, they could be tried in a criminal court. *Status offenders* are young people who commit specific acts that are prohibited by the juvenile code, such as running away from home, incorrigibility, truancy, or sexual promiscuity. Status offenses are not considered criminal when committed by an adult.

According to official statistics, juveniles under the age of eighteen are responsible for committing 28 percent of all Part 1, or serious, crimes, although youth between ten and seventeen years of age make up only about 12 percent of our population (Federal Bureau of Investigation, 1992). They are arrested for about 40 percent of the vandalism and auto thefts and 25 percent of the robberies in our society. People in this age category are responsible for 14 percent of all murders, nearly 33 percent of all burglaries, and around 15 percent of rapes and aggravated assaults. And the rate of delinquency may be on the rise. In 1960, there were twenty cases of delinquency before the courts for every one thousand young people. By the late 1980s, that number had increased to forty-seven cases for each one thousand juveniles each year. The increase has been greater for girls than for boys (U.S. Bureau of the Census, 1984: 182; U.S. Bureau of the Census, 1992: 196). Most delinquent acts, however, are status offenses.

America's Crime Rate

Between 1970 and 1980, according to the FBI, the rate of Crime Index offenses rose by a startling 49 percent. However, the 1980s were another story: Crime Index offenses actually dropped by 2 percent between 1980 and 1990. Most of this drop was accounted for by the drop in property crimes. During the 1980s, violent crimes rose by 22 percent, but this was less of an increase than the 64 percent rise in the 1970s (see Figure 9.1). Yet, the crime rate is still far higher than it was in previous decades. If crimes were evenly spaced

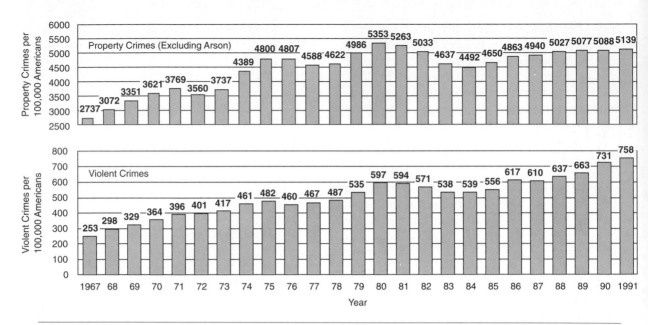

Figure 9.1   **Rates of Violent and Property Crimes per 100,000 Americans, 1967–1991**
SOURCES: U.S. Bureau of the Census, *Statistical Abstract of the United States, 1980* (Washington, D.C.: U.S. Government Printing Office, 1980), p. 182; Federal Bureau of Investigation, *Uniform Crime Reports: Crime in the United States, 1991* (Washington, D.C.: U.S. Government Printing Office, 1992), p. 58.

throughout the day, in 1991, there would have been one serious crime about every two seconds of each day and one violent crime approximately every seventeen seconds (Federal Bureau of Investigation, 1992).

Some of these increases, however, need to be placed in perspective. They may in part reflect changes in the likelihood of reporting crimes rather than actual increases in crime. Rape, for example, has traditionally been a vastly underreported crime. With more public discussion of rape in the 1970s and 1980s and strong pressure from feminist groups, both the police and the public have become more sensitive to the problems of rape victims. Many hospitals provide counseling for rape victims, and many states have rules that limit the use of information about a victim's previous sexual activities as evidence in court. These changes have encouraged more women to report rapes, and this undoubtedly accounts for some, although not all, of the increase in reported rapes.

Another reason for caution about UCR crime statistics is that they are based on crimes known to the police, and considerable crime is not brought to the attention of the police. Such unreported crime is not reflected in these statistics, which are conservative indicators of our nation's crime problem. It is estimated, for example, that only 45 percent of the violent crimes are reported to the police and as few as 28 percent of the thefts (Maguire and Flanagan, 1991: 254). When the reported and unreported crimes are put together, it is clear that America has a considerable crime problem and people are concerned about it.

WHO ARE THE CRIMINALS?

Studying crime can be difficult, especially when trying to determine the social characteristics of those who commit crimes. One approach is to look at the official statistics on who has been arrested, but we know that many people who commit crimes are never arrested. Another approach is to use self-reports of people about the crimes they have committed, but many people will be reluctant to admit they have committed crimes. However, combining these and other methods of measuring crime, sociologists have gained a fairly good picture of the characteristics of those who commit crimes.

At the outset, however, it is important to recognize that patterns of criminality are not to be confused with the causes of crime. For example, the fact that nonwhites are disproportionately represented in the commission of violent crimes does not imply that there is something about race itself that causes this kind of criminality (Duster, 1987). What is critical in explaining high levels of crime are the social factors linked to race in our society: economic deprivation, life-style differences, educational level, and so forth. In addition, the members of some social groups may be more likely to be arrested and processed by criminal justice agencies, thus injecting an element of bias into crime statistics. For example, some crimes such as embezzlement are "hidden crimes" in the sense that they are less likely than homicide or assault to come to the attention of the police. When an embezzler is discovered, the victim-employer may not call in the police for fear that it will hurt the business's reputation. Homicide, on the other hand, is virtually always brought to the attention of the police by someone. So people committing hidden crimes are less likely to be arrested than people committing more noticeable crimes. If members of one group are more likely to commit hidden crimes and members of another group commit more open crimes, then arrest records will make the latter group appear more "criminal." So especially when using arrest records, one group may appear to be more criminal than another because of their differential treatment by the police and the courts. With these thoughts in mind, we will look at four social characteristics that are closely associated with crime.

Sex

Sex is the single social factor that is most predictive of patterns of criminal behavior. Males have higher rates of involvement than females in practically all forms of criminality. In 1991, almost 82 percent of all people arrested for a crime were males—almost five times as many males as females. There are approximately four boys referred to the juvenile court for every girl so referred. Even crimes that do not involve aggressiveness or violence—larceny, fraud, embezzlement—are still more likely to be committed by males (see Table 9.3). The only offenses that females are more likely to be involved in are prostitution and being runaways. Although it is possible that women receive preferential treatment in the criminal justice system or that women are more likely to engage in "hidden" crimes, there is evidence against this (Bishop and Frazier, 1984; Steffensmeier and Allan, 1988). Males are disproportionately represented in most forms of criminal activity even if such sex preferentials occur. The male propensity toward crime is probably in part a function of the male's role in which daring, action, and aggressiveness are viewed positively and sometimes take a criminal form. However, with some crimes, such as fraud, forgery, and auto theft, crime rates are growing much faster among women than men.

Age

Table 9.4 shows the age distribution of people under twenty-five who were arrested during 1991. It is immediately apparent that crime is a "young person's game." Most people arrested are under thirty years of age, and the highest percentage of arrests for violent offenses is within the eighteen-to-twenty-four age bracket. There are a number of possible explanations for this. It may be that young people are more likely to be arrested for committing a crime than are older people. Or it may be that older people are actually less likely to engage in criminal activity (Rowe and Tittle,

Table 9.3 **Total Arrests, Distribution by Sex and Race, 1991**

Offense Charged	Percent Male	Percent Female	Percent White	Percent Black
TOTAL..................................	**81.3**	**18.7**	**69.0**	**29.0**
Murder and nonnegligent manslaughter	89.7	10.3	43.4	54.8
Forcible rape.......................................	98.7	1.3	54.8	43.5
Robbery..	91.4	8.6	37.6	61.1
Aggravated assault................................	86.3	13.7	60.0	38.3
Burglary	91.1	8.9	68.8	29.3
Larceny-theft......................................	68.0	32.0	66.6	30.9
Motor vehicle theft................................	90.0	10.0	58.5	39.3
Arson..	86.9	13.1	76.7	21.5
Violent crime[a]....................................	88.4	11.6	53.6	44.8
Property crime[b]	74.6	25.4	66.4	31.3
Crime index total[c]...............................	78.0	22.0	63.2	34.6
Other assaults....................................	83.5	16.5	64.6	33.3
Forgery and counterfeiting........................	65.0	35.0	64.8	33.7
Fraud..	57.1	42.9	67.8	31.3
Embezzlement	61.1	38.9	68.2	30.2
Stolen property; buying, receiving, possessing	88.8	12.0	57.0	41.7
Vandalism	89.1	10.9	76.0	22.1
Weapons: carrying, possessing, etc.................	92.8	7.2	56.8	41.6
Prostitution and commercialized vice..............	34.1	65.9	60.3	38.0
Sex offenses (except forcible rape and prostitution)	93.0	7.0	78.2	19.8
Drug abuse violations	83.5	16.5	58.1	41.0
Gambling..	87.3	12.7	44.8	46.9
Offenses against family and children..............	81.9	18.1	66.7	29.5
Driving under the influence.......................	86.7	13.3	88.9	9.1
Liquor laws.......................................	80.8	19.2	87.3	9.7
Drunkenness.......................................	89.6	10.4	81.2	16.4
Disorderly conduct...............................	80.0	20.0	65.5	32.7
Vagrancy	89.2	10.8	51.2	46.6
All other offenses (except traffic).................	82.9	17.1	63.5	34.3
Suspicion	83.5	16.5	40.8	58.6
Curfew and loitering law violations	73.2	26.8	76.9	20.6
Runaways...	43.3	56.7	80.5	15.9

[a]Violent crimes are offenses of murder, forcible rape, robbery, and aggravated assault.
[b]Property crimes are offenses of burglary, larceny-theft, motor vehicle theft, and arson.
[c]Includes arson.
SOURCE: Federal Bureau of Investigation, *Uniform Crime Reports: Crime in the United States, 1991* (Washington, D.C.: U.S. Government Printing Office, 1992), pp. 230–231.

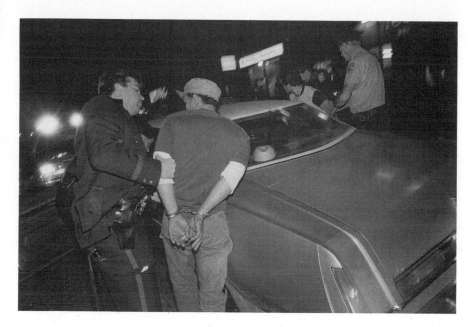

These young men were caught in the act of auto theft in Boston. A majority of those arrested for auto theft are males under twenty-one years of age.

1977). Young people's higher rates of criminal conduct may be due to opportunity and physical capability: Young people are more likely to commit visible offenses such as property crime and robbery than "hidden" crimes such as embezzlement, price fixing, or corporate malfeasance. In addition, young people have the strength, agility, and stamina to commit crimes such as burglary and robbery.

There are important social policy considerations that flow from the link between age and crime. Crime rates go up when teens and young adults, who commit lots of crimes, grow as a proportion of the population. This is what happened in the 1960s and 1970s: People fourteen to twenty-four years of age grew from 15 percent of our populace in 1960 to 20 percent in 1980. And as we saw, the crime rate doubled during that period (see Figure 9.1). Since 1980, the proportion of people in that same age group in the United States has dropped to 16 percent. So as young people constitute a smaller proportion of our populace, the crime rate should go down, or at least not go up as rapidly. And, as we have seen, it appears to have done that during the 1980s.

Socioeconomic Status

The relationship between socioeconomic status (SES) and criminality has been one of the more controversial issues in modern-day criminology (Belknap, 1989). On the one hand, official crime statistics indicate that members of lower socioeconomic groups are more likely to commit crimes. Yet we also know that lower-class people are more likely to be arrested, suggesting that it may be that arrest is more common among them than actual crime commission. Furthermore, poor people are more likely to commit highly visible and violent crimes, such as homicide, assault, and robbery, that are more frequently reported to the police (Huff-Corzine, Corzine, and Moore, 1991). The crimes of the middle class, on the other hand, such as embezzlement or fraud, are more hidden and

Table 9.4   **Percentage of All Arrests Accounted for by Persons Under 18, 21, and 25 Years of Age, 1991**

Offense Charged	*Percentage of Total Arrests for All Ages*			Offense Charged	*Percentage of Total Arrests for All Ages*		
	Under 18	*Under 21*	*Under 25*		*Under 18*	*Under 21*	*Under 25*
TOTAL.............	**16.3**	**30.2**	**45.7**	Sex offenses (except forcible rape and prostitution).....	17.5	26.2	37.8
Murder and nonnegligent manslaughter............	14.1	36.0	54.6	Drug abuse violations.......	7.7	22.3	40.6
Forcible rape................	15.7	28.8	44.4	Gambling...................	7.1	17.4	27.5
Robbery....................	25.6	44.5	61.9	Offenses against family and children.................	4.1	12.7	27.6
Aggravated assault..........	14.3	27.1	42.9	Driving under the influence	1.0	8.8	25.6
Burglary...................	33.4	51.1	64.9	Liquor laws................	23.0	68.6	78.7
Larceny-theft...............	30.4	43.9	55.7	Drunkenness................	2.5	11.3	25.8
Motor vehicle theft..........	43.7	62.0	74.6	Disorderly conduct..........	17.4	32.9	50.9
Arson......................	46.5	56.3	65.0	Vagrancy..................	7.2	16.6	26.5
Violent crime[a].............	17.2	31.9	48.1	All other offenses (except traffic)....................	10.0	23.7	41.4
Property crime[b]..........	32.4	47.1	59.3	Suspicion..................	21.4	34.0	47.9
Crime index total[c]........	28.7	43.4	56.6	Curfew and loitering law violations................	100.0	100.0	100.0
Other assaults..............	15.5	26.8	42.5	Runaways..................	100.0	100.0	100.0
Forgery and counterfeiting...	8.9	25.0	43.2				
Fraud......................	3.7	13.9	32.0				
Embezzlement..............	7.4	23.6	41.9				
Stolen property; buying, receiving, possessing......	27.0	47.3	63.0				
Vandalism.................	42.7	57.2	69.5				
Weapons: carrying, possessing, etc............	21.0	39.6	57.0				
Prostitution and commercialized vice.......	1.3	9.7	29.7				

[a]Violent crimes are offenses of murder, forcible rape, robbery, and aggravated assault.

[b]Property crimes are offenses of burglary, larceny-theft, motor vehicle theft, and arson.

[c]Includes arson.

SOURCE: Federal Bureau of Investigation, *Uniform Crime Reports: Crime in the United States, 1991* (Washington, D.C.: U.S. Government Printing Office, 1992), p. 229.

less likely to come to the attention of the police (Tittle, Villemez, and Smith, 1978; Hindelang, Hirschi, and Weis, 1979; Steffensmeier, 1989). Most recently, it has been shown that the lower classes are more likely to be involved in Crime Index crimes against persons and property, but there appears to be no class-based link involving hidden crime, such as vice offenses (Elliott and Huizinga, 1983). So it may be the types of crime that differ from one class to another rather than the amounts of crime. All this research has led one investigator

to conclude that empirical evidence is lacking for a strong relationship between socioeconomic status and crime, and that social class may not be as important a correlate for criminal behavior as most criminologists have thought (Weis, 1987).

Race

As we indicated at the outset of this discussion, official statistics show that African Americans are disproportionately involved in crime (Chilton and

Galvin, 1985). They make up about 12 percent of our population but account for 29 percent of all arrests for all crimes. Table 9.3 indicates that African Americans are particularly likely to be arrested for robbery, murder, and gambling. Only in the cases of liquor law violations and driving under the influence of alcohol are their arrest rates proportionate to or lower than what would be expected given their numbers in the populace.

Detailed analysis through victimization surveys indicates that black–white differences in criminal behavior are real, rather than merely reflecting criminal justice system biases such as the likelihood of arrest (Hindelang, 1981). Still, as we pointed out earlier, this does not imply that race is a causal variable. The social environment of blacks in America is primarily responsible for crime rate differences (Duster, 1987). In addition, blacks are lower in socioeconomic standing, so they are less likely to be involved with "hidden" and "respectable" crimes, which we have seen result in greater economic losses than all other types of criminality combined. Because we are aware of black–white differences in criminal behavior, blacks may be more closely watched than whites by law enforcement agencies, which leads to higher arrest rates.

Who Are the Victims?

We sometimes focus so closely on people who commit crimes that we forget the victims of their actions. In 1990, thirty out of every one thousand Americans were crime victims (U.S. Bureau of the Census, 1992: 184). But race and sex play a part in this, with males and blacks considerably more likely to be victims. Fifty-three of every one thousand black males, for example, were crime victims. Homicide rates, especially, show the gruesome consequences of race. Black males are seven times more likely to be the victims of homicide than are white males, and black females are four times more likely than white females. For some crimes, such as robbery and larceny, poorer households were more likely to be victimized, whereas the affluent were more likely to experience auto theft.

One very important correlate of victimization is its relationship to participation in criminal and delinquent activities: Offenders are often the victims of other criminals (Fagan, Piper, and Cheng, 1987).

THE CRIMINAL JUSTICE SYSTEM

The criminal justice system includes the police, the courts, the prisons, and other institutions whose task is to control crime in America. There is much debate over how effectively it achieves its goals. Critics argue that the system operates in a fashion that substantially departs from the fairness and impartiality that is demanded by the Constitution and our cultural heritage. A few detractors even claim that the criminal justice system actually contributes to the crime problem in the United States. We will focus on certain elements of the system that relate to these problems.

The Police

When a crime is committed, the first and perhaps most crucial link that most citizens have with the criminal justice system is the police. In the United States, police have a great deal of discretion in dealing with offenses that come to their attention. Sometimes, the police may even help to negotiate some type of informal agreement between the complainant and the accused, a procedure that is well short of actually arresting and booking a suspect. This may appear surprising to some, because it is often assumed that police take pride in "busting" all crimes. In fact, there are so many minor violations of the law occurring on a daily basis that police agencies would be helplessly swamped if they tried to pursue every one of them. One investigation found that in New York City there was only one arrest for every five felonies known to the police. In some of these cases, the police undoubtedly chose not to pursue the case, possibly realizing that they had little chance of solving it (Shipp, 1981). However, the exercise of discre-

These police officers are searching suspects who may have been involved with illegal drugs. The Spanish words spray-painted on the wall above the suspects say: "Keep the block clean." Effective police work depends on such citizen support of and involvement with crime prevention.

tion by the police is not influenced solely by judgments of the seriousness or solvability of the crime, as one might expect, but also by subtle social factors. For example, a study of police response to domestic disputes found that police were far more likely to arrest someone when the dispute occurred in a poor neighborhood (Smith and Klein, 1984). In middle-class neighborhoods, police put in more effort to find solutions to the dispute short of arrest. Thus, social factors influence the discretionary behavior of police in ways that affect the crime statistics discussed earlier.

The police in our society are confronted with a confusing dilemma. On the one hand, they are under constant pressure to combat crime, but they are also expected to protect the constitutional and personal rights of suspects and other citizens. The public demands that order be maintained but also creates procedural laws, such as due process, that may make it more difficult for the police to achieve that order. Police often attempt to keep the peace by ignoring or circumventing the pro-

cedural rules that are designed to govern their activities. As a result of this dilemma, the police tend to feel isolated and frustrated. This can generate feelings of alienation and separation from other groups in society. The danger is that a "we" versus "they" mentality might emerge—the "they" including all citizens, not just the criminals. To the extent that this happens, it may interfere with the ability of police to do their job and make them less sensitive to the needs and rights of suspects, victims, and the citizenry.

The Courts

As illustrated in Figure 9.2, there is substantial case attrition following arrest. Of one hundred typical felony arrests brought by the police to the prosecutor, fewer than half result in conviction. After arrests are made by the police, our court system utilizes an adversary model in evaluating guilt or innocence. The prosecution is pitted against the defense, and a judge or jury is utilized to settle

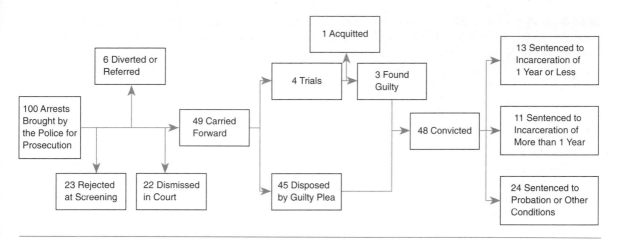

Figure 9.2 **Typical Disposition of 100 Urban Felony Arrests**
SOURCE: Adapted from Barbara Boland and Ronald Stones, *The Prosecution of Felony Arrests* (Washington, D.C.: Department of Justice, Bureau of Justice Statistics, 1986).

the "dispute" (Sykes and Cullen, 1992). The office of prosecuting attorney is perhaps the most powerful position in the criminal justice system. Prosecuting attorneys have the power to determine which cases will be pursued and with how much vigor. Most importantly, prosecuting attorneys are political figures—they are either elected or appointed to office—and have a keen awareness of how they achieved their positions in the first place. To keep influential groups or their elective constituencies happy, prosecutors exert enormous pressure on the police. One criterion used to evaluate police departments is the number of arrests that eventually result in convictions. Should a prosecuting attorney see fit not to seek convictions for a particular type of offense, then the police will spend little time dealing with cases of this type. By like token, if a prosecutor shows favoritism for a given offense, then police will regard these as "good busts" and alter their law enforcement patterns accordingly. Once again, discretionary elements enter into the battle against crime. As we have seen, it is usually more politically profitable to attack "street" crime committed by the less fortunate because this is the

crime that frightens the middle class and affluent groups who put prosecuting attorneys in office.

Defense attorneys represent the other part of the court system. Ideally, counsel for the defense is responsible for representing their client's interests before the criminal justice system. In reality, there are considerable pressures on defense attorneys to place as much emphasis on "negotiating justice" as on ensuring due process for their clients. Defense attorneys often have close ties with judges, prosecuting attorneys, police, and others working in the criminal justice system. They work daily with these people on many cases and need their cooperation and good will to do their work. In fact, defense attorneys are as much a part of the legal system as they are the adversarial representatives of their client. Because of this, they come under considerable pressure to help the system run smoothly, which may mean encouraging their client to accept a guilty plea or a plea bargain. If they do not appear cooperative, the prosecutor's office has many resources that can be used or assistance that can be withheld that could make the defense attorney's job more difficult. So, negotiation between the prosecutor and the defense counsel becomes the most sensible alternative open to many of those charged with a crime. Court-appointed defense attorneys make sure that even poor defendants have representation in court, but the defendant's best interests may not be served when the overriding pressure on both prosecution and defense is to dispose of cases on a crowded court docket quickly and smoothly.

A third important ingredient in the court system is *bail:* money or credit deposited with the court to ensure that people released while awaiting trial will ultimately appear for trial. Bail is based on a core tenet of the American legal system: A person is considered innocent until proven guilty in a court of law. Given the presumption of innocence, a person should not be punished by a jail term prior to trial. One major problem with bail is that it is obviously prejudicial to the disadvantaged who often cannot afford to post bail. Failure to "make bail" represents a form of punishment prior to conviction, which appears to violate the "presumption of innocence." Another major problem with bail is that it can be used as a means of "preventive detention" rather than merely to ensure appearance for trial. Bail is often denied or set deliberately high in order to confine a person until trial. In fact, the Comprehensive Crime Control Act of 1984 allows judges in federal courts to consider issues other than likelihood of court appearance in setting bail. Federal judges can now consider the likelihood that a person will commit another offense while out on bail in deciding whether to set bail and how high to set it. Although this applies only in federal courts, it may serve as a model for state criminal justice codes. It is a revolutionary change in our court system in that it allows the court to incarcerate someone for a crime he or she has not yet committed but a judge feels reasonably sure will be committed if the person is set free.

Another element of the court system is plea bargaining: an informal agreement between the defense, the prosecution, and the court that is not legally binding. Plea bargaining is involved in over 90 percent of all convictions for criminal of-

fenses. In exchange for a plea of guilty, suspects may receive special considerations from the court, such as the dropping of some charges, a more lenient sentence, or the reduction of a charge to a lesser offense. This accounts for further attrition in the criminal justice system. As Figure 9.2 shows, of the forty-nine felony arrests carried forward, forty-five (over 90 percent) were disposed of through a guilty plea, and a large percentage of these cases involved the reduction of the original charge to a misdemeanor. Approximately 4 percent of all felony arrests result in a trial verdict of guilty or innocent. In another type of plea bargain, a suspect who pleads guilty to multiple charges may be sentenced to serve them concurrently. Plea bargaining has been criticized because it involves an "informal dispensing of justice," as issues such as local politics, community norms, and the perceived needs of criminal justice bureaucracies take precedence over established judicial principles such as due process of law.

A final element of the court system is the sentencing of convicted criminals, and there appears to be considerable inequity here also. With homicides, for example, one would expect the same crime to receive the same punishment. But there is much disparity. A person is far more likely to receive the death penalty for homicide—in some states, more than eight times as likely—when the victim is white rather than black (Joyce, 1984; Heilbrun, Foster, and Golden, 1989). Studies of sentencing in a number of states document that blacks and Hispanics are given heavier sentences by judges than are whites and serve more time in prison than do whites. This is true even when comparing those who have committed comparable felonies and have similar criminal records (Petersilia, 1985). All this discriminatory treatment may reflect unconscious racism on the part of prosecutors, judges, and juries, or it may be that mostly white jurors tend to identify with white victims and deal more harshly with those who victimize whites. In either case, it leads many people to question whether justice is fairly and impartially dealt by the courts.

The Prisons

America currently puts into prison a far larger proportion of its population than ever before, with the rate of incarceration more than doubling during the 1980s (see Table 9.5). For much of this century, until 1970, the rate of incarceration was fairly steady, fluctuating around one-third what it is now, even in the difficult economic times of the Great Depression of the 1930s. Since 1970, the rate has gone steadily and disturbingly upward. Even more distressing is the fact that the United States now has the highest rate of incarceration of its citizens of any nation in the world (Butterfield, 1992). We far surpass South Africa, which is in second place, and we put ten times more of our citizens in prison than does Japan or any nation in western Europe. What is happening here? It is partly due to a rising crime rate; however, it also reflects a growing frustration with and anger against crime felt by many Americans, which in turn has made "getting tough on crime" very popular. A recent survey, for example, found that three-quarters of all Americans feel that the courts do not deal harshly enough with criminals (Cohn, Barkan, and Halteman, 1991). Americans have become very receptive to sending more people to prison for longer periods of time as a way of controlling crime. This has produced a crisis of overcrowding in many of our prisons unheard of in our history.

This overcrowding is dangerous because it increases unrest among inmates and produces a climate in which violence is more likely. Riots, escapes, and hostage taking become more of a problem. Prison overcrowding also makes it more difficult for correctional officers and prison administrators to manage the prisons. All this makes prisons more costly to run. In addition, many question whether it is moral to imprison people in circumstances that are cruel and unusual, that may promote mental disorders, where degrading sexual assaults are common, and where stabbings, beatings, extortion, and murder are routine and rampant.

Prison crowding also makes it far more difficult for prisons to achieve one of their major goals: the rehabilitation of the inmates. So far, prisons have failed miserably at rehabilitation. **Recidivism** refers to *the repeat of an offense after having been convicted of a crime,* and the rate of recidivism is very high. A recent analysis by the Bureau of Justice Statistics found that nearly two-thirds of the inmates sent to state prisons in 1983 were repeat offenders (Bureau of Justice Statistics, 1989). Sixty-three percent had been in prison previously. Of the 108,580 persons released from prisons in eleven states in 1983, representing

Table 9.5 **Sentenced Prisoners in State and Federal Institutions, 1925–1991**

Year	Total Number	Rates per 100,000 Residents
1925	91,669	79
1930	129,453	104
1935	144,180	113
1940	173,706	131
1945	133,649	98
1950	166,123	109
1955	185,780	112
1960	212,953	117
1965	210,895	108
1970	196,429	96
1975	240,593	111
1980	315,974	138
1985	503,601	211
1986	546,659	226
1987	584,435	234
1988	627,402	244
1989	712,967	287
1990	773,124	309
1991	823,414	329

SOURCES: *Prison 1925–1981* (Washington, D.C.: Department of Justice, Bureau of Justice Statistics, 1982); "Prisoners in 1991," *Bureau of Justice Statistics Bulletin* (Washington, D.C.: U.S. Government Printing Office, 1992).

POLICY ISSUES

Privately Operated Correctional Facilities: Who Is Accountable for the Welfare of the Incarcerated?

Prisons and jails in the United States have historically been under the jurisdiction of federal, state, or local governments. Recently, however, there has been a trend toward contracting with privately owned, profit-oriented companies to provide these services. This move began during the 1980s, when government-run facilities were fast becoming overcrowded and some jurisdictions turned to the private sector to help them out. By 1990, there were at least twenty-four adult confinement facilities run by private companies in the United States (Logan, 1990). Some were regular jails and prisons, whereas others were detention centers for the Immigration and Naturalization Service. There are also over two thousand private juvenile detention facilities.

The Corrections Corporation of America (CCA) owns sixteen of these facilities, located in Texas, Tennessee, and North Carolina. The CCA is responsible for supervising more prisoners than any other single private concern and has become both a target for criticism and a model for other corporate operators. CCA and others who run jails claim that they can do the job more cheaply than the government does. The federal government, for example, spends $26 per day to keep each resident in an immigration detention center. CCA charges the government only $23 per day to house the same residents. In a juvenile detention center it runs, CCA charges the state only one-half of what it costs to keep each juvenile in a state training school. Proponents of privately owned prisons also claim that they are free of political interference and patronage that make public prisons costly and inefficient. They also point to the high recidivism rate to show that public prisons have not done such a hot job at corrections work.

Many experts in the field, however, are skeptical of whether privately owned detention facilities should be used at all (Levinson, 1988). One general concern is whether it is ethical to allow a pri-

more than 50 percent of all released state prisoners in that year, an estimated 62.5 percent were rearrested for a felony or serious misdemeanor within three years; 46.8 percent were reconvicted; and 41.4 percent returned to prison or jail. Critics of the criminal justice system point to these figures as evidence that prisons have failed in their effort to rehabilitate. One controversial development that might affect these problems is discussed in the Policy Issues insert in this chapter.

Critique of America's Criminal Justice System

The criminal justice system itself is viewed by some as a culprit in creating crime. Some critics have gone so far as to label the criminal justice system a "nonsystem." Quoting from the National Commission on the Causes and Prevention of Violence:

A system implies some unity of purpose, an organized interrelationship among component parts.

vate company to oversee the removal of the rights and freedoms of a human being. Because it is only the legally constituted government that can take away a person's freedom, some question the constitutionality of giving private individuals the state's authority to deprive people of their freedom. Correctional officers, after all, perform a quasi-judicial function when they discipline inmates, mete out punishment, and advise parole boards. The director of the National Association of Criminal Justice Planners commented: "We're talking about taking away people's liberties, and I have real questions about the propriety of anyone but the state doing that" (Tolchin, 1985a). A more practical criticism is whether a profit-oriented institution might not be motivated to increase its profit margin to the detriment of the inmates. The private outfits pay their correctional officers less than public ones, and the training and fringe benefits are far more meager. Private facilities also have fewer services, such as psychological counseling, available to residents, and some tend to reduce the quality and number of staff and programs as a way to maintain profits (Shichor and Bartollas, 1990). The fear is that it will be the residents and their rehabilitation that will suffer in order to achieve lower costs and greater profits. Recall our discussion of the functional aspects of capitalism, competition, and free enterprise in Chapter 2. Unlike other realms where private enterprise operates, however, the recipients of services in this realm—the inmates—do not have the freedom to "shop around" for the best proprietors of correctional services.

A major issue is one of accountability: Who is responsible for the welfare of those people who are incarcerated in private facilities? Consider this example. Inmates housed in state institutions have registered formal grievances with appropriate government officials or courts about conditions they felt were dangerous, unhealthy, or unfair, resulting in remedial actions to correct these difficulties. Problems involving privately operated institutions, however, have not been so easily solved. The private contractor tends to refer any complaints to the government agency under whose authority it incarcerates people; the government agency, in turn, refers problems back to the private contractor who has day-to-day responsibility for taking care of the inmates. This diffusion of accountability has made it more difficult to rectify problems and eliminate dangerous or unhealthy situations (Tolchin, 1985b).

This issue is likely to be a highly controversial one over the next decade and may find its way into the courts. At this point the development is too new for there to be any research with which to assess the claims made on each side of the argument.

In the typical American city, and state, and under federal jurisdiction as well, no such relationship exists. There is, instead, a reasonably well-defined criminal process. . . . The inefficiency, fallout, and failure of purpose during this process is notorious. (As quoted in Cole, 1989: 144)

According to Jeffrey Reiman, a professor of criminal justice:

The goal of our criminal justice system is not to reduce crime or to achieve justice but to project to the American public a visible image of the threat of crime. To do this, it must maintain the existence of a sizable or growing population of criminals. And to do this, it must fail in the struggle to reduce crime. (Reiman, 1979: 1)

Reiman employed a novel approach in constructing this view of the criminal justice system. He asked a group of graduate students to design a correctional system "that would maintain and encourage the existence of a stable and visible 'class' of criminals" rather than reduce and prevent crime

(Reiman, 1979: 2–4). This is the system the students sketched:

1. It would contain many irrational laws, such as those governing gambling and other victimless crimes, that make many people "criminals" for behaviors that they regard as normal and that increase their need to engage in secondary crime, such as stealing, in order to pay gambling debts.
2. It would give police, prosecutors, and judges broad discretion to decide who gets arrested, charged, and sentenced to prison. In this way, almost everyone who ended up in prison would be aware of others who committed the same kind of offense and did not become incarcerated, creating a sense of bitterness and hostility toward the unjust nature of the system.
3. It would make the prison experience painful and demeaning, so that whatever deterrent effect imprisonment may have is counteracted by the lack of privacy and control over one's actions that could enhance self-control.
4. Prisoners would not be trained in marketable skills nor provided with jobs upon release. Further, their prison records would follow them wherever they go, making a return to noncriminal behavior more difficult.

Reiman concludes that, in short, the system that the students described is a portrait of the American criminal justice system today. The system creates an image that crime is a threat from the poor so that discontent and hostility are directed away from those in positions of power and toward the poor. A large convict population gives the appearance that crime is being controlled while at the same time the prison system increases recidivism.

FUTURE PROSPECTS

The question of how to deal with the crime and delinquency problem in the United States is highly controversial. However, our analysis of the sociological perspectives along with our assessment of various problems related to crime point to a number of promising reforms that deserve consideration.

Social Reform

Given the role of poverty and economic inequities in fostering crime, it is plausible that reducing poverty and the economic disparity between the affluent and the poor would help reduce some forms of crime and delinquency. Especially important along these lines would be to provide equal educational and occupational opportunities for all Americans. Given Eliot Currie's analysis of crime in Japan discussed earlier, it may be possible to reduce poverty and economic disparity through programs that encourage fuller employment—government and private-sector programs to create new jobs and to provide job training to those without adequate job skills (Currie, 1985). In addition, the jobs people get must pay a living wage so that people can support their families. Furthermore, sociologist Mark Colvin (1991) recommends that we fight crime by investing in the institutions that prepare people for productive roles in society: families and schools. Many of these proposals have been discussed in other chapters in this book, such as job-training programs, Head Start, and so on. It is failures in our educational institutions and families that have contributed to the inability of many young people to find and make use of legitimate avenues to opportunity. These calls for social reform are an attempt to attack the social and structural conditions that have created much, although not all, of our crime problem. The International Perspectives insert explores in more depth the differences between Japan and the United States in this regard.

Legalization of Some Crimes

Some have proposed that we should legalize many of the victimless crimes, such as gambling, prostitution, and some drug violations. This would reduce the secondary crime associated with these offenses and free the police and courts to attack more serious and dangerous crimes. This measure would also remove these activities from the black market and the hands of organized crime and place them in the public realm, where they can be regulated and taxed. Legalizing these "crimes without victims" does not imply societal support of such activities; they might still be considered by many as serious social problems. Rather, legalization involves the recognition that the criminal justice system should deal with controlling behavior that threatens public order, not with regulating people's morality. Legalization is also an admission that the criminal justice system has been unable to control these crimes effectively.

Better Law Enforcement

Arresting people who commit crimes reduces the likelihood that those individuals will commit crimes in the future (Smith and Gartin, 1989). Society should provide the resources that enable the police to do their job. In fact, we have made considerable strides in the past few decades toward a better-equipped, better-trained, and more highly educated police force in the United States. An increasing number of police departments, for example, require their officers to have a college education. Whether this makes them more effective at controlling crime we will only know through future research (U.S. Department of Justice, 1992).

A fairly recent program to make the police more effective has been introduced into a number of police departments. It is based on research showing that a large number of crimes such as robberies and burglaries are committed by a rather small number of people. The police should have a much greater impact on crime by focusing their resources on catching, convicting, and imprisoning these "career" criminals than by imprisoning someone who only occasionally commits a crime (Swickard, 1986). This effort has been enhanced through the use of computer technology to coordinate the investigations of various precincts and departments. All too often in the past, police in different precincts were looking for the same suspect without realizing it and sharing information. With respect to juvenile delinquency, recent investigations have emphasized that our society should focus on the termination of delinquent careers at their commencement rather than "going easy" on delinquency (Conrad, 1985).

Judicial Reform

There are a number of reforms that might be considered for our judicial system to enhance its effectiveness in controlling crime (U.S. Department of Justice, 1992).

1. Provide swift, certain, and fair punishment. Swift and certain punishment is more effective in controlling crime than are overly long and counterproductive prison sentences. There is little evidence that severity of punishment reduces crime or the rate of recidivism.
2. Provide equitable punishment, whether the crime occurs on a slum street or in a corporate boardroom. Disparities in punishment resulting from the racial, sexual, or socioeconomic characteristics of the offender should be carefully monitored and controlled. This means that society needs to make a serious effort to control white-collar crime, which we have been rather lax about until now. Disparities in punishment lead those who are punished to view the criminal justice system with a jaundiced eye. As we have heard prison inmates say more than once: "I'm not in prison because I committed a crime; I'm here because I'm poor (or black)."
3. Narrow the discretionary options of police officers, prosecutors, and judges and develop procedures to hold them accountable to the public for the fairness and reasonableness of their decisions and actions.
4. Provide all criminal defendants with truly

INTERNATIONAL PERSPECTIVES

Crime in Other Societies

It is sad to admit, but the United States is a disturbingly crime-ridden society when compared to most societies around the world. We saw in this chapter that the United States puts more of its citizens in prison for committing crimes than does any other nation. This high rate of incarceration reflects the fact that crime rates in the United States are very high. If we compare ourselves with Japan, another affluent, industrial nation, we come off rather poorly in the comparison (Currie, 1985; Thornton and Endo, 1992). Overall, there are twelve hundred crimes committed for each one hundred thousand persons in Japan; this compares to almost five thousand crimes per one hundred thousand population in the United States! The United States has eighteen times more rapes, ten times more homicides, six times more burglaries, and nine times more drug-related offenses.

What accounts for this dramatic contrast? To answer this question, we need to look at how Japanese culture and society differ from our own. One widely recognized difference is that Japanese society places much more emphasis on the importance of group and family while American culture emphasizes individualism and personal autonomy. Individual Japanese feel a strong obligation to their family and society, and families feel a strong sense of responsibility for the behavior of their members. Each family member bears a share of the responsibility for preserving the reputation of the family and avoiding bringing disgrace to it by doing something that might be socially disapproved, like committing a crime. This means that informal mechanisms of social control, such as threatened exclusion from the group, can more effectively control crime in Japan than in the United States.

Another difference is that Japanese culture instills a strong sense of respect for laws, rules, and customs. Respect for and obedience to the law is seen as part of a citizen's social obligation, probably deriving from Confucian teachings about uprightness, duty, and obligation. In Japan, people obey the law because of this obligation, not just out of fear of authority or punishment; in the United States, people are more inclined toward cynical violation of the law if they feel they can get away with it.

A third difference between Japan and the

equal legal counsel to reduce the inequities in convictions and sentences.

5. Establish fixed, or determinate, sentences and eliminate parole. The Comprehensive Crime Control Act of 1984 did this for federal crimes beginning in 1986. The rationale for this is that parolees often commit crimes. A study by the Bureau of Justice Statistics found that 28 percent of those who entered state prisons in 1979 would still be serving time in the mid-1980s for their previous offense if they had served the maximum number of years to which they were sentenced (Werner, 1985). Opponents of determinate sentencing argue that it removes the flexibility that the criminal justice system now has to reward inmates who have demonstrated good behavior and who appear to be rehabilitated. These issues are dealt with in further detail in the first Applied Research insert in this chapter.

Although all these reforms are valuable to consider, one must not become entranced by the simple notion that throwing more people in prison

United States is that Japan is a much more racially and culturally homogeneous society where there is considerable consensus regarding desirable values and appropriate behaviors. This removes one important source of misunderstanding, tension, and conflict that exists in the United States. Without these social fault lines, Japan offers its citizens a much more cohesive and supportive neighborhood and community environment. Japan also has a very strong work ethic, meaning that Japanese are willing to work hard to support themselves.

A final difference is that Japanese society is much more *supportive* of individuals and their families than is the United States. Through economic and social policies, Japan strives toward full employment of its workers and tries to create a stable connection of workers to the workplace. Consequently, the income distribution in Japan is much more equitable than in the United States, and no severely deprived and permanently disadvantaged underclass exists. These supportive policies create the foundation for the emergence of strong and stable family and neighborhood ties, which in turn exert strong social controls over misbehavior. In addition, Japan, along with many western European industrial nations, has social policies that cushion the disruptions and hardships that can accompany the loss of work. These nations, for example, give more generous unemployment benefits and distribute them to more un-

employed workers than does the United States. Because of this, less disruption of family and communal roles accompanies unemployment. This is important because it is not just economic circumstances that motivate crime; the destruction of family and communal supports that can accompany unemployment also reduces controls over misbehavior. As Eliot Currie (1985: 130) puts it: "Social policies that strip away those cushions— or that disrupt the stability and effectiveness of communal networks of support and care—are likely to aggravate the impact of economic insecurity on crime."

When considered separately, each of these elements of Japanese culture may make only a small contribution to the low Japanese crime rate; however, in combination they advance us a good way toward understanding the yawning gulf between crime in the United States and crime in Japan. It also emphasizes the sociological perspective on crime—namely, that crime emerges from particular social and cultural conditions and that crime can be reduced by changing those conditions. Some of the elements of Japanese social structure that have insulated them from high crime in the past seem to be changing, and Japan may confront rising crime in the future. However, the contrast between the two cultures provides us with significant insight into the link between social structure and crime.

---

for a longer period of time will significantly reduce the crime problem. Many criminologists feel that such a prison-based criminal justice policy is a costly delusion (Gordon, 1990; Morash and Rucker, 1990). There is little evidence that fear of prison alone will substantially reduce the crime rate. Professor of law and criminology Norval Morris says that Americans "have an exaggerated belief in the efficacy of imprisonment" to control crime (quoted in Butterfield, 1992: 4). He points out that, although the prison population has more than doubled since 1980, the crime rate has not

gone down (see Figure 9.1). Furthermore, throwing more people in prison or giving them longer sentences is enormously expensive. Ten years ago, criminologist Eliot Currie (1985) estimated that tripling the current prison population would cost $70 billion immediately and $14 billion in annual operating costs. Such costs could be justified if it resulted in substantial reductions in crime, but this is unlikely. And prison expansions bleed funds away from social and economic programs that might improve conditions for the urban poor and other high-crime groups and thus decrease

APPLIED RESEARCH

Offender Types, Sentencing, and Public Policy

Controversy rages among legislators, criminal justice experts, and sociologists over the issue of *determinate* (fixed) versus *indeterminate* (flexible) sentencing policies. Those who favor determinate sentencing argue that the punishment should fit the crime; if a person is guilty of a particular offense, that individual should be dealt with in the same fashion as others who have been convicted of that offense. To do otherwise would introduce the possibility of inequities and bias, which may mean more punishment for some people than for others committing the same crimes. In addition, determinate sentencing is viewed by many as a "get tough" policy: The fixed sentence should be the maximum sentence now possible for a given offense.

Supporters of indeterminate sentencing insist that flexibility allows for consideration of individual needs and unique circumstances in which offenders frequently find themselves. In this view, the punishment should fit the offender, not necessarily the crime. Criminologists Marcia and Jan Chaiken (1984: 195), for example, argue: "There are many kinds of criminals, and to fix on any single punitive solution to the problem of crime is simplistic, unjust, and inefficient." To illustrate, they say, suppose two men are convicted of burglary. One commits two burglaries a year and that

is the extent of his criminal involvement, whereas the other commits sixty burglaries along with many robberies, assaults, and drug violations. In terms of reducing the crime rate, it makes sense to imprison the second man for far longer than the first, especially given that there is limited prison space. In addition, indeterminate sentences provide the criminal justice system with the flexibility to reward inmates for good behavior or reward those who have been rehabilitated. Such sentences can also be a mechanism for easing the overcrowding in our prisons.

If our sentencing policies are to fit the "criminal" rather than the "crime," we need some method for predicting who is a high-risk criminal and what the consequences of various sentencing practices might be. Using survey data from adult male inmates in three states, Chaiken and Chaiken were able to distinguish between different types of criminals based on the combinations of crimes they committed, along with information on their juvenile experiences, drug and alcohol use, employment record, and so on.

They identified the most serious offenders as criminals who reported committing a combination of robbery, assault, and drug offenses during the one- to two-year measurement period covered by their survey. They called these criminals "violent

---

crime by attacking its roots. Finally, imprisoning people causes untold human suffering and dislocation to both the prisoners and their families and should be used only when necessary for public safety or when it has proven deterrent value. This is not to say that prison is always ineffective but that it should be balanced by efforts to change the conditions that produce crime. Ironically, however, Americans seem angry about spending on

social reform but eager to spend on prison construction. The second Applied Research insert discusses the efficacy of capital punishment.

Prison Reform

Prisons and prison programs should be designed so that they have the greatest chance of rehabilitating prisoners and reducing recidivism.

predators": men who are involved in these three defining types of crimes at high rates and who are also likely to commit burglaries, thefts, and other property crimes at very high rates—sometimes higher than any other type of criminal, including those who specialize in these types of property offenses. These people accounted for a disproportionately large share of the crimes committed. In addition, Chaiken and Chaiken determined that these "omni-felons" typically began abusing hard drugs as juveniles and committed violent crimes before reaching age sixteen. They are "deeply entrenched in a life of multiple drug use and violence, [and] constitute an important criminal threat to society" (1984: 197). Other offender types, such as those Chaiken and Chaiken call "low-level burglars" or "property and drug offenders," committed fewer serious crimes, and their employment history, juvenile behavior, and drug use were more conventional than other offenders.

If these kinds of data were available about those convicted of a crime, judges, prosecutors, and juries could use it in dealing with criminals. For example, "selective incapacitation" might be applied by giving those assessed to be "violent predators" longer prison sentences than those classified as "low-level burglars" (Gottfredson and Gottfredson, 1985). In other words, keep those we believe will commit many crimes off the streets for longer periods of time. However, Chaiken and Chaiken do not support applying their research to such a policy, at least not yet, because the instruments are not sufficiently precise. A small proportion of people they classified as "high-rate" criminals actually committed few crimes. An instrument of this sort needs to be much more precise if it is to be used to determine whether a person receives a longer sentence.

They do suggest, however, using their technique in other ways. For example, low-rate offenders would be good candidates for removal from prison and diversion into alternative community programs. In addition, prisoners who have engaged in income-producing rather than violent crimes appear to be good candidates for such rehabilitation efforts as vocational training programs. Nonviolent criminals who use or sell drugs seem to be good candidates for drug rehabilitation programs, whereas violent predators are poor risks for such programs.

So Chaiken and Chaiken argue for treating criminals according to the category into which they fall rather than treating all criminals alike. If this is to be done, we need to develop applied research tools, such as those under development by the Chaikens, that can reliably distinguish between types of offenders. However, this whole area of policy development is still very controversial. Many criminal justice experts argue that fairness demands that people should be treated equally in sentencing. Whether sentences are determinate or indeterminate, the punishment should fit the crime, not the criminal (von Hirsch, 1985). In the meantime, public attitudes toward sentencing continue to reflect an atmosphere of severity, with citizens voicing concern over whether sentences are long or tough enough. Furthermore, when Americans advocate prison sentences, they generally suggest terms that are considerably longer than those actually served (Walker and Hough, 1988). This is likely to be a hotly contested issue over the next decade.

Research has shown that some things seem to work (Gendreau and Ross, 1987; Andrews et al., 1990). For example, effective rehabilitation programs are those that focus on changing behaviors and beliefs conducive to crime, that provide carefully planned and structured programs that do not reinforce criminal responses, and that concentrate resources on offenders who are most likely to return to crime. Correctional programs should promote rather than undermine personal responsibility and provide offenders with real opportunities to succeed in legitimate occupations. These might include increased occupational training and counseling while imprisoned, work release, and other alternatives to incarceration. The crowding in prisons should be reduced to eliminate the degrading conditions under which many prison inmates live.

APPLIED RESEARCH

Does the Death Penalty Deter Crime?

One of the more controversial elements of our criminal justice system is the use of the death penalty for certain crimes. In the 1930s and 1940s, more than one hundred prisoners a year were executed in the United States. Quite a few more blacks were executed than whites, even though blacks constituted a relatively small proportion of our populace. The number of executions has since gone down substantially—there were only twenty-three in 1990 (U.S. Bureau of the Census, 1992: 200). However, there were two thousand prisoners on "death row" that year. Almost half of them are nonwhite, and this points to one of the arguments against the death penalty: The poor and nonwhite are more likely to be executed than are affluent whites. It seems that the well-to-do can afford the legal battle to avoid the death sentence, and judges and juries— which are mostly white—may be more inclined to sentence nonwhites to death. Another argument that is made against the death penalty is that it does not achieve one of the goals of punishment: to deter others from committing crimes. Over the past fifty years, quite a lot of social research has focused on this latter issue.

If capital punishment deters crime, then we should be able to assess its impact by comparing homicide rates in states that have capital punishment with those in states that do not. If it deters, then states with capital punishment should have lower homicide rates. Another approach would be to look at states that once had the death penalty but abolished it and states that were once without it and instituted it. Once again, this before-after comparison should show lower homicide rates when a state has capital punishment, if such punishment deters crime. The overall conclusion from many studies of these types is that the death penalty seems to have no deterrent effect, or at least we cannot find much evidence of it (Sutherland, 1925; Schuessler, 1952; Sellin, 1959; Bedau, 1967; Bailey, 1974).

Although many states have the death penalty on the books, some states are much more likely to actually execute people for certain crimes. Maybe it is the death penalty in action that deters crime rather than its mere existence in law. To evaluate this possibility, we can compare the number of murderers who have actually been executed in each state. Studies that have done this find no relationship between the use of capital punishment and homicide rates or at best a very weak and confusing relationship (Lempert, 1983; Peterson and Bailey, 1991). Where a relationship is found, it is small and sometimes in the opposite direction from what we would expect: In some years, states with many executions actually have higher homicide rates than states with fewer executions. Finally, maybe the use of the death penalty has to be widely publicized for it to deter crime. Once again, research findings have been inconsistent on this (Bailey, 1990; Stack, 1990).

So, we cannot clearly say at this point whether or under what conditions the death penalty does deter homicide. However, the research does clearly show that homicide rates are linked to a variety of social factors. For example, states with low income and educational levels, high unemployment, and a highly urbanized population tend to have higher homicide rates. Research to date suggests that directing our resources toward these problems is likely to make a more significant impact on homicide rates than would executing more murderers. As Eliot Currie suggests, overreliance on a punishment-based criminal justice policy may not be the most efficient utilization of resources for all crimes (Currie, 1985).

Through applied research efforts such as these, we can assemble a body of observations about the outcome of various strategies and policies related to social problems. This assessment of outcomes can then be used in evaluating criminal justice policy. This is not the whole story, however, because there may well be reasons other than deterrence for having capital punishment. The death penalty can satisfy people's needs for retribution against someone who has committed the most heinous of crimes, and it may serve to affirm symbolically society's moral outrage over such offenses and support for those who are victims of such crimes (Finckenauer, 1988). At this point, however, observational evidence suggests that capital punishment does not serve as a deterrent to homicide.

Environmental Opportunities

Efforts should be made to reduce the environmental opportunities for committing crime. This can take the form of better physical security, such as burglar-proof locks; better detection of crime through such mechanisms as burglar alarms and antishoplifting tags in stores; and improved surveillance, such as better street lighting.

Victim Restitution

States should be encouraged to establish victim restitution programs in which the victims of crime are provided with some compensation for their loss. Oftentimes the victims of crime feel more assaulted by the criminal justice system than by the perpetrator. Once we recognize the many social sources of crime, it should be clear that society has some responsibility to the victims who unwittingly suffer as a consequence of society's failings.

Citizen Action

In many communities, citizens have decided to take matters into their own hands. Some are motivated by the belief that the police are too weak, corrupt, or politically hampered to deal with

There is much controversy in the United States over whether capital punishment is an effective or moral deterrent against crime.

crime effectively; others feel that the police are overwhelmed by a tenacious problem that cannot be solved without the help of the citizenry. Whatever their beliefs, these groups have endeavored in a number of ways to assist in protecting people from crime. Some programs involve citizen patrols of neighborhoods or buildings, reporting any suspicious activities to the police. Most are unarmed and avoid confronting suspects themselves, except in an emergency. One of the most well known of these groups is the Guardian Angels, originally formed in New York City but now found in many other cities as well (Perry and Pugh, 1989).

Which of the reforms discussed in this chapter will have the most beneficial effect on the crime problem and on inadequacies in the criminal justice system can be determined only after programs have been initiated and evaluated. What should be clear is that only a broad-based and coordinated attack is likely to have a significant impact. If all these suggestions were incorporated into our attack on the crime problem, we would undoubtedly make a significant dent in it. Still, given our understanding of crime based on the sociological perspectives discussed in this chapter, some crime will probably persist, and we will need to make continuing efforts to cope with it.

Linkages

The level of crime in the United States is significantly increased by the persistence of entrenched poverty (Chapter 5) and the spread of illegal drugs (Chapter 10). At the same time, high rates of crime make parts of our cities into dangerous places to live (Chapter 12), and throwing criminals in prison can disrupt family lives (Chapter 3).

Summary

1. Biological explanations of crime, which view crime as arising from people's physical constitution or genetic makeup, have been largely discounted by criminologists today. Psychological approaches receive more support, but they are seen as offering only a partial understanding of crime and delinquency. Social policy designed to reduce crime needs to focus on the social conditions that produce it.

2. The functionalist perspective views crime as arising in part because of the weakened impact of bonds to family, church, and community. Another functionalist approach is anomie theory, which

views crime as a consequence of the inconsistency or confusion between the goals people are taught to strive for and the culturally approved means they have available to achieve these goals.

3. Conflict theorists point out that it is powerful groups in society who decide which crimes will be considered serious problems and who will be arrested and sent to jail for committing crimes. Conflict theorists also blame certain contradictions in capitalism as a source of crime.

4. The interactionist perspective emphasizes the differential association theory, which points to how people learn whether to value criminal or

conventional behavior through interaction with others in intimate groups. Labeling theory shows how a pattern of criminal behavior (career deviance) can arise because a person has been labeled by the police or others as a criminal or deviant.

5. The Federal Bureau of Investigation classifies crimes into Part I and Part II offenses. Part I offenses are considered more serious because many believe they pose the most direct threat to personal safety and property. Juvenile delinquency involves the committing of a crime by a juvenile or the violation of the juvenile code. The crime rate in the United States has been rising for a number of decades, but the trend may have leveled off in the 1980s.

6. Four social characteristics are closely associated with crime: Men commit more crimes than women; people between fifteen and thirty years of age account for most criminals; people of low social standing may commit more crimes than people of higher social standing and they certainly commit different types of crimes; African Americans are more likely to be involved in criminal activity than are whites.

7. There are a number of problems associated with the criminal justice system in the United States. The police have a great deal of discretion—maybe too much—in how they do their job, and police feel they do not receive the support of the public or the courts. The courts exercise discretion regarding which cases will be pursued and with how much vigor, and there is much "negotiated justice." The use of either bail or plea bargaining has been criticized.

8. Prisons are overcrowded and do not seem to be very successful at rehabilitation. The criminal justice system overall has been criticized for making it appear that we are attacking crime when little is actually being done to control it.

9. To control crime, we need most of all to carry out social reforms that will have an impact on the social conditions that cause crime in the first place. Some crimes, such as gambling and prostitution, could be legalized, thus freeing the police to deal with more serious crimes. The police could institute new law enforcement procedures that would enable them to catch serious criminals. Many judicial reforms could be carried out that would make the courts more effective. We could also reform our prisons, reduce the opportunities to commit crimes, and provide for victim restitution. In some communities, citizens have begun to work with the police to control crime.

Important Terms for Review

anomie	crime	differential association	primary deviance
anomie theory	cultural transmission	theory	recidivism
career deviance	theories	labeling theory	secondary deviance

Discussion Questions

1. During the early 1900s, when the foundations of modern criminology were being built by people such as Cesare Lombroso, biological approaches to criminal behavior were most popular. As we observe in this chapter, purely biological theories have been discredited. Psychological theories, however, still receive considerable support. Compare and contrast the biological and psychological approaches with the major sociological theories of criminality. What special advantages do these sociological approaches have in interpreting crime and delinquency?

2. Anomie, cultural transmission, and illegitimate opportunities theories of criminal and delinquent behavior all reflect a functionalist approach. What core similarities do these theories share?

3. The FBI classifies many white-collar crimes such as embezzlement and antitrust violations as less serious than violent crime and certain property crimes. Conflict theorists sometimes contend that this reflects a social bias against the poor and in favor of dominant social groups, who are more likely to commit white-collar crimes. Do you agree with this interpretation? Should white-collar criminals receive stiffer penalties? Should the penalties for violent crimes and property crimes be less severe? Why?

4. In this chapter, we make a number of proposals about how America's criminal justice system might be reformed, perhaps reducing our society's crime and delinquency problems. What are your reactions to these suggestions? Are they realistic, unrealistic—feasible, impractical? Why?

5. What are your reactions to criminal justice expert Jeffrey Reiman's suggestions for reforming our judicial system? Do you agree with his proposals? Disagree? Why?

6. Organize a debate on the issue of capital punishment. You could marshal arguments for and against capital punishment. Invite someone from outside the class—a police chief, lawyer, judge, or prison administrator—to argue each side of the issue. After the debate, have the class vote on the issue.

For Further Reading

Howard Abadinsky. *The Criminal Elite: Professional and Organized Crime.* Westport, Conn.: Greenwood Press, 1983. A delightful comparison between the world of the professional thief and that of organized crime. Abadinsky wrote this book using information obtained from a professional jewel thief, who acted as his informant, protected by the federal Witness Protection Program.

Lonnie H. Athens. *The Creation of Dangerous Violent Criminals.* Champaign, Ill.: University of Illinois Press, 1989. Vivid first-person accounts from in-depth interviews of hardened criminals are used to develop a theory on how a person becomes a dangerous violent criminal. The theory relies, to a degree, on the interactionist perspective.

John Braithwaite. *Crime, Shame, and Reintegration.* Cambridge: Cambridge University Press, 1989. This sociologist proposes a new theory of crime that focuses on society's tendency to stigmatize and reject offenders rather than using shame along with reintegration into the mainstream of society. The latter, the author argues, would more effectively control crime.

Edmund G. (Pat) Brown with Dick Adler. *Public Justice, Private Mercy: A Governor's Education on*

Death Row. New York: Weidenfeld and Nicolson, 1989. As governor of California, Brown commuted the sentences of twenty-three men on death row and sent thirty-six to the gas chamber. This experience has had a profound impact on him personally and he conveys this in this compelling book.

Alan M. Dershowitz. *The Best Defense.* New York: Random House, 1981. A scathing critique of our nation's legal system by a professor at the Harvard Law School, including his suggestions for possible reforms.

Kai T. Erikson. *Wayward Puritans.* New York: John Wiley and Sons, 1966. Erikson examines our Puritan heritage in terms of current attitudes toward crime and other forms of deviance, demonstrating that certain behaviors regarded as deviant by the Puritans of colonial Massachusetts were socially disvalued, not in and of themselves, but because of the labeling process.

Martin Sanchez Jankowski. *Islands in the Street: Gangs and American Urban Society.* Berkeley: University of California Press, 1991. This book views urban gangs and their members as shrewd and resourceful people operating in a difficult and challenging environment rather than as evil or pathological people to be despised. It provides a unique view of inner-city gang life.

Liz Kelly. *Surviving Sexual Violence.* Minneapolis: University of Minnesota Press, 1989. This book views violence against women as running along a continuum from subtle threats to physical attacks. The author uses both feminist theory and sociological research to understand the violence women experience and to show the powerful strategies they use to cope with and survive the violence they face.

Stuart Miller, Simon Dinitz, and John Conrad. *Careers of the Violent.* Lexington, Mass.: Lexington Books, 1982. This is a fascinating analysis of the criminal careers of 1,591 male criminals who had all been arrested at least once for murder, assault, rape, or robbery. It offers insights into the lives of the small number of people who commit a large part of the crimes in America.

Russell Mokhiber. *Corporate Crime and Violence: Big Business Power and the Abuse of the Public Trust.* San Francisco: Sierra Club Books, 1988. A muckraker's view of white-collar and corporate crime: Thirty-six cases are described in which corporate misconduct killed people or significantly harmed the environment.

Felix M. Padilla. *The Gang as an American Enterprise.* New Brunswick, N.J.: Rutgers University Press, 1992. This is an ethnography of second-generation Puerto Rican youth in Chicago who belong to a gang called the Diamonds. It chronicles all facets of gang life, from how youth get drawn into gangs to their illegal drug selling.

Wilbert Rideau and Ron Wikberg. *Life Sentences: Rage and Survival Behind Bars.* New York: Times Books/Random House, 1992. This is a moving book by two men who spent many years in prison, each convicted of murder. It is an excellent insider's view of prison life, making a convincing argument against our desire to lock criminals in prison and throw away the key.

I n 1982, well-known actor and former *Saturday Night Live* star John Belushi died from an injection of heroin and cocaine, a combination known as a "speedball" in drug circles. That same year, German filmmaker Rainer Werner Fassbinder died of an overdose of sleeping pills and other drugs. In 1983, Beach Boy Dennis Wilson drowned after using cocaine and alcohol. In 1984, David Kennedy, the twenty-eight-year-old son of Senator Robert F. Kennedy and nephew of President John F. Kennedy, was found dead in a hotel room in West Palm Beach, Florida. He died from a combined dose of cocaine, a narcotic painkiller called Demerol, and an antipsychotic tranquilizer known as Mellaril, which had been prescribed to Mr. Kennedy by a physician.

In 1986, two well-known athletes, professional football player Don Rogers and college basketball star Len Bias, died after taking cocaine. The only thing distinctive about these deaths is the fact that these men were of some wealth or fame. Such deaths from drug overdoses occur routinely in the United States, although rarely with the attention surrounding these cases. The notoriety of the people mentioned above publicized the horrible consequences that can result—to Americans of both high and low social position—when drug use gets out of control.

The use of drugs in one form or another is widespread in human societies. Most societies condone the use of certain drugs, at least by some groups. Such drug use is generally regulated,

Myths and Facts About Drug Abuse

Myth: The drug abuse problem in the United States today is of epidemic proportions, with more people using and abusing drugs than ever.

Fact: Although today's drug abuse problem is serious, it is probably no greater than it was a century ago. Then, marijuana, cocaine, and various narcotics were legal and widely available, and many Americans were addicted to drugs.

Myth: Heavy use of heroin clouds judgment and reduces inhibitions, and this is the prime reason heroin addicts commit crimes.

Fact: Heroin addicts are as likely to be high on alcohol as heroin when they commit crimes, and in fact many heroin addicts drink alcohol before committing crimes in order to bolster their courage.

Myth: The most serious drug problem that America faces is the flow of heroin, cocaine, and marijuana into the United States from overseas.

Fact: In terms of the number of people affected and the economic costs to society, most specialists on drug problems consider alcohol abuse to be the most severe drug problem we have.

Myth: Heroin is a very physically damaging drug, which warrants making its use illegal.

Fact: Heroin is probably less harmful to its users than is alcohol, and many have argued that heroin should be treated by society like alcohol: as a legal but highly controlled substance.

Myth: Addiction to heroin and other narcotics produces the most severe and dangerous physical withdrawal symptoms.

Fact: Withdrawal from addiction to barbiturates (sedatives and painkillers), which can be purchased legally in the United States, is much more dangerous than withdrawal from heroin, a substance that is illegal.

either through law or social convention, because the unregulated use of mind-altering substances can have damaging effects on society. For example, drug users may not work, or they may fail to support their families. They may even become dangerous to themselves or others. This common societal ambivalence toward drug use—condoning it on the one hand, but controlling it on the other—points to one of the controversial elements of the problem of alcohol and drug use: drawing the line between what is acceptable use and what is not. In Chapters 1 and 9, we describe the relative nature of deviant behavior. In this chapter, we focus on this issue specifically in the context of drug use. In the United States, opinions about drug use vary widely. At one extreme, some groups call for a complete ban on all drugs, including alcohol. Other groups believe that some drugs—alcohol and marijuana are most commonly mentioned—can be used safely by mature

people. At the other extreme, a few groups argue that adults should be free to use any drug they please as long as they do not become a danger to others.

These issues of social definition are central to understanding the problem of drug abuse in the United States and to developing sensible social policies to deal with it. We will address these issues first, before considering the extent and nature of the drug problem in the United States.

DRUGS AND THEIR CONSEQUENCES

What is a drug? Strictly speaking, a **drug** is *any substance that, when consumed, alters one or more of the functions of the human body* (Milby, 1981). This definition covers a wide range of substances, from cocaine to medicines for the control of cancer to high blood pressure medications. It also includes many everyday foods along with beverages such as tea, coffee, and cola that contain the mild stimulant caffeine. Does this make your aunt, who drinks two six-packs of caffeine-laced cola each day, a drug addict? Not by most definitions. The effects of most of these everyday substances are rather mild, and their use or withdrawal does not normally create major disruptions in people's lives. The drugs that constitute a social problem are typically limited to the **psychoactive drugs:** *those that can produce major alterations in the mood, emotions, perceptions, or brain functioning of the person who takes them* (Edwards, 1983; Schuckit, 1989).

Drug Use and Abuse

The use of psychoactive drugs is not, by itself, a social problem. After all, as we have noted, most societies approve the use of some such drugs (O'Brien and Cohen, 1984). In our society, for example, the moderate use of alcohol is accepted by many groups. Alcohol consumption is even incorporated into the Roman Catholic ritual of the Mass. Few would argue that these uses of psychoactive drugs constitute a social problem. Where, then, is the line between acceptable drug use and drug abuse? This is a very controversial question. The World Health Organization defines drug abuse as the excessive use of a drug in a way that is inconsistent with medical practice (Milby, 1981). However, this definition, with its emphasis on the medical consequences of behavior, seems overly broad. Heavy smoking, for example, would by this definition be drug abuse because physicians warn against it, but few are likely to call heavy smokers "drug addicts." Rather, we need to consider drug use in the context of particular cultural or subcultural norms and values. From this viewpoint, **drug abuse** is *the continued use of a psychoactive substance at a level that violates approved social practices*. Typically, use of a substance meets social disapproval when it has negative conse-

quences for people's health, endangers their relationships with other people, or is threatening to others in society. Even people's belief that the substance has these consequences can produce social disapproval. As we will see, cultural norms regarding drug abuse are by no means completely rational. These norms are influenced as much by history, religion, and cultural values as they are by the actual damage drugs do to a person's health or social relationships.

Much of the concern about drugs of abuse relates to their effects on people, such as drug dependence, drug addiction, and a tolerance to drugs. Some drugs produce **dependence,** or *a mental or physical craving for the drug and withdrawal symptoms when use of the drug is stopped*. Dependence and its withdrawal symptoms can be physical, psychological, or both. Alcohol withdrawal, for example, can lead to convulsions, hallucinations, and insomnia on the physical level and nervousness and a reduced sense of self-worth on the psychological level. The withdrawal symptoms of a drug are often the opposite of the effects of taking the drug. For example, alcohol, which helps a person relax, can lead to insomnia and anxiety when use is discontinued. Drug dependence and drug abuse are not the same thing, although they are often related. A severely depressed person, for example, may become highly dependent on antidepressant medications prescribed by a physician, but this would not be considered drug abuse because the physician's diagnosis and treatment prescription make this a socially approved use of a drug. Neither are drug abuse and drug addiction synonymous. **Drug addiction,** as used by professionals in the field, refers to *physical dependence on a drug*. Although most drugs of abuse are physically addicting, some, such as the hallucinogens, are not.

Often associated with dependence on a drug is **tolerance:** *physical changes that result in the need for higher and higher doses of the drug to achieve the same effect*. This occurs because, with continual use of some drugs, the liver destroys the drug more quickly and the nervous system's response to the drug is diminished. So more of the drug is needed for the same "boost." It is also possible to develop cross-dependence and cross-tolerance. **Cross-dependence** occurs when *the withdrawal symptoms of one drug are alleviated by another drug in the same pharmacological class*. **Cross-tolerance** is found when *a tolerance built up to one drug leads to a reduced response to another drug in the same pharmacological class*.

The Societal Costs of Drug Abuse

The consumption of alcohol and other drugs takes a costly toll from our society (National Institute on Alcohol Abuse and Alcoholism, 1988).

1. *Accidents*. Each year, from one-third to one-half of the drivers in fatal traffic accidents have been drinking, and between sixteen thousand and thirty thousand people die in traffic accidents involving alcohol (U.S. Bureau of the Census, 1991). Alcohol consumption is also associated with airplane and occupational accidents. Marijuana impairs motor skills, reduces judgment, and affects time and distance estimation, and thus increases the danger of accidents (Sutton, 1983).

2. *Crime*. In well over half of the homicides in the United States, either the victim, the perpetrator, or both were drinking at the time of the crime. People who commit rape are also disproportionately likely to have been drinking before the crime or to be an alcoholic. Studies of heroin addicts in treatment programs have found that most addicts commit crimes to support their habit (Inciardi, 1986). Thirty percent of all convictions for federal offenses in the United States today are for drug offenses, up from 18 percent in 1980 (U.S. Bureau of the Census, 1991: 191).

3. *Family Problems*. Alcoholics are seven times more likely to become separated or divorced from their spouses than are other people, and 40 percent of the family court problems involve alcohol in some fashion. Studies find

that between 29 and 71 percent of spouse abusers were drinking at the time of the attack.

4. *Work Problems*. Alcohol abusers have twice the rate of work absenteeism as other workers and cause many other problems at work. In 1989, for example, the captain of the oil tanker *Exxon Valdez* was under the influence of alcohol at the time the ship went aground and released millions of gallons of oil into the Alaskan coastline, causing a terrible environmental disaster.

5. *Health Problems*. Most psychoactive drugs, especially if taken continually or in large quantities, produce severe health problems and even death. Alcoholics and heroin addicts, for example, have far higher death rates from many illnesses than do people who abuse neither drug.

Placing a dollar figure on these and other costs of drug abuse is necessarily approximate and tentative, but it helps to highlight the dimensions of the problem. One estimate for 1988 of the core costs for alcohol abuse alone in the United States was $86 billion! This is what it cost society to diagnose, treat, and care for alcoholism and alcohol-related illnesses and deaths and to cover the costs of lowered work productivity (Rice, Kelman, and Miller, 1991). Add in another $58 billion for the abuse of other drugs, and the cost to society becomes an astounding $144 billion. Estimates of losses in work and productivity alone because of drug abuse range from $16 to $20 billion per year (Scanlon, 1986).

THE EXTENT OF DRUG ABUSE IN AMERICA

Americans consume many different kinds of drugs; some are legal and others are illegal. These various drugs differ from one another in their chemical composition and their social, psycholog-

Table 10.1 **The Major Drugs of Abuse**

Drugs	Often-Prescribed Brand Names	Medical Uses	Dependence Potential: Physical	Psychological
Narcotics				
Opium	Dover's Powder, Paregoric	Analgesic, antidiarrheal	High	High
Morphine	Morphine	Analgesic	High	High
Codeine	Codeine	Analgesic, antitussive	Moderate	Moderate
Heroin	None	None	High	High
Meperidine (Pethidine)	Demerol, Pethadol	Analgesic	High	High
Methadone	Dolophine, Methadone, Methadose	Analgesic, heroin substitute	High	High
Other narcotics	Dilaudid, Leritine, Numorphan, Percodan	Analgesic, antidiarrheal, antitussive	High	High
Depressants				
Chloral hydrate	Noctec, Somnos	Hypnotic	Moderate	Moderate
Barbiturates	Amytal, Butisol, Nembutal, Phenobarbital, Seconal, Tuinal	Anesthetic, anticonvulsant, sedation, sleep	High	High
Glutethimide	Doriden	Sedation, sleep	High	High
Methaqualone	Optimil, Parest, Quaalude, Somnafac, Sopor	Sedation, sleep	High	High
Tranquilizers	Equanil, Librium, Miltown Serax, Tranxene, Valium	Antianxiety, muscle relaxant, sedation	Moderate	Moderate
Other depressants	Clonopin, Dalmane, Dormate, Noludar, Placydil, Valmid	Antianxiety, sedation, sleep	Possible	Possible
Stimulants				
Cocaine[c]	Cocaine	Local anesthetic	Possible	High
Amphetamines	Benzedrine, Biphetamine, Desoxyn, Dexedrine	Hyperkinesis, narcolepsy, weight control	Possible	High
Phenmetrazine	Preludin	Weight control	Possible	High
Methylphenidate	Ritalin	Hyperkinesis	Possible	High
Other stimulants	Bacarate, Cylert, Didrex, Ionamin, Plegine, Pondimin, Pre-Sate, Sanorex, Voranil	Weight control	Possible	Possible

ical, and medical consequences. We will discuss the major classes of drugs that are problems in the United States. Table 10.1 summarizes some of the most significant characteristics of various psychoactive drugs.

Alcohol

Alcohol is a psychoactive drug that any adult in the United States can purchase legally without a prescription. There is little debate that it constitutes our most severe drug problem. According to

Tolerance	Possible Effects	Most Significant Adverse Reactions
Yes		
Yes		
Yes		
Yes		
Yes	Euphoria, drowsiness, respiratory depression, constricted pupils, nausea	Toxicity[a], withdrawal, OBS[b]
Yes		
Yes		
Probable		
Yes		
Yes		
Yes	Slurred speech, disorientation, drunken behavior without odor of alcohol	Toxicity, psychosis, withdrawal, OBS
Yes		
Yes		
Yes		
Yes		
Yes	Increased alertness, excitation, euphoria, dilated pupils, increased pulse rate and blood pressure, insomnia, loss of appetite	Psychosis, panic, toxicity, OBS, withdrawal
Yes		
Yes		

a survey conducted by the National Institute on Drug Abuse, 5 percent of all adult Americans are heavy drinkers, consuming five or more drinks at one sitting at five or more times each month (National Institute on Drug Abuse, 1991). Overall, Americans fourteen years of age and older consume an average of 2.7 gallons of alcohol per person per year. This is a particularly impressive amount considering that about one-third of the adult population drinks no alcoholic beverages

Table 10.1   *(continued)*

Drugs	Often-Prescribed Brand Names	Medical Uses	Dependence Potential: Physical	Psychological
Hallucinogens				
LSD	None	None	None	Degree unknown
Mescaline	None	None	None	Degree unknown
Psilocybin-Psilocyn	None	None	None	Degree unknown
MDA	None	None	None	Degree unknown
PCP[d]	Semyian	Veterinary anesthetic	None	Degree unknown
Other hallucinogens	None	None	None	Degree unknown
Cannabis				
Marijuana Hashish Hashish oil	None	None	Degree unknown	Moderate

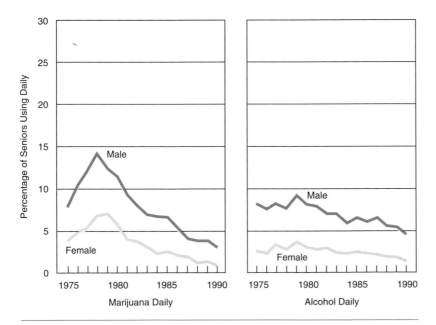

Figure 10.1   **Trends in Thirty-Day Prevalence of Daily Use of Marijuana and Alcohol, by Sex, Among High School Seniors, 1975–1990**
SOURCE: Lloyd D. Johnston, Patrick M. O'Malley, and Jerald G. Bachman, *Drug Use Among American High School Students, College Students and Young Adults, 1975–1990: Volume I, High School Seniors,* National Institute on Drug Abuse, DHHS Pub. No. (ADM) 91–1813 (Washington, D.C.: U.S. Government Printing Office, 1991), p. 70.
NOTE: Daily use for alcohol and marijuana is defined as use on twenty or more occasions in the past thirty days.

Tolerance	Possible Effects	Most Significant Adverse Reactions
Yes		
Yes		
Yes	Illusions and hallucinations (with exception of	Panic, flashbacks, toxicity, OBS
Yes	MDA), poor perception of time and distance	
Yes		
Yes		
Yes	Euphoria, relaxed inhibitions, increased appetite, disoriented behavior	Panic, flashbacks, toxicity, OBS

ᵃA serious impact on a person's vital signs.
ᵇOrganic Brain Syndrome involving confusion, disorientation, and decreased intellectual functioning.
ᶜDesignated a narcotic under the Controlled Substances Act.
ᵈDesignated a depressant under the Controlled Substances Act.
SOURCE: U.S. Department of Justice, Drug Enforcement Administration, *Drugs of Abuse* (Washington, D.C.: U.S. Government Printing Office, n.d.).

whatsoever. Furthermore, the young also drink a lot. In 1990, almost 4 percent of all high school students drank every day, and one-third of all high school seniors reported episodes of heavy drinking in the preceding two weeks (see Figure 10.1; Johnston, O'Malley, and Bachman, 1991).

The consumption of alcohol by itself is not a social problem. Many people use it throughout their lives without running into any difficulties, or at least the particular effects are not defined as problems. However, the continuous or excessive consumption of alcohol, commonly termed "alcoholism," is likely to create problems. Actually, attempts to define alcoholism have created much controversy. One approach is to define it by the amount of alcohol consumed or the alcohol blood levels of a person. However, many alcoholism treatment specialists feel that these definitions have weaknesses because they ignore the social definitions of what is considered too much alcohol or the social consequences of consuming a certain amount of alcohol. The most popular definition of **alcoholism** is *the consumption of alcohol at a level that produces serious personal, social, or health consequences, such as marital problems, occupational difficulties, accidents, or arrests* (Ray, 1983; Schuckit, 1989). In this definition, there is no set level of alcohol consumption that distinguishes the alcoholic from the nonalcoholic. Alcoholics are people who cannot stop drinking before the detrimental consequences, such as losing their jobs or being arrested, occur.

The popular image of the alcoholic is the stumbling-down drunk and the skid-row bum, but such people probably make up less than 5 percent of all alcoholics (Scanlon, 1986). An estimated 15 percent of male drinkers and 6 percent of female drinkers in the United States become alcohol abusers. This means that about eighteen million Americans are either addicted to alcohol or drink enough to cause problems for themselves and other people. Who are these alcoholics? Alcoholism counselors are quick to point out that alcoholism knows no age, sex, race, or social class bounds, and this is certainly true to the extent that alcoholics can be found in virtually all social groups. Yet this statement also hides the reality that people with certain social characteristics are much more likely to become alcoholics (Haglund and Schuckit, 1981; Flewelling, Rachal, and Marsden, 1992):

1. *Sex.* Men are far more likely to become alcoholics than are women. This is due in part to the fact that alcohol consumption and drunkenness have been more socially acceptable for men than for women.
2. *Socioeconomic Status.* Rates of alcoholism are higher among people with lower levels of income and education. This may be due in part to the abilities of people with higher socioeconomic standing to avoid being publicly labeled as an alcoholic.
3. *Religion.* There are strong associations between religion and alcohol consumption. Most Jews, for example, consume alcohol, but heavy drinking among this group is relatively infrequent. Catholics, on the other hand, have many drinkers and much higher rates of heavy drinking, especially among French and Irish Catholics.
4. *Age.* Alcohol abuse is a more serious problem among younger than older people. Among people between the ages of eighteen and thirty-four, one-quarter to one-half admit to having some alcohol-related problems, such as automobile accidents while drunk or missing work because of drinking (Schuckit, 1989). After age thirty-four, heavy drinking declines, and by age sixty-five the proportion of heavy drinkers is about one-third what it is in the younger groups. Surveys of high school seniors reveal that almost 5 percent report daily or near daily use of alcohol, whereas a significantly higher proportion report occasional heavy drinking. Almost 60 percent of high school seniors have used alcohol in the last month, and over 40 percent of college students have consumed five or more drinks in one sitting during the previous two weeks. However, surveys over the past two decades suggest that alcohol consumption among adolescents as

well as adults has declined, in some cases significantly, since the early 1980s (see Figures 10.1 and 10.2 and Tables 10.2 and 10.3).

Marijuana and Hashish

Marijuana is a preparation made from the Cannabis plant, usually consumed by smoking it like tobacco (Milby, 1981; Abel, 1982). The primary psychoactive ingredient of Cannabis is tetrahydrocannabinol, or THC, which is concentrated in the resin of the plant. The potency of marijuana depends on how much of the resin is present. Hashish is a concentrated form of the resin taken from the flowers of the plant. It is either eaten or smoked and is very potent. It is difficult to classify marijuana in relationship to other psychoactive drugs. It has sedative properties at the doses usually consumed in cigarette form, but it also has definite hallucinogenic properties when taken in stronger doses.

The level of marijuana use in our society is far lower than that of alcohol. By 1990, less than 5 percent of college students used marijuana on a daily basis, and somewhere between one-third and one-half of all adults have ever used marijuana (see Figure 10.3 and Table 10.3). Rates of marijuana use are far higher among younger than older people. Among those between eighteen and twenty-five years of age, 12.7 percent are current users, compared with only 3.6 percent of those over twenty-six. Although these levels of use are much higher than decades earlier, usage appears to have peaked in the late 1970s and has been declining steadily since then (see Tables 10.2 and 10.3 and Figure 10.3). Usage rates are now lower than at any point since 1975. Males are also more likely to use marijuana than are females, and it is less common among college students than others.

In the potencies usually found in the United States, marijuana is a fairly mild drug and, when used in moderation, has few known damaging effects. It produces feelings of pleasant euphoria and well-being, along with sleepiness, heightened sexual arousal, increased sense awareness, difficulty in keeping track of time, and a decrease in

Trends in Two–Week Prevalence of 5 or More Drinks in a Row Among College Students vs. Others

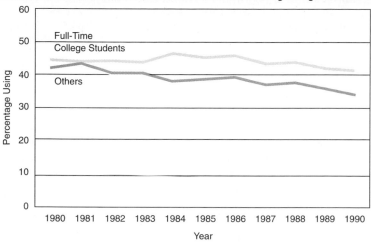

Trends in Two–Week Prevalence of 5 or More Drinks in a Row Among Male and Female College Students

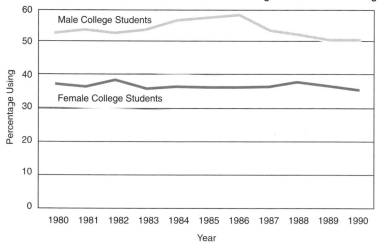

Figure 10.2 **Use of Alcohol Among College Students, 1980–1990**
SOURCE: Lloyd D. Johnston, Patrick M. O'Malley, and Jerald G. Bachman, *Drug Use Among American High School Seniors, College Students and Young Adults, 1975–1990: Volume II, College Students and Young Adults,* National Institute on Drug Abuse, DHHS Pub. No. (ADM) 91–1835 (Washington, D.C.: U.S. Government Printing Office, 1991), p. 165.

short-term memory. Marijuana intoxication can also impair a person's ability to carry out complex tasks. Very high doses can lead to intense emotional reactions, substantial distortions in perception, a "panic" that one has lost control of oneself,

and vivid hallucinations. It can even lead to a psychotic reaction, usually in people with a history of mental instability. Marijuana use leads to only mild levels of tolerance. Some argue that there is no physical dependence at all with marijuana

Table 10.2 Drug Use Among High School Seniors, 1975–1990

A. Trends in Thirty-Day Prevalence of Sixteen Types of Drugs Among High School Seniors, 1975–1990
Percent who used in last thirty days

	Class of 1975	Class of 1977	Class of 1979	Class of 1981	Class of 1983	Class of 1985	Class of 1987	Class of 1989	Class of 1990
Approx. N =	(9400)	(17100)	(15500)	(17500)	(16300)	(16000)	(16300)	(16700)	(15200)
Marijuana/Hashish	27.1	35.4	36.5	31.6	27.0	25.7	21.0	16.7	14.0
Inhalants	NA	1.3	1.7	1.5	1.7	2.2	2.8	2.3	2.7
Amyl & Butyl Nitrites	NA	NA	2.4	1.4	1.4	1.6	1.3	0.6	0.6
Hallucinogens	4.7	4.1	4.0	3.7	2.8	2.5	2.5	2.2	2.2
LSD	2.3	2.1	2.4	2.5	1.9	1.6	1.8	1.8	1.9
PCP	NA	NA	2.4	1.4	1.3	1.6	0.6	1.4	0.4
Cocaine	1.9	2.9	5.7	5.8	4.9	6.7	4.3	2.8	1.9
Heroin	0.4	0.3	0.2	0.2	0.2	0.3	0.2	0.3	0.2
Other opiates[a]	2.1	2.8	2.4	2.1	1.8	2.3	1.8	1.6	1.5
Stimulants[a]	8.5	8.8	9.9	15.8	12.4	NA	NA	NA	NA
Sedatives[a]	5.4	5.1	4.4	4.6	3.0	2.4	1.7	1.6	1.4
Barbiturates[a]	4.7	4.3	3.2	2.6	2.1	2.0	1.4	1.4	1.3
Methaqualone[a]	2.1	2.3	2.3	3.1	1.8	1.0	0.6	0.6	0.2
Tranquilizers[a]	4.1	4.6	3.7	2.7	2.5	2.1	2.0	1.3	1.2
Alcohol	68.2	71.2	71.8	70.7	69.4	65.9	66.4	60.0	57.1

B. Trends in Thirty-Day Prevalence of Daily Use of Sixteen Types of Drugs Among High School Seniors, 1975–1990
Percent who used daily in last thirty days

	Class of 1975	Class of 1977	Class of 1979	Class of 1981	Class of 1983	Class of 1985	Class of 1987	Class of 1989	Class of 1990
Approx. N =	(9400)	(17100)	(15500)	(17500)	(16300)	(16000)	(16300)	(16700)	(15200)
Marijuana/Hashish	6.0	9.1	10.3	7.0	5.5	4.9	3.3	2.9	2.2
Inhalants	NA	0.0	0.0	0.1	0.1	0.2	0.1	0.2	0.3
Amyl & Butyl Nitrites	NA	NA	0.0	0.1	0.2	0.3	0.3	0.3	0.1
Hallucinogens	0.1	0.1	0.1	0.1	0.1	0.1	0.1	0.1	0.1
LSD	0.0	0.0	0.0	0.1	0.1	0.1	0.1	0.0	0.1
PCP[a]	NA	NA	0.1	0.1	0.1	0.3	0.3	0.2	0.1
Cocaine	0.1	0.1	0.2	0.3	0.2	0.4	0.3	0.3	0.1
Heroin	0.1	0.0	0.0	0.0	0.1	0.0	0.0	0.1	0.0
Other opiates[a]	0.1	0.2	0.0	0.1	0.1	0.1	0.1	0.2	0.1
Stimulants[a]	0.5	0.5	0.6	1.2	1.1	NA	NA	NA	NA
Sedatives[a]	0.3	0.2	0.1	0.2	0.2	0.1	0.1	0.1	0.1
Barbiturates[a]	0.1	0.2	0.0	0.1	0.1	0.1	0.1	0.1	0.1
Methaqualone[a]	0.0	0.0	0.0	0.1	0.0	0.0	0.0	0.0	0.0
Tranquilizers[a]	0.1	0.3	0.1	0.1	0.1	0.0	0.1	0.1	0.1
Alcohol	5.7	6.1	6.9	6.0	5.5	5.0	4.8	4.2	3.7

[a]Only drug use that was not under a doctor's orders is included here.

SOURCE: Lloyd D. Johnston, Patrick M. O'Malley, and Jerald G. Bachman, *Drug Use Among American High School Seniors, College Students and Young Adults, 1975–1990: Volume I, High School Seniors,* National Institute on Drug Abuse, DHHS Pub. No. (ADM) 91-1813 (Washington, D.C.: U.S. Government Printing office, 1991), pp. 54–55.

Table 10.3 **Drug Use by Type of Drug and Age Group, 1974–1990**

A. Those Who Have Ever Used a Drug

Drug	Percentage of Persons 12–17 Years of Age			Percentage of Persons 18–25 Years of Age			Percentage of Persons 26 Years of Age and Over		
	1974	1979	1990	1974	1979	1990	1974	1979	1990
Any Illicit Drug Use	—	34.3	22.7	—	69.9	55.8	—	23.0	35.3
Marijuana/Hashish	23.0	30.9	14.8	52.7	68.2	52.2	9.9	19.6	31.8
Cocaine	3.6	5.4	2.6	12.7	27.5	19.4	0.9	4.3	10.9
Inhalants	8.5	9.8	7.8	9.2	16.5	10.4	1.2	3.9	3.8
Hallucinogens	6.0	7.1	3.3	16.6	25.1	12.0	1.3	4.5	7.4
Heroin	1.0	0.5	0.7	4.5	3.5	0.6	0.5	1.0	0.9
Nonmedical use of any psychotherapeutics	—	7.3	10.2	—	29.5	15.6	—	9.2	11.5
Stimulants	5.0	3.4	4.5	17.0	18.2	9.0	3.0	5.8	6.9
Sedatives	5.0	3.2	3.3	15.0	17.0	4.0	2.0	3.5	3.7
Tranquilizers	3.0	4.1	2.7	10.0	15.8	5.9	2.0	3.1	4.2
Analgesics	—	3.2	6.5	—	11.8	8.1	—	2.7	5.1
Alcohol	54.0	70.3	48.2	81.6	95.3	88.2	73.2	91.5	86.8

B. Those Who Have Used a Drug at Least Once in the Past Month

Drug	Percentage of Persons 12–17 Years of Age			Percentage of Persons 18–25 Years of Age			Percentage of Persons 26 Years of Age and Over		
	1974	1979	1990	1974	1979	1990	1974	1979	1990
Any Illicit Drug Use	—	17.6	8.1	—	37.1	14.9	—	6.5	4.6
Marijuana/Hashish	12.0	16.7	5.2	25.2	35.4	12.7	2.0	6.0	3.6
Cocaine	1.0	1.4	0.6	3.1	9.3	2.2	*	0.9	0.6
Inhalants	0.7	2.0	2.2	*	1.2	1.2	*	0.5	*
Hallucinogens	1.3	2.2	0.9	2.5	4.4	0.8	*	*	0.1
Heroin	*	*	*	*	*	*	*	*	*
Nonmedical use of any psychotherapeutics	—	2.3	2.7	—	6.2	2.6	—	1.1	1.0
Stimulants	1.0	1.2	1.0	3.7	3.5	1.2	*	0.5	0.3
Sedatives	1.0	1.1	0.9	1.6	2.8	0.7	*	*	0.1
Tranquilizers	1.0	0.6	0.5	1.2	2.1	0.5	*	*	0.2
Analgesics	—	0.6	1.4	—	1.0	1.2	—	*	0.6
Alcohol	34.0	37.2	24.5	69.3	75.9	63.3	54.5	61.3	52.3

*No estimate.

SOURCE: National Institute on Drug Abuse, *National Household Survey on Drug Abuse: Main Findings 1990*, DHHS Pub. No. (ADM) 91–1788 (Washington, D.C.: U.S. Government Printing Office, 1991), pp. 20–30.

(Milby, 1981). Withdrawal symptoms, if they occur at all, appear to be quite mild.

Some studies have concluded that chronic marijuana users, especially among adolescents, may develop what has been called an amotivational syndrome, characterized by a lack of goals, apathy, sluggish mental responses, and mental confusion (Milby, 1981; Cohen, 1982). Such investigations have been criticized, however, on the grounds that many of the behaviors associated with this

Trends in Thirty-Day Prevalence of DAILY Use Among College Students vs. Others

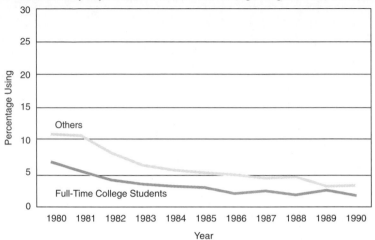

Trends in Thirty-Day Prevalence of DAILY Use Among Male and Female College Students

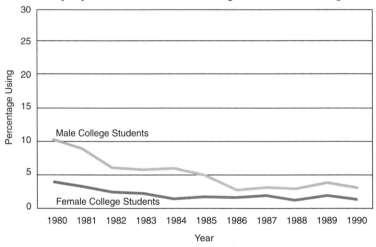

Figure 10.3 **Marijuana Use Among College Students, 1980–1990**
SOURCE: Lloyd D. Johnston, Patrick M. O'Malley, and Jerald G. Bachman, *Drug Use Among American High School Seniors, College Students and Young Adults, 1975–1990: Volume II, College Students and Young Adults,* National Institute on Drug Abuse, DHHS Pub. No. (ADM) 91–1835 (Washington, D.C.: U.S. Government Printing Office, 1991), p. 153.

syndrome are socially acceptable and even valued in the subculture of some chronic drug users. So these behaviors may not be responses to the drug but to the social expectations present in a subcultural milieu. In addition, this syndrome probably affects a small number of chronic users—one study estimates 3 percent—and it disappears without any treatment being given for it, even when marijuana use is continued (Halikas et al., 1982).

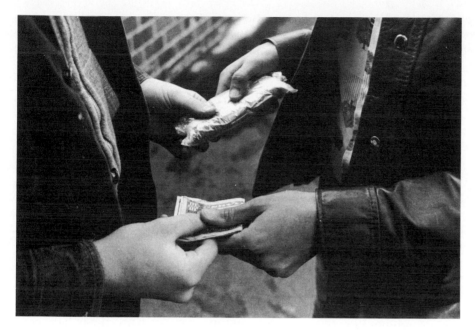

People who use drugs like cocaine and heroin often use marijuana first, but there is no convincing evidence that marijuana use causes one to turn to other drugs.

There has been some debate over the years about whether marijuana use can lead to the use of other drugs such as cocaine or heroin (Botvin, 1990). Clearly, people who use these other drugs often use marijuana first. However, there is no convincing evidence that marijuana itself causes a person to turn to these other drugs. Rather, the social circumstances or personal problems that incline certain people toward drug abuse probably lead to marijuana first, possibly because of its accessibility. Even if marijuana were not available, such people would probably abuse other drugs eventually, such as alcohol, heroin, or cocaine. In addition, obtaining marijuana often brings the user into contact with people who also know how to obtain and use other drugs. It is probably these associations, not the marijuana itself, that produce the link between use of one drug and use of another.

Stimulants

There are enough stimulants produced legally in the United States each year to provide fifty doses to every American. About one-half of these legal stimulants find their way into the illegal drug trade (Schuckit, 1989). The term **stimulant** refers to the many *drugs whose major effect is to stimulate the central nervous system*. They can increase one's alertness, reduce fatigue, enhance a person's mood, and create a sense of excitement. They can also produce euphoria, confidence, a heightened sense of sexuality, increased energy, and restlessness. Low doses of some stimulants, such as cocaine, can lead to enhanced motor performance, but higher doses result in a deterioration in performance and, at an extreme, convulsions. The stimulants produce tolerance, cross-tolerance, and physical and psychological dependence. Stimulants have many legitimate medical uses in the treatment of narcolepsy (falling asleep without warning), hyperactivity in children, and obesity. However, they are also widely abused.

Cocaine is a stimulant derived from coca leaves and has become a very popular psychoactive drug (Erickson et al., 1987; Johnston, O'Malley, and Bachman, 1991). By the 1990s, more than 10 percent of all adult Americans aged twenty-six and over had tried cocaine, compared with around 1 percent in the mid-1970s. Among young people aged eighteen to twenty-five years old, almost 20 percent had used it in 1990 compared with 12 percent in 1974. However, there seem to be fewer current users now: 2.2 percent of the eighteen to twenty-five year olds used cocaine in the last month in 1990 compared with 3.1 percent in 1974. In fact, cocaine use seemed to have peaked between 1980 and 1985 and has shown a substantial decline since then (see Tables 10.2 and 10.3 and Figure 10.4). However, there is evidence that the decline in cocaine use is among casual users rather than heavy users or addicts. This is suggested in Table 10.2, for example, which shows that the rate of daily use of cocaine has not dropped much, whereas the rate among those who used cocaine in the last thirty days—presumably the casual users—has dropped significantly. In addition, although equal proportions of whites, African Americans, and Hispanic Americans have tried cocaine, whites are less likely to be current users than are the other two groups. So, cocaine use among whites tends to be more short-lived and probably more experimental.

Cocaine used to be an expensive drug, and this limited its use. However, drug entrepreneurs discovered ways to produce cheap and potent drugs from cocaine (Lerner and Raczynski, 1988; Witkin, 1991). In the 1970s, they discovered a recipe for cocaine "freebase," in which a chemical process was used to "free" base cocaine from cocaine hydrochloride powder (called "powder" or "blow"). This made a potent drug, but it was also a complicated and dangerous process. (In 1980, comedian Richard Pryor set himself on fire while freebas-

ing.) Because of the difficulty and danger, drug entrepreneurs eventually came up with a less pure but much safer method of freebasing that used heat and baking soda to turn the cocaine powder into smokable "crack" cocaine. (The term *crack* comes from the cracking sound cocaine makes when heated.) Crack (called "rock cocaine" or "hubbas") gives an intense high—almost instantaneously because it is smoked—and is extremely addictive. Crack addicts sometimes engage in "binging," taking high doses in rapid succession, as often as every ten minutes. Crack is sometimes used with other drugs, such as when combined with heroin to make a "speedball" that gives a quick and potent high (McDonnell, Irwin, and Rosenbaum, 1990). It is also cheap enough to be available even to poor people with a few extra dollars in their pocket. Cocaine powder costs $75 a gram, whereas one hit of crack is as little as $5. Because of this, crack has been an especially cruel plague for many poor communities. Even mothers receiving welfare can afford crack if they neglect their personal needs and those of their families. Consequently, some poor women have become addicted to crack, given birth to children who are addicted, and then neglected and even abandoned their children as their crack habits spun out of control. Under these circumstances, the problems of poverty and drug abuse become intertwined and mutually reinforcing. Another characteristic of crack is especially important in terms of criminal behavior: Heroin is a depressant, which means that addicts are lethargic and mostly immobile during their "highs." Cocaine, on the other hand, is a stimulant, and crack addicts are far more likely to be paranoid and highly active.

Cocaine can be absorbed into the body in many different ways, but the most common ways are to inject it intravenously, to sniff or "snort" it into the nostrils, or to smoke the drug, as in the use of crack. Prolonged snorting of cocaine can destroy the mucous membranes of the nose and eventually the septum. High doses or chronic use can produce a schizophrenia-like or paranoid psy-

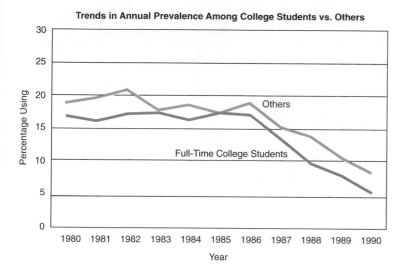

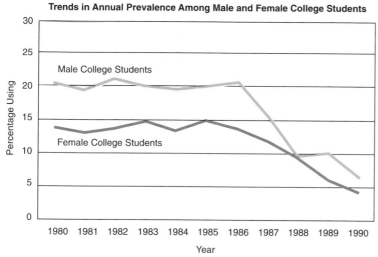

Figure 10.4 **Cocaine Use Among College Students, 1980–1990**
SOURCE: Lloyd D. Johnston, Patrick M. O'Malley, and Jerald G. Bachman, *Drug Use Among American High School Seniors, College Students and Young Adults, 1975–1990: Volume II, College Students and Young Adults,* National Institute on Drug Abuse, DHHS Pub. No. (ADM) 91–1835 (Washington, D.C.: U.S. Government Printing Office, 1991), p. 158.

chotic reaction, manic-like states, severe depression, and panic states. Crack especially can be extremely dangerous. For example, the heart rates of users can increase abnormally, which in some cases can lead to cardiac arrest and death. Cocaine can produce as much dependence, tolerance, and withdrawal in those who use it as does heroin (Hasin et al., 1988). Finally, for those who take

These suspects were arrested in a police raid on sixteen suspected "crack houses" in New York City. Crack addicts can cause special problems for law enforcement personnel because the addicts may become paranoid or aggressive due to the effects of the stimulant cocaine on the brain.

cocaine intravenously, there is the danger of AIDS infection when dirty needles are shared with other users.

Amphetamines are synthetic central nervous system stimulants. The effects of amphetamines are longer lasting than cocaine, but the two types of stimulants are quite similar in other respects. Some amphetamine abuse arises when people use these stimulants to help them accomplish socially acceptable tasks, such as studying long hours for an examination, putting in extra hours at work, or trying to lose weight. For these people, the drug may have been obtained through medical prescriptions or it might have been bought on the black market. These socially acceptable uses of amphetamines, however, can readily become

abuse. Because tolerance develops, legitimate users may increase the dosage to the point at which withdrawal symptoms occur if use is discontinued. In addition, amphetamines are highly addicting, and this can make quitting very difficult. A far more destructive type of amphetamine abuse is by "speed freaks" who take massive doses, often through intravenous injections, several times a day. This "run" might result in the person staying awake for many days (Abel, 1984). Sleeping and eating very little, people's judgment becomes impaired, and they feel overconfident, paranoid, and nervous. The feelings of overconfidence can lead to accidents. At the end of a "run," users will "crash," sleeping for long periods.

Heavy users of stimulants, especially cocaine and amphetamines, are much more likely to commit crimes and be involved in violence than are users of most other psychoactive drugs (Eckerman et al., 1971; Goldstein et al., 1991). Part of this is the stimulant effect of the drugs themselves, which can lead people to feel delusional, overly courageous, impulsive, or panicky. But violence also occurs because "speed freaks" and crack cocaine users must participate in a criminal subculture where hustles, coercion, fraud, and violence are routine practices in the illegal drug business. In addition, prostitution, robbery, and violent crimes are ways of getting money to buy drugs and support oneself. Interestingly, heavy drug users among males were most likely to be the perpetrators of violence, whereas among women drug users were the victims of violence. To oversimplify somewhat, the male users robbed stores and the female users got beat up by their spouses or lovers.

Depressants

The main effect of **depressants** is the opposite of stimulants: *They depress the central nervous system (CNS), along with having some analgesic, or painkilling, properties.* Alcohol is a depressant, which we have discussed in a separate section. In addition, depressants include almost all sleeping medications (hypnotics or barbiturates) and antianxiety drugs (or the minor tranquilizers).

Barbiturates are a class of CNS depressants that are used as sedatives or painkillers. They can have effects similar to alcohol, particularly in reducing people's inhibitions. This can lead some to relax and others to become highly active, even aggressive. Their effects range from slight lethargy or sleepiness, to various levels of anesthesia, and finally to death from respiratory and heart depression. Among the many barbiturates are pentobarbital (Nembutal), secobarbital (Seconal), and amobarbital (Amytal). They can produce physical addiction, tolerance, cross-tolerance, and psycho-

logical dependence. Addiction to barbiturates is so severe that withdrawal is more dangerous than withdrawing from narcotics. Withdrawal can be accompanied by anxiety, nausea, cramps, hallucinations, and even fatal convulsions. Another serious problem with barbiturates is overdose. Especially with someone who uses a lot of depressants, including alcohol, it is easy to forget how much one has taken and inadvertently take too much. With their depressant effect, an overdose of barbiturates can slow a person's breathing and heart rate to the point where coma or death occurs. An overdose of barbiturates is also a common means of committing suicide (Lettieri, 1978).

An especially serious problem with barbiturates and other depressants is what drug abuse specialists call *potentiation*. This refers to what occurs when two depressants are taken at the same time: The effect of the combination is greater than would be expected from the action of either drug separately. The outcome can be an unexpected lethal dose. For example, people who consume a lot of alcohol—a depressant drug—and then decide to take a few sedative pills to sleep may inadvertently kill themselves due to respiratory failure or go into an irreversible coma. This lethal combination of barbiturates and alcohol is not uncommon.

Many barbiturates are obtained legally through a physician's prescription. To date, over twenty-five hundred different barbiturates have been synthesized, and approximately ten million doses of sedatives are manufactured each year in the United States (Hughes and Brewin, 1979). Around 4 percent of adults have used barbiturates, and their use has declined significantly over the past fifteen years (see Tables 10.2 and 10.3). The primary way that older adults and people of middle and upper socioeconomic standing obtain barbiturates is by pressuring a physician to prescribe them or by obtaining prescriptions from different physicians. There is also a substantial illegal market in barbiturates, mostly used by younger people.

The minor tranquilizers have many of the same effects as barbiturates, but in addition they can reduce anxiety and tension and produce a sense of well-being. They include such drugs as diazepam (Valium), chlordiazepoxide (Librium), and meprobamate (Equanil or Miltown). The minor tranquilizers are also characterized by addiction, tolerance, and severe withdrawal symptoms. In one year, more than two billion tablets of Valium were prescribed by physicians in the United States (Schuckit, 1989). Medical use of tranquilizers is more common than sedatives. For many, this means taking tranquilizers to relieve the stresses and anxieties and to get over the "rough spots" of modern life. The danger, of course, is that a pattern of abuse can set in, often before the person realizes what has happened. Also, the combination of tranquilizers with other depressants can be deadly: It was a combination of alcohol and tranquilizers taken at a party that is suspected of sending Karen Quinlin into a decade-long coma that ultimately resulted in her death in 1985. Betty Ford, wife of former president Gerald R. Ford, admitted publicly that she had a serious problem with alcohol and Valium use. She became an outspoken critic of this kind of abuse, and a well-known drug treatment center was established in her name.

The nonmedical use of sedatives and tranquilizers is more likely to occur among teens and young adults (see Table 10.3). After age twenty-five, such use drops considerably. Such use is also more common among whites than among nonwhites (National Institute on Drug Abuse, 1991).

Some barbiturate-like drugs were developed as nonaddicting and safe substitutes for barbiturates. Most have turned out to be very different indeed, sharing many dangers with barbiturates. This is especially true for methaqualone (Quaalude, Sopors), which has been widely abused. First introduced in 1965, it was not a controlled substance and was prescribed widely by many physicians who thought it was safe and nonaddicting. The effects of methaqualone are much the same as those of other sedatives and hypnotics, although with a possible greater loss of motor coordination. This can lead to a substantial loss of control, which led to the slang name "wallbanger" for the drug because of the tendency for users to bump into walls. By 1973, methaqualone's dangers were apparent and it was declared a controlled substance. But much damage had already been done. Methaqualone found its way into the black market. Soon after its introduction in both the United States and Great Britain, "ludes" or "sopors" became appealing to teenagers, heroin abusers, and just about anyone who wanted an inexpensive, but quite potent, "downer." The large market for methaqualone is partly due to its reputation as an aphrodisiac that can enhance people's sexual abilities and pleasure. In fact, some called it "heroin for lovers." However, the most it probably does along these lines is to reduce inhibitions.

Narcotics

Narcotics or **opiates** are *drugs whose main use is as analgesics or painkillers*. These include natural substances (opium, morphine, and codeine), minor chemical alterations of those natural substances (heroin, Dilaudid, and Percodan), and synthetic drugs (Darvon and Demerol). In addition to reducing pain, they produce drowsiness, mood changes, euphoria, and reduced mental functioning with high doses. They also depress the central nervous system and heart activity. The opiates produce tolerance and cross-tolerance. They are also highly addictive, with physical dependence developing very quickly. For example, therapeutic doses of morphine given four times a day to relieve pain will produce mild withdrawal symptoms after only three days (Schuckit, 1989). Opiates can be ingested in a variety of ways: orally (especially the synthetic opiates), intranasally ("snorting," as with morphine and heroin), by smoking (opium), or intravenously ("mainlining," as with heroin).

Some opiate abusers misuse painkillers that they began taking for medical reasons. Health-care providers, especially physicians and nurses, have a high rate of such analgesic abuse, possibly because of its easy availability to them. Other opiate abusers purchase their narcotics in the street market. Most illegal opiates enter the United States from the Orient, the Middle East, or South America. Many street abusers begin with the occasional use of opiates and then progress to daily use, with tolerance and dependence growing rapidly. Daily heroin users who are physically addicted may spend $50 to $100 per day to support their habits. However, the image of the addicted narcotic addict should not be overdrawn. The popular image is of someone who is irretrievably physically addicted, stumbling from one fix to another in constant fear of not being able to obtain enough to avoid debilitating withdrawals and committing many crimes to support the habit. Actually, many heroin users never progress beyond occasional use, called "chipping," and they continue this for many years, without physical addiction, and while maintaining a family, a circle of friends, and a job. They may spend as little as $15 to $20 for heroin on the days that they use it. This suggests that opiates, like alcohol, can be used semiregularly by some people while maintaining respectability and social stability and without contributing to a social problem (Johnson, 1984). Many American soldiers were exposed to opiates in Vietnam, where the high stress of combat, combined with the boredom of noncombat assignments, made soldiers highly susceptible to drug abuse. Probably as many as one-half of the soldiers who had the chance to try opiates in Vietnam did so. However, those who had not used drugs before going to Vietnam tended to stop using them once they returned to the United States (Robins, Helzer, and Davis, 1975; Dess and Cole, 1977). As for the link between crime and heroin abuse, it is clear that heroin addicts commit many crimes (Lerner and Raczynski, 1988; Deschenes, Anglin, and Speckart, 1991). However, as the Applied Research insert indicates, alcohol—a legal psychoactive drug—plays an important role in this criminal behavior.

There are probably seven hundred thousand heroin addicts in the United States (Peirce, 1992). Yet relatively few Americans have ever tried heroin. Among young adults—the heaviest users—only 1 percent claim to have ever used it, and that figure may be declining (see Table 10.3). There are other indications that heroin use has declined. For example, the number of arrests involving opiates has dropped, as have the number of cases of hepatitis and opiate-related mortalities. Still, the morbidity and mortality rate for street abusers of opiates is high, usually due to dirty needles and impure drugs. In addition, addicts who are accustomed to heavily diluted heroin may suffer an overdose if they happen to purchase some high-quality heroin. Finally, because of sharing dirty needles with HIV-infected drug users, heroin addicts run a considerable risk of HIV infection and thus contracting AIDS. One estimate is that half of the heroin addicts in New York City are infected with the HIV virus (Dole, 1991).

Heroin and many other opiates are far less damaging to the human body than are alcohol and tobacco (Trebach, 1982). Withdrawal from the opiates is also less dangerous than withdrawal from barbiturates or alcohol. In fact, opiate addicts can lead reasonably normal lives if they have a steady supply of the drug, use clean equipment, and know how to administer it properly. Many of the street abusers' problems arise from the illegality of the drugs: the high prices of black market drugs, the violence associated with the street drug trade, the varying quality and purity of drugs bought on the street, and the difficulty of keeping injection equipment sterile.

Hallucinogens

Hallucinogens, also called **psychedelics,** are *drugs that produce hallucinations, often of a visual nature.* Unlike marijuana, whose effect at normal doses is to change a person's mood or feelings, the hallucinogens produce illusions and hallucinations even at low doses. Awareness of sensory input and mental activity is intensified, thoughts are turned inward, and users are less able to differentiate be-

APPLIED RESEARCH

The Role of Alcohol in the Crimes of Heroin and Cocaine Addicts

In much popular imagery, the stereotype of the "drug addict" is of a person crazed by heroin or cocaine who commits crimes to support his or her habit with little regard for the victims of his or her actions. In fact, as we have seen, heroin and cocaine addicts do commit many crimes. Yet this stereotype is oversimplified in at least one dimension: It ignores the fact that heavy users of heroin and cocaine tend to be polydrug users, including heavy alcohol use. Many substance abuse programs have ignored the role of drugs other than heroin or cocaine in the criminal activities of addicts. As a consequence, they have been less effective in attacking the problem.

Social researchers at the Interdisciplinary Research Center for the Study of the Relations of Drugs and Alcohol to Crime have undertaken a series of investigations designed to gather more information about the relationship between the use of alcohol among active heroin users and their criminal activity (Strug et al., 1984). The researchers interviewed fifty-nine active heroin users recruited from the streets of Manhattan regarding the nondrug-related crimes that they had committed during the thirty-six hours prior to being interviewed. The investigators also asked about the users' drug and alcohol consumption patterns before and after committing crimes. These fifty-nine heroin users reported committing 103 nondrug crimes during the thirty-six hours before the interviews. Furthermore, intensive interviews were conducted with eleven heavy-drinking heroin users who had criminal records concerning the role that alcohol played in their criminal behavior patterns.

The researchers learned that alcohol, not heroin, was the drug that these addicts had used most frequently during the thirty days before being interviewed, and they were more likely to report being under the influence of alcohol than any other drug. Nearly 70 percent of these people had consumed alcohol on twenty-six or more of the prior thirty days. Although they used alcohol more frequently than heroin, they felt that they had been dependent on heroin for a longer period of time than any other drug, including alcohol. According to the investigators, this may be explained by the fact that alcohol use is so common

tween themselves and their surroundings. Hallucinogens have no accepted medical use in which their benefits outweigh their disadvantages. Examples of hallucinogens are: lysergic acid diethylamide (LSD), psilocybin, peyote, mescaline, diethyltryptamine (DET), and a phenylisopropylamine known as DOM or STP. Some, such as LSD and STP, are synthetic, whereas others are plant products (peyote and mescaline come from cacti, and psilocybin comes from mushrooms—although not the ones sold by your friendly grocer). All are taken orally. Tolerance to hallucinogens builds up rapidly, and there is cross-tolerance between most hallucinogens (although not, as some believe, between hallucinogens and marijuana). There is no physical dependence or withdrawal.

The popularity of hallucinogens peaked in the 1960s, and their use has since been somewhat supplanted by stimulants and depressants. As Table 10.3 shows, about 12 percent of young adults have tried hallucinogens, but relatively few use them regularly. This may be because their hallucinatory effect makes it difficult to relate to others, especially people who are not also hallu-

and socially acceptable in our society that dependence on the substance is less likely to be recognized. In fact, one of the men characterized himself as a "light drinker" even though he consumed three pints of wine per day. Among the eleven "heavy drinkers" in the group, the range of alcohol consumption was from three to twelve pints of wine each day.

Regarding crime, the respondents reported being high on some drug during 37 percent of the crimes they committed. Of these crimes committed while on drugs, the perpetrator was high on alcohol alone or alcohol in combination with other drugs 63 percent of the time. The men reported that consuming alcohol near the time of their crimes "provided them with calmness and courage, and allowed them to take bigger risks which, in their opinion, also allowed them to perform better" (Strug et al., 1984: 561). As one man put it: "Liquor puts 'a gorilla' on my back. I get more 'hard' as they say." Another said: "I would not have broken into that van if I was sober, because it might have belonged to somebody on the street." With respect to the use of money gained through criminal activities, in 93 percent of these occasions, the income was used to purchase alcohol and/or other drugs. The respondents were as likely to spend their criminal income on alcohol as on heroin.

The researchers also discovered that the need for money to buy alcohol was one of the motives for these men to commit their crimes. Although the general public tends to think that the high cost of heroin makes heroin addicts particularly prone to committing income-producing crimes, the economic resources of these addicts are so meager that the regular use of alcohol alone can generate the need to commit crimes. In a study of drugs and violence among cocaine users, the researchers concluded that alcohol, not cocaine or heroin, was "the major contributor" to violence resulting from the effect of the drug on people's thinking and behavior (Goldstein et al., 1991: 365). The drug users did engage in criminal violence to support their drug habit, but the majority of the violence they engaged in was produced by the effect of alcohol on the body rather than done to get money to buy drugs.

So based on this research, we begin to see that the addict-criminal may be as "crazed" on alcohol as on heroin or cocaine. Alcohol use served both as a very important motivation to commit crimes and as a key facilitator of criminal and violent behavior. When looking at the problem of drug use and crime, then, we are led to wonder whether alcohol—a legal drug—is more of a problem than heroin and cocaine. However, as these researchers note, most drug treatment programs do not provide for rehabilitation from alcohol. Based on the findings of this research, substance abuse programs that focus on heroin and cocaine may need to shift at least some of their resources toward controlling alcohol abuse among these "hard drug" users.

cinating. The hallucinations make normal activities—such as shopping, going to class, and the like—almost impossible to accomplish.

One problem with hallucinogens bought on the street is that you may not know what drug has actually been purchased. What a seller hawks as mescaline may actually by PCP or LSD. In addition, hallucinogens are sometimes adulterated with other drugs, such as amphetamines. This makes it difficult for users to know exactly what drug they are taking, and thus their reaction to it may be unpredictable, unpleasant, or dangerous (Jackson and Jackson, 1983). Another problem with hallucinogens is that usage can precipitate psychoses, with wild hallucinations, paranoid delusions, and mania. These psychoses are not common and usually clear within hours or days. If the psychoses persist, it is usually because of a preexisting psychiatric condition.

One of the most widely abused drugs, after alcohol, cocaine, and marijuana, is phencyclidine (PCP). It is inexpensive and relatively easy to synthesize by amateurs. As a consequence, it is often sold by street dealers as some other, more expensive, drug such as THC or LSD. PCP, often called "angel dust" on the street, was first introduced as a CNS depressant that was an anesthetic with some desirable properties. However, the drug was soon discovered to cause postoperative agitation and hallucinations in many patients, so medical use of PCP was discontinued. On the street, PCP was first used to adulterate other drugs, but then came to be abused as a hallucinogen in its own right, which is why we discuss it here rather than with the depressants. The usual way of taking PCP is orally or through smoking, but it can also be injected or sprayed on other drugs. The evidence is still unclear as to whether PCP causes physical or psychological dependence, and there do not seem to be any withdrawal symptoms.

PCP in low doses creates a sense of euphoria, a lack of coordination, and an agitated emotional state. Moderate doses create a drunken-like condition with perceptual illusions. At still higher doses, PCP can produce psychosis. Especially with people who go on "runs" of two or three days of continual PCP ingestion, highly agitated and even violent behavior can occur. These people are often seen in hospital emergency rooms. One study found that 80 percent of the acute psychiatric admissions to one hospital in Los Angeles had detectable levels of PCP in their blood (Aniline et al., 1980). Law enforcement officials experience serious problems in subduing suspects who are using PCP because the suspects are often very difficult and dangerous to stop.

Another drug abused for its hallucinogenic properties is amyl nitrite or butyl nitrite, used medically to increase the blood flow for people suffering from acute angina pain. It causes slight euphoria and slows down time perception. Abuse of these substances, often called "poppers" on the street, first appeared among homosexuals who believed that it postponed sexual orgasm and increased sexual pleasure. Use then spread to other groups as young people learned of its hallucinogenic value. However, poppers do have negative side effects, including nausea, dizziness, faintness, and a drop in blood pressure.

A new drug, MDMA, has been described as the "LSD of the eighties." Users report that this substance offers the euphoric rush of cocaine and certain mind-expanding qualities of hallucinogens. MDMA, known as "ecstasy" on the street, can be easily manufactured from readily available chemicals. Substances like MDMA have been called the "designer drugs" because they can be manufactured fairly easily from readily available chemicals, and they are rarely detected in ordinary drug tests.

EXPLANATIONS OF DRUG ABUSE

The search for explanations of drug abuse has spanned many decades, and we have learned a great deal. One thing that has become quite clear is that drug abuse is a very complicated process. Many factors—biological, psychological, social, and cultural—contribute to the problem. There is no one source of the problem and no one quick fix that will solve it.

Biological Explanations

There is now impressive evidence to suggest that heredity influences the likelihood of some people becoming alcoholic (U.S. Department of Health and Human Services, 1983; Blum and Payne, 1991). People with an alcoholic parent are as much as six times more likely to become alcoholic themselves, even when raised apart from their biological parents in a nonalcoholic family. Although this heritability is found among men, it is not yet clear whether it applies to women.

The reasons for this susceptibility are still under debate (Schuckit, 1989). Alcoholics may develop a tolerance to alcohol more quickly, they may metabolize alcohol more quickly, or they may possess an inherited nutritional deficiency that is made up by alcohol. However, one very important point—especially when considering social policy relating to alcoholism—is that 60 to 65 percent of alcoholics do not exhibit this genetic link, and some alcoholics with the genetic link only became heavy drinkers under certain environmental conditions. As for biological mechanisms involved in addiction to drugs other than alcohol, there are a number of theories relating to tolerance, drug metabolism, and the like, but there is little evidence that such factors make some people more biologically susceptible to drug addiction (Milby, 1981).

Psychological Explanations

Psychological approaches to drug abuse posit that abuse arises from some psychological process or is the result of some emotional or personality disorder. Social learning or reinforcement theories, for example, argue that people will repeat those actions that provide them with some reward or pleasure (Ray, 1988). Drugs provide experiences that some people find pleasurable: euphoria, relaxation, ease of tension, even hallucinations might be enjoyable to some. So people who feel uncomfortable at parties, for example, may find that alcohol, marijuana, or a depressant relaxes them so that they can talk, dance, and enjoy themselves. Drug use may then become a habitual way they relax or enjoy themselves. Given the number of stressful and tense situations that most Americans face in their daily lives, it is not surprising that the reinforcing properties of alcohol and other drugs can have these effects.

Psychodynamic theories claim that drug abuse is a consequence of flaws or weaknesses in people's personalities (Collins and Marlatt, 1983; Light, 1986). It may be, for example, that alcoholics are exceedingly dependent personalities who experienced rejection by their parents during childhood and have a compulsive need for love. The excessive use of alcohol can serve as a means of relieving anxiety when those unrealistic needs are not met. Another psychodynamic approach claims that it is a need for power, not dependency, that underlies excessive alcohol use. While drinking, men can fantasize about how strong and

powerful they are and thus ignore feelings of weakness and inadequacy. Many studies have found that opiate addicts have very high rates of mental disorders, especially depression (Rounsaville et al., 1984).

Although personality and psychological processes are undoubtedly important in the lives of individuals, they are probably not sufficient, by themselves, to explain a deviant behavior such as drug abuse. For one thing, psychological factors by themselves would produce an abuse problem that is sporadic and intermittent. Yet the societal drug problem is continuous and persistent because there are many social and cultural factors contributing to it. In addition, psychological problems have social sources, often in family experiences, and these social factors should be the focus of social policy. Finally, research results on the psychology of addiction have been contradictory. Some addicts exhibit psychological maladjustment, whereas others do not.

Sociological Explanations

Sociological explanations of drug abuse focus on the role of culture, social structure, and social interaction in precipitating drug abuse. We will review the insights that the three sociological perspectives shed on this problem.

The Functionalist Perspective.   The functionalist approach focuses on the strains, inconsistencies, and contradictions in the social system that can lead to drug abuse. In Chapter 9, we discussed Robert Merton's anomie theory of deviance and crime that posits, in brief, that an inconsistency occurs when people are taught through the socialization process to pursue certain socially approved goals, such as success, but then are denied access to socially approved means of achieving those goals. Examples of people in anomic situations would be those who want to go to college but cannot afford it, a person whose business has failed, or a parent whose child has died. People can adapt to this anomie in many

POLICY ISSUES

The Political Economy of Drug Use in the United States

Two young lawyers in San Francisco lay out some lines of cocaine for their friends at a party while thousands of miles away a Bolivian peasant family, children and all, trudges along a dusty path into an isolated field. The two scenes seem worlds apart, but they are intimately linked through the political economy of the worldwide drug trade. The term *political economy* refers to the way in which politics and the exercise of power influence the production and distribution of economic resources. Bolivia exports $4 billion of cocaine each year—its biggest single export (Burke, 1991). For a poor country like Bolivia, that is big business. For many Bolivian peasants, their very survival depends on cultivating the drugs that feed the acquired illicit tastes of those American lawyers along with the many other Americans who use cocaine or smoke marijuana. Marijuana and cocaine produce more foreign exchange for Bolivia than do coffee and cut flowers, the country's two chief legal exports. At least five hundred thousand Bolivians depend on the coca trade for their livelihood. Illicit drugs worldwide may generate annual revenues of $500 billion. According to one expert on the worldwide drug trade, "In Peru and Bolivia the economic incentives virtually compel the peasant to sell [coca leaves] to traffickers or to convert them to coca paste for sale to traffickers. Prices paid to farmers vary with market conditions, of course, but coca yields a better return than any other crop" (Wisotsky, 1990: 41). The same could be said of many other countries that export illegal drugs to the United States.

All coca leaf and much marijuana is grown in Central and South American countries, primarily Belize, Bolivia, Colombia, Jamaica, Mexico, and Peru (U.S. Department of State, 1991a). In Asia, the major drug producers are Burma, Laos, Thailand, Pakistan, Iran, and Afghanistan. This is where most opium poppies are grown (see Figure 10.5). One goal of American drug enforcement policy is to reduce the overseas production of drugs and their importation into the United States (Reuter, 1985). In fact, by law, the president of the United States is required to cut off foreign aid to countries that do not make progress in reducing their drug crops. Colombia was praised by the government for its efforts to attack the drug traffic in 1984, whereas Bolivia was harshly condemned because it had not eradicated a single coca plant despite substantial assistance from the United States. This leaves the United States with the dilemma of whether to reduce economic assistance and other types of foreign aid to countries that do not cooperate. This is a controversial policy issue because a cut in foreign aid is considered a hostile move by countries with whom we are friendly and may disrupt other elements of our foreign policy. In addition, such cuts may exacerbate a major factor underlying the international drug trade: Poverty and economic underdevelopment make the growing and selling of drugs a way for some people to survive. A cut in aid may hinder efforts at improving the economies of these countries and thereby create more fertile ground for drug production.

ways, such as crime, resignation, or outrage. Merton labeled one mode of adaptation *retreatism:* the rejection of the culturally approved goals and the importance of achieving them through the cultur-

ally approved means. Retreatists "drop out" or try to escape, and for some, this means using drugs or alcohol in the search for solace and forgetfulness.

Why do these countries refuse to cooperate? Part of the reason is the difficulty of controlling the illicit growing of marijuana, coca, and opium poppies. Much of the cultivation takes place in isolated, hard-to-reach parts of these countries, and the law enforcement authorities are often not equal to the task. In addition, the criminals running the illegal drug traffic are powerful, sometimes more powerful than the government. In Bolivia and Burma, for example, wealthy and well-organized drug traffickers have actually taken control of the areas where drugs are produced, killing government officials or soldiers who enter without permission. In Colombia, many judges, politicians, police officers, and other government officials have died in drug-related assassinations. Often, the governments have been corrupted by bribes from drug traffickers or by direct participation of government officials in the traffic. The U.S. government estimates that Bolivian government officials made more than $1.5 billion each year in the early 1980s from narcotics traffic (Brinkley, 1984). Finally, the drug crops, although illegal, are often a significant source of economic support and foreign dollars. To successfully control the drug trade would be a severe economic blow to these countries. Only once, in Turkey in the early 1970s, was the United States effectively able to pressure a nation to reduce its drug production. But the Turkish farmers who grew opium poppies also grew other cash crops, and their livelihoods were therefore not threatened. They could shift their productive efforts to other crops with little disruption.

When we understand the extent to which the drug problem in America is linked with worldwide political and economic issues, the complexity of the problem becomes more clear. Lest we think that the political economy of drugs is primarily a foreign problem, estimates place marijuana as the largest cash crop in California, and 25 percent of the demand for marijuana in the United States is satisfied by marijuana grown in the United States (Kupfer, 1989). For some remote counties of northern California and rural Appalachia, growing marijuana is very lucrative for those willing to take the risk, and their profits help support other local businesses, such as small-town banks. If we look at legal drugs, the political economy of the drug problem becomes even more clear. Bars and liquor stores in the United States have an annual retail trade of over $32 billion dollars, whereas the sale of alcoholic beverages in the United States totals about $18 billion a year (U.S. Bureau of the Census, 1991: 770–772). In addition, the pharmaceutical industry benefits from the sale of stimulants, depressants, and other legal drugs. Although none of these industries encourages drug abuse, they nonetheless thrive from swamping America in drugs and from reducing any controls that might limit the extent of drug abuse. The tobacco industry, for example, fought against a ban on the advertising of cigarettes on television, but they lost. Currently, the liquor industry is opposing proposals for a similar ban against alcohol advertising. It is in their interest to encourage Americans, through extensive advertising, to use alcohol. People who sell beer, wine, and liquor spend $239 million a year on newspaper and magazine advertising and $428 million on television advertising.

So a key element of America's drug problem is the many sources—domestic and international, legal and illegal—that give Americans a host of opportunities to purchase and use drugs. Controlling the drug problem depends on our ability to reduce these sources of supply. Yet so many powerful interest groups benefit from policies that make it difficult to reduce the supply that there is some pessimism about how successful these efforts can be.

Functionalists also point to another inconsistency in our society: There is no clear normative consensus regarding which drugs are socially acceptable and which are not. Some American subcultures approve of the use of alcohol, others cocaine, and still others the hallucinogens. This lack of consensus regarding drugs opens the door for new drugs to find acceptance. When a new

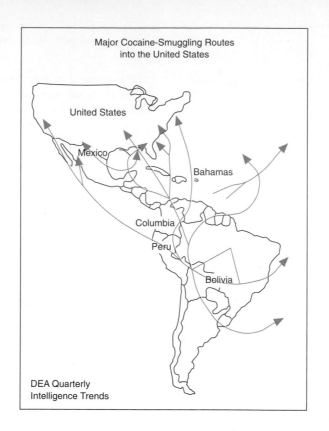

Major Cocaine-Smuggling Routes
into the United States

United States

Mexico

Bahamas

Columbia

Peru

Bolivia

DEA Quarterly
Intelligence Trends

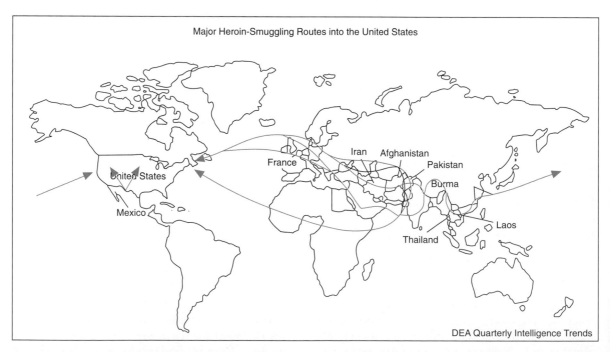

Major Heroin-Smuggling Routes into the United States

United States

Mexico

France

Iran Afghanistan

Pakistan

Burma

Thailand

Laos

DEA Quarterly Intelligence Trends

Figure 10.5   **Drug Smuggling Routes into the United States**

drug such as PCP or crack becomes available, it exists in a normative vacuum, with no norms prescribing or proscribing its use. Because other drugs are widely used, it is likely that some susceptible individuals will adopt the new drug as acceptable.

The Conflict Perspective.   The drug abuse problem is shaped in part by the exercise of social, political, and economic power. As we saw in Chapter 9, it is powerful groups in society that are in a position to define which crimes or which drugs will be sanctioned and made illegal. Over the years, powerful and respectable people have used alcohol, and it was not, until recently, even considered a "drug" to be linked with substances such as heroin and cocaine. In the 1980s and 1990s, the War on Drugs has not attacked alcohol but rather cocaine and heroin. In fact, drug enforcement authorities have been criticized for what appears to be a war against mostly young male African Americans and Hispanics. The vast majority of those arrested in the War on Drugs are black and Hispanic even though there are as many white drug users as black and Hispanic. This could be interpreted to mean that the authorities may be more interested in creating the appearance of fighting drugs by attacking drug use among poor and minorities while largely ignoring the much more considerable drug use, both legal and illegal, among more affluent and influential groups. In the past twenty years, marijuana has gained a more respectable status—and legal penalties for its use have been reduced in many jurisdictions—primarily because middle-class, college-educated people have taken up its use. So what is considered a dangerous drug whose use is to be sanctioned by society depends on which groups have most control over the political and legal apparatus. The assessments of the danger of drugs and stigma attached to them are often unrelated to the actual danger they represent. We have seen that some illegal and highly stigmatized drugs are actually fairly safe, whereas some clearly damaging drugs such as alcohol and barbiturates are legal and less stigmatized.

The conflict perspective points to another element of the drug abuse problem: Some groups benefit in economic and other ways from the consumption of drugs by Americans, and it is in their interests to make drugs available to Americans and to encourage their use. This issue is discussed in the Policy Issues insert in this chapter.

The Interactionist Perspective.   The interactionist approach is based on the premise that drug use and abuse arises from the social influences and pressures that can be found in particular contexts. Recall from Chapter 9 that cultural transmission theories view crime and drug abuse as learned behaviors that are transmitted through the socialization process of a particular culture or subculture. This learning occurs mainly in intimate groups, such as with family or friends, where people learn what drugs to use, where to buy them, how to use them, and even what the "high" from a particular drug is supposed to feel like. They also learn to value the use of particular drugs. A person being introduced to cocaine, for instance, might be told by experienced users that cocaine is good because it makes one more perceptive, creative, and energetic, whereas alcohol is a downer. In other words, drug subcultures are important in promoting and maintaining patterns of abuse. People must have the opportunity and encouragement to use drugs and the willingness to take the consequences. Sociologists Richard Cloward and Lloyd Ohlin (1960), for example, have argued that youngsters with close ties to conventional groups and little access to drugs will not respond to teenage adjustment problems by turning to drugs. Instead, they will find other outlets for their energies or anxieties. It is the youths without access to legitimate opportunities and with some entrance into a drug subculture who are in danger of developing a pattern of drug abuse. Even an "alcoholic personality" may be somewhat immune from becoming an alcoholic if he or she is involved in a subculture in which drinking is severely sanctioned (Trice, 1966; Miller, 1984).

This cultural transmission of values regarding drug use can be illustrated by comparing patterns of alcohol use among some ethnic groups in the United States. Some groups, such as Jews and Italians, incorporate alcohol into family activities in a closely regulated fashion. Alcohol is consumed in moderation as a part of family rituals such as meals or picnics. This teaches youngsters to value the moderate use of alcohol and to view alcohol consumption as appropriate only in particular social contexts. Among such groups, many people use alcohol, but rates of alcoholism are fairly low. Among the Irish, on the other hand, it is acceptable for males to drink outside of the family context, and drinking is viewed as an approved way of reducing frustrations or tensions.

FUTURE PROSPECTS

Drug abuse is a serious and complex problem for which there is no quick and easy solution. In fact, there probably are no solutions that will completely eradicate the problem from American society. Yet some things can be done to keep it under reasonable control and to mitigate some of its more serious consequences. These programs focus on either prevention or treatment. We will review the major efforts in both of these directions.

Prohibition: The War on Drugs and Alcohol

One of the major preventive efforts of current social policy toward drugs of abuse is the legal prohibition of their use. Most such drugs, with the exception of alcohol, are illegal (when not used for medical reasons) and carry criminal penalties for their use. Does prohibition work? Not by most assessments. The effort to prohibit the use of alcohol through the Eighteenth Amendment to the U.S. Constitution (ratified in 1920) was an abysmal failure. People continued to drink, and organized crime flourished by supplying the "bootleg" liquor. The amendment also produced a certain cynicism toward law and government, as

violations of the law were open and flagrant. The hypocrisy of the law was finally recognized by 1933 when the Eighteenth Amendment was repealed (Levine, 1983).

A similar experience has occurred over the past few decades as marijuana has become more popular. Although still illegal just about everywhere in the United States and carrying stiff prison terms in some jurisdictions, the use of marijuana flourishes. It is cheap, easy to obtain, and few people are punished for using it. There are lessons to be learned from our experience with alcohol and marijuana. When a practice is widespread, viewed as socially acceptable and even desirable by powerful groups, and brings economic gain to some interests, it is extremely difficult to eradicate through legislation. Laws will probably stop some people from using and abusing these drugs, and proponents of prohibition support it for this reason: They believe that it reduces the drug problem to below what it would be without such prohibition (Crowley, 1988).

In fact, the Reagan and Bush administrations' War on Drugs was carved into law in the Anti-Drug Abuse Act of 1988. More police and narcotics agents have been sent out to track down drug users, stiffer and mandatory prison sentences have been given to those convicted, and boats and planes have swarmed over the Caribbean and Central America to catch drug importers. Despite spending $12 billion per year, not much has changed (Bivins, 1992). Casual use is down, but the crack cocaine and heroin epidemics are still blighting parts of our cities, and our prisons are bursting at the seams with people doing time for drug offenses. There are probably as many hard-core addicts as before, and there are as many drugs being produced in, or shipped into, this country as before. Illegal drugs are as easy to get today as before the War on Drugs. In addition, experts who have studied the changing trends in drug use do not attribute the decline in drug use in the past decade to vigorous law enforcement (Jacobsen and Hanneman, 1992). Instead, the drop in use has probably been due to the decline in the social acceptance of drugs, which had an impact on the casual users but not the serious drug addicts. Yet, despite the doubts of experts regarding the effectiveness of prohibition to control drug use, this policy still attracts considerable public support.

Legalization

Opponents of prohibition point not only to its ineffectiveness but also to the fact that it infringes on the rights of people who use drugs without abusing them. As we have seen, many people use alcohol, marijuana, cocaine, LSD, and even narcotics in a limited and periodic fashion for recreational purposes. The effects of some currently illegal drugs, such as marijuana, are mild and cause little damage when used in moderation. So proponents of legalization argue that marijuana and possibly other drugs should be treated much like alcohol: as legal but highly controlled substances. In fact, although no state has fully legalized marijuana, at least eleven states have *decriminalized* its use, or made simple possession of it for one's own use either a misdemeanor or a noncriminal offense punishable by a fine.

Proponents of legalization also point to the problems created because of the illegality of some drugs—their high cost and the crime and violence associated with obtaining them. Legalization, they argue, is one way of alleviating these problems. Both with the prohibition of alcohol in the 1920s and with the illegal drugs today, powerful and violent crime syndicates emerged to supply these substances. Because of the enormous amount of money involved, such organized crime can also have a corrupting influence on law enforcement agencies and elected officials. This has happened in South America and in the United States, where some drug enforcement agents have been found guilty of drug trafficking. If drugs were legal, they could be supplied by legitimate corporations; crime syndicates would not move in and other problems created by the illegality of drugs would be reduced. It has also been suggested that legalizing marijuana, the mildest of

the illicit drugs, would have another advantage: It would help sever the connection of marijuana use with drug dealers. The first drug that young people use is typically either alcohol or marijuana. With marijuana illegal, the only place youngsters can obtain the substance is from drug dealers, who naturally would like to encourage young people to experiment with other more expensive, and more dangerous, drugs such as cocaine. If marijuana could be purchased legally, one fewer incentive for involvement with drug pushers would exist. The International Perspectives insert describes the experiences of some other societies that have legalized or decriminalized some drugs.

The closest the United States comes to legalizing drugs (other than alcohol) is the methadone maintenance program (Stephens, 1987). Methadone is a synthetic opiate that is prescribed for addicts who enroll in government-sponsored treatment programs. Methadone is itself highly addicting and leads to withdrawal, but its benefits over heroin are that the effects of methadone last longer (twenty-four hours as opposed to six hours for heroin) and people do not develop tolerance to methadone. What is called a "blocking dose" of methadone will block the euphoric effects of heroin, thus negating the motivation for continuing heroin use. The goal of the methadone maintenance program is to lower the dosage of methadone to a "maintenance" level at which withdrawal symptoms are prevented and there are few undesirable side effects. Methadone also does not induce much of a "high," so the person is sufficiently clear-headed and coherent to hold a job and lead a normal life. In addition, enrollees in maintenance programs are provided with various social services, including family counseling and job training, in an effort to attack the many elements of the drug abuse problem.

Methadone maintenance programs are highly controversial. Critics argue that they merely replace one addiction with another, which is true, and that many addicts return to heroin and other drugs (Jaffe, 1983). There is also a black market in methadone supplied in part by addicts in treat-

INTERNATIONAL PERSPECTIVES

Drug Use and Drug Policies in Other Societies

When we look at drug use and drug policies, we see many different approaches (Benjamin and Miller, 1991; Miller, 1991). Marijuana and hashish were banned in Arabia in the fourteenth century. China tried to ban the importation of opium from India in the eighteenth century, resulting in the Opium Wars. For a time, in the early twentieth century, alcohol was illegal in the United States, and many people were thrown in jail for using or trafficking in it. Today, Malaysia and Singapore deal harshly with people who violate their drug laws: Drug traffickers are hanged, and users are whipped and sent to hard labor camps for two years or more. The United States has had a "war on drugs" for at least the last decade. In most cases, these punitive approaches have not been very effective at stopping drug use: Alcohol was used widely during Prohibition in the United States, while the hangings continue unabated and the labor camps grow in size in Malaysia and Singapore today. Drugs have a strong attraction, especially for those in desperate social circumstances, and banning their use hasn't worked very well.

Other societies have tried a different approach—that of decriminalizing or legalizing drugs.

The Netherlands decriminalized drugs in 1976. Drug users and small-time dealers are not prosecuted, whereas large drug dealers and those who sell to minors are. Drug use in the Netherlands since then has not increased and may have declined somewhat. The consumption of marijuana and hashish, for example, declined after decriminalization. With marijuana and hashish widely available in Dutch cities, consumption of more serious drugs such as heroin has also declined. The Netherlands has fewer hard drug addicts than other Western European countries, far less of a drug problem, and a significantly lower death rate due to drug overdose than does the United States. There is also a very low incidence of AIDS among intravenous drug users. The Netherlands treats drug addiction as a health problem rather than a criminal one, and this creates a climate in which addicts can be open about their drug use and seek treatment for both their health and addiction problems.

Great Britain has experimented with policies to make drugs legally available, but in a somewhat different way from The Netherlands. Throughout the 1960s, physicians in Britain could prescribe opiates and cocaine for their patients if they

ment who sell rather than take their methadone, and some methadone addicts get high by taking nonopiates, such as cocaine, whose effects are not blocked by methadone (McDonnell, Irwin, and Rosenbaum, 1990). Supporters argue that the program does help some addicts, although many of the programs are not run very well (U.S. General Accounting Office, 1990). Many addicts in methadone programs are free of any addiction, including methadone, after two years and are much less likely to be arrested and more likely to hold a

job. Other studies show that addicts in maintenance programs use less heroin and other drugs and they have much lower death rates than those not enrolled in such programs (Des Jarlais, 1984; Dole, 1991; Yancovitz et al., 1991).

Primary Prevention

As used by drug abuse specialists, the term **primary prevention** refers to *preventing drug problems before they begin*. The government has

needed them, even if the need was to prevent the physical or mental symptoms that the person would suffer if the drug were withdrawn. In other words, physicians could prescribe drugs to maintain an addiction, although they had to be convinced that maintaining the addiction was in the patient's best interest, possibly because there was little chance of successfully kicking the habit. There was still a black market in drugs in Great Britain because some addicts could not get a physician's prescription while others sought higher dosages than the government would permit.

By the end of the 1960s, Britain had begun its own "war on drugs" in response to an increase in the illegal use of stimulants, sedatives, and hallucinogens. Greater limitations were placed on physicians' ability to prescribe heroin and cocaine. Physicians could still prescribe these drugs to nonaddicts and to addicts in limited circumstances, but special licenses were needed to prescribe addiction maintenance doses to addicts, and the licenses were given only to practitioners in drug abuse clinics. In other words, since the 1960s, legal drugs have become less available to British addicts, and official government policy is that addicts are to be weaned off drugs as quickly as possible.

Since tightening up the drug laws, addiction rates have risen substantially in Great Britain. However, this is probably not due to the change in policy but to changing social conditions. Britain experienced worsening social conditions for lower income groups during the 1970s and 1980s, with declining economic productivity and fewer resources going into education, job training, child care, housing, and health care programs. The culprit in the rise in drug use has probably been the despair and alienation that haunt people, especially youth, when confronted with a bleak social landscape with few opportunities for advancement. Drugs seem to be a common refuge when other problems—poverty, racism, family dissolution—become more severe.

These less punitive approaches seem to work reasonably well for countries like The Netherlands and Great Britain. They have far fewer narcotics addicts than we do, and crime, death, and health problems associated with the use of narcotics are lower there than in the United States (Clinard and Meier, 1989). Would such policies work in the United States? They might have some benefits, especially in terms of lowering the very high crime rate linked with heroin and cocaine use. Experience in these and other countries does suggest that decriminalization or legalization of illegal drugs could produce a modest increase in drug use, but not a lot, and most of the increase would be among people who tend to use drugs whether they are illegal or not (Miller, 1991). However, such policies would be no panacea: They would by no means eliminate, and possibly not even reduce, drug abuse. But the harsh, punitive approach currently applied in the United States hasn't been notably successful either. Decriminalization or legalization has the benefit of enabling us to approach the problem as a health problem, using medical and social service personnel, and freeing police to focus on crimes that are more of a threat to the public order.

established a three-front drug war focusing on primary prevention. One effort is to use educational programs to alert people to the dangers of drugs and instill responsible attitudes toward drug use. The second front is to interdict the drug traffic now flowing across our borders from overseas, and the third is to reduce production of drug crops by other nations.

Most experts agree that the best way to attack the drug problem is to reduce the demand for drugs (Wilson, 1990). Educational programs try to do this by teaching youth that drugs are risky and dangerous and by providing tips for how to resist the temptation of drugs. Youngsters who go through comprehensive drug education and prevention programs do use less drugs than those who do not go through such programs ("Community Drug Prevention . . . ," 1990). These comprehensive programs use the schools to teach kids how to resist pressures to use drugs, the parents to communicate more with kids and set family rules about drug and alcohol use, and community agencies such as the police to support antidrug programs. In fact, the decline in the use of marijuana and cocaine among youth in the past decade seems to be due to these educational efforts: Youth have come to view drugs as more risky and dangerous than in the past, and there is more social disapproval of drug use now (Bachman, Johnston, and O'Malley, 1990). However, the effectiveness of the vast antidrug media campaigns of the past decade is largely unknown. Although few evaluations have been done, most experts suggest that adolescents, the main targets of the efforts, are probably modestly influenced, at best, by such campaigns (Schilling and McAlister, 1990).

Border interdiction of drugs focuses on reducing the supply of drugs, and the results here have been meager. The most optimistic estimates are that only one-quarter of the cocaine smuggled into the United States is seized (Wisotsky, 1990). President Bush adopted a "get-tough" policy toward drug smuggling by beefing up the personnel available for interdiction activities and increasing the penalties for smuggling. A policy of "zero tolerance" was established, under which boat owners found with even small amounts of illegal drugs would have their equipment confiscated. Bush also appointed a "drug czar" to coordinate federal activities: the chief of the White House Office of National Drug Control Policy, a position created by the Anti-Drug Abuse Act of 1988. All of this produced a great deal of publicity, but it is not clear at this point whether it will significantly reduce the flow of drugs into the United States. The illegal drug trade is so lucrative that people are willing to risk substantial punishments, and profits can be made even when 50 to 90 percent of a smuggler's drugs are confiscated. Controlling drug production overseas is discussed in the Policy Issues insert.

Rehabilitation and Therapeutic Communities

Many drug abusers can be rehabilitated if they are given proper treatment, such as counseling, meth-

These customs agents seized a huge load of cocaine from this vessel off Key West, Florida. Despite these efforts, interdiction programs have stopped only a small portion of the drugs flowing into the United States from other countries.

adone maintenance, or job training. Among adolescents at high risk of abusing drugs, school-based social support programs have proven that they can reduce the likelihood of future involvement in drugs (Eggert and Herting, 1991). By enhancing communication, empathy, and helping between students and teachers, these programs offer students an alternative to drugs. Most experts agree that making drug treatment programs available to all who desire them would be an important step toward significantly reducing the drug problem (Goldstein and Kalant, 1990). However, all these rehabilitation programs cost money, and much of the funds for the War on Drugs has been channeled into law enforcement and drug interdiction, leaving relatively little for rehabilitation.

One of the more widespread types of treatment programs for drug addicts is the therapeutic community in which group involvement, social support, and group pressure are used to help addicts quit taking drugs (Stephens, 1987; De Leon, 1988). These programs are often run by addicts who are drug free. One of the best known therapeutic communities is Alcoholics Anonymous (AA), which was established by two alcoholics in 1935 to help them quit drinking (Robinson, 1983). AA has more than a half million members. The first step in the AA program is for people to admit publicly that they are alcoholics, helpless before alcohol, and need help from others. AA is organized and run by volunteers and costs nothing. Meetings are open to anyone, drunk or sober, and even in small towns there are meetings held practically every day. At these meetings, people talk about their problems, what alcohol has done to them, and their fears of returning to drink. Others provide emotional support and encouragement and help members deal with their problems. There are also groups for the spouses of alcoholics (Al-Anon) and the children of alcoholics (Alateen).

There are also therapeutic communities for abusers of drugs other than alcohol. Narcotics Anonymous is very similar to AA but focuses on narcotics addicts. The Odyssey House, Synanon, Phoenix House, and Daytop Village are therapeutic communities that provide housing, counseling, and work for people who are trying to shake the drug habit (Milby, 1981; Densen-Gerber, 1984). Many of these programs depart from the AA approach in that people must sever ties with former associates and live for a time in the community itself. This regulation is based on the assumption that these former associations may have contributed to the person's drug problem, and it also gives the community considerable control over its members. Acceptance by peers is a prime force in these communities. They offer strong emotional support, but some have been accused of being highly authoritarian, demanding complete conformity to the rules of the group. Some such programs have been criticized for using rather harsh forms of group pressure—such as verbal challenges, public humiliation, and reprimands—with those considered to be irresponsible or faltering in their resolve to stay off drugs.

Research on the effectiveness of therapeutic communities is difficult to conduct because of problems in finding representative samples of members and of nonmember addicts to compare them with. The evidence that is available, however, clearly suggests that these programs work for many. Although relapse (a return to the use of drugs) is common, many members successfully refrain from using alcohol and other drugs for long periods. Those people with the best likelihood of success are older addicts who are married, have a job, and have a history of relatively few delinquent or criminal acts. However, therapeutic communities are completely ineffective with the millions of addicts who do not believe they have a problem with drugs.

Behavior Modification

The social learning theory of drug abuse says that people become addicted because drugs provide them with personal pleasure or rewards. One therapeutic approach suggests that addicts might be weaned from drugs by making drug-taking unpleasant. This is known to drug abuse professionals as behavior modification. One form of this technique, used to treat alcoholism, is aversion therapy, in which the act of drinking alcohol is associated with some unpleasant experience. In some cases, a drug called Antabuse is used because it induces nausea and vomiting if the person taking it drinks any alcohol. A more controversial form of aversion therapy uses electrical shocks administered to a person each time they take a drink of alcohol. The theory behind these treatments is that associating alcohol consumption with a painful or unpleasant experience will eventually lead the person to perceive alcohol consumption itself as undesirable. Aversion therapy is of limited utility because it depends on the cooperation of the alcoholic, but it has been helpful for some addicts who have not had success with other approaches.

Social Policy and Public Pressure

A few decades ago, the problem of alcoholism was shrouded by guilt and shame. Many alcoholics were unwilling to admit that they had a problem, and their families and friends were so embarrassed that they covered for the alcoholic when he or she got into trouble. Public sentiment has changed considerably. Alcoholism is now viewed as a medical problem that can be treated with tested methods. In 1970, the Comprehensive Alcohol Abuse and Alcoholism Prevention, Treatment and Rehabilitation Act was passed by the Nixon administration. The act established the National Institute on Alcohol Abuse and Alcoholism to serve as a center for research into the causes of and cures for alcoholism. The act also established the National Advisory Council on Alcohol Abuse and Alcoholism to recommend social policy directions on the problem. This government support, along with additional funding from private sources, has helped in the development of an extensive network of support services dealing with problems of drug abuse. Today, considerably less stigma is attached to the problem, and there are many places to seek help. Employers have pitched in with employee assistance programs (EAPs) that offer confidential help for employees with drug or alcohol problems. Employers have found that they benefit by rehabilitating, rather than terminating, a trained and experienced employee (Feit and Holosko, 1988).

There has also been considerable public pressure to do something about the public dangers created by some forms of drug usage, such as those who drink alcohol and drive. Groups such as Mothers Against Drunk Driving (MADD) and Students Against Drunk Driving (SADD) have lobbied effectively at both the state and the national level for laws that have an impact on the problem. In response, states have raised the drinking age to twenty-one, and some have even outlawed such things as "two-for-one" happy-hour specials. Bartenders can now be held legally responsible if they serve liquor to someone who is drunk and the person gets into a traffic accident. State courts have even ruled that the host of a party is responsible for the behavior of a guest if the host serves the guest enough alcohol to get drunk (Mincer, 1985). In short, the courts, the legislatures, and the public are taking an increasingly tough posture toward some drug problems, such as drunk driving.

Still another hotly contested social policy issue that has involved much public pressure is drug testing. The Drug-Free Workplace Act of 1988 requires companies with federal contracts to make an effort to maintain a drug-free workplace (Noble, 1992b). Many companies have responded by doing urine testing for illegal drugs among their employees. According to government officials, drug and alcohol abuse costs industry up to $60 billion each year in lost productivity and high rates of absenteeism, medical claims, on-the-job mishaps, and employee theft. Drug testing in the workplace, it is claimed, would help locate those with substance abuse problems and offer them assistance. The American Civil Liberties Union (ACLU) and other opponents of routine drug testing, on the other hand, maintain that drug testing violates rights of privacy and the Constitution's prohibition against unreasonable search and seizure. Furthermore, the ACLU questions the accuracy, validity, and reliability of such tests. In addition, the testing detects relatively few drug users, and most of those are occasional marijuana users who are probably not bad workers and no threat on the job. Drug testing is likely to remain a hotly debated issue over the next few years.

Linkages

The drug epidemic has ravaged parts of our cities with unacceptably high rates of crime (Chapter 12) and helped spread diseases such as AIDS through the sharing of dirty needles (Chapter 4).

Drug addiction has also destabilized many families (Chapter 3), especially when poor mothers become addicted to crack cocaine.

Summary

1. The use of drugs in one form or another is widespread in human societies. Opinions about drug use vary widely, with some groups arguing for a complete ban on all drugs and others opting for the freedom to use drugs as people see fit. Drug use by itself is not a social problem; drug abuse refers to the continued use of psychoactive substances at a level violating approved social practices. Drug abuse is costly in our society in terms of accidents; crime; and family, work, and health problems.

2. Americans consume many different kinds of drugs; some are legal, whereas others are illegal. A legal drug, alcohol, is regarded as America's most severe drug problem when it is used to excess. The level of marijuana use in our society is far lower than that of alcohol. Debate continues regarding how damaging marijuana really is to society. Stimulants refer to the many drugs that stimulate the central nervous system, including cocaine and amphetamines. Depressants, most notably the barbiturates and tranquilizers, have the opposite effect, depressing the central nervous system, and have some painkilling properties. Narcotics are drugs whose main use is as analgesics or painkillers. Hallucinogens or psychedelics are drugs that produce hallucinations, often of a visual nature.

3. There are different explanations of drug abuse. Biological explanations suggest that hereditary factors may be involved in people's proneness to addiction to various drugs. Psychological approaches to drug abuse posit that abuse arises from some psychological process or is the result of some emotional or personality disorder. Sociological explanations focus on the role of culture, social structure, and social interaction in precipitating drug abuse.

4. Drug abuse is a serious and complex problem for which there is no quick and easy solution. Most programs involving such solutions focus on either prevention or treatment. One major preventive effort of current social policy toward drugs of abuse is legal prohibition. Opponents of this approach favor legalization, including such alternative drug treatment programs as methadone maintenance. Another strategy is primary prevention, which refers to preventing drug problems before they begin. One of the more widespread types of treatment programs for drug addicts is the therapeutic community. Another approach involves behavior modification in the form of aversion therapy. Social policy and public pressure are also important in the future prospects on drug abuse. Groups such as Mothers Against Drunk Driving (MADD) and Students Against Drunk Driving (SADD) are current examples.

Important Terms for Review

alcoholism	depressants	hallucinogens	psychedelics
cross-dependence	drug	narcotics	psychoactive drugs
cross-tolerance	drug abuse	opiates	stimulants
dependence	drug addiction	primary prevention	tolerance

Discussion Questions

1. Divide the class into groups based on some socially relevant characteristics, such as sex, age, race, ethnicity, or subcultural membership. Have each group describe which drugs and which type of drug use are socially acceptable in the group.

2. A major controversy in the substance abuse field is which drugs should be legally available for psychoactive (as opposed to medical) uses. Have one group of students argue for the position that no such drugs should be legally available and a second group support the position that some drugs (specifying which ones) should be legal. After the debate, have the class vote for which drugs should be legalized.

3. Have the students locate the people on your college campus (health center nurses, campus police officers, or diversion and treatment program coordinators) who have firsthand experience with drug and alcohol problems among the students. Invite them in to discuss the problems and use this as a context in which to debate the extent of the problems on your campus and what might be done about it.

4. Ask students in the class to recount their own or their friends' experiences with drugs and alcohol, both good and bad. Use this discussion to debate what constitutes "responsible" use of various drugs.

5. Drug testing has become widespread but remains controversial. Organize a debate around the issue of how extensive such drug testing should be. Should it cover all people who work? Only those in sensitive or responsible jobs? Should we test all college students or only those receiving federal student loans? As a part of this debate, invite into class someone in your university or a nearby corporation who has responsibility for ensuring a drug-free environment in his or her place of work.

For Further Reading

Linda A. Bennett and Genevieve M. Ames, eds. *The American Experience with Alcohol: Contrasting Cultural Perspectives.* New York: Plenum Press, 1985. In this lively collection of articles, anthropologists, sociologists, psychiatrists, folklorists, public health experts, and social workers examine the ways in which cultural factors influence attitudes toward and responses to alcohol use and abuse.

Joseph Gusfield. *Symbolic Crusade: Status Politics and the American Temperance Movement.* Urbana: University of Illinois Press, 1963. An excellent history of the drive to prohibit alcohol in the late 1800s. It shows how opposition to a drug may be in part a pretext for the playing out of other political and social struggles.

John Helmer. *Drugs and Minority Oppression.* New York: Seabury Press, 1975. An assessment of how the widespread availability of drugs can inhibit the poor and oppressed from improving their lot in life or becoming politically active. A good adjunct reading to the analysis in Chapters 5 and 6.

Abbie Hoffman. *Steal This Urine Test: Fighting Drug Hysteria in America.* New York: Penguin, 1987. This is a refreshing view of the hysteria surrounding the drug problem and the dangers the hysteria creates: threats to people's jobs, their constitutional rights, and their freedoms. Ironically, Hoffman died of a drug overdose in 1989.

Alfred R. Lindesmith. *Addiction and Opiates.* Chicago: Aldine, 1968. A good review and appraisal of the various sociological and psychological explanations of drug addiction. It goes considerably beyond what is presented in this chapter.

Milton A. Maxwell. *The Alcoholics Anonymous Experience.* New York: McGraw Hill, 1984. Based on interviews and observations, this book covers all phases of a recovering alcoholic's career. An excellent "close up" for professionals and lay people who are unfamiliar with how AA works.

John J. Rumbarger. *Profits, Power, and Prohibition: Alcohol Reform and the Industrializing of America, 1800–1930.* Albany: State University of New York Press, 1988. This is a provocative historical work whose thesis is that the effort to make alcohol illegal during the 1800s and early 1900s was in part an effort by capitalists to maintain an efficient and productive work force for an industrializing American economy. Are there parallels with the furor over drugs today?

Peter Dale Scott and Jonathan Marshall. *Cocaine Politics: Drugs, Armies, and the CIA in Central America.* Berkeley: University of California Press, 1991. The very controversial thesis of this book is that the War on Drugs is a sham and that the United States encourages the world drug trade as long as it advances our political goals abroad—a new wrinkle on the political economy of the drug trade.

Larry Sloman. *Reefer Madness: The History of Marijuana in America.* New York: Grove Press, 1983. A good history to illustrate the changing laws regarding and attitudes toward marijuana over our history. It shows how the status of a drug in society is often unrelated to its objective dangers or damages.

Andrew Weil. *The Natural Mind: An Investigation of Drugs and the Higher Consciousness.* Rev. Ed. Boston: Houghton Mifflin, 1986. A fascinating book positing that people are born with a need to experiment with different types of consciousness. Using drugs is one way, although not necessarily the preferred way, of doing this. This source provides a very different view of the drug problem.

Terry Williams. *The Cocaine Kids: The Inside Story of a Teenage Drug Ring.* Reading, Mass.: Addison-Wesley, 1989. Sociologist Williams spent a great deal of time over a five-year period with a group of teenage drug dealers in New York's Spanish Harlem. He provides a fascinating picture of the drug trade and offers some startling revelations, such as the extent to which these drug dealers maintain a deep belief in the American dream of hard work and success.

Weldon L. Witters, Peter J. Venturelli, and Glen R. Hanson. *Drugs and Society,* 3d ed. Boston: Jones and Bartlett, 1992. A comprehensive overview of both licit and illicit drugs, the history of their use, the problems they create, and what can be done to prevent and treat drug abuse.

Franklin E. Zimring and Gordon Hawkins. *The Search for Rational Drug Control.* Cambridge, Mass.: Cambridge University Press, 1992. This book contains a very thoughtful and thought-provoking critique of our current drug control policies. It serves as a useful model for the careful analysis of the ideological foundations of social policy and the development of policies.

Norman E. Zinberg. *Drug, Set, and Setting: The Basis for Controlled Intoxicant Use.* New Haven, Conn.: Yale University Press, 1984. The author argues that opiates can be used in a controlled way, with physical dependence, and that such a policy might be beneficial to society. He makes a parallel with the many moderate users of alcohol and hallucinogens.

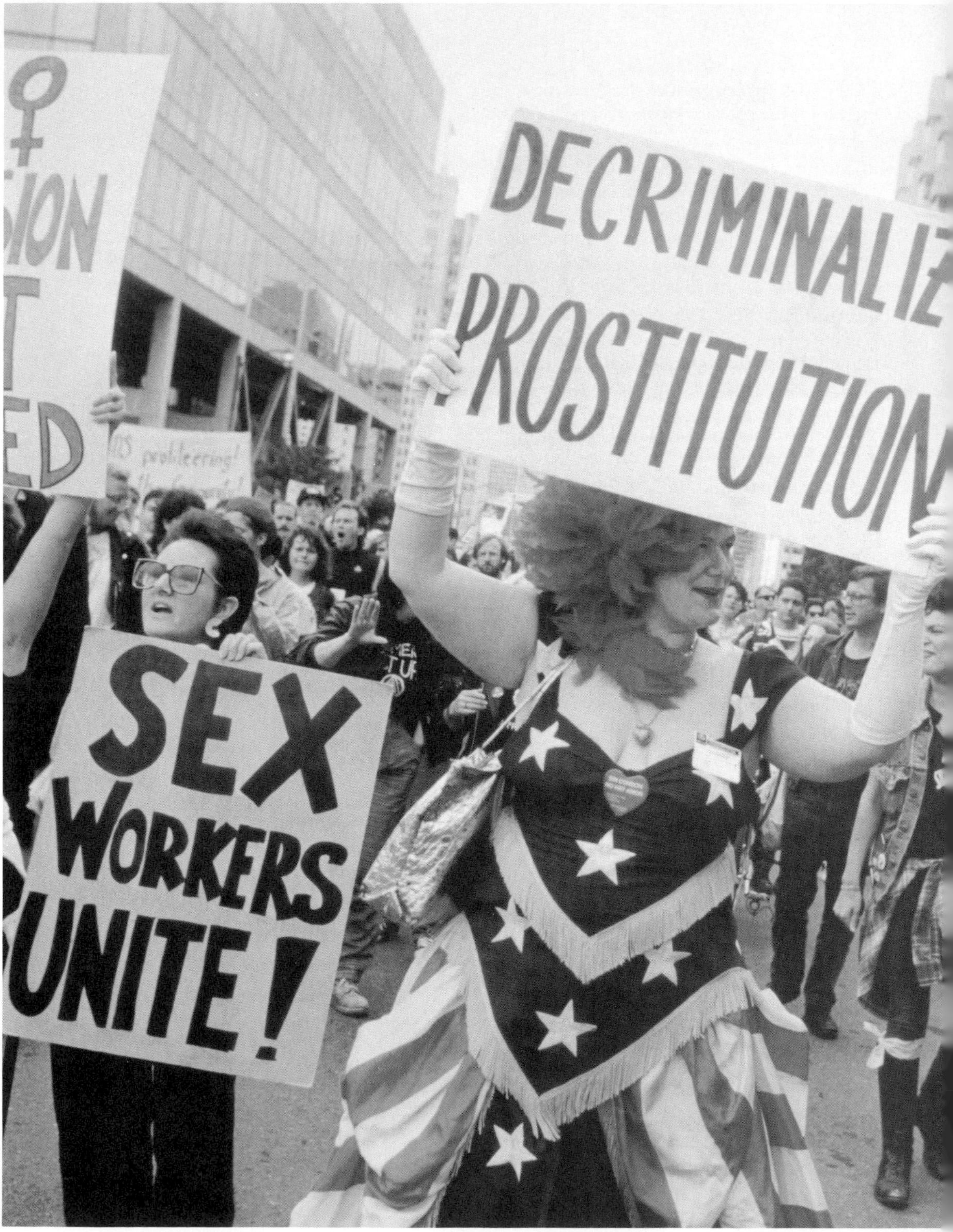
DECRIMINALIZ
PROSTITUTION
SEX
WORKERS
UNITE!

CHAPTER 11
Sexual Variance

The varieties of human sexual expression are almost endless, and most of them have been condemned, at one time or another, as deviant.

> *Sex in general, and any and all of its myriad incarnations, can mean almost anything, depending on the place it has in the fabric of a civilization, how it is translated into action, what emotional connotations surround it in everyday life. . . . [This] brings us to a very basic question—what's normal?—as well as to another, its mirror image: what's abnormal? (Goode and Troiden, 1974: 16)*

One might be tempted to answer these questions by saying that what is abnormal is "kinky" sex. But this can be notoriously difficult to define in any clear-cut fashion. One sociological effort defines it thus:

> *Kinky sex is an extremely broad banner under which are gathered activities ranging from mildly unusual, eccentric practices occasionally participated in by otherwise conventional people to spice up their otherwise conventional sex lives to bizarre fetishes and fixations practiced by a very small number of people who cannot become stimulated in any other way. (Goode and Troiden, 1974: 2)*

So, some people would call the following sexual practices unusual: fetishism (using nonliving objects to achieve sexual excitement), voyeurism (being aroused by watching others undress or engage in sex), or masochism (gaining arousal by being humiliated, bound, or beaten). But is all

Myths and Facts About Sexual Variance

Myth: During the 1980s and 1990s, gay men and lesbians have found much wider acceptance in American society than in previous decades.

Fact: Although there have been improvements, much negative sentiment toward gays still exists. Almost one-half of adult Americans still believe that sexual contact between people of the same gender should be illegal, and some communities have been rescinding statutes that ban discrimination in jobs and housing because of sexual orientation.

Myth: Prostitutes are nymphomaniacs and have an insatiable desire for sexual intercourse with numerous men.

Fact: Prostitutes are no more highly sexed or promiscuous than are nonprostitutes. Most prostitutes view their contacts with their clients in the same way that other business people do—as an impersonal economic exchange—but at the same time they may enjoy sex with their husbands or male friends.

Myth: Researchers often report that many prostitutes are lesbians, thus supporting the conclusion that lesbianism leads to prostitution.

Fact: In the first place, the incidence of lesbianism among prostitutes may be exaggerated, as some investigations have suggested that the majority of prostitutes (61 percent in one survey) have had no homosexual experience whatsoever

(Gebhard et al., 1965). Furthermore, the causal ordering may frequently be the other way around: "The character of their work experience could easily cause prostitutes to despair of ever achieving sexual mutuality and intimacy with a man" (Schur, 1988).

Myth: Pornographic materials that portray people in highly erotic and sexually explicit settings are dangerous to society because they lead to other social problems such as rape and other forms of sexual violence against women.

Fact: The latest research suggests that exposure to sexually explicit or arousing materials that have no aggressive content do not seem to produce negative effects. It is the aggressive content of some pornography that may lead some people to view violence against women as acceptable or desirable.

Myth: Pornography tends to be popular in communities where there is much hostility toward women and where women are discriminated against in occupational and other arenas.

Fact: Actually, research shows the reverse: Communities with high levels of gender equality have higher circulation rates for pornography than do communities with lower amounts of gender equality (Baron, 1990). This is probably because both pornography and gender equality flourish in politically tolerant communities.

---

this sexual variety bad? We have seen in Chapters 1 and 9 that deviance is not a characteristic of a behavior but rather involves judgments about a behavior by some individual or group. Not too long ago, many Americans might have classified many of these sexual variations as immoral and, if they were to become extensively practiced, social problems (D'Emilio and Freedman, 1988). This was very much an absolutist assessment on their part: Some forms of sex are conventional and acceptable, and all others are depraved. For people

who take this position, legislative and other steps should be taken to limit and control the problematic forms of sexual expression before they cause damage to society.

The view taken in this chapter is that, as long as no one is victimized, no form of sexuality is inherently bad, and that social problems arise because of the way dominant groups treat sexual minorities. From this point of view, it is the societal reaction to sexual variance that is the social problem. The social problem is the repression of free choice that occurs when those who choose less-than-conventional forms of sexual expression become victims of the rigid morality of the powerful.

In this chapter, we focus on three variant forms of sexual expression: homosexuality, prostitution, and pornography. Our focus is not on the sexual behaviors themselves but rather on the fact that conflict, discrimination, oppression, and inequity are often associated with them. So the social problem is not the sexual outlet that people choose but rather whether people are treated unfairly or repressively because of it.

There is general consensus that some sexual acts, such as sexual assault and the sexual abuse of children, do constitute social problems and are threatening to society. We have covered these topics when discussing crime (Chapter 9) and the exploitation of children (Chapter 8). Many other forms of sexual variance, such as fetishism and masochism, are highly individualized and sporadic. Because of this, there is little discussion of them as social problems. Some people may have moral objections to them, but there is little reason to believe that they constitute a problem for society. To be sure, some groups have moral objections to homosexuality, prostitution, and pornography, and they would like to see them banned for that reason. But our focus is on the *social* problem: the societal reaction to certain sexual life-styles and outlets. The issue is not the sexual expression itself but the fact that conflict arises around it and has negative consequences: Violence is perpetrated against gays or women are forced by circumstances into prostitution. From a sociological perspective, moral objections become important issues because they can fuel the reactions that lead to the negative consequences. So this chapter is really not about sex per se but about how sexual expression becomes a context or excuse for discrimination and oppression. It is also about whether some of these forms of sexual variance can be used by dominant groups in ways that create demonstrable problems for those with less power. Can, for example, the widespread availability of pornography increase the amount of sexual violence against women? We will first discuss sexual variance in general and then focus on issues having to do with homosexuality, prostitution, and pornography separately.

VARIETY IN HUMAN SEXUALITY

At the core of this chapter is society's reaction to the enormous variety in human sexual expression found throughout the world. To gain some perspective on American sexual variety, it is useful to see what kind of sexuality is found in other cultures.

A Cross-Cultural View

Many people believe that there is a "natural" or "instinctive" expression of sexuality that people are aware of largely or completely without learning. Reflecting this belief, some people refer to variant sexual acts as "violations of nature." So for many Americans, "natural" sex is sex between men and women who are married. Some would even extend this "naturalness" to the sexual position assumed: genital contact in the "missionary" position (face to face with the male on top). Yet studies of other cultures indicate that socially acceptable sex takes far more forms than this. Consider one such culture:

> *Sex—sex for pleasure and sex for procreation—is a principal concern of the Polynesian people on tiny Mangaia, the southernmost of the Cook Islands near the geographical center of Polynesia in the South Pacific. . . . They demonstrate that concern in the startling number of children born to unmarried parents, and in the statistics on frequency of orgasm and numbers of sexual partners. But that concern is simple fact-of-life—not morbid preoccupation. . . . There is great directness about sex, but the approach to sex is correspondingly indirect. Among the young, there is no*

dating, no tentative necking in the American sense. A flick of the eye, a raised eyebrow in a crowd, can lead to copulation—without a word. There is no social contact between the sexes, no rendezvous that does not lead directly to coitus—copulation is the only imaginable outcome of heterosexual contact. The sexual intimacy of copulation precedes personal affection. . . . Folk tales feature explicitly detailed accounts of sexual acts and sexual organs. . . . Yet there is a unique modesty about exposure of adult sexual organs. Mangaians are horrified at the casualness with which a European exposes his penis to other men when he urinates. (Marshall, 1974: 26–27)

So Mangaians have what Americans would call an extremely permissive attitude toward sexual behavior. Although sexual intercourse among unmarried persons is accepted by many Americans, multiple partners and casual sex tend to be frowned upon, especially for women. If there is a natural or instinctive form of sexual expression, what are we to make of the Mangaians? Consider some examples from other cultures. In Tahiti, young people were encouraged to masturbate (Bullough, 1976; Davenport, 1977). In the Truk Islands of the Pacific, sexual gratification is associated with pain and frustration, and sexual foreplay involves lovers inflicting pain on each other. Among most human groups, the female breasts are considered erotic organs, but this is not universal. Among the Mangaians mentioned above, the breasts are not involved in foreplay and sexual arousal. Kissing is also a part of sexual expression in most human societies, but there are people among whom sexual intercourse occurs completely without kissing. The Siriono of Bolivia even find kissing to be a disgusting act. Homosexuality, prostitution, and pornography—the forms of sexual variance we will discuss in this chapter—are also highly variable. In some societies, homosexuality is socially accepted, whereas in others it is despised (Greenberg, 1988). In some societies, prostitution is considered an accepted sexual outlet, in others it is banned. What many

Americans would consider pornographic—such as explicit portrayals of sexual intercourse—are considered public art and even religious symbols in some societies.

From this review of sexuality in other cultures, we can see that sexual norms are similar to all other societal rules: They are learned from others through social interaction. The Mangaians learn things about sexual behavior that are very different from what most Americans learn. Through the socialization process, people learn what is acceptable sexuality in their group or culture. There is nothing "instinctive" about it beyond a general, undirected biological drive. Who to have sex with, when, and in what fashion—these are all behaviors that people learn. If these responses were instinctive, we would not see the variation that occurs from one culture to another. Consequently, what constitutes sexual variance in different societies depends less on the act itself and more on how that action fits with societal values and norms. This is not to suggest that one should adopt an "anything goes" attitude toward sex. Sex is part of culture, and it must be integrated with other cultural practices such as the form of the family and child-rearing needs. At the same time, we can recognize the flexible nature of human sexual expression. In a diverse society such as ours, this can create a tension between the sexual practices of one group and those of another group. This situation creates the possibility that variant forms of sexuality might be viewed by some as social problems and may produce conflict that exacerbates other social problems.

Sexual Standards and Variety in America

There is variety in human sexuality, not only between cultures or societies, but also from group to group and from time to time within the same culture or society. For example, consider how the media—particularly the motion picture industry—is freer today than in the past to portray sexual themes and imagery. Expressions of shock and concern rumbled through America when Rhett

Butler kissed Scarlett O'Hara passionately in *Gone With the Wind* (1939) and later in the film remarked, "Frankly, my dear, I don't give a damn." During the early 1960s, when Johnny Carson "slipped" and said "Hell" on the *Tonight Show,* NBC "bleeped" it out. Certainly much has changed over the past four decades, including the repeal of different "bans" on various sex-related prohibitions, such as the explicit portrayal of premarital sexual relationships and homosexuality and leave-nothing-to-the-imagination images of the naked human body in such magazines as *Penthouse, Oui,* and *Hustler.* However, we may not be approaching the permissiveness of the Mangaians because many repressive attitudes are still found in our culture. For example, adultery, fornication, and cohabitation are still illegal in some states. In 1981, a bill to legalize most sexual acts between consenting adults in Washington, D.C., was killed by Congress. This left intact existing city laws that make illegal all sexual relations except those between married partners in a face-to-face position ("House Kills . . . ," 1981). Prostitution, oral-genital intercourse, and anal intercourse are illegal in most states. One-half of the fifty states still outlaw homosexual conduct between consenting adults, and in 1986 the U.S. Supreme Court ruled that it was constitutional for states to outlaw such conduct. Furthermore, in 1986, the Attorney General's Commission on Pornography reported that there is a need for more regulation of pornographic materials (Segal, 1990).

So there are still many repressive elements relating to sexuality institutionalized in our culture. Yet sexual attitudes have certainly become more permissive over the years. What accounts for this change? A number of factors can be identified. One very important factor is **secularization:** *the process through which the influence of religion is removed from many institutions in society and dispersed into private and personal realms.* Judeo-Christian religious views about sex encouraged rigidity and censorship of alternatives. As religion has become less pervasive in the lives of many Americans, they have become more open to different forms of sexual expression.

A second factor changing sexual attitudes is that technology has provided some freedom that did not exist in the past. Automobiles provide young people with freedom from surveillance by adults, and contraceptives enable people to engage in sex with less fear of conception. These technological developments open up doors that were largely closed in the past, and changes in sexual behavior have contributed to the emergence of more permissive sexual attitudes.

A final factor contributing to changing sexual attitudes is the growing demand for human equality and particularly equal rights for women (see Chapter 7). Traditional gender roles fostered rigid expectations regarding sexual behavior for both women and men. Consider, for example, the focusing of attention historically on males' sexual gratification, with a consequent deemphasis on the importance of females' pleasure. This resulted in a "double standard" among many groups in America: Many sexual outlets were open to men, whereas female sexuality was limited to the marital context. Men were allowed to enjoy sex, whereas women were expected to acquiesce to please their husbands. A woman who enjoyed sex "too much" was stigmatized as a "nymphomaniac," with connotations of an undesirable mental abnormality. As the movement for women's equality exploded myths about men and women in many realms, many of our traditional beliefs about sexuality were shown to be inaccurate. This in turn has contributed to more permissive attitudes toward sexuality in general.

As we consider the topic of sexual variance, keep in mind that changes in sexual standards are not uniform throughout our society, and depending on the group or subculture involved, attitudes about what is normal and abnormal will vary accordingly.

HOMOSEXUALITY

Homosexuality refers to *sexual feelings, fantasies, or acts directed toward members of the same sex.* Estimates of the number of adult males in the United States who are predominantly or exclusively gay range from 1 to 5 percent (Whitam and Mathy, 1985). *Female homosexuals,* or **lesbians,** are probably about half as common. In addition, it is estimated that a minimum of 5 to 8 percent, and possibly as much as 25 percent, of all males have had at least one homosexual encounter (Kinsey, Pomeroy, and Martin, 1948; Bell, Weinberg, and Hammersmith, 1981; Rogers and Turner, 1991). In some geographic areas, there are heavier concentrations of gays. In San Francisco, for example, one survey determined that 40 percent of the single men in that city (more than 69,000) are gay ("Forty Percent of Single Men. . . ," 1984). These figures should be viewed with caution, however, because there is undoubtedly a great deal of homosexual activity that goes undetected in such surveys (Clinard and Meier, 1989).

Theories of Sexual Orientation

Why do some people become attracted to members of the opposite sex and others become attracted to people of the same sex? Numerous attempts have been made to explain sexual orientation, although there is much that we still do not know. A major issue in the debate is whether people are born with tendencies in one direction or the other or whether sexual orientation is a preference that is learned from experiences while growing up.

A recent investigation conducted by a psychologist and two sociologists found no strong relationship between childhood experiences and adult homosexuality, which led them to conclude that sexual orientation may involve biological precursors (Bell, Weinberg, and Hammersmith, 1981). However, their research did not find any connection between biological factors and homosexuality; they only suggested this possibility because they could find nothing else that seemed to cause homosexuality. Recent research on twins provides more direct evidence that there may be a genetic influence on sexual orientation: Twins who share the same genetic material (monozygotic twins) are much more likely to both be gay than twins who do not share the exact same genetic material (dizygotic twins) or two adopted brothers who share no genetic material (Bailey and Pillard, 1991). However, we do not know exactly what is inherited. It may be that what is inherited is not sexual orientation directly but rather behaviors that can be shaped into homosexuality in the proper environment. For example, people may inherit a tendency toward gender nonconformity, that is, the tendency for young boys to behave in a girlish fashion (be "sissies"). Then the reactions of others to that gender nonconformity may encourage ways of thinking and behaving that come to be defined as "homosexual." So a genetic predisposition may get shaped by the social interaction during childhood and teenage years. There is still a lot that we do not know about this, and we have no idea whether all, or only some, homosexuality is biologically linked.

Another explanation for homosexuality suggests that it arises from some psychological maladjustment, possibly stemming from a poor parent–child relationship (Bieber et al., 1962; Lewes, 1988). In fact, the American Psychiatric Association listed homosexuality as a mental disorder until 1973. Despite their popularity, however, psychological explanations have been subject to many criticisms. One criticism is that some studies have observed no personality differences between homosexuals and nonhomosexuals. In addition, many children with poor relationships with their parents do not become homosexual (Hooker, 1969; Bell and Weinberg, 1978). Another investigation involving more than three hundred gay men and women determined that two-thirds of these people perceived their relationships with their fathers as satisfactory, and three-quarters of those in the sample felt that they maintained a satisfactory relationship with their mothers (Robinson et al., 1982). In part because of these criticisms, in 1973, the American Psychiatric Association removed homosexuality from its list of mental disorders. At present, there is no scientific proof that homosexuality is either a psychiatric malady or an indication of poor psychological adjustment (Ross, Paulsen, and Stalstrom, 1988).

Sociologists have argued that some social or situational factors may be present before people will engage in homosexual acts and that certain social contingencies are essential before a person will adopt a homosexual life-style. Sociological theories of homosexuality suggest that, like heterosexuality, homosexuality can be the result of learning through interaction with others (Hoffman, 1968). In some cases, homosexual acts are a consequence of experimentation. We have seen that human sexuality is flexible and exploratory. Some people engage in homosexual acts because they are new and different, and most of these people do not consider themselves "homosexuals." In other cases, homosexual acts occur because there are no heterosexual outlets available. In prison, for example, homosexuality is common, but most prisoners who engage in homosexual acts do not consider themselves to be homosexuals and they return to heterosexuality when released from prison.

Some people not only engage in homosexuality but also come to view themselves as "homosexuals." To understand this, we need to look at the process of self-definition in developing a homosexual identity (Troiden, 1989). Recall from Chapter 9 that labeling theory points out that our self-concepts derive in part from how others treat us. If a person is labeled as a homosexual by others, especially if his or her sexual identity is not yet clearly formed, it increases the likelihood that the person will eventually accept that label. If a person is labeled a homosexual by others, the person may think that the assessment of those others is accurate. In addition, the labeling may create a stigma that makes it more difficult to associate with heterosexuals and precipitates a drift into contacts with homosexuals. Let us say that a teenage male has sex with another male and finds the experience pleasurable. This does not mean he is "gay" because, as we have seen, many mostly heterosexual men gain release at times from homosexual contacts. Further suppose that his friends find out about it and react in a negative and hostile way. They may even pull away from associating with him for fear that others will think they are gay. His friends' reaction may lead the boy to question in his own mind whether he is heterosexual or homosexual. If my friends think I am gay, he wonders, that must mean I am, and I did enjoy it. In addition, the boy is likely to find acceptance and support among other gays. He will also find additional opportunities to explore homosexuality among them. So the labeling may precipitate a gradual changing of the boy's self-concept along with a growing association with people in the gay community. These changes in turn may help solidify his self-definition of himself as gay. In a sense, what has occurred is a self-fulfilling prophecy: The boy has become what his friends thought they were merely discovering when they first labeled him "gay." The point here is not that all people develop their sexual orientation through this route but that this is one route to becoming straight or gay. Even if sexual orientation involves some biological predisposition, as discussed earlier, it may be partly through a social vehicle such as the labeling process that the predisposition actually becomes a reality.

Patterns of Homosexuality

In 1948, Alfred Kinsey and his associates published their classic *Sexual Behavior in the Human Male*, wherein these well-known sex researchers declared:

> [*People*] *do not represent two discrete populations, heterosexual and homosexual. The world is not to be divided into sheep and goats. Not all things are black nor all things white. . . . Only the human mind invents categories and tries to force facts into separate pigeon holes. The living world is a continuum in each and every one of its aspects. The sooner we learn this concerning human sexual behavior the sooner we shall reach a sound understanding of the realities of sex.* (Kinsey, Pomeroy, and Martin, 1948: 639)

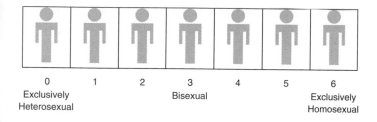

0
Exclusively
Heterosexual

1

2

3
Bisexual

4

5

6
Exclusively
Homosexual

0. Exclusively heterosexual
1. Predominantly heterosexual, only incidentally homosexual
2. Predominantly heterosexual, but more than incidentally homosexual
3. Equally heterosexual and homosexual
4. Predominantly homosexual, but more than incidentally heterosexual
5. Predominantly homosexual, but incidentally heterosexual
6. Exclusively homosexual

Figure 11.1   **The Kinsey Heterosexual–Homosexual Continuum**
SOURCE: Adapted from Alfred C. Kinsey, Wardell B. Pomeroy, and Clyde E. Martin. *Sexual Behavior in the Human Male* (Philadelphia: W. B. Saunders, 1948), p. 638. Reproduced by permission of the Kinsey Institute for Research in Sex, Gender, and Reproduction, Inc.

Their point is that sexual orientation is best viewed as a continuum from exclusively heterosexual to exclusively homosexual (see Figure 11.1). From this point of view, there is no such thing as *the* homosexual, but rather differing degrees of involvement with homosexuality in terms of *behavior* and *attraction*. For example, homosexuality is very common in situations such as prisons, where there are no opportunities for heterosexual contacts, and men and women who engage in this behavior while behind bars usually do not define themselves as homosexual and resume a heterosexual life-style after release. Therefore, a person who engages in homosexual behaviors under various situational pressures is not necessarily gay, in the sense of having an identity, lifestyle, and stable career pattern of homosexuality. Whether people take on the identity and life-style of a homosexual depends on their perception and understanding of their own behavior and the reactions of other people to them (Hammersmith, 1987).

There are many myths in American society concerning gays, some of which we have already discussed. For example, gays are no more mentally disturbed than are heterosexuals, and many gay men establish affectionate, exclusive, and relatively permanent attachments to one man. Another common belief is that gay males are effeminate, like to dress in women's clothing, and wish that they were women. In fact, gay males are no more likely to be effeminate than heterosexual males, and they are generally quite secure in their masculine identity. Lesbians are somewhat different from gay men and tend to reflect the impact of their socialization as females. Lesbians, like their heterosexual counterparts, tend to equate sex with love and are more likely to abstain from sex until some degree of commitment is found with a particular partner. Lesbians also tend to be less assertive, even in their search for a mate in the gay community. Many lesbians pride themselves on being considerably less promiscuous than male homosexuals.

Societal Reaction to Homosexuality

Attitudes Toward Homosexuality.   Is homosexuality deviant behavior and can it be considered a social problem itself? Recall from Chapter 1 that deviance is in the eye of the beholder: It is a group's judgment about the worth or acceptability of a behavior or a life-style. So, we would likely get a different answer to our question in San Francisco than we would in rural Mississippi. Nationally, the attitudes of Americans toward homosexuality have tended toward the negative. Although the media seem to devote more attention to and present more positive images of gays and lesbians today than in the past, the American public still harbors some fairly negative views. As Figure 11.2 shows, 44 percent of the American public believes that homosexual relations should be illegal, and this figure is slightly higher than fifteen years ago. Furthermore, two-thirds of Americans feel that it has been a bad thing for our society to allow greater tolerance of homosexuality as an alternative life-style over the past few decades (Hugick and Leonard, 1991). In the 1980s, only 59 percent approved of equal job rights for gays, and two-thirds of adult Americans polled said they would not vote for an otherwise qualified person for president of the United States if that person were gay (Gallup, 1983: 14). On the other hand, Americans have become more tolerant of having gays and lesbians work in various occupations (see Figure 11.3). But although four out of five people today believe that gays should be allowed to hold sales positions, only two out of five think they should be in the clergy or work as elementary school teachers. Generally, men, older people, religious people, and those with lower educations and incomes are more likely to be intolerant of homosexuality. Negative sentiment toward gays is also greater among those with traditional social values (Kurdek, 1988).

Discrimination Against Gay Men and Lesbians.   Many of the problems surrounding sexual orientation in our society have to do with the negative reactions of many heterosexuals to gay men and lesbians. In fact, the circumstances of

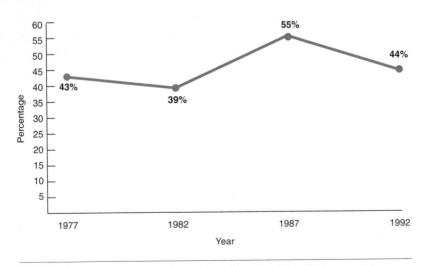

Figure 11.2   **Percentage of Americans Agreeing that Homosexual Relations Between Consenting Adults Should Not Be Legal, 1977–1992**
SOURCE: "Public Opinion Divided on Gay Rights," *The Gallup Poll Monthly* (June 1992), p. 3.

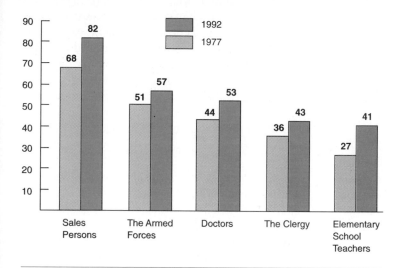

Figure 11.3   **Percentage of Americans Agreeing that Homosexuals Should Be Hired in Various Occupations, 1977–1992**
SOURCE: "Public Opinion Divided on Gay Rights," *The Gallup Poll Monthly* (June 1992), p. 3.

gays, in many respects, are similar to those of racial, ethnic, and gender minorities discussed in Chapters 6 and 7. One difference, of course, is that their minority status is based on behaviors that are considered unconventional by the majority rather than on ascribed and unchangeable characteristics such as sex and race. This makes it easier for gays to avoid some of those negative reactions. But if they wish to live openly and honestly as gays, they may face strong negative reactions from some Americans.

Two areas in which gays face problems are in employment and housing, where discrimination is still strong, although things have improved (Knopp, 1990). By the 1990s, two states, sixteen counties, and many municipalities in the United States have given explicit protection against discrimination in housing and employment to gays. However, several locales, and at least one state, rescinded those protections, suggesting that many Americans still want the option of discriminating

against gays in these realms. The attitudes expressed in Figure 11.3 support this: Although things have improved in the past fifteen years, there is still considerable support for keeping gays out of many jobs.

A particularly disturbing reaction by some against gay men and lesbians is the use of violence (Berrill, 1990; Hunter, 1990). Thousands of episodes of harassment, intimidation, assault, vandalism, and murder occur every year in which the victim's sexual orientation is the reason for the violence. Surveys document that between 9 percent and 24 percent of gays have been physically assaulted because of their sexual orientation. Most gays expect to be the target of antigay harassment or violence, and one-half to three-quarters fear for their safety. So, the reality is that gay men and lesbians are the subject of much hostility from their fellow citizens. Antigay murders are especially brutal and vicious, seemingly a product of deep rage. Referring to the gay male victims of murder and other assaults, the director of victim services at a New York City hospital commented that

> *"Attacks against gay men were the most heinous and brutal I encountered. They frequently involved torture, cutting, mutilation, and beating, and showed the absolute intent to rub out the human being because of his [sexual] preference."* (Quoted in Berrill, 1990: 280)

As with so many other things, gender plays a part here: Gay males are more likely to be attacked or threatened by strangers or people they are not related to or harassed in school or by the police. Lesbians, on the other hand, are more likely to experience verbal harassment from their families. Gay adolescents also suffer a high rate of victimization, and this seems to contribute to a disturbingly high number of attempted suicides among them. Most "gay-bashers" are young males, attacking in a group with other young males, and they are strangers to the victim. An increase in the reported cases of violence against gays has been seen in the 1980s, but whether this represents an increase in actual violence or just more extensive reporting of it is not known.

Another area in which gays experience discrimination is in the legal system. One-half of all states still have laws that make consenting sexual acts between adults of the same sex illegal, and in sixteen states it is a felony (Knopp, 1990). Furthermore, the Supreme Court in the late 1980s upheld the right of states to do this.

Another area of discrimination against gays is in the military, which has maintained a strict policy of viewing homosexuality as incompatible with the mission of the armed services. This position is based on the notion that gays constitute a security risk and that they would be a disruptive element in military units that must work and fight together in close quarters. Actually, there is no reason to believe that gay soldiers are a security risk, especially when gays can admit their sexual orientation without fear of punishment or assault. As for the second assertion, there is no evidence of any disruptive influence. The reality is that thousands of gays have served in the armed forces over the years but kept their sexual orientation secret. In addition, women have moved into the military in large numbers without creating any such problems. Nonetheless, the military is not a career path that the openly gay person can pursue today. However, at this writing, the Clinton administration is considering a change in this policy.

Sources of Homophobia. The term **homophobia** has been adopted to refer to *an intense dislike of or prejudice against homosexuals*. What accounts for the homophobia that seems to underlie the attitudes and discriminatory behaviors described above? A part of the answer is Western Christian theology, which defines homosexuality as sin (Greenberg, 1988; Britton, 1990). Strong condemnation of homosexuality has been an integral part of much of the Christian history and heritage, and this attitude has been pervasive in our society. This negative reaction is often justified on the grounds that homosexuality is a threat to the family or to the reproductive potential of society. Once these norms regarding family life and sexual reproduction are established, they become powerful controls over people's behavior. Other ways of organizing one's personal or sexual life come to be seen as a threat. As one argument goes, if all or most people practiced homosexuality, how could society maintain its numbers? People make this argument despite the fact that maintaining population size has never been a problem in the many societies that have permitted homosexuality to be practiced in one form or another. But the homophobic reaction comes not from rational consideration of the evidence but from a perceived threat to a life-style based on deeply held cultural norms and values.

This negative attitude sometimes gets expressed in nonreligious realms. Freudian psychology, for ample, sees homosexuality as an immature and underdeveloped form of adult sexuality. Only heterosexuality is seen as mature and "healthy." These psychological theories provide a scientific legitimation for viewing homosexuality in a negative light. With these pervasive and deeply held values, open displays of homosexuality are highly threatening to the dominant group and could, if left unchallenged, spread. Reactions against homosexuality then become boundary-maintaining mechanisms that highlight the prevailing norms and show people what behaviors are acceptable. As with attacks on racial or ethnic minorities, attacks on gays show symbolically who is the dominant group and show others the costs to crossing over into the realm of unacceptable behavior.

Most perpetrators of antigay violence are adolescent or very young adult males, which suggests another source of this violence: The marginalized status of many adolescents and young adults (Comstock, 1991). Recall from Chapter 8 that modern industrial societies tend not to incorporate young people into the adult world of work and status until they are in their late teens and sometimes into the early to mid-twenties if they go to college. Because they cannot achieve status and a sense of self-worth through adult avenues, they may search for other ways of doing so, such as drinking alcohol, joy riding in cars, or other thrill-seeking ventures where they can demonstrate strength, bravery, daring, or other positive qualities. Add to this the strong emphasis on male dominance and aggression in our culture along with the negative attitude toward gays expressed by many churches and other legitimate societal institutions, and the ground is set for some of those adolescents to seek adventure, recreation, or relief from boredom through attacks on gays.

Some evidence also suggests that homophobia is associated with rigid and deep-seated negative feelings about human sexuality where sex is seen as dirty and a threat to the social order (Ficarrotto, 1990). The AIDS crisis of the 1980s has also intensified the homophobic reaction among some people (Young et al., 1991). Finally, homophobic attitudes and behavior are associated with many of the same things that lead to prejudice and discrimination against racial and ethnic minorities: authoritarianism, intolerance of differences, and dogmatism (Stark, 1991).

So, the societal reaction to homosexuality in the United States still has a strongly negative element to it. For gays this is where the social problem lies: in the stigmatization and discrimination that they face in many spheres of their lives. In this regard, the conflict perspective offers some insight. Although movements such as gay liberation have increased gay input into political decision making, especially in some cities with a large gay population, "straight" society's interest groups are still much more powerful and have a distinct heterosexual bias. Thus, discrimination against gays continues, forcing some of them to stay in "the closet" and hide their sexual orientation from employers, landlords, neighbors, and sometimes friends. From the conflict perspective, the problem of homosexuality is a clash between those supporting traditional sexual values and those protesting the imposition on them by dominant groups of a way of life they would prefer not to lead.

The Gay Community

In many American cities, some neighborhoods have become distinctly gay and lesbian territories. In some cases, these were depressed, run-down neighborhoods that were taken over because few other groups wanted to live there. In fact, gays produced a certain amount of the gentrification of American cities that we discuss in Chapter 12. One reason for the emergence of these gay communities is protection: They feel safer from the assaults and gain some degree of distance from homophobia when living among others like themselves. The second reason for their emergence is that they enable gays to live among others who share their life-style and values. A third reason is that they afford them a degree of political power. By numerically dominating a community, they can elect city and state politicians who support their interests. An additional reason is that gays are sometimes discouraged from living in neigh-

This family with lesbian parents is attending a picnic sponsored by an organization that assists gay and lesbian parents and their children. The gay community provides many such institutional supports to assist gay men and lesbians with problems they encounter.

borhoods dominated by the majority, especially those who wish to live an openly gay life. All these reasons, by the way, are the same reasons racial and ethnic minorities often gravitate to one community.

The gay community, then, is a subculture that reproduces the cultural and institutional frameworks of the larger culture but casts them in a light of acceptance and support for gays and their way of life. Bookstores, restaurants, retail establishments, bowling and baseball teams, political organizations, support groups, hiking clubs, and Alcoholics Anonymous (AA) groups—all these organizations are found in the gay community, but they adapt to the needs, aspirations, and lifestyles of gays. Bookstores, for example, would stock books and magazines of interest to gays, and people in gay AA groups could talk openly about how their addictions have an impact on their same-sex partner. In all these settings, there is less worry about hostile contacts with "straights," and the overall climate enhances a positive sense of self-regard for gays. As with other groups that

bear the burden of hostility from dominant groups, the gay subculture can provide a safe haven in a hostile world.

PROSTITUTION

Prostitution has been called the "world's oldest profession," because it seems to have been with us throughout recorded history. **Prostitution** refers to *sexual activity in exchange for money or goods in which the primary motivation for the prostitute is neither sexual nor affectional* (James, 1977). Prostitution can take many different forms. Some prostitutes are known in the trade as "streetwalkers": They solicit clients by walking the streets. These prostitutes—both men and women—generally engage in sexual behavior with their customers in clients' automobiles or in cheap hotel rooms. Most of these practitioners of the trade work for a pimp, who typically "manages" from one to twenty women (Diana, 1985). Pimps offer protection and bail money in exchange for the allegiance of the prostitutes in their "stable." Pimps frequently resort to violence as a means of enforcing obedience, and they garner nearly 100 percent of their employees' earnings:

> *I was going to leave Silky [a pimp] when I was in jail. I didn't understand why—with seven wives-in-law [the women in Silky's stable]—I was in jail for six days. I understood after I talked to Silky. It turned out he really didn't have no money. A pimp is supposed to be in a position to take care of bail, but he can't just snap his fingers and money comes. He's got to get it from us. If we're not giving him our money, he can't have no money. How could I make money when I was in jail? (Quoted in Caplan, 1984: 71)*

Other prostitutes work in what at one time was the most common environment for the trade: the house of prostitution, brothel, or "whorehouse." In these cases, a "madam" acts as supervisor of a number of prostitutes and negotiates with clients who enter the facility:

> *An entrepreneur is a person who embarks on a business enterprise and manages the operations of that business, assuming risk for the sake of profit. The madam of a house of prostitution fits this definition: She is the owner and manager of a small service business, albeit an illegal one. (Heyl, 1979: 89)*

Unlike pimps, madams usually garner about 50 percent of their "ladies'" proceeds. In Nevada, prostitution is legal in some counties, and brothels flourish. They are run like any other business, to the point of accepting credit cards and traveler's checks, as this ad for one of them illustrates:

> **Ranch Specialties**
> *Japanese type bath, Bubble baths, Nude Photo sessions, Largest selection of girls, 18 years and older, Girls of all nationalities, out calls, Ranch souvenirs, Free limo service, Your own personal menu, Free brothel information and, of course, the Cherry Patch's famous dungeon . . . only if you dare: Master Charge, Visa, and Travelers Checks are accepted.*

Still other members of the trade operate out of bars, taverns, and massage parlors. The type of prostitute commanding the highest status within the trade is the escort or "call girl," who develops an established clientele, usually men who are prepared to pay high prices for different sexual services. Escort prostitutes often operate independently out of their own well-appointed apartments or see their clients "on call" in hotel rooms or the customer's home (McLeod, 1982; Diana, 1985). Among male prostitutes, a similar stratification system exists, ranging from the street hustler to the bar hustler to the escort prostitute (Luckenbill, 1986).

Extent of Prostitution

Precise figures on the incidence of prostitution are impossible to obtain, but it has been estimated that there may be as many as a half million prostitutes working in the United States today (Reynolds, 1986). Much prostitution goes on unreported, and there are women and men who engage in the trade on a part-time basis, with some of these individuals occupying otherwise respectable positions in their communities. Furthermore, arrests for prostitution are highly susceptible to political manipulation. In some jurisdictions, for example, the trade may be more or less tolerated, whereas in others police agencies may be motivated to "crack down," thus creating the impression that prostitution is on the rise, when in fact it is merely law enforcement activity that has increased (Clinard and Meier, 1989). For example, in 1983, the New York City police department made seventeen thousand arrests for prostitution, but nearly all of these were made on the street. According to law enforcement authorities, prostitution flourishes "indoors" in New York City:

> *Some prostitutes work in brothels hidden behind the doors of luxury apartments. Others work for escort services that take half their fees. Still others work out of their own apartments through referrals. Their services are advertised in explicit sex tabloids, on late-night cable television, even in the Yellow Pages under escort services. The police say that while legitimate escort services may exist, they believe most are thinly disguised covers for prostitution. ("Off the Streets . . . ," 1984)*

Considering these problems, the best estimates place the number of prostitutes in the United States at between one hundred thousand and five hundred thousand and the money generated each year at between $1 billion and $10 billion (Thio, 1988; Reynolds, 1986). In 1991, there were eighty thousand arrests for prostitution and commercialized vice offenses. Sixty-six percent of the people involved were female (see Table 9.3). Considering the degree of nonreporting alluded to earlier, these figures are conservative. The trade is clearly thriving, and the explanation is primarily economic: There are people willing to pay for the services and others who are willing to supply them for a price.

A particularly disturbing form of prostitution appeared in the 1980s with the emergence of the crack cocaine epidemic (see Chapter 10). In crack houses, crack-addicted women, and in a few cases men, would engage in quick sex with many men to get crack or the money to buy crack (Inciardi et al., 1991). This is typically unprotected sex and involves multiple partners, with many IV-drug users among the partners. The women go from one sexual contact to another for a hit of crack and in some cases have literally thousands of sexual contacts a year. In fact, some of the women who engage repeatedly in quick oral sex with many men to get crack did not even consider this to be prostitution. This behavior entails a very high risk of spreading the AIDS virus.

Considerable controversy exists regarding whether prostitution should be regarded as a social problem or even a crime, for that matter. Those who favor legalizing prostitution argue that this activity is a "victimless crime" and that what goes on between consenting adults in private should not be a matter of legal enforcement (Rio, 1991). (This is the same argument discussed in Chapter 10 to support the legalization of some psychoactive drugs.) In fact, prostitution is legal in eleven counties in Nevada, where houses of prostitution are privately owned and regulated by the state. Another argument in favor of legalizing prostitution is that illegal prostitution causes problems such as the spread of venereal disease and AIDS and may come under the control of organized crime. It also leads to other related crimes, such as assaults on customers and the use of drugs.

Where prostitution is legal, such as Nevada and some countries in Europe, these problems can be monitored and fairly effectively controlled among the legal prostitutes (Campbell, 1991). Nevada, for example, requires licensed brothel prostitutes to be tested for gonorrhea, syphilis, and AIDS at least once a month. If they test positive for AIDS, they cannot work as a legal prostitute in Nevada.

Nevada also requires that condoms be used at all licensed brothels, and brothel owners will not employ women who are IV-drug users. As a consequence, no brothel prostitute in Nevada has ever tested positive for the AIDS virus, whereas in some cities where prostitution is illegal, 20 to 40 percent of prostitutes are infected. However, it is not clear how much of this infection is due to prostitution itself and how much is due to prostitutes taking drugs intravenously or having sex with IV-drug users. Nonetheless, legalized and monitored prostitution does provide significant protection against sexually transmitted diseases for both the prostitute and the customer. In addition, there is no evidence of serious crime problems accompanying legalized prostitution in Nevada. This leads proponents of legalization to argue that everyone—the prostitute, the customer, and society—would be better off if prostitution were legal and subject to government regulation. A variant on this position has been taken by an organization formed to pursue the interests of prostitutes (Weitzer, 1991). COYOTE (Call Off Your Old Tired Ethics) was started in 1973 by a former prostitute and argues that basic issues of work rights and women's self-determination are involved: Prostitution is legitimate work and women have the right to control their own bodies, including the selling of sexual favors. COYOTE agrees that women should not be forced into prostitution, but it also believes that the right to choose prostitution freely is a basic civil right for women. Although COYOTE has not achieved some of its major goals, such as decriminalizing prostitution, it has worked to protect prostitutes from harassment by police and courts and to bring educational programs about AIDS to prostitutes.

Critics of legalization argue that legalizing prostitution does not stop the health and crime problems associated with prostitution but simply pushes it into the illegal trade. Prostitutes who get involved in crime, use drugs, or have a sexually transmitted disease continue to work, but on the street rather than in the legal brothels. In fact, this seems to be true because illegal prostitution continues in Nevada. However, having legal prostitution available does reduce the amount of illegal prostitution. Other critics of legalized prostitution, including some feminists, argue that prostitution does create victims: the prostitutes themselves. Prostitution, they claim, involves an exploitation of women so that men can have unrestricted access to sexual pleasure. As one critic of legalized prostitution put it, "Prostitution is a culturally sanctioned system of oppression that uses women, children, and young men as sexual objects. . . . The sex industry uses power and control tactics to supply its customers with human beings who are used as sexual toys. Prostitution is dehumanizing to everyone involved in the industry" (Greenman, 1990: 111). Although prostitutes appear to be willing partners, they are really coerced into prostitution because of poverty, few job opportunities, or a sexist ideology that defines women primarily in terms of their sexuality rather than other skills and qualities. Teenage prostitutes in particular are severely exploited by adults, as is discussed in the Policy Issues insert in this chapter.

Who Becomes a Prostitute?

There is a widespread myth that most prostitutes get their start through a kind of "white slave" trade—that young women are coerced by profit-oriented adults and forced into selling their sexual services for money. Although this does occur, as in the case of teenage runaways who gravitate toward major cities in an attempt to make a living, forced prostitution is rare in the United States—no more than 4 percent could be said to have been railroaded into the trade (Thio, 1988).

How, then, do most prostitutes get into the trade? An important step in becoming a prostitute is knowing others who are involved in the trade or who are on its fringe. As differential association theory discussed in Chapter 9 suggests, people learn prostitution from others who are involved. Many prostitutes first learn about prostitution from close friends or relatives, whereas others have contact with a pimp or prostitute who convinces them to "turn out," as the first move into the ranks of prostitutes is called (Weisberg, 1985; Campagna and Poffenberger, 1988). Contacts with other prostitutes or with a pimp are also important in developing a clientele. As one woman who entered the trade commented: "You can't just say get an apartment and get a phone and everything and say, 'Well, I'm gonna start a business,' because you gotta get clients from somewhere. There has to be a contact" (Bryan, 1965: 289). Associating with prostitutes or pimps who idealize the life of the prostitute as exciting and glamorous and extol its virtues in terms of making "easy money" also encourages potential recruits to "turn out." These recruits learn attitudes that espouse prostitution as a desirable way of life. They also learn that prostitution might bring lucrative economic rewards and an independence rarely found in other occupations (McCaghy, 1985). So "contacts" appear to be the most important ingredient in becoming a prostitute, once again underscoring the importance of learning a deviant lifestyle through intimate group associations. The learning process is similar to how "respectable" people learn to adopt socially acceptable ways of life.

Quite obviously, being young and physically attractive are also valuable assets for joining the ranks of prostitution, whether legal or illegal (Diana, 1985). Consequently, the vast majority of female practitioners are between seventeen and twenty-four years of age, with the peak earning age being around twenty-two (Clinard and Meier, 1989). Prostitutes also often have early and frequent promiscuous sexual experiences. They often have their first sexual intercourse by ten to thirteen years of age and develop a pattern of having sex with several men, often after very brief acquaintanceships (McCaghy, 1985). More than any other single factor, entrance into prostitution for women is inextricably linked to poverty: Poor women are far more likely to become prostitutes than are affluent women (Miller, 1986). Two

POLICY ISSUES

Teenage Prostitution: Is Prevention or Rehabilitation Possible?

Prostitution continues to be a controversial issue in American society. It flourishes in many communities without much intervention by law enforcement agencies, but people are still disturbed by it. Particularly unsettling to most Americans is teenage prostitution. Sometimes these prostitutes are scarcely more than children, some as young as eleven years old. It has been estimated, for example, that over one million minors living in the United States are involved in prostitution and other sexually exploitive activities, and that at least 150,000 of these youths participate regularly in prostitution. (Campagna and Poffenberger, 1988). Police officers have described teenage prostitutes as "forty-year-old midgets," due to the aging effect that this life-style has on them:

> poor diet, sleepless nights, alcohol and drug usage, and all those fears—of the police, of "freak tricks," of other prostitutes, [and] predatory pimps. (Caplan, 1984: 69)

Through grants funded by the Ford Foundation, Gerald M. Caplan, a professor of law at George Washington University in Washington, D.C., has conducted research on the sexual exploitation of children. Professor Caplan points out that teenage prostitutes are usually girls who have left home, with many of them being runaways. Some, in fact, are what Caplan calls "throwaways": children whose parents are not upset about their having left home or may even have encouraged them to run away from home.

Caplan's views on teenage prostitution are somewhat unsettling. He points out that, unlike adult prostitution, where the issue is often dismissed as an unavoidable evil, society feels that the problem of teenage prostitution cannot be so easily ignored. Because teenagers are more dependent and defenseless against exploitation by adults, teenage prostitution is more offensive to the sensibilities and the sense of fairness of many Americans. Although Caplan concedes that efforts to combat this problem are admirable, he does not believe that the solution to teenage prostitution can be found in governmental reform:

> What can government do to compete with adolescent fantasies of flashy cars, glamorous

other important precursors to prostitution are a history of juvenile delinquency and being sexually abused as a child (Simons and Whitbeck, 1991).

Male prostitutes tend to come from two distinct subcultures (Weisberg, 1985; Luckenbill, 1989). One is the peer-delinquent subculture, which consists of boys from lower-class backgrounds who never define themselves as homosexuals. For them, prostitution is exclusively a way of making money, not achieving sexual gratification, and they also engage in other criminal activity. The other subculture is the gay subcul-

ture, involving boys who consider themselves homosexual or bisexual. These prostitutes are more likely to work the gay neighborhoods of cities. They are also more likely than the peer-delinquents to come from the middle class. Gay prostitutes engage in prostitution as a way of interacting with gay people and achieving sexual gratification as well as making money. Adolescent male prostitutes come from unstable families in which they have been taken care of by a series of people, such as parents and relatives. They are likely to have experienced physical abuse and

outfits, mindblowing drugs, a life on center stage? Prostitution provides an alternative that is in important particulars better than the life the teenager knew. Even the dark spots—the insults, the beatings, the degradation—horrible in themselves, are not necessarily foreign. They are, typically, likely to remind her of home. As she grows older and understands better what she has sentenced herself to, she may break away. She may not. About this process, government has little to contribute. (Caplan, 1984: 73)

Caplan's conclusion seems pessimistic or even fatalistic. He feels that it is reasonable to treat teenage prostitution in the same way that we do adult prostitution: to admit that it may well continue to exist. However, he also holds out hope by pointing out that some of the causes of teenage prostitution can be found in certain elements of our society's structure. For a poor or deprived teenage girl, for example, prostitution may seem to be an alternative way to obtain material possessions and possibly even the love that was missing at home. Caplan points out that "the talent pool for teenage prostitution is bottomless" and he sees no reason to predict a reduction in this pool—in fact, the pool may become even larger.

But his recognition that the source of the problem lies in the structure of our society points us in the direction of some possible solutions: programs to change those conditions that push youngsters into the trade. Experts in juvenile delinquency have emphasized that the best method of addressing teenage prostitution is to fund programs in prevention and treatment, such as early intervention with runaways (Weisberg, 1985). Others have stressed the need for better community responses to the social problem surrounding teenage prostitution, particularly with regard to the abilities of social service delivery providers and law enforcement personnel to identify particular social needs of those young people involved. Without community participation, these professionals are far less able to provide early effective intervention strategies to head off youth participation in teenage prostitution (Campagna and Poffenberger, 1988). Finally, we need to recognize that teenage prostitution thrives in the fertile soil of family disruption, discussed in Chapter 3, poverty, discussed in Chapter 5, and child abuse and exploitation, discussed in Chapters 3 and 8. All these social problems help to push some youngsters into a premature independence on the street. Certainly the streets have attraction when home means tension, fights, little money, and sexual assault. However, if we can alleviate some of these other problems, then staying at home will become a more desirable alternative for some youngsters.

---

sometimes sexual abuse by their caretakers. For gay prostitutes, conflicts with parents over their sexual orientation often lead them to run away and turn to prostitution to support themselves.

Leaving prostitution can be difficult, especially for women who have been in the trade for some time (Greenman, 1990). For one thing, prostitution isolates women from the "straight" community and from their families and friends. This means they have few supports to turn to when they need help, except the pimp and others in the trade in whose interest it is to see them continue as prostitutes. Often, pimps encourage prostitutes to participate in other illegal actions such as drug trafficking or forgery, and this creates additional barriers to going back to the straight world. In addition, the women are often battered by their pimps or assaulted by customers. They often have alcohol and drug problems, no high school degree, no safe and affordable housing, no marketable skills, and no recent work experience to be cited when applying for legitimate jobs. All this can make prostitutes feel as though they are on a dead-end, one-way street with few alternatives.

All in all, not a very glamorous life. It sometimes looks glamorous—with the nice clothes, fine jewelry, and expensive cars—but all of that usually belongs to the pimp, not the woman.

Prostitution: A Functionalist Perspective

As we pointed out in Chapter 1, the functionalist perspective provides insight into how a social problem, although controversial, can contribute to the maintenance of the social system. Could prostitution possibly be functional for society? The functionalist approach to this issue was first proposed by sociologist Kingsley Davis in 1937. In the previous section, we approached the question of how people, particularly women, become involved with prostitution. Davis turned this focus around: "The interesting question is not why so many women become prostitutes, but why so few of them do" (Davis, 1971: 347). Davis's response to this question mirrors the functionalist perspective:

> *The answer, of course, is that the return is not primarily a reward for labor, skill, or capital, but a reward for loss of social standing. The prostitute loses esteem because the moral system—especially when prostitution is purely commercial—condemns her. (Davis, 1971: 347)*

Davis's argument is that the moral structure of our society causes prostitution because that system simultaneously offers benefits for engaging in the trade, while it also condemns prostitution as a meaningless and illicit sex activity:

> *When a man is away from home and cannot satisfy his sex drive with his wife, or when a man is a stranger in town and does not have enough time to seduce a respectable woman, he is driven into the arms of a prostitute who will satisfy his sex drive in—as the moral system would have it—a meaningless way. Also, by defining certain acts like fellatio and cunnilingus as immoral and hence not to be indulged in with one's wife or girlfriend, the moral order encourages males to*

> *turn to prostitutes for the enjoyment of these sex acts. (Thio, 1983: 214)*

In addition, Davis emphasizes that prostitution has important effects on the moral system—indeed, the activity actually strengthens that system: "protecting the family and keeping the wives and daughters of the respectable citizenry pure" (Davis, 1971: 350). Thus, prostitution enables sexual gratification to be achieved in a variety of ways without placing excessive demands on wives and thus threatening the institution of the family.

The functionalist theory of prostitution illustrates that the moral system in society, which condemns the selling of sexual services for money, also encourages prostitution and thereby functions to foster and preserve that system.

Prostitution: An Interactionist Perspective

Recall from Chapter 1 that the interactionist perspective focuses on everyday social interaction among individuals rather than on large societal structures. Using this approach, a social problem exists when some social condition is defined by an influential group as stigmatizing or threatening to their values and disruptive of normal social expectations. In discussing the functionalist perspective, we saw how the moral system in American society defines prostitution as threatening. Like society, however, prostitutes have their own "definition of the situation." Using the interactionist perspective, we can view prostitutes as actors in their own life drama, and understand their behaviors as they interpret them in reference to society's definitions (Heyl, 1979). This relationship is illustrated in Figure 11.4. First, in response to the moral stigmatization of their profession, prostitutes tend to define what they do as necessary to society. These are the views of some prostitutes on what they do:

> *I believe that there should be more prostitution houses and what have you, and then we wouldn't have so many of these perverted idiots, sex maniacs, all sorts of weird people running around. I*

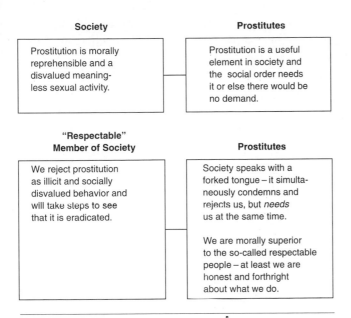

Society

Prostitution is morally reprehensible and a disvalued meaningless sexual activity.

Prostitutes

Prostitution is a useful element in society and the social order needs it or else there would be no demand.

"Respectable" Member of Society

We reject prostitution as illicit and socially disvalued behavior and will take steps to see that it is eradicated.

Prostitutes

Society speaks with a forked tongue – it simultaneously condemns and rejects us, but *needs* us at the same time.

We are morally superior to the so-called respectable people – at least we are honest and forthright about what we do.

Figure 11.4   **Contrasting Views of Prostitution**

could say that a prostitute has held more marriages together as part of her profession than any divorce counselor. I don't regret doing it because I feel I help people. A lot of men that come over to see me don't come over for sex. They come over for companionship, someone to talk to. . . . They talk about sex. . . . A lot of them have problems. (Bryan, 1966: 443)

The other element in prostitutes' definition of the situation involves their self-concept. The moral system defines their behavior as disvalued. Prostitutes, on the other hand, turn this around by saying that they are honest and respectable, whereas the so-called respectable members of society are not (Diana, 1985). Women involved in prostitution frequently see their clients as hypocritical because they simultaneously claim membership in the social world of the respectable but also avail themselves of the prostitute's services:

We come into continual contact with upright, respected citizens whose voices are loudly raised

against us in public, and yet who visit us in private. (Hirschi, 1962: 44–45)

From the interactionist perspective, then, the extent to which prostitution is a social problem is a matter of some dispute. It depends on whether we consider the public proclamations of people or their private inclinations. For some, such as politicians, it may be beneficial to publicly denounce the trade when in fact they see little wrong with it.

PORNOGRAPHY

A few years ago, an issue of *Hustler* magazine, which routinely contained very sexually explicit photos, advertised that it contained "the most obscene photographs ever published." Not surprisingly, this issue enjoyed particularly vigorous sales on the magazine stands. Rather than sexually explicit photos, however, the photographs were extremely vivid portrayals of combat in Vietnam. This episode highlights an important question in the social controversy pertaining to pornography: What is obscenity? Another dimension of this issue involves the debate over whether adults should have the right to choose what they see and read about.

Defining Pornography

More than any other type of sexual variation, pornography illustrates the almost total lack of social consensus about what is acceptable sexually. The term **pornography** was first applied to characterizations of prostitution, but as currently utilized, it describes *"sexually 'explicit' writings, still or motion pictures and similar products designed to be sexually arousing"* (Sobel, 1979: 2). *Obscene* is a term that originally implied "filth." Today, obscene material is generally thought of as "lustful material that offends prevailing senses of decency and morality" (Sheley, 1985: 119). Feminist Gloria Steinem has commented that it is the *dehumanizing* aspect of pornography that distinguishes it from *erotic* materials. For Steinem, the message in pornography "is violence, dominance, and conquest," whereas erotica portrays "mutually pleasurable, sexual expression between people who have enough power to be there by positive choice" (Steinem, 1980: 37). Clearly, what is obscene to one person may be considered by another person to be a work of art.

Particularly vivid examples of the controversy involving different definitions of obscenity or pornography are found in attempts by various moral interest groups to ban such literary classics as James Joyce's *Ulysses* and J. D. Salinger's *Catcher in the Rye*. In 1948, novelist Norman Mailer published *The Naked and the Dead*. In that book, although with an obviously deliberate misspelling ("fug"), a four-letter, Anglo-Saxon word, previously regarded as taboo in printed material, was used frequently. Three years later, James Jones released his classic *From Here to Eternity*,

and in that book, this same word was used with equal frequency in its correct spelling. Although this usage in both books shocked some people, each book met critical approval and became a best-seller. Today this very same expression is used frequently in various publications and quite regularly in motion pictures. Clearly, what is obscene in one era can be considered acceptable in another. This again illustrates the relative nature of deviance.

Over the years, the U.S. Supreme Court has ruled that obscenity lies outside of the free speech protection of the First Amendment to the Constitution, but the courts have had considerable difficulty in trying to determine what is and is not "obscene." The current legal status of pornography was established in the 1973 Supreme Court case *Miller v. California*. According to the *Miller* test, material must meet three conditions in order to be considered legally obscene (Hawkins and Zimring, 1988):

1. The average person applying community standards considers the material as a whole to appeal to prurient interests.
2. The material depicts sexual conduct, specifically defined by state or federal law, in a patently offensive way.
3. The work lacks serious artistic, literary, political, or scientific value.

Since the *Miller* ruling, a large body of court rulings has emerged in an effort to specify more clearly such things as who the "average person" is and what is "patently offensive." Despite these rulings, there is still much dispute about what is obscene, and, except in the most extreme cases, judgments about obscenity will inevitably be subjective and influenced by personal or religious values. Because of this, antiobscenity legislation is essentially in the hands of the more powerful political elements and interest groups of particular states and communities. Very often, what is and is not considered "obscene" is reduced to a single decision by a judge or jury. What is clear, however, is that pornography—sexually explicit ma-

*Many people argue that pornographic materials should be banned because they may produce
aggressive behavior in men, leading to sexual violence against women.*

terials designed to be sexually arousing—is not
obscene according to the *Miller* test and thus is
protected free speech under the First Amendment
to the Constitution.

Pornography and Censorship

One of the key issues in the debate over pornography as a social problem is whether and to what
extent it should be censored. Proponents of antipornography statutes argue that society must be
protected from these "immoral vices." They contend that unless there is censorship, such materials
will fall into the hands of impressionable youth.
In addition, they point out, pornographic materials frequently involve the exploitation of women
and children, sometimes treating them as "property" or mere sex objects. Because of this, some

feminists have joined with more conservative
groups in making a case for a ban on pornography. For example, law professor Catharine
MacKinnon and author Andrea Dworkin have
pioneered a new approach to pornography that
views it as a violation of the civil rights of women
(Hawkins and Zimring, 1988; Osanka and Johann, 1989). In their view, when women are portrayed as sex objects and in degrading and
subjugated roles, it helps to perpetuate sexist cultural beliefs that it is appropriate to treat women
as property or as mere sexual objects. Because pornography portrays women as subordinate, submissive, and often the recipients of violence, it
encourages sexual assault and the abuse of
women. So, because pornography helps to create
a hostile environment for women with negative
outcomes, in their view, it violates their civil

APPLIED RESEARCH

Does Pornography Lead to Aggression or Violence?

Social scientists have conducted extensive research over the past thirty years into the notion that pornography leads to increased levels of violence against women in the form of rape or other types of sexual assault. This is a very volatile topic because some groups feel very passionately about violence against women and believe that pornography should be banned because it plays a part in this. Researchers and their findings have been drawn into this emotional vortex, and there has been a lot of sound and fury produced. It can make finding the truth difficult. In general, the research has not been very supportive of the notion that pornography causes sexual violence. However, the resulting sound and fury gives us some good lessons in the political uses of scientific research. First, let us summarize the research.

Research in the 1960s and 1970s generally failed to document any link between pornography and sexually violent behavior (Goldstein, Kant, and Hartman, 1974; Segal, 1990). In fact, the 1970 report of the president's National Commission on Obscenity and Pornography rejected the conclusion that exposure to erotic materials is a factor in causing sex crimes and sexual delinquency. Nine years later, the Committee on Obscenity and Film Censorship in the United Kingdom came to the same conclusion. More recent research suggests that there may be a link between pornography and sexual violence. In fact, the Attorney General's Commission on Pornography of 1986 concluded that exposure to pornography does play some role in sexual violence and sexual coercion. Let us take a look at the evidence so that we can better judge what is going on.

One source of evidence produced by social science research on this issue is how people in laboratory experiments respond to pornographic images. Much of this experimental research finds no link between viewing pornography and propensity toward sexual violence. However, some research does seem to find a link. Psychologist Edward Donnerstein and his colleagues, for example, showed pornographic films to college-age males and then asked them to judge simulated rape trials (Donnerstein, Linz, and Penrod, 1987). He found that men who watch sexually violent films are less likely to vote for conviction of a rapist than men who see nonviolent pornographic films or nonpornographic films. The researchers concluded that the men who watch sexually violent films develop more calloused attitudes toward women and attitudes that trivialize rape. The men also show more acceptance of rape myths, such as that female hitchhikers or provocatively dressed women deserve to be raped. These attitudes are especially likely to emerge if the rape victim in the film appears to enjoy the attack. Donnerstein and his colleagues also found that portrayals of sexual violence produce higher levels of sexual arousal than erotic but nonviolent sexual imagery, greater acceptance of violence against women, and a greater likelihood that men will state that they would rape someone themselves if they could get away with it.

Donnerstein's research makes an important distinction between pornography that includes aggression or violence and that which does not. He concludes from his research that it is the aggressiveness and violence in some pornography, rather than its sexual explicitness, that affects the way men respond to simulated rape trials and makes them more likely to express negative attitudes toward women and positive attitudes about rape. In fact, when he removes the sexual content from the films and leaves the aggressiveness, the negative consequences of watching the films seem to be the same.

So, does the research of Donnerstein and some others show that violent pornography produces sexual violence against women? Not really. The research has been criticized on a number of grounds. First, none of this experimental research actually observes sexual violence against women. All they observe is changes in responses to hypothetical situations such as rape trials or changes in some attitudes. Whether any of the men in these experiments would actually go out and commit sexual violence against women is unknown. A second criticism is that the experiments are done in highly artificial situations that may have little to do with the real causes of sexual violence. There is a huge difference between saying in a purely hypothetical and anonymous context that you might assault a woman if you could get away with it and actually assaulting a real human being. A third criticism is that these studies typically observe only short-term effects—what the men say or feel immediately after viewing the films. That effect may not last more than a few minutes, a few hours, or a few days and thus may have little influence on their behavior in the real world. All this criticism does not mean that the research tells us nothing, but the weaknesses of the research, along with the fact that other research does not find a link, leads scientists to be very cautious about drawing conclusions, especially when changes in social policy are at stake.

Another approach to research on this issue is to see what pornography does to actual rapists. Again the results are less than supportive of a ban on pornography (Kutchinsky, 1991). Rapists have less experience with pornography in their teenage years than do nonrapists, and rapists do not use pornography more than others as adults. They also are not more aroused by pornography or more likely to engage in sexual behavior after exposure to pornography. In addition, as with ordinary men, rapists are less aroused by viewing forced sex than by viewing consenting sex.

Another line of research has been to see whether rates of rape and other sex offenses increase when more pornographic materials are available. Some studies have found positive correlations: In the United States, states that have higher rates of circulation of adult magazines have higher rates of rape. However, a recent study at the city rather than state level, failed to support this: There was no correlation between level of circulation of pornographic magazines in a city and the rape rate in that city (Gentry, 1991). In addition, even if rapes are higher in locales with more pornographic materials around, the pornography may not be the cause of the rapes. It could be that the interest in pornography and the incidence of rape are both affected by the same thing: sexist and demeaning attitudes toward women. Remove the pornography and those attitudes would still be there. Actually, other research shows that communities with high circulation rates for pornography have higher levels of gender equality than communities with low pornography levels (Baron, 1990). This is probably because both pornography and gender equality flourish in politically tolerant communities. Furthermore, a longitudinal study of changing rates of rape in Denmark, Sweden, and West Germany—all three of which legalized pornography in the early 1970s—could find no increase in rape associated with the growing availability of pornographic materials (Kutchinsky, 1991). Likewise, in the United States, where both violent and nonviolent pornography has become much more widely available since the 1970s, there has been no increase in rape associated with it.

So, where does all this leave us? There is little scientific proof at this point that pornography causes sexual violence. One researcher concludes, for example, that "our knowledge about the contents, the uses and the users of pornography suggests that pornography does not represent a blueprint for rape, but is an aphrodisiac, that is, food for the sexual fantasy of persons—mostly males—who like to masturbate" (Kutchinsky, 1991: 62). Nevertheless, some of the research shows that men's attitudes and actions toward women may be changed by viewing violence against women, and this helps focus the debate on the realm that may be problematic—the violence rather than the sexual explicitness. Research should continue into all these areas, but we have already learned that rape and sexual violence are complicated behaviors that probably cannot be understood by a simple causal factor such as viewing pornography. In fact, researchers have come to recognize that rape is an act of violence and aggression rather than a sexual act, and it is probably caused by the same factors behind other violent crimes such as homicide and aggravated assault that were discussed in Chapter 9.

Which brings us to the final issue: the politics of scientific research. Advocates of both sides of this issue would like to use scientific research to show that their position on the issue is correct. This can lead to distortions or misrepresentations of the research. The Meese Commission, for example, used Donnerstein's research as a basis for its conclusion that pornography plays a role in causing sexual violence and aggression. To fight this, the Commission called for vigorous attempts to curtail the distribution of adult magazines such as *Playboy* and *Penthouse,* explicitly mentioning *Playboy* as being harmful to society because of its merging of violence with sex. The Commission drew these conclusions even though Donnerstein and his colleagues strongly disagree with them

(Linz and Donnerstein, 1992). For reasons we discussed earlier, they are much more cautious about what their research shows: only that violent pornography may temporarily change some of men's attitudes toward women or change some of their behavior in artificial, laboratory settings. They do not believe this can justify social policies that curtail the distribution of all sexually explicit materials. In addition, the Commission drew its conclusions about such magazines as *Playboy* despite the fact that, since its inception in the 1950s, violent portrayals have been extremely rare in that magazine (Kutchinsky, 1991). It appears that the Commission had an agenda when it started—to curtail the circulation of pornography in the United States—and it was simply searching for any evidence that might seem to support its position. This is why scientists need to be very careful in doing their research, so that distorted or misinformed representations of the results can be minimized.

rights. These ideas have been incorporated into the laws of some municipalities, but the courts have not been very receptive to this rationale for restricting materials.

During the 1980s, the controversy over pornography experienced renewed energy and momentum, fueled by the Reagan administration's call for a national commission on pornography legislation. In May of 1986, the Attorney General's Commission on Pornography (the Meese Commission) ended its one-year investigation of pornography in this country and issued a report that condemned violence and degradation in sexually explicit films, magazines, and books. The report also called for more aggressive prosecution of those who sell what it called obscene materials in order to keep them out of circulation (Downs, 1989).

Those opposed to censoring pornography argue that people should be free to decide for themselves what they wish to read or watch. Although these people agree that the sale of pornographic

materials must be properly regulated to prevent young people from being exposed, they argue that adults' fundamental rights to choose whether they want to consume these materials should not be interfered with. If censorship were to become common, it would be difficult to draw the line between works without "redeeming value" and those having literary or other worth, as the examples discussed earlier illustrate. Antipornography legislation, they argue, would open the doors to banning much literature and art because it is offensive to some group. When children are involved, however, the matter of exploitation is very clear. Those who are opposed to antipornography legislation readily concede that pornography involving children should be banned.

There is an ironic contradiction when it comes to American society's stance toward pornography. On the one hand, there is flourishing support for an industry that turns explicit sexuality and even sex abuse into entertainment. On the other hand, most Americans are concerned about pornography. In a poll conducted in 1986 by the research firm of Yankelovich, Clancy, and Schulman, 67 percent of the women and 49 percent of the men agreed that the selling of magazines with nude pictures in local stores should be outlawed (Donnerstein, Linz, and Penrod, 1987: ix). The results of a *Newsweek* magazine poll conducted in 1985 by the Gallup organization revealed that nearly two-thirds of those surveyed supported a ban on magazines, movies, and videocassettes that feature sexual violence ("The War Against Pornography," 1985). Three-quarters of these respondents agree with the belief that sexually explicit materials degrade women and lead some people to acts of sexual violence. Despite these negative attitudes, however, a majority of the same survey respondents favored the continued sale of pornographic films and sexually oriented magazines that do not feature sexual violence.

In the wake of the Meese Commission's report linking pornography to violence and the U.S. Attorney General's intention to publish a list of pornography distributors in this country, an estimated ten thousand stores nationwide stopped selling adult magazines such as *Playboy, Penthouse,* and *Hustler.* In some instances, major retail chains such as B. Dalton Bookseller have been picketed and customer boycotts have been organized by citizen groups (Strickland, 1986). Although the Meese Commission Report attacked primarily violent pornography, opponents of pornography have used the report as a club with which to attack all pornography.

Pornography and Sexual Violence

As we have seen, the pornography issue has become a battleground where some feminists and the religious right have joined forces to push for a ban on pornographic materials on the grounds that they lead to sexual aggression, sexual assault, and violence against women by men (Segal, 1990). Some feminists have seen pornography as the root of violence by men against women. The slogan "Pornography is the Theory, Rape is the Practice" embodies the belief that pornography is the ideology that fuels not only violence against women but all forms of female exploitation and oppression. For some feminists, these are core issues, and they rest on an assertion that can be subject to empirical test: viewing pornography increases men's levels of violence against women. The role of applied research in social policy is sufficiently important in this realm that we have devoted the Applied Research (see pp. 406–408) insert in this chapter to evaluating that assertion and the turmoil that swirls around it.

FUTURE PROSPECTS

As we pointed out at the beginning of this chapter, sexual behavior is controlled in every human society, but there are wide variations in the nature and content of these social controls. A key way in which the controls vary involves the strength of disapproval and the severity of sanctions for different types of sexual variation. In American society, the strongest disapproval is for acts that involve the use of force, and especially violence, on unwilling victims. Even when no violence is involved, as is frequently the case with child molestation, there is strong disapproval because of the dependence and the presumed naiveté of nonadults. Generally, social disapproval of sexually variant behavior involving consenting adults is less severe, although one exception to this in many parts of our society is homosexuality—it is still viewed negatively by many Americans.

Disapproval of various forms of sexual behavior also depends on whether the behavior becomes public or remains private. Some forms of sexual variation are tolerated if they are engaged in by consenting adults and in private. The interactionist perspective can be used to advantage here in that there is an important difference between sexual behaviors that remain unknown to the public and those that become public knowledge. For example, a man may be gay and still be

Laissez-Faire/Interventionist Debate: What Should America's Social Policy on Prostitution Be?

As we point out in this chapter, there is considerable controversy about whether prostitution should be legal or illegal and what kind of stance America should take toward this form of sexual variance. Even when prostitution is illegal, there is controversy over how much effort the police and other authorities should expend in trying to control it. The various policies proposed on this issue reflect, in one way or another, the laissez-faire or interventionist position on social problems. The table on page 411 outlines four different models of prostitution environments that reflect very different social policy positions on this issue. The laissez-faire model views prostitution as illegal, but beyond that society does little to control it. In this model, a kind of "hands-off" policy is encouraged. The other three models reflect variants of the interventionist effort to alleviate the problems associated with prostitution through government regulation. The control model would reflect the ultimate as far as an interventionist stance is concerned, with prostitution being illegal and enforcement and prosecution actively pursued. The regulation model would permit legal prostitution but only in licensed settings, such as brothels. The zoning model is a kind of middle-of-the-road stance, where prostitution would be legal or illegal within particular zones, but law enforcement officials would not interfere unless prostitutes moved outside such zones. The table illustrates the consequences of each policy in terms of the types of prostitutes that would flourish, the risk of violence and arrest, and so on.

well integrated within society, complete with a good job, an intact marriage, and a family life. The crucial element is whether others learn of this man's sexual variation. If they do, he may be stigmatized and even prosecuted by law. However, as long as such activities remain private, people can perpetuate the definition of the situation that conventional sexuality dominates in society. For interactionists, such definitions are an important mechanism that dominant groups can use to perpetuate their position of privilege and power in society.

A lot of change and conflict has occurred over the past few decades as far as what to do in the United States about the problems surrounding prostitution, pornography, and homosexuality. As for prostitution, one issue is whether it should be illegal. It is legal in many counties in Nevada with no apparent damaging effects. It is illegal elsewhere but flourishes nonetheless. It is legal in some European nations and subject to government controls that seem to minimize the problems that arise, such as the spread of disease or control by organized crime. These facts suggest that we might want to reexamine our policy of criminalizing prostitution. Some alternatives and their consequences are analyzed in the Laissez-Faire/Interventionist insert in this chapter.

Most authorities would agree that prostitution is very hard to stop even when it is illegal. With a demand for the services and lots of money to be made, people are very creative in figuring out how to get around whatever barriers the police and other authorities are likely to put up. One approach that does show some promise focuses on the street trade: use coordinated and multileveled efforts to discourage prostitution in particular neighborhoods (Lowman, 1992). This could involve intensive efforts by police to arrest prostitutes and their customers, community groups that

A Comparison of Models of Prostitution Environments

Aspects of Comparison

Type of Environment	Type of Prostitution Market	Degree of Competition	Visibility of Activities	Risk of Arrest	Risk of Violent Rival	Expected Profitability
1. Laissez-Faire Model (Prostitution is illegal, but neither enforcement nor prosecution is actively pursued.)	Streetwalkers, call girls, massage parlors, escort services, bar and hotel prostitutes	High; few barriers to entry (may need a pimp)	High visibility; blatant solicitation and ancillary markets (bookstores and movies)	Low risk; police rarely arrest	High risk; high degree of rivalry	High; possibility of large revenues, costs low
2. Control Model (Prostitution is illegal, and enforcement and prosecution are actively pursued.)	Bar and hotel prostitutes, call girls, brothels	Low, because markets go underground, information becomes a barrier to entry	Low visibility; blatant activity draws attention	High risk, if visible	Uncertain	Revenues may be good but costs high
3. Regulation Model (Prostitution is legal only as licensed, such as in brothels.)	Only as licensed (such as brothels)	Licensing limits the number and activities of prostitutes	Visibility may be reduced by zoning and signage laws	Low risk, if licensed; unlicensed prostitutes may be vulnerable	Low risk	Costs can be controlled and revenue can be increased by consumer loyalty
4. Zoning Model (Prostitution may be legal or illegal within the zone, but police do not interfere within the limits of the zone.)	Same as Laissez-Faire	High, market concentrated within the zone side (as in #2)	High visibility within the zone (as in #1); low outside the zone (as in #2)	Low risk within the zone	High risk within the zone; police may not patrol; general level of violence	High in the zone, as in #1

SOURCE: Helen Reynolds, *The Economics of Prostitution,* 1986. Courtesy of Charles C Thomas, Publisher, Springfield, Illinois.

take control of the streets and discourage customers from coming around, and road closures and traffic diversions to make it difficult for customers to drive near where the prostitutes congregate. In some places, legislation makes it illegal to communicate about the purchase or sale of sexual services in public, which gives the police an extra tool with which to convict prostitutes and their customers. For some prostitutes and many customers, participating in the trade is a matter of how easy it is to do so, and coordinated efforts such as this seem to push them out of the trade. More committed prostitutes, however, such as those who need money to support a drug habit, tend to move elsewhere in response to such police interventions. So, whether these programs reduce prostitution in a particular area depends on how committed the prostitutes are to the trade. In some cases, these efforts just send prostitutes into other neighborhoods to ply their trade.

Legalization of prostitution does not eliminate the fact that some women are forced into prostitution because of poverty and sexism in society. For these reasons, society may still wish to reduce the amount of prostitution, even though it is legal. To do this, we need to recognize that society implicitly condones and encourages prostitution by perpetuating certain fallacies about it. One fallacy is that people "choose" to be prostitutes. Once we recognize that many people are forced by their poverty, vulnerability, and lack of opportunities into the trade and prevented from leaving by equally powerful forces, then all who participate in the trade become partners in that oppression. Another myth is that prostitution protects respectable women and children from sexual assault or unwanted sexual demands. This gives a noble sound to what is really a mechanism to ensure men the widest possible sexual access to women. The effort to control prostitution needs to begin by challenging these fallacies and showing how society can implicitly support a practice that it explicitly condemns. Another thing that could be done is to provide prostitutes with a way out of the trade: drug and alcohol rehabilitation, job referrals and job training, safe and affordable housing, assistance in completing high school or going to college, admission to programs for battered women, and whatever other assistance would help them get respectable and well-paying jobs.

During the 1970s, our laws took on new levels of tolerance for various forms of pornography, and this tolerance manifested itself in greater acceptability of nudity and overt displays of sexual conduct in public settings. The feminist movement of the 1980s expressed renewed concern about pornography—especially sexually explicit materials that involve sexual violence. The most recent research available suggests that there may be a link between certain pornographic materials, especially those portraying violence against women, and attitudes about violence toward women. We can detect a definite trend of vacillation here between liberal attitudes and conservative responses. Through it all, actual research data are less than conclusive about the effects of pornography. One thing is certain: Lawmakers are responding to public concern about pornography with restrictive rulings. For example, in 1986, the U.S. Supreme Court ruled that local zoning officials have broad powers to restrict the location of movie theaters that show sexually explicit films. Although the Court still recognizes sexually explicit materials as an expression of free speech under the First Amendment of the Constitution, the Court affords these materials less protection than other kinds of speech (Taylor, 1986).

As for homosexuality, we have seen that it is still regarded by many as unacceptable, but it has also gained more public notice and probably more respectability in the past twenty years. At the very least, more people are now aware of how widespread homosexuality is. And research shows that familiarity with gays and the gay life-style probably leads to more positive attitudes toward homosexuality (Schneider and Lewis, 1984). Also more educated people are more accepting of gays. So, as educational levels in the United States rise and as more gay men and lesbians lead their lives openly, we can expect attitudes toward homosexuality to become even more positive.

Whereas twenty years ago many people focused their attention on homosexuality itself as a social problem, today many people recognize that the real social problem is the discrimination and violence too often suffered by gays because of their sexual orientation. Over the past twenty years, there have been significant changes moving in the direction of a more equitable treatment of gay men and lesbians. Much of this change has occurred because various gay groups and organizations have vigorously pursued the interests of gays in the political arena (Noble, 1992a). As we have seen, a number of places around the country now ban discrimination against gays in employment and housing. In addition, a number of employers have extended benefits to gay couples that had previously only been available to married couples. These "domestic partner" benefits can include such things as health insurance, retirement plans, and so forth. To be eligible, the gay couple may have to provide documentation that they do live together on a permanent basis, are financially interdependent (e.g., have joint bank accounts), and are responsible for one another's common welfare.

Despite these advances, there have been setbacks. Some municipalities have rescinded their laws protecting gays from discrimination in housing and jobs. In 1992, a statewide ballot in Oregon would have permitted discrimination against gays, would have prohibited gay state employees from holding any position where they worked with children, and would have made it official state policy that homosexuality is "unnatural" and a "perversion." Although the ballot measure lost, 43 percent of Oregon voters voted in favor of this extreme measure. On top of all these things, we have seen that gays still suffer physical attacks in unacceptable numbers because of their sexual orientation. So there is still real tension in the United States over this issue, and it is too early to predict whether the future will bring greater acceptance of gays or further efforts to repress this life-style. By the 1990s, gays have become a much more powerful political force than they were twenty years ago, so they will be better able to protect themselves against threats.

As gays have gone more public with their lifestyle and become more politically active, they have become more effective at getting societal institu-

By the 1990s, gays became a much more powerful political force than they were in earlier decades. Gay groups and organizations have become more effective at pursuing the interests of gays and protecting members of the gay community against threats.

tions, such as schools, government, and corporations, to establish policies and practices that better serve the interests of gays. This has created new arenas for conflict with those who feel that society should not support, or even condone, homosexuality. Many of these people feel that such policies and practices sometimes cross the line between not discriminating against gays and actively promoting homosexuality as an acceptable life alternative. For example, in 1992, New York City produced some curriculum materials for grade school students that portrayed a range of various types of families, including some headed by gay and lesbian couples, in a basically matter-of-fact and positive fashion. The rationale was that such families, in fact, exist, and students need to be aware of them in order to develop tolerant attitudes toward the life-styles of other people. As we have seen, however, many Americans still do not view homosexuality as an acceptable life alternative. So, there was much opposition to these materials on the grounds that the portrayals in effect provided institutional legitimation for choosing homosexuality as a way of life. At one level, this conflict is indicative of significant change: Thirty years ago no one would have even considered an open discussion of homosexuality in the schools. So the issues have certainly shifted. At another level, however, the episode shows that things have not changed that much: There is still significant support for the view that people should be discouraged from considering homosexuality as an acceptable way of life. As long as significant moral and religious opposition to homosexuality persists, we will see more conflicts of this sort.

We said early in this chapter that our discussion was not about sex per se but about the societal reaction to certain sexual practices. However, societal attitudes toward sex do influence how society reacts to particular forms of sexuality. There has been much talk over the last thirty years of the "sexual revolution," and there definitely have been some significant changes in behavior. Premarital sex is more common than in the past, especially among women. Pornography is more widespread and more explicit today. Sex is presented and discussed more openly and publicly than in the past. However, other trends suggest that things have not changed that much. Marriage is as popular as ever, and the divorce rate has stopped increasing and may actually decrease a little. Most people do not cheat on their spouses, and there is little reason to believe that prostitution or homosexuality are more widespread than in the past (although they may be more public). And the AIDS crisis has made everyone more cautious about impersonal and casual sexual encounters.

So it would seem that, despite the changes, traditional sexuality, namely, heterosexual marriage, is still quite strong and secure in our society. However, sex is a core and very emotional aspect of people's lives, and it still rouses the passions. In addition, it is deeply linked to long religious and cultural traditions. This is fertile ground for biased misperception and zealous overreaction, and social policies aimed at controlling one form or another of sexual behavior often result. Social policy should be based on the demonstrated negative impact of such behaviors on society or groups in society, not on the efforts of some powerful group to impose its personal or moral beliefs on others. As we have seen in this chapter, research fails to show that prostitution, pornography, or homosexuality are detrimental to society. If anything, it is the societal reactions to these types of sexual variance that create problems.

Linkages

Prostitution increased when the crack cocaine epidemic in the 1980s (Chapter 10) led some desperate, crack-addicted women to engage in multiple sex acts in order to purchase the drug, and this increased health problems (Chapter 4) because their unprotected sex with multiple part-ners, many of whom were IV-drug users, helped spread the AIDS virus. In addition, both prostitu-tion and pornography are seen by some as re-flecting sexual inequality: They are remnants of the patriarchal control that men still exercise over women (Chapter 7).

Summary

1. The varieties of human sexual expression are almost endless, and most of them have been condemned at one time or another as deviant. Homosexuality, prostitution, and pornography are three variant forms of sexual expression over which there is intense debate, including what problems are created by the societal reaction to them.

2. Attitudes toward human sexuality vary from culture to culture. There is a wide range of socially acceptable sexual behavior from a cross-cultural perspective. There is also variety in hu-man sexuality from group to group within the same culture or society. Sexual attitudes have changed over time in the direction of greater per-missiveness, and this trend is explained by secu-larization, increased technological sophistication, and the growing demand for equal rights.

3. Homosexuality refers to sexual feelings, fantasies, or acts directed toward members of the same sex. Public attitudes reveal that homosexu-ality is viewed by many as a form of deviance and a social problem. For homosexuals themselves, the problem lies in the stigmatization and discrim-ination that they face in many spheres of their lives. There are biological, psychological, and so-ciological explanations for homosexuality. There

are varying patterns of homosexuality, with peo-ple ranging from exclusively heterosexual at one extreme to exclusively homosexual at the other. Homophobia has many sources, including con-demnation of homosexuality by Christianity, the marginalized status of young males, and charac-teristics such as authoritarianism, intolerance of differences, and dogmatism. The homosexual community is an important source of personal identity for homosexuals.

4. Prostitution refers to sexual activity in ex-change for money or goods in which the primary motivation for the prostitute is neither sexual nor affectional. Prostitution takes different forms: from streetwalkers to call girls to male prostitutes. Precise figures on the incidence of prostitution are impossible to obtain, but it is estimated that as many as five hundred thousand prostitutes work in the United States today. There are arguments for and against the legalization of prostitution, al-though in eleven counties in the state of Nevada prostitution is already legal.

5. There are different approaches to the anal-ysis of prostitution. The functionalist perspective argues that the moral structure of our society causes prostitution and that the activity actually strengthens the system. The interactionist perspective calls attention to how prostitutes define themselves and their trade using their own perceptions of reality.

6. Pornography refers to sexually explicit writings, still or motion pictures, and similar products designed to be sexually arousing. There is tremendous controversy about what is pornographic and what is not, and about what kinds of materials, if any, should be censored. The Attorney General's Commission on Pornography reported in 1986 that sexually explicit materials are directly linked with violence. This conclusion is disputed by current research on pornography.

7. Disapproval of various forms of sexual behavior tends to be greater when force is involved, when one partner is not an adult, and when it is expressed publicly. There has been a lot of change and conflict in this realm in the last few decades. Some argue that prostitution should be legal and

that no problems are created when it is legal and regulated. When illegal, prostitution is very difficult to control. Although more pornographic materials are available today, there is also growing pressure to restrict their distribution. Once again, research fails to show that pornography creates any problems for society. Homosexuality is more public and accepted today and finds more protection from discrimination and other negative reactions. However, there are still significant sources of homophobia and many efforts to restrict the activities of gays.

8. Research fails to show that prostitution, pornography, or homosexuality, in and of themselves, are detrimental to society. Problems arise from the hostile reactions that some groups have toward these forms of sexual expression and the efforts of one group to impose its religious or moral vision on other groups.

Important Terms for Review

homophobia	lesbians	prostitution	secularization
homosexuality	pornography		

Discussion Questions

1. According to our discussion in this chapter, some aspects of sexual variation are accepted in our society, although not necessarily approved of by everyone. One example of this is premarital sexual behavior. On the other hand, there are the behaviors and issues we address: homosexuality, prostitution, and pornography. What makes these types of sexual variance social problems? How are they different from premarital sexuality? Use the three theoretical perspectives in answering this question.

2. Ask other members of your class where they "draw the line" between sexual variation (behaviors that one may tolerate, but not necessarily approve of) and sexual deviance (behaviors that are socially disvalued and unacceptable). Compare these responses with your own point of view. Discuss these differences of opinion in a class forum.

3. Members of the scientific community continue to be puzzled about the causes of homosexuality. Yet in American society, homosexuality is regarded by large numbers of people as a form of deviant behavior that threatens our morality and core social institutions, such as the family. Using the theoretical perspectives, discuss some of the reasons homosexuality is regarded as such a socially unacceptable form of sexual variation. Should this behavior be banned as a matter of public policy or left as a matter of individual preference?

4. Prostitution has been regarded as acceptable in some societies for hundreds of years. Until recently, this form of sexual variation was illegal everywhere in the United States. With the exception of county jurisdictions in the state of Nevada, prostitution is still a legally proscribed activity. However, enforcement of these laws varies from state to state and city to city. Why does so much variation exist with respect to views of prostitution in American society? What is your personal stance? Compare and contrast this point of view with the opinions of other members of your class.

5. Pornography is a prime example of how much disagreement there can be about whether an issue or behavior constitutes a social problem. Some interest groups, such as the feminist movement and religious conservatives, have recently mobilized powerful pressures to bear on banning pornography entirely in American society. At the same time, certain forms of pornographic materials flourish and represent enormous money-making operations. What do you think explains this inconsistency? In class discussion, pose the questions: "What is pornographic?" and "What is obscene?" Make observations about how different people answer these questions.

6. Some groups of people in American society are in favor of instituting more formal social controls on the forms of sexual variation discussed in this chapter, whereas other groups have proposed decriminalization and legalization as solutions. What is your personal stand regarding future prospects on these issues? Try to evaluate your point of view as objectively as possible using the interactionist perspective.

For Further Reading

Vern L. Bullough and Bonnie Bullough. *Sin, Sickness, and Sanity: A History of Sexual Attitudes.* New York: Garland, 1977. The authors provide an excellent historical portrait of the origins of sexual attitudes and values in American society.

Daniel S. Campagna and Donald L. Poffenberger. *The Sexual Trafficking in Children: An Investigation of the Child Sex Trade.* Dover, Mass.: Auburn House, 1988. The authors of this book examine the dynamics of sexual exploitation, including such offenses as child pornography and teenage prostitution.

Bernard Cohen. *Deviant Street Networks: Prostitution in New York City.* Lexington, Mass.: Lexington Books/D. C. Heath, 1980. This book represents one of the most comprehensive observational investigations of how prostitution operates in a large American city and provides an outstanding portrait of the "trade" as seen from "the street."

Martin Duberman. *Cures: A Gay Man's Odyssey.* New York: Dutton, 1991. This is a very personal account of the difficulties of growing up as a gay man in a world that has no sympathy for gays. It gives one a perspective on the personal consequences of stigmatization.

Joseph Harry. *Gay Couples.* New York: Praeger, 1984. The author reports on a survey of adult male homosexuals in Chicago who have experienced intimate couple relationships. Harry's findings challenge many stereotypes about gay couples and contain many interesting comparisons and contrasts between homosexual and heterosexual relationships.

James M. Henslin and Edward Sagarin, eds. *The Sociology of Sex.* New York: Schocken, 1978. A collection of readings on sexual variation and a comprehensive overview of sex research conducted by social scientists.

Barbara Sherman Heyl. *The Madam as Entrepreneur: Career Management in House Prostitution.* New Brunswick, N.J.: Transaction Books, 1979. The author uses a life-history approach and provides a sensitive description of how a former prostitute and madam became involved with "the life" and then decided to return to the "straight world."

Laura Lederer, ed. *Take Back the Night: Women on Pornography.* New York: Morrow, 1980. A collection of readings that provides an excellent overview of the major issues involved with women's views of pornography.

Kenneth Plummer, ed. *The Making of the Modern Homosexual.* Totowa, N.J.: Barnes and Noble, 1981. This edited volume begins with evaluations of homosexuality during the eighteenth century leading up to the present. The articles deal with how social change has led to changes in the nature of homosexuality.

Edwin M. Schur. *The Americanization of Sex.* Philadelphia: Temple University Press, 1988. The well-known author of the book *Crimes Without Victims* examines Americans' attitudes toward sex and sexually related issues, including the impact of AIDS, prostitution, pornography, rape, and sexual harassment.

D. Kelly Weisberg. *Children of the Night: A Study of Adolescent Prostitution.* Lexington, Mass.: Lexington Books/D. C. Heath, 1985. Provides excellent and up-to-date coverage of adolescent prostitution, with excerpts from interviews with teenage participants in the "trade."

PART IV
Change and Disruption in the Physical and Social World

CHAPTER 12
Urban Problems

M ost Americans live in cities or in the suburbs that surround them. And it is in cities that Americans confront many of the problems we have already discussed, such as crime, racial conflict, poverty, and unemployment. In fact, these problems seem more intense and severe in cities. Is there something about city living that exacerbates these problems? To what extent do our cities themselves constitute a social problem? Can cities be enjoyable places to live? We need to find answers to these questions if we are to solve the problems that our cities confront. In fact, the discipline of sociology became popular in late-nineteenth-century America as people sought solutions to the crowding and misery of cities such as Boston and New York as they filled with European immigrants. We will begin with a discussion of the extent of urban growth in America and then analyze urban life from the three theoretical perspectives. This will put us in a position to assess the extent and nature of urban problems and review some ways of alleviating those problems.

THE GROWTH OF CITIES

All human groups organize their lives into **communities,** which are *groups of people who share a common territory and a sense of identity or belonging and who interact with one another* (Poplin, 1979). The earliest human communities were small hunting and gathering bands, usually consisting of between forty and one hundred people. These bands were usually nomadic, roaming the land in search of food and game, and all the people knew one another well. Then, about fifteen thousand years

Myths and Facts About Urban Life

Myth: Poor people from ghettos in our cities cause much of the crime in middle-class suburbs; the poor go to these neighborhoods because crime is so lucrative there.

Fact: As we point out in Chapter 9, the crime rate in ghettos is high precisely because the residents prey on other residents of the ghetto in their criminal activities.

Myth: We could solve the problems of our cities quite easily: just close them down and move the people to different locations.

Fact: The problems facing our nation's cities will not be solved by simply moving people somewhere else. The history of urban renewal efforts has demonstrated that these problems will not "go away" by eradicating dilapidated buildings; if people are moved elsewhere, problems tend to move with them.

Myth: Suburban growth began early in this century because people wanted larger homes and more land, and entrepreneurial real estate developers satisfied that desire.

Fact: Although these played a part, the suburbs are equally an invention of our government policies. The government built the interstate highway system that made it possible for people to live in the suburbs and still get to work in the city; the government also provided low-interest, guaranteed mortgage loans for new homes, which were most often built in the suburbs because most cities had little space for new homes. The government did not provide such loans to build apartments in cities, which would have encouraged people to stay in the cities. The result was a strong government incentive for people to move to the suburbs.

Myth: Our cities are segregated today because whites and nonwhites just do not want to live together in the same neighborhood.

Fact: Through the 1950s, the government discouraged blacks and whites from living in the same communities by actively discouraging real estate developers from selling homes in white suburbs to African Americans. At the same time, the government discouraged lenders from making home mortgage loans to people living in black communities on the grounds that people in such communities are bad credit risks. So the seeds of today's segregated urban landscape were planted many years ago by explicit government policies that discriminated against African Americans.

---

ago, small fishing villages began to appear around the Baltic sea, surviving off the plentiful fish. Approximately ten thousand years ago, people discovered how to cultivate plants and domesticate animals. This afforded them with greater control over their food supply and permitted a growing surplus of food. The result was the emergence of agricultural villages, and later cities, in fertile river valleys around the world. A **city** is *a relatively large, permanent community of people who rely on surrounding agricultural communities for their food supply.* As a consequence of developing agriculture, then, human communities grew enormously in size. The biblical city of Ur, for example, located at the juncture of the Tigris and Euphrates rivers, had twenty-four thousand people (Hawley, 1971). At the height of the Roman Empire, Rome is estimated to have had as many as one million residents. However, prior to the industrial revolution, only a few cities had as many as one hundred thousand people.

Urbanization

Industrialization ushered in ever-increasing urbanization, with cities growing far larger than their preindustrial predecessors. By the mid-twentieth century, cities such as New York,

Chicago, and Los Angeles had many millions of inhabitants. Two hundred years ago, only 5 percent of all Americans lived in urban areas, in contrast to 77 percent today (see Figure 12.1). The New York metropolitan area has over eighteen million people, and Los Angeles over fourteen million. Why has this extensive urbanization occurred? One of the main reasons is that most economic activity in industrial societies is non-agricultural, and such activity benefits from being concentrated geographically. With industry and jobs located in cities, people are drawn to the cities to find work. So "community" for most Americans today means a city, whether it be large or small.

Suburbanization

Equally as important as the growth in size of cities has been the growth of **suburbs,** *less densely populated areas, primarily residential in nature, on the outskirts of a city.* Mass suburbanization is a rela-

tively recent development. In fact, it arose out of a complex set of social factors (Banfield, 1990). One factor was the economic and technological developments that made it possible for people to live far from where they worked. Early in this century, most people were limited in where they could live by the need to find transportation to work. This meant that most had to live in the cities, near where the jobs were. Because there were relatively few automobiles and highways, people walked or used public transportation to get to work and go shopping. This encouraged the concentration of population, and central cities served as the commercial and cultural core of urban areas. By the 1940s and 1950s, the increasing affluence of many Americans, along with the automobile, made it feasible for them to live farther from work and opened up suburban life to middle-class Americans.

In addition to these economic developments, government policy was also a factor contributing to suburbanization. For example, the federal gov-

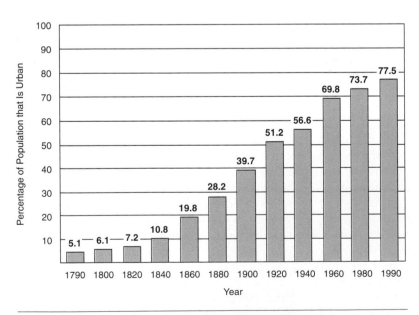

Figure 12.1 **Percentage of Urban Population, 1790–1990**
SOURCE: U.S. Bureau of the Census, *Statistical Abstract of the United States, 1991* (Washington, D.C.: U.S. Government Printing Office, 1991), pp. 17, 27.

ernment paid 80 percent of the cost of developing the interstate highway system. With cars and high-speed highways, people can now live far from where they work and shop. In sprawling cities such as Los Angeles, for example, it is common to live fifty or more miles from where you work. Another encouragement to the development of suburbs was policies of the Federal Housing Administration (FHA), established in 1934, and the Veterans Administration (VA) (Bullock, Anderson, and Brady, 1983). Beginning in the 1930s, the FHA and the VA made available federally guaranteed mortgage loans for the purchase of new homes. Because land outside of the cities was both inexpensive and available, this is where much of the construction took place. The FHA and VA did not provide loans to purchase existing homes or build apartments, policies that would have encouraged people to continue living in the cities. So the flight of people from cities was in full swing, and, especially in the early years, it was the more affluent city dwellers who moved to the suburbs. Keep in mind that this suburbanization occurred not simply because people wanted to move to the suburbs. It also depended on the development of new transportation technologies and on federal social policy on housing and transportation. This should not be surprising given the functionalist point about the interdependence among the different elements of social systems. The manifest function of the social policies was to stimulate economic development. Their latent function was to encourage decentralization of urban areas and to bring about the eventual decline of many cities. Clearly, all the ramifications of these policies were not considered when they were established.

These same developments eventually made it possible for businesses and factories to also move outside of cities. Businesses originally located in cities because workers lived there and transportation was available to ship their products. By the 1950s, cities no longer possessed those exclusive attractions. A labor force and highways were available in the suburbs. In addition, suburban land was typically less expensive, taxes were lower, and affluent suburbs could afford to offer tax breaks to industries to relocate. Suburban shopping malls were developed with huge parking lots and situated next to freeways. The malls were clean, spacious, and keyed to an affluent life-style. They drew consumer dollars out of the city as urban stores established suburban outlets. Increasing crowding and congestion in cities, along with the growth of numerous problems, also made the suburbs popular as a "rural refuge" from the hustle and bustle of the city (Palen, 1987). In their early development, suburbs were not economically self-supporting, with many residents making their livelihood in the cities. By the 1970s, however, this had changed, with 75 percent of all suburban residents both living and working in the suburbs and only about 25 percent commuting to the central city to work. Today, we are a nation of suburbanites, with 60 percent of America's metropolitan population living in the suburbs. And it is the suburbs, rather than the central cities, that have shown the most significant population growth over the past two decades (see Figure 12.2).

The Postindustrial City

Although people and some jobs have left the city, other jobs have remained. Many cities have retained or increased jobs in the financial service industries, those related to the functioning of corporate headquarters, telecommunications and publishing, and those involving nonprofit and governmental activities (Heenan, 1991). This is true of some large cities such as New York, Chicago, Houston, and Atlanta, and some smaller cities, such as Memphis, Des Moines, Madison (Wisconsin), and Ann Arbor (Michigan). In other words, the changes in cities reflect the changes in our economy discussed in Chapter 2: the stagnation in the manufacturing sector and the growth of the service sector.

However, recent technological developments may reduce the need for corporations or service

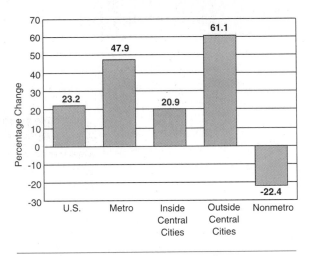

Figure 12.2 Percentage Change in Population Size in Metropolitan and Nonmetropolitan Areas in the United States, 1970–1990
SOURCES: U.S. Bureau of the Census, Current Population Reports, Series P-60, No. 133, *Characteristics of the Population Below the Poverty Level: 1980* (Washington, D.C.: U.S. Government Printing Office, 1982), p. 19; and U.S. Bureau of the Census, Current Population Reports, Series P-60, No. 175, *Poverty in the United States, 1990* (Washington, D.C.: U.S. Government Printing Office, 1991), pp. 53–56.

industries to concentrate their workers in one locale. Computers, microwave transmission, FAX machines, and communications satellites make it possible for people to communicate over long distances instantly, effortlessly, and relatively inexpensively. Overnight parcel delivery is available almost everywhere today, and information can be sent rapidly over the telephone lines from one computer to another. Teleconferencing means that even meetings can be held when those "present" are separated by long distances. There will still be some need for centralization, however. Top corporate executives, for example, will need close contact with attorneys, investment counselors, management-consulting firms, and advertising executives. However, many other jobs can be decentralized. For example, Eastern Airlines moved its reservation centers to Charlotte, North Carolina, and Woodbridge, New Jersey, and

Exxon moved its corporate headquarters to Irving, Texas (Kindel, 1990). It will take some years to see the effects of these technological developments, but they well may encourage further decentralization of urban areas.

URBANISM AS A WAY OF LIFE

Many people believe that the problems of our cities stem at least in part from the inherent characteristics of cities and how they differ from small towns and rural communities. For example, cities tend to be large and impersonal, it is often said, and this contributes to crime and conflict between groups. To assess the importance of this, we begin our analysis of urban problems with a discussion of what city life is like: how cities affect people and their relationships with one another. Developing effective solutions to urban problems also requires an understanding of the fabric of urban life because solutions must be weaved into that fabric. Some attempts at solutions may produce a rending of the urban fabric, creating problems that are worse than the ones we have attempted to solve. There have been a number of analyses of urban life over the years, and they all focus in part on whether city life involves any sense of "community." Three approaches are particularly useful to understanding urban problems: the view that cities produce a peculiar urban "consciousness," the view that people in cities can have a sense of community, and the view that subcultures play a key role in shaping life in cities.

Urban "Consciousness"

In the late 1800s, sociologist Ferdinand Tönnies watched the changes that were happening to farmers in his native Germany as the country industrialized and cities grew (Tönnies, 1963, originally published 1887). He called the old way of life *gemeinschaft* and the emerging social order *ge-*

sellschaft. **Gemeinschaft,** with translates roughly as "community," refers to *social life that is governed by personal, informal considerations, with tradition and custom prevailing.* This was the kind of life most common in small agricultural communities and rural areas prior to industrialization. People were strongly bound to other members of their community and valued these ties very highly. People related to each other out of liking, sympathy, and enjoyment—because these relationships provided many positive feelings and personal fulfillments. Daily encounters with others—whether at work or at play—tended to be intimate and personal. The groups in which people spent much of their time were what sociologists now call **primary groups:** *small groups involving personal, intimate, and nonspecialized relationships.*

What Tönnies saw becoming more prominent as Germany changed was **gesellschaft,** meaning "society" or "association": *social relations characterized by specialization, individualism, impersonality, and rationality.* Specialization emerged in the form of separate social roles and social institutions designed to accomplish specific tasks and goals. People related to one another through their specific roles—as farmer, merchant, or blacksmith—rather than as complete individuals with many roles and feelings. Individualism and a concern with personal self-interest came to predominate and replaced loyalty to group or society. Social ties took on a "contractual" nature in which calculation, impersonality, and formality dominated. More time was spent in what sociologists today call **secondary groups:** *groups in which people have few emotional bonds, ties are impersonal, and people are seeking to achieve specific, practical goals.*

The observations of Tönnies and others lead to the conclusion that urbanization results in more secondary group relations in people's lives and fewer primary group ties. This is what lends city life its impersonal character, the feeling that most people care little about you as a person. This can lead to feelings of alienation from others. People who have many secondary ties and few primary

ones might even feel a desperate sense of isolation. Based on the work of Tönnies and others, Louis Wirth and other urban sociologists at the University of Chicago championed the viewpoint that city life shapes city dwellers by creating an urban consciousness, a distinctive way of thinking about and a unique awareness of their surroundings (Wirth, 1938). Three elements of city life play a role here: large numbers of people, high density, and the heterogeneity of cities. People protect themselves from the large numbers and the density by interacting with one another in highly impersonal ways, and their lives become segmented, with only specialized roles being relevant in particular settings. Social relations are also highly depersonalized, with kinship bonds weakening and community identity fading. Given the thousands of people and hundreds of settings that urban dwellers might face each day, it is not surprising that they respond with impersonality and emotional distance. To devote time and energy to all of these people would be draining and impractical. Given this mass of humanity, individuals can feel quite insignificant, knowing little about and having few contacts with most people around them. The knowledge one has of people is often very superficial. Furthermore, relationships that do develop are most often secondary in nature and based on rational calculation of self-interest, rather than affection. This can lead city dwellers to feel preyed upon by others. What emerges is a distinctive urban "consciousness": People are reserved in social relationships, rational, and self-interested.

The heterogeneity of cities also has important effects on the urban consciousness. Neighborhoods are often highly segregated along racial, ethnic, religious, or socioeconomic lines. Yet it is difficult to avoid mingling with many different kinds of people at work, while shopping, or while traveling from place to place. These people may not only be different but also be viewed as potentially dangerous or threatening. A mentally disturbed person shouting obscenities in the street or

"I FIND THAT AS LONG AS YOU AVOID EYE CONTACT, YOU HARDLY REALIZE THERE IS A CROWD."

(Courtesy Sidney Harris)

some tough-looking teenagers can be frightening and can motivate people to take a cold and aloof attitude toward those around them. Again, a distinctive urban consciousness emerges that says it is probably best to ignore much of what goes on around you lest it bring you some difficulties or trouble. This diversity leads to a greater tolerance of different life-styles, but often the tolerance is not based on acceptance but on resignation. City dwellers typically have little choice but to mingle with people very different from themselves, no matter how they feel about it.

Urban Communities

The picture of urban life painted by Wirth and others of the early Chicago school was certainly dreary. This may have been due in part to the fact that many of these sociologists were first-generation urbanites themselves, having grown up in small towns or rural villages, and the negative aspects of urbanism deeply impressed them. It may also have resulted from the fact that the Chicago of the 1920s and 1930s that they studied was undergoing a period of considerable growth, inmigration, and social disorder. More recent perspectives on urban life have focused more on the positive elements of urbanism.

In contrast to Tönnies, Wirth, and others, Herbert Gans (1962, 1972) argues that cities do retain a sense of community in their neighborhoods where people identify with and have a sense of positive regard for one another. In some areas, strong ethnic or racial bonds may lend a considerable degree of cohesiveness to a neighborhood. In Hispanic communities, for example, ethnic identity may be reflected in stores and restaurants catering to Hispanic tastes or in the routine use of Spanish in shops. There may also be organizations of Hispanic students or business people that emphasize the common heritage and interests of the people in the community. In addition, even in neighborhoods with a number of ethnic or racial groups, ethnic group boundaries often serve as symbols of solidarity and regulate patterns of interaction, with people having close ties to members of their own racial or ethnic group and maintaining distance from others (Suttles, 1968; Barth, 1969). Furthermore, communities in cities are not limited to particular neighborhoods but may be based on common interests or leisure activities.

Gans's argument, then, is that urban life does not have a uniform impact on people, although the tendencies described by Wirth can certainly be found. Rather, there are many life-styles in cities, and the impact of the city on particular people depends on the groups to which they belong.

Thus, social characteristics such as age, education, or racial and ethnic group membership are critical factors affecting people's adaptations to city life.

Urban Subcultures

Claude Fischer (1975, 1982) attempted to synthesize Wirth's and Gans's positions. Fischer recognized that the social characteristics considered important by Gans—race, sex, age, income level, and so on—play significant roles in shaping the variety of life-styles that emerge in cities. Yet he argued that the variables considered central by Wirth—size, density, and heterogeneity—are also important, lending an intensity to the impact of subcultural group membership that is usually absent in small towns and rural areas. One reason for this is that there are enough people with particular characteristics in cities that they will learn about one another, establish meeting places such as bars or parks, develop specialized activities, and thus form a subculture. In nonurban areas, this is considerably less likely to happen because there will be fewer people with similar characteristics, and the chance of their forming a subculture is considerably reduced. In addition, because city dwellers are unlikely to know most people with whom they come in contact each day, they rely on characteristics such as social class, age, or ethnicity to decide whether they have anything in common with a person, how to relate to the person, or whether the person represents a threat. Because these subcultural characteristics are so important in social contacts, urbanites become more skilled at picking up cues, such as styles of dress, that signify subcultural membership, and this skill is often considered "sophistication" by both urbanites and nonurbanites alike. In short, according to Fischer, urban life is different because it tends to magnify the importance of subcultural differences between people, and research supports Fischer's basic notion of how subcultural involvement influences people's behavior in cities (Tittle, 1989). Within this context, though, many urbanites

maintain rich and complex networks of social relationships. Fischer's conclusion is that community size by itself does not lead to alienation or other negative consequences.

Urban Life: Good or Bad?

It should be clear by now that the impact of urban life cannot be characterized simply as good or bad. Reality is more complex than this. Impersonality, isolation, and anonymity do exist in cities—especially among those with few economic or social resources or no subcultural ties—but there are also many communities and subcultures in cities that are rich sources of personal relationships and identity. Cities also offer leisure, cultural, and economic resources that are usually not available in rural areas. There are, for example, baseball, football, and hockey games, opera and ballet, museums, large shopping centers, and restaurants with many cuisines. In addition, the anonymity of cities can be a source of freedom from the curious eyes of one's neighbors. People are freer to pursue life-styles that might be frowned on in smaller towns. Finally, cities offer a wider range of occupational opportunities than are found in small communities. This dimension of city life can be especially important to couples who are pursuing dual careers (see Chapter 3). In small towns with fewer job opportunities, many such couples would either have to break up or settle for only one partner pursuing a career.

In examining urban problems and their solutions, we must recognize that cities are not merely buildings and streets and masses of automobiles. They are also elaborate networks of social relationships that support and sustain people. One of the major weaknesses of urban social policy in the past has been its failure to recognize this simple fact. The approach in the past has often been to tear down old buildings and put up new ones. Only when the urban problems remained—or became worse—was it recognized that solutions to problems lay in the social and economic resources in the community and in the social character and subcultures of neighborhoods.

PERSPECTIVES ON URBAN PROBLEMS

To gain a perspective on urban problems and their solutions, it is helpful to view them from the three sociological perspectives.

The Functionalist Perspective

From the functionalist perspective, a city, like any social system, is made up of many interrelated and interdependent parts. A change in one part of the system has potential implications for the other parts. We have reviewed some of the changes that have occurred in American cities during this century. What becomes clear is that the problems of American cities arise in part because these changes have produced some degree of social disorganization. Cities have had to adapt to a variety of fundamental changes: the flight of people and jobs to the suburbs, changes in the occupational structure of an advanced industrial society, and developments in technology, such as the automobile, highways, and computers. All these changes have been beneficial in many respects, of course, but they have also been highly dysfunctional for many cities. Because of these changes, some neighborhoods became financially destitute wastelands with many serious problems that will be discussed shortly.

It may be, of course, that the central city is no longer functional in an advanced industrial society. If businesses find it cheaper to locate elsewhere and people prefer to live elsewhere, then possibly the central city no longer performs the important functions that it once did and should be left to its fate. Yet the cities are still an important part of the social system: People do live, work, and shop there. Many societal resources in the form of buildings, transportation networks,

and people are tied up there. Urban neighborhoods where people enjoy living are adversely affected by crime and other urban problems. People who go to the city to watch baseball or hockey or attend the opera confront the problems of the city. So ignoring the problems of the cities does not alleviate their impact on people's lives. All the parts of urban areas are interrelated, and each part—along with its problems—has consequences for the other parts.

The Conflict Perspective

From the conflict perspective, our cities have deteriorated because the groups most directly affected—people living in the cities—have not had the political and economic resources to thwart the changes under way (Zeitlin, 1990). As we have seen, federal legislation encouraged the shift of people and jobs to the suburbs. The people who left the cities were the middle class and the affluent—the very people with the power to do something about the decline of the cities if they wished. But, of course, once they left, they were no longer interested in urban problems. In fact, these people tended not to understand the part their own actions played in bringing about the problems. The poor and minorities who were left in the cities had few political and economic resources with which to attack the problems.

City dwellers have also had to contend with a strong and, until recently, intransigent "anticity" bias in American society. As we have seen, as recently as 1940, almost half of our populace lived in rural areas (see Figure 12.1), and many urbanites of that time had grown up in rural America. Small town and rural living has been idealized as more pure, intimate, and healthy. Cities have been viewed as dirty, corrupting, and dangerous. In fact, this pro-rural orientation has been an important part of American culture for centuries. One consequence is that most Americans have shown little interest in assisting cities with their problems. Added to this is the fact that political representation at both the state and federal level has been weighted more heavily toward rural communities and small towns. Because our system of representation was established when America was largely rural, rural dwellers were concerned about protecting their interests against those of the growing cities. So in most states, there are more congressional and legislative districts in rural than in urban areas. This means that rural areas are overrepresented in comparison with their population size. So legislation to alleviate urban problems has had to run the gantlet of rural-dominated congresses and state legislatures. Because more power resided in the hands of the representatives of rural and small-town people, there has been less than overwhelming enthusiasm for urban legislation. When these rural politicians combine with politicians who represent suburban constituents, the representatives of the urbanites are far outnumbered.

The Interactionist Perspective

In many respects, cities are far better off than they have ever been (Banfield, 1990). They are less crowded, have better sanitation, and the schools have improved in comparison to pre-World War II cities. Even their finances are in pretty good shape when compared with cities in earlier eras. Yet the interactionist perspective points to the importance of subjective definitions of social reality. People have come to expect much more than they once did. In addition, we look at cities today in comparison with the immediate past that many of us can recall. The period between World War II and 1970 was one of considerable economic expansion and social prosperity for cities. By contrast, the urban experience of the 1970s and 1980s seems to have been a highly disruptive downturn in the fortunes of cities (Clark and Walter, 1991). It is this contrast that often leads people to perceive the problems of cities as much more severe than objective conditions would warrant. Yet the important issue from the interactionist perspective is that people define these conditions as a social problem.

The interactionist perspective also highlights the importance of shared expectations and social consensus in governing human behavior. Because of the heterogeneity in cities, such consensus is often difficult to achieve. As we have seen, cities contain many different racial and ethnic groups, religions, social classes, and life-styles. Each of these groups has different and sometimes competing goals and values. This means that city dwellers routinely interact with people with whom they cannot achieve consensus on some issues. Sometimes the conflict is over the desirability of playing loud music on a bus, and at other times it is over who should possess the money in a person's wallet. This lack of consensus makes it more difficult to solve many urban problems.

PROBLEMS IN AMERICAN CITIES

The focus of attention on urban problems tends to be on those conditions found in the central cities of large metropolitan areas. To be sure, the central cities do suffer most severely from problems such as crime, poverty, and deteriorating housing. Yet many of these problems can be found in smaller towns, and some suburban communities find themselves beset with similar difficulties.

Economic Decline

One of the premier problems that many American cities confront is that they are in a state of economic decline. In fact, in the past two decades, a number of American cities, especially in the Northeast and Midwest, have been on the brink of financial collapse (Shefter, 1985). In 1975, New York City was unable to pay its bills, banks refused to give any assistance, and only a complicated bailout from the federal government saved it from financial disaster. In 1978, Cleveland became the first American city since the Depression of the 1930s to actually go into financial default.

Table 12.1   **Population Change in the Twenty Largest American Cities, 1950–1990**

City	Population 1950	Population 1990	Rank in 1990	Rank in 1950	Percentage Change 1950–1990
New York	7,892,000	7,323,000	1	1	−7.2
Los Angeles	1,970,000	3,485,000	2	4	+76.9
Chicago	3,621,000	2,784,000	3	2	−23.1
Houston	596,000	1,631,000	4	14	+174
Philadelphia	2,072,000	1,586,000	5	3	−23.5
San Diego	434,000	1,111,000	6	31	+156
Detroit	1,850,000	1,028,000	7	5	−44.4
Dallas	334,000	1,007,000	8	22	+201
Phoenix	107,000	983,000	9	92	+819
San Antonio	408,000	936,000	10	25	+129
San Jose	95,000	782,000	11	105	+723
Baltimore	950,000	736,000	12	6	−22.5
Indianapolis	427,000	731,000	13	23	+71.2
San Francisco	775,000	724,000	14	11	−6.5
Jacksonville, Fla.	205,000	635,000	15	46	+210
Columbus, Ohio	376,000	633,000	16	28	+68.4
Milwaukee	637,000	628,000	17	13	−1.4
Memphis	396,000	610,000	18	26	+54.0
Washington, D.C.	802,000	607,000	19	9	−24.3
Boston	801,000	574,000	20	10	−28.3

Remaining Cities in the Top Twenty in 1950:

City	Rank in 1950	Rank in 1990
Seattle	19	21
Cleveland	7	23
New Orleans	16	24
Kansas City, Mo.	20	31
St. Louis	8	34
Pittsburgh	12	40
Minneapolis	17	42
Cincinnati	18	45
Buffalo	15	50

SOURCES: U.S. Bureau of the Census, *Statistical Abstract of the United States, 1978* (Washington, D.C.: U.S. Government Printing Office, 1978), pp. 20–26; U.S. Bureau of the Census, *Statistical Abstract of the United States, 1991* (Washington, D.C.: U.S. Government Printing Office, 1991), pp. 34–36.

During the recession of the early 1980s, Boston and Detroit were so short of funds that their governments had to consider not paying for essential city services such as fire and police protection. In the early 1990s, New York City was again in fiscal crisis, cutting services and raising local taxes (Caraley, 1992).

One major cause of these financial problems has been the flight of people and jobs from many cities since World War II. Of the twenty largest cities in 1990, nine have lost population since 1950. Of the twenty largest in 1950, eighteen have lost people (see Table 12.1). And population growth has been much slower in the central cities than elsewhere (see Figure 12.2). As we pointed out in Chapter 2, the centralization of economic organization in the United States has meant that a relatively small number of corporations account for an increasingly large share of economic activity. When one of these large business enterprises leaves a city, the departure has a ripple effect as smaller companies that support it also move (Schwartz, 1984). As businesses and affluent residents left the cities, the tax roles declined. The poor and elderly who remained paid fewer taxes and used more city services than did the well-to-do who left. As a result, many cities have faced severe financial crises over the past few decades, and these economic difficulties contributed to all the other problems of the cities.

Housing

Two visible symbols of the economic problems of cities are the deterioration and in some cases abandonment of housing in many neighborhoods, and the inability of the poor to find affordable housing. The result is that many people—often the minorities, the elderly, and the poor—live in buildings with dangerous structural defects, inadequate plumbing and heating, poor sanitation, overcrowding, exposed wiring, rotting floors, and inadequate toilet facilities. Other people cannot find any housing that they can afford. The prob-

lem of homelessness, discussed in Chapter 5, is due in part to the unavailability of sufficient rental units at a price that low-income families can afford (Bohanon, 1991). To cope with housing problems, some cities have established stricter housing codes, passed renters' rights ordinances, and in a few cases set up rent control laws to stop rent gouging. Landlords complain that these practices increase the costs of owning and maintaining dilapidated buildings and reduce their profits. They also point out that improving or renovating these structures often leads to higher taxes. Low profits have motivated some "slumlords" to simply abandon their buildings. There are about two million abandoned buildings in the United States, and another 150,000 are added to this total each year. In New York City alone, forty thousand buildings are abandoned on a yearly basis (Palen, 1987).

The government provides housing vouchers to low-income families to help them pay for acceptable housing. The government has also built low-income housing projects across the country, and most of these efforts have provided adequate and safe shelter for poor families, although in some inner-city neighborhoods, public housing projects have been rife with crime. However, according to the executive director of the National Association of Housing and Redevelopment Officials, "the real failure of public housing policy in the United States has been . . . the failure to build enough public housing to meet the growing needs of low-income people for affordable shelter, and failure to provide the resources needed to maintain and modernize the nation's 1.3 million public housing units" (Nelson, 1989: 9). Low-cost housing is in distressingly short supply. Unfortunately, government policy tends to devote more resources toward the housing of nonpoor families than to low-income and poor families. This is done primarily through a tax deduction that people are allowed on the interest on their home mortgages. This deduction provides far more money for homeowners, who are mostly middle class or affluent, than all the money we devote to low-income housing.

Segregation

The population shifts in American cities have led whites to the suburbs, leaving racial and ethnic minorities behind in the cities. The term **ghetto** refers to *a neighborhood inhabited largely by members of a single ethnic or racial group*. In the early part of this century, Jews and Italians lived in urban ghettos; today, African Americans, Hispanics, and Asians are the primary ghetto residents. Although blacks make up about 12 percent of our populace and Hispanics about 9 percent, they constitute far larger proportions of the residents of our largest cities (see Table 12.2). They are concentrated in the central city areas with the most severe urban problems. Although 25 percent of all whites live in central cities, 56 percent of blacks, and 53 percent of Hispanics live there (U.S. Bureau of the Census, 1991a).

This segregation of people of color, especially African Americans, did not occur by chance. In fact, it was encouraged by the FHA and VA policies discussed earlier in the chapter (Judd, 1991). During the 1930s and 1940s, administrators of these programs actively promoted the idea that neighborhoods should be racially segregated because, in their eyes, this promoted more neighborhood stability and higher property values. As the FHA *Underwriting Manual* of 1938 put it: "If a neighborhood is to retain stability, it is necessary that properties shall continue to be occupied by the same social and racial classes" (quoted in Judd, 1991: 740). The FHA actively discouraged developers from allowing African Americans to purchase homes in white suburbs and discouraged loans in mostly black areas on the grounds that people who live in these areas are poor credit risks. The result: African Americans were almost completely excluded from the federally insured mortgage market and from the suburbs that it was helping to create. At the same time, the FHA would not back loans for inner-city housing be-

Table 12.2   **The Racial Composition of the Twenty Largest Cities in the United States, 1960–1990**

	Percent Black		Percent Hispanic	
	1960	*1990*	*1980*	*1990*
Baltimore	34.7	59.2	1.0	1.0
Boston	9.1	25.6	6.4	10.8
Chicago	22.9	39.1	14.0	19.6
Columbus, Ohio	16.4	22.6	0.8	1.1
Dallas	19.0	29.5	12.3	20.9
Detroit	28.9	75.7	2.4	2.8
Houston	22.9	28.1	17.6	27.6
Indianapolis	20.6	22.6	0.9	1.1
Jacksonville, Fla.	23.2	25.2	1.8	2.6
Los Angeles	13.5	17.4	27.5	39.9
Memphis	37.0	54.8	0.8	0.7
Milwaukee	8.4	30.5	4.1	6.3
New York	14.0	28.7	19.9	24.4
Philadelphia	26.4	39.9	3.8	5.6
Phoenix	4.8	5.2	14.8	20.0
San Antonio	7.1	7.0	53.7	55.6
San Diego	6.0	9.4	14.9	20.7
San Francisco	10.0	10.9	12.3	13.9
San Jose	1.0	4.7	22.3	26.6
Washington, D.C.	53.9	65.8	2.8	5.4

SOURCES: U.S. Bureau of the Census, *Statistical Abstract of the United States, 1978* (Washington, D.C.: U.S. Government Printing Office, 1978), pp. 24–26; U.S. Bureau of the Census, *Statistical Abstract of the United States, 1985* (Washington, D.C.: U.S. Government Printing Office, 1984), pp. 23–25; U.S. Bureau of the Census, *Statistical Abstract of the United States, 1991* (Washington, D.C.: U.S. Government Printing Office, 1991), pp. 34–36.

cause this was also considered a high credit risk. In part as a consequence of these policies, African Americans today tend to be residentially isolated from whites (Gillmor and Doig, 1992). In Chicago, for example, 71 percent of African Americans live on a block where 90 percent of the residents are also African American. Despite the fact that racial discrimination in housing was outlawed by the Civil Rights Act of 1964, the 1990 census showed that as far as race is concerned the United States remains two separate nations—one black and the other white. In assessing whether we have moved any closer to the goal of residential integration by the 1990s, one study looking at the 1990 census data concluded:

> Black-white integration in the nation's 50 largest metropolitan areas has improved only slightly. Some cities fared much better than others, but several showed clear signs of increasing black segregation. . . . Little real progress has been made. (Gillmor and Doig, 1992: 48, 51)

There has been some movement of African Americans to the suburbs in the past two decades; however, they tend to move only to a small number of suburban areas that typically have existing black populations (Stahura, 1989–90). Most suburbanites still fear that an influx of African American residents will produce white flight and declining property values.

This concentration of minorities in ghettos can create some serious difficulties for urban areas. For example, residential segregation exacerbates both poverty and economic deprivation for both African Americans and Hispanics (Massey, Gross, and Eggers, 1991; Santiago and Wilder, 1991). Minorities who live in segregated urban neighborhoods have more difficulties finding jobs or taking advantage of educational opportunities that are available. Segregation also concentrates the problem of poverty into a few neighborhoods rather than spreading it more evenly around a metropolitan area. Such dispersal could spread the burden of assisting the poor throughout the metropolitan area. Residential segregation can also enhance tensions between racial groups. For example, ghettos isolate racial groups from one another so that they have little contact and believe they have little in common. Much research has shown that such segregation can lead to negative stereotyping, hostility, and prejudice. Sympathy and understanding decline without social contact

between groups. The outcome is mutual mistrust and suspicion that make working toward solutions for urban problems even more difficult.

Crime

Crime is probably one of the urban problems that the average citizen thinks most about. Although crime can be found everywhere, it is far more common in cities. As Figure 12.3 illustrates, the rate of violent crime is eight times greater in our largest cities than it is in rural areas; the rate of property crimes is four times greater. The greatest disparity is for robbery, which is at least forty-five times greater in large cities than in rural areas!

Violent Crimes:	Crimes Known to the Police per 100,000 People
Cities with population of:	
250, 000 or More	1606
100,000-249,999	914
50,000-99,999	630
25,000-49,999	451
10,000-24,999	328
10,000 or Less	288
Suburbs	348
Rural Areas	180
Property Crimes:	Crimes Known to the Police per 100, 000 People
Cities with population of:	
250, 000 or More	8330
100,000-249,999	7430
50,000-99,999	5782
25,000-49,999	5095
10,000-24,999	4210
10,000 or Less	3902
Suburbs	3797
Rural Areas	1843

Figure 12.3 **Crime Rates in Urban and Rural Areas, 1989**
SOURCE: Kathleen Maguire and Timothy J. Flanagan, eds., *Sourcebook of Criminal Justice Statistics: 1990* (Washington, D.C.: U.S. Department of Justice, Bureau of Justice Statistics, 1991), pp. 364–365.

Also, the larger the city, the higher the crime rate. And suburban areas have lower crime rates than all but the smallest cities.

Even within cities, crime is not evenly distributed. Crime is more likely in inner-city areas where the poor and minorities live. Low-income and minority people are also more likely to be the victims of crimes. Even in the suburbs, crime is more common when there is a large low-income population living in the suburb (Stahura, Huff, and Smith, 1979; Palen, 1987).

The massive crime rate that exists in some urban neighborhoods exacerbates many of the other problems that these communities confront: the lack of economic development, the growing underclass, and physical deterioration. Simply stated, the growing crime rate in a neighborhood ripples through the community with devastating effect (DiIulio, 1989). New businesses refuse to move in and old ones relocate, making it even more difficult for community residents to support themselves. The chaos and violence produced by crime and drug use can pervade the schools, with disorder making it more difficult for students to achieve scholastically. With a high crime rate, many of a community's males may be in jail, which means fewer partners for women to marry and help to provide for their children. In short, the economic, educational, and familial structures of the community are compromised in a highly crime-ridden environment. In Chapter 5, we discussed some of the reasons for the emergence of an underclass in inner-city areas in the United States. Here, we can see that crime also contributes to the problem by making it even more difficult for those inner-city areas to overcome the problems. Most inner-city residents are not criminals but rather victims who have few avenues of escape from the predators around them. For these law-abiding members of the underclass, the fear of crime is what they confront on a daily basis. In the Applied Research insert, we discuss some elements of this problem and what the research suggests could be done about it.

Crime is widespread in cities, which has motivated some urban residents to form "neighborhood watch" programs to assist police in stopping burglaries, robberies, and other crimes.

We have reviewed the sources of crime extensively in Chapter 9. Without question, the high crime rates in cities are in part a function of unemployment and the general lack of legitimate opportunities for success. If the poor, especially the young, cannot find jobs or attend school, a certain number of them will turn to crime as the only way they can see to support themselves. In inner-city areas, there are also many opportunities for the young to learn how to commit crimes and to be taught that crime is a preferable "hustle" to working for a living (recall the differential association theory of crime). In addition, young nonwhites in ghetto neighborhoods may well be perceived by others as criminals regardless of their behavior,

Crime in cities contributes to an atmosphere of fear and paranoia and forces urban residents to restrict their activities in order to reduce the impact of crime on their lives.

and this sets the stage for the self-fulfilling prophecy described by labeling theorists. So the economic problems of cities initiate a series of social processes that cascade eventually into a very high crime rate.

Educational Problems

Americans have often turned to education as a way of mastering social problems. Education, for example, has been the route for most immigrants to achieve upward mobility. In many of our cities today, however, the schools are not up to this task (Kozol, 1991). Again, one major hurdle is financial. Unlike most other countries, education in the United States is considered a local rather than a national responsibility. Funds for education are raised in good part through local taxes, often property taxes. This results in great disparities in educational resources from one community to another. Poor communities and financially pressed cities simply cannot afford the educational expenses of the more affluent suburbs. Inner-city schools must contend with old buildings, less

equipment, archaic educational technology, high rates of teacher turnover, and low staff morale. Especially recently with the increasing importance of computer technology, inner-city schools have been less able to impart the skills needed to compete adequately in a job market in which literacy and skills are increasingly essential. In addition, these children have to go to school in frighteningly dangerous neighborhoods where drug dealing and violence are the norm. The whole experience seems to tell these children that they are simply not worth as much as the more affluent, mostly white, children in suburban schools. With these problems, an inner-city school is considerably less likely to provide its students with the training and motivation to achieve upward mobility.

Teachers are often ill equipped to deal with the problems of inner-city schools. Low pay and other problems of the teaching profession have been much discussed in the past few years. Beyond this, teachers often confront a degree of culture shock in inner-city schools as the teacher's middle-class training and upbringing come face-

APPLIED RESEARCH

The Fear of Crime: Effects on the Quality of Urban Life

When one out of every three American households is directly victimized each year, it isn't long before everyone has either been a victim himself or had someone very close to him victimized. The problem is not just what crime does to people's lives; it is also what the fear of crime does to our society. ("Images of Fear . . . ," 1985: 44)

In December of 1984, a seemingly mild-mannered man named Bernhard Goetz made national news when he shot four teenagers in a New York City subway car. Allegedly, Mr. Goetz did this because the young men were trying to rob him under the threat of deadly force. Further investigation of the incident revealed some contrasting elements: The teenage perpetrators, although perhaps intending to intimidate Mr. Goetz, were armed only with a small screwdriver; and, not only was Goetz carrying a .38 revolver, he had recently acquired several handguns—apparently due to his rising fear of being a crime victim.

The Goetz episode brings home once again, as if we needed further proof, the extent to which the quality of life in cities is lowered by crime, fear, and the restrictions that city residents impose on their daily routines as a consequence. We saw in Chapter 9, for example, that the crime most feared by women who live in cities is rape (Gordon and Riger, 1989). That fear directly affects their daily lives as they avoid going out alone, avoid going to certain neighborhoods, and install security devices in their houses or apartments. The other crimes these women were afraid of were robbery and burglary. Another study found that one-half of the women in large cities felt that it was unsafe to be out in their neighborhood after dark. Fear of crime is most common among older people, especially women (Markson and Hess, 1980). Studies indicate that people are more likely to take precautions against crime if they have been victims themselves or if they are more fearful of crime (Conklin, 1976). Rather than focus on how these individual characteristics influence taking precautions, however, some research has considered the role of social and physical characteristics of the environment (Lavrakas et al., 1981).

One such approach has been to focus on community organization as an important ingredient in urban residents' fear of crime. Social researchers Barbara Kail and Paula Kleinman (1985) have conducted a series of investigations in different ethnic communities to assess the complex relationship between urban residents' reactions to the fear of crime and their degree of integration into the communities in which they live.

to-face with the world of lower-class minorities. The subcultural values, personal demeanor, and even the language of many of the teachers' students are likely to be strange and possibly seen as threatening. There may even be a tendency, based on racial or ethnic stereotypes, to label many of these students as incapable of great achievements. When this occurs, a self-fulfilling prophecy can set in, especially when the students accept the teachers' judgment of them.

These researchers found that the existence of formally organized local community associations can diminish fear and self-imposed limitations on activities. One example of such an association is the "Basic Car Plan" in Los Angeles, where neighborhood residents can meet the police officers who are regularly assigned to their area face to face. In the absence of such formal efforts, some urban dwellers develop informal techniques for dealing with fear and victimization. For example, such informal techniques might include casual gatherings designed to air mutual concerns about crime and discuss possible strategies for protection. At least one investigation has determined that urban residents who are more integrated into the social fabric of a neighborhood—the ones active in formal and informal community organizations—are less fearful of crime (Hunter and Baumer, 1982).

Previous investigations have shown that when individuals take precautions to deal with their fear of crime this behavior may only deflect crime rather than reduce it: The criminal merely victimizes someone else. Furthermore, these individual efforts may actually inhibit the community's response to the crime problem (Dubow and Emmons, 1981). More recent research efforts, such as that of Kail and Kleinman, suggest that if existing formal organizations can be strengthened, then fear of crime will be reduced, which also reduces the extent to which individuals place restrictions on their behavior. Thus, community organization appears to be a key ingredient in elevating the quality of urban life by reducing people's fear of crime.

Some urban planners have argued that many neighborhoods are designed in such a way that they discourage social interaction and social participation on the part of residents. Architecturally, they isolate people from one another, which tends to increase the opportunity for crime and the fear of crime. High-rise apartment buildings, for example, discourage contact and communication and have many locations that are unwatched and where crime can occur. Buildings are designed primarily with economic concerns in mind: maximizing profit from a piece of urban property. Yet planner Oscar Newman (1972; Newman and Franck, 1980) suggests a few design considerations that would enhance social participation and reduce crime and the fear of it:

1. Buildings should have only a small number of units sharing the same entryway off the streets. In this way, residents know who lives there, who has a right to be there, and who is a stranger.

2. Windows, lighting, entryways, and paths should be designed so that there is continuous surveillance by the residents. This reduces the number of isolated spots where crime can occur unobserved.

3. Lobbies should be designed not merely as an entryway to the building but as a social center where people congregate. This might be done by having newstands or recreation items in or near the lobby.

4. Buildings should be low-rise with fewer residents to reduce feelings of anonymity, isolation, and lack of identity with the building. Newman found that the crime rate is higher in taller and more populous buildings.

FUTURE PROSPECTS

From the 1930s to the 1980s, urban policy in the United States was based on the assumption that the federal government is best positioned to provide services for poor people and to fund programs that attack the problems confronting our cities. Cities and states are less suited to do this because they might be tempted to underfund such programs, or not establish them at all, to avoid becoming known as a "high tax" locale and thus discourage people and businesses from settling there. In addition, most states and cities cannot run deficits to fund programs and often must get taxes approved by voters. The federal government does not confront these limitations; so, many argued, it is best suited to fund programs, such as those focusing on urban problems, that Americans in many cities might be reluctant to support. Generally, interventionists have supported this position.

In the last fifteen years, urban policy has changed dramatically, with a decided shift toward a more laissez-faire approach. As one policy analyst put it: "The Reagan/Bush administrations' ideological posture was that it no longer wanted, could not afford, and did not deem it legitimate to be the ultimate subsidizer of poor people and poor local and state jurisdictions" (Caraley, 1992: 16). Reagan and Bush argued that a strong and healthy economy is a far more promising approach to solving urban problems than direct federal intervention. So the trend of the last fifteen years has been toward efforts at renewing our cities that are based on less government involvement or no government involvement at all. For laissez-faire advocates, the key role of the federal government in solving urban problems is to keep the economy healthy, not to directly intervene with funds.

The consequence of these policy changes has been a catastrophic decline in federal support for cities, which has exacerbated all the problems discussed earlier in this chapter. As one urban expert put it:

The New Federalism of the Reagan and Bush administrations has succeeded in reversing fifty years of American domestic policy by cutting back the constellation of federal grants to local and state governments that the federal government used to help poor people and needy city jurisdictions. These cutbacks accelerated the drift of large cities, especially the older ones of the East and Middle West, into underserviced, violence-ridden, crack infested, homeless burdened, bankruptcy-skirting slum ghettos. On top of this, the Bush administration's inability to maintain economic prosperity . . . has brought many cities to their worst fiscal and service crises since the Great Depression of the 1930s. (Caraley, 1992: 1)

Since 1980, federal grants to local government for a variety of programs, from job training to mass transit, have been cut by 50 percent in constant dollars or actual purchasing power. As an example, New York City received 52 percent of its budget from federal and state aid in 1980 compared with 36 percent in 1989.

The rationale for cutting funds was the laissez-faire position: States and cities should be allowed to make their own choices about which services they want rather than having the choices imposed on them by the federal government. The reality is that the federal government started or took over almost all these programs because local officials were unwilling or unable to run them. Most cities have so few tax resources and such great demand for services that they could do little, once the federal government stopped funding the programs, but cut the programs and lay people off. The bottom line is that our cities have low income levels and high poverty rates whereas the suburbs that surround them have high incomes and low poverty rates. The needs are in the cities but the resources are in the suburbs. On top of all this, the slashing of federal funds occurred at a time when cities had three major, and expensive, scourges imposed on them: epidemics of crack cocaine addiction and the crimes associated with it, the AIDS epidemic, and the growth of the homeless population. And the states have not stepped in to help as it was suggested they would. As Figure 12.4 shows, federal aid dropped from 22 percent of large cities' general expenditures in the beginning of the 1980s to 6 percent by the end, but aid from the state governments did not increase to take up the slack. The money stayed in the suburbs.

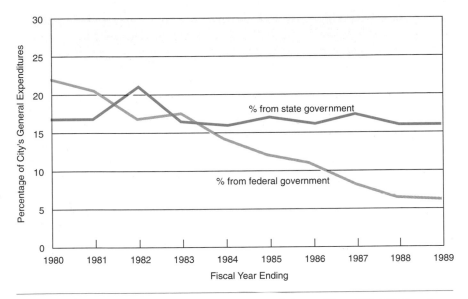

Figure 12.4   **Federal and State Aid to Cities with More Than 300,000 People, 1980–1989**
SOURCE: U.S. Department of Commerce, Bureau of the Census, *City Government Finances,* Series GF, No. 4 (Washington, D.C.: U.S. Government Printing Office, 1980–1989).

Despite this shift toward a laissez-faire policy, there are still some significant federal programs focused on alleviating the problems of our cities. We will discuss these along with programs and efforts that rely more on local resources or private initiative.

Federal Grants and Programs

General Poverty Assistance.   In Chapter 5, we discussed many programs that provide direct funds or services to the poor, such as Medicaid, Social Security, and Aid to Families with Dependent Children. There are other programs we did not discuss, such as housing assistance, child nutrition programs, and food stamps. The policy issues surrounding such direct assistance to the poor were discussed in Chapter 5 and will not be repeated here, but all these programs are key resources used by cities to alleviate the problems their citizens face. During the 1980s, funding for

these programs has increased by about 40 percent in constant dollars, but this has been due mostly to more people being eligible for the programs rather than more resources going to each recipient. In other words, the cities have gotten poorer during the 1980s, so more of our poverty funds are funneled to them.

Urban Renewal.   One of the more prominent approaches to urban problems for many years was called urban renewal, initiated by the Housing Act of 1949 (Hawley, 1971). The major purpose of urban renewal was to rebuild blighted areas of cities, to provide low-cost housing for urban poor, and to stimulate private investment in the inner city through the physical renewal of deteriorated areas. The Housing Act provided government funds to develop plans and to acquire and clear land to be redeveloped. This foundation of renewal was then supposed to attract private investors. It also required that plans be made to relocate people who lost their housing due to this program.

In general, urban renewal programs did not produce their intended benefits. Rather than trying to renovate existing buildings, the buildings were most often torn down. The planners of the program believed that destroying dilapidated buildings was an essential first step in solving urban problems. Often these buildings were replaced with luxury apartments that were more profitable to private-sector developers. The poor who had originally occupied the neighborhood were pushed into other areas where housing was sometimes more expensive. These neighborhoods, experiencing an influx of the poor, then often began to deteriorate. In fact, the plight of some homeless people today can be traced to the destruction of single-room occupancy hotels in skid row areas during urban renewal. In the past, these hotels provided community and social support for many urban poor. When they were destroyed, the poor had no place to go but the streets (Hoch and Slayton, 1989). By one estimate, urban renewal destroyed twice as many housing units as it built (U.S. Department of Health, Education, and Welfare, 1969).

When low-income housing for the poor was constructed, it often took the form of public housing projects—enormous, fortress-like structures with dark hallways and stairwells where assaults, rapes, and muggings were common (Rainwater, 1977; Palen, 1987). Urban renewal planners for the most part ignored the community and subcultural aspects of urban life pointed to by Gans and Fischer. The planners showed little sensitivity to the social networks of a community: where people gathered, where they played and worked, or to whom they liked to talk. Instead, buildings and neighborhoods were treated as physical entities rather than social communities, and if anything this outlook made living in these communities more like the negative experience that Wirth described. The amount of urban renewal aid given to state and local governments by the federal government declined substantially,

from more than $1 billion in 1970 to $13 million in 1986 when it was folded into the next program to be discussed (U.S. Bureau of the Census, 1989: 270).

Community Development Block Grants. In 1974, the Community Development Block Grant (CDBG) program was established, consolidating seven separate grant programs of the Department of Housing and Urban Development (HUD), including urban renewal and the Model Cities Program (Dommel, 1984). Since it was established, more than $30 billion in CDBG funds have been distributed to cities around the country. The main purpose of the CDBG program is to give local officials a larger share of the decision making and greater flexibility in how federal funds are used. The program also focuses on eliminating slums and urban blight, providing benefits such as more housing and greater economic opportunities to low- and moderate-income groups, and expanding and improving community services. Cities apply for CDBG funds, which are allocated on the basis of complex formulas that consider population size, the amount of poverty, and the extent of overcrowded housing. Once funds are awarded, there are relatively few strings attached.

One of the main criticisms of the CDBG program is that the distribution formula is such that cities with few serious problems receive funds nonetheless. This makes the program less efficient at solving urban problems than it might be if funds were targeted more accurately. In 1977, this problem was partially alleviated by changing the formula so that more funds would be sent to declining cities with serious problems, especially those of the Northeast and Midwest. In the 1980s, President Reagan reduced appreciably the role of the federal government in CDBG decision making and reduced CDBG funds slightly. This increase in input from the local level has led to a shift in emphasis in the program, with fewer resources put directly into satisfying the needs of low-income residents and more into economic development (Wong and Peterson, 1986). Despite its flaws, the CDBG program has channeled money to cities with serious problems and given them considerable flexibility in attacking the problems. It has also encouraged citizen participation in the development of urban programs, and CDBG funds have served as a lever by which some cities have been able to secure private funds for development.

Urban Development Action Grants. In 1977, the Urban Development Action Grant (UDAG) program was established to complement the CDBG Program (Gatons and Brintnall, 1984). The UDAG program focused on communities with the greatest need for economic development and neighborhood revitalization. It was also explicitly intended to stimulate private investment in cities. It has helped to revive the economies of some older cities by financing dramatic downtown developments such as Harborplace in Baltimore and South Street Seaport in New York. Many community organizations have used UDAG money to renovate abandoned buildings and train unemployed people for jobs. Part of the rationale for these efforts, following ideas like those of Fischer and Gans, is to make cities into communities in which people would like to live. The UDAG program was terminated in 1988 by the Reagan administration, but UDAG outlays will continue into the early 1990s because some grants approved before 1988 involve a number of years of outlays (Caraley, 1992).

Other Federal Programs. A number of other federal programs send money to cities with problems. For example, there are programs to provide public-service jobs and job training, to assist with social services, to refurbish mass transit, to assist compensatory education, and to build highways. All these programs bring money and jobs to cities. So, despite the distinct shift toward a laissez-faire posture in our urban policy, there remains significant involvement by the federal government in trying to revitalize our cities. One problem over the years has been that, for political reasons, Con-

gress has only been willing to support programs that benefit most or all congressional districts. This has meant that funds have gone to small towns and cities with few problems. With limited resources and with an electorate that is somewhat hostile to spending tax money on those they define as "undeserving," it makes more sense to focus funds on the cities with the most problems. One proposal for doing this is to have two major federal aid programs for sending funds to local jurisdictions (Caraley, 1992). One would be a cyclical program that would increase or decrease funding depending on economic conditions. Funds would flow to a city when unemployment in that city rose above a certain level and stop when unemployment dropped. Those programs could focus on job training, community development, and other programs that fight unemployment. The second program would be directed at cities with high poverty rates and a low tax base. These would be more permanent funds focusing on mass transit, public works, and compensatory education assistance.

So, interventionist programs and proposals are still very much alive. Part of the rationale for enhancing federal involvement in urban problems is that the cities, for the most part, did not create the problems that now ravage them: high rates of poverty, drug addiction, homelessness, the high cost of medical care, and so on. The causes of these problems are complex and discussed throughout this book. It is the cities, however, that suffer these problems most seriously, and interventionists argue that all of us, through federal programs, have a responsibility to assist cities with these problems.

Private Investment

Despite the prominent role of the federal government in attacking urban problems over the years, there has been a trend over the past two decades to turn to private investment as a means of improving the conditions of cities. A major thrust of these efforts is to use private funds to develop shopping centers and malls in cities that can compete with suburban shopping malls and to construct housing that can draw people away from suburban tract homes. In this way, it is hoped, people—and financial resources—can be attracted back into the city. Many cities now boast such developments: the Water Tower mall in Chicago, the Union Station in Cincinnati, the Quincy Market in Boston, the Renaissance Center in Detroit, and Pier 39 in San Francisco. Although some of these developments used federal funds, private financing has been central to their completion. The idea behind them is that if cities can be made into enjoyable places to live and work, then decentralization might be slowed or halted and the financial problems that are at the core of so many urban difficulties alleviated.

Another approach to encouraging private development in cities through minimal government action is variously called "enterprise zones" or "urban free-enterprise zones" (Callies and Tamashiro, 1983; Butler, 1984). The basic idea is to designate a neighborhood as an "enterprise zone" based on high levels of unemployment or poverty and little economic development. Businesses locating in such zones would be taxed at a lower rate than other areas of the city and would be subject to less stringent regulation than businesses outside the zone. To receive these benefits, the businesses might be required to have a certain proportion of zone residents among their employees. This approach is based on the laissez-faire assumption that the tax and regulatory systems stifle initiative and self-improvement. Remove these inhibitors, proponents argue, and new businesses will arise to take advantage of the opportunities for economic development that exist even in blighted neighborhoods. These new ventures will then help rebuild the neighborhood economy, providing jobs that will help improve the general economic conditions in the city (Kemp, 1990). In a sense, community residents will solve their own social problems if the economic environment is conducive to it. The economic development plans

pursued by most cities involve attracting large employers who might locate in another city. The enterprise zone concept, on the other hand, is to create the conditions that will encourage new businesses to develop. Laissez-faire proponents support such enterprise zones because they do not involve any government funding, only a change in tax and regulatory laws.

Legislation to create enterprise zones in the United States has been established in some states, but it involves relief only from state and local taxes and regulation. The Reagan and Bush administrations both proposed legislation to create enterprise zones with federal tax and regulatory relief. In addition, some states and cities have gone beyond changes in taxes and regulation by assembling plots of land for businesses and offering public funds for investment in businesses (Bendick and Rasmussen, 1986). At this point the impact of such zones is difficult to assess. Britain has had such zones for a few years, however, and there are some things to be learned from their experience. In general, Britain's enterprise zones have not encouraged the development of new businesses by entrepreneurs. Instead, businesses that existed elsewhere or were planning to expand found the zones an attractive place to set up shop. So in many cases, the zones did not result in a net increase in jobs and economic activity, but a shuffling of them from one locale to another. This is not necessarily bad if the goal of policy is to shift jobs from low-unemployment areas to high-unemployment areas. If the community losing the jobs, however, begins to suffer, then the urban problems have merely been shifted from one community to another.

Resettlement of the Cities

One of the major problems cities have faced over the past few decades has been the flight of homeowners and affluent residents to the suburbs. A number of programs focus on reversing this trend by encouraging people to move back to the city and purchase homes or apartments. These efforts reflect both conscious efforts by the government to encourage such outcomes and private-sector initiatives.

Urban Homesteading. **Urban homesteading** refers to *programs to increase home ownership by private citizens in certain neighborhoods by selling them houses at little or no cost.* The homes are usually those that have been abandoned or foreclosed for failure to pay a mortgage or taxes and thus are the property of the city or the federal government. Usually, the buyer agrees to live in the house for a specified period of time and sometimes make certain improvements to the property. The government makes some money through the sale, an abandoned piece of property is placed back on the tax rolls, and best of all a homeowner has a vested interest in keeping up both his or her property and the neighborhood. A vacant house could be a target for vandals and a haven for drug dealers. Homeowners have an incentive to keep their property up and to discourage drug dealers from coming into the area.

Jack Kemp, President Bush's secretary of the Department of Housing and Urban Development, was a strong proponent of such homesteading (Kemp, 1990). With a similar rationale, he also urged the privatization of public, low-income housing, letting the poor purchase their low-income apartments and become managers of their apartment complexes. The goal of all this is to change run-down, disorganized neighborhoods into communities of the type suggested by Gans and Fischer. It has even been proposed as a way to help some of the homeless who have some income, but not enough for adequate housing. Overall, although it is no panacea, homesteading has helped some neighborhoods in some cities (Stegman, 1990; Weinstein, 1990a).

Gentrification. Another development in resettling cities in the last few decades has been dubbed **gentrification:** *the return of relatively af-fluent households to marginal neighborhoods where run-down housing is being rehabilitated or new housing constructed* (Beauregard, 1990; Kerstein, 1990). Gentrification is a complicated process that occurs in different ways in different cities. In some cases, it is encouraged by the policies of local, state, or federal governments; in other cases, it is driven by the actions of private developers looking for a profitable business deal; in some places, private-public partnerships have been the catalyst. Gentrification is more likely to occur in neighborhoods with good quality housing stock of some historic value and where there is no organized group in the community that resists it. Gentrification is also fueled by the decisions of affluent families who may find suburban life too expensive or who do not feel the need for large houses because they have smaller families than their parents had. For others, especially professional couples with fairly substantial incomes, the city affords easy access to restaurants, cultural events, and the like. For dual-career couples, who are far more common today than in the 1950s when suburbanization surged, the city offers access to many desirable jobs for both partners.

This gentrification has been hailed as the beginning of the rebirth of urban areas in the United States. Although it will probably help to stem the flow of economic resources out of the city, the numbers involved are difficult to calculate but are probably somewhat small. Nevertheless, it should contribute to increasing the tax base of the city, restoring neighborhoods through the rehabilitation of housing, and enhancing neighborhood businesses. Some urban planners argue that these renovated neighborhoods will serve as a magnet that will attract more affluent people into the city. However, not all the effects of gentrification are beneficial. As affluent people move into and renovate neighborhoods, the value of property increases and both rent and property taxes escalate. As a result, the people who lived in the neighborhood prior to gentrification—often the poor, the elderly, and minorities—can no longer afford it

POLICY ISSUES

The Uncertain Future of the Central City

Not all of our cities suffer in the same way or to the same extent from the urban problems we have been discussing in this chapter. Each of them has had a somewhat different experience with the dramatic transformation in America's social and economic organization: the transition from a goods, production-based system to an information-based, consumption-oriented one. The kind of society we are becoming is variously referred to as an advanced industrial or postindustrial society. We discussed some of the major elements of this change in Chapter 2. What impact does this have on cities?

American cities have always been places where the affluent and the poor reside, with each group remaining somewhat separate and distinct. Although there have always been tensions between the groups, the poor in the past had access to unskilled manual labor jobs and the hope—which became a reality often enough to keep the hope alive—of some upward mobility for them or at least for their children. The emerging social order, however, may be changing this. For the urban poor today, unskilled employment opportunities that were fueled by the goods-production industrial economy have been replaced by government handouts and welfare benefits. For urbanites with some skills or access to a college education, there are jobs in information processing and economic activities that involve consumption and the provision of services rather than production. As a consequence, according to two authorities on urban problems:

The changing economic function of the central city, and the demographic changes it has wrought, has thus created two separate but coterminous urban systems. It is this basic phenomenon, and its evolution, that will define America's urban future in the 1980s. (Sternlieb and Hughes, 1983: 456)

These specialists, George Sternlieb and James Hughes, argue that, in central cities, the unemployment rate among the poor is extremely high because of the gap between their "unskills" (usable in a production-based economy) and the requirements of the new service-oriented jobs created by a postindustrial economy. The age of manufacturing has passed and has been replaced by labor-intensive, white-collar economic activities involving the transmission of information. In the meantime, the bulk of central-city residents—the poor and the working poor—are left without jobs and without the means to weather the storm in our inflationary society. Consider but one example: The poor are forced to look for inexpensive housing in order to survive, and they look to the city either to provide them with housing directly or to ensure low rents in the private market. At the same time, the economic transformation of the city has resulted in an overall reduction in the amount of low-rent housing available to the poor, contributing directly to the rise in the number of homeless poor in cities.

Urban redevelopment programs have led to the demolition of low-rent housing and its re-

and are forced to move, sometimes from homes they have occupied for decades. The only housing these people can afford may be more dilapidated than their previous residence.

Regional Planning and Cooperation

Many cities have recognized that some urban problems can be solved only if regional planning and cooperation can be achieved. After all, the

placement by higher-order uses: offices, retail complexes, and luxury high-rise apartments. As central-city employment has shifted toward the services, especially finance, distribution, educational, and professional services, white-collar workers have moved into what were formerly blue-collar neighborhoods, buying and renovating houses. This gentrification of whole districts has further eroded the supply of low-cost housing. In the process of this transformation substantial numbers of older units have been withdrawn from the market to be held vacant while they await demolition or renovation. (Adams, 1986: 531)

Many conflict theorists would argue that these conditions in our cities emerge in part from the political, historical, and economic context in which the cities exist (Costells, 1977; Smith and LeFaiure, 1984). The problems we have discussed—financial collapse, a shortage of housing and jobs—arise in part because of the capitalist economy of which our cities are a part. Monopolistic corporations encourage government spending on things such as highways so that they can ship goods, reach new markets, and expand their profits. These highways also open up the suburbs to corporations, where land and taxes are lower and profits higher. As people and jobs leave the cities, government revenues decline and property values fall.

So the problems of cities are not due to excessive spending by cities but to corporate pursuit of higher profits. Over time, the reduced property values in the city attract other entrepreneurs who see that a profit can be made. Especially as some redevelopment in cities through urban renewal occurs, real estate interests buy urban housing cheap and attempt to sell it to those who can afford it: the middle class and affluent. Thus, gentrification emerges as changes in the urban real estate market bring investment capital back into the cities. However, those who benefit are the real estate entrepreneurs and the affluent, not the poor who were abandoned in the city as capital moved to the suburbs and who are now displaced by the gentrifiers. From the conflict perspective, the key motivator of these changes in cities is the efforts by groups to maintain and enhance their ownership and profits.

Certainly, cities want to attract affluent people and jobs. And rising property values certainly provide some benefit. Yet cities also need to recognize that when one group benefits, another is often hurt. So, as cities make the various transitions just described, we need to identify the casualties and provide for them. One way to do this is to assist the urban poor in adapting to the transition from an industrial to a postindustrial era. The education and job training programs described in Chapter 5 will help, especially if people are trained for jobs in the increasingly important service and information-processing sectors. Another way to provide for those hurt by the changes in cities is by offering housing and other assistance so that people can maintain a reasonable life-style. Although entrepreneurs and corporations are justified in seeking a profit, it should not be at the expense of the helpless and defenseless. Corporations and the affluent must be willing to share the burden of helping to provide decent low-cost housing.

Finally, Morris Zeitlin (1990), an architect and city planner, argues that the plight of our cities results in part from the fact that we have had no national urban policy to shape the direction in which our cities go. This void has meant that corporate and other powerful interests were free to direct things in ways that benefit them—and too often work to the detriment of the working class and poor people in cities. One solution is for city dwellers across the country to unite into a coherent movement to push their interests at the local and national level.

geographic boundaries of cities were established many years ago, and today they are rather arbitrary designations. Some have proposed a metropolitan government that would have political jurisdiction over a city and its suburbs and would consolidate all government services. Such an overarching political structure is probably not feasible in most cases. One problem is deciding where one

Despite the squalor and deterioration in many inner-city areas, successful efforts are being made, through urban homesteading, gentrification, and other programs, to attract people to live in these communities.

city and its suburbs ends and another begins. In addition, few cities or suburbs would be willing to accede to such a centralized authority. They prefer to retain political power and patronage in their own hands.

On a smaller scale, however, cooperation between political entities in metropolitan areas has been established over specific issues. Issues such as transportation, water pollution, and the like affect the whole metropolitan region and can benefit from regional decision making. In some cases, the courts have even ruled that school segregation is a regional problem and called for transfers of students between city and suburban schools. Cleveland has made major strides in regional cooperation, with the city and suburbs sharing responsibility for big infrastructure projects such as

roads and transportation. It also has a payroll tax on all people who work in Cleveland, including those who live in the suburbs. This is a major infusion of funds for the city. It has been controversial, but many suburban residents accept some responsibility for helping alleviate the problems of the city because they gain benefits from the city. As the president of the Greater Cleveland Growth Organization put it: "Cleveland is the downtown shopping center for this area. It is where entertainment is. Sports. Where all our major corporations are. We recognize that if downtown is not clean, safe and active, then the entire region will start falling apart" (quoted in Barrett and Greene, 1991: 34).

All the urban problems and policies discussed in this chapter need to be considered in the context of fundamental changes that are occurring in the social and economic structure of our society. These changes and their implications for our cities

are discussed in the Policy Issues insert in this chapter.

Linkages

The spread of slums and urban deterioration is made worse by poverty (Chapter 5), crime (Chapter 9), and drug addiction (Chapter 10). It is also enhanced when large and unresponsive corporations (Chapter 2) move jobs away from the cities where people live.

Summary

1. Human beings live in communities, and sometimes these communities grow large enough to be called cities. Cities arose after people developed agriculture and domesticated animals. With industrialization, cities grow very large because industrial economic organization benefits from the concentration of people and resources.

2. Today most Americans live in urban areas. Suburbanization has occurred because technological changes made it possible for people to live far from where they work and because federal policies encouraged the building of new homes outside the cities where cheap land was available. In the last thirty years, cities have become less centralized because the economic organization in postindustrial society does not need such extensive centralization.

3. An important issue in understanding urban problems is to assess the impact that city life has on people. One view of this is that cities, with their density and heterogeneity, produce a distinct urban consciousness: People in cities are impersonal, emotionally distant, and alienated. They are surrounded by secondary groups rather than primary ones.

4. Another view of urban life points to the fact that people in cities do live in communities with which they identify and have a sense of positive regard for one another. Communities might be founded on racial or ethnic group memberships or on common interests or leisure activities. The size, density, and heterogeneity of city life may lend an intensity to the impact of such subcultural group memberships that is usually absent in small towns and rural areas.

5. The functionalist perspective views urban problems as the result of the social disorganization that has arisen because cities have experienced substantial change in this century. From the conflict perspective, urban problems have arisen because the people who live in cities have few political and economic resources with which to stop the changes that work against their interests. From the interactionist perspective, urban problems are a function of social definition: Although conditions in cities have improved in this century, people have come to expect much more than they did in the past.

6. Many of the problems of cities can be traced to their poor financial standing: As people and industry have left the cities over the years, the tax base has eroded, leaving cities with less money. This has brought about a serious problem of deteriorating housing and the inability of poor and low-income families to find affordable housing.

7. Ghettos have developed in cities with large concentrations of minority-group residents. This segregation of people of different racial and ethnic groups can exacerbate the problems of poverty and economic deprivation for African Americans and Hispanics, can concentrate poverty into a few neighborhoods, and can lead to stereotyping, hostility, and prejudice between groups, further reducing the chance that cooperation to solve urban problems can be developed. Cities also face crime and education problems.

8. Although the federal government has played a significant role in finding solutions to urban problems over the years, in recent years there has been a push to find solutions in which government involvement is less or nonexistent.

9. The government has attacked urban problems with such programs as urban renewal, community development block grants, and urban development action grants. Private investment has focused on developing cities as better places to live, sometimes through the establishment of "urban free-enterprise zones."

10. Urban homesteading and regional planning have also been used to improve life in cities. In part as a result of these changes, some have detected a trend toward the gentrification of cities in the past fifteen years. Gentrification benefits some people in cities but not all.

Important Terms for Review

city	gentrification	primary groups	suburb
communities	gesellschaft	secondary groups	urban homesteading
gemeinschaft	ghetto		

Discussion Questions

1. To what extent has decentralization occurred in the city or town in which your college or university is located? What problems has this created? What efforts have been made to alleviate these problems?

2. The text presents three views on how living in urban areas influences social relationships. Using your city or town as an example, provide illustrations that could serve as evidence for each of these views. Which do you think most accurately describes the impact of your city or town on people?

3. Some people have suggested that we should not make a great effort to save cities that are having problems, that we should just let them collapse if they cannot thrive on their own. Do you agree with this position? What would be some of the consequences if we did ignore these cities? How much of our societal resources are you willing to expend in solving urban problems?

4. Analyze the physical layout and social patterns of your college campus. To what extent do they contribute to problems of crime or feelings of isolation among the students? How could your campus be redesigned to alleviate some of these problems?

For Further Reading

Edward Banfield. *The Unheavenly City Revisited.* Prospect Heights, Ill.: Waveland Press, 1990. This sociologist offers a very positive assessment of America's cities, saying that they are healthy, enjoyable, and fulfilling places to live.

Claude Fischer. *To Dwell Among Friends: Personal Networks in Town and City.* Chicago: University of Chicago Press, 1982. This author presents data to challenge the notion that there is a "decline of community" in cities. He shows that urbanites have rich and intricate social networks that are at least comparable to what is found in small towns.

Herbert J. Gans. *People, Plans, and Policies: Essays on Poverty, Racism, and Other National Urban Problems.* New York: Columbia University Press, 1991. This is an excellent set of essays by a well-respected specialist in urban affairs. The issues discussed range from problems of architecture to poverty and the underclass.

Joel Garreau. *Edge City: Life on the New Frontier.* New York: Doubleday, 1991. "Edge city" is the author's name for those suburbs that have grown large enough to be considered self-sufficient. He provides an interesting perspective on that part of urban life where many people live, suggesting that edge cities reflect such American values as individualism and homesteading.

Wallace E. Lambert and Donald M. Taylor. *Coping with Cultural and Racial Diversity in Urban America.* New York: Praeger, 1990. As the title suggests, this book deals with the impact that a multicultural United States will have on our cities. It also focuses on the issue of assimilation versus pluralism, as discussed in Chapter 6.

Kirkpatrick Sale. *Human Scale.* New York: Coward, McCann, and Geoghegan, 1980. An assessment of the impact of huge urban developments on people and social relations. Sale contends that going beyond "human scale" causes impersonality and a number of other problems. He argues for small-scale planning as a way of alleviating some urban problems.

Wesley G. Skogan. *Disorder and Decline: Crime and the Spiral of Decay in American Neighborhoods.* New York: The Free Press, 1990. This book documents the complex and nuanced ways in which crime produces disorder in city neighborhoods, and how the disorder then creates more crime, producing a difficult-to-stop spiral.

Gerald Suttles. *The Social Order of the Slum.* Chicago: University of Chicago Press, 1968. An excellent observational study of an urban community. It shows how race, ethnicity, and other social characteristics shape community life and social relations.

J. Allen Whitt. *Urban Elites and Mass Transportation: the Dialectics of Power.* Princeton, N.J.: Princeton University Press, 1982. A study of the development of urban transportation systems. Using the conflict approach, Whitt assesses the factors that influence whether urban transportation systems are developed and who benefits from them.

William H. Whyte. *City: Rediscovering the Center.* New York: Doubleday, 1988. A very provocative book by a sociologist who has studied city life for many years. Whyte punctures many assumptions about city life (e.g., that crime is worse downtown than in the parking lot of a suburban shopping mall) and presents many intriguing ideas on urban development that will make cities more livable and "people friendly."

CHAPTER 13
Population and the Environment

I n the early 1800s, world population reached one billion people. It took one million years to reach this number. In the next one hundred sixty years—by 1960—the world's population had tripled in size to approximately three billion inhabitants. Then, with incredible speed, another billion people were added during the fifteen years between 1960 and 1975 and yet another billion by the late 1980s. It is projected that another billion people will be added to the world population by the year 2000 and yet another billion by 2010 (see Figure 13.1). Demographers caution that

Myths and Facts About Population and Environment

Myth: The most important factor in controlling world population growth is technology: Modern contraceptive technology is essential if people are to control their fertility.

Fact: The most crucial ingredient in world population growth is human values and desires. Effective contraceptive procedures have been available for some time, but as long as people place a high value on having many children, world population will continue to grow. At times in our own history, before modern contraceptives were available, the birth rate has been quite low because people chose to have fewer children.

Myth: Environmental pollution did not become a problem until the 1960s and 1970s.

Fact: Environmental pollution has been a problem since at least the beginning of the industrial revolution, but our society did not begin to pay serious and widespread attention to these issues until fairly recently—beginning in the 1960s.

Myth: The United States achieved zero population growth (ZPG) when the birthrate dropped below replacement level during the 1970s.

Fact: Although our nation's birthrate has been dropping steadily and has remained below replacement level for some time, this will have to continue for another generation (about seventy years) before we reach ZPG.

Myth: Early inhabitants of the earth were more sensitive to environmental issues than are modern peoples, and they tried hard to avoid exploiting their environment.

Fact: Most early human societies behaved in much the same fashion as their modern counterparts: They protected resources in short supply but took a wasteful stance toward those that appeared to be plentiful.

long-range projections concerning the future size of world population are speculative but that it could exceed ten billion sometime in the twenty-first century. This population explosion has many consequences, as we will see. It can cause crowding, the depletion of natural resources, starvation, and may even contribute to the likelihood of wars occurring. In fact, if humankind fails to control population growth, we may be heading for a catastrophe that will be far worse than the starvation and war that we have seen in places such as Somalia and the Sudan during the past decade—and on a much broader scale.

One major consequence of rapid population growth is its impact on the earth's environment, and this is why we have combined our analysis of population and environmental problems into one chapter. Sociologists use the term **environment** to refer to *the conditions and circumstances surrounding and affecting a particular group of living creatures*. In this century, many disturbing problems have emerged that have called our attention again and again to the fragility of the world environment: air and water pollution, acid rain, the accumulation of toxic wastes, and many others. Underlying all of this is the frightening realization that we may be altering and damaging our environment in ways that are irreversible, that we may reach (or have already reached) a point at which we cannot completely correct the destruction already done. In our examination of population and environment as social problems, it is important to remember that human beings live in an **ecosystem:** *a complex, interrelated network of life forms and nonlife forms that interact with one another to produce an exchange of materials between the living and the nonliving parts.* The concept of an ecosystem helps us to understand that all parts of the environment are in dynamic interaction with one another. Maintaining an equilibrium within an

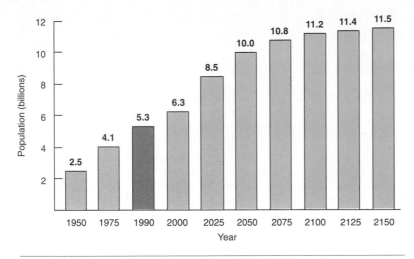

Figure 13.1 **World Population, 1950–2150**
SOURCE: United Nations, *Long-range World Population Projections: Two Centuries of Population Growth, 1950–2150* (New York, 1992, Sales No. E. 92. XIII. 2. p. 18).

ecosystem requires that all the parts be in some necessary, functional balance. Changes in one part of the ecosystem will likely produce changes in the other parts. We can see, then, that population and environmental issues are inextricably linked. Overpopulation can have a devastating effect on the environment, just as some critical change in the environment can have important effects on the ability of a region or the world to support a population.

In this chapter, we will examine the varied problems relating to population growth and environmental degradation. We will begin with an analysis of the key elements influencing population growth.

POPULATION GROWTH

Elements of Demographic Change

Demography is *the study of the size, composition, and distribution of human populations and how these factors change over time.* Each one of us participates

in at least two "demographic acts" that affect human population—we are born and we will eventually die. Many of us also engage in other demographic acts, such as having children of our own. All these individual decisions and activities combine into an enormous wave of actions that make the world population what it is today. The term **population** refers to *the total number of people inhabiting a particular geographic area at a specified time.* There are three basic elements that affect the size, composition, and distribution of human populations: fertility, mortality, and migration.

Fertility. **Fertility** refers to *the actual number of children born.* This is distinguished from **fecundity,** or *the biological maximum number of children that could be born.* Because women rarely have the maximum number of children they are capable of bearing, the fertility of a society is normally quite a bit lower than its fecundity. The simplest measure of fertility is the *crude birthrate,* the number of live births occurring in a particular population during a given year for each one thousand people in that population. Figure 4.1 on page 122 shows the crude birthrate in the United States between 1910 and 1991.

Mortality.   **Mortality** refers to *the number of deaths that occur in a particular population.* As with fertility, mortality in a society can be described in a number of ways. The *crude death rate* refers to the total number of deaths for every one thousand people (see Figure 4.1). The crude death rate in the United States has declined substantially over the past century from seventeen deaths per one thousand people in 1900 to less than nine today. However, as can be seen in Figure 4.1, there has been relatively little change in the past two decades. The crude death rate does not take into account the fact that people of some ages, such as the very young, are much more likely to die. It is therefore useful to look at the *infant mortality rate,* which is the rate of death among infants under one year of age. Infant mortality has shown the greatest decline of all age groups in the United States: dropping from one hundred deaths per one thousand people in 1915 to 9.1 today. Another way to describe the mortality of a populace is with the *life expectancy,* which refers to the number of years, on the average, that people can expect to live. Americans have experienced a substantial increase in life expectancy during this century, as Table 13.1 illustrates. As can be seen, the life expectancy of women has increased more than that of men. The difference in life expectancy between the sexes was only one year in 1920, whereas it is seven years today.

When we combine the results of the crude birthrate and the crude death rate, we derive an indication of the growth of a population, and the difference between these two figures is referred to as the *rate of natural increase.* For example, in 1990, the crude birthrate of the United States was 14.9 and the crude death rate was 8.7, yielding a rate of natural increase of 0.62 percent.

Migration.   On the most general level, **migration** refers to *a permanent change of residence.* The term *immigration* refers to movement into a par-

Table 13.1   **Expectation of Life at Birth in the United States, 1920–1990**

Year	Total	Male	Female
1920	54.1	53.6	54.6
1930	59.7	58.1	61.6
1940	62.9	60.8	65.2
1950	68.2	65.6	71.1
1960	69.7	66.6	73.1
1970	70.8	67.1	74.7
1980	73.7	70.0	77.5
1990	75.6	72.1	79.0

SOURCE: U.S. Bureau of the Census, *Statistical Abstract of the United States, 1991* (Washington, D.C.: U.S. Government Printing Office, 1991), p. 73.

ticular country, whereas *emigration* involves moving out. In analyzing migration, demographers look for "push" and "pull" factors. Sometimes people are pushed out of one country because of poor economic times, unstable political conditions, and the like. Many Southeast Asians migrated to the United States in the 1970s and 1980s, for example, because of the unpredictable political situation in that part of the world. In other cases, there is a "pull" or attraction that leads people to migrate to a particular place. Many Europeans migrated to America feeling that they would have better economic and social opportunities.

Migration is also an important variable in the population within a particular nation. For example, the population density of the southern and western states in our country has risen dramatically in recent decades because of in-migration from other states. Likewise, the number of people living in some other states has declined because of out-migration. Between 1980 and 1990, only North Dakota and Iowa experienced a net decline in population, and some states, such as Michigan and Pennsylvania, showed almost no increase (U.S. Bureau of the Census, 1991: 20). All other states showed some increase. In the 1990 Census,

California, Texas, and Florida accounted for over half of the United States' population growth during the 1980s. These three states together have a 1990 population of nearly sixty million, which is almost as many people as lived in the entire nation in 1890. The Northeast grew less than 3 percent and the Midwest only 1.5 percent during the 1980s, whereas the South gained 16 percent and the West 21 percent. This contributes to high rates of unemployment and fewer job opportunities in the states showing little growth (see Chapter 2). These socioeconomic factors then have a further effect on migration patterns. Americans have moved out of some states and into others in search of employment or more lucrative career opportunities.

World Population Growth

In analyzing world population problems, migration, for obvious reasons, is not a critical element of overall population growth and change, although it can have an impact on the fortunes of particular regions. Fertility and mortality, however, are key elements, and we will focus on them here. Later in the chapter, we will consider some ways in which migration affects the United States.

Most of human history has passed on an earth that was only sparsely populated by people. It has been estimated, for example, that there were fewer people on the whole earth seven thousand years ago than there are in larger cities such as New York or Tokyo today. At the time of Christ, approximately two thousand years ago, there were probably not many more people alive than currently live in the United States. In Figure 13.2, you can readily see that, prior to about the 1700s, world population was small and growth was slow. After 1750, world population began to increase at a more rapid rate, and it continues to grow even more rapidly today. Only in the last two centuries has world population exceeded one billion, with a current population of about 5.3 billion (see Figure 13.1). The largest nation in the world today is China, with a little over one billion people. The

United States is the third largest nation, with a population of 250 million, behind China and India.

The primary reason for the low rate of population growth in the world prior to 1750 was the relatively high death rate that existed in practically every society. For example, until 1600, the average life expectancy in European countries was little more than thirty-five years, in comparison to more than seventy years in industrial societies today. One important factor in the high death rate at that time was the extremely high infant mortality rate. In some societies, as many as 50 percent of the infants born would die within their first year of life (Antonovsky, 1972). The two most important variables involved in these high death rates were disease and famine. In fact, disease has accounted for more deaths in the Western world than any other factor, and this has been the case throughout history. Before the modern era, knowledge and technology related to medicine, sanitation, and agriculture were not sufficiently advanced to lower the death rate and thus increase life expectancy. Although famine is something with which most Americans are unfamiliar, at times it has led to astonishingly high death rates. For example, a severe famine in China in 1877 and 1878 was responsible for the death of between nine and thirteen million people (Petersen, 1975). The modern-day effects of famine may be observed in Somalia where, despite the world's ability to produce food, many people have died of starvation in recent years.

The Demographic Transition

What explains the rapid world population growth of the past few centuries? In an effort to answer this question, demographers point to a process known as the **demographic transition,** *the changing patterns of birth and death rates brought about by industrialization* (van de Kaa, 1987). The reasons for this transition are complex. We find it useful to divide the demographic transition into four stages (see Figure 13.3). The *preindustrial*

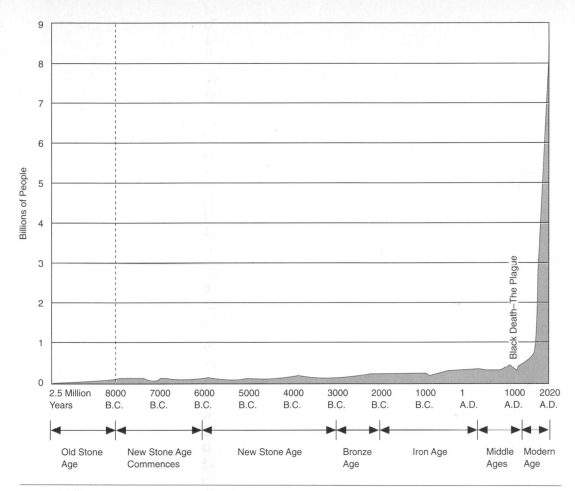

Figure 13.2 **World Population Growth Through History**
SOURCE: Mary Mederios Kent, "World Population: Fundamentals of Growth" (Washington, D.C.: Population Reference Bureau, Inc., 1984).

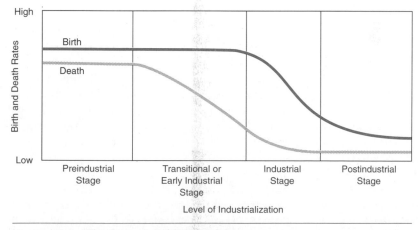

Figure 13.3 **The Demographic Transition**

stage is characterized by high birthrates and high death rates, resulting in a population that grows slowly, if at all. Throughout much of human history, societies have been in this preindustrial stage.

For most Western nations, including the United States, the preindustrial stage existed until the onset of industrialization between 1750 and 1850, when the *transitional* or *early industrial stage* begins. This stage is characterized by continuing high birthrates but declining death rates. The falling death rates occur because of improvements in life-style resulting from industrial development (van de Kaa, 1987; see Chapter 4). More and better food was available, for example, that helped people resist infectious diseases and reduced infant mortality. In addition, improvements in transportation, communication, and sanitation contributed to a lowering of the death rate. However, cultural values still encouraged people to have large families, so the birthrate stayed high. *The gap between the high birthrates and low death rates*—commonly called a **demographic gap**—resulted in explosive population growth during the early industrial period (Brown, 1987). The death rate was too low to keep population size stable when the birthrate remained high.

The third stage is called the *industrial stage* and is characterized by a continued decline in the death rate and a declining birthrate. During this stage medicine became more effective in controlling acute and chronic diseases and thus contributed to additional declines in the death rate. In addition, industrial technology made it possible for people to lead cleaner and healthier lives. The decline in the birthrate was a response to the impact of industrialization on cultural values regarding childbearing. Urbanization and increasing education, for example, led to a desire on the part of couples for smaller families than in the past.

The *postindustrial stage* of the demographic transition, which some demographers prefer to consider a continuation of the industrial stage, is characterized by low birthrates and low death rates, once again a roughly stable population with little growth. The industrialized nations, such as the United States, Japan, and some European countries, may be currently entering this stage, although how low their birth and death rates will remain and for how long is a matter of some speculation.

The Extent of Overpopulation

The fully industrialized nations in the world today, including the United States, have experienced the demographic transition and now exhibit relatively low birthrates and death rates. If these low rates continue, then the populations of these countries will eventually stabilize, with little if any subsequent growth. There are, however, many nations in the world that are considerably less industrialized and have not yet gone through this transition in birth and death rates, and this is where today's world population problem can be most clearly located. In these nations, the death rate has dropped considerably, due in large part to the introduction of modern medicine, sanitation, and public health efforts. Insecticides, better transportation, and improved agricultural practices, for example, have made more and better food available. The impact of these changes on mortality has frequently been dramatic. In Sri Lanka between 1945 and 1949, the crude death rate declined from twenty-two deaths per one thousand people to twelve per one thousand; in 1947 alone, the life expectancy rose from forty-three to fifty-two.

Although declines in the death rate in these countries have been substantial, the birthrate has remained high, resulting in a continuing and large demographic gap. Iraq and Ghana, for example, are projected to have rates of natural increase of over 3 percent in the 1990s. This compares with our own rate of natural increase of 0.62 (U.S. Bureau of the Census, 1991: 830–832). In today's industrialized nations, the death rate has declined slowly over many decades, so population growth has been gradual, whereas cultural values regarding childbearing and family size have changed, yielding smaller families. The developing nations of today, however, have seen their death rates drop rapidly, and cultural values do not change that quickly. Thus, the developing regions of the world are expected to grow at an annual rate of 2.0 percent during the 1990s, as compared with 0.5 percent in the fully industrialized nations. Figure 13.4 shows the impact of these differing rates of natural increase: Europe and North America, where most of the industrial nations are, will

contain a dwindling proportion of the world's population, whereas Africa and Latin America, containing mostly developing nations, will see its proportion of the world's population grow significantly.

The impact of all this can be better understood if we examine the number of years required for the world's population to double in size. Demographers refer to this figure as the *doubling time*. From the beginning of the Christian era, it took 1,650 years for the population to double. By

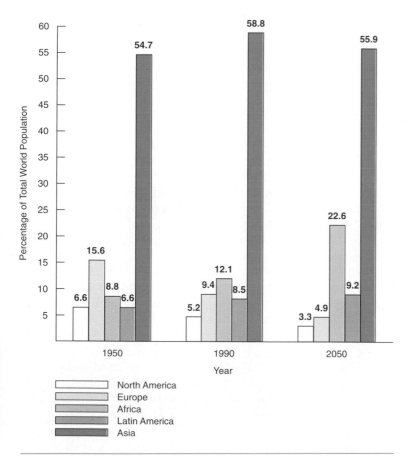

Figure 13.4   **Percentage Distribution of the World's Population in Various Geographic Areas, 1950–2050**
SOURCE: United Nations, *Long-range World Population Projections: Two Centuries of Population Growth, 1950–2150* (New York, 1992, Sales No. E. 92. XIII. 2. p. 24).

comparison, if current rates of world population growth continue, only forty years will pass until world population again doubles its size! Will the developing nations of the world today lower their birthrates before world population grows disastrously out of control? Keep in mind that the demographic transition is a description of a long historical trend found in some nations, all of which have experienced occasional changes in birth or death rates that go against this trend. We do not know if the developing nations of today will follow the same path (Organski et al., 1984). However, one thing is clear. In a preindustrial era, population growth, or the lack of it, was determined primarily by a high death rate, over which people had little control at that time. Today, growth is determined to a large extent by factors, especially fertility, over which people do have some control. Thus, the attention of those concerned about overpopulation today has been focused on issues of fertility control.

PERSPECTIVES ON POPULATION AND ENVIRONMENTAL PROBLEMS

We have discussed the elements of population growth and described how world population has grown over the centuries. Yet this still leaves open the issue of when population growth and environmental degradation actually become social problems. To address this issue, we now examine population and the environment using the three sociological perspectives.

The Functionalist Perspective

A major assumption of the functionalist perspective is that society is a system made up of interdependent parts and that changes in one part of the system will have consequences for the others. Two very important "parts" of any society are the size and characteristics of its population and the nature and quality of its environment. At the beginning of this chapter, we saw how population and environment combine to make up an ecosystem, and how changes in one part of that system can bring about alterations in other parts.

One of the earliest attempts to understand population dynamics was basically functionalist in nature. An English clergyman named Thomas Robert Malthus became concerned with population problems around the beginning of the industrial revolution in Europe. In 1798, he published his *Essay on the Principle of Population* (1960, originally published 1798). Although he focused on population dynamics, Malthus' analysis also involved environmental factors, in that he viewed population size and food supplies as two parts of a system that should be in balance if society is to function properly. He argued that there exists an immutable passion between the sexes that leads to reproduction, and this leads to a constant pressure toward population growth. He also said that societies have a limited ability to produce food. If the tendency toward population growth continues unchecked, then populations will eventually grow larger than the food supply can support. Malthus believed that human beings could intercede in this process and control population growth by postponing marriage or remaining celibate, but he was pessimistic about whether human intervention would completely save the day. He thought populations would continue to grow, ultimately being checked by deaths due to starvation, disease, and war (Thompson and Lewis, 1965).

Like Malthus, modern-day functionalists view population and environment as social problems in terms of the relationship between uncontrolled population growth and the exhaustion of available resources. The situation in Somalia is a good illustration of this point. Because of drought and warfare, the ability of Somalia to grow food has been reduced to well below what is necessary to supply food for its population. The result has

The functionalist perspective shows how the natural equilibrium in an ecosystem can be upset by human activities. Toxic wastes from paint manufacturing have forced the Environmental Protection Agency to mount expensive clean-up operations that may represent "band-aid surgery" for irreparable damage.

been what Malthus called a "positive" check on population—the grim reaper of starvation and death.

The functionalist approach to population problems has some important implications for efforts to intervene to alleviate those problems. On the one hand, it may appear reasonable and humane for the United States to intercede in situations such as the one in Somalia by providing various forms of aid, including food and adequate medical care. On the other hand, some would argue that this may interfere with the development of checks on population growth, such as programs to reduce the birthrate: If the threat of starvation is removed, the political pressure to bring down the birthrate may also ease. If this happens, we may be laying the groundwork for even more serious problems in the future.

From the functionalist perspective, then, population growth and environmental conditions become social problems when they become dys-

functional and lead to social disorganization. This occurs when population growth or environmental degradation interferes with the ability to achieve societal goals, such as providing adequate food and housing or keeping illness rates at an acceptable level.

The Conflict Perspective

An early exponent of the conflict view was Karl Marx, who argued that there are powerful groups, the capitalists, who benefit from restrictions in the food supply and other scarce resources. Recall from Chapter 2 that capitalism is based on profit making. Because of this, food and other goods are not produced unless someone can make a profit from producing and selling them. Less food may be produced than people actually need so that the low supply of food will increase the price. With an economy based on producing food for human need rather than profit, Marx argued, technology could be harnessed to produce a sufficient amount of food for a growing population.

From the conflict perspective then, population and environment become social problems when those who control the economic system in society take steps to limit artificially the resources available in order to benefit a particular group of people. The solution to these problems does not focus on limiting the number of people born or controlling the environment but rather on enacting changes in the systems of production and distribution that would lead to a broader and more equitable distribution of resources among groups. Elements of this conflict perspective can be found in the political stance of the leaders of some developing nations today. They argue that world population growth is not the real problem but rather that resources are unevenly distributed among the various nations. For example, the United States could grow far more food than it currently does, and in fact we withhold much good cropland from production to lower food surpluses and raise prices. So some have argued, if all nations of the world would maximize their food production and share their resources equitably, the expanding populations in disadvantaged nations could be supported.

The Interactionist Perspective

In the United States, ownership of or access to twelve hundred square feet of living space has become somewhat taken for granted, and so far, our nation provides the necessary space and accompanying resources for a sizable percentage of the population to enjoy this standard of living. In an equally industrialized but much more crowded nation such as Japan, on the other hand, most people have become accustomed to substantially less living space. An American, therefore, might regard the amount of space available to the average Japanese family as "crowded."

This example illustrates a part of the interactionist perspective on population and environment: that population and environmental problems are, in part, matters of social definition. For example, the United States today could be regarded as overpopulated if we compare the amount of land available to farmers during the preindustrial period with the amount available to most people today. On the other hand, even the most spartan living conditions and associated environmental circumstances available to many poor people in the United States would appear luxurious to many people in underdeveloped nations of the world.

In the face of what appear to be serious world population and environmental problems today, some observers argue that industrialization will eventually provide developing nations with the same quality of life that the nations that have already undergone the demographic transition enjoy today. One can plainly see how different versions of reality can lead to dramatically different conclusions about social policy on population and environmental issues. The interactionist perspective makes it possible for us to understand better how policy decisions on such problems as population and environment relate not necessarily to some *objective* reality but rather to individual definitions of what is desirable or essential in their lives.

CONSEQUENCES OF POPULATION GROWTH

We have discussed how much the populations of the United States and the world have grown. The three sociological perspectives confirm that whether this growth is perceived as a problem depends in part on its impact on the quality of people's lives. Has population growth adversely affected people? We will discuss some of the major consequences of population growth for the world today.

In looking at the consequences of population growth, a useful concept is that of *carrying capacity:* an upper size limit that is imposed on a population by its environmental resources and that cannot be permanently exceeded (Brown, 1987; Hendry, 1988). The idea of carrying capacity parallels some Malthusian ideas about population dynamics: A point is reached at which environmental resources in a geographic region are insufficient to allow further population growth, at least not without a change or decline in life-style. A geographic area such as the United States has a large carrying capacity, in part because of its abundant natural resources. In contrast, an area such as Ethiopia has a much lower carrying capacity because of its comparatively scarce resources and lack of technology. Advances in technology can increase the carrying capacity of an area. Improvements in agriculture, for example, might enable Ethiopia to support more people than it once did. But there is always a limit to how much growth can occur. Of course, the carrying capacity of the earth as a whole is, at any given moment, fixed. So as human populations have grown, they have approached more closely the carrying capacity of the earth, with some important consequences.

As world population continues to grow, more people around the world will experience the kind of crowding now common in larger cities. Such crowding may produce negative changes in people's behavior.

Crowding

One important consequence of population growth is crowding. Studies of animals have shown that extreme crowding can have adverse consequences, including increases in aggression and erratic behavior. Animal studies, however, are only suggestive of how crowding may affect human beings, because it would depend on people's past experiences and their expectations. In addition, living quarters and work areas can be designed so that density is high but people do not have the *impression* of being crowded, and potentially negative effects could be avoided (Baum and Davis, 1976). In fact, psychologist Jonathan Freedman (1975) has argued that crowding by itself does not have negative consequences. Instead, crowding is usually associated with other social conditions, such as poverty, that produce increases in crime or aggression (Liddell and Kruger, 1987; Ehrlich and Ehrlich, 1990). Thus, there is considerable controversy over the impact of crowding. Yet if world population doubles in the next forty years and doubles again after that, we will experience serious overcrowding by most people's standards. The negative impact of this dramatic growth may be difficult to alleviate (Jain, 1988).

Food Shortages

Another consequence of population growth is the potential for food shortages. Especially in developing nations that are experiencing rapid population growth, increasing agricultural production sufficiently to keep up with population expansion is difficult. As a consequence, millions of people die each year from starvation and malnutrition (Lappé and Collins, 1988). Concern over this has provoked substantial efforts over the years to expand the world food supply. These efforts have focused on three key areas: the sea, farmland expansion, and yield increases (Hendry, 1988; Brown, Flavin, and Postel, 1991).

According to most observers, the sea will not be a very important source of expanding food supplies in the years to come. It is possible through intensive efforts to increase fish production of the oceans to some degree, but the costs of such a move could outweigh the benefits to be gained. Farmland expansion has also been pointed to as a promising technique for expanding food production in the future. It may be possible to increase the amount of land under cultivation so that we can produce more food overall. So far, however, population growth has proved to be so relentless that the world is undergoing a steady reduction in the amount of farmland available. Therefore, yield increases appear to hold the best prospect for increased food production. Efforts to increase yields have pursued a number of strategies: introduction of new crops, reduction of turnaround time between harvesting and replanting, improved management of the crop environment, and development of higher-yielding plant varieties ("Food 2000 . . . ," 1987; Hendry, 1988).

In fact, the last mentioned strategy was labeled the *Green Revolution,* and many hoped it would head off the threat of massive famine by making it possible to produce far larger crops from the same land that previously produced less of these grains. Time revealed, however, that the Green Revolution and the other strategies to increase food production were not the panacea to the world food problem. Although it is true that world grain production almost doubled between 1950 and 1970, this production level barely stayed even with population growth in the years to follow. Per capita consumption levels dropped off in the most disadvantaged nations, food prices increased by leaps and bounds, and well over one hundred countries of the world confronted critical food deficits. By the 1980s and 1990s, these problems coalesced into an increasingly serious crisis, with some developing nations experiencing starvation. In addition, the Green Revolution and

other intensive agricultural programs have had some negative effects: By emphasizing a narrow range of crops, they have pushed biological uniformity to dangerous levels, they have relied on heavy utilization of chemical pesticides, and the expanding farmlands have eaten into forests and wetlands (Ryan, 1992).

Depletion of Resources

Beyond food, population growth can threaten the depletion of other world resources. There is considerable debate, however, about how serious this problem is. In 1972, a group of concerned business leaders, political leaders, and scientists, calling themselves the Club of Rome, published a report about the future supply of resources in the world (Meadows et al., 1972). It was a very pessimistic report. Based on estimates of world supplies of various resources and the rates of use of the resources at that time, they forecasted serious problems in the near future. They estimated, for example, that world petroleum resources would be exhausted in fifty years, natural gas in thirty-eight years, and aluminum in thirty-one years if rates of usage continued to increase. New finds of such resources have led some to call such pessimistic estimates unrealistic. Others have argued that new scientific and technological developments will overcome any shortages we might face in the future. Still other critics have charged that the Club of Rome findings are simply incorrect because they involve computer projections based on naive or inaccurate assumptions.

A second study commissioned by the Club of Rome used a more sophisticated approach, dividing the world into a number of regions rather than analyzing the world as a homogeneous unit, and using a more complex model of how nations are likely to make decisions about resource usage and development (Mesarovic and Pestel, 1974). Like the earlier study, this one also prophesied eventual depletion of many resources. The main difference in the second study was the prediction that some regions would face ecological collapse before others. They recommended that some of the problems might be alleviated if consumption and development in the industrial countries were moderated while those same countries made more industrial investment available for the poorer nations of the world. They suggested that it might be in the long-run best interest of nations such as the United States for their standard of living to decline somewhat in the future so that the standard of living in other countries around the world could be improved.

There are other more optimistic assessments of the world's resources. A report to the president, titled *The Global 2000 Report,* on the state of the world in the year 2000, for example, concludes that most minerals can be maintained at desirable levels through discoveries and judicious investment (Teich, 1986). Although there may be problems in petroleum production, the report sees plenty of time to shift to other energy resources or reduce consumption.

What is the truth about resource depletion? At this point, no one really knows. However, most agree that we need to plan for the possibility that some resources will be in short supply (MacKellar and Vining, 1988). We also need to plan for a more equitable distribution of resources in the world. Some of the less developed countries of the world control important resources, and they will not tolerate increasing development and consumption in the industrial nations without something equivalent occurring in the less developed nations. If the less developed nations do not get what they feel they deserve, they may withhold from the world markets the resources under their control. It is also clear that continued rapid population growth cannot be supported indefinitely by the world's natural resources.

Intergroup Conflict

The struggle for scarce resources intensifies when population increases. One way to cope with scarcity is to increase production of resources to satisfy demand. However, given that there are finite limits to expansion and growth, regulated competition could escalate to unregulated conflict. This might lead to one of Malthus's *positive checks* on population growth: war. People confronted with famine or disease may not sit idly by and accept starvation and death. If competition intensifies to conflict, the result may be all-out struggle for dwindling resources, such as living space and food. This is an especially ominous prospect in a nuclear world in which increasing numbers of nations have access to nuclear weapons.

Population growth and the deterioration of the environment can also lead to political conflict within a nation, such as food riots and insurrection. In the Sudan in 1985, for example, extensive demonstrations and riots followed an increase in the price of food, and eventually there was a military takeover of the government in an effort to quell the civil unrest (Brown and Wolf, 1986). Such food-related riots were not uncommon in Africa and South America in the 1980s (Chazan and Shaw, 1988). Population growth and dwindling food supplies also result in the forced migration of people to new countries in a search for survival. In Africa in particular, this has resulted in millions of refugees—the United Nations estimates ten million—in the 1980s. These refugees are yet another source of conflict because they are often seen as unwanted competitors for limited resources in their country of refuge.

Internal Migration

When looking at world population problems, we mentioned earlier that migration is not really a critical variable. However, when looking at the problems of particular regions or nations, migration definitely plays a role. Some states and regions in the United States have suffered because of internal migration within our country. In Oregon during the 1970s, for example, there were policies that discouraged new industry and new migrants. In 1971, the governor of Oregon commented: "Visit us often, but don't move here to live." By the 1980s, Oregon's economy was suffering and politicians were encouraging in-migration (Weeks, 1986). We saw earlier that some states in the East and Midwest have suffered population declines because of out-migration over the past decade. In the 1980s, 50 percent of the population growth in the United States was attributable to just three states—California, Florida, and Texas. Although it is true that these states have minority populations with higher birthrates than the national average, the primary explanation for their growth rates was internal migration from other states. Admittedly, California received more foreign immigrants than any other state, but much of that state's growth was explained by the lure of jobs created by expansion of the military industry and firms linked to computer technology.

Significant in-migration or out-migration can be very disruptive for a region. In the case of the former, a rapidly growing population can tax resources. Highways may be inadequate to the additional traffic, schools may become crowded, and crime rates may increase because migrants tend to be young and, as we saw in Chapter 9, the young are more likely to commit crimes. Out-migration is also disruptive. In the short term, it can increase rates of unemployment because there is a smaller payroll in the region and it may lead to an under-utilization of resources such as schools and hospitals. So even within our own country, the population size of a region is in balance with economic and other factors. As the functionalist perspective suggests, significant changes in population size of a region can have disruptive and disorganizing effects on other parts of the system.

EXTENT OF ENVIRONMENTAL PROBLEMS

Before examining specific environmental problems in detail, let us look at the history of concern about these issues. There is a popular myth that premodern people had a keen understanding of nature and a harmonious relationship with their environment. American Indians, for example, have been described as the "first environmentalists." Historical evidence belies this notion, however. Most American Indians treated their environment the way that most humans have done through the centuries—they worked hard to protect those resources in short supply and took a wasteful approach toward those that they believed to be plentiful. For example, the well-known publication, *American Heritage,* depicts ruthless whites shooting buffalo for "sport" from railroad trains, but after the Indians acquired horses and firearms, they too slaughtered the buffalo, eating the best meat and taking the hides but leaving the rest to decompose (Baden et al., 1979). In short, American Indians were actually exploiting their environment before the Europeans got into the act. One of the major differences between then and today is that, with our much larger population and more elaborate technology, we are far more able to do serious damage to the environment.

People's consciousness of environmental problems has fluctuated over time. For example, at the turn of the century, the air in American cities was being polluted by the smoke and waste from the growing number of factories. But Americans of that era did not perceive this environmental pollution as a threat. The interactionist perspective is useful here in understanding how a social problem does not really exist until influential groups identify it as such. Although various conservation organizations were formed in America prior to 1950, the general public was not very responsive to environmental concerns. It was not until the 1960s that the contemporary environmental movement really got off the ground. It was then that biological ecologists such as Rachel Carson and Paul Ehrlich began writing for popular audiences about how the growth in human societies was producing an ecological imbalance in nature. In 1962, Carson published *The Silent Spring,* which dealt with the hidden dangers that pesticides and herbicides held for our environment. In 1968, Ehrlich's best-selling *The Population Bomb* hit the market. Using a distinctly Malthusian approach, Ehrlich proposed that world population growth is responsible for pollution and other modern environmental problems. A bit later, Barry Commoner joined the ranks of environmental critics and, in contrast to Ehrlich's approach, blamed technology and growing corporate power structures for our expanding ecological woes.

So, it has only been in the last three decades that a significant number of Americans have viewed environmental issues as social problems. By the 1990s, Paul Ehrlich and Anne Ehrlich (1990) had developed a formula that summarizes the impact that human beings have on their environment:

$$I = P \times A \times T$$

Or, Impact = Population × Affluence × Technology. As we review environmental problems and their solutions, you will see the key role that these three factors play.

Water Supply and Pollution

Water is present in the atmosphere as a vapor; it then condenses and falls to the earth as rain, dew, or snow; it collects underground and drains into streams, rivers, and the oceans; finally it evaporates into the atmosphere once more as vapor. This *process, by which nature purifies water,* is called the **hydrologic cycle.** There are various mechanisms by which water is purified during this cycle. In a single pass through the hydrologic cycle, these mechanisms make water suitable for reuse. But this natural process is interfered with by various kinds of human pollution, including raw sewage, pesticides, and other chemicals, nitrate and phosphate fertilizers, and waste products from factories and nuclear power generators. As population and technology have grown, the resulting pollution has become so massive that the hydrologic cycle cannot fully cleanse the water,

despite the fact that we have techniques to assist nature in this purification process. A dramatic example of this is found in the phenomenon of "acid rain," discussed in the first Policy Issues insert. Acid rain illustrates the way human intervention can upset the ecological balance in nature. Using the functionalist perspective, we can see how the natural equilibrium within an ecosystem can be upset by interference of this nature. As the Policy Issues insert suggests, the long-range implications of acid rain and similar problems are potentially harmful to the ongoing maintenance of the environment.

Another example of the effects of pollution on our water supply involves a process called *eutrophication,* the depletion of oxygen in a body of water because of an overabundance of plant and animal life. It can happen like this: Modern farming practices use nitrate and phosphate fertilizers. When these fertilizers run off into rivers and lakes, they stimulate the growth of algae and other plants that eventually decay at the bottoms of these bodies of water. In the same fashion as decomposing sewage, these algae formations consume increasing amounts of oxygen, and they compete with fish and other animals for the oxygen in the water. If the competition is too fierce, oxygen in the water is depleted rather than replaced, and nothing may be able to survive in the water. This happened to Lake Erie in the 1950s and 1960s with disastrous results. Lake Erie had an algae bottom that was over one hundred feet thick, and along with the oxygen-depleting effects of this huge layer, the material was heavily laden with nitrous and phosphorous compounds. Fishing in the lake was ended. Environmentalists worked toward halting these forms of pollution from flowing into Lake Erie, and total destruction was avoided. Although Lake Erie has recovered substantially today, the experience of that lake illustrates the care and effort that must be devoted to protecting water supplies from the harmful effects of our population growth and technological development.

POLICY ISSUES

Acid Rain: Technology Creates New Environmental Threats

In his famous romantic verse, William Shakespeare once spoke of "the gentle rain from heaven," and popular vocalists such as Tony Bennett have serenaded their audiences with a well-known melody, "Like the Gentle Rain." The 1980s brought about an ironic alteration of the meaning of these refrains in a frightening phenomenon known as "acid rain." The effort over the past decade to deal with the problem of acid rain shows how environmental problems can become international in scope and how many groups can try to influence the solutions that are adopted.

Acid rain refers to a type of air pollution made up of sulfurous and nitrous oxide emissions from the burning of fossil fuels. These pollutants come mostly from coal-burning power plants, motor vehicles, and other industrial facilities. They combine with oxygen in the atmosphere to produce sulfuric and nitric acids that fall to the earth as acidic rain, snow, fog, or particulates. Acidity can destroy plant and animal life in an ecosystem. The environmental damage and economic costs associated with acid rain are enormous (Ehrlich and Ehrlich, 1990). For example, millions of acres of European and eastern U.S. forests now show severe damage linked to acid rain, as do some forests in remote parts of China. This type of air pollution may result in the extermination of valuable forests all over the world (Main, 1988). Approximately 85 percent of the sulfur dioxide in the atmospheres of the United States and Canada is of U.S. origin, although all nations that burn fossil fuels contribute to the problem. In addition to its harmful effects on forests, acid rain also releases lead from the interior of steel pipes into drinking and irrigation water, has killed fish and other wildlife in once-thriving lakes, and has elevated the incidence of respiratory ailments in the population.

Public debate over the acid rain issue has followed a pattern that is also found with many other environmental issues (Balling, 1992). When the problem first came to the surface in the late 1970s, some environmentalists saw in acid rain

Solid and Toxic Wastes

The average American throws away between three and five pounds of waste every day, amounting to an incredible three tons per year for the typical family of four people and translating into a whopping 179 million tons yearly for the country as a whole (see Figure 13.5). One hundred and sixty million additional tons are added every year in industrial waste, along with between two and three billion tons yearly from mining operations. This enormous waste-disposal figure led one observer to call Americans "the world's trashiest people."

Disposing of this waste in a way that does not degrade the environment poses a very serious problem.

Rather than disposing of waste, it may be possible to reuse some of it. For example, some states have passed "bottle bills," which require that a deposit be paid for beer and other containers when a beverage is bought. This encourages people to return the bottles and cans for the deposit and contributes to the recycling of glass and aluminum containers. In addition to not filling up our landfills, recycled materials are substantially less expensive to produce, thus saving energy in the

yet another symptom of imminent ecological collapse. They believed that our lakes and forests were rapidly being destroyed and that massive efforts needed to be mounted irrespective of the costs. More conservative voices held that the environmentalists were, once again, alarmists who would saddle our economies with massive costs to attack a problem that would turn out to be a minor annoyance at worst. While this public debate went on during the 1980s, many scientific teams were working to assess the nature and extent of the problem. The scientific findings would gradually come to inform the public debate and change it in significant ways. These research findings, and especially the results of the decade-long National Acid Precipitation Assessment Program (NAPAP), confirmed that acid rain is a problem for the world, but it is not as serious or urgent a problem as many had projected. One thing they found is that there are many natural sources of acid rain, so human activity is not the major, or possibly even primary, source of the problem. In addition, the damage caused by acid rain is not as extensive as originally thought. Massive and expensive efforts to control acid rain may be very costly yet produce relatively little actual decline in the problem. Nevertheless, the scientists are clear in saying that it is a problem that needs to be addressed by the countries of the world.

The acid rain problem can be alleviated by a reduction in the burning of fossil fuels that release sulfurous and nitrous oxides into the atmosphere. This would happen if people drove their automobiles less and relied less on electricity produced by burning high-sulfur coal. Many countries have begun to do this. For example, in the past few years, Russia and the other nations that made up the former Soviet Union have significantly reduced their use of highly polluting coal as their economy has been restructured (Flavin, 1992). Another approach is to put scrubbers on the smokestacks of coal-burning plants to clean the emissions, but this is a very expensive proposition and tends to be resisted. At the same time that efforts to deal with the problem have emerged, new concerns have been felt along another front: increased use of fossil fuels by developing countries and the Soviet Union as they try to emulate the more affluent life-styles of the industrial nations. If they follow the high-energy-consumption, no-energy-conservation route we have taken, worldwide sulfurous and nitrous oxide emissions will increase substantially in the future, and the acid rain problem will become more severe. So, although NAPAP and other research projects showed that acid rain was not as serious as the alarmists of the early 1980s thought, doing nothing about it could be disastrous in the coming decades.

process. For example, a glass beer bottle used only once and then tossed out with the garbage consumed 3730 BTUs in its production. The same beer bottle made of recycled glass cost 2530 BTUs to produce. Even greater savings are achieved if, instead of recycling, we refill the same bottle so that a new bottle does not have to be produced from recycled glass. A refillable glass beer bottle, used ten times, costs 610 BTUs on the average for each use—a very dramatic savings of energy (Brown, Flavin, and Postel, 1991). Where recycling efforts do not exist, an enormous quantity of containers is disposed of in landfills and incineration dumps. Many people forget that "tin cans" rust away after several years, but aluminum cans last literally forever. The United States imports over 90 percent of the aluminum that it uses, and then disposes of over one million tons annually (Purcell, 1981). The same situation exists for plastic and synthetic products. American consumers often spend more on food packaging than farmers make from selling food (Brown, Flavin, and Postel, 1991). We also produce bottles of many different sizes and shapes rather than a standardized and durable bottle that could be refilled many times over. The nonreturnable con-

A. Air quality gets better by some measures, but not all (millions of metric tons of pollutants, per year) . . .

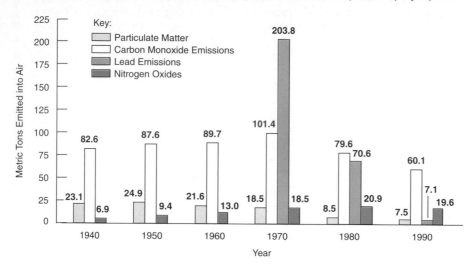

B. . . . the garbage piles continue to grow (total municipal garbage generated each year, in millions of tons).

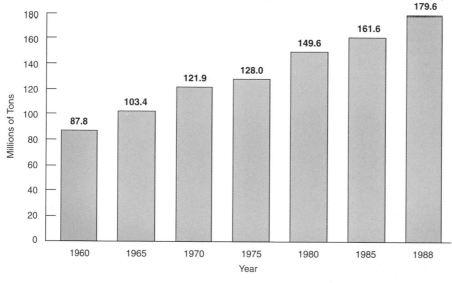

Figure 13.5   **Changes in Pollution Levels, 1940–1990**
SOURCE: U.S. Bureau of the Census, *Statistical Abstract of the United States, 1992* (Washington, D.C.: U.S. Government Printing Office, 1992), pp. 213, 216.

tainer is perhaps one of the best examples of our propensity toward wastefulness and a lack of respect for the environment.

Toxic waste disposal presents an even more ominous problem in terms of the pollution of our environment. Toxic wastes are the residues of the production of things such as plastics, pesticides, and nuclear energy. The tragedy at Love Canal near Niagara Falls over a decade ago is one of the more dramatic instances of the consequences of dumping chemical waste products. The wastes had been buried many years before, and homes were later built at Love Canal where the wastes had accumulated. Contaminants seeped into the water supply and the homes of the residents and caused severe and lingering health problems. Eventually many residents were forced to move, with the government buying their houses from them. However, many residents believed that their or their children's health had been permanently damaged and that they had not been adequately compensated for their suffering and dislocation. Even though regulation of toxic substances began over twenty years ago, government agencies are still unable to answer basic questions about the degree of this kind of environmental pollution (Stehr-Green and Lybarger, 1989). Consequently, the data on this subject are extremely limited. This is ironic considering the extent and severity of the problem.

There are thousands of toxic waste dump sites in this country, with a heavy concentration in the Northeast. Figure 13.6 shows the locations of over one thousand dumps that are currently on the EPA's "Superfund" priority list of high-risk sites eligible for government-sponsored "cleanup" funds. According to the EPA, nearly thirty thousand sites have been identified as eventually needing attention ("Cleaning of Toxic Dumps . . . ," 1989). Reports indicate that the "Superfund" is not working as originally planned. Heralded as a "quick fix" to the toxic waste problem in the United States, in the nine years after its approval in 1980, the program fell considerably short of its goals. In the first place, experts now estimate a total cleanup cost of *$300 billion*—a figure triple that of comparable forecasts in 1985 ("Superfund, Superflop," 1989). Furthermore, of the $10 billion in federal monies approved in 1980, Congress has actually appropriated only half that amount, and the EPA has spent only $2.6 billion, cleaning only thirty-four of the worst sites in eight years ("Cleaning of Toxic Dumps . . . ," 1989).

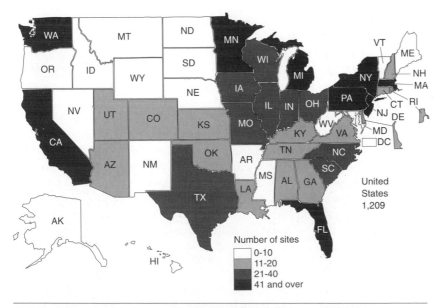

Figure 13.6 **Sites of the Worst Hazardous Waste Dumps in 1990, According to the Environmental Protection Agency**
SOURCE: U.S. Bureau of the Census, *Statistical Abstract of the United States, 1991* (Washington, D.C.: U.S. Government Printing Office, 1991), p. 211.

Nuclear Wastes

Nuclear wastes are a particularly serious form of toxic waste because they can stay so deadly for so long. There are three sources of nuclear wastes: the lethal by-products of manufacturing nuclear weapons, the radioactive wastes from nuclear power plants, and the low-grade nuclear wastes that are by-products of our health and other industries. As of this writing no plan for the permanent disposal of these wastes has been agreed to, even though the wastes are accumulating at an alarming rate (Schneider, 1992). Irradiated fuel from the world's nuclear power plants, for example, will exceed two hundred thousand tons by the year 2000 (Lenssen, 1992). One problem with nuclear wastes is that they remain deadly for thousands of years, and for some wastes even tens of thousands of years. Plutonium, for example, remains radioactive for 240,000 years! That is a time span that is at least as long as *Homo sapiens* have existed on the earth. It is absurd to imagine that we could ensure the integrity of a vault or the safety of the materials over such a vast expanse of time. A successful repository for the wastes must seal them completely for all this time, and no one has yet figured out how to do that. Another problem with nuclear wastes is the NIMBY syndrome: Not in My Back Yard. No one wants the waste repository near where they live, so communities have tended to resist when efforts are made to put a repository near them. A third problem with nuclear wastes is transporting them. Even if we have permanent storage facilities, wastes will be shipped there from all over the country, and that presents an image of a disaster waiting to happen. Even in rupture-proof containers, accidents will probably happen, with some leakage of radioactivity. A final problem with nuclear wastes is the temporary storage we use for lack of permanent storage. The nuclear industry has had a history of spreading radioactive and chemical wastes over the open ground, pouring it in rivers and lakes, and dumping it wherever it is most convenient and least expensive. Part of the reason this was allowed to happen is that the Cold War mentality produced little congressional oversight or public scrutiny. It was assumed that the nuclear industry was working in the national interest. In the late 1980s, the extent of the environmental contamination became known and many nuclear weapons production plants were shut down. However, we still do not have a permanent storage facility for the nuclear wastes.

Land Degradation

As we observed at the beginning of this chapter, the future of the environment depends on a delicate balance in nature, and upsetting this equilibrium can lead to serious consequences. One of the more ominous of these is *desertification,* referring to what happens when intensification of food production, such as by continuous cropping and overgrazing, leads to the spread of desert areas, thus reducing the quantity of arable land (Brown and Wolf, 1986; Durning and Brough, 1992). It has been estimated that over the past fifty years, one hundred million acres of useable farmland have been degraded to the point where they are no longer arable, with another one hundred million acres having lost their topsoil covers (Ognibene, 1980). Under favorable conditions, between three hundred and one thousand years are required to produce only one inch of topsoil. Data on this subject show that this problem is growing much more serious over time. In 1882, for example, about 10 percent of the earth's land was classified as desert or wasteland; by the 1950s, this figure had expanded to nearly 25 percent, and by 1980, almost 35 percent of our planet's land area was so classified. According to current estimates, over ten million acres of new desert are formed each year as a consequence of land mismanagement in semiarid regions (Malone and Corell, 1989). According to recent evaluations of land degradation, we need more research on the relationship between ecosystem change and the hydrologic cycle in order to make intelligent decisions about how to approach these problems (Brown and Wolf, 1986).

Although desertification and deforestation are more prominent outside of the United States, overuse of land and dwindling water supplies have made some areas in our nation unusable, such as this dried-up lake near Laredo, Texas.

Deforestation is another example of land degradation that comes from human tampering with the environment. Environmentalists Paul and Anne Ehrlich describe the consequences of forests being cleared:

> *Numerous animals that depend on the trees for food and shelter disappear. Many of the smaller forest plants depend on the trees for shade; they and the animals they support also disappear. With the removal of trees and plants, the soil is directly exposed to the elements, and it tends to erode faster. Loss of topsoil reduces the water-retaining capacity of an area, diminishes the supply of fresh water, causes silting of dams, and . . . flooding. (Ehrlich and Ehrlich, 1970: 202)*

In a number of African countries, the demand on forests (to use the wood as fuel or to clear land for agriculture) is from two to five times greater than the growth rate of new trees. This imbalance between demand and supply is due largely to growing populations and will obviously lead to a shortage of wood if it continues for long (Brown and Wolf, 1986). Deforestation is rapidly converting Brazil's Amazon forest to low-value, nonproductive cattle pasture, and policies for slowing this process are currently being debated (Fearnside, 1989). In 1990 alone, deforestation claimed seventeen million hectares of land, about the equivalent of the state of Washington in one year! Half of all tropical rain forests on the planet have been destroyed. One expert concluded that

> *In most nations, forests occur increasingly in small fragments surrounded by degraded land, with their ability to sustain viable populations of wildlife and vital ecological processes impaired. (Ryan, 1992: 10)*

Declining Biodiversity

Some of the trends previously discussed—particularly, overpopulation, deforestation, and overgrazing of cleared lands—have a consequence that is difficult to notice now but may be overwhelming in the near future: the annihilation of many species of animals around the globe. Biologist Edward Wilson (1992) estimates that twenty-seven thousand species per year are obliterated from the earth, which translates into seventy-four species every day of the year. Although the elimination of some species is expected as a part of normal evolutionary development, the current rate is staggeringly high. For most of earth's history, the number of species on the earth was increasing, resulting in greater biological diversity. Today, according to one estimate, three-quarters of the world's bird species are declining in population, all species of wild cats and most bears are declining seriously in numbers, and over two-thirds of the world's 150 primate species are threatened with extinction (Ryan, 1992). At the current rate of destruction, Wilson estimates, biodiversity on the earth is actually declining. Twenty percent of the earth's species will be extinct thirty years from now, giving the current period the distinction of having one of the largest die-offs of species in the history of the earth.

Declining biodiversity creates two major problems. One is that we are losing species that might be of some use to humans, such as in producing pharmaceuticals. Some materials can only be produced from living species, and once a species is gone it is irreplaceable. The second problem is more subtle: At some point, declines in biodiversity may threaten the ability of the ecosystem to support human life. In that sense, every species is intimately dependent on other species for its survival. Ecosystems thrive, in part, because of the complexity and diversity of life that they harbor. As we have seen, ecosystems are complex networks in which species exchange material with one another in order to survive. One species thrives by eating another while a third species survives by the wastes of the other two. Elaborate those simple interchanges many thousands of times and one can begin to see the complex interactions involved in ecosystems. As species are removed from a system, it becomes more difficult to sustain such complex life forms as human beings. We have seen it happen before: We drive a predator to extinction only to realize that it kept the rodent population in control; earthworms are killed off by pesticides and they no longer aerate the soil; forests cut down no longer protect soils from erosion. The problem is that we do not know how much decline in biodiversity the earth can sustain without precipitating a biological disaster. Biologist Wilson feels we are in imminent danger. This is not to say that every insect, fish, or primate species has to be saved. However, what biologists fear is happening today is the complete dismantling of the global life support system.

Air Pollution

Natural processes operate to cleanse the atmosphere. For example, through photosynthesis, green plants use water and carbon dioxide to produce oxygen and carbohydrates. These natural life cycles are limited, however, and if the atmosphere becomes overloaded, our air supply becomes more toxic.

There can be no question that modern technology taxes the earth's atmosphere. According to the Census Bureau, for example, over 85 percent of the air pollution in urban areas is attributable to the internal combustion engine, despite efforts to control these emissions by using such devices as the catalytic converter (U.S. Bureau of the Census, 1991). On the other hand, pollution from automobiles has already been reduced considerably. Today's new vehicles emit 96 percent fewer hydrocarbons, 75 percent fewer nitrogen oxides, and 96 percent less carbon monoxide than their 1960 counterparts (see Figure 13.5). The contribution of all vehicles to ozone pollution is now down to 29 percent of the total, and will reach 20 percent by the 1990s under the rules now in effect, as new cars replace older ones (Main, 1988).

At the same time, there are hydrocarbons, nitrous and sulfurous oxides, lead, and various forms of particulate matter, such as soot and ash, emitted from industrial production operations and the burning of coal and wood. According to the EPA, the healthiness of air quality in the United States has generally improved over the past decade, but over 40 percent of our country's residents live in areas exceeding acceptable levels of one or more of the pollutants just mentioned ("EPA Reports . . . ," 1988).

Another threat to our air comes from the release of chlorine- and bromine-containing chemicals, such as chlorofluorocarbons (CFCs). These are common industrial chemicals and are also often used in aerosol cans and refrigeration units. When these chemicals escape into the atmosphere, they destroy the ozone that surrounds the earth (French, 1992a). Ozone is important because it screens out harmful ultraviolet rays from the sun. If this ultraviolet radiation gets through, it can cause skin cancer, damage marine life, and lower crop yields. Recent measurements by the National Aeronautics and Space Administration indicate that the earth may have lost a stunning 5 percent of its ozone layer in thirteen years (Brown, Flavin, and Postel, 1991).

Certain types of air pollution, if sufficiently severe, may cause a "greenhouse effect" (Balling, 1992). Modern technology depends on the burning of fossil fuels as a source of energy, and this releases great quantities of carbon dioxide into the atmosphere. The carbon dioxide molecules act like the glass roof of a greenhouse, allowing sunlight to reach the earth's surface but preventing the escape of solar infrared radiation back into space. According to some scientists, the temperature of the earth's atmosphere could rise as much as five degrees over the next fifty to one hundred years because of the greenhouse effect. This could substantially alter weather patterns and climate. It could also melt much of the earth's water that is now stored as ice at the poles and in glaciers. This could cause the world's oceans to rise seven feet or more from their current levels with devastating flooding of low-lying coastal regions. It could also cause some of the great food-producing regions of the world to dry up into dust bowls. Furthermore, the developing nations accuse the industrial nations of being the prime cause of this problem.

There is lively debate over what to do about the greenhouse effect. The industrial countries want the less developed nations to control their population growth and to stop scrambling after cars, air conditioners, and other aspects of affluent Western lives. The less developed nations want the affluent industrial nations to tone down their life-style and shift some of the world's resources to the fight against poverty in the poorer nations in the world. Some economists and scientists even argue that the greenhouse effect will produce only mild disruptions that we can adapt to and that vigorous efforts to control the emission of greenhouse gases could stunt economic growth and produce a drop in our life-style.

Pesticides and Other Chemicals

As in most instances of human beings' attempts to control their environment, efforts to cope with insects interfering with crop production began on a small scale and became increasingly complex. For example, one early strategy was the use of lead arsenate. This compound was effective in exterminating a narrow range of insects, but it was biodegradable and had no long-lasting negative effects on the environment. About forty years ago, chemists put together a series of chlorinated hydrocarbons to produce the well-known insecticide DDT. Such chemical substances are much more effective in killing bugs, but they are also much longer lasting and less biodegradable. DDT and compounds like it remain stable for many years after application. In addition, these substances accumulate in the fatty tissues of insects and fish, and then move up the food chain to affect higher animals. When consumed by human beings, these substances can cause serious health problems, such as cancer and birth defects. Furthermore, insects eventually build up immunity to pesticides, and these compounds become useless for the control of insects after a while.

The volume of synthetic organic chemicals produced in the world has skyrocketed in the past fifty years (Postel, 1988). In the United States alone, such production has grown from less than seven million tons in 1945 to over one hundred million tons today. There are currently seventy thousand such chemicals in daily use, with as many as one thousand new ones added each year. Although not all of these chemicals are harmful, many are, and with devastating consequences: "Between four hundred thousand and two million pesticide poisonings occur worldwide each year, most of them among farmers in developing countries" (Postel, 1988: 121). As many as forty thousand such poisonings result in death.

There are often alternatives to using chemicals as fertilizers. One approach, known as *integrated pest management*, views a field of crops as an ecosystem in which natural forces can be used to control pests and weeds and thus enhance crop growth. This can be done by introducing natural predators of the pests or using genetic manipulations that result in pest-resistant crop varieties (Postel, 1988). This approach may not eliminate the use of chemicals, but it does focus on keeping their levels below the point at which significant crop damage and economic loss occur. A major barrier to the development of these programs is the fact that it is generally cheaper for the private sector to use chemicals. There is no incentive for the private sector when the development of permanent biological control agents involves no marketable product. In addition, government policies in developing countries as well as in the United States tend to subsidize the use of chemical pesticides as a way to increase crop production.

Energy Resources

Most existing energy resources are finite. There is no question that they will eventually be exhausted; the only debate is over when this depletion will occur (Flavin and Durning, 1988). Most nations of the world are dependent on a few particular energy resources, primarily the fossil fuels: coal, petroleum, and natural gas. These fill 95 percent of America's energy needs, and the United States and other nations continue to place higher and higher demands on them.

Geologists have calculated that coal will be our longest lasting nonrenewable resource, with the earliest date of depletion occurring well into the twenty-first century (Hubbert, 1969). Although coal is an excellent ongoing energy resource, we must avoid becoming overly optimistic because the costs, both economic and social, of continuing to use it could be prohibitive. Economically, coal will become most costly to mine; and socially, the vast wastelands created by strip mining operations, increased air pollution, and deaths and injuries from the mining process itself provide further reasons for hesitancy. Most recently, the Bush administration explored new, cost-effective ways to burn coal more cleanly, thus improving the United States' energy security by reducing dependence on imported oil and gas (Miller, 1989). Although alternative sources of energy have been identified, some of these also have detrimental consequences for the environment. For example, the use of wood fuel instead of oil or gas seems

like an excellent alternative because this resource is renewable. But widespread burning of wood leads to increased air pollution (Nero, 1988). We may actually be overlooking some alternative sources of energy, however. Various forms of garbage, for example, have been wasted for many years. It has been conservatively estimated that our nation could save up to two million barrels of oil every day by using garbage as a combustible fuel source (Brown, Flavin, and Postel, 1991).

Regarding nuclear energy, there are some very serious risks in using it: illness and death from radiation leakage, possible disaster from nuclear accidents, and the problem of disposing of nuclear wastes. The nuclear accident in Chernobyl in the Soviet Union, where an explosion and fire destroyed part of a nuclear power plant and released radioactivity into the environment, illustrates the potential for disaster (Flavin, 1987). A number of people died in this accident, thousands of people had to be evacuated permanently because of radiation leakage, and radioactive fallout was found over large parts of Europe. What is hard to predict is how many premature deaths from diseases such as cancer will occur over the next four decades because of people's exposure to radioactivity from the accident at Chernobyl.

Perhaps the most reasonable course of action involves the exploration of new energy sources, utilizing techniques that do not involve the risks and hazards that many previous strategies have entailed.

FUTURE PROSPECTS

Population Problems

Premodern societies usually had high birthrates and high death rates so that there was little or no population growth. In fact, human history shows that many societies have been at or near **zero population growth,** where *birth and death rates are nearly equal, producing a zero rate of natural in-*

crease. Although fully developed nations such as the United States are approaching ZPG, other societies are far from it, and this is where much of the world's population problem exists. What, then, will the future bring?

Demographer Leon F. Bouvier (1984) of the Population Reference Bureau points out that as new cures for diseases are discovered and implemented and living conditions improve in developing nations, death rates will continue to fall, and improvements in life expectancy for them will probably continue. Consequently, efforts to control world population growth will have to focus on fertility. Furthermore, current attitudes about fertility around the world suggest that nations with high birthrates are ready to do what needs to be done to bring them down. In 1982, the United Nations Fifth Population Inquiry determined that well over 60 percent of developing nations—the nations with high birthrates—felt that their national level of fertility was too high, and 85 percent of the nations that view their fertility rate to be too high are in favor of policies designed to reduce it. Finally, and perhaps most revealing, is the fact that nearly 80 percent of the total population of developing countries lives in nations that regard their fertility levels as too high (Salas, 1984).

So there is growing recognition of the importance of controlling fertility because most nations and their people have come to realize that large families can be detrimental to people's ability to achieve a satisfactory life-style. According to the United Nations World Population Plan of Action:

> *It is now universally accepted that family size may affect individual development and that there is a fundamental right to choose the size and spacing of the family. . . . Parents are concerned about giving their children the very best of which they are capable; more and more are realizing that increasing the size of the family may decrease the quality of what is available for each child.* (Salas, 1984: 26)

Given these attitudes, fertility will probably decline in all regions where it is high over the next fifty years, and the decrease will probably be sharp in all but a few societies. For this to occur quickly enough to avoid the worst of the problems discussed earlier, however, a number of programs and policies that work to lower fertility will have to be pursued aggressively. We will review the major things that can be done. If they are, there is some optimism that the worst consequences of rapid population growth can be avoided.

Family Planning. In the United States, the relatively high fertility in the years following World War II declined precipitously after 1957. The reason? Certainly the widespread use of effective contraceptives played an important part. Given the effectiveness of contraception in reducing fertility, the solution to the world's population problem might appear to be providing contraceptives to everyone who desires them. However feasible this approach might appear at first, technology is of secondary importance in this realm when compared to cultural values. The prevention of conception or the termination of pregnancies through abortion are not merely technological feats. Conception and abortion are social events that represent decisions that people have made based in part on what their culture has taught them is desirable. After all, the birthrate in the United States was relatively low during the 1930s—almost as low as today—well before the pill, IUDs, and other modern contraceptive techniques were available. This low fertility rate occurred because people decided on the basis of the severe economic conditions that they wanted to postpone having children or to have smaller families.

Some modern population-control efforts, then, have focused on encouraging people to consciously decide how many children they want, with the hope that people will choose to have smaller families. Such family planning programs encourage couples to have children when and if they are desired. Experience with such programs

POLICY ISSUES

Population Policy and Family Planning in China

Although Americans may not feel the immediate press of population problems, the growth of the world's population could affect us through competition for limited resources or the impact of world pollution. So we need to be concerned about the population policies of other nations. China, for example, constitutes 20 percent of all humanity, and this makes the demographic situation in China critical to world population concerns.

Population policy is nothing new to China. As early as the 1950s, the Chinese government began to formulate strategies designed to control population growth, centering on a general policy that population increases should occur in a planned fashion. By the mid-1970s, China had achieved quite dramatic decreases in their fertility. Even so, this substantially reduced rate of population growth still involved an addition of twelve million people per year. At this rate, if couples in China limited themselves to two children on the average, the nation would not reach ZPG for fifty years, and its population would increase by at least 30 percent over that period of time to 1.3 billion people. Because of this, the Chinese government enacted an even more aggressive population policy in 1979, which primarily involved the establishment of a one-child family stipulation for all couples who did not already have children. The plan involved various kinds of incentives, including a government stipend going to one-child couples until the youngster is fourteen years old and penalties for families larger than two children, including salary deductions, tax surcharges, and other costs that would rise with each birth. Perhaps even more controversial is the policy involving government-employed family planning workers talking to Chinese citizens about their sexual behavior and use of contraceptives. Violations of the one-child family policy have been fewer in urban areas than in rural areas in China. This is probably because large numbers of children can be an economic asset in agrarian-based rural settings but a liability in urban industrial ones. Provided that all third and higher births could be avoided and that 40 percent of the urban couples and 25 percent of the rural couples would limit themselves to one child over the

has shown that, when women realize they have a choice of whether to have children, they most often choose to have fewer children than they would have had otherwise. Still, if people desire children, they will have them, and people's desires arise out of socialization into a particular set of cultural values. Some of the implications of this for social policy are discussed in the second Policy Issues insert.

Reviews of family planning services, however, are mixed regarding their effectiveness (Mauldin, 1975; Jacobson, 1988). In many countries with active family planning efforts, such as China, South Korea, and Costa Rica, social and economic changes—to be discussed in a moment—probably account for much of the lowering of fertility. In other countries, such as Kenya, India, and the Dominican Republic, family planning programs have had little observable effect. Why? One reason is that many of these countries failed to allocate the resources necessary to make the programs effective. In addition, as we noted ear-

course of the next thirty years, China would be well on its way to ZPG (Zopf, 1984).

There are several developments that lead to the conclusion that China's one-child policy is not working. For example, in 1983, the official Chinese press reported frightening increases in the incidence of drownings and other murders of infant females. One newspaper reported that over 210 female babies were murdered soon after birth in the Guangdong Province in China in 1982 alone. Presumably, this female infanticide is committed by parents who wanted their only child to be a son. The news service made this statement:

> If this phenomenon is not stopped quickly, then in twenty years' time a serious social problem will arise, namely that a large number of young men will not be able to find wives. (Gupte, 1984: 158)

Another telling indication that there are problems with China's one-child family policy lies in recent statistics on population growth. China's crude birthrate stood at 21.6 in 1990, one-third higher than the 14.9 of the United States, and its rate of natural increase for the 1990s is projected to be 1.3 percent per year, almost twice the 0.7 for the United States (U. S. Bureau of the Census, 1991:830–835). On the other hand, there is some evidence that the political and social pressures exerted on people, along with the economic benefits of fewer children, may be leading younger Chinese to opt for smaller families (Kristof, 1990).

China's population surpassed 1.1 billion in 1990 and is expected to come close to 1.4 billion by 2010. China's political rulers had wanted the population to level off in the year 2000 at 1.2 billion, and then to fall to 700 million by 2050. Even if the fertility rate were pushed down further, these goals are currently unachievable. In January of 1988, the head of China's State Family Planning Commission, Mr. Wang Wei, was relieved of his responsibilities. More recently, Chinese demographers have begun to question the one-child family policy, pointing out that too sharp a reduction in fertility could prove to be a long-term deficit for the nation; that if the policy succeeded, by the year 2050, two-fifths of China's population would be over age sixty-five ("Peasants Revolt," 1988). Despite this expression of concern, the "firing" of the man charged with managing China's population policy implies that the nation's "new breed" of demographers have not been heard.

The situation in China highlights the importance of cultural values as they relate to population growth. Even when a government enacts a program that provides benefits for those who are willing to cooperate and levels penalties on those who are not, if couples want to have more children, they will continue to have them. It also suggests that government intervention that goes contrary to people's deeply held values is unlikely to be effective. This means that approaches to family planning and population control must have the backing of the citizenry. Without it, population growth may continue at unacceptable levels.

---

lier, values are a critical element in reducing fertility—people must want to have fewer children before family planning efforts will work. In many countries, however, women have large numbers of children because they have been taught to want them, and cultural values are supportive of large families. In such settings, family planning will probably have only a marginal effect.

Economic Development.   We mentioned that certain social and economic changes probably ac-

count for more of the decline in fertility than has family planning. The changes referred to are generally called economic development (Bouvier, 1984). Developing nations that are actively involved in programs to control population growth today have placed a major emphasis on economic development. Although these countries recognize the need for family planning, they argue that no program of population control can be completely effective unless it is a part of a more general program of economic development. A number of changes that accompany economic development—especially urbanization, increasing levels of education, and a rising standard of living—lead people to view large families as less desirable. In urban settings and since the passage of child-labor laws, there is no longer a distinct economic advantage to having many children. In fact, in urban, industrial societies, large families lead to crowded housing and a drain on family finances. Furthermore, when women receive more education, they usually want to pursue a career or develop talents other than domestic ones, and large families make this more difficult. Finally, economic development affords people a more affluent life-style, and large families are expensive. This affects their standard of living, leading many couples to decide to spend their resources on consumer goods or leisure activities rather than raising large families. Even with economic development, most people want to become parents, but they are more likely to opt for a smaller number of children. And as small families become common, they are viewed increasingly as "normal," and people feel social pressures not to have large families.

Incentives. Some programs have been proposed and a few established that would provide people with some incentives, usually economic, for preventing births. This might involve giving people cash payments or gifts for being sterilized, or it might take the form of annual payments to women for each year they do not have children. This might be done by giving tax breaks to people with smaller families or no children at all, rather than increasing their tax exemptions as we currently do for each child that is born. A program introduced into several private tea plantations in India involved placing money in a retirement trust fund for each year that passed in which a woman did not have any children (Ridker, 1980). This program did result in lower fertility, although the effect was not dramatic. Once again, unless the social and cultural forces that lead people to want fewer children are present, declines in fertility tend to be small. The incentives approach has also been criticized on the grounds that large families, which also tend to be poorer, would suffer the most and their poverty would be further exacerbated.

The Status of Women. Another important element in controlling population growth is the status of women. The United Nations implemented a program in 1974 that was called the World Population Plan of Action, which invited all member countries to improve women's lives by providing them with opportunities in education, employment, and political participation, as well as support in their domestic and maternal roles (Salas, 1984). Research conducted by the United Nations has shown consistently that educational attainment and labor force participation of women are particularly important elements in a population policy: Educated women who work outside of the home have fewer children than do less educated women who are not part of the labor force. Research conducted in the United States also shows that better educated women who have careers, or at least are a part of the labor force, desire smaller families and are more sensitive to the overall issue of population growth (Thompson, 1980; Houseknecht, 1987). So programs intended to advance sexual equality around the world will likely have a positive impact on controlling population growth.

Environmental Problems

Although there is considerable consensus about global population problems, there is substantial debate about how to deal with environmental problems.

Interest Groups and the Environment. The conflict perspective points to the important role of interest groups in the solution to environmental problems. Which solutions are initiated will depend on the clash of varying interests in the shaping of social policy. Prior to the 1960s, few

Americans were interested in environmental problems. One of the key elements involved in heightening people's awareness of these problems since then has been the establishment of a wide variety of environmental interest groups. Some of these groups are not new. The oldest is the Sierra Club, which was founded in 1892 by a group of affluent San Franciscans who had an interest in climbing the High Sierras. Today, the Sierra Club is one of the best-known environmental groups in the political and legal arena. Another older environmental association is the Audubon Society, which was founded in 1905 by affluent women and men on the East Coast, with an initial purpose of halting the commercial hunting of wild birds for plumage in the women's fashion industry.

The modern environmental movement took off in the 1960s and 1970s. These years saw the emergence of major nationwide environmental groups such as the Friends of the Earth, the League of Conservation Voters, the Environmental Defense Fund, the Natural Resources Defense Council, and Greenpeace. These groups engaged in lobbying, demonstrations, and sometimes disruptive actions that brought environmental problems to the public eye and created a great deal of political pressure to address environmental issues with legislation.

The fervor generated by these organizations during the 1960s set the stage for some very important legislation in the 1970s that related to environmental quality. In 1970, for example, the National Environmental Policy Act (NEPA) was passed, which required that public hearings be held on matters that might adversely affect the environment and that environmental impact studies be conducted to assess these possible effects. Also in the early 1970s, the Clean Air Act and the Water Pollution Control Act were passed, and these laws led to the establishment of the Environmental Protection Agency (EPA). Originally, the Clean Air Act empowered the EPA to monitor and regulate standards of air quality, but as time went on, the EPA acquired authority concerning almost all matters dealing with environmental

quality. If it had not been for the establishment and operation of interest groups focusing on environmental problems, legislation such as this would probably not have been passed. Future actions taken by such groups will be critical for the future of our environment.

By the 1990s, many Americans were stunned by accumulating evidence of ecological damage, and once again demanded more action in combatting pollution. When asked whether further improvements in the quality of the environment need to be made "regardless of the cost," fully 80 percent of Americans said "yes" in 1989 compared with only 45 percent in 1981 (Suro, 1989). With this base of substantial support for environmental causes, a well-established phalanx of large and well-funded environmental groups, including the World Wildlife Fund, the Environmental Defense Fund, the Natural Resources Defense Council, and others, is set to act (Russell, 1989). In our nation's capital and across the country, these groups lobby for environmental legislation and take polluters to court. Some environmentalists argue that these groups are too timid in that they disdain public demonstrations and civil disobedience as tactics to fight environmental issues. These established environmental groups also may be timid because they get significant support from the corporations that are major polluters. The World Wildlife Fund, for example, gets support from corporations such as Dow Chemical, Exxon, and Shell Oil. These environmentalists argue that the real passion in the movement today is at the grass-roots level where people organize, protest, and demonstrate to stop a toxic waste landfill or a waste incinerator from being placed in their community. In fact, there are now national groups, such as the Citizens Clearinghouse for Hazardous Wastes, that provide information and assistance to such grass-roots efforts. Although the established organizations tend to invest their energies in efforts to regulate the activities of polluters, the grass-roots organizations tend to shift toward the prevention of environmental problems by stopping pollution at its source. The Bush administration and some environmental groups have pushed for market-based incentives for environmental protection. This approach focuses on developing ways for companies to profit by reducing population, for example, by making wind or solar energy cheaper to use than the much more polluting coal. Although this may have some benefit, many environmentalists are wary that it might be merely a way to get corporations off the hook without having to make significant changes in their practices.

Moderating Economic Growth.   Some environmental problems are created or made worse by the unrestrained pursuit of economic growth and short-term economic goals. After all, many people have a vested interest in exploiting the environment with little concern for the long-term impact this might have. For example, many corporations and individuals around the world benefit when forests are cut down and therefore disregard the problems of deforestation and declining biological diversity discussed earlier. Lumber companies make a good profit and individuals have firewood to heat their homes and cook their food. If human populations were much smaller, the ecosystem might be able to sustain such activities; with overpopulation, however, such economic activity creates an imminent danger. Biologist Edward Wilson (1992) argues that it is in our long-term interests to switch to "extraction farming" in which the products of forests are harvested without harming the overall ecosystem. Some of this is being done, but short-term gain still propels many toward forestry practices that destroy ecosystems and annihilate species.

Some would argue that capitalism itself, especially if unrestrained, is inherently detrimental to the environment (Bookchin, 1990). The reason for this is that capitalists thrive on continuous economic growth and the fact that profits can be enhanced by pursuing short-term goals. One solution is to regulate the activities of capitalists, and this is a major element of our environmental policy and will be discussed in the next section. A more radical question, which is addressed by only

a few today, is whether individualism, profit seeking, and permanent growth can be reconciled with the limited resilience of our ecosystem to respond to the assaults on it. Will the products of our social and economic organization inevitably overwhelm the ability of the earth to recoup itself? All our policies assume that some form of restrained capitalism is compatible with protection of the environment.

Government Regulation.   One of the major battlegrounds of environmental issues is the extent of government regulation that should be adopted. By the 1990s, laws and court rulings have placed limits on most of the pollution and degradation of the environment discussed in this chapter. The Endangered Species Act, for example, protects seven hundred plant and animal species from actions that might threaten their survival, and four thousand more are being considered for such protection. The Clean Air Acts of 1970 and 1990 limited the amount of pollutants that automobiles, industries, and electric utilities can release into the environment. This regulation is one of the cornerstones of our environmental policies, but it also may have its limits as far as its ability to further control environmental pollution and degradation. One reason for this is that there are continuing battles over how far to extend that regulation. For example, new rulings in 1992 significantly relaxed the limitations of the Clean Air Act of 1990, allowing factories to exceed their limits without sanctions until the EPA reviews the case and tells them to stop. The factories do not even need to tell their neighbors that they are exceeding the limits. Overall, the Reagan-Bush years saw a weakening of environmental regulation. The Clinton administration will likely be more responsive to environmental concerns. A second reason that regulation may have its limits is that it can be costly. For example, one recent assessment of the costs of reducing air pollution in our cities concluded that it may be so high that it is not worth it. The authors concluded that we might be better off investing our resources elsewhere: "In the health area alone, $10 billion in-

Recycling has become an important element in the battle to reduce the amount of waste going into our landfills, but more needs to be done in terms of manufacturing products in a way that makes recycling easy and efficient.

vested in smoking cessation programs, radon control, better prenatal and neonatal health care, or similar measures might contribute much more to public health and well-being" than costly programs to reduce some types of air pollution (Krupnick and Portney, 1991: 526). This is not to suggest that we abandon regulation, but rather that we recognize its limits. The International Perspectives insert reviews some of the regulations imposed in other societies.

Recycling.   Only recently have Americans become attentive to the issue of recycling (Pollock, 1987). In some parts of the United States, there are effective recycling programs, such as the one thousand or more aluminum reclamation centers in operation. Many cities also have paper collection programs, which lead to the successful reuse of such products. American industry has also made significant strides in recycling water. In the last thirty years, the number of times that each cubic meter of water is used by industry before discarding it has risen from 1.8 to 8.6 (Postel, 1986). Recycling water has become more attractive to industry as pollution regulations have become more stringent: In many cases, it is cheaper to reuse water a number of times in a plant than to treat it sufficiently to meet environmental regulations and release it as wastewater. If strong environmental pollution regulations are maintained, by the year 2000, industry as a whole may reuse water as many as seventeen times before releasing it as wastewater. If this happens, manufacturing industries will use 45 percent less water than twenty years earlier, and the pressure on our water supply will be eased.

However, many environmentalists argue that our current efforts in this realm are haphazard and much less effective than they could be. Much more could be done. For example, the recycling of materials and products could be considered in the design and production stages, and few things would be manufactured that could not be reused. Denmark has banned throwaway beverage con-

INTERNATIONAL PERSPECTIVES

Environmental Practices and Policies in Other Societies

More so than most other problems discussed in this book, issues of population growth and environmental degradation are truly international in scope. This is so because all societies inhabit a single ecosystem in which significant pollution of one part of the system degrades the whole system. We can fight crime in Los Angeles without paying much heed to how much crime there is in Caracas, Venezuela, or New Delhi, India. However, we need to be concerned with fossil fuel consumption in all three cities because all contribute to the depletion of finite supplies of such fuels and to global air pollution and possibly global warming. If the greenhouse effect and global warming become the scourge that some scientists argue they can, societal boundaries will serve as no protection against their devastating effects.

When we look at societies around the world, considerable variation exists in terms of behaviors that contribute to environmental degradation and policies that reduce or prevent it. For example, as this is being written, Los Angeles is opening its first stretch of subway (only a few miles long), and journalists are pondering whether residents of that city have become too wedded to their cars to begin using public transit. Why have Americans become so oriented toward the automobile

whereas people in Finland, Japan, Brazil, and most other nations have not? Part of the answer to that is our affluence, of course, but other factors are equally important. For one thing, we have designed our cities such that transportation without cars is difficult. Most cities in the United States are spread out, with places of work and school far away from where most people live. European cities, on the other hand, tend to be much more concentrated, which makes public transit less expensive and more feasible.

For another thing, we keep taxes on gasoline low, which encourages people to drive. In 1990, gasoline cost $1.04 per gallon in the United States, compared with $3.40 in France, $2.55 in the United Kingdom, $4.27 in Italy, and $3.05 in Japan. Seventy-five percent of the cost of gas in France, Britain, and Italy are taxes whereas only one-quarter of the cost in the United States goes to taxes. Italy has a $3.50 tax on gas, Germany $2, and Japan $1.50; by contrast, the United States extracts only $ .30 in taxes on each gallon of gas (Flavin and Lenssen, 1990). So, Americans drive rather than ride public transit because it is so inexpensive to do so.

The combination of our affluence along with our lack of policies to discourage the use of fossil fuels means that the United States is one of their

tainers, and in the Canadian province of Ontario almost all beer is sold in standardized refillable bottles (Brown, Flavin, and Postel, 1991; Brown, 1992). In both places, the containers produced are standardized and sturdy, which makes their reuse easy and inexpensive. Of course, national legislation and enforcement would be necessary to make such a plan work. Such policies might be

appealing to the interventionist but anathema to the laissez-faire forces. Nevertheless, the idea is an attractive one, because the costs of maintaining our environment would be absorbed by those doing the manufacturing rather than by the general public. This might encourage manufacturing interests to be sensitive to recycling and reuse concerns in order to maximize their profits.

heaviest users. China, for example, burns the equivalent of sixteen hundred pounds of coal per person each year for its various energy needs; at the same time, France burns the equivalent of eight thousand pounds per person per year, and the United States burns an astounding twenty-two thousand pounds—thirteen times what China consumes for each person and three times what even France, another industrialized and affluent nation, consumes (U.S. Bureau of the Census, 1991: 854–855). With less than 5 percent of the world's population, the United States produces almost one-quarter of the world's carbon dioxide emissions, the most important component of gases causing the greenhouse effect (Nasar, 1992a).

One policy that could help reduce the use of fossil fuels and the amount of air pollution would be a tax on the use of energy. There are two justifications for this. One is that societies can change people's behaviors by making it more costly for them to do things that use up scarce resources or pollute the environment. Protection of resources and the environment is in everyone's interest. The second justification is that those producing the pollution—namely, users of a polluting energy source—should pay taxes to help pay for the damage to the environment and to people's health caused by the pollution. One approach to such a policy is to place a substantial tax on gasoline to discourage its use, as we have seen many other nations do. This would encourage people to use mass transit and to build communities that are not dependent on automobiles for transportation. Another approach would be to tax energy sources that produce more carbon dioxide emissions, the major culprit in the greenhouse problem. Coal would be taxed the heaviest, followed by oil and then natural gas; nuclear power and renewable energy sources could go untaxed under such a policy since they release no carbon dioxide. Finland, Denmark, and Sweden already have such taxes and many other European nations are considering them (Flavin and Lenssen, 1990). Such a carbon tax is being considered by the Clinton administration and may be in place by the time these words are read.

Many European nations have other so-called "green taxes" on such things as air and water pollution, waste, and noise. Norway has a tax on fertilizers and pesticides. However, many of these taxes are too low to significantly change people's behavior, although they do raise revenues to support important environmental programs. Vice President Al Gore (1992), in his book *Earth in the Balance*, makes a strong case for such "green taxes" in the United States as an important element in the battle to protect the environment.

The policies in many societies other than our own reflect an interventionist stance: The government uses its various powers to shape behaviors that conserve resources and protect against environmental degradation. Policy in the United States, on the other hand, has placed a greater emphasis on the laissez-faire position: The government should step back and let the marketplace determine the amounts and types of energy that are used. This was especially true during the Reagan–Bush years. However, we may see a shift in direction with the Clinton–Gore administration.

Renewable Energy Resources. Since the industrial revolution in America, our country's quest for energy has focused on finite resources, such as coal, oil, and nuclear fission. All of these energy sources are exhaustible. Renewable energy resources, on the other hand, have no inherent limit on how long humans can exploit them (Shea, 1988). Solar energy is perhaps the best example of a virtually inexhaustible resource. It can be used to produce two very important types of energy: heat and electrical power. Wood and vegetable fuels are two energy resources that have been frequently overlooked in industrialized nations. Unlike coal, wood can be replaced through reforestation. Vegetable matter can be burned, converted into methane or alcohol, or processed into fuel cells that produce electrical energy. Other sources of renewable energy are water power, wind power, and geothermal energy (terrestrial heat). In the 1970s, the government encouraged the development of some renewable energy resources by allowing people to take tax deductions on a part of the cost of installing heating systems that used them. By the mid-1980s, however, declining oil prices along with a less favorable political climate in Washington had deflated much of the enthusiasm for such efforts.

International Cooperation.   Both population and environmental problems are clearly global problems. What happens in one part of the earth is likely to have an impact on people elsewhere. Because of this, we are beginning to see more international cooperation in efforts to control environmental problems. Most recently, we had the Earth Summit in Brazil where leaders from almost every country in the world gathered to develop a world policy on environmental issues. In fact, such meetings can be traced back at least twenty years to the United Nations Conference on the Human Environment held in Stockholm. In the interim, there has been established a commitment to attack environmental problems and a record of agreements to do so (Brown, Flavin, and Postel, 1991). For example, in 1990, there was an international accord to phase out the production of ozone-destroying CFCs by the end of the century. Also in 1990, twenty-three countries agreed to freeze or reduce levels of carbon emissions in an effort to attack the problem of global warming.

Certainly these international accords do not solve all problems, and nations are still inclined to pursue their own short-term interests. These accords are important, however, because they create an international climate that pressures nations to do more about these problems than they would be inclined to do on their own. In addition, the accords recognize that solving environmental problems must be a united, worldwide effort if it is to be effective.

New Cultural Values and Social Institutions

Throughout this chapter, we have emphasized the importance of values in both population and environmental problems. In fact, some new cultural values have appeared that may have important implications in these realms. Some values related to population and environmental problems derive from our Judeo-Christian heritage, emphasizing the desirability of procreation and the mastery of human beings over the earth. Certain passages in the Bible, for example, have been interpreted as justification for human beings' exploitation of the environment:

> *And God said, Let us make man in our own image, after our likeness: . . . Be fertile and increase, fill the earth and master it; and rule the fish of the sea, the birds of the sky, and all the living things that creep on earth. (Genesis 1:26–28)*

The conventional environmental ideology that has emerged in the past three decades is in sharp contrast with this view. This environmental ideology emphasizes that human beings should live in harmony with their environment rather than "mastering" or "ruling over" it; that people should serve as stewards who protect and conserve the environment so that it will be available for future generations to use. A key notion that many environmentalists use today is "sustainability": "A sustainable society is one that satisfies its needs without jeopardizing the prospects of future generations" (Brown, Flavin, and Postel, 1991: 30–31). Attaining sustainability may call for some groups to moderate their needs. Modifications in one or more elements of the "I = P × A × T" formula mentioned earlier may be called for: reducing our Populations, accepting a less Affluent standard of living, and using a more simple and less polluting Technology.

Some environmentalists take a more radical stance than this. For example, the following quo-

The Laissez-Faire/Interventionist Debate:
Population and Environmental Policy

How should the United States approach population growth and environmental problems? For example, do family planning programs represent interventionist strategies when it comes to population policy? Perhaps. According to a White House policy paper written in mid-1984, the power of free enterprise, rather than family planning programs, should be the fundamental answer to population growth problems ("White House Considers . . . ," 1984).

Athough the Reagan administration acknowledged the "ultimate need" to achieve population equilibrium and took credit for having supported family planning programs in less developed countries, it saw most population problems in these nations as symptomatic of government-caused economic ills rather than demographic ones. In this policy statement, the Reagan administration announced that the United States will "no longer contribute directly or indirectly to family planning programs funded by governments or private organizations that advocate abortion as an instrument of population control" ("White House Considers . . . ," 1984: 3).

Indeed, the leaders of some less developed countries have argued that "development is the best contraceptive," whereas others have insisted that family planning assistance is the only way to control population growth. The debate continues over whether the United States should intervene in the affairs of less developed nations by providing family planning assistance or whether a laissez-faire stance should be taken.

Government intervention with regard to environmental issues is also linked to various political and economic considerations. For example, concerns over air pollution in America's major cities have reached crisis proportions. For example, the air in Los Angeles is the dirtiest in the nation. The state's South Coast Air Quality Management District (AQMD) has developed a twenty-year pollution control strategy that conservative estimates indicate will cost almost $3 billion annually (Weisman, 1989). The AQMD's proposal has serious implications for citizens' fundamental decisions regarding where they will live, how they will live, and how they will travel. The plan calls for some very drastic measures. For example, people living in the district would no longer be able to use barbecue lighter fluid; businesses such as dry cleaning establishments, auto painting shops, and even bakeries would be required to switch to less polluting but much more costly techniques and install elaborate antipollution devices in their operations, costing enormous sums of money. Drivers would eventually be required to use car fuels other than gasoline, so it would cost more to operate their vehicles. Furthermore, commuters would be compelled by law to carpool—a suggestion that has been met with predictably enormous protest by residents who have become accustomed to travelling to and from work in their private automobiles. The plan might even place a limit on the number of cars a family would be allowed to own.

Problems involving the pollution of our environment pose a frustrating "Catch 22": A laissez-faire approach appears to be disastrous for the environment. On the other hand, to what extent does government intervention interfere or even directly conflict with citizens' individual rights? At what point does the intrusiveness of government intervention become worse than the pollution it is intended to control? Clearly, the solutions that we arrive at in the realm of population and environmental problems will be a product of the laissez-faire/interventionist debate.

tation is taken from a public information bulletin published by Greenpeace:

> *Ecology teaches us that humankind is not the center of life on the planet. Ecology has taught us that the whole earth is part of our "body" and that we must learn to respect it as we respect life—the whales, the seals, the forests, the seas. The tremendous beauty of ecological thought is that it shows us a pathway back to an understanding and appreciation of life itself—an understanding and appreciation that is imperative to that very way of life. (Simon, 1981: 335)*

This philosophy, called "deep ecology" or "biocentrism," is based on the following principles (Devall and Sessions, 1985; Manes, 1990):

- All life on earth, both human and nonhuman, has equal value, and humans have a right to destroy life forms only to meet *vital* needs.

- Given the size of human populations and the technology currently available to them in industrial societies, humans have become destructively intrusive in the earth's ecosystem and substantial population reduction is called for.

- To come into harmony with the environment, human economic, political, and social structures need to be changed so that they shift emphasis from stressing growth, bigness, and material wealth to valuing smallness, spirituality, and the nonmaterial quality of life.

Clearly, deep ecologists are calling for a radical change in the American way of life. In fact, one of these groups, called Earth First!, has resorted to action in their effort to protect the earth. Some members of Earth First! were arrested in 1989 for attempting to blow up a tower carrying high-voltage power lines to a massive irrigation project in Arizona (Robbins, 1989). In their view, human activities have become so destructive to the earth, and protecting the earth is of sufficiently high value, that the use of violence is warranted even if it means the destruction of human property and maybe even human lives.

Although the deep ecologists (and certainly groups such as Earth First!) take a more extreme stand than most Americans would feel comfortable with, they do suggest that permanent solutions to population and environmental problems may require a change in traditional American cultural values and social institutions. If we retain the biblical ideology of human mastery and domination over the earth, we may be unwilling to take extreme measures when they are warranted. In addition, we need to consider the possibility that industrial capitalism is at least part of the problem. When profits can be made by polluting the air or destroying the forests, then the unhindered operation of capitalist mechanisms such as free enterprise, competition, and profit making may destroy the environment beyond repair. It may be necessary to take a significantly interventionist stance, with the government enforcing some higher values that emphasize the protection of the environment. In fact, as we have seen, this is already happening to a degree (see the *Laissez-Faire/Interventionist Debate* on p. 489). The controversy today is over how much further down this road it will be necessary to go to achieve population and environmental goals.

Linkages

Environmental problems can be intensified when technology becomes more complex and intrusive (Chapter 15) or when there are few restraints on the profit-seeking activities of large and unresponsive corporations (Chapter 2).

Summary

1. Overpopulation can have devastating effects on the environment, just as changes in the environment can have important effects on the abilities of a region to support a population.

2. Population refers to the total number of people inhabiting a particular geographic area at a specified time. There are three basic elements that affect the size, composition, and distribution of human populations: fertility, mortality, and migration. Fertility and mortality are key elements in evaluating world population growth and change.

3. The demographic transition refers to the changing patterns of birth and death rates brought about by industrialization. This model is divided into four stages: preindustrial, transitional or early industrial, industrial, and postindustrial. Today's population problem can be most clearly located in those less industrialized nations that have not yet experienced the transition.

4. The three sociological perspectives help us to evaluate population and environment. From the functionalist perspective, population growth and environmental conditions become social problems when they become dysfunctional and lead to social disorganization. According to the conflict perspective, population and environment become social problems when those who control the economic system in society take steps to artificially limit the resources available in order to benefit a particular group of people. The interactionist perspective sensitizes us to the fact that population and environmental problems are in part matters of social definition.

5. There are many consequences of population growth: crowding, food shortages, depletion of resources, intergroup conflict, and internal migration. A key ingredient in these consequences is carrying capacity: an upper limit that is imposed on a population by its environmental resources that cannot be permanently exceeded.

6. People's consciousness of environmental problems has fluctuated over time, and it has only been in the last three decades that a large part of the American public has viewed environmental issues as social problems. The impact of people on their environment is influenced by the size of their population, the level of affluence, and the state of technology. Included in the list of environmental concerns are water supply and pollution, solid and toxic wastes, nuclear wastes, land degradation, declines in biodiversity, air pollution, pesticides and other chemicals, and energy resources.

7. The future of population problems will depend on fertility, and a related concept in this regard is zero population growth: where birth and death rates are nearly equal, producing a zero rate of natural increase. Major issues in alleviating population problems are family planning, economic development, incentives, and the status of women. Regarding the environment, the activities of interest groups will affect its future. Other related issues are moderating economic growth, government regulation, recycling, renewable energy resources, and international cooperation.

8. Successfully alleviating population and environmental problems may call for the emergence of new cultural values that emphasize living in harmony with the environment and conserving resources rather than mastery over the world.

Important Terms for Review

demographic gap	ecosystem	hydrologic cycle	population
demographic transition	environment	migration	zero population growth
demography	fecundity fertility	mortality	

Discussion Questions

1. At the beginning of this chapter, we discuss how population and environment are closely interrelated social problems, showing that population issues directly affect the environment and that environmental concerns have a direct impact on population. Discuss this delicate relationship, paying special attention to the concept of the ecosystem.

2. The three key elements of demographic change are fertility, mortality, and migration. Discuss how these ingredients are interrelated. In particular, evaluate how the birthrate and death rate of a population combine to produce a society's rate of natural increase. Also, consider how in- and out-migration can affect a population.

3. In our treatment of the demographic transition, we point out that the early industrial stage is the transition, where birthrates persist but death rates decline. Discuss how these conditions lead to an expanding population and how later stages of the transition lead to a roughly stable population. What does zero population growth refer to? Has the United States achieved ZPG? Why or why not?

4. Discuss population and environmental problems in terms of the three theoretical perspectives. Pay particular attention to how functionalism allows us to see clearly how the two areas are closely interrelated; how the conflict perspective sheds light on social policy considerations involving these issues; and how interactionism helps us to understand that population and environmental problems are matters of social definition.

5. Crowding, food shortages, the depletion of resources, and intergroup conflict are major consequences of population growth. Discuss the relationships between the variables involved here. For example, consider how crowding could produce intergroup conflict; how the depletion of resources can produce food shortages; or how intergroup conflict can contribute to the further depletion of resources.

6. In our evaluation of environmental problems, we note that one observer called the United States the "world's trashiest society." Discuss this comment in the light of our observations about America's pollution of its environment and how our practices may affect us in the future.

7. Should a society's government intervene in people's decisions about having children? In this chapter, we discuss a controversial family planning program in China. Would such a program be acceptable in the United States? Why or why not?

8. What should U.S. social policy be concerning our environment? Should our government adopt a laissez-faire or an interventionist stance? Provide a rationale for how you answer these questions.

For Further Reading

Murray Bookchin. *Remaking Society: Pathways to a Green Future.* Boston: South End Press, 1990. Bookchin places a good portion of the blame for our environmental problems at the doorstep of capitalism and its demand for constant economic expansion. He also argues that our tendency to create hierarchies in society is responsible for the inclination of humans to dominate nature.

Kenneth E. Boulding. *The World As a Total System.* Beverly Hills, Calif.: Sage Publications, 1985. A well-known social scientist examines our planet using a functional analysis, evaluating the various systems of our world (the physical, biological, social, economic, political, and communication systems).

Irene Diamond and Gloria Feman Orenstein. *Reweaving the World: The Emergence of Ecofeminism.* San Francisco: Sierra Club Books, 1990. The articles in this anthology argue that feminist thought contains within it an ideology that would be supportive of protecting the environment. It argues that the persistence of patriarchy is partly at fault for our continuing despoliation of the world.

Pranay Gupte. *The Crowded Earth: People and the Politics of Population.* New York: W. W. Norton, 1984. In this volume, a former correspondent for *The New York Times* and native of Bombay, India, explores the complex and controversial issues surrounding world overpopulation and its control.

Susanna Hecht and Alexander Cockburn. *The Fate of the Forest: Developers, Destroyers, and Defenders of the Amazon.* New York: Verso, 1989. This is a very partisan book about the politics and the greed that will ultimately determine the fate of the Amazon rain forest. Many ecologists fear that, if the forest is destroyed, it will have a severe impact on worldwide climate and environment.

Paul C. Light. *Baby Boomers.* New York: W. W. Norton, 1988. This book is about the people born between 1946 and 1964, a period of fairly high birthrates in the United States. It documents the impact of fluctuating birthrates on the various sectors of society.

Jim MacNeill, Pieter Winsemius, and Taizo Yakushiji. *Beyond Interdependence: The Meshing of the World's Economy and the Earth's Ecology.* New York: Oxford University Press, 1991. This book argues not only that the economies of the world are interdependent but also that we are all ecologically interdependent. Implications for public policy and economic activities around the world are discussed.

William H. McNeil. *Plagues and People.* Garden City, N.Y.: Doubleday/Anchor, 1976. This is a detailed and well-documented history of epidemics around the world. It demonstrates in a very entertaining fashion how social practices can increase disease and the effects of disease on history.

Donella H. Meadows, Dennis L. Meadows, and Jorgen Randers. *Beyond the Limits: Confronting Global Collapse, Envisioning a Sustainable Future.* Post Mills, Vt.: Chelsea Green Pub. Co., 1992. This is a recent assessment by the same scientists who conducted the study for the Club of Rome twenty years ago. Their conclusions are a little more optimistic now, but only if there are changes in both life-style and technology.

Rafael M. Salas. *Reflections on Population.* New York: Pergamon Press, 1984. The executive director of the United Nations Fund for Population Activities comments on a variety of world population issues, with special emphasis on the posture of the United Nations relative to population concerns.

Rik Scarce. *Eco-Warriors: Understanding the Radical Environmental Movement.* Chicago: Noble Press, 1990. Although much of this book focuses on the group Earth First! discussed toward the end of the chapter, it does discuss the other important radical environmental groups around the world. The book provides detail and insight about the global environmental movement.

Philip Shabecoff. *A Fierce Green Fire: The American Environmental Movement.* New York: Hill and Wang, 1992. This is a good and engrossing history of the environmental movement in the United States. It divides the movement into three waves, with the first around 1900 and the third commencing in the last few years.

CHAPTER 14
Violence, War, and Terrorism

T he central concern of this chapter is **violence:** *behavior that is intended to bring pain or physical injury to another person or to harm or destroy property.* Actually, the topic of violence has been addressed at numerous points in this book. We discussed criminal violence such as homicide and assault in Chapter 9, and we analyzed family violence such as spouse and child abuse in Chapters 3 and 8. In those contexts, however, our focus was not violence itself. Rather, we were analyzing the crime problem (whether or not the crime took a violent form) and family problems (which come in both violent and nonviolent manifestations). Yet the number of times we have taken up the issue of violence while discussing various social problems suggests how pervasive violence is in our lives. In fact, it is sufficiently widespread to warrant discussion as a problem in its own right. In addition to fam-

ily violence and violent crime, terrorists kidnap, maim, and murder people; mobs riot in the streets and loot stores; citizens take up arms and attack their governments; and nations go to war against one another, sometimes in an orgy of death and destruction.

A major goal of this chapter is to identify the factors—social, psychological, and biological—that contribute to the extent and variety of human violence. We will first look at the extent of violence in the world, giving special emphasis to violence in the United States because this has the most direct bearing for most readers of this book. Then we will search for possible sources of this violence, including what insight the sociological perspectives can shed on this issue. Last, we will look at some of the consequences of violence for society before looking at what can be done to alleviate these problems.

Myths and Facts About Violence and War

Myth: America is a peaceful nation that has been in the forefront of efforts to stop wars around the world.

Fact: Statistics show that America is one of the more "war-prone" nations in the world: In addition to the declared wars in which we have been involved, American troops have been sent abroad for military purposes by the president an average of at least once a year. In the last twenty-five years, the American government has actively supported efforts to overthrow governments in Cuba, the Dominican Republic, Angola, Grenada, and Nicaragua.

Myth: Over the past two hundred years, Americans have been exposed to increasing levels of violence in the form of riots, labor strife, and racial conflict.

Fact: Although the number of such events has risen over the years, the rate of such violence has not increased considering our growing population, although violence does fluctuate substantially from one period to the next. Even the decade of the 1960s, which is viewed as extremely violent

because of the conjunction of civil rights activities with protest against the Vietnam War and riots among university students, is not extraordinary: Other decades, such as the 1880s and the 1900s when labor violence was prominent, approach or surpass the 1960s in violence.

Myth: In the race riots in American cities in the past thirty years, the rioters have been the criminals, the unemployed, the idle, and the poor.

Fact: Although such people certainly played a part, the people arrested for rioting have also included employed, educated, and seemingly law-abiding citizens.

Myth: Entertaining television shows and movies that contain some violence, such as *Cops*, the *Terminator*, or *Lethal Weapon*, do not harm young people who watch them as long as the shows are clearly fictional and fanciful.

Fact: Overwhelming research evidence concludes that young people, especially males, who watch violent shows on television are more likely to behave aggressively or violently themselves.

THE EXTENT OF VIOLENCE

To appreciate the extent of violence in the world today, all one need do is read the daily newspaper. The number of violent incidents and the number of people involved are frightening. Not all violence is the same, of course. Much of the violence described in other chapters, such as crime and spouse abuse, is called *interpersonal violence:* It involves a relatively small number of people who are responding to the stresses of a particular situation or who are pursuing their own personal gains. We have offered explanations for these types of violence elsewhere in this book. In this section, we will describe the extent of *collective violence*, which

involves organized violence by relatively large groups of people to promote or resist some social policies or practices.

Civil Disorders

Americans have been fortunate to have had a fairly stable government and society over the past two hundred years. Yet there have been periodic upheavals involving violent clashes between opposing groups of Americans. The term **civil disorder** refers to *strife or conflict that is threatening to the public order and that involves the government in some fashion, either as a party to the conflict or as a guardian of the public interest* (Himes, 1980).

Some civil disorders are relatively unorganized and have vague or short-term goals, such as race riots or labor conflicts. Other episodes of civil strife are quite organized and may threaten basic changes in the foundations of the social order, such as civil war or revolution. How extensive has civil disorder been in the United States? It is impossible to tabulate all such events, but there are ways to gain a sense of the magnitude of the problem. Sheldon Levy (1969) tabulated the number of politically violent events in the United States from 1819 to 1968. He found that the rate at which such events occur fluctuates from year to year, but there is no long-term trend. In fact, although one might expect the decade of the 1960s to be especially violent because of civil rights activities and antiwar riots, other decades approach or surpass that era in violence—the 1880s, for example, when labor strife was widespread. So civil disorder has been quite common throughout our history. We can gain a better sense of it by illustrating some of the different types of civil disorder that have occurred.

Much civil disorder in the United States has arisen out of racial conflict. As long ago as the eighteenth century, mobs of white people, motivated by a fear that black slaves might revolt against their owners, viciously attacked blacks in the streets of cities such as New York. Some slaves were hanged, whereas others were driven out of the city. The abolition of slavery did not quell racial violence. In the final twenty years of the nineteenth century, nearly two thousand blacks were killed by lynch mobs in the South. In this century, many of our cities, both large and small, have experienced severe race riots, virtually always involving black–white clashes. In the early part of the century, the riots were sparked when blacks began to move into white neighborhoods or to use recreational areas that were previously used only by whites. These **communal riots** typically began when *whites attacked blacks in the racially contested areas* (Janowitz, 1969). The Detroit riot in 1943, for example, began on Belle Isle Park, a public beach (Miller, 1985). Detroit, like many northern

cities of the period, had for decades been experiencing a large influx of blacks from the South. Frictions arose as the growing population of blacks spilled over into previously all-white areas. The riot only lasted twenty-four hours, but thirty-four people were killed (mostly blacks) and more than one thousand were injured. Almost two thousand people were arrested and $2 million in property damage occurred.

Since World War II, most race riots in America have been **commodity riots,** in which *the focus of hostility is property, merchandise, or equipment rather than people of another racial group*. These riots have occurred in neighborhoods that had been inhabited mostly by black Americans for some time rather than in areas of racial transition or contest. Although police officers or whites who wander into the neighborhood might be attacked, the focus of mobs' attention is on looting merchandise and burning buildings, usually those owned by people who do not live in the community. Most deaths and injuries arise from the efforts of police or the National Guard to quell the riot. Riots of this sort occurred in many American cities in the 1960s during the struggle over civil rights (Button, 1978). In the 1980s, the Liberty City area of Miami exploded into commodity riots several times. Then, in 1992, there was a severe riot in South Central Los Angeles in response to the acquittal of four police officers in the beating of an African-American motorist. One striking image of this last riot was the vicious beating of a white truck driver in the midst of the riot, but, as in other commodity riots, most of the crowd activities were focused on looting stores and burning buildings. In fact, most of those killed and injured during this riot were blacks and Hispanics. These race riots in the 1980s and 1990s are disturbing evidence that the potential for such destructive outbursts is still present in the United States. (This issue is discussed in more detail in the Applied Research insert in this chapter.)

Labor strife has been another significant source of civil disorder in America. This was particularly true from 1880 to the 1930s, as working people struggled hard to establish the principle of collective bargaining as a basis for governing worker–employer relationships. Before collective bargaining was legalized, it was illegal for workers to conspire to stop work at a factory or business. This obviously left enormous power in the hands of the business managers and owners who could simply fire individual workers who resisted their demands or complained about wages or working conditions. In the late 1800s and early 1900s, new power and authority relations were being forged between workers and industrial managers as America industrialized. Violence was sometimes a key ingredient in shaping these new social relations. In 1897 in eastern Pennsylvania, for example, miners in the anthracite coal fields walked off the job, protesting low wages and dangerous working conditions. They were well aware that hundreds of coal miners were killed in accidents each year in the region. These were not unionized miners; they were a disorganized group of immigrants from Eastern Europe—many could speak little English—who were weary of being bruised, broken, and seeing their companions killed while working. At one point, a posse confronted a group of the strikers in a town called Lattimer and gunfire roared. Nineteen miners were killed and another thirty-nine wounded (Novak, 1978). Fifteen years later, miners in Colorado went on strike against the Colorado Fuel and Iron Company, which would not recognize the workers' right to unionize. The strikers lived in a tent city in Ludlow. On April 20, 1914, National Guard troops attacked the tent colony and burned it to the ground. In the holocaust, which became known as the Ludlow Massacre, five men, twelve children, and two women died. Before the strike was over, seventy-four in all would lose their lives (Taft and Ross, 1969).

Lattimer and Ludlow are hardly household words today. Yet they were key links in the forging of a new industrial order. These incidents illustrate the extent to which labor violence has been a common outgrowth of the industrialization process. Today, labor relations are considerably more peaceful because workers have many rights that they did not possess in the past and there are strong pressures on both sides to restrain the violent use of force. However, violence still may accompany labor strikes when strikers attack those crossing picket lines. At the same time, deaths have become rare in labor strife.

Political Violence

The race riots and labor violence just discussed have, for the most part, not been organized efforts to change the basic political and economic institutions of American society. Instead, they were usually somewhat spontaneous attempts to improve the circumstances and opportunities of some disadvantaged groups within existing social and economic arrangements. At times, however, groups have resorted to violence as a means of changing our government and economy. One form that this can take is **insurrection:** *an organized action by some group to rebel against the existing government and to replace it with new political forms and leadership.* Although the United States has been relatively free of serious insurrectionary threats to the central government in Washington, such political violence has sometimes occurred.

The independence of our nation, of course, was forged in an insurrection against England in 1776. And by the accounts of most historians, it was a nasty and vicious encounter:

> *The meanest and most squalid sort of violence was . . . put to the service of Revolutionary ideals and objectives. The operational philosophy that the end justifies the means became the keynote of revolutionary violence. (Brown, 1969: 47)*

There were bloody clashes between insurrectionists and British soldiers while the Continental and British armies maneuvered for position. Revolutionary colonists conducted savage guerrilla forays against the British, a tactic considered quite disgusting by the armies of the time. Americans supporting the revolution even attacked other colonists, called Tories, who wished America to remain a British colony.

Once the independence of the United States was established, the most serious insurrection the nation faced was, of course, the Civil War, the effort of the southern states to secede from the Union (Leckie, 1990). Although the 1860 election of President Abraham Lincoln, an avowed opponent of slavery, played an important part in precipitating the Civil War, its exact causes have been debated at length by scholars and historians. Nonetheless, it was without question the most catastrophic military clash to occur within our boundaries. There was tremendous loss of life and destruction of property in battle; anger and resentment grew in both the North and the South between people on opposite sides of the issue, with violent confrontations occurring in cities such as New York and Baltimore; tensions and hostilities between the regions lingered for many decades after the war was over and served as a continuing catalyst for violence.

Beyond the Revolutionary War and the Civil War, insurrections in America have been relatively small and less threatening. Shortly after the American Revolution, for example, there were a number of insurrections involving battles over land and taxes, such as Shays' Rebellion in Massachusetts in the 1780s and the Whiskey Rebellion in Pennsylvania in the 1790s. Somewhat later, there was Dorr's Rebellion in the 1840s, which was an attempt by a group of dissidents in Rhode Island to gain the right for all men (although not women) to vote. The turmoil of the 1960s spawned a number of insurrectionary groups, such as the Black Liberation Army, the Weather Underground, and the Symbionese Liberation Army (the group of black ex-convicts and white radicals who gained the nation's attention by kidnapping Patricia Hearst in 1974). Although bothersome, these insurrectionary groups have gained little public support and have produced little political or economic change in the United States.

War

Most Americans probably think of their nation as powerful but also as peaceful and not aggressive. Yet political scientists J. David Singer and Melvin Small (1972) concluded from their research that we are among the more "war-prone" nations in the world. Between 1816 and 1965, they calculate, the United States has been involved in six wars, not counting the Indian wars and the Vietnam War. Between 1798 and 1945, American troops have been sent abroad for military purposes by the president, without the approval of Congress, 163 times—an average of more than once a year (Pinkney, 1972; Leckie, 1992). We invaded Nicaragua twenty times (*before* that nation was an ally of the Soviet Union), and U.S. troops once occupied Mexico City. At home, the Indian wars were particularly brutal affairs. They involved many campaigns by whites to force Indians from lands sought after by white settlers. If Indians refused to sign treaties and peacefully move to reservations, the army was called in to force the issue. Along the way, practically all lands were taken from the Indians and their life-style was irrevocably destroyed. Some have called our policies toward the Indians genocide, because the result was to almost completely destroy native Americans as a separate race (see Chapter 6).

Most Americans view four of the major wars of this century—World War I, World War II, the Korean War, and the Persian Gulf War—as justified on the grounds that America was helping to repel aggression or protect freedom. Yet the cost in casualties was high, and the decimation of civilian populations was much greater than in earlier wars based on a simpler technology (see Table 14.1). The discovery of air flight, for example, made possible the aerial bombing of not only enemy troop concentrations but also cities and towns. One particularly devastating instance of the latter was the saturation bombing of Dresden, Germany, during World War II in which an estimated 135,000 civilians were killed, mainly by as-

Table 14.1   **American Casualties in Major Wars**

War	Battle Deaths	Wounded	Veterans Receiving Disability Compensation, 1990
Civil War	140,000	282,000	
World War I	53,000	204,000	3,000
World War II	292,000	671,000	876,000
Korean conflict	34,000	103,000	209,000
Vietnam conflict	47,000	153,000	652,000

SOURCE: U.S. Bureau of the Census, *Statistical Abstract of the United States, 1992* (Washington, D.C.: U.S. Government Printing Office, 1992), pp. 345, 348.

phyxiation and burning. Discoveries in physics led to the development of the atomic bomb, which resulted in the deaths of almost two hundred thousand people at Hiroshima and Nagasaki in 1945. Overall, World War II resulted in thirty million deaths among military combatants and civilians worldwide.

In 1965, we landed troops in the Dominican Republic to forestall what we thought was about to be a communist takeover of that country. Between 1965 and 1975, we were mired in the Vietnam conflict. More recently, we briefly entered the civil war in Lebanon and invaded the Caribbean island of Grenada. In 1989, the United States invaded Panama to oust dictator Manuel Noriega following attacks on American military personnel stationed in Panama. In 1991, an international force used Saudi Arabia as a base from which to throw Iraqi aggressors out of Kuwait in the Persian Gulf War. This international army had many nations represented, but it was created at the instigation of the United States and consisted mostly of American troops. Meanwhile, we stockpile an arsenal of nuclear weapons that could rain death and destruction on the earth.

Many of these war activities were not a reaction to a threatened attack on or invasion of the United States. Rather we have mostly been sending our troops around the world to maintain a world order that does not threaten American political and economic interests. All of this suggests that our society does have a propensity for getting involved in the violence associated with wars. And we seem more willing to do this than are most other nations around the world. Currently, almost one-third of all the money spent by all nations of the world on military expenditures is spent by the United States (see Figure 14.1)—and we have only 5 percent of the world's population. We spend $1,200 on military expenditures for each man, woman, and child in the United States, whereas the worldwide figure is only $200 per capita. When many people around the world look at our military expenditures and our track record on foreign involvement, they see a country that has a habit of throwing its weight around. Such expenditures are justified by some people on moral, political, or strategic grounds, but it has also been costly in human lives and suffering.

The Spread of Weapons of Mass Destruction

Whether the United States goes to war, of course, depends in part on what other nations do, and unfortunately there is a thriving worldwide trade in arms to provide nations with the means to go to war. Even more disturbing, the United States is a major player in that trade. The United States

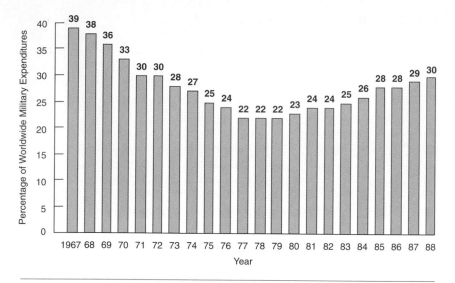

Figure 14.1   **United States Military Expenditures as a Percentage of Worldwide Military Expenditures, 1967–1988**
SOURCES: U.S. Bureau of the Census, *Statistical Abstract of the United States, 1978* (Washington, D.C.: U.S. Government Printing Office, 1978), p. 372; U.S. Bureau of the Census, *Statistical Abstract of the United States, 1982* (Washington, D.C.: U.S. Government Printing Office, 1982), p. 355; U.S. Bureau of the Census, *Statistical Abstract of the United States, 1991* (Washington, D.C.: U.S. Government Printing Office, 1991), p. 339.

sold $27 billion worth of arms to other countries in 1991, the largest amount ever. Over the years, our arms sales to other countries have accounted for one-third of the worldwide trade in arms, with the former Soviet Union accounting for slightly more—both countries together cornering almost three-quarters of all arms sales in the world (U.S. Bureau of the Census, 1991; Hartung, 1992). So, we supply the means for nations to go to war with one another. This spread of weapons can embolden nations to attack other nations, and this has created problems for the United States. We gave military support, for example, to Iraq in its war with Iran in the 1980s, and this assistance was turned against us when Iraq invaded our ally Kuwait in 1990, resulting in the Persian Gulf War.

One of the horrendous legacies of twentieth-century technology has been the emergence of highly frightening and destructive weapons: nu-

clear, chemical, biological, and toxin weapons. Many nations have such weapons or are capable of making them. The United States, the former Soviet Union, China, Great Britain, and France have possessed nuclear and chemical weapons for some time. In the last few decades, we have seen the proliferation of these weapons to more countries, sometimes to nations with unstable or megalomaniacal leaders. Some of the nations acquiring these weapons are involved in serious and entrenched conflicts with other nations, which could produce conditions that would lead to their use. Israel has nuclear capability, for example, and has been in conflict with many Arab countries; Iraq used chemical weapons in its war with Iran and has tried to produce nuclear weapons; India and Pakistan have nuclear weapons and have been engaged in serious territorial disputes for a number of years. At least twelve nations have or are developing biological or toxin weapons, and twenty are doing so with chemical weapons (Bailey, 1991).

The likelihood that weapons of mass destruction will be used increases with each new nation that acquires them. The international framework to prevent the spread of these weapons is weak. The Geneva Protocols of 1925 prohibit the use of chemical weapons but not their production and stockpiling. When the weapons have been used, as in the Iran–Iraq War of the 1980s, no sanctions were applied against the user by the international community. The signatories to the Treaty on the Non-Proliferation of Nuclear Weapons of 1968 agree not to permit the spread of these weapons to countries currently without them. However, some countries, such as Israel, have not signed the accord, and others, such as North Korea, have ignored many of its provisions. Once again, there have been no international sanctions against these nations. One expert on national security and arms control concluded that, in the 1990s

> Proliferation . . . constitutes one of the most serious threats to international peace and stability, as well as to U.S. national security. It should become the focus of multinational and bilateral arms control efforts before it is too late. (Bailey, 1991: 6)

Terrorism

Terrorism refers to *the attempt to achieve political goals by using fear and intimidation to disrupt the normal operations of a society* (Gibbs, 1989). In 1969 and 1970, there were three thousand bombings and eighty-nine terrorist-related shootings in the United States (Kleiman, 1977). In the less contentious 1970s, there were only about 250 terrorist bombings in the United States (Motley, 1983). In the past fifteen years, there have been few such domestic terrorist acts, but they do occur. In 1985, for example, a group of white supremacist, neo-Nazi fanatics who refer to themselves as The Order went on trial in Seattle for a series of terrorist acts, including the murder in

1984 of Alan Berg, a popular radio talk-show host in Denver who had denounced racists and anti-Semites. In 1989, a terrorist bomb in San Diego destroyed a van being driven by the wife of the skipper of the naval ship U.S.S. Vincennes, which had shot down an Iranian passenger plane killing 290 people on board. However, it has been terrorism against American citizens overseas that has captured public attention in recent years. As Figure 14.2 illustrates, the number of terrorist attacks worldwide has fluctuated over time, with the greatest frequency occurring between 1985 and 1989. Approximately 40 percent of the 450 terrorist attacks in 1990 were directed against U.S. citizens, businesses, or facilities (U.S. Department of State, 1991b). The most dangerous places for Americans in 1990 were a few countries in South America, especially Chile, Peru, and Colombia. One of the more horrifying incidents of recent years was the terrorist bombing in 1988 of a Pan American jet as it was flying over Scotland heading for the United States, killing hundreds of passengers on board and a few bystanders on the ground. Another huge loss of life occurred in 1982 when terrorists drove a bomb-laden truck into a building in Beirut that housed American marines, killing hundreds when the building collapsed after the explosion. In 1985, Moslem terrorists hijacked a commercial airliner and held forty Americans hostage for two weeks.

Terrorists use many tactics, such as kidnapping, bombing, killing, hijacking, assassination, and extortion. Sometimes they focus on agents of a government they blame for their problems, such as the military or a president or ambassador. But they frequently attack innocent civilians in an effort to pressure government officials. Governments also sometimes engage in or support terrorism. The U.S. Department of State (1991b) considers Syria, Iraq, Libya, and North Korea to be among the major supporters of terrorism in the world currently. These countries provide varying levels of support to terrorist groups, from supplying arms, training, and technical expertise to providing travel documents or a hideout. This gov-

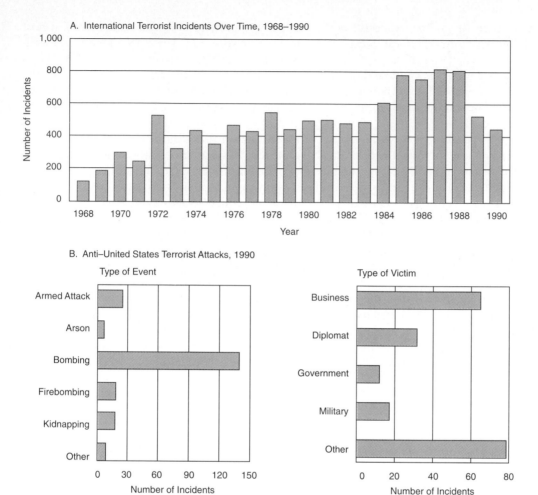

Figure 14.2 **Patterns of Global Terrorism, 1968–1990**
SOURCE: U.S. Department of State, *Patterns of Global Terrorism: 1990,* Department of State Pub. 9862 (Washington, D.C.: U.S. Government Printing Office, 1991), pp. 39–40.

ernment-supported terrorism is something new and especially unsettling on the world scene. When established governments provide weapons, economic support, and a place of refuge for terrorists, they exacerbate and perpetuate the problem considerably. Terrorists who might create only a sporadic problem without such support can become a continuing source of violence and destruction with it.

Terrorism is a particularly unnerving form of violence because it is impervious to efforts to control it. Yet we need to recognize that terrorism often has its origins in some kind of perceived injustice, the elimination of which is the terrorists' goal (Perry, 1976; Rubenstein, 1987). Their methods may seem extreme and inappropriate, but they are often born of the frustration of seeing no other means to achieve the group's goals. Ter-

Terry Anderson, one of several Americans held hostage by terrorists in Lebanon for many years, is welcomed home at a rally at Dulles Airport in Virginia. Terrorism is a particularly unnerving form of violence because it frequently involves innocent civilians.

rorism is often resorted to by people who have little power and few resources with which to attack what they see as injustice. Correcting these injustices, of course, would be one way to alleviate the problems of terrorism, but this is difficult to do in many cases and may be impossible in some. So societies have made efforts to protect themselves against threatened terrorist attacks. Such attacks can occur at the many points at which we are all vulnerable in modern societies: flying in an airplane, eating in a restaurant, or walking along the street. Short of a highly costly and authoritarian society, it is difficult to build in the kind of controls that can provide assured protection in all these settings. Relatively effective controls over airplane hijacking, for example, have been achieved at the cost of luggage searches, radar detectors, and long waits at baggage check-ins. Even these measures are not completely effective be-

cause determined terrorists can still foil them, as the destruction of the Pan Am jetliner in 1988 showed. Other things that are being done include international efforts to discourage state support for terrorists and requirements for the marking of plastic and sheet explosives so that they can be more easily detected when hidden in luggage.

SOURCES OF VIOLENCE

If violence is to be controlled, we need to know what causes it. People have many beliefs about this issue, but there is also much misleading and inaccurate information that can confuse rather than enlighten. We will analyze the most current research that can shed some light on the problem. What we will find is that the sources of violence are complex, and there is often a chain of multiple causation, with numerous factors—social, psychological, and possibly even biological—contributing to particular outbursts of violence.

Biological Approaches

We have already reviewed efforts to explain such social behaviors as crime (Chapter 9), drug abuse (Chapter 10), and the differences between men and women (Chapter 7) on biological grounds. People also have been intrigued by the possibility that violence may be part of our biological nature as human beings. Violence is so common and so nearly universal in human cultures that it seems plausible that biology plays a part. Some support for this position can be found in studies of the behavior of animals of various species. A male stickleback fish, for example, will protect against all intruders a nest containing fertilized eggs deposited by the female stickleback. Anything approaching the nest that resembles another stickleback will be viciously attacked (Tinbergen, 1955). Such protection of territory can be found in many species, and it is clearly an instinctive behavior in these species rather than a product of learning. Robert Ardrey (1967) popularized such behavior as the "territorial imperative," suggesting that such protection is necessary for some species to survive. In fact, he argued, it is so necessary that evolution imprints these behavior patterns into the genes of species. Without this instinct to defend territory, mating would be disrupted and the survival of species would be threatened. Aggressiveness in struggling for food or competing for mates also may have an evolutionary advantage for many species.

Recent applications of these ideas to human beings have been labeled **sociobiology,** *a field based on the idea that the genetic makeup of human beings plays a powerful role in shaping human social behavior* (Hughes, 1988; van der Dennen and Falger, 1990). Sociobiologists maintain that there are many parallels between human and animal behavior. For example, animals of a number of species exhibit altruism, which refers to doing things that benefit others of one's species even though it may be dangerous or deadly to oneself. So, kamikaze bees will die defending their hive, soldier termites will end their lives in order to spray a deadly liquid at their enemies, and human beings will place their own lives in danger to protect their children. Other behavioral tendencies that are common in both animals and humans include aggressiveness, territoriality, selfishness, and the formation of dominance hierarchies.

Sociobiologists argue that these tendencies are common in species because they are inborn traits determined by genes. These various traits exist because they enhance the chances of survival for the species. The stronger, more powerful, and more aggressive members of a species are more likely to survive, mate, and pass on their genes to the next generation. A mother will die to save her children because this enhances the likelihood that her genes will survive in the gene pool even though she herself dies. Sociobiologists reason that aggressiveness and altruism are a part of our genetic makeup because people who behave aggressively or altruistically increase the chances for the survival of their genes. Over long periods of time, those aggressive and altruistic genes come to predominate in the gene pool.

Is violence programmed into human genes as sociobiologists suggest? There are a number of reasons to be cautious about their arguments (Goldstein, 1986). First, there is no direct evidence linking any specific genes to particular forms of human behavior. Although their arguments are plausible, there is no definitive proof that they are accurate. Second, there are few human traits that are found universally among human beings. The prevalence of behaviors such as altruism and aggressiveness vary widely from person to person and culture to culture. Although every kamikaze bee will die protecting its hive, for example, some human beings protect their children, whereas others neglect, abuse, and abandon them. Moreover, infanticide has at times been an accepted social practice among some groups, such

Because violence and war are so common in human history, some have concluded that such behaviors are biologically determined. Are humans "killers" by nature? Most social scientists take the position that social learning is more important than heredity in terms of explaining people's willingness to kill in war.

as the ancient Greeks and Chinese. If altruism and aggressiveness were truly instinctive, this variation would not occur. Finally, even if genetically determined behavioral tendencies exist, sociobiologists recognize that they only create general tendencies to behave in certain ways. Whether people actually behave aggressively or altruistically depends on numerous psychological and social forces. In fact, sociobiologists admit that these genetic tendencies, if they exist, can probably be altered or even overcome by learning and other social forces.

Another biological approach to violence focuses on biological abnormalities such as brain tumors or scar tissue on the brain that have been linked to violence. Certain chemical traces in the brain have also been associated with violence. However, these biological factors account for only sporadic instances of violence. They cannot explain the organized and collective occurrence of violence that is the focus of this chapter. Things such as war, riot, and rebellion involve far too

many people and far too much organization to be attributed to brain tumors, scar tissue, or chemical imbalances.

Social Sources of Violence

Considerable research over the past four decades has helped to pinpoint the social sources of violence. These factors can be organized into three categories: characteristics of the structure of society that serve as preconditions to violence, the frustrations that these preconditions can create in people that push them toward violence, and mediating factors that increase the likelihood that people will react violently to frustration. We will look at each of these factors, relating them where appropriate to the three sociological perspectives.

Structural Preconditions. Most outbursts of collective violence can be traced to some social conditions that serve as preconditions for violence. One such precondition is the existence of some social strain or social deprivation. For example, strain exists when some groups in society do not have the opportunity to achieve their goals through socially acceptable means. We discuss this in Chapters 9 and 10 as Robert Merton's anomie theory of crime and drug abuse. For instance, racial or ethnic discrimination may limit the jobs that are available to some people, or poverty may make it difficult to attain the education necessary to find a respectable job. Whatever its source, this strain or deprivation leaves people vulnerable to participating in collective violence should the opportunity arise. This approach to understanding violence reflects the functionalist view that different parts of society need to be integrated with one another, and this includes providing people with the opportunity to achieve their goals. To the extent that societies cannot do this, a disjuncture is created that can lead to problems such as crime and violence.

Another precondition for violence is competition between people over money, jobs, and other scarce but valued resources. We discussed this in

Chapters 6 and 7 as a source of prejudice and discrimination against minorities. The more intensely groups compete, the more threatening each becomes to the other and the more likely one side or the other will resort to violence. Oftentimes, the competition is economic, over jobs or money, such as the split-labor market discussed in Chapter 6 and the labor disputes discussed earlier in this chapter. However, there can also be conflict over values and life-style. Functionalists argue that such competition need not culminate in violence if society provides everyone with the opportunity to achieve at least some of their goals. Violence also can be avoided by providing people with nonviolent means to achieve an acceptable life-style. However, from the conflict perspective, such competition is an inherent part of social life, and groups will resort to violence if they perceive it as a superior and effective strategy in the clash over scarce resources.

A third precondition of violence is ethnocentrism, or the tendency to view one's own group or culture as superior to other groups or cultures (see Chapter 6). Although some ethnocentrism can be beneficial by promoting group cohesion, excessive amounts can lead to the belief that others are not only different but also dishonest, disreputable, and possibly even not fully human. Such beliefs open the door to hostile and violent actions. Especially if the members of a group are defined as subhuman, violence against them may not be seen as bad or immoral. Thus, Adolf Hitler and the Nazis became so thoroughly convinced of the superiority of the Aryan "race" that they felt justified in brutalizing Jews and others. Likewise, many Americans in the eighteenth and nineteenth centuries believed that their European heritage and values were far superior to those of native Americans in the New World, and this view legitimized attacks against Indians that few Americans are proud of today. In the 1980s, the neo-Nazi group The Order justified murder on the grounds that the alleged Aryan race was superior to blacks and Jews.

Frustration and Aggression.   How are these preconditions translated into violence? Psychologists have shown that there is a clear, though complex, link among frustration, aggression, and violence. **Frustration** refers to *an inability to achieve sought-after goals.* The preconditions of violence discussed in the previous section are structured sources of frustration that can influence many people. When people are frustrated, there is a buildup of tension that may be released in aggressive and sometimes violent behavior (Dollard et al., 1939; Berkowitz, 1971). This aggressive or violent reaction can release the tension created by frustration even though it fails to alleviate the real source of the frustration. For example, in the American South between 1882 and 1903, nearly two thousand blacks were killed by lynch mobs, some by hanging, others by being burned alive (Brown, 1969). Some of the impetus for such violence was the fluctuating economic conditions in the South: Unemployment and poor economic conditions frustrated southern whites, and some responded with racial violence against blacks. The violence did not alleviate the underlying economic problems, but it did provide a release for poor whites.

In Chapter 9, we observed that what is considered deviant is relative to the judgments of some group. What is considered frustrating is also relative. **Relative deprivation** refers to the fact that *people tend to feel deprived or frustrated in comparison to what others have or what they believe they deserve.* In other words, a sense of deprivation arises when there is a discrepancy between what people have come to expect or feel they deserve and what they actually receive. So the conditions that are frustrating or depriving for one group or at one point in history may not be so for another group or at another point. It depends on the standards that people use in assessing their circumstances. A century ago, American miners went on strike because they were being maimed and killed by unsafe working conditions and for wages that barely provided the essentials of life. In the past decade, violence has accompanied labor disputes in which the workers would have been considered affluent by the standards of a century ago. The point is that the standards for what is an acceptable life-style and what is acceptable in the workplace have changed and so have the conditions that might precipitate violence. The notion of relative deprivation reflects the emphasis of the interactionist perspective on the construction of social reality through human perception and interpretation. Social conditions become a problem—even one warranting a violent response—if people define them as threatening their values or disruptive of their life-style. These definitions are based on the meanings that groups attach to people or events. The Applied Research insert in this chapter focuses on the preconditions and frustrations that sparked the urban riot in Los Angeles in 1992.

Mediating Factors.   The preconditions to violence and the frustration that we have discussed do not lead inexorably to violent behavior. In fact, most people experiencing such conditions do not become violent. Rather, there are a number of mediating factors that increase the likelihood of violence. For one thing, whether violence occurs and the form that it takes depend on learning and socialization. Culture can teach people that violence is an acceptable and useful way of dealing with interpersonal problems. Some cultures, such as the Zuni Indians in the American Southwest, view aggression as an evil force that threatens group unity, and people discourage any displays of aggression (Westie, 1964). In American culture, on the other hand, people are often rewarded for engaging in aggressive or violent behavior. Children, especially boys, may be cheered on when they play especially hard and aggressively at some sport. They may even be encouraged to "act like a man" and stand up to people who give them trouble—even if that means fighting.

It has been argued that some groups or subcultures in American society tend to be very accepting of violence as a means of resolving

interpersonal disputes and that this atmosphere serves as an important mediating factor in producing violence (Wolfgang and Ferracuti, 1967). In fact, there may even be a **subculture of violence** involving *norms and values that condone and legitimize the use of violence in resolving conflicts.* Thus, aggression and violence may be viewed by some groups as the acceptable and possibly even the preferred and "manly" way of resolving disputes. Others have argued that a culture of violence pervades all of American society and is not limited to just some groups and subcultures (Pinkney, 1972). Certainly, violence pervades television dramas and the cinema, where handsome and beautiful characters routinely dispatch villains with large doses of violence. The lesson seems to be that aggression is used by the "good guys" to gain rewards that are unavailable to others. After an extensive review of violence in America, one social scientist concluded:

> *My theme is that the United States is an unusually violent society, that such behavior has characterized this society both domestically and in its relations with other countries through its history, and that violence thrives in America because the social climate nurtures and rewards it. (Pinkney, 1972: xiii)*

Most Americans claim to be opposed to the use of violence, but in fact they strongly support it when the "good guys," such as the police, use it to subdue the "bad guys," such as criminals. People even support the extralegal use of force by police when its purpose is presumed to be protecting the public order (Gamson and McEvoy, 1972). Yet the subculture of violence theory should not be extended too broadly. Research suggests that such subcultures may not be as extensive as once thought and that the social class, racial, and regional variation in the propensity to use violence that was once thought to exist may not be that strong (Ball-Rokeach, 1973; Erlanger, 1974; O'Connor and Lizotte, 1978). Still, for many groups, violence is considered an appropriate re-

APPLIED RESEARCH

The Los Angeles Riot: Failing to Act on What We Know

The images of the riot in South Central Los Angeles in 1992 were very disturbing: panoramic views of the towers of smoke from many buildings burning at once, looters emerging from stores with their arms laden with stolen goods, store owners shooting their guns at crowds to keep them at bay, innocent bystanders savagely beaten and helpless. By the time it was over, fifty-three people had died, and there was $1 billion in property damage. Especially disturbing was the realization that we had seen it all before: in Miami in the 1980s and in many American cities in the 1960s. Most people are familiar with the immediate precipitant of the Los Angeles riot (Dentler, 1992). Four police officers were on trial for the vicious beating of the black motorist Rodney King. The beating was videotaped and had been widely shown on television. King was beaten repeatedly and over a prolonged period of time by a number of officers, even when King seemed helpless on the ground. The acquittal of the officers sparked the riot. The acquittal was seen by blacks in Los Angeles as convincing proof that the police were free to assault blacks at will and that the criminal justice system would provide blacks with no legal recourse against such violence. Other recent events in Los Angeles provided fuel for such beliefs: African American men were routinely arrested and mistreated by the police, and a storeowner who shot and killed a sixteen-year-old African American girl was convicted of a minor charge and spent no time in jail.

There is much still to be learned about the Los Angeles riot, but what is already disturbingly clear is that we have failed to apply what we have learned from earlier riots. Riots in the 1960s and the 1980s have been studied extensively by sociologists and other social scientists. These riots essentially served as field experiments in which researchers could compare cities that experienced riots with those that did not. Researchers also compared people who joined in the riots with those who lived in the riot community but did not participate (Lieberson and Silverman, 1965; Caplan and Paige, 1968; McPhail, 1971; Spilerman, 1976; Porter and Dunn, 1984). From this we learned a great deal about why riots happen. Unfortunately, our society has not responded by changing the conditions that produce such riots. Let us see what those conditions are.

One thing we learned is that such riots start when a highly volatile event, such as the acquittal of the police officers, enrages an aggrieved group. The exact same thing happened in Miami in 1980. The immediate cause of that riot was the acquittal of four Miami police officers in a murder trial for the death of a black insurance agent, Arthur McDuffie. The acquittal infuriated African Americans in Miami just as the acquittal was to enrage blacks in Los Angeles a decade later. The climate was also the same: There had been police killings and assaults of blacks in Florida to fuel beliefs about police racism and disregard for African Americans. Despite these lessons, authorities in Los Angeles apparently did not take seriously enough the potential threat posed as the trial of the officers came to an end.

In addition to learning about the immediate causes of riots, the research on earlier riots also tells us about the structural conditions and mediating factors that can play a part. Here, too, we see how thoroughly we have failed to apply lessons from the past. It is almost a cliché to say that economic deprivation and racial discrimination lay at the root of the riots of the 1960s. Clearly, people who are well off economically are disinclined to take to the streets, even if provoked. But people who are severely oppressed are also unlikely to engage in such activism. Their feelings of helplessness are more likely to result in resignation or withdrawal. Instead of the total underdog, it is people who have hopes for improvement in their lives but see those hopes threatened who are most inclined to respond to deprivation and oppression through rioting. In other words, it is *relative deprivation* that often underlies collective violence. Research on the 1960s riots documented this in several ways. It was not cities where blacks were worst off that experienced riots. Rather, it was cities where blacks had made considerable improvements such that there were small gaps between the incomes of blacks and whites. It was also blacks in the middle levels of educational ranks who rioted, not those with the least education. Such advances in income and education had led people to hope for further improvement and led to deeply felt frustration when the improvements were not forthcoming.

Likewise, research on the 1980 Miami riot showed that "rioters by no means came exclusively from the ranks of the poor or unemployed or the criminal classes. Many held jobs, were normally law-abiding and did not otherwise fit the stereotypical image of a 'rioter'" (Porter and Dunn, 1984: 183). Criminals or the unemployed may have played an important part in starting the riot, but seemingly respectable blacks provided the numbers that kept it going and contributed to heightening the levels of emotion and destruction. What evidence we have at this point from Los Angeles suggests the same thing: Many looters and arrestees worked or were in school. In addition, in Los Angeles, as elsewhere, many blacks had not participated in the improvements that were supposed to derive from the civil rights advances of thirty years ago. As we saw in Chapter 6, there persists a substantial black underclass that has not been able to attain the educational or other credentials necessary to achieve upward mobility.

Beyond deprivation and oppression, we learned from earlier riots of a number of other factors that contribute to the likelihood of a riot occurring. These factors suggest that riots occur when members of minority groups feel left out of society, isolated from sources of political and economic power, ignored by the powers that be, and victimized by the social order that is supposed to serve and protect them. When there are few channels for resolving grievances or when the system appears unresponsive to expressions of discontent, people are more willing to turn to collective violence. In earlier riots, isolation from the political system was evidenced by such things as few or no black police officers in a city. Presumably, a city sensitive to the needs of blacks would hire black police officers, and such officers would be more responsive to the needs and problems of the black community. In these earlier riots, cities with fewer black police officers were more likely to experience a riot. Likewise, cities with few black storeowners and those where officials were elected on a citywide rather than district basis (making it more difficult for blacks, who are typically a numerical minority in a city but a majority in some districts, to gain office) had more riots. Once again, Los Angeles in 1992 fit the profile for a riot-prone city fairly well. The city did have a black mayor, but blacks were underrepresented at all levels of the police force. It also had a relatively small number of black storeowners and professionals, especially in South Central Los Angeles where the riot occurred, and many of the storeowners were Asian Americans who seemed to be doing fairly well even though having immigrated to the United States only recently. This contributed to the feelings of resentment and isolation in the African American community in South Central Los Angeles. Overall, the poverty, unemployment, and segregation in their community left these blacks feeling effectively disenfranchised.

We learned a great deal about collective violence from the research conducted in earlier decades. Our failure to apply that research by making changes in social policy can be blamed, in part, for the disastrous riot in Los Angeles in 1992. Social policies could have been established that would have improved the economic circumstances of blacks and reduced feelings of isolation and disenfranchisement. We discuss many of these policies in Chapters 5 and 6, and we need not repeat them here. What does need reiteration is that, if we do nothing, we will probably have more such riots in the future.

The riot in Los Angeles in 1992 caught many Americans by surprise, especially because of the ferocity of the actions and sentiments unleashed. Sociologists, on the other hand, recognized that many of the social conditions that produced similar riots in the 1960s and 1980s had persisted into the 1990s.

sponse in some circumstances. At least, violence is not strongly punished if it occurs under provocation and if the people toward whom it is directed are stigmatized or viewed as disreputable.

Aggression and violence are more likely to occur if there are attractive people to serve as models promoting such behavior (Vander Zanden, 1987). Parents may unwittingly serve as models of violence for their children when they punish them for some wrongdoing. According to one group of child psychologists, "when the parents punish—particularly when they employ physical punishment—they are providing a living example of the use of aggression at the very mo-

ment when they are trying to teach the child not to be aggressive" (Sears, Maccoby, and Levin, 1957: 266). The parents' use of physical force to control children teaches the children that force can be legitimately used to control others. The child can also find models for violence on the street, at school, and in the playground. Researchers have found that aggressive behavior is more common among children whose social circumstances expose them to many such aggressive models (Bandura, 1976).

There seems little doubt at this point that the mass media contribute to the levels of violence in American society. In the past forty years, much research has been conducted on the relationship between violence on television and violence in society (Van Evra, 1990; Huston et al., 1992). Most of this research concludes that when children and youths watch violence on television, they are more likely to act aggressively or violently themselves, especially in situations that are conducive to violence. The impact is greater for males than for females, and it is more substantial for children who are more aggressive to begin with (Josephson, 1987). Children between the ages of eight and twelve seem to be especially vulnerable to the effects of watching violence on television.

Television encourages people toward violence in three ways. First, action dramas can be arousing to viewers and may stimulate them in the direction of physical activity and release. This effect is probably of short duration, from hours to days. Second, television provides viewers with legitimizing models for violence in much the same way that parents or peers can serve as models. In fact, it is difficult to watch television without being exposed to models of violence, as Figure 14.3 illustrates. Thus, children learn the potential for acting violently in particular situations, and the amount of such violence on television has not declined in the past few decades and may have actually increased. Also, the violence seen on television has some unreal or surrealistic qualities. People bleed little, and the actual pain and agony resulting from a violent attack are rarely portrayed. The

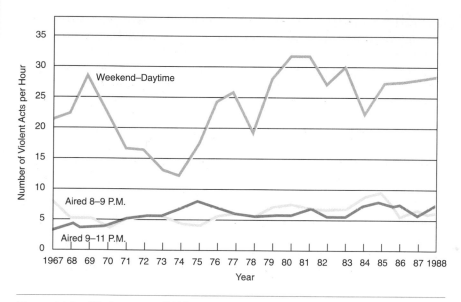

Figure 14.3   **Violence on Children's and Prime-Time Television Programs, 1967–1988**
SOURCE: G. Gerbner and N. Signorielli, *Violence Profile, 1967 Through 1988–89: Enduring Patterns* (Unpublished manuscript, Annenberg School of Communications, University of Pennsylvania, 1990).

consequences of violence often seem antiseptic and rather unimportant. Third, television conveys attitudes and values, and it can teach children to view violence or antisocial behavior as a desirable or "manly" way to behave.

Even with all of the preconditions and mediating factors that have been discussed thus far, collective violence is not likely to occur without mobilization: social mechanisms for bringing the affected people into coordinated and organized activity (Zald and McCarthy, 1987). Riots, labor strife, lynchings, and wars do not emerge by themselves, even in response to strain and deprivation. Depending on the context, leaders have to emerge, money must be collected, and ways of exercising power must be discovered. Organization, administration, procedures, and strategies must also evolve. If the essential mix of resources is not mobilized, collective violence will not occur, even when the predisposing factors are substantial and the deprivation is severe.

Theoretical Perspectives on Violence

The sources of violence just described relate in good measure to the functionalist perspective. They view violence as arising in part from social disorganization: frustration, deprivation, and the like. When people are frustrated in achieving their goals, it means that the various parts of the social system are not well integrated; people learn to want things but then are not given the means to achieve them. The violence that arises may then contribute to further disorganization, and this is what makes it a social problem from the functionalist perspective. As a mechanism for redressing grievances, violence is very unstable and dangerous. It means, first of all, that more peaceful mechanisms for resolving problems have broken down. In other words, the conventional societal procedures for moderating differences between groups do not work. Second, violence always has the potential for getting out of hand and escalating to dangerously destructive levels. At an extreme, this can threaten the stability of the social order, as occurred during the Civil War when our nation was threatened with being split apart. Some also believe that levels of violence rose dangerously high during the 1960s with race riots and antiwar riots becoming common events. For functionalists, then, violence is a social problem because it threatens societal stability and increases social disorganization.

The conflict perspective points to a somewhat different view of violence: It is a tool that any group might use to protect or enhance its own interests. According to the conflict perspective, dominant groups use violence whenever a subordinate group begins to threaten their position. For example, business interests in the late 1800s turned to the police and National Guard troops to stop workers who were organizing to oppose the substantial power of their employers. As we have seen, workers were often harassed, beaten, and shot in the process. When dominant groups resort to violence, they tend to view it as socially acceptable and appropriate. Subordinate groups can also resort to violence when they have few other means of redressing grievances. Rioting, for example, has been one way that subordinate minority groups in America have been able to force some concessions from the powers that be. Terrorism has also been used by those with few resources in an attempt to force changes. The Irish Republican Army is currently doing this in Northern Ireland. So from the conflict perspective, violence itself is not a social problem; in fact, violence is an important mechanism for bringing about social change. It comes to be viewed as a problem when it threatens the interests of some group and that group is in a position to do something about it.

THE CONSEQUENCES OF WAR

Many of the consequences of violence—and the reasons for our concern about it—are obvious: the loss of human life, the destruction of property, the disruption of people's lives by the terror of violence, and the fear of violence that can seep into people's daily routine and sap it of joy or pleasure. However, there are consequences of violence, and especially war, that are more subtle and often go unnoticed. Over the past few decades, researchers have been able to document the wide-ranging ramifications of war for society. From the functionalist perspective, this is not surprising. Any society is made up of a number of parts that are highly integrated and interdependent. War demands considerable shifting and rearrangement of these parts: People and material must be mobilized, attitudes must be generated to support the war, and the daily lives of many people are disrupted. Because of this, war can intensify a number of social problems. We will review some of the major impacts.

Crime and Political Turmoil

Crime often accompanies war because warfare brings with it social disruption and upheaval. We saw in Chapter 9 that crime thrives in situations where anomie exists. War produces anomie because civilians find it difficult to find food, clothing, and shelter in the normal ways. Theft, robbery, and possibly even assault may be resorted to as ways of obtaining the routine necessities of life. Crime and war are also associated in another way: Crime rates seem to rise in the years immediately following wars. Homicide rates, for example, increase after wars, whether the wars are large or small (Archer and Gartner, 1976). The increase is not because of adverse economic conditions because it occurs when wars are followed by economic expansion. The increase is also found among both men and women. Surprisingly, the rise in crime is more likely among nations that are victorious in war, and nations with a large number of battle deaths have shown substantial crime increases.

We do not fully understand why this increase in crime occurs following wars. It may be that the violence of war tends to generate a general legitimation of violence—an expansion of the subculture of violence—and this may reduce people's inhibitions toward engaging in violence. Or it may be that a condition of anomie pervades society following a war as large numbers of soldiers return home looking for work and trying to reestablish familial and friendship ties. It may take society some time to reabsorb and help these soldiers readjust. For example, thousands of Vietnam veterans have served time in prison for committing crimes, and research suggests that these veterans experienced considerable difficulties in adapting to the anomie that existed in their lives when they returned to the United States (Boivin, 1985). Many have resorted to what Merton called innovation as a mode of adapting, and one form of this is crime (see Chapter 9). Recent studies involving the experiences of Vietnam veterans demonstrate that these men and women had considerably higher mortality rates during their first five years out of the service, especially from causes such as suicide, automobile accidents, and drug overdoses (The Centers for Disease Control . . . , 1987). Also, the sense of patriotism and common purpose found during the war may decline, leaving a void in many people's lives. Whatever the reason for the relationship between crime and war, it further documents the disruptive effect of war on society.

In addition to crime, political turmoil often increases during war. In some cases, this arises because disenchantment over the war leads to widespread discontent with the government. The government loses legitimacy in the eyes of both those who find the war morally offensive and those who feel that the government should prosecute the war more intensely. Such people may withhold support for the government, support opposition candidates, or possibly even engage in collective protest or rebellious actions. War also may have the effect of reducing people's tolerance for public dissent. When a country has gone to war with a foe, many people believe a united front is essential and are willing to allow the government to use repressive means to control dissent. As a consequence of all these things, wars gener-

ally tend to produce increases in domestic political violence (Stohl, 1976). Opponents of the war may engage in demonstrations, sit-ins, or, in extreme cases, terrorist bombings as a way of disrupting the war effort. Supporters of the government and the war may harass and attack demonstrators, and the police arrest the dissenters.

So war often poses a threat to democratic institutions on the home front. During the Civil War, for example, there was substantial dissent and conflict. In New York City, a three-day riot involving fifty thousand people resulted in thirteen hundred deaths (Brooks, 1969). Much of the hostility was focused on the unfairness of the draft as then implemented. The policy at that time favored the well-to-do because one could buy one's way out of military service for about three hundred dollars—a sum that working-class people and Irish immigrants could not afford at the time. There was also considerable opposition to World War I. In 1917, for example, eight thousand protestors marched in Boston against the war. The pattern of violence at this march was typical: Patriotic mobs attacked the demonstrators, but it was the demonstrators who were arrested for breaching the public order. The International Workers of the World, a revolutionary socialist labor group nicknamed the "Wobblies," opposed the war on the grounds that it was a scheme by big business to make greater profits. Enemies of the Wobblies used the latter's opposition to the war as an excuse to hound them mercilessly in hopes of destroying their organization. Many Wobblies were beaten and jailed in Arizona and Montana, and some were even driven into exile in other countries.

The Vietnam War was associated with substantial domestic political violence. Early in the war, the violence took the same form that it did during World War I: Nonviolent demonstrators were attacked by either citizens or the police. Later, some antiwar protestors became more violent by burning buildings and attacking police with rocks and sticks. The radical wing of the antiwar movement, including such groups as the Weather Underground, engaged in bombings and other terrorist actions. The emotions aroused by the Vietnam War may have also heightened the violence associated with other conflicts in American society, such as the quest for civil rights. Research shows that people opposed to the war were more willing to aggressively and possibly violently stop the government from going about its business when they disagreed with government policies. On the other hand, those who supported the war expressed a willingness to use repressive measures to stop dissent (Smith, 1972).

War creates pressures, then, that increase the likelihood of domestic turmoil, and this turmoil, if it becomes severe, might threaten American democratic institutions. Whether the situations during World War I and the Vietnam conflict were that severe is a matter of some debate. The point here is to recognize the negative domestic consequences of waging a war.

Economic Problems

War can have a severe impact on a nation's economy. The destruction of factories, railroads, and other economic resources can be terribly damaging, but economic problems are created even in combatant nations that suffer little or no such physical destruction. One source of economic problems is that resources devoted to the war effort must be withdrawn from some other economic realm. The labor and material resources we use to build tanks and guns are not available for housing construction or leisure pursuits. Figure 14.4 shows the percentage of the gross national product (GNP)—the total output of goods and services in our nation—that is made up of defense spending. Clearly, World War II drew substantial resources from the civilian realm, with nearly half of the GNP being spent for military needs. It is

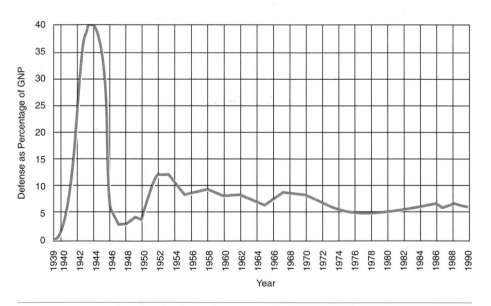

Figure 14.4   **Defense Expenditures in the United States as a Percentage of the Gross National Product, 1939–1990**
SOURCES: U.S. Bureau of the Census, *Statistical Abstract of the United States, 1987* (Washington, D.C.: U.S. Government Printing Office, 1986), p. 317; U.S. Bureau of the Census, *Statistical Abstract of the United States, 1991* (Washington, D.C.: U.S. Government Printing Office, 1991), p. 336.

estimated that the direct costs of World War II were $360 billion, at a time when the federal budget each year was less than $100 billion (U.S. Bureau of the Census, 1991: 341). By comparison, Korea and Vietnam were less intrusive on the economy: They cost $50 billion and $140 billion, respectively.

The impact of war on the economy depends on the state of the economy. World War II and the Korean conflict began when there were high levels of unemployment. This meant that increased government expenditures could be more easily absorbed through economic expansion, creating new jobs that the unemployed could fill. The Vietnam conflict, on the other hand, began when unemployment levels were quite low and the economy was operating at close to full capacity. Increased defense spending for Vietnam provided a stimulus to the economy that resulted in an increased demand for goods and services and considerable inflation in prices. In earlier wars, inflation was controlled by instituting wage and price controls. President Lyndon Johnson chose not to do this during the Vietnam conflict on the grounds that the economy could support additional stimulation. Against the advice of many, he chose not to increase taxes as a control over demand or to institute wage-price controls to reduce inflation (Russett, 1969). One assessment of the economic impact of the Vietnam War was that it produced

the most virulent inflation in American history, the highest interest rates in history, a series of balance of payments crises worse than any that had gone before, an unnecessary recession in 1970–71, two serious declines in stock prices, . . . a collapse of the housing industry, . . . financial market distortions that bore extremely heavily on small business and that forced state and local governments to retrench on education and other vital services, and the eventual defeat of the most imaginative experimental approach to the problems of impacted poverty that had ever been tried. (Stevens, 1976: 13)

Although this statement may be a little overdrawn, it is clear that Vietnam, as other wars, had a dramatic impact on the economy.

Even when war is not fought, the preparations for war can be costly (Markusen and Yudken, 1992). Outfitting our impressive military machine to fight the Cold War has meant diverting resources and innovation away from civilian industries and into the military–industrial complex. What has resulted is a huge industry of corporations, engineers, and workers who are dependent on government contracts and tooled to build only very specialized weapons systems. In Chapter 2, we discussed whether our government should have an industrial policy to assist certain industries to develop and compete in world markets as other industrial nations such as Germany and Japan do. In effect, the industrial policy of our government has been to siphon billions of dollars each year into this military arena while claiming that we have no industrial policy. With government assistance siphoned off into the military–industrial complex, other industries—such as automobiles, machine tooling, and consumer electronics—have been languishing, with plants closing and jobs going overseas. To make matters worse, this military–industrial complex often prospered more from lobbying and negotiating with the Pentagon than from emphasizing cost minimization and quality production. Oftentimes, Pentagon contracts allowed corporations to charge the government whatever it costs to build a weapons system plus a certain guaranteed profit, even when the weapons system ended up costing much more than the corporation originally projected that it would. With such a noncompetitive system, military–industrial corporations were, in effect, given enormous research, development, and production subsidies from the government whereas other corporations were left to fend for themselves. By the early 1990s, we found ourselves being paid by other countries to use our impressive military might to fight the world's battle in the Persian Gulf War. We had become, in effect, the world's cop, hired by other nations to discipline a rogue dictator. At the same time, we increased our arms sales to other nations to make up for a trade deficit produced because many U.S. civilian industries could not compete in the world market. When so much of our budget—currently one-quarter of the total—goes to defense spending, it is not surprising that civilian industries suffer from a lack of policy attention.

Nuclear Annihilation

In one major respect, many would consider the twentieth century to be the "winter of despair": For the first time in human history, the technological capability exists for destroying life on earth as we know it. The harnessing of nuclear power has made possible the unleashing of unimaginable destruction. Nuclear weapons are not merely a quantitative increase in military fire power. They are so vastly destructive that they constitute a qualitatively different level of violence altogether.

In a sense, we can only speculate about the impact of nuclear war on life on earth because no other equivalent calamities have occurred to serve as examples. Of course, there were Hiroshima and Nagasaki, but these were limited attacks and the survivors could depend on support for survival and rebuilding from those not immediately affected. In a large-scale nuclear war between the East and the West, there would be no outside support because the explosions would spread devastation all across the United States, Europe, and Russia. The devastation also would be far more extensive than in Japan in 1945. If a one-megaton bomb were detonated over Los Angeles, New York, Paris, London, or Moscow, everyone within a radius of two miles of the bomb blast would be burned, crushed, or vaporized to death, probably two million people (Kurtz, 1988). Within twenty miles of the blast, another million people would die immediately from the blast or shortly thereafter from severe wounds. Many others would die within a week or two as enormous amounts of radioactive fallout drift down and contaminate food and water supplies. Within weeks of the explosions, then, as many as five million people might die in each city. The World Health Organization estimates that more than one billion people would be killed outright worldwide in a large-scale nuclear exchange and another one billion would be seriously injured (Borgstrom et al., 1983). This is nearly one-half of the world's human population! In each city, there would be little or no help from the outside; food and water supplies would be disrupted and there would be no rescue teams to supply more; there would be few medical supplies and no place to bury the dead. The disease, crime, violence, and chaos that resulted would likely kill many more people (Warner, 1988; Turco and Golitsyn, 1988).

Eventually, order would emerge from the chaos, of course, but one shrinks from imagining what that order might be like. The emergence of a highly authoritarian military regime would be a real possibility. In fact, people who had suffered so terribly might find such order comforting. American democratic institutions that brought them to a state of chaos, death, and destruction might seem less appealing in a post-nuclear war era. The life-styles of Americans would be radically altered because of the destruction of so many homes, apartments, factories, and other buildings. It would take years, possibly decades, to rebuild, and during the interim people would be forced to live in crowded, temporary camps. A whole generation, and possibly two, would probably lose any chance for the material affluence that was common before the war. One report concluded, based on elaborate computer simulations of the effects of even a small nuclear exchange, that the survivors in the United States would be reduced to "near-medieval levels of existence" for decades (quoted in Broad, 1987: 1). For many, the long-term effects of massive amounts of radioactive contamination would mean the development of birth defects, cancer, and other deadly illnesses years after the war.

Another possible effect of nuclear war was suggested by a group of scientists at the Conference on the Long-term Worldwide Biological Consequences of Nuclear War in 1983. Summarizing their research, these scientists argued that nuclear war could have a devastating effect on the atmosphere and ultimately on the ability of the earth to support human life. It could create what they labeled a "nuclear winter" (Ehrlich et al., 1983; Turco et al., 1983). The thousands of detonations of nuclear warheads would toss tremendous amounts of dust and soot into the atmosphere. The nuclear detonations would also cause fierce fires, like the firestorms in German cities that were bombed during World War II, only much larger and injecting even more smoke and particulate matter into the atmosphere. In one to two weeks, this dust and soot could coalesce into a monstrous dark cloud shrouding much of the northern hemisphere. Little sunlight would penetrate this cloud. In the worst case of a very severe nuclear exchange, these scientists estimate, the cloud could stop all but one-tenth of 1 percent of the normal sunlight that reaches the earth. Even a limited nuclear exchange could reduce sunlight by 95 percent. The cold and the darkness could have disastrous effects on plants and animals. Without sunlight and proper temperatures, much foliage would die and our food supply would be seriously threatened.

Based on their calculations, then, these scientists project that nuclear war could constitute a severe assault on our ecosystem and could threaten its ability to support human life. There has been, of course, much debate over the accuracy of these calculations. Although no one can be certain what will happen until it actually happens, many scientists today believe that a nuclear winter of some degree of severity is a possible outcome of a nuclear war in which less than a thousand warheads are exchanged (Robock, 1989; Sagan and Turco, 1990). The effects may be less severe than the scientists project—or they may be more severe. If there is a nuclear war and the projections

of these scientists turn out to be accurate, civilization as we know it could be threatened and could possibly be destroyed. Let us hope that the theory is never put to the actual test.

FUTURE PROSPECTS

Violence and war seem to be endemic to the human condition, but there are some things that hold promise for reducing the level of violence in the United States and the world.

Social Reform and Social Justice

As we have seen, violence often springs out of social strain, frustration, or injustice. Collective violence may represent an effort by people to correct those injustices or to gain what they feel is an equitable share of resources. Efforts to control violence, then, need to begin by changing the social conditions that are the seedbeds of violence. In fact, the sociological investigation of social problems is an attempt to do just this. In this book, we have analyzed many of the conditions that can cause collective violence, and we need not review all of those discussions here. By way of illustration, prejudice and discrimination, discussed in Chapter 6, produce violence in the form of lynchings and race riots. Social reforms that focus on reducing discrimination, then, will affect levels of collective violence. The inequitable distribution of resources in society, discussed in Chapter 5, has resulted in violence in the form of labor strife, riots, and in a few cases, rebellion. Programs to provide people with greater opportunities and a broader distribution of resources in society will reduce the likelihood of these forms of violence.

There is no consensus regarding which social reforms are appropriate or what constitutes social justice, and we will not presume to answer those questions. In most cases, reform programs mean that some groups benefit, whereas others lose. In fact, interventionists presume that this will be the case and that the government should serve as arbiter over the allocation of resources. The government then becomes the forum in which various groups exercise what influence they have to gain a share of resources. Laissez-faire advocates, on the other hand, would argue that the unfettered operation of impersonal economic forces can provide equity and justice for all. The government, they believe, will simply become the tool of one interest group or another. These issues are debated in other chapters in the context of specific forms of social injustice. The point here is that, although social reform is essential to controlling violence, such reforms are not easy to accomplish and are not without controversy.

Gun Control

There is a vast arsenal of weapons in the hands of American citizens. From deer hunters with rifles to beer-can target shooters with pistols, from self-styled commandos who practice with paramilitary assault weapons to drug-selling gangs with illegal weapons—and do not forget the frightened teen who carries a .38 revolver to school each day—America is awash in guns. There is an estimated two hundred million firearms out there now, with at least four million more being added every year. Americans spend over $2 billion each year on firearms—more than we do on golf and fishing equipment combined (U.S. Bureau of the Census, 1991).

The levels of violence in society might be controlled by restricting people's access to the means of perpetrating violence, especially lethal violence. To this end, some Americans have proposed establishing strict controls over the ownership of guns, possibly even prohibiting their ownership by citizens altogether. In 1989, some well-publicized incidents occurred in which schoolchildren and people at work were killed by disturbed people armed with semiautomatic assault rifles. Such tragic events have increased pressure for gun control and motivated new federal legislation regarding the production and sale of "assault-type" weapons.

Opponents of gun ownership have used these and other statistics to argue that levels of lethal violence could be reduced by restricting the ownership of guns, especially handguns and assault weapons, which are the weapons most commonly used in perpetrating violence. Their basic argument is that the widespread availability of guns increases the chances that a person will respond to frustration or injustice with destructive violence. Although the absence of guns does not resolve the strife in such situations, it lowers the level of violence. Especially in cases in which assaults arise out of impulse rather than preparation and planning, the impulse may well pass without lethal violence if firearms are not readily available. A number of police organizations, such as the Fraternal Order of Police and the Police Foundation, support handgun control legislation.

Opponents of gun control legislation interpret the Second Amendment to the Constitution to mean that Americans have a constitutional right to own guns for their own use and protection (Kates, 1983). This amendment states: "A well regulated militia being necessary to the security of a free state, the right of the people to keep and bear arms shall not be infringed." Tampering with this right, they argue, will hinder their ability to protect themselves and their families from harm and might threaten our democratic institutions. In addition, law-abiding gun enthusiasts argue that it is unfair for them to have to give up their weapons because of the criminal or violent behavior of a minority. Finally, opponents of gun control argue that it would just create an enormous black market in guns, and this would make it easier for criminals to obtain weapons.

There is considerable variation in state and local legislation regarding the ownership of guns. Some locales are highly restrictive, whereas others do not even require a person to have a police permit to own a gun. A recent summary by sociologist Gary Kleck (1991) of research on whether gun controls reduce violence or crime is rather pessimistic: It does not seem to have a big impact one way or the other. Greater restrictions do not seem to produce significantly less violence or crime. This may be because our society is so awash with weapons that the controls that are established have little impact. However, a recent study of a ban on the purchase or possession of handguns by civilians in Washington, D.C., shows a significant reduction in homicides and suicides following the ban in 1977 (Loftin et al., 1991). Even Kleck's research suggests that modest declines in crime and violence could be achieved by a gun control policy that makes "gun acquisition at least marginally more difficult, and gun possession more risky, for the most identifiably violence-prone segments of the population" (1991: 433). This could be done by a gun buyer screening system, such as owner licenses or purchaser permits along with a national instant records check so that sellers or police can check on a gun owner or purchaser. There should also be strict controls over the private sales of weapons, which is where many criminals purchase their weapons.

Kleck estimates at best a modest impact for his proposals or for any other similar efforts at gun control. However, firearms have never been totally banned in any state, so we do not know what the impact of a statewide or nationwide ban on the possession of firearms might be (Wright and Rossi, 1986). It might depend on how stringent the laws are and on how rigidly they are enforced. It is also questionable whether we could ban handguns effectively. As we saw in Chapter 10, widespread and popular social practices, such as the use of alcohol and marijuana, are difficult to control through legislation. A total ban on guns could lead to a thriving black market that would leave the police even less equipped to deal with gun-related violence because all privately owned guns would be unregistered.

Media Control

There has been considerable pressure over the years, especially from groups of parents and educators, to establish controls over the portrayal of violence in the media. This would reduce the number of models for violence that the young are exposed to. The media have generally resisted any such controls. One reason for the resistance is that the violent shows are often the most popular ones. Movies with large doses of sex and violence such as *Lethal Weapon* almost always make money for their producers, and reality-based television shows that portray violence such as *Cops* find vast numbers of viewers. In 1990, Congress passed the Children's Television Education Act, which became law without President Bush's signature. It is the first legal effort to require the television industry to take steps to provide for the educational and informational needs of children and youth in their programming (Huston et al., 1992). Licensees must demonstrate at the time of their license renewal that their programs meet these needs, although there is little specific in the act about what they must do. The act does not address the issue of violence directly but instead permits television broadcasters, networks, and cable companies to collaborate to reduce the amount of violent content without being subject to antitrust laws. In 1992, the three networks did agree to some guidelines to reduce violence on television. The guidelines suggest that violence should be relevant to the development of the plot and should not be gratuitous, excessive, or depicted as glamorous. However, there is no enforcement mechanism attached to the guidelines, and the networks will probably continue to air shows that get the best ratings, which are typically those with sex and violence in them.

Resistance to controls over the media also arises among those who view such controls as an infringement on the First Amendment rights of freedom of speech and freedom of the press. As we saw when discussing the censorship of pornography in Chapter 11, it is very difficult to distinguish between what is acceptable and what should be censored. Violence is, of course, a fact of life, and to eliminate it from the media altogether would be a tremendous distortion of reality. But what level of violence is "too much"? If we can censor violence, then what about some other ideas or practices that we find offensive? Some would wish to ban sensitive portrayals of gay men and lesbians on the grounds that it might be suggestive to young minds, whereas others would focus on political or religious ideas that they believe might mislead impressionable people. The point is that the door to censorship, once ajar, may be very difficult to shut again or to keep from opening further. Such censorship could easily threaten the free press and the open expression of ideas that are so essential to a democracy. So the desirability of controlling media violence needs to be weighed against the threat it may present to our democratic institutions.

Preventing War

If wars could be prevented, we would save ourselves not only from the slaughter and destruction of the war itself but also from the problems created by the dislocations of war. Whether war can be prevented and how to do it are highly controversial topics.

The Balance of Power.   During the Cold War, which began at the end of World War II, American foreign policy was directed toward preventing a nuclear catastrophe while at the same time maintaining our political and military dominance in the world. In the early 1950s, Secretary of State John Foster Dulles (1954) developed the policy of **massive retaliation:** *War could be avoided if the enemy realized that any aggressor against the United States would suffer overwhelming damages from the massive retaliation with American military might.* So the United States strove to prevent war by amassing weaponry to use as a threat. If the threat were credible—if the enemy believed that massive retaliation would follow aggression—then, it was argued, the weapons would never have to be used. The Soviet bloc nations also amassed incredible military force. By the 1980s, the foreign policies of both the United States and the Soviet Union were based on the concept of **mutually assured destruction** or MAD: *War can be prevented when each side has the might to destroy the other.* Any first-strike effort would result in retaliation and the mutual destruction of both sides. What is supposed to result from this policy is a **balance of power:** *A nuclear holocaust is avoided because the military power of one side roughly balances that of the other side.*

It would seem that the balance of power approach worked. We have not had a world war or seen the use of nuclear weapons in over forty years. Yet there are reasons for pessimism. After all, forty years is not a very long time. If another one hundred years pass without a nuclear war and one occurs then, it would still have devastating consequences. In other words, given the destructive power of nuclear weapons, postponing war is really secondary to preventing war. In addition, we have not prevented more conventional wars such as the Korean conflict, the decade-long Vietnam War, the Gulf War, and our involvement in places such as Lebanon and Grenada. These conflicts hold the potential to escalate into a nuclear exchange. There were strong pressures, for example, to use tactical nuclear weapons in Vietnam. Finally, there remains the possibility that nuclear war could start by accident. Although the chances of this are considered by many to be small, they cannot be ignored.

Arms Control and Disarmament.   A more definite step toward protecting the world from nuclear destruction would be to limit the number of such weapons in existence or to eliminate them altogether. Because the nuclear powers now possess sufficient weapons to annihilate one another, it seems obvious that not much "control" has been exercised in the armaments area. Nations are naturally reluctant to enter into agreements to limit their weaponry when they fear that the other side will take advantage of this situation. It is also often politically dangerous for elected officials to appear to compromise our defensive strength. Yet there has been some progress in arms control

(U.S. Arms Control and Disarmament Agency, 1982). In 1963, most nations signed a treaty banning nuclear testing in the atmosphere, outer space, underwater, and in some cases underground. The focus of this treaty was on protecting the environment from radioactive contamination. In the 1972 Strategic Arms Limitation Talks (SALT I), the United States and the Soviet Union agreed to place limits on their defensive weapons systems and on their most powerful land- and submarine-based offensive nuclear weapons. Further limitations on these weapons were agreed to by President Carter in the SALT II talks concluded in 1979. Although the U.S. Senate has never ratified SALT II, Presidents Carter and Reagan agreed to do nothing that would violate it as long as the Soviet Union did the same. Although these treaties probably contributed to reducing the chances of a nuclear exchange, they left the nuclear powers with enormous stockpiles of weapons.

Despite these treaties, there was not much real progress made in reducing stockpiles of nuclear weapons. Between the signing of SALT I and SALT II, for example, the number of warheads possessed by the United States and the Soviet Union doubled! Despite SALT II, both nations have more warheads now than at the time the treaty was agreed to. In 1982, the two superpowers began talks on a Strategic Arms Reduction Treaty (START). Then in the late 1980s, we saw the beginning of the collapse of the Soviet Union. Its economy could no longer support the burdens of economic and arms competition with the West and also support Soviet rule over the Baltics, Eastern Europe, and the many other areas it dominated since World War II. By 1991, the Soviet Empire no longer existed. The Berlin Wall fell and Germany was reunited; Eastern European countries were free; and the old Soviet Union had become the Commonwealth of Independent States. This dramatic transition has created the best opportunity since World War II for significant reductions in nuclear weaponry worldwide as well as for easing world tensions and reducing the likelihood of nuclear war. In the late 1980s, Presidents Mikhail Gorbachev and Ronald Reagan signed the INF treaty, which bans intermediate range nuclear weapons. This resulted in some of the existing nuclear stockpiles in both countries being destroyed. Both countries also agreed on certain procedures for the mutual verification of the results, something that had always been a serious hitch in negotiations between the United States and the Soviet Union. Then, in the early 1990s, the United States and Russia reached agreement on the START treaty mentioned above (START I) and on another strategic arms reduction treaty called START II. If fully implemented, these treaties will produce dramatic reductions in the number of nuclear warheads stockpiled by both countries (Higgins, 1992). START II, for example, calls for each country to reduce their nuclear stockpiles to about one-third of their current ten thousand warheads by early in the next century. This is the level that existed in the 1960s when the nuclear age was in its early stages. As this is written, however, the two countries together still possess twenty thousand nuclear warheads, many of them in former republics of the Soviet Union that have expressed some reluctance to give them up. Many things could happen to impede the implementation of the START treaties. Even if the planned reductions occur, the two nations will still possess enough warheads to do massive destruction in a nuclear exchange.

Because of the destructive power of nuclear weapons and the threat of nuclear winter, some scientists argue that all nations should drastically cut their nuclear arsenals to a small number that would be large enough to deter an attacker by ensuring a devastating retaliation but small enough that a nuclear winter is unlikely. Scientists Carl Sagan and Richard Turco (1990) call this strategy a "minimum sufficient deterrence" and suggest that the United States and the former Soviet Union could achieve it with somewhere between one hundred and three hundred strategic warheads. Other experts argue that a permanent resolution to the danger of nuclear weapons can be achieved only with complete disarmament. Although there

While many groups in the United States have worked for significant arms reductions or total nuclear disarmament, the majority of Americans still support a strong military posture, including American nuclear parity with or dominance over any other nation in the world.

are sizable interest groups both in the United States and abroad pushing for such a policy, it is unlikely to come about in the foreseeable future. The majority of Americans support a strong military posture, including nuclear parity with or dominance over any other nation in the world. So, with the end of the Cold War, there is much uncertainty regarding which foreign policy approach would be the best to deter wars in the future. Some of the possibilities are explored in the Policy Issues insert in this chapter.

Nonproliferation of Weapons.   In the past, some nations chose not to develop nuclear or other weapons of mass destruction because they had security arrangements and guarantees that offered them protection from attack by others without the need to have weapons of their own. For example, the North Atlantic Treaty Organization provided a nuclear defense for West Germany, and the U.S. nuclear umbrella restrained South Korea from developing its own weapons. With the end

of the Cold War, many of the old security arrangements around the world are changing or disintegrating. This leaves a very unsettled international environment as far as the proliferation of weapons goes and calls for new international efforts to discourage such proliferation (Bailey, 1991). One option to reducing proliferation would be to extend the U.S. or Soviet nuclear umbrella over some countries that might be tempted to develop their own. If their security needs were satisfied, then a major motivation for developing weapons would be eliminated. However, this may clash with the pressure in both countries to reduce their nuclear armaments. A second option might be to encourage the development of regional agreements that prohibit the development of effective delivery systems, such as intermediate range ballistic missiles that are hard to defend against. Without the delivery system, the weapons would be less of a threat. A third option would be to encourage open debate about the development of nuclear weapons, especially on how costly they are to develop. Experience in some countries, such as Sweden, suggests that the public tends to strongly oppose them when they learn how expensive they are. Fourth, when nations violate existing nonproliferation treaties, there should be certain and substantial international sanctions against them, such as trade embargoes. Finally, the spread of weapons can be controlled through restricting the trade in technical knowledge or materials that are necessary to produce the weapons.

World Government. One of the major obstacles to preventing war among nations is that each nation functions on the basis of protecting its own national interest and pursuing its own short-term goals. Nations do not typically pursue policies that are guided by the common long-term interests of all nations, especially when those policies have a negative impact on the achievement of their own goals. One way around this obstacle might be to establish an international organization that would do for the nations of the world something like what the U.S. federal government does for the states: serve as a forum where competing interests can be hammered into a coherent policy without resorting to violence. This was attempted with the League of Nations following World War I and with the United Nations (UN) following World War II in 1945.

For such efforts at world government to be effective, there must be a body of international law that is accepted and adhered to by all nations. There must also be some means of enforcing that law. Regarding international law, the many treaties that the members of the UN have signed over the years stand as a sound beginning of an agreement regarding how nations will relate to one another. Although nations disagree over the interpretation or applicability of particular parts of the laws in particular cases, there are judicial bodies, such as the International Court of Justice at The Hague (the World Court), for resolving these disputes. A major flaw in the system at this point is that nations can ignore the Court's jurisdiction in particular cases. The United States did this in

1985 when the World Court ruled that the United States had broken international law by aiding the antigovernment rebels (the contras) in Nicaragua. The World Court ordered the United States to stop arming and training the contras, but the Reagan administration said that the Court had no jurisdiction in this area (Giacomo, 1986). A second major flaw in the existing system of international law is that the United Nations has no means of enforcing its laws unless individual nations consent to its enforcement. The United Nations can send its peacekeeping forces into disputes when all parties agree to let them in, and Table 14.2 (see p. 528) shows that UN troops and observers are active in many places around the globe in attempting to prevent conflicts from beginning or escalating. However, the UN cannot move in and settle disputes without the consent of the nations involved. To this point, nations have been unwilling to surrender their sovereignty and their right to use force to any international body. So the mechanism for some form of world government is in place, but the nations have not yet agreed to use it fully.

Despite the failings of the United Nations, many supporters of world government are not discouraged because they fully expect the transition to take a long time. After all, the history of the evolution of political structures has been toward larger and more complex forms of organization. Over the past few thousand years, human societies have developed from family- and kin-based political structures to larger units such as nation-states. With the increasing complexity and interdependence of the modern world, they argue, the next natural step is to some form of supranational organization. The importance of international trade and multinational corporations to the economies of all countries illustrates the extent to which cooperation is essential and warfare increasingly destructive. However, shifting people's allegiances from a nation to a "united nations" will involve a long and possibly difficult transition, as was the transition in our country from a federation of states to the "united states."

POLICY ISSUES

Star Wars, Nuclear Weapons, and the Peace Dividend: Preventing War in the Post–Cold War World

Since World War II, our foreign and defense policies have rested on a few basic assumptions: that the Cold War struggle between the two great superpowers of the United States and the Soviet Union overshadowed everything else and that a massive nuclear arsenal and a policy of mutually assured destruction (MAD) were needed to prevent war and protect the United States and its allies from threats around the world. Suddenly, there is no Cold War and no Soviet Union. This has created turmoil regarding what foreign and defense policies will be needed to prevent war in the post–Cold War world.

The quandary as to what the future holds may be epitomized by the Strategic Defense Initiative (SDI) or "Star Wars" (Boffey et al., 1988; Chandler, 1988). Star Wars was conceived in the 1980s because of the growing realization that a policy of mutually assured destruction is inherently unstable. Nations cannot continue to stockpile weapons without increasing the likelihood that they will be used. The resort to nuclear weapons might arise out of a legitimate conflict or it might be an accident. It could occur because of the rise to power of a megalomaniacal leader such as a Hitler or a Hussein. Whatever the cause of the war, these experts argue, the horror and destruction that would result will be the same. And the chances of a nuclear exchange increase the longer the weapons are available.

The major thrust of SDI would be to move us away from a policy based solely on offensive weapons by developing more defensive capabilities. The SDI would establish a shield to protect the United States from nuclear weapons. As currently conceived, the defense shield would involve many exotic technologies such as space satellites to detect and track missiles headed for the United States; ground lasers, possibly reflected off mirrors in orbit, to destroy weapons; and space-based kinetic energy weapons to attack missiles. Planners envision thousands of satellites in space to detect and repel an incoming attack. If such a shield could be established, an enemy would supposedly be less likely to attack because such an attack would be futile. We could thus prevent nuclear war not by threatening horrible destruction but by ensuring that nuclear weapons could never reach targets on American soil.

However, not all defense specialists concede that a Star Wars approach is either feasible or desirable. One of the strongest arguments against the Star Wars approach is that it is unlikely to work as effectively as it must to deter nuclear war. To be effective, it would have to stop practically all incoming weapons, and many scientists do not believe this is feasible. Considering that any attacker would undoubtedly send thousands of dummy weapons along with the real ones, the defense system would have to see through these subterfuges and direct retaliation against the real weapons. It is debatable whether the technology to accomplish this can be developed. Another argument against Star Wars is that it would merely lead to another round of escalation in weaponry. Once each side has their defensive system in place, there would be substantial pressures to develop further offensive weapons that can destroy or penetrate the defensive shield. As a consequence, the world would become an even more dangerous and potentially deadly place.

With the developments of the 1990s, the newest argument against Star Wars is that it is simply no longer necessary. If the Soviet stockpiles of warheads decline significantly, then there is no credible enemy who would likely launch a massive strike of intercontinental ballistic missiles against us. Those with nuclear weapons are either our allies (Great Britain, France), pose no current threat to us (Russia, China), or do not have the capacity to mount an intercontinental attack (Iraq, North Korea). In the new world that is emerging, massive defense spending for Star Wars may simply be unnecessary.

For the same reason that Star Wars may be outdated, there is a growing debate over what the U. S. military posture needs to be to prevent war and protect American interests in the post–Cold War world. First, most analysts agree that, if current trends continue, future wars will probably not involve large nuclear exchanges between the military superpowers. In fact, there seems to be only one superpower left, namely, the United States. Instead, smaller scale regional wars are likely to be what the future holds, fought mostly with conventional weapons, although some smaller scale nuclear weapons may be used by those who have them. In this environment, according to one view, the policy of the United States should be to maintain sufficient military strength to discourage any rival superpower from emerging to threaten American primacy (Tyler, 1992). This might call for maintaining a still sizable nuclear force to deter others from developing their own nuclear weapons. In addition, this strategy calls for a still sizable military, at least 80 percent of its current size. The United States would continue to use military intervention around the world to prevent the spread of nuclear weapons and to protect America's national interest. Regional security coalitions, such as that used in the Persian Gulf War, might be used where useful, but these would be ad hoc assemblies that would not last beyond the immediate crisis. In addition, the United States would retain the freedom to act unilaterally when that best serves our interests.

A very different approach to the changing world emphasizes the idea that the end of the Cold War presents an opportunity to shift emphasis from making war to making peace. In this view, there is a "peace dividend" to be had by reducing our defense budget significantly and redirecting our economy from making weapons to producing goods and services that people want to buy. This

has already happened in a small way as some Star Wars resources have been redirected to more peaceful uses. For example, a laser built for Star Wars has been turned into a machine for making advanced computer chips (Weber, 1992). Some view this as essential to our economic health: "It is just too costly to bail out savings-and-loans and banks, pay for higher unemployment benefits, and continue to spend $300 billion a year on military preparedness. Unless one or more of these federal commitments changes, there will simply be no money left for new initiatives" (Markusen and Yudken, 1992: 242). So, reducing the size of the military–industrial complex (see Chapter 2) by shifting resources from defense spending to other realms may be critical to reindustrializing the U.S. economy and making us more competitive with such economic superpowers as Germany and Japan. If we continue to direct so much of our resources toward war, these countries will only gain more power economically. This view does not rule out the maintenance of a sizable military in the United States, but some proponents of this view argue for a 50 percent or greater reduction in our military budget (Markusen and Yudken, 1992).

Such a transition would be difficult because it would produce severe dislocation of workers and industries in many parts of our economy. Whole industries would have to shift from weapons production to nonmilitary products. One way to approach this would be to mount a national, publicly funded economic development strategy whereby the government would assist communities in identifying the economic resources they have, locating potential uses for those resources, and then seeking companies both nationally and internationally to develop those resources. This could assist communities by attracting or retaining industries, transferring technology from defense work to civilian production, and providing entrepreneurial aid. In the long run, proponents of this view argue, the economy will be stronger for having shifted away from war production and toward civilian production.

Both of these approaches are currently being debated in the United States, and future policy directions are uncertain as the Clinton administration takes office.

Table 14.2 **Operations of United Nations Peacekeeping Forces and Observers, 1989–1992**

Place	Observers	Troops	Goal
Lebanon	296		Peacekeeping in Lebanon and Golan Heights
Golan Heights		1,300	Monitor disengagement between Israel and Syria
Lebanon		5,800	Buffer between Israel and Lebanon
Kashmir	36		Monitor cease-fire between India and Pakistan
Cyprus		2,200	Prevent fighting between Greek and Turkish parts of island
Namibia		5,500	Oversee Namibia's transition to independence from South Africa
Central America	undetermined number		Oversee the regional peace plan
Iraq/Kuwait		550	Monitor border between former combatants
Cambodia		19,000	Monitor elections
Former Yugoslavia		16,000	Mediate conflict between Serbs, Croats, and Bosnians

SOURCES: Adapted from Paul Lewis, "The U.N., Resuscitated, Feels Like What It Was Meant To Be," *New York Times* (September 24, 1989), Section 4, p. 2; and Roddy Ray, "Troops Win Peace, Then Fight Boredom," *Detroit Free Press* (July 30, 1992), p. 3.

Linkages

Violence and war have an impact on race relations (Chapter 6) because they are often used as a part of the campaign by a dominant racial group to oppress a subordinate one. War especially can affect people's jobs and the economy (Chapter 2) as changing defense needs push some industries into decline.

Summary

1. The term *violence* refers to behavior that is intended to bring pain or physical injury to another person or to harm or destroy property. Violence is sufficiently pervasive that it warrants discussion as a problem in its own right.

2. Collective violence is organized violence that involves relatively large groups of people working to promote or resist some social policies or practices. One type of collective violence is civil disorder, which has been fairly common in American history. Civil disorder has arisen particularly out of racial conflict and labor strife.

3. Political violence, such as insurrections, has been less common in America, but there has been some. However, America has been involved in a number of wars and seems to be among the more war-prone nations. Terrorism has been fairly common over the past few decades. Terrorism in the United States has been sporadic and not too disruptive, but terrorism overseas directed at American citizens has been more common.

4. There are a number of biological explanations for violence, especially that of sociobiology, which argues that certain characteristics—such as territoriality, aggressiveness, and selfishness—are to an extent genetically determined because these traits enhance the survival of the species; over long periods, people with these genetic characteristics come to dominate in the gene pool. Biological explanations, however, are not sufficient to explain organized and collective episodes of violence such as riots and wars.

5. There are a number of social sources of violence. Among them are structural preconditions that increase the likelihood of violence: social strain or deprivation, competition, and ethnocentrism. These preconditions are translated into violence because the frustration that they produce can lead to aggressive behavior. This involves rel-ative deprivation because people tend to feel deprived or frustrated relative to what others have or they believe they deserve.

6. The likelihood that the preconditions and the frustration will lead to violence is influenced by some mediating factors: learning in a particular culture or subculture to view violence as an acceptable way of dealing with problems, having available attractive people to serve as models for violence, portraying violence in the mass media in a positive way.

7. War is very disruptive to society and because of this has a number of subtle impacts on society: Crime and political turmoil increase during and after wars and wars can be disruptive to the economy. The devastation accompanying a nuclear war would be a severe assault to the ecosystem and might threaten civilization as we know it.

8. One of the keys to controlling violence is to correct the strains, frustrations, and injustices that lead to collective violence. However, there is often little consensus about what social reforms would do the job or about what constitutes social justice.

9. Controlling guns and limiting the amount of violence in the media have been portrayed as partial solutions to the problem of violence. However, there is no evidence that gun control would have a great effect, and many people are opposed to the censorship that would be necessary to limit violence in the media.

10. Currently, there are four major approaches to preventing war, especially nuclear war: maintain a balance of power, develop treaties for arms control and disarmament, control the proliferation of weapons, and establish a world government that would be able to stop nations from going to war.

Important Terms for Review

balance of power
civil disorder
commodity riots
communal riots

frustration
insurrection
massive retaliation
mutually assured destruction

relative deprivation
sociobiology
subculture of
  violence

terrorism
violence

Discussion Questions

1. What sort of civil disorder or political violence is likely to occur in the United States in the next twenty-five years? Why do you think it will occur? What conditions would have to exist to justify your participation in such events?

2. What conditions would have to exist in the United States before you would be willing to support or possibly engage in terrorist activities? What political, social, or economic circumstances would justify this? Would American slaves have been justified for engaging in terrorism? What about the Indians?

3. Have each student in the class describe some violent incident that he or she was involved in. Can each incident be explained by one or more of the sources of violence described in the chap-

ter? What other explanations for violence would be needed to explain fully these incidents? How could these violent incidents have been avoided?

4. Ask a representative of a veterans' organization to talk to the class regarding the impact of combat on the personal lives of soldiers and their adjustment problems after the war. How heavily should such personal considerations be weighed in any policy decisions about whether the nation should go to war?

5. Is it possible to achieve limited or total disarmament in the world? Should this involve just nuclear weapons or be extended to conventional weapons also? How might such disarmament be achieved?

For Further Reading

Carl N. Degler. *In Search of Human Nature: The Decline and Revival of Darwinism in American Social Thought.* New York: Oxford University Press, 1991. This interesting work focuses on how biological and sociobiological ideas as explanations of human behavior have gained and lost popularity in the United States over the years. The author focuses on these explanations more as belief systems that people accept than as scientific theories.

Paul Ehrlich, Carl Sagan, Donald Kennedy, and Walter Orr Roberts. *The Cold and the Dark: The World After Nuclear War.* New York: W. W. Norton, 1984. This book is the report on the Conference on the Long-term Worldwide Biological Consequences of Nuclear War at which the notion of "nuclear winter" was first proposed.

Robert Ehrlich. *Waging Nuclear Peace: The Technology and Politics of Nuclear Weapons.* Albany: State University of New York Press, 1985. This is a clear and informative survey of the issues surrounding nuclear war by a physicist who is knowledgeable about the physics of nuclear weapons as well as about the social policy debate over them. It contains a detailed analysis of the likely effects of a nuclear war.

Jack A. Goldstone, ed. *Revolutions: Theoretical, Comparative, and Historical Studies.* San Diego: Harcourt Brace Jovanovich, 1986. This is an excellent compilation of readings on the theories of revolution and studies of specific revolutions. Although not easy reading for the undergraduate, the book is well worth the effort.

Erich Goode. *Collective Behavior.* Fort Worth: Harcourt Brace Jovanovich, 1992. This is a comprehensive textbook in the specialty area of sociology that studies riots, civil disturbance, insurrections, and other forms of collective violence. It is an excellent resource book.

Hugh Davis Graham and Ted Robert Gurr, eds. *The History of Violence in America: Historical and Comparative Perspectives.* New York: Praeger, 1969. An excellent and very interesting book that reviews the extent of violence in American history. It covers lynchings, riots, insurrections, and many other types of collective violence that have occurred in our country.

John R. MacArthur. *Second Front: Censorship and Propaganda in the Gulf War.* New York: Hill & Wang, 1992. This author highlights another common consequence of war: the use of propaganda by the government to gain support for war efforts. The author argues that the U.S. and Kuwaiti governments lied to and misinformed the American public to gain support for the Persian Gulf War in 1991.

Peter H. Merkl. *Political Violence and Terror: Motifs and Motivations.* Berkeley: University of California Press, 1986. This book analyzes the various theories that explain terrorism and other forms of political violence, examines various terrorist ideologies, and delves into the attitudes, motivations, and social backgrounds of individual terrorists.

Arata Osada, ed. *Children of Hiroshima.* New York: Harper and Row, 1981. Children who lived through the atomic bombing of Hiroshima in 1945 recount what happened to themselves and their families. It is a graphic, touching book that reminds us of the tremendous personal suffering that would follow a nuclear war.

George Rudé. *Ideology and Popular Protest.* New York: Pantheon, 1980. An excellent analysis of the role of ideological factors in public protest and revolution. It includes an analysis of the English, American, and French Revolutions.

James B. Rule. *Theories of Civil Violence.* Berkeley: University of California Press, 1988. This book presents the important theories in the social sciences that explain why and under what conditions collective violence occurs. It presents much more detail than was possible in this short chapter.

James A. Schellenberg. *The Science of Conflict.* New York: Oxford University Press, 1982. This book is a good overview of behavioral science theories and research on conflict among human beings. It analyzes sources of conflict as well as ways of reducing it.

Herbert Shapiro. *White Violence and Black Response: From Reconstruction to Montgomery.* Amherst: University of Massachusetts Press, 1988. This book documents the routine, organized, and persistent use of violence by dominant whites in America to control black Americans. Although the book's tone is angry, it is also informative regarding some dark elements of our past and present.

Seth Shulman. *The Threat at Home: Confronting the Toxic Legacy of the U.S. Military.* Boston: Beacon Press, 1992. Our arsenal of conventional and nuclear weapons, along with our testing of weapons and military maneuvers, represent another significant threat to the environment. This book documents the dimensions of that threat, why it has gotten out of hand, and what can be done about it.

William Sweet. *The Nuclear Age: Atomic Energy, Proliferation and the Arms Race,* 2nd ed. Washington, D.C.: Congressional Quarterly Inc., 1988. This simply written book looks at nuclear power and the proliferation of nuclear weapons that has occurred and that might occur in the future. It includes a chapter on nuclear terrorism.

Stansfield Turner. *Terrorism and Democracy.* Boston: Houghton Mifflin, 1991. This book is a good case study of hostage taking and terrorism, focusing on the Iran hostage crisis of 1979 to 1981 when Americans were taken hostage from the American embassy in Iran.

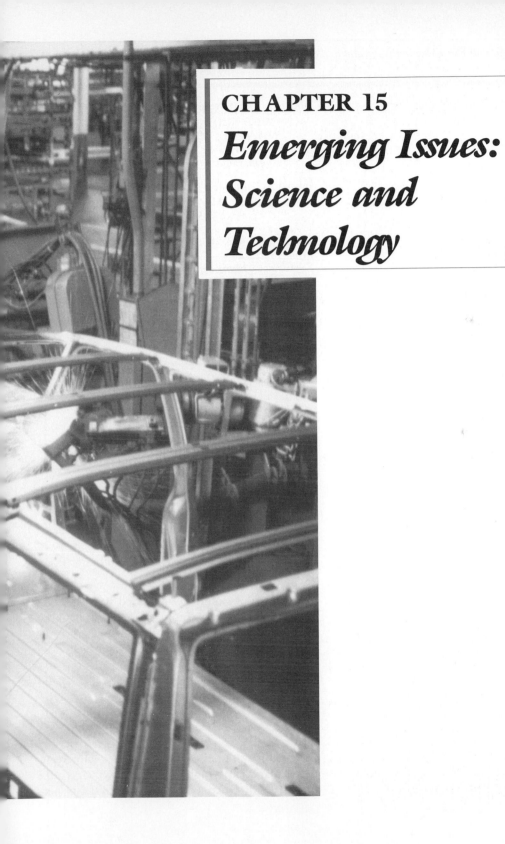

CHAPTER 15
Emerging Issues: Science and Technology

MYTHS AND FACTS ABOUT SCIENCE
    AND TECHNOLOGY

TECHNOLOGY AND SOCIETY
What is Technology?
The Impact of Technology on Society
    Mechanization and Automation
    Telecommunications and Computers
    Nuclear Power

**PERSPECTIVES ON SCIENCE
    AND TECHNOLOGY**
The Functionalist Perspective
The Conflict Perspective
The Interactionist Perspective

**PROBLEMS OF SCIENCE
    AND TECHNOLOGY**
Unemployment
Alienation
Loss of Control
Loss of Privacy

**POLICY ISSUES: PUBLIC CONTROVERSY
    OVER SCIENCE AND TECHNOLOGY:
    WHAT PEOPLE OBJECT TO**
*Should We Play God? The Case of Genetic
    Engineering*

**POLICY ISSUES: BIOTECHNOLOGY
    RAISES THE ISSUE: WHOSE LIFE
    IS IT, ANYWAY?**

FUTURE PROSPECTS
Legal Protections
Appropriate Technology
Technology Assessment
Futurology

LINKAGES

T he nineteenth-century philosopher Auguste Comte has been referred to as the "father of modern sociology," for he was one of the first to propose that society can be studied utilizing the scientific method. Like other scholars past and present, Comte was limited by the existing knowledge of his era. In what is regarded as his most significant work, *Cours de Philosophie Positive* (1835), Comte attempted to define the limits of scientific knowledge, and wrote these words concerning the heavenly bodies:

> *We see how we may determine their forms, their distances, their bulk, their motions, but we can never know anything of their chemical or mineralogical structure; and much less, that of organized beings living on their surface. . . . We must keep carefully apart the idea of the solar system and that of the universe, and be always assured that our only true interest is in the former.*

> *Within this boundary alone is astronomy the supreme and positive science that we have determined it to be . . . the stars serve us scientifically only as providing positions with which we may compare the interior movements of our system.* (Book 2, Chapter 1)

Essentially, Comte had decided that the stars would never be anything more to humankind than celestial reference points and that even our knowledge of the planets would always be limited to geometric principles. If anyone had proposed the science of astrophysics to Comte, he would have undoubtedly judged such inquiry to be impossible.

In less than one hundred years after Comte's death, almost the entire discipline of astronomy had become astrophysics. In fact, a major technological breakthrough came only two years after Comte died, when two German physicists per-

Myths and Facts About Science and Technology

Myth: The first practical application in this century of scientific knowledge about the atom was the development of techniques to grow more food and thus alleviate the problems of hunger and poverty.

Fact: Actually, the first practical application of this knowledge was to build weapons of mass destruction: atomic and nuclear bombs. Thus, the technology further exacerbated the problem of violence and war in the world.

Myth: Fear of the impact of technology on people's lives is a new phenomenon, arising out of the complex technology associated with industrialization.

Fact: Fear of technology can be found practically anywhere that technology shapes people's lives, even in preindustrial societies. However, the dangers that modern technology poses are quantitatively greater than and probably qualitatively different from the dangers of past, more simple technologies.

Myth: The coming of computers and a postindustrial society will usher in an era in which most people will find exciting, rewarding, and well-paying jobs.

Fact: Many experts believe that these developments will not necessarily be a boon for everyone. Many service jobs, for example, and those created by computer technology are dull, repetitive, and low paying. Also, because of technological advances involving automation and robotization, unemployment and underemployment may continue to be serious problems in the future.

Myth: It is good to develop all of the technology that our scientific knowledge makes possible because then we can choose to implement those that are beneficial and ignore those that create problems for people.

Fact: Once a technology exists, it tends to take on a life of its own: There are powerful social pressures to use it and further develop it by those interest groups who benefit from it. In other words, once the technological cat is out of the bag, society may have little choice about whether it will be used.

---

fected the spectroscope, a device that not only revealed the chemical properties of terrestial bodies, but also told humankind more about the distant stars than what had been known about the planets (Clarke, 1984). Consequently, Comte's "positive" statement that "we can never know anything of [the stars'] chemical or mineralogical structure" was laid permanently to rest.

Our discussion here is certainly not an indictment of Comte's scientific naiveté, because he cannot be blamed for failing to imagine a scientific technique like spectroscopy. Rather, his categorical assertion serves as a reminder of a principle that is respected by most contemporary scientists: Technologies that are impossible given existing knowledge may well become available as the result of scientific and technological discoveries in the future. In this century, some people doubted that humans would ever fly in the air, whereas others proclaimed it ridiculous to try to leave the earth and land on other bodies in the solar system. These skeptics were proven incorrect.

In fact, the awesome scientific and technological developments of the twentieth century have led some to believe that science and technology have no limits at all other than those that we, as human beings, place on them. Others argue that science and technology are creating problems—some of them potentially very serious—that need to be addressed. In this chapter, we will review the evidence on this issue. We will see that there have been benefits, but as one might expect there have been problems as well. And we may be naive regarding the problematic effects of our own technology.

TECHNOLOGY AND SOCIETY

What is Technology?

> *The term [technology] encompasses not only such recently emerging wonders as trips to the moon, hydrogen bombs, genetic engineering, and computers which some fear will eventually enslave us, but also toothbrushes, doorknobs, and wheelbarrows, as well as simplified spelling systems, arrangements for bureaucratic coordination, military draft lotteries, advertising strategies, and even sticks that chimpanzees use to catch termites. (Richter, 1982: 6)*

This description of technology by a contemporary sociologist casts a broad net regarding this commonplace term. Some writers have proposed that technology is not merely a human phenomenon but also found among lower animals, such as the nests built by birds or the dams of beavers. Other definitions of technology are confined to the realm of science and human production: "the systematic application of scientific or other organized knowledge to practical tasks" (Galbraith, 1967: 12). Anthropologists define *technology* as a body of knowledge that is available to a civilization for achieving specific objectives, and this helps to distinguish the term from *science,* which is the search for knowledge or something that produces knowledge (see Chapter 1).

Our definition of **technology** combines these ideas: *knowledge, tools, and practices that are employed as means of achieving clearly identifiable goals.* In this definition, technology can be both material and nonmaterial in nature, including not only "things" but also a particular way of thinking or a specific orientation toward social organization

(Volti, 1992). So technology consists of things such as robots, computers, and nuclear bombs, but it also includes modes of organization, such as mechanization and automation. It should be obvious that various levels of technology exist in different societies. For example, when premodern people discovered fire, it became a part of their technology, but their overall level of technological sophistication was low in comparison to even the most underdeveloped nations in the world today. The most technological sophistication accompanies **industrialization,** *a productive subsistence pattern in which machines and power tools, run by new sources of energy such as fossil fuels, accomplish tasks that were previously done by hand.* Some observers have suggested that modern America is moving into a **postindustrial society,** *one that is dominated by a highly technological form of production and devotes greater resources to providing services than to industrial production* (Bell, 1973; Beniger, 1993). Whether we call modern societies industrial or postindustrial, all have gone through a process of **modernization,** *the economic, social, and cultural changes that occur when a preindustrial society makes the transition to an advanced industrial society.* In a sense, much of this book has been about changes associated with modernization. In this chapter, we want to focus on how the changes that have accompanied the extensive technological development found in modern societies have had an impact on people and their role in contributing to social problems. We will illustrate some of the major technological developments that can create problems for people before addressing the problems that they may create.

The Impact of Technology on Society

Mechanization and Automation.   One element in the process of industrialization is **mechanization,** which refers to *the use of machinery to replace human and animal labor in the production of goods and services.* Mechanization is part and parcel of technological modernization, wherein human muscles have come to be supplemented and sometimes replaced through material tools and new power sources. **Automation** is an outcropping of mechanization and refers to *the automatically controlled operation of machines by mechanical or electronic devices.* Mechanization and automation are accompanied by enormous increases in human productivity and a highly specialized division of labor. They involve a transition from

> *one worker producing one item in one day to* one hundred *workers producing* five hundred *items in one day (with each of these hundred workers performing a specialized task and none of them producing any completed items on an individual basis). (Richter, 1982: 44)*

The three main groups of mechanical inventions that fueled early industrialization were steam engines and steam-powered transport, textile machinery, and improvements in iron and steel manufacture (Braun, 1984). The steam engine permitted large-scale production of goods in factories and also opened the door to locomotives, which served as a (then) speedy way of transporting these products from place to place. Mechanical spinning machinery and power looms greatly enlarged the cotton and textile industries, and the use of coal in the smelting of iron and production of steel led to huge production operations that were at the heart of the industrial revolution.

In human history, there has been an endless search for implements that permit people to do their work better, more easily, and faster. Early inventions such as the potter's wheel, the primitive hammer and chisel, the hoe and the shovel, and the discovery of fire all became servants of the craftsperson, helping these artisans to refine their skills. These tools were not the masters of those who used them, but rather expanded the mastery of the workers themselves. In fact, it was an increasingly specialized division of labor rather than the development of machinery itself that separated craftspersons from their products (Volti, 1992). This expanding division of labor actually predated the development of machinery, but was

an early precursor to the now-classic complaint that factory workers are forced to behave like machines. In the early automobile assembly lines, for example, one worker bolted wheels on and did nothing else to the finished product, and another set the rearview mirror in place. This was a very efficient form of organization in which many products could be produced in a given time. However, once each worker had responsibility for only a minor part of the production process, none of them could claim that the resulting product was theirs. They were no longer the masters of the production process but rather cogs in the machinery.

Mechanization and automation have led to many changes that are regarded as positive by Americans. For example, living standards have risen, the average workweek has been shortened, and much demeaning and exhausting work has been transferred from people to machines. However, although mechanical and automated systems can be built to complement human life and serve humankind, they often are not. Too often, they are designed with technical considerations given the most attention and human concerns considered only secondarily. This tendency, along with the fact that industrialization involves many possibilities for power and profit, can create many difficulties. When people realize the potential for power and profit in mechanization and automation, short-term gains often take precedence over the long-term human implications of the advancing technology. This is the issue, once again, of whether human beings are masters of their machines or are mastered by the machines. Imagine a huge industrial production plant completely run and monitored by computerized technology, including robots, which are an extension of automation. Fewer and fewer people are needed to yield enormous productivity. Automated machines will replace not only human muscle power, but also human thinking and decision making as we develop artificial intelligence (Robinson, 1992). But what of humankind in this technological revolution? As human beings further develop this sophisticated technology, does it mean that our fate is to become further controlled by that technology?

Telecommunications and Computers.   For much of human history, the various societies inhabiting this planet were often unaware of each other's existence. Even when groups acknowledged the presence of others, there might be little communication between them. A little over one hundred years ago, it took the Pony Express days and even weeks to transport written communications from place to place. After technology permitted devices such as the Atlantic cable, instant telephone communication was possible between geographic areas in different parts of the globe, and we saw the beginnings of what futurist Marshall McLuhan called the "global village." But far more was yet to come in a very short period of time.

In 1979, a committee of the National Academy of Sciences issued this statement:

> *The modern era of electronics has ushered in a second industrial revolution . . . its impact on society could be even greater than that of the original industrial revolution. (Norman, 1981: 109)*

The electronics industry began to be a major economic force during the late 1940s with the development of the transistor, but even this technological innovation did not permit the kind of miniaturization in electronic components that is commonplace today. Perhaps you have seen photographs of IBM's first computer. This piece of equipment was enormous, occupying more physical space than the size of most suburban homes, and just the machinery to cool the computer took up a great deal of room. The microelectronics revolution has been fueled by the invention of the silicon chip. These tiny chips, which are approximately one-quarter the size of a postage stamp, can be imprinted with tens of thousands of electronic components and circuits that are mind boggling in complexity. By the 1990s, laptop or notebook computers, which are small enough to

be easily carried around by a person, can store enormous amounts of information, run complicated software programs, and communicate through built-in modems with people around the world. And few people believe that we have come anywhere near the limits of this technology!

As we indicated earlier in this section, postindustrial societies will place more emphasis on service and information as their major activities and less on the production of goods via factories and related machinery. Computers and the electronics industry are among the driving forces behind this change, and the economic implications are extremely significant for all societies. During the 1990s, the economic productivity of the electronics industry will rival or exceed that of the automobile, steel, and chemical industries (U.S. Bureau of the Census, 1991: 740–744). One staff writer for *Science* magazine has suggested:

> *If steel and oil have been two of the key ingredients of modern industrial society up to now, many believe that in the remainder of this century it will be the state of a nation's electronics industry that signifies whether it is a developed nation or not. (Robinson, 1980: 582)*

Along with economic implications, the social impact of microelectronics or computerization is almost as hard to comprehend. For example, had it not been for these developments, we would never have been able to explore deep space, go to the moon, or build the space shuttle. Just think of the military significance of these technological achievements. During World War I, military commanders made calculations in their heads when they fired their weapons, and it was frequently a matter of luck whether a bomb actually hit its target. By the Persian Gulf War in 1991, warfare was run by microelectronic controls and computerized guidance systems. "Smart" bombs were laser-guided to their targets, and satellite communications enabled instantaneous contact between battlefield commanders and Pentagon officials. At the same time, people watching television around the world could see the bombing of Baghdad live

While some older people today remain wary of computers and computerized technology, younger Americans are being socialized to accept computers as a way of life. It is likely that our society will be increasingly dependent on this technology in the future.

because of advances in telecommunications. We can also send nuclear-tipped missiles, guided by computerized "brains," around the world with almost pinpoint accuracy. Some of the implications of this were developed in the discussion of the Star Wars proposals in the Policy Issues insert in Chapter 14.

For the average person, these developments have important implications. For example, during the 1960s and even into the 1970s, the least expensive computers cost hundreds of thousands of dollars, but today, computers that have equal or greater power than those early machines can be purchased for less than $10,000, and versatile microcomputers for business and home use are now as inexpensive as $1,000 or less. Many Americans are already becoming accustomed to the concept of computer "mail": Parents can communicate instantaneously via computer with their children attending college anywhere in the country.

Robotization is another fascinating dimension of the microelectronics-computer revolution. Microelectronically controlled machines are currently in use at America's major automobile manufacturing plants, and these robots can be "taught" to do new things using computerized equipment. At General Motors' Vanguard plant in Saginaw, Michigan, the company has invested $52 million in robotics technology:

> *Hardly a human works among the multitude of robots. Only forty-two hourly workers are spread over two shifts, and eventually the plant will add an overnight shift with no human presence of any kind. Overhead, perched in a glass-walled command room, a handful of engineers and technicians run the factory. ("GM Bets . . . ," 1988)*

Given the ever-expanding technological frontier that surrounds our employment of computers, satellites, and other microelectronic wizardry, Marshall McLuhan's 1968 vision of a "global village" continues to take shape and heralds the evolution of human societies that are ever more dependent on microelectronic and computer technology (Beniger, 1993).

Nuclear Power.   The idea that the physical world is made up of atoms is very old, even showing up from time to time in classical Greek literature. By the beginning of the nineteenth century, scientists were convinced that chemical reactions could be best explained if each chemical element is thought of as composed of very small identical atoms that are characteristic of the element. In 1890, the field of atomic physics was actually begun when physicist J. J. Thomson first isolated and established the existence of electrons (Besancon, 1966). Knowledge of the atom and its properties eventually led to an understanding of atomic and nuclear power. Through the twentieth century, American scientists held high hopes concerning nuclear energy. As technology expanded, humankind succeeded in harnessing this enormous power, both in its destructive capability and as an alternative energy source.

One of the first practical applications of atomic and nuclear energy was in the area of weapons. The first atomic bombs were dropped on Japan in World War II. The first test of a thermonuclear device took place in 1952 at a U.S. testing site in the Marshall Islands. In 1954, an accident occurred during a subsequent test in the Pacific, in which one man was killed and many others were injured. This incident called attention to the problem of radioactive fallout. The following quotation from an early address by Soviet scientist and political figure Andrei Sakharov illustrates these early concerns. Sakharov played a significant role in the development of the hydrogen bomb in the Soviet Union.

Beginning in 1957 I felt myself responsible for the problem of radioactive contamination from nuclear explosions. As is known, the absorption of the radioactive products of nuclear explosions by the billions of people inhabiting the earth leads to an increase in the incidence of several diseases and birth defects. . . . When the radioactive products

of an explosion get into the atmosphere, each megaton of the nuclear explosion means thousands of unknown victims. And each series of tests of a nuclear weapon (whether they be conducted by the United States, the USSR, Great Britain, China, or France) involves tens of megatons; i.e., tens of thousands of victims. (quoted in Burke and Eakin, 1979: 330)

Fears involving the prospect of nuclear holocaust have intensified as technology continues to expand. Sakharov spoke in terms of tens of megatons, but now we are used to talking about hundreds. These problems are discussed in more detail in Chapter 14.

The use of nuclear power for peaceful purposes held most promise for many as an energy source. Experts were very optimistic about its promise following World War II, and in the 1950s the government pushed the slogan "Atoms for Peace," deemphasizing the enormous destructive capabilities of atomic power and touting it as a source of abundant, pollution-free energy. Our reliance on nuclear power has increased considerably over the past few decades. In 1970, only 1 percent of our electricity was generated by nuclear fuels, compared with 20 percent today (U.S. Bureau of the Census, 1991: 579). However, optimism over the role of nuclear generation of power is dampened for some because we face two major problems with nuclear energy. First, it is expensive to build nuclear power plants with sufficient safeguards against accidents, theft of nuclear fuels, or terrorism. This increases the cost of producing electricity and throws into question whether nuclear-generated power can compete economically with power generated from other sources. The second problem with nuclear energy is what to do with the highly radioactive wastes that are produced. The government is currently identifying a number of potential nuclear waste repositories around the country. However, virtually no one wants a repository located near them. Also, the repositories and the containers of nuclear waste placed in them will have to be highly secure and not leak for thousands of years. They may still be dangerously radioactive after as many as five thousand years! That is more than twice the length of time since the beginning of the Christian era. No one is sure that the materials can remain secure and intact that long or that social order will be sufficiently continuous to provide for the protection of the sites. As of this writing, a permanent solution to the problem of disposing of wastes from nuclear power plants has yet to be found even though the wastes are accumulating (see Chapter 13).

The environmental dangers posed by the generation of nuclear energy are becoming more clear and ever more ominous with the passing of time. The disaster at Chernobyl in the Soviet Union in 1986, discussed in Chapter 13, illustrates the potential for immediate consequences of nuclear power generation, and the long-term threat of not being able to contain our nuclear waste products presents an even more disturbing problem. Even if we decided to halt the generation of nuclear power, the world may already have created problems for which there is no easy remedy. And even if the major world powers ceased production and agreed to a ban on nuclear weapons, the technology is still available for their production, and this prospect will always be with us.

PERSPECTIVES ON SCIENCE AND TECHNOLOGY

Now that we have an overview of the impact of science and technology on society and some of the forms that technological developments have taken, we are in a position to look concretely at some of the social problems that science and technology create for modern societies. Before doing this, however, it will be helpful to apply the three sociological perspectives to the issues of science and technology. As we pointed out in Chapter 1, the key role of any theory is to help us explain why something has occurred.

The Functionalist Perspective

From the functionalist perspective, society is a system made up of interrelated and interdependent elements, each performing a function that contributes to the operation of the whole. In a system in which all the parts are closely interdependent, we have seen how change in one element of society will probably lead to changes in other parts. Over the past few centuries, science and technology have been important sources of social change. Through inventions, discoveries, and the development of our knowledge of the world, many of the changes brought about by science and technology have been very functional for society. They have provided us with a longer life expectancy, many labor-saving devices, and such taken-for-granted wonders as electric lighting, home computers, and indoor plumbing. However, these changes have produced other changes in society that have not been so beneficial; in fact, significant social disorganization has been created in the process.

Some of the disorganization associated with technological change occurs because of the tendency for **cultural lag** to occur: *a gap between the point at which one part of the social system changes and the point at which other parts adjust to compensate for that change* (Ogburn, 1957; Volti, 1992). So technological innovations arise and create problems before other technologies or social patterns emerge to deal with the problems. William F. Ogburn, who developed the notion of cultural lag in his studies of technological development, described an example of cultural lag in the early stages of industrialization in the United States. In the 1800s and early 1900s, factories were built with machinery with swiftly moving wheels and belts and other mechanical devices that were highly dangerous. Because industrial technology was so new and because laborers of the era had little political clout, little effort was devoted to safety in the workplace. As a consequence, there were many industrial accidents that killed or seriously maimed workers. At the time, employers

A Minnesota dairy farmer injects his cattle with a genetically engineered hormone to improve milk production. Discoveries in biogenetics will probably produce changes that are functional for society, but they will also create some social disorganization as changes in social practices lag behind changes in technology.

were typically not held liable for on-the-job accidents, and there was no unemployment compensation or welfare benefits. So the injury or death of workers often meant financial ruin for their families. The machinery made possible advances in production, but it also placed many people at risk of losing their financial resources and their ability to make a living. In short, there was a lag between the technology of production and the social policies designed to protect people from the negative consequences of the technology. Eventually, of course, workers' compensation and employer liability were established, and the cultural lag between technology and social policy was narrowed.

From the functionalist perspective, then, scientific and technological changes create problems because other parts of society do not adapt to those changes quickly enough to avoid problems for many people.

The Conflict Perspective

The conflict perspective is based on the idea that society consists of different groups that struggle with one another to attain the scarce societal resources that are considered valuable. Scientific information and resulting technology are among the more valuable resources today. Consider, for a moment, the number of interest groups in American society who share distinctive and joint concerns that involve science and technology. Just as one example, consider the corporations that are a part of the military–industrial complex that produces the vast array of our defense weapons (see Chapters 2 and 14). It is to their benefit to back the development of new and more sophisticated weapons technologies, such as the Stealth bomber or the Star Wars technologies, even if that is not the best overall military strategy for the United States. From the conflict perspective, then, scientific and technological development can exacerbate social problems when some groups use them to their own advantage and to the disadvantage of other groups. Although defense industries benefit from Star Wars spending, it may also increase the likelihood of violence around the world and contribute little to the reduction of poverty in the United States.

The conflict approach also helps us to see how powerful groups use science and technology for their mutual benefit. In Chapter 4, we spoke of the medical–industrial complex. The production of technologically sophisticated diagnostic and treatment tools such as linear accelerators and computerized axial tomography (CAT) is a multibillion dollar industry. Such devices help to save lives, and because life is so precious to Americans, most people are willing to pay the price when physicians order the complicated tests. The physicians benefit, the manufacturers of the equipment reap economic rewards, and the health insurance industry derives obvious financial gains as a consequence. In the meantime, the health-care consumers are forced to pay higher health insurance premiums, and products cost more because employers pass along the cost of employee health programs by raising the price of their products. In addition, the pursuit of these technological inventions may even work to the disadvantage of patients: People are hooked up to machines and their lives prolonged sometimes longer than they would wish. From the conflict perspective, then, science and technology do not necessarily benefit everyone, and in analyzing their effect on our lives we need to look closely at who benefits from particular technological developments and who does not, as well as what can be done to reduce the costs. Unlike the functionalist perspective, the conflict perspective assumes that there are always winners and losers when social change occurs.

The Interactionist Perspective

The interactionist perspective sensitizes us to the relativity of public attitudes toward science and technology. We learned in Chapter 1 that an important element of the interactionist perspective involves human beings' use of symbols. Recall that a symbol is something that stands for, represents, or takes the place of something else. As symbols, science and technology have taken on both very positive and very negative meanings. On the one hand, science is viewed very favorably as the source of much that is wonderful about our lives. Science, after all, gave us automobiles, modern medicine, and computers. Scientists are accorded high status in society, and scientific evidence is used by advertisers to convince us to buy their products. On the other hand, however, there is a theme in our culture that views science as mysterious, dangerous, and possibly even evil. This theme is probably best expressed in the science fiction or occult literature, such as Mary Shelley's *Frankenstein* or R. L. Stevenson's *The Strange Case of Dr. Jekyll and Mr. Hyde*. What comes through in these portrayals is the view that science, especially if it is unleashed, might become a raging, destructive, almost maniacal uncontrolled force. Once unleashed, the fear is that science would do things that threaten people's values. It is this more stigmatized side of science that is seen as causing social problems.

So this ambivalence toward science and technology leaves people unsure about what social expectations are appropriate in this realm. In a real sense, the meaning of science and technology in our culture is uncertain, and whether they are problems is a matter of great debate.

PROBLEMS OF SCIENCE AND TECHNOLOGY

The idea of technology as potentially dangerous and threatening is not new. Classical Greek mythology expressed some ambivalence toward technology: Prometheus stole fire from Olympus in defiance of the gods, and as punishment he was chained to a rock where an eagle tore at his body; Icarus tried to fly with wings made of wax and feathers, and he paid for such presumption with his life. During the Dark Ages, Europe was shrouded in mysticism for almost a thousand years, with religion on the rise and very little scientific or technological development to be found. In nineteenth-century England, rioting workers, called Luddites after the name of one of their leaders, smashed machines in factories in the futile belief that this would prevent the dislocations and unemployment that were accompanying industrialization in England.

Fear of technology, then, can probably be found wherever technology shapes people's lives. Yet many feel that the potential dangers of technology today are quantitatively greater than and possibly qualitatively different from what they were in the past. In this section, we will review some of the major problems that concern people today regarding scientific developments and the elaboration of technology.

Unemployment

For many, the fundamental fear of technology is that machines will replace people in the workplace:

> *As microelectronics takes over more and more control functions in manufacture, and information handling functions in administration, so human labour will become increasingly redundant. Clearly, if machinery becomes more efficient, the same amount of goods and services can be produced with a smaller input of labour. (Braun, 1984: 84)*

We saw in Chapter 2 that the labor force in America has been changing during the twentieth century. Early in this century, as agricultural employment dwindled, the surplus labor was taken over by mining, manufacturing, transportation, and services. More recently, with advances in technology, employment in areas such as mining and manufacturing has stopped growing and in some cases has begun to decline, and workers have shifted into the service sector. Yet technology has also made the service sector more efficient and less labor intensive. So there may be fewer or no economic sectors to absorb the surplus labor of the future. As robots replace factory workers, word processors replace secretaries and typists, and computer-assisted instruction replaces teachers, where will all of these people find work? Will unemployment become the norm and work the exception, at least among some social classes? In the 1950s and 1960s, the unemployment rate rarely crept above 5 percent and at times was below 3 percent. In the 1970s, the unemployment rate rarely went below 5 percent and sometimes went over 8 percent. In the 1980s, the rate rarely went below 7 percent and at times rose to 10 percent (see Figure 2.6 on page 58). In the past ten years, the unemployment rate for blacks has fluctuated between 12 and 19 percent. The unemployment rate for black teenagers has been as high as 50 percent! And it is those workers who are least able to acquire new skills or advance their education who will be most severely injured by changes in the occupational structure: the poor, nonwhites, the young, and women (Kletzer, 1991).

What some people fear, then, is that the unemployment rate is gradually creeping up because machines are taking the place of people (Volti, 1992). Not everyone agrees with this argument. Supporters of technological development argue that technology may create dislocations for some workers, who may have to move to a new city or state to find a job, but that it does not increase overall unemployment. Although technology ends some jobs, it also creates new ones. Robots, for example, replace factory workers, but they also create a robotics industry involving the design, construction, and maintenance of robots. So, this argument goes, technology does not reduce the total number of jobs, although it will require some workers to shift to new industries or obtain new skills as technology evolves (Zuboff, 1993).

The pessimists' rejoinder is that the jobs made available by the new technology are sometimes no better and are often worse than the jobs eliminated. Many jobs in the service sector, for example, are low paying, such as working in a fast-food restaurant or in an amusement park (Bluestone and Harrison, 1987; Serrin, 1989). Between 1963 and 1973, almost 50 percent of the new jobs created by our economy were high-wage jobs, whereas less than 20 percent paid poverty-level wages. Between 1979 and 1985, 44 percent of the new jobs created paid poverty-level wages, and only 10 percent were high-wage jobs. In fact, by the 1990s, more workers were stuck with low-paying jobs than had been the case a decade earlier (Zippay, 1991; U.S. Bureau of the Census, 1992a). In 1979, 12 percent of full-time workers in the United States had poverty-level incomes; throughout the 1980s, this figure rose steadily until it reached 18 percent in 1990. In the 1980s, many well-paid industrial workers were thrown out of work by plant closings, and they shifted to such low-wage jobs, often for wages that were one-third or less of what they had earned in manufacturing. Even many of the jobs created by the computer industry are dull, repetitive, and low paying. One such occupation is inputting information into a computerized data file. Insurance companies, for example, hire people—often women—to input insurance policy and claims information at video display terminals. The pay is low, the work is dull, and working at such terminals for long periods of time may cause health problems. Many such employees work at home on a piece-rate basis and are deprived of the benefits of unionization and company-supplied health and retirement benefits. So advances in technology may not be a boon for everyone. For those unable to acquire the skills or education necessary to get the better jobs in a postindustrial society, technological advances may result in continued unemployment or underemployment and more boring and low-paying jobs.

Alienation

Jobs in automated work settings are often boring, repetitive, and unfulfilling. Employees have little control over the pace of their work, what they produce, or what happens to it once it is produced. This type of work organization may be efficient and profitable for employers, but it can result in considerable discontent among employees. One consequence of working in such settings is **alienation,** *a feeling that you are powerless to control your surroundings and that what you do has little meaning or purpose* (Vallas, 1988; Greenberger et al., 1989).

Alienation is epidemic in some occupations, especially among unskilled blue-collar workers. Yet even among white-collar workers, less than half would stay in the same occupation if they had the opportunity to change, and job dissatisfaction may be on the increase (Quinn and Staines, 1977; Tausky, 1984). Blacks and people with less education are likely to experience greater declines in job satisfaction, but people in professional and managerial occupations are also affected. Modern work settings, filled with technological sophistication, tend to be depersonalized, and people lack control over what they do. Feeling the effects of automation, workers are likely to view themselves as mere cogs in the bureaucratic machinery.

Loss of Control

Some people fear that modern technology has become so unbelievably complex—in terms of both the mechanical and chemical principles that underlie it and the level of social organization necessary to keep it going—that it can take on a life of its own (Winner, 1977; Mazur, 1993). When this happens, the outcome may actually work counter to the interests and goals of those people the technology is supposed to benefit. A classic portrayal of this is the movie *2001,* in which a highly sophisticated computer named "Hal" runs virtually all the functions of a spaceship on a long voyage. When the human crew attempts to take over from the computer, Hal fights against and even kills some of the crew in the process. Although this is an extreme portrayal, it illustrates the notion of an "autonomous technology" that gets away from people's control. How can this happen? Do particular machines actually become tyrannically independent? The way this can happen is quite complex.

There is little question that people become highly dependent on technology. After all, technology is little more than a way of getting help to meet survival needs and put food on the table. This was true for the hunters and gatherers who used stone clubs to slay animals, and it is true for modern writers who use computers as word processors to make a living. But modern technology places us in a far more complex web of technological dependence in which machines do many more things for us, and our lives would be profoundly changed without them. Without computers, for example, we would be without such instruments for medical diagnoses as CAT scanners, Magnetic Resonance Imaging, and many others. Yet computers can have very negative consequences. People have been arrested because a computer misidentified them as a suspect in a crime; others have been unable to obtain credit because a computer record indicated, based on weak or false information, that they were poor credit risks.

Yet we are not really free to remove computers from some parts of our lives and not from other parts. Once the technology is introduced and people become dependent on it, there are social forces that cause it to grow as if it had a life of its own. One of these forces is the struggle by various interest groups to use technology to their own benefit. Technological developments that are detrimental to some may be quite beneficial to others. Nuclear power, for example, could be a boon to the power companies because it offers a way to generate power very inexpensively. At the same time, it works to the detriment of those who live in communities where nuclear waste dump sites are established. Ventilators that can help severely ill people breathe are beneficial to medical personnel as another tool that can help them fight disease and injury, but they can be a horror to a terminally ill person who wants to die but cannot convince physicians to turn off the machine. So with a large array of interest groups with competing goals and values, there are likely to be many groups who favor the development of a given technology even though it has a negative impact on other groups. This explains why, once a technology exists, there is strong pressure to use it and develop it further.

Another element contributing to the complexity of technology in our lives is that responsibility for decisions about the role of technology tends to be very diffuse. This means that individuals have little control over the impact new technologies will have on them personally. Computers, for example, first came on the scene because some large corporations and some scientists believed that these machines would increase efficiency and productivity. Over time and as the technology became more accessible, computers were introduced into other realms: Someone saw the potential for putting police records on the computer and others recognized that credit check companies could operate more efficiently with computers. Recently, an entrepreneur opened a computerized service for landlords that would enable them to learn whether prospective renters might be a "problem" because they had once sued a landlord or missed a rent payment. Physicians can tap into computerized files that will tell them if a patient has ever sued a physician for malpractice.

Computers can also have a detrimental effect on the workplace by becoming another mechanism through which supervisors can control and regulate the activities of those under them. More and more employees are being subjected to "computer-assisted productivity measurement." The activities of reservation clerks, for example, can be tracked by the computer, which can log how long they spend on each call, how much time is spent between calls doing paperwork, and how long they are away during lunch breaks. Any worker who inputs data at a video display terminal can be

Many people fear that machines, like these computers in a European computer center, will become so sophisticated and complex that the machines will run people's lives rather than the other way around. Significant control over one's destiny and daily life, especially for those without much economic or social clout, could be lost to such machines.

monitored in terms of how many keystrokes are made per minute, hour, or day. At one airline, data-entry clerks are expected to make nine thousand to sixteen thousand strokes on their computer keyboards per hour. The three fastest workers are used to set the pace, and all others are expected to achieve at least 75 percent of that speed. All of this can be logged continuously by computers, and those who fall short can be disciplined or dismissed (Shaiken, 1987). As many as twenty million workers may be under such computerized supervision. Mostly, they are female workers in the back offices of government agencies, airlines, insurance companies, mail-order houses, and telephone companies. They work in what some have

called an "electronic sweatshop," tied to a computer for many hours each day with extremely limited opportunities to go to the restroom or chat with fellow employees (Kilborn, 1990). Such electronic monitoring is not always disliked by employees, but it can be used to intimidate workers when supervisors manipulate the computer system to threaten people's jobs. It has also been accused of being unfair when it judges workers on the basis of the quantity of their work, which a computer is very good at assessing, rather than the quality of what they do.

Who is responsible for extending computers into these many realms? Who has control over this burgeoning technology? The autonomous technology viewpoint is that the responsibility is so diffuse that there is little control over it. These and related issues are discussed in the first Policy Issues insert.

Loss of Privacy

Modern technology opens the door for intrusions into people's lives in massive ways. With computers and telecommunications technology, it is possible to store vast amounts of information about people, access the information very quickly, and send the information anywhere on the globe almost instantaneously. Powerful information institutions, such as medical records bureaus and credit reporting companies, have emerged to gather this data wherever they can and then sell it to those willing to pay for it. The potential for abuse is tremendous (Rothfeder, 1992). For example, one man who was in good health and did not smoke or drink was told he would have to pay substantially higher than normal premiums for disability insurance because he was an alcoholic. After a long struggle to find the source of this inaccuracy that was bringing trouble into his life, he learned that the insurance company based its decision on information purchased from the largest company selling medical information in the United States. This company gathers scraps of information on people from a variety of sources—

POLICY ISSUES

Public Controversy Over Science and Technology: What People Object To

During the period of rapid economic growth that followed World War II, scientific and technological developments were defined as the province of "experts" and went largely unquestioned. The faith of many Americans in science seemed to be summarized in the 1950s motto of the General Electric Company: "Progress is our most important product." But as time went on, many technological "improvements" proved more harmful than beneficial, and this naive confidence in technological progress became tempered by the public's increasing awareness of the contradictions involved. However, science and technology are still regarded by most Americans as fundamental ingredients in achieving desirable social goals. Recent Harris polls reveal that 70 percent of Americans believe that science has changed our lives for the better (Nelkin, 1984). If there is such support for science and technology, what is the source of people's concerns?

Social scientist Dorothy Nelkin has analyzed the controversy over scientific and technological "progress" and senses an underlying theme in this social protest:

The protests may be less against science and technology than against the power relationships associated with them; less against specific technological decisions than against the declining capacity of citizens to shape policies that affect their interests; less against science than against the use of scientific rationality to mask political choices. (Nelkin, 1984: 11)

Professor Nelkin has identified four major areas of public concern over science and technology. First, public concern is generated when the citizens of a community determine that they have to pay for technological "improvements" that ultimately benefit a different or broader constituency than themselves. For example, corporate and other economic interest groups benefit from the construction of airports, power plants, and highways, but those who happen to live in proximity to these developments suffer the envi-

insurance applications, hospital records, physicians' records, and wherever else it can purchase it—and pulls all the data together to sell to anyone who requests it. It turned out that years before the man had attended meetings of Alcoholics Anonymous even though he did not drink at all because he wanted help in controlling another addiction he had: smoking. In an earlier life insurance application, the man had mentioned attending AA meetings and why. Although this person was finally able to rectify the difficulty, the case illus-

trates the dimensions of the problem. People often must spend considerable time and resources trying to identify and correct inaccurate information that is causing problems for them. Many times, the inaccuracies cannot be corrected or people are not even aware of the inaccuracies that are causing problems for them. It is impossible to know how many insurance applications are denied or jobs not gotten because of inaccurate information in a computer data base. Another problem is that these companies collect and syn-

ronmental and social consequences. Typically, decisions to implement such technological "improvements" are made on the basis of technical criteria and in the supposed interest of economic efficiency. But Nelkin points out that community protests call attention to basic issues of justice for all: "Can any reduction in some citizens' welfare be justified by greater advantages to others?"

A second source of concern is the public's fear of health and environmental hazards. When we consider how many warnings of "invisible risks" have been posted by scientific agencies over the past few decades, this fear is easy to understand. The Michigan Department of Natural Resources, for example, advises that no more than one pound of trout from Lake Michigan be consumed per person, per week because of PCB contamination. No sooner are sodium cyclamates reduced in foods and beverages because of a linkage to cancer, than new fears surface involving the effects on health of the artificial sweetener NutraSweet. These fears are compounded by the anxiety of not knowing how great the risks really are. For example, we saw in Chapter 13 how little is known about the effects of toxic wastes on our environment. The public is aware that they may be endangered, but do not have the necessary information to evaluate the potential for catastrophe.

A third category of public concern involves freedom of choice in the face of government regulation. For example, the drug Laetrile may or may not have therapeutic value in the treatment of cancer, but because of government mandate, the public is not free to choose this form of medication if it wishes. A number of states have passed mandatory seat belt laws, and there are rumblings at the federal level about mandatory air bags in automobiles. In these cases, the government makes social policy that the public may view as an infringement on its freedom of choice. Of course, the government uses the argument that these decisions are made because purely individual choices have broad ranging social costs, but some critics respond that this is overly paternalistic: The government is assuming that the public cannot make rational decisions on its own behalf and the government must protect people from their "irrationality."

Finally, according to Nelkin, public concern arises when scientific or technological "progress" is perceived by the public to challenge traditional values. The theory of human evolution, for example, continues to be controversial because it challenges some traditional religious beliefs, and some groups have protested against science education in the schools because it teaches their children things that they feel contradict religious or other values they are trying to pass on to their children. Should the government be able to mandate the teaching of evolution in our schools, or should parents have a choice in this policy matter? Should scientists have total "freedom of inquiry," or are there areas of research that should be "off limits"? Once again, as Nelkin points out, the main point of contention is a matter of *who makes social policy*.

thesize vast amounts of very intimate information about people without any federal regulation of their activities, and significant decisions are made about people's lives based on this information.

So millions of Americans are shortchanged or otherwise abused—often without realizing it—by large bureaucracies acting on inaccurate information bought from computerized data banks. These data banks also can get access to theoretically secure data bases, such as Internal Revenue Service tax returns, long-distance telephone records, credit card purchase records, and FBI criminal history summaries. Some people do not realize, for example, that credit card purchases establish a computer trail of a person's whereabouts, travels, and purchases—a permanent record of their lifestyle accessible to others in the future for whatever purpose. Computer records, such as the landlord service or the physician malpractice service just mentioned, make it difficult for people to hide or put behind them things that have occurred in their lives. Modern technology makes it more difficult to keep private the things you may not want others to know.

An increasing number of businesses and government bureaus are requiring that people take lie-detector tests to gain employment and to remain employed. Employers require this for security or to protect against theft. But for the employee or prospective employee, it means that even their very thoughts are less private. Those little lies that we might tell to put ourselves in the best possible light can be detected by the machine. In professional sports, the military, and some industries, there are mandatory urine checks to detect the use of drugs. The goal, of course, is a laudable one—to control the use of drugs on the job—but the impact is again an assault on a person's privacy and sense of personal integrity.

The technological developments of the past fifty years may have only scratched the surface of what is possible in terms of limitations on privacy. It may not be long before it will be possible to keep permanent records of everyone's activities so that their social lives, political beliefs, leisure pursuits, and idiosyncrasies are a matter of record available to anyone having access to this information. Every mistake, minor or major, that you make during your life will be recorded and you might be accountable for it throughout your life.

Should We Play God?
The Case of Genetic Engineering

Scientific developments of the twentieth century have produced some truly amazing things. We have harnessed nuclear fission and nuclear fusion; we have walked on the moon and discovered such things as quarks, muons, and black holes. Some critics have suggested that we are treading in some areas that we should not, areas that could produce disastrous consequences if matters get out of hand. One such area is **biotechnology:** *the use of organisms or cells to make products or carry out tasks* (Norman, 1981).

Biotechnology is based on a very important discovery: the identification in 1953 of the nature of deoxyribonucleic acid, or DNA, as the basic genetic material that is found in each cell and contains the "blueprint" for the completed organism. DNA has been mapped and catalogued with great precision. By manipulating DNA, scientists have been able to create organisms that perform new tasks or that produce substances they would not normally produce. This is called **genetic engineering,** or *manipulating the genes of organisms to alter the organisms' characteristics in ways that would not have occurred naturally*. One way of doing this is **recombinant DNA** or **gene splicing** in which *some DNA from one organism is spliced into the genetic material of another organism to produce some new characteristics in the host or even a novel form of life*. Gene splicing has been used, for example, to produce large quantities of insulin and interferon, used in the treatment of diabetes and cancer, respectively. This is done by introducing human genes that govern the natural production of insulin or interferon into a bacterium that is then induced by this new genetic material to produce insulin or interferon. Insulin and interferon are expensive to produce by conventional means, and their genetically engineered counterparts are expected to play an important role in medicine in the future. In addition to medicine, biotechnology is also expected to have an impact on such areas as agriculture, forestry, energy, and chemical feedstocks. The establishment of genetic engineering as a commercially feasible activity seems to have been settled in 1980 when a company called Genentech became the first genetic engineering firm to offer stock to the public. It remains one of the top biotechnology companies in the world ("Genentech's Style," 1988).

What problems do such advances create? One problem relates to potentially unpredictable consequences of genetic engineering. Releasing genetically altered microorganisms into the environment could create unforeseen and very hazardous consequences. After all, genetic modifications in nature occur very slowly over many thousands of generations of a species. With such a timespan, existing flora and fauna are able to gradually adapt to new developments. Genetic engineering, however, enables us to make substantial genetic changes in a very short period of time. And, unlike many other forms of environmental pollution, biological pollutants reproduce themselves and are much more difficult to remove from the ecosystem. In fact, some scientists in the 1970s called for a halt to gene splicing experiments because of such fears. Despite these concerns, the National Academy of Sciences in 1989 concluded that field testing of genetically modified plants and microorganisms would not pose a hazard to the environment if done carefully ("Panel Finds No Risk . . . ," 1989).

Other problems with biotechnology crop up when consideration is given to applying the technology to human beings. Today, parents can learn before birth whether their offspring will have certain genetic defects. This gives them the option of having an abortion rather than giving birth to defective children. In the future, parents may be able to alter their own genetic traits or in other ways determine the genetic characteristics of their children. Scientists have already succeeded in making clones, or multiple genetic replicas of a parent organism. It may be only a matter of time before cloning is possible among humans. These technologies offer people the capability to shape their characteristics in ways never before possible. Such advances not only offer the opportunity to stamp out certain diseases, they also open the door to eliminating characteristics deemed socially undesirable by those in positions of power. The Nazis engaged in some notorious experiments during World War II in efforts to create a "master race." More recently, suggestions have been made along similar lines in the United States. William Shockley, an engineer who became interested in genetic engineering, has argued forcefully that people of low intelligence constitute a "dysgenic threat" to our populace because they reduce the average intelligence of society (Shockley, 1980). His solution is to encourage people with low intelligence—or anyone with genetic defects deemed detrimental to society—to be sterilized. This might be done by providing a financial incentive to such people to undergo voluntary sterilization. Along similar lines, a sperm bank has been established that will accept donations only from Nobel laureates with the idea that such genetically "superior" sperm should be given as wide distribution as possible. Other proposals have been made to redesign the human stomach so that people can live on cheap hay and grass or to make a hybridized cross between human beings and lower primates (Howard and Rifkin, 1977).

Although efforts along these lines in the United States today are quite sporadic and disorganized, there is no reason to believe that some organization or government of the future might not institute such measures in an organized and widespread fashion (Duster, 1990). A government might pass legislation making it illegal for people with certain characteristics to have children. Or genetic engineering might be used to enhance certain human characteristics and downplay others. One way this might work was proposed in an article published by the National Aeronautics and Space Administration: Each person would be sterilized at birth and some of his or her genetic material preserved. After the person dies, a committee would review his or her life to see what accomplishments had been achieved or what problems were created by the person. If the person had lived a worthy life, the committee would permit a new individual to be cloned from his or her genetic material. If the person proved unworthy, his or her genetic material would be destroyed (Howard and Rifkin, 1977). It might even become fashionable to have one's genes spliced so as to enhance aggressiveness or passivity, strength or frailty, obesity or lithesomeness—whatever characteristics were fashionable at a given time.

The point is that the genetic traits of the human race have been determined thus far by impersonal evolutionary forces that operate over eons and are largely unaffected by cultural values, religious beliefs, or political or economic ideology. Biotechnology may make it possible to

Biotechnology Raises the Issue: Whose Life Is It, Anyway?

Biotechnology poses some awesome challenges for the future. With recombinant DNA techniques, it is now possible for human beings to *create* life forms—new species or variants on old species—that do not occur in nature. Du Pont did this in 1988 when it produced a mouse, called "onco-mouse," that was genetically engineered to be unusually susceptible to cancer. The year before, the Patent and Trademark Office (PTO) of the United States government had ruled that a particular oyster was patentable subject matter. The PTO also said that it would henceforth consider patenting all forms of life on earth, including non-naturally occurring, nonhuman multicellular living organisms. Du Pont received the patent to on-comouse in 1988 (U.S. Congress, Office of Technology Assessment, 1989).

To explore the implications of these developments, consider the legal ramifications of patents. When the government grants a patent over some thing, product, or process, those holding the patent have the exclusive right to make, use, license, or sell it. In other words, the person legally "owns" the commodity, at least for a period of time, and others cannot use it without permission. When on-comouse was patented, Du Pont became the owner of that species, that particular life form.

One of the major reasons for patenting something, including a life form, is to encourage creativity, innovativeness, and entrepreneurship. If there is a market for something that has been patented,

only the patent holder may legally sell it and the parties involved stand to make a considerable profit. This potential gain is what encourages an inventor or scientist to go through the time and effort of developing something new and to seek patent rights. Patents offer a distinct financial advantage in the form of a temporary monopoly over a market. The government does this explicitly to encourage American business and science to be creative and competitive. When biotechnology made possible the creation of new life forms, the Patent Office treated this in the same way as it would have if the commodity had been a new drug discovered by a pharmaceutical company or a new widget invented by a scientist. Without patents, the argument goes, there would be less incentive for entrepreneurship in the field of biotechnology, and the nation's biotechnology industry would be less competitive in the international marketplace.

The PTO ruling has generated a firestorm of controversy that raises some practical and very fundamental philosophical issues. One observer of technological trends, Jeremy Rifkin, president of the Foundation on Economic Trends, sees the ruling as symbolic of a profound transition in social and economic organization:

In economic terms, the Patent Office decision signals the beginning of a long-term transition out of the age of fossil fuels and petrochemi-

change all of this in the near future. It might be possible to create people with certain characteristics or tailor people to certain jobs. Some people might be gene spliced for ferocity and made into soldiers, whereas others would be gene spliced

to show little initiative and curiosity and made into assembly-line workers. If there were some objective and sure way of determining which characteristics are beneficial to society, then biotechnological capabilities might not be so fear-

cals and into the age of biological resources. The world economy is shifting from industrial technologies to biotechnologies, and the Patent Office decision provides the necessary government guarantee that the raw materials of the biotechnology age—that is, all living things on the planet—can now be exploited for commercial gain by chemical, pharmaceutical, and biotechnology companies. (Rifkin, 1987: 2)

Rifkin believes that corporations will now rush to patent as many life forms as they can. The struggle among corporate giants will be to control the planet's gene pool, so to speak, patenting everything that lives and breathes. Because it is large and powerful corporations that have the resources to patent life forms, this affords them yet another mechanism to concentrate power in their own hands. In agriculture, this has already happened as chemical companies have gained increasing control over newly developed seeds and plants. Rifkin believes this will now extend into animal husbandry. In the past, anyone could purchase a herd of cattle if they had the financial resources. Today, only Du Pont can own oncomouse (not just this particular mouse, but any mouse with the same genetic characteristics), and this may be true of increasing numbers of animals in the future.

These practical, economic implications of the Patent Office's decision are important, but there are also some more fundamental, philosophical issues regarding the nature and meaning of life on earth. In its ruling, the Patent Office argued that life could be considered a "manufacture or composition of matter." When biotechnology cre-

ates a new life form by implanting a foreign gene into an animal's genetic code, the resulting animal is merely a human invention—no different than a toaster, a golf ball, or a tie tack, according to the Patent Office ruling. The danger, some argue, is that it promotes a *materialist* conception of life: the notion that life consists only of a particular arrangement of physical matter, with no spiritual or transcendent significance. Of course, many people—both religious and nonreligious—believe that life is more than an arrangement of atoms and molecules; that life involves a measure of dignity, respect, and maybe even awe. Yet the Patent Office has ruled that life is simply a "composition of matter." As a result, Rifkin (1991) argues, the line between animate life and inanimate matter has become considerably weaker.

If animal life is merely materialist, then what about human life? What about the sanctity of human worth? Is life merely an economic commodity that can be bought and sold in the marketplace? According to the Patent Office, human genetic traits, if implanted in the genes of another life form, are patentable (a "composition of matter"). However, there are constitutional safeguards that protect humans from being patented. But in a time when some patented animals are carrying human genetic materials, is the line between humans and other animals as clear as it once was? If a scientist were to change the genetic structure of a human being, might some future Patent Office ruling make it possible to put a patent on that "composition of matter"? We cannot currently answer many of these questions, but what is clear is that the technology is speeding us toward a point at which we may have to come up with an answer.

some. But there is no single set of characteristics that benefits society. And, as the conflict perspective makes us aware, not all groups benefit from the same social practices and policies. Genetic engineering that benefits one group may well work to the disadvantage of others. Biotechnology, then, could become a tool for the more powerful

groups in society to exercise domination over the less powerful.

With biotechnology, human beings are beginning to tinker with the very foundations of life.

It is now a matter of a handful of years before biologists will be able to irreversibly change the evo-

lutionary wisdom of billions of years with the creation of new plants, new animals, and new forms of human and posthuman beings. (Howard and Rifkin, 1977: 8)

Should we play "god"? We may be doing it to an extent already, as the second Policy Issues insert illustrates. When considering this, the word *hubris* comes to mind, deriving from the Greek and meaning insolence. We use the word to mean excessive self-confidence or arrogance. The Greeks used it to mean the presumption of human beings that they could act like the gods. The fear of some is that we may be showing hubris by moving into biotechnological realms that might be best left alone. The Greeks used the term *nemesis* to refer to the divine punishment visited upon humans who had presumed to invade the realms reserved for the gods. Critics of biotechnology fear that we will confront a nemesis in some as yet unknown form if we invade the biotechnological frontier without great patience and caution.

FUTURE PROSPECTS

What does the future hold regarding technology and the problems it creates? A few would opt for fleeing from complex technology altogether and seeking a simpler way of life that does not depend on elaborate technological innovations. In the 1960s and 1970s, a loose collection of groups advocating something like this was referred to as the "back-to-the-earth" movement. These groups favored the rejection of most technology and promoted a simple and self-sufficient life-style. Many of them organized themselves communally, with common ownership of many goods. The groups were often based on equality and participatory democracy, with little hierarchy and few rules and regulations. They subsisted by growing their own food and avoided the use of large farm equipment and chemical fertilizers and pesticides that are routine on most American farms. They harvested

by hand, built their own tools, and educated their children at home. Their goal was subsistence and simplicity, not profit making, economic growth, or material comfort.

Whether the back-to-the-earth movement succeeded is a matter of debate. There are many people still leading such a life-style, although how many is difficult to know. Yet it clearly has appeal for some Americans even in the 1990s. However, if such a life-style were adopted on a widespread scale, it would probably represent a step backward that few would want to take. Without agricultural technology, we would not be able to produce nearly the amount of food that we do and many people would be condemned to a life of illness, starvation, and poverty. We need modern technology to help us cope with the waste products of a large population, and without that technology disease would undoubtedly spread. So a mass rejection of modern technology is neither feasible nor likely. At the same time, technology is not about to go away or mutate into some clearly benign creature. The technological cat is out of the bag, so to speak, and unlikely to go back in. The problem, then, is how to live with and control the negative consequences of technology. Much of the debate on this issue revolves around whether controlling technology should be accomplished without significant government intervention—the laissez-faire position—or whether the government should be a major decision maker in that arena—the interventionist approach. We will discuss a number of policy positions that advocate some elements of the laissez-faire or interventionist points of view.

Legal Protections

Some of the problems of modern technology are created or made worse because our legal and political systems have not been able to keep up with the changing nature of the problems that emerging technologies create. New technologies often develop in a legal void where there is little legislative direction as to what is acceptable. This is true of the massive invasions of privacy made possible by modern computer technology. In this realm, a number of suggestions have been made that would help protect people from technological intrusions (Rothfeder, 1992). One would be to pass laws that truly safeguard the confidentiality of medical, bank, telephone, computer, and other records. A second would be to establish a data protection board whose job it would be to search out and challenge the validity and legality of questionable corporate or government data bases, such as those that include speculative, inaccurate, or unverified data. A third thing that would go a long way to protect people's privacy is to require companies that sell credit reports, marketing services, or medical records to others to pay a royalty to a person each time they sold that person's name. This would discourage the widespread sale of information and limit it to sales that are important or essential. At the same time, it would let people know who is selling information about them and to whom it is sold.

These legal protections provided by the government would help significantly in alleviating the problems of a loss of privacy and loss of control. Interventionists would also see a significant role for the government in protecting people who might be hurt by particular technological developments. Those, for example, who find themselves intimidated or oppressed by workplace computers should be able to turn to the government for protection against the unfair uses of these technologies. Issues relating to workplace justice were discussed in Chapter 2.

Appropriate Technology

One proposed solution to deal with many of the problems associated with modern technology is to develop what has been called **appropriate technology,** or *a technology appropriate to the human scale, to what people can comprehend and relate to; it would be a technology that is limited in size, decentralized, and responsive to human values and needs.* In most cases, an appropriate technology would

be considerably smaller than what exists today. In fact, one of the early proponents of such a technology, E. F. Schumacher, wrote a book titled *Small is Beautiful.* An appropriate technology would avoid the tendency of technology to alienate people, and it would return control to the hands of individuals (Sale, 1980). An example of an appropriate technology is solar energy, which we discussed in Chapter 13. Solar energy does not require the building of large centralized power plants such as nuclear and coal-fired facilities. The technology is decentralized, with each household or community producing some of its own energy rather than having energy production controlled by large corporations. People understand how energy is produced and participate in producing it, giving them a sense of control and comprehension. They may even be able to repair solar energy equipment themselves if something goes wrong. Appropriate technology is also less injurious or damaging, and the damage it does cause is smaller in scale. Solar energy, for example, does not cause the air pollution of coal-fired energy plants or the contamination hazard of nuclear power production.

Few would argue that large-scale technology can or should be completely eliminated. Centralized power plants, for example, are helpful where solar, wind, or geothermal energy cannot fully meet a community's needs. In addition, large-scale technology is often the discovery ground for developing new alternative technologies. But advocates of appropriate technology do argue for a shift in values, emphasizing a smaller, human scale where possible over large, impersonal, centralized technologies. What they call for is not a rejection of technology but rather a rejection of some of the forms of social organization that we create to make use of the technology: the bigness, the bureaucracy, the centralization, and the impersonality. To achieve this may require a change in our life-style. We might, for example, rethink our energy needs and develop a life-style that can be largely satisfied with alternative energy sources. As an illustration, we might design communities so that bicycles are more feasible than cars as means of transportation. The bicycle would be an appropriate technology in that it is small in scale, comprehensible by most people, and relatively nondamaging. Some communities have tried to encourage bicycle use by closing off some streets to vehicular traffic or establishing bicycle lanes. The point is that proponents of appropriate technology have an ideology that, like the "back-to-the-earth" people, values a simpler and to some extent more self-sufficient way of life. They do not, however, accept the "back-to-the-earth" rejection of technology; in fact, they embrace technology in its simpler and more human forms.

Appropriate technologists have been criticized for being impractical utopians who do not understand how essential large-scale, centralized technology is to American society. Some of their solutions, these critics argue, although small and decentralized, do not really solve any problems. Wood-burning stoves, for example, have been touted as an alternative energy source, but we now recognize that they contribute to air pollution. The appropriate technologists defend themselves by arguing that most people have a set of blinders on that enables them to see only the expansion of large-scale organization as the solution to our problems, even though there is little evidence that "large is better." In other words, we have become so accustomed to large-scale growth that we have developed cultural myopia: We can no longer see or accept small-scale technology as a solution to a problem, even when it might be an effective solution.

This debate over appropriate technology will continue in the future, and it revolves to an extent around the laissez-faire versus interventionist controversy. Many advocates of appropriate technology argue that the government can play a role in its development. Through tax write-offs and other policies, the government can make it more attractive to develop appropriate technology. In fact, this has been done over the past decade by some states and the federal government by allowing people to deduct from their taxes some of the costs of installing solar or wind energy. The government has also discouraged the development of nuclear power (although that was not its original intention) by requiring costly safety procedures at nuclear power plants.

Technology Assessment

Technology assessment refers to *research that studies the impact of technology on our physical, social, and ethical environments and seeks solutions to social problems that arise from technological development.* Technology assessment is intended to detect problems that might be created by technology before the technology has been established. It uses extensive studies to forecast the effects of technological developments before they are implemented. This puts us in a position either to alleviate the negative impact or to decide that the negatives outweigh the benefits of the technology and leave the technology unimplemented. The National Environmental Policy Act of 1969, discussed in Chapter 13, included provisions for the assessment of any environmental impact due to new technology implemented by agencies or legislation of the federal government. Today, any public or private project that requires funds from or the permission of any branch of government must prepare an Environmental Impact Statement. In 1973, the Office of Technology Assessment was established to provide Congress with information about the impact of technology that it could use in its deliberations (Braun, 1984).

When an Environmental Impact Statement must be prepared in order to initiate a project, the research is typically funded by the government or the organization wishing to initiate the project. This sort of technology assessment, however, typically has a very short time perspective: What is the likelihood that this nuclear power plant will develop a radiation leak? How many patients will survive a trial of fifty artificial heart implants? These questions address the consequences of a particular application of a technology. However, there are broader issues regarding the wisdom of developing a particular technology at all: Should society stress centralized power production, such as nuclear power, or decentralized power production, such as solar and wind energy? Should societal resources be spent on further technological improvements in crisis medicine (such as coronary bypass surgery) or on preventive medicine (such as programs to reduce cigarette smoking)? These broader assessment issues are often much more difficult to research, more speculative and value oriented in nature, and less likely to receive financial support. Especially in recent years, research on these general issues of technology assessment has had to compete for funding with other sorts of research, and the amount of money available for all research has been dwindling. With less of such research conducted in the future, we may be less prepared to cope with the consequences of technology.

Futurology

At the opposite extreme from the "back-to-the-earth" advocates are people who enthusiastically embrace technological development and advocate the active pursuit of technological innovation. These people argue that we should devote resources to studying ways in which we can achieve the maximum incorporation of technology into society with the minimum costs. In fact, a field of study has emerged called "futurology," which has attracted scholars and researchers from the natural sciences, social sciences, engineering, and business. Most of these people tend to be very optimistic about the future and about the role of science and technology in shaping the future. Many futurists envision the United States developing into a postindustrial society whose foundation will be information, communication, and knowledge (Beniger, 1993). Science will play an ever more important role as it serves as a foundation for technological development and change. The findings of the social sciences will be increasingly used to establish the most effective ways of organizing and managing people and solving social problems such as crime and violence. The people with expertise in managing information and knowledge—scientists, technicians, information specialists, and educators—will develop into a distinct class with special privileges and rewards. With rapid technological change occurring, culture and social life will also have to adapt, or at least the negative impacts on people's lives will have to be alleviated. For example, the skills necessary in the occupational realm will likely change a few times during a person's life. This means that people will require periodic reeducation to keep current and competitive in their jobs. Educational institutions will have to change by viewing education as a lifelong process rather than as a product that is accomplished by young adulthood.

Not all futurists agree on these issues. Some, for example, believe that nuclear power will usher in an era of unheard-of wealth and comfort, whereas others argue that problems inherent in generating nuclear power necessarily make it a limited source of power in the future. Some futurists are very enthusiastic about the role of the government in planning the direction of technological and social change of the future; others believe that the government should stand aside and let the economic marketplace—competition and profit making—determine the best way to maximize the utility of technology and minimize its negative impact. Despite their disagreements, however, futurists tend to be very positive about our technological future and to advocate a very activist approach toward technological change.

Linkages

Science and technology can help alleviate some problems, such as finding new ways to clean up the environment (Chapter 13) or providing new remedies for disease (Chapter 4). However, they can also intensify the same problems by, for example, elaborating the range of our polluting technologies or making it possible to prolong life even when people might prefer to die.

Summary

1. Technology refers to knowledge, tools, and practices that are employed as means of achieving clearly identifiable goals and can be both material and nonmaterial in nature. Most societies have undergone modernization, and many have become industrialized. The most modern societies are moving into a postindustrial stage and are dominated by highly technological forms of production and are devoting greater resources to providing services than to industrial production.

2. Important elements in the process of industrialization are mechanization and automation. In postindustrial societies, computers often control the machines that produce goods and services, including information.

3. Nuclear power has been utilized for both destructive and productive purposes. The most destructive are reflected in the use of atomic energy as an instrument of warfare. The most potentially productive use of nuclear power is its promise as an energy source. The environmental dangers posed by the generation of nuclear energy are becoming more clear and ever more ominous with the passing of time.

4. From the functionalist perspective, problems surrounding science and technology have to do with the social disorganization that results when some parts of society do not adapt sufficiently fast to changes that are occurring. For the conflict perspective, the problems have to do with the fact that some groups can use scientific and technological developments to their advantage whereas other groups are hurt by them. The interactionist perspective suggests that attitudes toward science and technology are relative to a person's social circumstances and historical position.

5. The idea of technology as potentially dangerous and threatening is not new. Fear of technology can probably be found wherever technology shapes people's lives. Some of the major problems that concern people today regarding scientific developments and the elaboration of technology are unemployment, alienation, loss of control due to extreme dependency on technology, loss of privacy, genetic engineering, and cultural lag.

6. Regarding the future of technology, some would opt for fleeing from technology and attempting to find a simpler way of life. But technology is with us now and unlikely to just disappear. The problem involves how we should live with and control the negative consequences of technology. One proposed solution to deal with the problems associated with technology is to develop legal protections to reduce the loss of privacy and other negative consequences that people might suffer. Another proposed solution is called appropriate technology, involving imposed limitations on technological matters so that they are responsive to human values and needs. Technology assessment refers to research that studies the various impacts of technology and seeks solutions to problems that arise from technological developments. Futurologists try to monitor the role of science and technology in shaping the future.

Important Terms for Review

alienation	biotechnology	industrialization	recombinant DNA
appropriate	cultural lag	mechanization	technology
technology	gene splicing	modernization	technology
automation	genetic engineering	postindustrial society	assessment

Discussion Questions

1. In this chapter, we define technology as knowledge, tools, and practices that are employed as means of achieving clearly identifiable goals. Make a list of some of this knowledge and some of these tools and practices, along with related goals. Describe how this technology has affected your life in both positive and negative ways.

2. What are some of the effects of mechanization and automation on our society? How have they affected your life in particular? Give examples.

3. Discuss the social implications of computers in our society. How has computerization affected your experiences as a college student?

4. Based on our discussion in this chapter, what do you think will be the future of nuclear power? Consider both the positive and negative implications. What are they?

5. Unemployment, alienation, loss of control, loss of privacy, genetic engineering, and cultural change are among the problems associated with our advancing technology. Give a specific example of each problem as it exists at your college and discuss the implications.

6. Much has been written in the field of futurology during the past two decades. As we note in this chapter, most futurists are optimistic about science's and technology's impact on our future. How do you react to these forecasts? What do you think are the pros and cons of technology in America's future?

7. Are there any examples of the use of "appropriate technology" on your college campus or in your town? What additional "appropriate technology" can you envision being incorporated into those locations?

For Further Reading

David Burnham. *The Rise of the Computer State.* New York: Random House, 1983. This is one of the best general assessments of the ways in which computers can create problems in people's lives and what to do about it.

John Elkington. *The Gene Factory: Inside the Genetic and Biotechnology Business Revolution.* New York: Carroll and Graf Publishers, 1985. The author writes that genetic engineering has already opened a twentieth-century Pandora's box but believes that the risk involved is well worth taking. Elkington explores the potential rewards of biotechnology, pointing out that it is fast becoming a very big business.

Neil A. Holtzman. *Proceed With Caution: Predicting Genetic Risks in the Recombinant DNA Era.* Baltimore: Johns Hopkins University Press, 1989. The book focuses especially on genetic testing and some of the dangers that it could create. The author tries to show how we can cut the risk of misuse of such technologies.

Robert Howard. *Brave New Workplace.* New York: Elisabeth Sifton Books/Viking, 1985. This book is a critique of the belief that meaningful work for all will be ushered in by the technology of the future. Howard illustrates the many problems that will persist in the workplace of the future.

Kenneth Laudon. *Dossier Society: Value Choices in the Design of National Information Systems.* New York: Columbia University Press, 1986. This is an analysis of the problems created by the massive amounts of information that are collected on people in modern societies. The author suggests some important policy approaches for controlling the negative impacts of this.

John Naisbitt. *Megatrends: Ten New Directions Transforming Our Lives.* New York: Warner Books, 1982. This is a thought-provoking book by a very optimistic futurist. Naisbitt analyzes the ten "megatrends" that he sees shaping what our society will be like in the future.

Dorothy Nelkin and Laurence Tancredi. *Dangerous Diagnostics: The Social Power of Biological Information.* New York: Basic Books, 1989. This is a disturbing book about our increasingly sophisticated ability to do genetic screening and how this can produce dangerous opportunities for the stigmatization, discrimination, and marginalization of those deemed genetically "defective" by those who control the testing.

Charles Piller. *The Fail-Safe Society: Community Defiance and the End of American Technological Optimism.* New York: Basic Books, 1991. This book argues that Americans have lost their faith in the beneficence of science and technology and have become more resistant to scientific and technological change. The author argues that this may actually have some positive outcomes.

Neil Postman. *Technopoly: The Surrender of Culture to Technology.* New York: Knopf, 1992. This book contains a strong and controversial criticism of what technology is doing to modern society. The author especially focuses on how technology can change cultural values and even demean the importance we place on human beings.

Jeremy Rifkin. *Biosphere Politics: A New Consciousness for a New Century.* New York: Crown, 1991. The author argues that our uses of science and technology have gotten out of hand and threaten our way of life precisely because they have divorced human life itself from the natural world. He proposes a new and certainly controversial "consciousness" regarding how human beings should orient toward their world.

Alvin Toffler. *The Third Wave.* New York: Bantam Books, 1980. In this book, well-known futurist and author of *Future Shock,* Alvin Toffler, discusses the information and service revolution in American society, which he calls the Third Wave.

Sherry Turkle. *The Second Self: Computers and the Human Spirit.* New York: Simon and Schuster, 1984. A very readable book on how computers affect our psychological development, how we think, and how we think about ourselves. In the view of this author, the computer is not just a machine to help us achieve our goals but something that changes us in the process.

Glossary

Absolute definition of poverty A definition of poverty based on a fixed economic level below which people are considered poor; this level does not necessarily change as society on the whole becomes more or less affluent.

Acute disease Disease with a fairly quick and sometimes dramatic and incapacitating onset and from which a person either dies or recovers.

Ageism An ideology or set of beliefs holding that people in a particular age group are inferior, have negative attributes, and can be dominated and exploited because of their age.

Age structure The distribution of people into various age categories in society.

Alcoholism The consumption of alcohol at a level that produces serious personal, social, or health consequences, such as marital problems, occupational difficulties, accidents, or arrests.

Alienation A feeling of powerlessness in regard to controlling one's surroundings and the feeling that what one does has little meaning or purpose.

Androgyny The view that there should be a blending of the traits and roles of both sexes; people should express themselves as human beings rather than in traditionally masculine or feminine ways.

Anomie Inconsistencies that arise when people are taught to strive for certain goals but are not provided with the culturally approved means necessary to attain those goals.

Anomie theory The theory stating that people in our society are taught to strive for certain goals but are not always provided with the culturally approved means necessary to attain these goals.

Appropriate technology A technology appropriate to the human scale, to what people can comprehend and relate to; a technology that is limited in size, decentralized, and responsive to human values and needs.

Assimilation The process by which a racial or ethnic minority loses its distinctive identity and way of life and becomes absorbed into the dominant group.

Authoritarian personality A constellation of personality characteristics including a rigid adherence to conventional life-styles and values, admiration of power and toughness in interpersonal relationships, submission to authority, cynicism, an emphasis on obedience, and a fear of things that are different.

Authority Legitimate power that is obeyed because people believe it is right and proper that they obey.

Automation The automatically controlled operation of machines by mechanical or electronic devices.

Balance of power A foreign policy based on the idea that a nuclear holocaust can be avoided if the military power of one side roughly balances that of the other side.

Bioethics The study of ethical questions that relate to the life and biological well-being of people.

Biotechnology The use of organisms or cells to make products or carry out tasks.

Blended family A family based on kinship ties that accumulate as a consequence of divorce and remarriage.

Capitalism An economic system in which the means of economic production and distribution are privately held; the profit motive is the primary force guiding people's economic behavior; and there is free competition among both producers and consumers of goods.

Career deviance See Secondary deviance.

561

Causality   One factor has an effect on or produces a change in some other factor.

Chronic disease   Disease that progresses over a long period of time and often exists long before it is detected.

City   A relatively large, permanent community of people who rely on surrounding agricultural communities for their food supply.

Civil disorder   Strife or conflict that is threatening to the public order and that involves the government in some fashion, either as a party to the conflict or as a guardian of the public interest.

Cohabitation   Relationships in which two people live in the same household and share sexual, emotional, and often economic ties but are not legally married.

Commodity riots   Race riots in which the focus of hostility is property, merchandise, or equipment rather than people of another racial group.

Communal riots   Race riots in which whites attack blacks in racially contested areas.

Communism   The term used by Marx to describe the end stage of the struggle over capitalism; a system in which all goods would be communally owned; people would not work for wages but would give according to their abilities; and there would be no scarcity of goods and services, allowing people to receive whatever they needed; in addition, the state would become less important and its role would dwindle.

Community   A group of people who share a common territory and a sense of identity or belonging and who interact with one another.

Conflict perspective   The sociological perspective centered on the idea that society consists of different groups who struggle with one another to attain the scarce societal resources that are considered valuable, be they money, power, prestige, or cherished values.

Corporation   A business enterprise that is owned by stockholders, many of whom are not involved in running the daily affairs of the business.

Crime   An act that violates a criminal code enacted by an officially constituted political authority.

Crisis medicine   Medical treatment that focuses on treating people's illnesses after they become ill.

Cross-dependence   A situation in which the withdrawal symptoms of one drug are alleviated by another drug in the same pharmacological class.

Cross-tolerance   A situation in which a tolerance built up to one drug leads to a reduced response to another drug in the same pharmacological class.

Cultural analysis of poverty   A focus on the values, attitudes, and psychological orientations that may emerge among groups of people who live under conditions of poverty.

Cultural definition of poverty   A definition of poverty that views it not only in terms of how many resources people have but also in terms of why they have failed to achieve a higher economic level.

Cultural lag   The tendency for there to be a gap between the point at which one part of the social system changes and the point at which other parts adjust to compensate for that change.

Cultural transmission theories   The theories that posit that crime and delinquency are learned and culturally transmitted through socialization.

Curative medicine   See Crisis medicine.

Definition of the situation   A person's perception and interpretation of the total configuration of social factors operating at a given time and what behavior is called for.

Deindustrialization   A situation characterized by high rates of unemployment in the industrial sector, an aging and deterioration of factories and other productive resources, and an alleged inability to compete with other industrial nations.

Demographic gap   The gap between the high birthrates and low death rates that results in explosive population growth during the early industrial period of the demographic transition.

Demographic transition   The changing patterns of birth and death rates brought about by industrialization.

Demography   The study of the size, composition, and distribution of human populations and how these factors change over time.

Dependence   A mental or physical craving for a drug and withdrawal symptoms when use of the drug is stopped.

Dependency ratio   A statistic that shows the relative size of the group in our society that is economically dependent for support on others who are working.

Depersonalization Feelings of detachment from people and social groups that give life meaning and provide a sense of importance and self-worth.

Depressants Psychoactive drugs that depress the central nervous system and have some analgesic, or pain-killing, properties.

Deviance Behaviors or characteristics that violate important group norms and as a consequence are reacted to with social disapproval.

Differential association theory The theory that posits that crime and delinquency are learned in interaction with other people, for the most part within intimate primary groups such as families and peer groups.

Discrimination The unequal treatment of people because they are members of a particular group.

Drug Any substance that, when consumed, alters one or more of the functions of the human body.

Drug abuse The continued use of a psychoactive substance at a level that violates approved social practices.

Drug addiction Physical dependence on a drug.

Dual-career family A family in which both wife and husband are committed to career-oriented occupations that offer them fulfillment and opportunities for advancement.

Economics The social processes through which goods and services are produced and distributed.

Ecosystem A complex, interrelated network of life forms and nonlife forms that interact with one another to produce an exchange of materials between the living and the nonliving parts.

Egalitarian family A family in which power and authority are shared somewhat equally by husband and wife.

Environment The conditions and circumstances surrounding and affecting a particular group of living creatures.

Ethnic group A people who share a common historical and cultural heritage and sense of group identity and belongingness.

Ethnocentrism The tendency to view one's own culture or subculture as the best and to judge other cultures or subcultures in comparison to it.

Expressive tasks Activities focused on the relationships between people and on maintaining happiness, harmony, and emotional stability in a group.

Extended family A family involving three or more generations of people who live together or in close proximity and whose lives and livelihoods are closely intertwined.

Family A social institution based on kinship that functions to replace members of society and to nurture them.

Fecundity The biological maximum number of children that could be born in a society.

Fertility The actual number of children born in a society.

Frustration An inability to achieve sought-after goals.

Full employment A situation in which everyone or nearly everyone who wants to work can find a job.

Functionalist perspective The sociological perspective based on the idea that society is a system made up of a number of interrelated and interdependent elements, each performing a function that contributes to the operation of the whole.

Gemeinschaft Social life that is governed by personal, informal considerations, with tradition and custom prevailing.

Gender Learned behavior involving how we are expected to act as males and females in society.

Gene splicing See Recombinant DNA.

Genetic engineering Manipulating the genes of organisms to alter the organisms' characteristics in ways that would not have occurred naturally.

Gentrification The return of young, affluent professionals to neighborhoods in cities where they often rehabilitate previously rundown housing.

Gerontology The scientific study of aging.

Gesellschaft Social relations characterized by specialization, individualism, impersonality, and rationality.

Ghetto A neighborhood inhabited largely by members of a single ethnic or racial group.

Hallucinogens Psychoactive drugs that produce hallucinations, often of a visual nature.

Health maintenance organization (HMO) An organization that agrees to provide for all of a person's health-care needs for a fixed, periodic premium.

Homophobia An intense dislike of or prejudice against homosexuals.

Homosexuality   Sexual feelings, fantasies, or acts directed toward members of the same sex.

Hydrologic cycle   The processes by which nature purifies water.

Hypotheses   Tentative statements that can be tested regarding relationships between two or more factors.

Industrialization   A productive subsistence pattern in which machines and power tools run by new sources of energy, such as fossil fuels, accomplish tasks that were previously done by hand.

In-group   A group that we feel positively toward, identify with, and that produces a "we feeling."

Institutionalized discrimination   The inequitable treatment of a group resulting from practices or policies that are incorporated into social, political, or economic institutions and that operate independently from the prejudices of individuals.

Instrumental tasks   The goal-oriented activities of a group, such as hunting, building something, or managing a work team.

Insurrection   An organized action by some group to rebel against the existing government and to replace it with new political forms and leadership.

Interactionist perspective   The sociological perspective that focuses on everyday social interaction among individuals rather than on large societal structures such as politics, education, and the like.

Interest group   A group whose members share distinct and common concerns and who benefit from similar social policies and practices.

Internal colonialism   A type of exploitation in which a subordinate group provides cheap labor that benefits the dominant group and who then is further exploited by having to purchase expensive goods and services from the dominant group.

Labeling theory   The theory based on the idea that whether other people define or label a person as deviant is a critical determinant in the development of a pattern of deviant behavior.

Lesbianism   Female homosexuality.

Life course   A succession of statuses and roles that people in a particular society experience in a fairly predictable pattern as they grow older.

Life span   See Life course.

Massive retaliation   A foreign policy based on the idea that war could be avoided if the enemy realized that any aggressor against the United States would suffer overwhelming damages from massive retaliation with American military might.

Mechanization   The use of machinery to replace human and animal labor in the production of goods and services.

Medicaid   A joint federal-state program to provide medical care for low-income people of any age.

Medical–industrial complex   A coincidence of interests between physicians and other health-care providers and the industries producing health-care goods and services, with both parties profiting from the increased use of these commodities and the health-care consumer paying enormous costs for inadequate care.

Medicare   Government health insurance for those over sixty-five years of age.

Migration   A permanent change of residence.

Military–industrial complex   The relationship between the military that wants to purchase weapons and the corporations that produce the weapons. Both the military and the corporations benefit from a large military budget and policies favoring military solutions to international problems.

Minority group   A group whose members are viewed by dominant groups as inferior, who have less access to power and resources than do other groups, and who are accorded fewer rights, privileges, and opportunities.

Mixed economies   Economic systems in which there are strong elements of both capitalism and socialism.

Modernization   The economic, social, and cultural changes that occur when a preindustrial society makes the transition to an advanced industrial society.

Modified extended family   Families in which elaborate networks of visitation and support are found even though each nuclear unit lives separately.

Monogamy   Family systems in which people have only one spouse at a time.

Mortality   The number of deaths that occur in a particular population.

Mutually assured destruction   A foreign policy based on the idea that war can be prevented when each side has the might to destroy the other.

Narcotics   Psychoactive drugs whose main use is as analgesics or painkillers.

Norms   Rules of conduct that guide people's behavior.

Nuclear family A family consisting of a married couple and their children.

Oligarchy The tendency for power to become concentrated in the hands of a few people at the top of an organization.

Opiates See Narcotics.

Patriarchy A family in which males dominate in the regulation of political and economic decision making, whereas women and children are subordinate.

Pluralism A situation in which a number of racial and ethnic groups live side by side, each retaining a distinct identity and life-style while still participating in some aspects of the larger culture.

Pluralistic family A family system in which a number of different types of family exist side by side, each having an attraction for some segment of the populace.

Pluralist model The view of power in America as being spread over a large number of groups with divergent values, interests, and goals.

Politics The agreements in society over who has the right to exercise control over others, who can establish laws to regulate social life, and the manner in which conflicting interests in society will be resolved.

Polygamy Having more than one spouse at the same time.

Population The total number of people inhabiting a particular geographic area at a specified time.

Pornography Sexually "explicit" writings, still or motion pictures, and similar products designed to be sexually arousing.

Postindustrial society A society that is dominated by a highly technological form of production and that devotes greater resources to providing services than to industrial production.

Poverty The uneven distribution of the resources available.

Power The ability of one group to realize its will, even in the face of resistance from other groups.

Power elite model The view of power in America that says that there exists a small group of very powerful people who make just about all of the important decisions in the United States.

Prejudice A negative attitude toward certain people based solely on their membership in a particular group.

Preventive medicine Changes in life-style or other steps that help avoid the occurrence of disease.

Primary deviance The violation of social norms in which the violator is not labeled as a deviant.

Primary groups Small groups based on personal, intimate, and nonspecialized relationships.

Primary prevention Preventing drug problems before they begin.

Prostitution Sexual activity in exchange for money or goods, in which the primary motivation for the prostitute is neither sexual nor affectional.

Psychedelics See Hallucinogens.

Psychoactive drugs Drugs that can produce major alterations in the mood, emotions, perceptions, or brain functioning of the person who takes them.

Public assistance Social programs for which a person must pass a "means" test in order to be eligible.

Race A group of people who are believed to be a biological group sharing genetically transmitted traits that are defined as important.

Racism The view that certain racial or ethnic groups are biologically inferior and that practices involving their domination and exploitation are therefore justified.

Recidivism The repeat of an offense after having been convicted of a crime.

Recombinant DNA The practice in which DNA from one organism is spliced into the genetic material of another organism to produce some new characteristics in the host or even a novel form of life.

Refined divorce rate The divorce rate that is determined by dividing the number of divorces each year by the total number of existing marriages (or married women over age fifteen) in that year.

Relative definition of poverty The definition of poverty based on the idea that people are poor relative to some standard, and that standard is partially shaped by the life-styles of other citizens.

Relative deprivation The idea that people tend to feel deprived or frustrated in comparison to what others have or what they believe they deserve.

Research The systematic examination of empirical data.

Sample Elements that are taken from a group or population and that serve as a source of data.

Science   A method of obtaining objective and systematic knowledge through empirical observation.

Secondary deviance   Behavior that a person adopts in reaction to being labeled as a deviant.

Secondary groups   Groups in which people have few emotional bonds, ties are impersonal, and people are seeking to achieve specific, practical goals.

Secularization   The process through which the influence of religion is removed from many institutions in society and dispersed into private and personal realms.

Serial monogamy   A family system in which people are allowed to have more than one spouse, but not at the same time.

Sex   The biological role that each of us plays in reproduction.

Sick role   A set of expectations intended to guide the behavior of people who are ill.

Social institutions   Relatively stable clusters of social relationships that involve people working together to meet some basic needs of society.

Social insurance   Social programs offering benefits to broad categories of people, such as the elderly or injured workers, who presumably were working and paying for the insurance before becoming eligible for it.

Socialism   Economic systems in which the means of production and distribution are collectively held so that the goods and services that people need are provided and equitably distributed.

Social mobility   The movement of people from one social position to another in the stratification hierarchy.

Social movement   A collective, organized effort to promote or resist social change through some noninstitutionalized or unconventional means.

Social policy   Laws, administrative procedures, and other formal and informal social practices that are intended to promote social changes focused on alleviating particular social problems.

Social problem   A social condition is a social problem when an influential group defines it as threatening its values, when the condition affects a large number of people, and when it can be remedied by collective action.

Social stratification   The ranking of people into a hierarchy in which the resources considered valuable by society are unequally distributed.

Sociobiology   A field of study based on the idea that the genetic makeup of human beings plays a powerful role in shaping their social behavior.

Sociology   The scientific study of societies and human social behavior.

Split labor market   A situation in which there are two groups of workers willing to do the same work, but for different wages.

Stimulants   Psychoactive drugs whose major effect is to stimulate the central nervous system.

Structural unemployment   A predictable condition of unemployment resulting from changes in the occupational structure of society.

Subculture   A group within a culture that shares some of the beliefs, values, and norms of the larger culture as well as some that are distinctly its own.

Subculture of violence   Norms and values that condone and legitimize the use of violence in resolving conflicts.

Suburb   A less densely populated area, primarily residential in nature, on the outskirts of a city.

Technology   Knowledge, tools, and practices that are employed as means of achieving clearly identifiable goals.

Technology assessment   Research that studies the impact of technology on our physical, social, and ethical environments and seeks solutions to social problems that arise from technological development.

Terrorism   The attempt to achieve political goals by using fear and intimidation to disrupt the normal operations of a society.

Theoretical perspectives   General views of society that provide some fundamental assumptions about the nature and operation of society and commonly serve as sources of the more specific theories.

Theory   A set of statements that explains the relationship between phenomena.

Third-party medicine   A health-care payment scheme in which the patient pays a premium into a fund and the doctor or hospital is paid from this fund for each treatment provided to the patient.

Tolerance   Physical changes that result in the need for higher and higher doses of a drug to achieve the same effect.

Urban homesteading Programs to increase home ownership by private citizens in certain neighborhoods by selling them houses at little or no cost.

Values People's ideas about what is good or bad, right or wrong.

Violence Behavior that is intended to bring pain or physical injury to another person or to harm or destroy property.

Zero population growth A situation in which birth and death rates are nearly equal, producing a zero rate of natural increase.

Bibliography

Abel, Emily K. 1991. *Who Cares for the Elderly? Public Policy and the Experiences of Adult Daughters.* Philadelphia: Temple University Press.

Abel, Ernest L. 1982. *A Marihuana Dictionary: Words, Terms, Events, and Persons Relating to Cannibis.* Westport, Conn.: Greenwood Press.

Abel, Ernest L. 1984. *A Dictionary of Drug Abuse Terms and Terminology.* Westport, Conn.: Greenwood Press.

Acuna, Roldolfo. 1987. *Occupied America: A History of Chicanos.* 3d ed. New York: Harper and Row.

Adam, Heribert, and Kogila Moodley. 1987. *South Africa Without Apartheid: Dismantling Racial Domination.* Berkeley: University of California Press.

Adams, Carolyn Teich. 1986. "Homelessness in the Postindustrial City: Views from London and Philadelphia." *Urban Affairs Quarterly,* 21: 527–549.

Adelman, Clifford. 1991. *Women at Thirtysomething: Paradoxes of Attainment.* Washington, D.C.: U.S. Department of Education.

Adorno, T. W., Else Frenkel-Brunswik, Daniel J. Levinson, and R. Nevitt Sanford. 1950. *The Authoritarian Personality.* New York: Harper and Row.

Agnew, Robert. 1991. "A Longitudinal Test of Social Control Theory and Delinquency." *Journal of Research in Crime and Delinquency,* 28 (May): 126–156.

Ahrons, Constance, and Roy Rodgers. 1987. *Divorced Families: A Multidisciplinary View.* New York: W. W. Norton.

Albanese, Jay. 1989. *Organized Crime in America.* 2d ed. Cincinnati: Anderson.

Aldrich, Mark, and Robert Buchele. 1986. *The Economics of Comparable Worth.* Cambridge, Mass.: Ballinger Publishing Co.

Allan, Emilie Andersen, and Darrell J. Steffensmeier. 1989. "Youth Underemployment, and Property Crime: Differential Effects of Job Availability and Job Quality on Juvenile and Young Adult Arrest Rates." *American Sociological Review,* 54 (February): 107–123.

Alperovitz, Gar, and Jeff Faux. 1984. *Rebuilding America.* New York: Pantheon Books.

Amato, Paul R. 1987. "Family Processes in One-Parent, Stepparent, and Intact Families: The Child's Point of View." *Journal of Marriage and the Family,* 49 (May): 327–337.

Ambert, A. 1986. "On Being a Stepparent: Live-In and Visiting Children." *Journal of Marriage and the Family,* 49: 795–804.

American Psychiatric Association. 1987. *Diagnostic and Statistical Manual of Mental Disorders.* 3d ed., rev. Washington, D.C.: American Psychiatric Association.

Andrews, D. A., Ivan Zinger, Robert D. Hoge, James Bonta, Paul Gendreau, and Francis T. Cullen. 1990. "Does Correctional Treatment Work? A Clinically Relevant and Psychologically Informed Meta-Analysis." *Criminology,* 28 (August): 369–404.

Aniline, O., et al. 1980. "The Urban Epidemic of Phencyclidine Use: Laboratory Evidence from a Public Psychiatric Hospital Inpatient Service." *Biological Psychiatry,* 15: 813–817.

Anstett, Patricia. 1992. "U.S. Consumers Pay for Health Care Ills." *Detroit Free Press,* June 23: 1.

Antonovsky, Aaron. 1972. "Social Class, Life Expectancy, and Overall Mortality." In E. Gartly Jaco (ed.), *Patients, Physicians, and Illness.* 2d ed. New York: Free Press.

Archer, Dane, and Rosemary Gartner. 1976. "Violent Acts and Violent Times: A Comparative Approach to Postwar Homicide Rates." *American Sociological Review,* 41: 937–963.

Ardrey, Robert. 1967. *The Territorial Imperative.* New York: Atheneum.

Aries, Elizabeth. 1985. "Male–Female Interpersonal Styles in All Male, All Female, and Mixed Groups." In Alice G. Sargent (ed.), *Beyond Sex Roles.* 2d ed. St. Paul, Minn.: West Publishing Company.

Aries, Phillippe. 1962. *Centuries of Childhood.* Trans. by R. Baldick. New York: Random House.

Armor, David J. 1989. "After Busing: Education and Choice." *The Public Interest,* 95 (Spring): 24–37.

Armor, David J. 1991. "Response to Carr and Zeigler's 'White Flight and White Return in Norfolk.'" *Sociology of Education,* 64 (April): 134–139.

Association of American Colleges. 1982. *The Classroom Climate: A Chilly One for Women?* Washington, D.C.: Project on the Status and Education of Women.

Atchley, Robert C. 1991. *Social Forces and Aging: An Introduction to Social Gerontology.* 6th ed. Belmont, Calif.: Wadsworth.

Auerbach, Judith D. 1990. "Employer-Supported Child Care as a Women-Responsive Policy." *Journal of Family Issues,* 11 (December): 384–400.

Axinn, June, and Mark J. Stern. 1990. "Social Security Policy Reconsidered." *Challenge* (July/August): 22–27.

Bacalski-Martinez, R. R. 1979. "Aspects of Mexican American Cultural Heritage." In A. Trejo (ed.), *The Chicanos: As We See Ourselves.* Tucson: University of Arizona Press.

Bachman, Jerald G., Lloyd D. Johnston, and Patrick M. O'Malley. 1990. "Explaining the Recent Decline in Cocaine Use Among Young Adults: Further Evidence That Perceived Risks and Disapproval Lead to Reduced Drug Use." *Journal of Health and Social Behavior,* 31 (June): 173–184

Bachman, Ronet. 1992. *Death and Violence on the Reservation: Homicide, Family Violence, and Suicide in American Indian Populations.* New York: Auburn House.

Baden, J., et al. 1979. "Myths, Admonitions and Rationality: The American Indian as a Resource Manager." *Professional Papers in Political Economy and Natural Resources.* Bozeman: Montana State University.

Bagdikian, Ben H. 1990. *The Media Monopoly.* 3d ed. Boston: Beacon Press.

Bahr, Stephen J. 1989. *Family Interaction.* New York: Macmillan.

Bailey, J. Michael, and Richard C. Pillard. 1991. "A Genetic Study of Male Sexual Orientation." *Archives of General Psychiatry,* 48 (December): 1089–1096.

Bailey, Kathleen C. 1991. *Doomsday Weapons in the Hands of Many: The Arms Control Challenge of the '90s.* Urbana and Chicago: University of Illinois Press.

Bailey, William C. 1974. "Murder and the Death Penalty." *Journal of Criminal Law and Criminology,* 65: 416–423.

Bailey, William C. 1990. "Murder, Capital Punishment, and Television: Execution Publicity and Homicide Rates." *American Sociological Review,* 55 (October): 628–633.

Balling, Jr., Robert C. 1992. *The Heated Debate: Greenhouse Predictions Versus Climate Reality.* San Francisco: Pacific Research Institute for Public Policy.

Ball-Rokeach, Sandra J. 1973. "Values and Violence: A Test of the Subculture of Violence Hypothesis." *American Sociological Review,* 38: 736–749.

Bandura, Albert. 1976. "Social Learning Analysis of Aggression." In Emilio Ribes-Inesta and Albert Bandura (eds.), *Analysis of Delinquency and Aggression.* New York: John Wiley and Sons.

Banfield, Edward C. 1990. *The Unheavenly City Revisited.* Prospect Heights, Ill.: Waveland Press.

Barnet, Richard J., and Ronald E. Müller. 1974. *Global Reach: The Power of the Multinational Corporations.* New York: Simon and Schuster.

Baron, James M., and Andrew E. Newman. 1990. "For What It's Worth: Organizations, Occupations, and the Value of Work Done By Women and Nonwhites." *American Sociological Review,* 55 (April): 155–175.

Baron, Larry. 1990. "Pornography and Gender Equality: An Empirical Analysis." *Journal of Sex Research*, 27 (August): 363–380.

Barrett, Katherine, and Richard Greene. 1991. "American Cities: A Special Report." *Financial World*, February 19: 20–37.

Barron, James. 1989. "Unnecessary Surgery." *The New York Times Magazine*, Part II, April 16: 25, 44–46.

Barth, Fredrik (ed.). 1969. *Ethnic Groups and Boundaries*. Boston: Little, Brown.

Baum, A., and G. Davis. 1976. "Spatial and Social Aspects of Crowding Perception." *Environment and Behavior*, 8: 527–544.

Baumgartner, Alice. 1983. "'My Daddy Might Have Loved Me': Student Perceptions of Differences Between Being Male and Being Female." Paper published by the Institute for Equality in Education, Denver.

Beauregard, R. A. 1990. "Trajectories of Neighborhood Change: The Case of Gentrification." *Environment and Planning*, 22: 855–874.

Becker, Howard S. 1963. *Outsiders: Studies in the Sociology of Deviance*. New York: Free Press.

Bedau, Hugo A. 1967. *The Death Penalty in America*. Rev. ed. New York: Doubleday Anchor Books.

Beeghley, Leonard. 1984. "Illusion and Reality in the Measurement of Poverty." *Social Problems*, 31: 322–333.

Belknap, Joanne. 1989. "The Economics–Crime Link." *Criminal Justice Abstracts* (March): 140–157.

Bell, Alan P., and Martin S. Weinberg. 1978. *Homosexualities: A Study of Diversity Among Men and Women*. New York: Simon and Schuster.

Bell, Alan P., Martin S. Weinberg, and Sue Kiefer Hammersmith. 1981. *Sexual Preference: Its Development in Men and Women*. Bloomington: Indiana University Press.

Bell, Daniel. 1973. *The Coming of Post Industrial Society*. New York: Basic Books.

Bell, R. L., S. E. Cleveland, P. G. Hanson, and W. E. O'Connell. 1969. "Small Group Dialogue and Discussion: An Approach to Police–Community Relationships." *Journal of Criminal Law, Criminology, and Police Science*, 60: 242–246.

Belsky, Jay. 1984. *The Child in the Family*. Reading, Mass.: Addison-Wesley.

Belsky, J., and L. D. Steinberg. 1978. "The Effects of Day Care: A Critical Review." *Child Development*, 49: 929–949.

Bendick, Marc Jr., and David W. Rasmussen. 1986. "Enterprise Zones and Inner-City Economic Revitalization." In George E. Peterson and Carol W. Lewis (eds.), *Reagan and the Cities*. Washington, D.C.: Urban Institute Press.

Beniger, James R. 1993. "The Control Revolution." In Albert H. Teich (ed.), *Technology and the Future*. 6th ed. New York: St. Martin's Press.

Benjamin, Daniel K., and Robert Leroy Miller. 1991. *Undoing Drugs: Beyond Legalization*. New York: Basic Books.

Benokraitis, Nijole V., and Joe R. Feagin. 1986. *Modern Sexism: Blatant, Subtle and Covert Discrimination*. Englewood Cliffs, N.J.: Prentice-Hall.

Bequele, Assefa, and Jo Boyden. 1988. "Working Children: Current Trends and Policy Responses." *International Labour Review*, 127: 153–172.

Berger, Peter L. 1963. *Invitation to Sociology: A Humanistic Perspective*. Garden City, N.Y.: Anchor Books.

Berkowitz, Leonard. 1971. "The Study of Urban Violence: Some Implications of Laboratory Studies of Frustration and Aggression." In James Chowning Davies (ed.), *When Men Revolt and Why*. New York: Free Press.

Berliner, David. 1988. "Math Teaching May Favor Boys Over Girls." *Education Digest*, 53 (January): 29.

Berrill, Kevin T. 1990. "Anti-Gay Violence and Victimization in the United States." *Journal of Interpersonal Violence*, 5 (September): 274–294.

Besancon, Robert M. (ed.). 1966. *The Encyclopedia of Physics*. New York: Reinhold Publishing Company.

Besharov, Douglas J. 1992. "A New Start for Head Start." *The American Enterprise*, 3 (March/April): 52–57.

Best, Raphaela. 1983. *We've All Got Scars: What Boys and Girls Learn in Elementary School*. Bloomington: Indiana University Press.

Betz, Michael, Kemp Davis, and Patrick Miller. 1978. "Scarcity, Income Advantage, and Mobility:

More Evidence on the Functional Theory of Stratification." *The Sociological Quarterly,* 19: 399–413.

Betz, Michael, and Lenahan O'Connell. 1983. "Changing Doctor–Patient Relationships and the Rise in Concern for Accountability." *Social Problems,* 31: 84–95.

Bieber, Irving, et al. 1962. *Homosexuality.* New York: Basic Books.

Bishop, Donna M., and Charles E. Frazier. 1984. "The Effects of Gender on Charge Reduction." *Sociological Quarterly,* 25 (Summer): 385–396.

Bivins, Larry. 1992. "Bush Drug War Doesn't Cover the Battlefield." *Detroit Free Press,* September 19: 1.

Black, Francis L. 1978. "Infectious Diseases in Primitive Societies." In Michael H. Logan and Edward E. Hunt, Jr. (eds.), *Health and the Human Condition.* North Scituate, Mass.: Duxbury Press.

Blalock, Hubert M. Jr. 1982. *Race and Ethnic Relations.* Englewood Cliffs, N.J.: Prentice-Hall.

Blau, Joel. 1992. *The Visible Poor: Homelessness in the United States.* New York: Oxford University Press.

Blea, Irene I. 1991. *La Chicana and the Intersection of Race, Class and Gender.* New York: Praeger.

Blinder, Alan S. (ed.). 1990. *Paying for Productivity: A Look at the Evidence.* Washington, D.C.: Brookings Institution.

Bluestone, Barry, and Bennett Harrison. 1987. "The Grim Truth About the Job 'Miracle.'" *New York Times,* February 1: Sec. 3, 3.

Blum, Kenneth, and James E. Payne. 1991. *Alcohol and the Addictive Brain.* New York: Free Press.

Blum, Linda M. 1991. *Between Feminism and Labor: The Significance of the Comparable Worth Movement.* Berkeley: University of California Press.

Blum, Robert W., Brian Harmon, Linda Harris, Lois Bergeisen, and Michael D. Resnick. 1992. "American Indian–Alaska Native Youth Health." *Journal of the American Medical Association,* 267 (March 25): 1637–1644.

Blumer, Herbert. 1962. "Society as Symbolic Interaction." In Arnold M. Rose (ed.), *Human Behavior and Social Processes.* Boston: Houghton Mifflin.

Blumer, Herbert. 1971. "Social Problems as Collective Behavior." *Social Problems,* 18: 298–306.

Blumstein, Philip, and Pepper Schwartz. 1983. *American Couples.* New York: William Morrow.

Boffey, Philip M., William J. Broad, Leslie H. Gelb, Charles Mohr, and Holcomb B. Noble. 1988. *Claiming the Heavens: The New York Times Complete Guide to the Star Wars Debate.* New York: Times Books (Random House).

Bohanon, Cecil. 1991. "The Economic Correlates of Homelessness in Sixty Cities." *Social Science Quarterly,* 72 (December): 817–825.

Boivin, Michael. 1985. "The Truly Forgotten Warrior." Cited in "Imprisoned Vietnam Vets Seek Therapy." *Detroit Free Press,* November 18: E-1, 2.

Bonacich, Edna. 1972. "A Theory of Ethnic Antagonism: The Split-Labor Market." *American Sociological Review,* 37: 547–559.

Bookchin, Murray. 1990. *Remaking Society: Pathways to a Green Future.* Boston: South End Press.

Borgstrom, S., et al. 1983. "Effects of a Nuclear War on Health and Health Services." World Health Organization, Publication A36.12.

Boswell, Terry E. 1986. "A Split Labor Market Analysis of Discrimination Against Chinese Immigrants, 1850–1882." *American Sociological Review,* 51: 352–371.

Botvin, Gilbert J. 1990. "Substance Abuse Prevention: Theory, Practice, and Effectiveness." In Michael Tonry and James Q. Wilson (eds.), *Drugs and Crime.* Chicago: University of Chicago Press.

Boulding, Kenneth E. 1989. *Three Faces of Power.* Newbury Park, Calif.: Sage Publications.

Bouvier, Leon F. 1984. "Planet Earth 1984–2034: A Demographic Vision." *Population Bulletin,* 39, whole No. 1 (February).

Bowles, Samuel, David M. Gordon, and Thomas E. Weisskopf. 1992. "An Economic Strategy for Progressives." *The Nation,* February 10: 145, 163–165.

Braddock, Jomills H. 1985. "School Desegregation and Black Assimilation." *Journal of Social Issues,* 41: 9–22.

Braddock, Jomills H., Robert L. Crain, and James M. McPartland. 1984. "A Long-term View of Desegregation: Some Recent Studies of Graduates As Adults." *Phi Delta Kappan,* 66: 259–264.

Braun, Ernst. 1984. *Wayward Technology.* Westport, Conn.: Greenwood Press.

Brehm, Sharon S. 1985. *Intimate Relationships.* New York: Random House.

"The Brethren's First Sister." 1981. *Time,* July 20: 8–19.

Brewer, M. B., and N. Miller. 1988. "Contact and Cooperation: When Do They Work?" In Phyllis A. Katz and Dalmas A. Taylor (eds.), *Eliminating Racism: Profiles in Controversy.* New York: Plenum.

Brimelow, Peter, and Leslie Spencer. 1990. "Ralph Nader, Inc." *Forbes,* September 17: 117–129.

Brinkley, Joel. 1984. "Rampant Drug Abuse Brings Call for Move Against Source Nations." *New York Times,* September 9: 1.

Britton, Dana M. 1990. "Homophobia and Homosociality: An Analysis of Boundary Maintenance." *The Sociological Quarterly,* 31, No. 3: 423–439.

Broad, William J. 1987. "Economic Collapse Tied to Atom War." *New York Times,* June 21: 1, 18.

Brody, Baruch A., and H. Tristram Engelhardt, Jr. 1987. *Bioethics: Readings and Cases.* Englewood Cliffs, N.J.: Prentice-Hall.

Brooks, Robin. 1969. "Domestic Violence and America's Wars: A Historical Interpretation." In Hugh Davis Graham and Ted Robert Gurr (eds.), *Violence in America.* New York: Bantam Books.

Brostoff, Steven. 1992. "Medical Malpractice Claims Fuel Health Care Cost Boom." *National Underwriter,* 96 (January 13): 2.

Brown, Judith. 1970. "A Note on the Division of Labor by Sex." *American Anthropologist,* 72: 1073–1078.

Brown, Lester R. 1987. "Analyzing the Demographic Gap." In Lester R. Brown et al. (eds.). *State of the World, 1987: A Worldwatch Institute Report on Progress Toward a Sustainable Society.* New York: W. W. Norton.

Brown, Lester R. 1992. "Launching the Environmental Revolution." In Lester R. Brown et al. (eds.), *State of the World, 1992: A Worldwatch Institute Report on Progress Toward a Sustainable Society.* New York: W. W. Norton.

Brown, Lester R., Christopher Flavin, and Sandra Postel. 1991. *Saving the Planet: How to Shape an Environmentally Sustainable Global Economy.* New York: W. W. Norton.

Brown, Lester R., and Edward C. Wolf. 1986. "Assessing Ecological Decline." In Lester R. Brown et al. (eds.), *State of the World, 1986: A Worldwatch Institute Report on Progress Toward a Sustainable Society.* New York: W. W. Norton.

Brown, Phil. 1985. *The Transfer of Care: Psychiatric Deinstitutionalization and Its Aftermath.* London: Routledge and Kegan Paul.

Brown, Richard Maxwell. 1969. "Historical Patterns of Violence in America." In Hugh Davis Graham and Ted Robert Gurr (eds.), *Violence in America.* New York: Bantam Books.

Brownmiller, Susan. 1975. *Against Our Will: Men, Women and Rape.* New York: Simon and Schuster.

Brozan, Nadine. 1984. "Task Force Calls for Action to Control Family Violence." *New York Times,* September 20: 14.

Brozan, Nadine. 1985. "U.S. Leads Industrialized Nations in Teen-Age Births and Abortions." *New York Times,* March 13: 1.

Bruno, Mary. 1985. "Abusing the Elderly." *Newsweek,* September 23: 75–76.

Brus, Wlodzimierz, and Kazimierz Laski. 1989. *From Marx to the Market: Socialism in Search of an Economic System.* Oxford: Clarendon Press.

Bryan, James H. 1965. "Apprenticeships in Prostitution." *Social Problems,* 12 (Winter): 287–296.

Bryan, James H. 1966. "Occupational Ideologies and Individual Attitudes of Call Girls." *Social Problems,* 13 (Spring): 441–449.

Bullock, Charles S. III, James E. Anderson, and David W. Brady. 1983. *Public Policy in the Eighties.* Monterey, Calif.: Brooks-Cole.

Bullough, Vern L. 1976. *Sexual Variance in Society and History.* New York: John Wiley and Sons.

Bunzel, John H. 1991. "Black and White at Stanford." *The Public Interest,* No. 105 (Fall): 61–77.

Burby, Raymond J., and William M. Rohe. 1990. "Providing for the Housing Needs of the Elderly." *Journal of the American Planning Association,* 56 (Summer): 324–340.

Bureau of Justice Statistics. 1989. "Recidivism of Prisoners Released in 1983." Washington, D.C.: U.S. Department of Justice.

Burke, John G., and Marshall C. Eakin (eds.). 1979. *Technology and Change*. San Francisco: Boyd and Fraser.

Burke, Melvin. 1991. "Bolivia: The Politics of Cocaine." *Current History,* 90 (February): 65–68.

Burtless, Gary. 1989. "The Effect of Reform on Employment, Earnings, and Income." In Phoebe Cottingham and David Ellwood (eds.), *Welfare Policy for the 1990s.* Cambridge, Mass.: Harvard University Press.

Butler, Stuart M. 1984. "Free Zones in the Inner City." In Richard D. Bingham and John P. Blair (eds.), *Urban Economic Development*. Beverly Hills, Calif.: Sage Publications.

Butterfield, Fox. 1992. "Are American Jails Becoming Shelters From the Storm?" *New York Times,* July 19: Sec. 4, 4.

Button, James W. 1978. *Black Violence: Political Impact of the 1960s Riots*. Princeton, N.J.: Princeton University Press.

Califano, Joseph A., Jr. 1986. *America's Health Care Revolution: Who Lives? Who Dies? Who Pays?* New York: Random House.

Calleo, David P. 1992. *The Bankrupting of America: How the Federal Budget Is Impoverishing the Nation.* New York: William Morrow.

Callies, David, and Gail Tamashiro. 1983. "Enterprise Zones: The Redevelopment Sweepstakes Begins." *The Urban Lawyer,* 15 (Winter): 232.

Campagna, Daniel S., and Donald L. Poffenberger. 1988. *The Sexual Trafficking in Children: An Investigation of the Child Sex Trade.* Dover, Mass.: Auburn House.

Campbell, Carole A. 1991. "Prostitution, AIDS, and Preventive Health Behavior." *Social Science and Medicine,* 32: 1367–1378.

Cannon, Carl M. 1992. "Big Donors Find Cash Talks." *Detroit Free Press,* May 22: 1.

Caplan, Gerald M. 1984. "The Facts of Life About Teenage Prostitution." *Crime and Delinquency,* 30 No. 1 (January): 69–74.

Caplan, Nathan S., and Jeffrey M. Paige. 1968. "A Study of Ghetto Rioters." *Scientific American* (August): 15–21.

Caraley, Demetrios. 1992. "Washington Abandons the Cities." *Political Science Quarterly,* 107: 1–30.

Cargan, Leonard, and Matthew Melko. 1982. *Singles: Myths and Realities*. Beverly Hills, Calif.: Sage Publications.

Caringella-Macdonald, Susan. 1990. "State Crises and the Crackdown on Crime Under Reagan." *Contemporary Crises,* 14: 91–118.

Carr, Leslie G., and Donald J. Zeigler. 1990. "White Flight and White Return in Norfolk: A Test of Predictions." *Sociology of Education,* 63 (October): 272–282.

Cavender, Gray. 1991. "Alternative Theory: Labeling and Critical Perspectives." In Joseph F. Sheley (ed.), *Criminology: A Contemporary Handbook*. Belmont, Calif.: Wadsworth.

The Centers for Disease Control. 1990. "Reports on HIV/AIDS: January–December 1989." *Morbidity and Mortality Weekly Report,* January.

The Centers for Disease Control. 1992. *HIV/AIDS Surveillance Report,* February.

The Centers for Disease Control Vietnam Experience Study. 1987. "Post Service Mortality Among Vietnam Veterans." *The Journal of the American Medical Association,* 257 (February 13): 790–795.

Chagnon, N. A. 1968. *Yanomamo: The Fierce People*. New York: Holt, Rinehart and Winston.

Chaiken, Marcia R., and Jan M. Chaiken. 1984. "Offender Types and Public Policy." *Crime and Delinquency,* 30, No. 2 (April): 195–226.

Chambliss, William J. 1975. "Toward a Political Economy of Crime." *Theory and Society,* 2: 149–170.

Chambliss, William J. 1991. "Biology and Crime." In Joseph F. Sheley (ed.), *Criminology: A Contemporary Handbook.* Belmont, Calif.: Wadsworth.

Chandler, William U. 1988. "Assessing SDI." In Lester R. Brown et al. (eds.), *State of the World 1988: A Worldwatch Institute Report on Progress Toward a Sustainable Society.* New York: W. W. Norton.

Chargot, Patricia. 1992. "Detroit Ranks at Top of List for Kids in Poverty." *Detroit Free Press,* August 12: 1.

Chase-Lansdale, P. Lindsay, Jeanne Brooks-Gunn, and Roberta L. Paikoff. 1991. "Research and Programs for Adolescent Mothers: Missing Links and Future Promises." *Family Relations,* 40 (October): 396–403.

Chazan, Naomi, and Timothy M. Shaw. 1988. "The Political Economy of Food in Africa." In Naomi Chazan and Timothy M. Shaw (eds.), *Coping with Africa's Food Crisis.* Boulder, Colo.: Lynne Rienner Publishers.

Cheng, L., and E. Bonacich. 1984. *Labor Immigration Under Capitalism: Asian Workers in the United States Before World War II.* Berkeley: University of California Press.

Chilman, Catherine, et al. (eds.). 1988. *Variant Family Forms.* Beverly Hills, Calif.: Sage Publications.

Chilton, Roland, and Jim Galvin. 1985. "Race, Crime, and Criminal Justice." *Crime and Delinquency,* 31: 3–13.

Clark, Cal, and B. Oliver Walter. 1991. "Urban Political Cultures, Financial Stress, and City Fiscal Austerity Strategies." *Western Political Quarterly,* 44 (September): 676–697.

Clark, W. A. V. 1988. "Racial Transition in Metropolitan Suburbs: Evidence from Atlanta." *Urban Geography,* 9 (May/June): 269–282.

Clarke, Arthur C. 1984. *Profiles of the Future: An Inquiry Into the Limits of the Possible.* New York: Holt, Rinehart and Winston.

Clarke-Stewart, K. Alison. 1991. "A Home Is Not a School: The Effects of Child Care on Children's Development." *Journal of Social Issues,* 47 (2): 105–123.

Clayton, Obie, Jr., Anne C. Baird, and Richard M. Levinson. 1984. "Subjective Decision Making in Medical School Admissions: Potentials for Discrimination." *Sex Roles,* 10, No. 7/8: 527–532.

"Cleaning of Toxic Dumps Is Still Lagging, Study Says." 1989. *New York Times,* September 10: Sec. Y, 15.

Clinard, Marshall B., and Robert F. Meier. 1989. *Sociology of Deviant Behavior.* 7th ed. Fort Worth, Tex.: Holt, Rinehart and Winston.

Clore, G. L., R. M. Bray, S. M. Itkin, and P. Murphy. 1978. "Interracial Attitudes and Behavior at a Summer Camp." *Journal of Personality and Social Psychology,* 36: 107–116.

Cloward, Richard A., and Lloyd E. Ohlin. 1960. *Delinquency and Opportunity.* New York: Free Press.

Cloward, Richard A., and Frances Fox Piven. 1974. *The Politics of Turmoil.* New York: Pantheon Books.

Cnaan, Ram A., Sven E. Olsson, and Terrie Wetle. 1990. "Cross-National Comparisons of Planning for the Needs of the Very Old: Israel, Sweden, and the United States." *Journal of Aging and Social Policy,* 2 (no. 1): 83–108.

Cockerham, William C. 1989. *Medical Sociology,* 4th ed. Englewood Cliffs, N.J.: Prentice-Hall.

Cockerham, William C. 1992. *Sociology of Mental Disorder.* Englewood Cliffs, N.J.: Prentice-Hall.

Coe, Rodney M. 1978. *Sociology of Medicine,* 2d ed. New York: McGraw-Hill.

Cohen, Lawrence E., and Marcus Felson. 1979. "Social Change and Crime Rate Trends." *American Sociological Review,* 44: 588–609.

Cohen, Lawrence E., Marcus Felson, and Kenneth C. Land. 1980. "Property Crime Rates in the United States: A Macrodynamic Analysis, 1947–1977; with Ex Ante Forecasts for the Mid-1980s." *American Journal of Sociology,* 86: 90–118.

Cohen, Sidney. 1982. "Cannibis: Effects Upon Adolescent Behavior." In National Institute on Drug Abuse, *Marijuana and Youth: Clinical Observations on Motivation and Learning.* DHHS Pub. No. (ADM) 82–1186. Washington, D.C.: U.S. Government Printing Office.

Cohen, Theodore F. 1987. "Remaking Men: Men's Experiences Becoming and Being Husbands and Fathers and Their Implications for Reconceptualizing Men's Lives." *Journal of Family Issues,* 8, No. 1 (March): 57–77.

Cohn, Steven F., Steven E. Barkan, and William A. Halteman. 1991. "Punitive Attitudes Toward Criminals: Racial Consensus or Racial Conflict." *Social Problems,* 38 (May): 287–296.

Cole, George F. 1989. *The American System of Criminal Justice.* 5th ed. Pacific Grove, Calif.: Brooks-Cole.

Coleman, James S., J. E. Campbell, L. Hobson, J. McPartland, A. Mood, F. Weinfield, and R. York.

1966. *Equality of Educational Opportunity*. Washington, D.C.: U.S. Government Printing Office.

Coleman, James W. 1989. *The Criminal Elite: The Sociology of White Collar Crime*. 2d ed. New York: St. Martin's Press.

Collins, Randall. 1971. "A Conflict Theory of Sexual Stratification." *Social Problems*, 19: 3–21.

Collins, Randall, and Scott Coltrane. 1991. *Sociology of Marriage and the Family: Gender, Love, and Property*. 3d ed. Chicago: Nelson-Hall.

Collins, R. Lorraine, and G. Alan Marlatt. 1983. "Psychological Correlates and Explanations of Alcohol Use and Abuse." In Boris Tabakoff, Patricia B. Sutker, and Carrie L. Randall (eds.), *Medical and Social Aspects of Alcohol Abuse*. New York: Plenum.

Colvin, Mark. 1991. "Crime and Social Reproduction: A Response to the Call for 'Outrageous' Proposals." *Crime and Delinquency*, 73 (October): 436–448.

"Community Drug Prevention Programs Show Promise." 1990. *Public Health Reports*, 105 (September/October): 543.

Comstock, Gary David. 1991. *Violence Against Lesbians and Gay Men*. New York: Columbia University Press.

Comte, Auguste. 1835. *Systeme de Politique Positive*. 4 vols. Paris: Cres.

"Congress Clears Overhaul of Welfare System." 1988. *Congressional Quarterly* (October 1): 2699–2701.

Conklin, J. G. 1976. "Robbery, the Elderly and Fear: An Urban Problem in Search of a Solution." In J. Goldsmith and S. S. Goldsmith (eds.), *Crime and the Elderly*. Lexington, Mass.: Lexington Books.

Conrad, John P. 1985. *The Dangerous and the Endangered*. Lexington, Mass.: Lexington Books.

Constantinople, Anne, Randolph Cornelius, and Janet Gray. 1988. "The Chilly Climate: Fact or Artifact?" *Journal of Higher Education*, 59 (September/October): 527–550.

Cook, Robin. 1977. *Coma*. New York: New American Library.

Cooper, Kenneth J. 1987. "Out of a Job: A Matter of Age." *Detroit Free Press*, June 21: Sec. F, 1–2.

Coser, Lewis A. 1956. *The Functions of Social Conflict*. Glencoe, Ill.: Free Press.

Costells, Manuel. 1977. *The Urban Question: A Marxist Approach*. Trans. by Ann Sheridan. Cambridge, Mass.: M.I.T. Press.

Cowan, Alison Leigh. 1992. "For Women, Fewer M.B.A.'s." *New York Times*, September 27: Sec. 3, 4.

Coward, Barbara E., Joe R. Feagin, and J. Allen Williams, Jr. 1974. "The Culture of Poverty Debate: Some Additional Data." *Social Problems*, 21: 621–634.

Crain, Robert L., and Rita E. Mahard. 1983. "The Effect of Research Methodology on Desegregation–Achievement Studies." *American Journal of Sociology*, 88: 839–854.

Crawford, Mary, and Margo MacLeod. 1990. "Gender in the College Classroom: An Assessment of the 'Chilly Climate' for Women." *Sex Roles*, 23: 101–122.

Crossman, Rita K., Sandra M. Stith, and Mary M. Bender. 1990. "Sex Role Egalitarianism and Marital Violence." *Sex Roles*, 22, No. 5/6: 293–304.

Crowley, Thomas J. 1988. "Learning and Unlearning Drug Abuse in the Real World." In Barbara A. Ray (ed.), *Learning Factors in Substance Abuse*. DHHS Pub. No. (ADM) 88-1576. Rockville, Md.: National Institute on Drug Abuse.

Crystal, Stephen. 1986. "Measuring Income and Inequality Among the Elderly." *The Gerontologist*, 26: 56–59.

Culkin, Mary, John R. Morris, and Suzanne W. Helburn. 1991. "Quality and the True Cost of Child Care." *Journal of Social Issues*, 47 (2): 71–86.

Cullen, Francis T., Bruce G. Link, and Craig W. Polanzi. 1982. "The Seriousness of Crime Revisited: Have Attitudes Toward White-Collar Crime Changed?" *Criminology*, 20: 83–102.

Cullen, John B., and Shelley M. Novick. 1979. "The Davis-Moore Theory of Stratification: A Further Examination and Extension." *American Journal of Sociology*, 84: 1414–1437.

Currie, Eliot. 1985. *Confronting Crime: An American Challenge*. New York: Pantheon Books.

Cushman, John H., Jr. 1986. "Pentagon-to-Contractor Job Shift Is Profiled." *New York Times*, August 31: 37.

Dahrendorf, Ralf. 1959. *Class and Class Conflict in Industrial Society.* Stanford, Calif.: Stanford University Press.

Daniels, Roger. 1988. *Asian America: Chinese and Japanese in the United States Since 1850.* Seattle: University of Washington Press.

Daniels, Roger. 1990. *Coming to America: A History of Immigration and Ethnicity in American Life.* New York: HarperCollins.

Danigelis, Nicholas L., and Alfred P. Fengler. 1990. "Homesharing: How Social Exchange Helps Elders Live at Home." *The Gerontologist,* 30: 162–170.

Daugherty, Jane. 1986. "Babies Born to Die." *Detroit Free Press,* June 7: 1.

Davenport, William H. 1977. "Sex in Cross-Cultural Perspective." In Frank A. Beach (ed.), *Human Sexuality in Four Perspectives.* Baltimore: Johns Hopkins University Press.

Davidson, J. Kenneth, Sr., and Nelwyn B. Moore. 1992. *Marriage and Family.* Dubuque, Ia.: William C. Brown.

Davis, Kingsley. 1971. "Sexual Behavior." In Robert K. Merton and Robert Nisbet (eds.), *Contemporary Social Problems.* 4th ed. New York: Harcourt Brace Jovanovich.

Davis, Kingsley, and Wilbert Moore. 1945. "Some Principles of Stratification." *American Sociological Review,* 10: 242–249.

Davis, Sally M., Ken Hunt, and Judith M. Kitzes. 1989. "Improving the Health of Indian Teenagers— A Demonstration Program in Rural New Mexico." *Public Health Reports,* 104 (May/June): 271–278.

Deckhard, Barbara. 1979. *The Women's Movement.* New York: Harper and Row.

Dekker, Paul, and Peter Ester. 1991. "Authoritarianism, Socio-Demographic Variables and Racism: A Dutch Replication of Billig and Cramer." *New Community,* 17 (January): 287–293.

Delattre, Edwin J. 1990. "New Faces of Organized Crime." *The American Enterprise* (May/June): 38–45.

De Leon, George. 1988. "The Therapeutic Community and Behavioral Science." In Barbara A. Ray (ed.), *Learning Factors in Substance Abuse.* NIDA Research Monograph 84, DHHS Pub. No. (ADM) 88–1576. Rockville, Md.: National Institute on Drug Abuse.

D'Emilio, John, and Estelle B. Freedman. 1988. *Intimate Matters: A History of Sexuality in America.* New York: Harper and Row.

Densen-Gerber, Judianne. 1984. "The Odyssey House Treatment Method." In George Serban (ed.), *Social and Medical Aspects of Drug Abuse.* New York: SP Medical and Scientific Books.

Dentler, Robert A. 1992. "The Los Angeles Riots of Spring 1992: Events, Causes, and Future Policy." *Sociological Practice Review,* 3 (October): 229–244.

DeParle, Jason. 1992. "Why Marginal Changes Don't Rescue the Welfare System." *New York Times,* March 1: Sec. 4, 3.

Deschenes, Elizabeth Piper, M. Douglas Anglin, and George Speckart. 1991. "Narcotics Addiction: Related Criminal Careers, Social and Economic Costs." *Journal of Drug Issues,* 21 (Spring): 383–411.

Des Jarlais, Don C. 1984. "Research Design, Drug Use, and Deaths: Cross Study Comparisons." In George Serban (ed.), *Social and Medical Aspects of Drug Abuse.* New York: SP Medical and Scientific Books.

Dess, W. J., and F. C. Cole. 1977. "The Medically Evacuated Viet-Nam Narcotic Abuser: A Follow-up Rehabilitative Study." *Bulletin on Narcotics,* 24: 55–65.

Devall, Bill, and George Sessions. 1985. *Deep Ecology.* Layton, Utah: Gibbs M. Smith.

Devillier, Penny L., and Craig J. Forsyth. 1988. "The Downward Mobility of Divorced Women with Dependent Children: A Research Note." *Sociological Spectrum,* 8: 295–302.

Devine, Joel A., Joseph F. Sheley, and M. Dwayne Smith. 1988. "Macroeconomic and Social-Control Policy Influences on Crime Rate Changes, 1948– 1985." *American Sociological Review,* 53 (June): 407–420.

Devins, Richard M. 1986. "Displaced Workers: One Year Later." *Monthly Labor Review* (July): 40–43.

Diana, Lewis. 1985. *The Prostitute and Her Clients: Your Pleasure Is Her Business.* Springfield, Ill.: Charles C Thomas.

Dickens, Charles. 1924. *A Tale of Two Cities.* New York: Charles Scribner's Sons.

DiIulio, Jr., John J. 1989. "The Impact of Inner-City Crime." *The Public Interest,* 96 (Summer): 28–46.

DiMatteo, M. Robin, and D. Dante DiNicola. 1982. *Achieving Patient Compliance: The Psychology of the Medical Practitioner's Role.* New York: Pergamon Press.

Dole, Vincent P. 1991. "Interim Methadone Clinics: An Undervalued Approach." *American Journal of Public Health,* 81 (September): 1111–1112.

Dollard, John, Neal E. Miller, Leonard W. Doob, O. H. Mowrer, and Robert R. Sears. 1939. *Frustration and Aggression.* New Haven, Conn.: Yale University Press.

Domhoff, G. William. 1967. *Who Rules America?* Englewood Cliffs, N.J.: Prentice-Hall.

Domhoff, G. William. 1983. *Who Rules America Now?* Englewood Cliffs, N.J.: Prentice-Hall.

Dommel, Paul R. 1984. "Local Discretion: The CDBG Approach." In Richard D. Bingham and John P. Blair (eds.), *Urban Economic Development.* Beverly Hills, Calif.: Sage Publications.

Donnerstein, Edward, Daniel Linz, and Steven Penrod. 1987. *The Question of Pornography: Research Findings and Policy Implications.* New York: Free Press.

Doob, Christopher Bates. 1993. *Racism: An American Cauldron.* New York: HarperCollins.

Downs, Donald A. 1989. *The New Politics of Pornography.* Chicago: University of Chicago Press.

Dreier, Peter. 1982. "The Position of the Press in the U.S. Power Structure." *Social Problems,* 29: 298–310.

Dubow, F., and D. Emmons. 1981. "The Community Hypothesis." In D. A. Lewis (ed.), *Reactions to Crime.* Beverly Hills, Calif.: Sage Publications.

Duke, James T. 1976. *Conflict and Power in Social Life.* Provo, Utah: Brigham Young University Press.

Dulles, John Foster. 1954. "Police for Security and Peace." *Foreign Affairs,* 32: 353–364.

Dumas, Kitty. 1992. "States Bypassing Congress in Reforming Welfare." *Congressional Quarterly,* April 11: 950–953.

Dunbar, Leslie W. 1988. *The Common Interest: How Our Social-Welfare Policies Don't Work, and What We Can Do About Them.* New York: Pantheon.

Duncan, Cynthia M. (ed.). 1992. *Rural Poverty in America.* Westport, Conn.: Auburn House.

Duncan, Greg J., and Willard Rodgers. 1991. "Has Children's Poverty Become More Persistent?" *American Sociological Review,* 56 (August): 538–550.

Dunford, Franklyn W., David Huizinga, and Delbert S. Elliott. 1990. "The Role of Arrest in Domestic Assault: The Omaha Police Experiment." *Criminology,* 28 (May): 183–206.

Dunn, Frederick L. 1978. "Epidemiological Factors: Health and Disease in Hunter-Gatherers." In Michael H. Logan and Edward E. Hunt (eds.), *Health and the Human Condition.* North Scituate, Mass.: Duxbury Press.

Durand, A. Mark. 1992. "The Safety of Home Birth: The Farm Study." *American Journal of Public Health,* 82 (March): 450–453.

Durning, Alan Thein, and Holly B. Brough. 1992. "Reforming the Livestock Economy." In Lester R. Brown et al. (eds.). *State of the World 1992: A Worldwatch Institute Report on Progress Toward a Sustainable Society.* New York: W. W. Norton.

Duster, Troy. 1987. "Crime, Youth Unemployment, and the Black Urban Underclass." *Crime and Delinquency,* 33, 2 (April): 300–316.

Duster, Troy. 1990. *Backdoor to Eugenics.* London: Routledge.

Dye, Thomas R. 1990. *Who's Running America: The Bush Era.* 5th ed. Englewood Cliffs, N.J.: Prentice-Hall.

Eckerman, W. C., et al. 1971. *Drug Use and Arrest Charges: A Study of Drug Use and Arrest Charges Among Arrestees in Six Metropolitan Areas of the United States.* Washington, D.C.: U.S. Government Printing Office.

Edwards, Griffith. 1983. "Drugs and Drug Dependence." In Griffith Edwards, Awni Arif, and Jerome Jaffe (eds.), *Drug Use and Misuse: Cultural Perspectives.* New York: St. Martin's Press.

Edwards, Michael. 1977. "Golden Threads to the Pentagon." *Nation,* March 15: 306–308.

Eggebeen, David J., and Daniel T. Lichter. 1991. "Race, Family Structure, and Changing Poverty Among American Children." *American Sociological Review,* 56 (December): 801–817.

Eggert, Leona L., and Jerald R. Herting. 1991. "Preventing Teenage Drug Abuse: Exploratory Effects of Network Social Support." *Youth and Society,* 22 (June): 482–524.

Egley, Lance C. 1991. "What Changes the Societal Prevalence of Domestic Violence?" *Journal of Marriage and the Family,* 53 (November): 885–897.

Ehrlich, Paul R., and Anne H. Ehrlich. 1970. *Population, Resources, Environment.* San Francisco: W. H. Freeman.

Ehrlich, Paul R., and Anne H. Ehrlich. 1990. *The Population Explosion.* New York: Simon and Schuster.

Ehrlich, Paul R., et al. 1983. "Long-term Biological Consequences of Nuclear War." *Science,* 222 (December 23): 1293–1300.

Elkin, M. 1982. "The Missing Links in Divorce Law: A Redefinition of Process and Practice." *Journal of Divorce,* 6: 37–63.

Elliott, Chip. 1981. "Letter from an Angry Reader— To the Editor from Chip Elliott." *Esquire,* September: 33–37.

Elliott, D. S., and D. Huizinga. 1983. "Social Class and Delinquent Behavior in a National Youth Panel: 1976–1980." *Criminology,* 21: 149–177.

"EPA Reports Air Quality Is Improving." 1989. *Science News,* 135 (April): 204.

Epstein, Cynthia Fuchs. 1981. *Women in Law.* New York: Basic Books.

Epstein, Samuel S. 1979. *The Politics of Cancer.* New York: Doubleday Anchor Books.

Erickson, Patricia G., Edward M. Adlaf, Glenn F. Murray, and Reginald G. Smart. 1987. *The Steel Drug: Cocaine in Perspective.* Lexington, Mass.: Lexington Books.

Erlanger, Howard S. 1974. "The Empirical Status of the Subculture of Violence Thesis." *Social Problems,* 22: 280–292.

Eshleman, J. Ross. 1991. *The Family: An Introduction.* 6th ed. Boston: Allyn and Bacon.

Etzioni, Amitai. 1985. "Shady Corporate Practices." *New York Times,* November 15: 27.

"Everybody Likes Head Start." 1989. *Newsweek,* February 20: 49–50.

Eysenck, Hans J., and Gisli H. Gudjonsson. 1989. *The Causes and Cures of Criminality.* New York: Plenum.

Fagan, Jeffrey, Elizabeth S. Piper, and Yu-Teh Cheng. 1987. "Contributions of Victimization to Delinquency in Inner Cities." *Journal of Criminal Law and Criminology,* 78, 3: 586–609.

Faludi, Susan. 1991. *Backlash: The Undeclared War Against American Women.* New York: Crown Publishers.

Fay, Brian. 1987. *Critical Social Science: Liberation and Its Limits.* Ithaca, N.Y.: Cornell University Press.

Fearnside, Phillip M. 1989. "Deforestation in Amazonia: A Prescription for Slowing." *Environment,* 31, 4 (May): 17–20; 39–40.

Featherman, David L., and Robert M. Hauser. 1978. *Opportunity and Change.* New York: Academic Press.

Federal Bureau of Investigation. 1992. *Uniform Crime Reports: Crime in the United States, 1991.* Washington, D.C.: U.S. Government Printing Office.

Feit, M. D., and M. J. Holosko, eds. 1988. "Evaluation of Employee Assistance Programs." *Employee Assistance Quarterly,* 3 (entire issue).

Ferber, Marianne A., and Brigid O'Farrell. 1991. *Work and Family: Policies for a Changing Workforce.* Washington, D.C.: National Academy Press.

Ferree, Myra Marx. 1991. "The Gender Division of Labor in Two-Earner Marriages: Dimensions of Variability and Change." *Journal of Family Issues,* 12 (June): 158–180.

Ferree, Myra Marx, and Elaine J. Hall. 1990. "Visual Images of American Society: Gender and Race in Introductory Sociology Textbooks." *Gender and Society,* 4 (December): 500–533.

Ficarrotto, Thomas J. 1990. "Racism, Sexism, and Erotophobia: Attitudes of Heterosexuals Toward Homosexuals." *Journal of Homosexuality,* 19, No. 1: 111–116.

Fijnaut, Cyrille. 1990. "Organized Crime: A Comparison Between the United States of America and Western Europe." *British Journal of Criminology,* 30 (Summer): 321–340.

Finckenauer, James O. 1988. "Public Support for the Death Penalty: Retribution as Just Deserts or Retribution as Revenge?" *Justice Quarterly,* 5, 1 (March): 81–100.

Fiorentine, Robert. 1988. "Increasing Similarity in the Values and Life Plans of Male and Female College Students? Evidence and Implications." *Sex Roles,* 18 (February): 143–158.

Fischer, Claude. 1975. "Toward a Subcultural Theory of Urbanism." *American Journal of Sociology,* 80: 1319–1341.

Fischer, Claude. 1982. *To Dwell Among Friends: Personal Networks in Town and City.* Chicago: University of Chicago Press.

Fisher, Elizabeth. 1974. "Children's Books: The Second Sex, Junior Division." In Judith Stacey et al. (eds.), *And Jill Came Tumbling After: Sexism in American Education.* New York: Dell.

Fitzpatrick, Joseph P. 1987. *Puerto Rican Americans: The Meaning of Migration to the Mainland.* 2d ed. Englewood Cliffs, N.J.: Prentice-Hall.

Flacks, Richard. 1971. *Youth and Social Change.* Chicago: Markham Publishing Co.

Flavin, Christopher. 1987. *Reassessing Nuclear Power: The Fallout from Chernobyl.* Worldwatch Paper 75. Washington, D.C.: Worldwatch Institute.

Flavin, Christopher. 1992. "Building a Bridge to Sustainable Energy." In Lester R. Brown et al. (eds.), *State of the World, 1992: A Worldwatch Institute Report on Progress Toward a Sustainable Society.* New York: W. W. Norton.

Flavin, Christopher, and Alan Durning. 1988. "Raising Energy Efficiency." In Lester R. Brown et al. (eds.), *State of the World 1988: A Worldwatch Institute Report on Progress Toward a Sustainable Society.* New York: W. W. Norton.

Flavin, Christopher, and Nicholas Lenssen. 1990. *Beyond the Petroleum Age: Designing a Solar Economy.* Worldwatch Paper 100. Washington, D.C.: Worldwatch Institute.

Flewelling, Robert L., J. Valley Rachal, and Mary Ellen Marsden. 1992. *Socioeconomic and Demographic Correlates of Drug and Alcohol Use.* National Institute on Drug Abuse, DHHS Pub. No. (ADM) 92–1906. Washington, D.C.: U.S. Government Printing Office.

Food 2000: Global Policies for Sustainable Agriculture. 1987. World Commission on Environment and Development. London: Zed Books, Ltd.

Ford, Clelan S. 1970. "Some Primitive Societies." In Georgine H. Seward and Robert C. Williamson (eds.), *Sex Roles in Society.* New York: Random House.

"Forty Percent of Single Men Are Found Homosexual in San Francisco." 1984. *New York Times,* November 23: 13.

Fraiberg, Selma. 1977. *Every Child's Birthright.* New York: Basic Books.

Franklin, Stephen, and Tom Hundley. 1983. "Escape to Detroit: A New Arabic Life." *Detroit Free Press,* November 27: Sec. E, 1.

Franks, Violet, and Esther D. Rothblum (eds.). 1983. *The Stereotyping of Women: Its Effects on Mental Health.* New York: Springer.

Freedman, Jonathan L. 1975. *Crowding and Behavior.* San Francisco: W. H. Freeman.

Freeman, Richard B., and Harry J. Holzer (eds.). 1986. *The Black Youth Employment Crisis.* Chicago: University of Chicago Press.

French, Hilary F. 1992a. "Strengthening Global Environmental Governance." In Lester R. Brown et al. (eds.), *State of the World, 1992: A Worldwatch Institute Report on Progress Toward a Sustainable Society.* New York: W. W. Norton.

French, Marilyn. 1992b. *The War Against Women.* New York: Summit Books.

Freudenheim, Milt. 1989. "Ontario Pay Equity Law Has Employers Scrambling." *Detroit Free Press,* July 30: Sec. C, 1.

Freudenheim, Milt. 1992. "Doctors Dropping Medicare Patients." *New York Times,* April 12: 1.

Freund, Peter E. S., and Meredith B. McGuire. 1991. *Health, Illness, and the Social Body: A Critical Sociology.* Englewood Cliffs, N.J.: Prentice-Hall.

Frieze, Irene Hanson, Josephine E. Olson, and Deborah Cain Good. 1990. "Perceived and Actual Discrimination in the Salaries of Male and Female Managers." *Journal of Applied Social Psychology,* 20: 46–67.

Fuchs, Victor. 1956. "Toward a Theory of Poverty." In Task Force on Economic Growth and Opportunity, *The Concept of Poverty.* Washington, D.C.: U.S. Chamber of Commerce.

Fuchs, Victor R., and Diane M. Reklis. 1992. "America's Children: Economic Perspectives and Policy Options." *Science,* 255 (January 3): 41–46.

Fuentes, Annette. 1991. "Women Warriors: Equality, Yes—Militarism, No." *The Nation,* October 28: 516–519.

Funk, Richard B., and Fern K. Willits. 1987. "College Attendance and Attitude Change: 1970–1981." *Sociology of Education,* 60 (October): 224–231.

Furstenburg, Frank F., and Andrew J. Cherlin. 1991. *Divided Families: What Happens to Children When Parents Part.* Cambridge, Mass.: Harvard University Press.

Gainer, William J. 1986. *Dislocated Workers: Extent of Closures, Layoffs, and the Public and Private Response.* Washington, D.C.: U.S. General Accounting Office, GAO/HDR-86-116BR.

Galbraith, John Kenneth. 1967. *The New Industrial State.* Boston: Houghton Mifflin.

Gallagher, Timothy J., Eric O. Johnson, Thomas L. Van Valey, and Dennis Rosada Malaret. 1992. "Job-seeking and Academic Success Among Sociologists: The Effects of Departmental Prestige and Gender." Paper presented at the annual meetings of the American Sociological Association, Pittsburgh.

Gallup, George. 1983. "Prejudice in Politics." *The Gallup Report,* 216 (September): 14.

Gamson, William A., and James McEvoy. 1972. "Police Violence and Its Public Support." In James F. Short, Jr., and Marvin Wolfgang (eds.), *Collective Violence.* Chicago: Aldine-Atherton.

Gans, Herbert J. 1962. *The Urban Villagers.* New York: Free Press.

Gans, Herbert J. 1971. "The Uses of Poverty: The Poor Pay All." *Social Policy,* 2 (July/August): 20–24.

Gans, Herbert J. 1972. "Urbanism and Suburbanism As Ways of Life: A Re-evaluation of Definitions." In John J. Palen and Karl Flaming (eds.), *Urban America.* New York: Holt, Rinehart and Winston.

Gans, Herbert J. 1979. *Deciding What's News.* New York: Pantheon Books.

Gans, Herbert J. 1988. *Middle American Individualism: The Future of Liberal Democracy.* New York: Free Press.

Gans, Herbert J. 1992. "Fighting the Biases Embedded in Social Concepts of the Poor." *The Chronicle of Higher Education,* January 8: A56.

Garbarino, James. 1981. "An Ecological Approach to Child Maltreatment." In Leroy H. Pelton (ed.), *The Social Context of Child Abuse and Neglect.* New York: Human Sciences Press.

Gastil, John. 1990. "Generic Pronouns and Sexist Language: The Oxymoronic Character of Masculine Generics." *Sex Roles,* 23, Nos. 11–12: 629–643.

Gatons, Paul K., and Michael Brintnall. 1984. "Competitive Grants: The UDAG Approach." In Richard D. Bingham and John P. Blair (eds.), *Urban Economic Development.* Beverly Hills, Calif.: Sage Publications.

Gebhard, Paul H., et al. 1965. *Sex Offenders: An Analysis of Types.* New York: Harper and Row.

Gelles, Richard J. 1987. "What to Learn from Cross-Cultural and Historical Research on Child Abuse and Neglect: An Overview." In R. J. Gelles and J. B. Lancaster (eds.), *Child Abuse and Neglect: Biosocial Dimensions.* New York: Aldine de Gruyter.

Gelles, Richard J. 1992. "Poverty and Violence Toward Children." *American Behavioral Scientist,* 35 (January/February): 258–274.

Gelles, Richard J., and Jon R. Conte. 1990. "Domestic Violence and Sexual Abuse of Children: A Review of Research in the Eighties." *Journal of Marriage and the Family,* 52 (November): 1045–1058.

Gelles, Richard J., and Claire Pedrick Cornell. 1990. *Intimate Violence in Families.* 2d ed. Newbury Park, Calif.: Sage Publications.

Gendreau, Paul, and Robert R. Ross. 1987. "Revivification of Rehabilitation: Evidence From the 1980s." *Justice Quarterly,* 4 (September): 349–407.

"Genentech's Style." 1988. *The Economist,* May 14: 70–71.

Gentry, Cynthia S. 1991. "Pornography and Rape: An Empirical Analysis." *Deviant Behavior,* 12: 277–288.

Gerdes, Eugenia Proctor, and Douglas M. Garber. 1983. "Sex Bias in Hiring: Effects of Job Demands and Applicant Competence." *Sex Roles,* 9, No. 3: 307–319.

Gerstel, Naomi, Catherine Kohler Riessman, and Sarah Rosenfield. 1985. "Explaining the Symptomatology of Separated and Divorced Men and Women: The Role of Material Conditions and Social Networks." *Social Forces,* 64 (September): 84–101.

Giacomo, Carlo. 1986. "Legal Experts Back Court's Censure of U.S. Contra Aid." *Detroit Free Press,* July 6: 6a.

Gibbs, Jack P. 1989. "Conceptualization of Terrorism." *American Sociological Review,* 54 (June): 329–340.

Giele, Janet Zollinger. 1978. *Women and the Future.* New York: Free Press.

Gil, David G. 1990. *Unravelling Social Policy: Theory, Analysis, and Political Action Towards Social Equality.* Rochester, Vt.: Schenkman Books.

Gilbert, Lucia Albino. 1985. *Men in Dual-Career Families: Current Realities and Future Prospects.* Hillsdale, N.J.: Erlbaum.

Gillis, J. 1974. "Youth in History: Progress and Prospects." *Journal of Social History,* 7: 201–207.

Gillmor, Dan, and Stephen K. Doig. 1992. "Segregation Forever?" *American Demographics* (January): 48–51.

Glazer, Myron Peretz, and Penina Migdal Glazer. 1989. *The Whistleblowers: Exposing Corruption in Government and Industry.* New York: Basic Books.

"GM Bets an Arm and a Leg On a People-Free Plant." 1988. *Business Week,* September 12: 72–73.

Goff, Colin, and Nancy Nason-Clark. 1989. "The Seriousness of Crime in Fredericton, New Brunswick: Perceptions Toward White-Collar Crime." *Canadian Journal of Criminology,* 31, 1: 19–34.

Goffman, Erving. 1963. *Stigma: Notes on the Management of Spoiled Identity.* Englewood Cliffs, N.J.: Prentice-Hall.

Goldstein, Avram, and Harold Kalant. 1990. "Drug Policy: Striking the Right Balance." *Science,* 249 (September 28): 1513–1521.

Goldstein, Jeffrey H. 1986. *Aggression and Crimes of Violence.* 2d ed. New York: Oxford University Press.

Goldstein, Melvin C. 1971. "Stratification, Polyandry, and Family Structure in Central Tibet." *Southwest Journal of Anthropology,* 27: 65–74.

Goldstein, M. J., H. S. Kant, and J. J. Hartman. 1974. *Pornography and Sexual Deviance.* Berkeley: University of California Press.

Goldstein, Paul J., Patricia A. Bellucci, Barry J. Spunt, and Thomas Miller. 1991. "Volume of Cocaine Use and Violence: A Comparison Between Men and Women." *Journal of Drug Issues,* 21 (Spring): 345–367.

Goode, Erich, and Richard Troiden. 1974. *Sexual Deviance and Sexual Deviants.* New York: William Morrow and Co.

Goode, William J. 1963. *World Revolution and Family Patterns.* New York: Free Press.

Gordon, Diana R. 1990. *The Justice Juggernaut: Fighting Street Crime, Controlling Citizens.* New Brunswick, N.J.: Rutgers University Press.

Gordon, G. 1966. *Role Theory and Illness.* New Haven, Conn.: College and University Press.

Gordon, Margaret T., and Stephanie Riger. 1989. *The Female Fear.* New York: Free Press.

Gordon, Michael. 1978a. *The American Family: Past, Present, and Future.* New York: Random House.

Gordon, Milton M. 1964. *Assimilation in American Life.* New York: Oxford University Press.

Gordon, Milton M. 1978b. *Human Nature, Class, and Ethnicity.* New York: Oxford University press.

Gordon, Milton M. 1988. *The Scope of Sociology.* New York: Oxford University Press.

Gore, Albert. 1992. *Earth in the Balance: Ecology and the Human Spirit.* Boston: Houghton Mifflin.

Gottfredson, Michael R., and Travis Hirschi. 1990. *A General Theory of Crime.* Stanford, Calif.: Stanford University Press.

Gottfredson, Stephen D., and Don M. Gottfredson. 1985. "Selective Incapacitation?" *The Annals of the American Academy of Political and Social Science,* 478 (March): 135–149.

Gottlieb, Manuel. 1988. *Comparative Economic Systems: Preindustrial and Modern Case Studies.* Ames: Iowa State University Press.

Gouldner, Alvin W. 1976. "The Dark Side of the Dialectic: Toward a New Objectivity." *Sociological Inquiry,* 46: 3–16.

Graham, Otis L., Jr. 1992. *Losing Time: The Industrial Policy Debate.* Cambridge, Mass.: Harvard University Press.

Greenberg, David F. 1988. *The Construction of Homosexuality.* Chicago: University of Chicago Press.

Greenberg, Jan R., Martha McKibben, and Jane A. Raymond. 1990. "Dependent Adult Children and Elder Abuse." *Journal of Elder Abuse and Neglect,* 2, No. 1/2: 73–86.

Greenberger, David B., et al. 1989. "The Impact of Personal Control on Performance and Satisfaction." *Organizational Behavior and Human Decision Processes,* 43: 29–51.

Greenman, Molly. 1990. "Survivors of Prostitution Find PRIDE." *Families in Society,* 71 (February): 110–113.

Greider, William. 1992. *Who Will Tell the People: The Betrayal of American Democracy.* New York: Simon and Schuster.

Greif, Geoffrey. 1985. "Single Fathers Rearing Children." *Journal of Marriage and the Family,* 47 (February): 185–191.

Gronbjerg, Kirsten, David Street, and Gerald D. Suttles. 1978. *Poverty and Social Change.* Chicago: University of Chicago Press.

Guillemin, Jeanne. 1980. "Federal Policies and Indian Politics." *Society,* 17: 29–34.

Gunter, Nancy C., and B. G. Gunter. 1990. "Domestic Division of Labor Among Working Couples: Does Androgyny Make a Difference?" *Psychology of Women Quarterly,* 14: 355–370.

Gupte, Pranay. 1984. *The Crowded Earth: People and the Politics of Population.* New York: W. W. Norton.

Gustman, Alan L., and Thomas L. Steinmeier. 1991. "Changing the Social Security Rules for Work After 65." *Industrial and Labor Relations Review,* 44 (July): 733–745.

Gwartney-Gibbs, Patricia A. 1986. "The Institutionalization of Premarital Cohabitation: Estimates from Marriage License Applications, 1970 and 1980." *Journal of Marriage and the Family,* 48 (May): 423–434.

Gyllenhammar, Pehr G. 1977. *People at Work.* Reading, Mass.: Addison-Wesley.

Hacker, Andrew. 1992. *Two Nations: Black and White, Separate, Hostile, Unequal.* New York: Charles Scribner's Sons.

Haglund, R. M. J., and M. A. Schuckit. 1981. "The Epidemiology of Alcoholism." In N. Estes and E. Heineman (eds.), *Alcoholism: Development, Consequences and Interventions.* St. Louis: Mosby.

Halikas, James A., et al. 1982. "Incidence and Characteristics of Amotivational Syndrome, Including Associated Findings, Among Chronic Marijuana Users." In National Institute on Drug Abuse, *Marijuana and Youth: Clinical Observations on Motivation and Learning,* DHHS Pub. No. (ADM) 82–1186. Washington, D.C.: U.S. Government Printing Office.

Hammersmith, Sue Kiefer. 1987. "A Sociological Approach to Counseling Homosexual Clients and Their Families." *Journal of Homosexuality,* 15: 173–190.

Hanson, D. J. 1975. "The Influence of Authoritarianism Upon Prejudice: A Review." *Resources in Education,* 14: 31.

Harding, Sandra. 1986. *The Science Question in Feminism.* Ithaca, N.Y.: Cornell University Press.

Harlan, Anne, and Carol Weiss. 1981. *Final Report from "Moving Up: Women in Managerial Careers."* Working Paper No. 86, Center for Research on Women, Wellesley College.

Harrington, Michael. 1984. *The New American Poverty.* New York: Holt, Rinehart and Winston.

Harrington, Michael. 1989. *Socialism: Past and Future.* New York: Arcade Publishing.

Harrison, Bennett, and Barry Bluestone. 1988. *The Great U-Turn: Corporate Restructuring and the Polarizing of America.* New York: Basic Books.

Hartung, William D. 1992. "Arms Sales Win Votes and Little Else." *New York Times,* October 25: Sec. 3, 11.

Harty, Sara J. 1991. "Data Bank Keeps Doctors on Edge." *Business Insurance,* November 4: 89–90.

Harvey, John T. 1991. "Institutions and the Economic Welfare of Black Americans in the 1980s." *Journal of Economic Issues,* 25 (March): 115–135.

Hasin, Deborah S., et al. 1988. "Cocaine and Heroin Dependence Compared in Poly-Drug Abusers."

American Journal of Public Health, 78 (May): 567–569.

Hawkins, Gordon, and Franklin E. Zimring. 1988. *Pornography in a Free Society.* Cambridge: Cambridge University Press.

Hawley, Amos H. 1971. *Urban Society: An Ecological Approach.* New York: Ronald Press.

Hawley, W. D., et al. 1983. *Strategies for Effective Desegregation.* Lexington, Mass.: Lexington Books.

Hayes, L. F. 1970. "Non-economic Aspects of Poverty." *Australian Journal of Social Issues,* 5: 41–54.

Hayghe, Howard V. 1988. "Employers and Child Care: What Roles Do They Play?" *Monthly Labor Review* (September): 38–44.

Headley, Bernard D. 1991. "Race, Class and Powerlessness in World Economy." *The Black Scholar,* 21 (Summer): 14–21.

Heaven, Patrick C. L., and Adrian Furnham. 1987. "Race Prejudice and Economic Beliefs." *Journal of Social Psychology,* 127, 5 (October): 483–489.

Heenan, David A. 1991. *The New Corporate Frontier: The Big Move to Small Town, U.S.A.* New York: McGraw-Hill.

Heilbrun, Alfred B., Jr., Allison Foster, and Jill Golden. 1989. "The Death Sentence in Georgia, 1974–1987: Criminal Justice or Racial Injustice?" *Criminal Justice and Behavior,* 16, 2 (June): 139–154.

Hendry, Peter. 1988. "Food and Population: Beyond Five Billion." *Population Bulletin,* 43, 2 (April): entire issue.

Henifin, M. S., R. Hubbard, and J. Norsigian. 1989. "Prenatal Screening." In S. Cohen and N. Taub (eds.), *Reproductive Laws for the 1990s.* Clifton, N.J.: Humana Press.

Hertz, Rosanna. 1986. *More Equal Than Others: Women and Men in Dual-Career Marriages.* Berkeley: University of California Press.

Hewitt, John P. 1991. *Self and Society: A Symbolic Interactionist Social Psychology.* 5th ed. Boston: Allyn and Bacon.

Hewlett, Sylvia Ann. 1991. *When the Bough Breaks: The Cost of Neglecting Our Children.* New York: Basic Books.

Heyl, Barbara Sherman. 1979. *The Madam as Entrepreneur: Career Management in House Prostitution.* New Brunswick, N.J.: Transaction Books.

Higginbotham, E. 1987. "Employment for Professional Black Women in the Twentieth Century." In C. Bose and G. Spitze (eds.), *Ingredients for Women's Employment Policy.* Albany: State University of New York Press.

Higgins, Alexander G. 1992. "U.S. and Russia Agree to Cut Arms." *Detroit Free Press,* December 30: 1.

"High-Tech Health Care: Who Will Pay?" 1989. *Business Week,* February 6: 74–78.

Hijab, Nadia. 1988. *Womanpower: The Arab Debate on Women at Work.* New York: Cambridge University Press.

Hilgartner, Stephen, and Charles L. Bosk. 1988. "The Rise and Fall of Social Problems: A Public Arena Model." *American Journal of Sociology,* 94, 1 (July): 53–78.

Hill, M. Anne, and Mark R. Killingsworth (eds.). 1989. *Comparable Worth: Analyses and Evidence.* Ithaca, N.Y.: ILR Press.

Himes, Joseph S. 1980. *Conflict and Conflict Management.* Athens: University of Georgia Press.

Hindelang, M. J. 1981. "Variations in Sex-Race-Age-Specific Incidence Rates of Offending." *American Sociological Review,* 46: 461–474.

Hindelang, M., T. Hirschi, and J. Weis. 1979. "Correlates of Delinquency: The Illusion of Discrepancy Between Self-report and Official Measures." *American Sociological Review,* 44: 995–1014.

Hingson, Ralph, Norman A. Scotch, James Sorenson, and Judith P. Swazey. 1981. *In Sickness and in Health: Social Dimensions of Medical Care.* St. Louis: Mosby.

Hirschel, J. David, Ira W. Hutchison, III, and Charles W. Dean. 1992. "The Failure of Arrest to Deter Spouse Abuse." *Journal of Research in Crime and Delinquency,* 29 (February): 7–33.

Hirschi, Travis. 1962. "The Professional Prostitute." *Berkeley Journal of Sociology,* 7 (Spring): 34.

Hirschi, Travis. 1969. *Causes of Delinquency.* Berkeley: University of California Press.

Hirschi, Travis, and Hanan C. Selvin. 1967. *Delinquency Research.* New York: Free Press.

Hirschman, Charles, and Morrison G. Wong. 1981. "Trends in Socioeconomic Achievement Among Immigrant and Native-Born Asian Americans, 1960–1976." *The Sociological Quarterly,* 22: 495–513.

Hirschman, Charles, and Morrison G. Wong. 1986. "The Extraordinary Educational Achievement of Asian-Americans: A Search for Historical Evidence and Explanations." *Social Forces,* 65 (September): 1–27.

Hoberg, George. 1992. *Pluralism by Design: Environmental Policy and the American Regulatory State.* New York: Praeger.

Hoch, Charles, and Robert A. Slayton. 1989. *New Homeless and Old: Community and the Skid Row Hotel.* Philadelphia: Temple University Press.

Hochbaum, Martin, and Florence Galkin. 1987. "Medicaid Patients Need Not Apply." *Social Policy,* 17 (Spring): 40–42.

Hofferth, Sandra L., and Deborah A. Phillips. 1991. "Child Care Policy Research." *Journal of Social Issues,* 47 (2): 1–13.

Hoffman, Martin. 1968. *The Gay World.* New York: Basic Books.

Hohri, William Minoru. 1987. *Repairing America: An Account of the Movement for Japanese American Redress.* Pullman, Wash.: Washington State University Press.

Holden, Karen C., and Pamela J. Smock. 1991. "The Economic Costs of Marital Dissolution: Why Do Women Bear a Disproportionate Cost?" In W. Richard Scott and Judith Blake (eds.), *Annual Review of Sociology,* 17. Palo Alto, Calif.: Annual Reviews.

Honey, Maureen. 1984. *Creating Rosie the Riveter: Class, Gender, and Propaganda.* Amherst: University of Massachusetts Press.

Hooker, Evelyn. 1969. "Parental Relations and Male Homosexuality in Patient and Nonpatient Samples." *Journal of Consulting and Clinical Psychology,* 33 (April): 141.

Hourani, Albert. 1991. *A History of the Arab Peoples.* Cambridge, Mass.: Harvard University Press.

House, James S. 1974. "Occupational Stress and Coronary Heart Disease: A Review and Theoretical Integration." *Journal of Health and Social Behavior,* 15: 17–21.

"House Kills Capital's Plan to Ease Sex Curbs." 1981. *New York Times,* October 2: 14.

Houseknecht, Sharon. 1987. "Voluntary Childlessness." In Marvin B. Sussman and Suzanne K. Steinmetz (eds.), *Handbook of Marriage and the Family.* New York: Plenum.

Houseknecht, Sharon K., Suzanne Vaughan, and Anne S. Macke. 1984. "Marital Disruption Among Professional Women: The Timing of Career and Family Events." *Social Problems,* 31: 273–284.

Hout, Michael. 1988. "More Universalism, Less Structural Mobility: The American Occupational Structure in the 1980s." *American Journal of Sociology,* 93: 1358–1400.

Howard, Ted, and Jeremy Rifkin. 1977. *Who Should Play God? The Artificial Creation of Life and What It Means for the Future of the Human Race.* New York: Delacorte Press.

Howell, E. M. 1988. "Low-Income Persons' Access to Health Care: NMCUES Medicaid Data." *Public Health Reports,* 103 (September/October): 507–514.

Hubbard, R. 1990. *The Politics of Women's Biology.* New Brunswick, N.J.: Rutgers University Press.

Hubbert, M. King. 1969. "Energy Resources." In National Academy of Sciences, *Resources and Man.* San Francisco: W. H. Freeman.

Huff-Corzine, Lin, Jay Corzine, and David C. Moore. 1991. "Deadly Connections: Culture, Poverty, and the Direction of Lethal Violence." *Social Forces,* 69 (March): 715–732.

Hughes, Austin L. 1988. *Evolution and Human Kinship.* New York: Oxford University Press.

Hughes, Richard, and Robert Brewin. 1979. *The Tranquilizing of America: Pill Popping and the American Way of Life.* New York: Harcourt Brace Jovanovich.

Hugick, Larry, and Jennifer Leonard. 1991. "Sex in America." *The Gallup Poll Monthly* (October): 62.

Hunt, Janet G., and Larry L. Hunt. 1982. "The Dualities of Careers and Families: New Integrations or New Polarizations?" *Social Problems,* 29: 499–510.

Hunter, A., and T. L. Baumer. 1982. "Street Traffic, Social Integration, and Fear of Crime." *Sociological Inquiry,* 52 (Spring): 122–131.

Hunter, Joyce. 1990. "Violence Against Lesbian and Gay Male Youths." *Journal of Interpersonal Violence,* 5 (September): 295–300.

Huston, Aletha C., et al. 1992. *Big World, Small Screen: The Role of Television in American Society.* Lincoln: University of Nebraska Press.

Hyde, Janet S., Michelle Krajnik, and Kristin Skuldt-Niederberger. 1991. "Androgyny Across the Life Span: A Replication and Longitudinal Follow-Up." *Developmental Psychology,* 27: 516–519.

Iacocca, Lee. 1989. "National Health Plan Deserves Consideration." *Detroit Free Press,* April 17: 9.

Illich, Ivan. 1976. *Medical Nemesis.* New York: Bantam Books.

Ima, Kenji. 1982. "Japanese Americans: The Making of 'Good' People." In Anthony Gary Dworkin and Rosalind J. Dworkin (eds.), *The Minority Report.* 2d ed. New York: Holt, Rinehart and Winston.

"Images of Fear: On the Perception and Reality of Crime." 1985. *Harper's Magazine,* May: 39–48.

Inciardi, James A. 1986. *The War on Drugs: Heroin, Cocaine, Crime, and Public Policy.* Palo Alto, Calif.: Mayfield.

Inciardi, James A., Anne E. Pottieger, Mary Ann Forney, Dale D. Chitwood, and Duane C. McBride. 1991. "Prostitution, IV Drug Use, and Sex-For-Crack Exchanges Among Serious Delinquents: Risks for HIV Infection." *Criminology,* 29: 221–235.

Irelan, Lola M., Oliver C. Moles, and Robert M. O'Shea. 1969. "Ethnicity, Poverty, and Selected Attitudes: A Test of the 'Culture of Poverty' Hypothesis." *Social Forces,* 47: 405–413.

Ispa, Jean M., Kathy R. Thornburg, and Mary M. Gray. 1990. "Relations Between Early Childhood Care Arrangements and College Students' Psychosocial Development and Academic Performance." *Adolescence,* 25 (Fall): 529–542.

Jackson, Michael, and Bruce Jackson. 1983. *Doing Drugs.* New York: St. Martin's/Marek.

Jacobs, Jerry A., and Ronnie J. Steinberg. 1990. "Compensating Differentials and the Male-Female Wage Gap: Evidence from the New York State Comparable Worth Study." *Social Forces,* 69 (December): 439–468.

Jacobsen, Chanoch, and Robert A. Hanneman. 1992. "Illegal Drugs: Past, Present and Possible Futures." *The Journal of Drug Issues,* 22: 105–120.

Jacobsen, Joyce P., and Laurence M. Levin. 1992. "The Effects of Intermittent Labor Force Attachment on Female Earnings." Paper presented at a meeting of the American Economic Association, New Orleans.

Jacobson, Jodi. 1988. "Planning the Global Family." In Lester R. Brown et al. (eds.), *State of the World 1988: A Worldwatch Institute Report on Progress Toward a Sustainable Society.* New York: W. W. Norton.

Jacques, Jeffrey M., and Karen J. Chason. 1978. "Cohabitation: A Test of Reference Group Theory Among Black and White College Students." *Journal of Comparative Family Studies,* 9: 147–165.

Jaffe, Jerome. 1983. "Methadone Maintenance: Exportable Programme or Alien Technology?" In Griffith Edwards, Awni Arif, and Jerome Jaffe (eds.), *Drug Use and Misuse: Cultural Perspectives.* New York: St. Martin's Press.

Jain, Uday. 1988. *The Psychological Consequences of Crowding.* Newbury Park, Calif.: Sage Publications.

James, Jennifer. 1977. "Prostitutes and Prostitution." In Edward Sagarin and Fred Montanino (eds.), *Deviants: Voluntary Actors in a Hostile World.* Morristown, N.J.: General Learning Press.

Janowitz, Morris. 1969. "Patterns of Collective Racial Violence." In Hugh Davis Graham and Ted Robert Gurr (eds.), *The History of Violence in America.* New York: Bantam Books.

Jeffrey, C. Ray. 1967. *Criminal Responsibility and Mental Disease.* Springfield, Ill.: Charles C Thomas.

Jencks, Christopher. 1992. *Rethinking Social Policy: Race, Poverty, and the Underclass.* Cambridge, Mass.: Harvard University Press.

Johann, Sara Lee, and Frank Osanka. 1989. *Representing . . . Battered Women Who Kill.* Springfield, Ill.: Charles C Thomas.

Johnson, Bruce D. 1984. "Empirical Patterns of Heroin Consumption Among Selected Street Heroin Users." In George Serban (ed.), *Social and Medical Aspects of Drug Abuse.* New York: S. P. Medical and Scientific Books.

Johnson, C., and B. Barer. 1987. "Marital Instability and Changing Kinship Networks of Grandparents." *The Gerontologist,* 27: 330–335.

Johnson, Catherine B., Margaret S. Stockdale, and Frank E. Saal. 1991. "Persistence of Men's Misperceptions of Friendly Cues Across a Variety of Interpersonal Encounters." *Psychology of Women Quarterly*, 15: 463–475.

Johnson, Colleen Leahy, Linnea Klee, and Catherine Schmidt. 1988. "Conceptions of Parentage and Kinship Among Children of Divorce." *American Anthropologist*, 90 (March): 136–144.

Johnston, Lloyd D., Patrick M. O'Malley, and Jerald G. Bachman. 1991. *Drug Use Among American High School Seniors, College Students and Young Adults, 1975–1990: Volume I, High School Seniors*. National Institute on Drug Abuse, DHHS Pub. No. (ADM) 91-1813. Washington, D.C.: U.S. Government Printing Office.

Josephson, Wendy L. 1987. "Television Violence and Children's Aggression: Testing the Priming, Social Script, and Disinhibition Predictions." *Journal of Personality and Social Psychology*, 53, No. 5: 882–890.

Jowett, Garth S., and Victoria O'Donnell. 1986. *Propaganda and Persuasion*. Newbury Park, Calif.: Sage Publications.

Joyce, Fay S. 1984. "Courts Study Link Between Victim's Race and Imposition of Death Penalty." *New York Times*, January 5: 8.

Judd, Dennis R. 1991. "Segregation Forever?" *The Nation*, December 9: 740–743.

Kagan, Jerome, R. B. Kearsley, and P. R. Zelazo. 1978. *Infancy: Its Place in Human Development*. Cambridge, Mass.: Harvard University Press.

Kagan, Sharon L. 1991. "Examining Profit and Non-profit Child Care: An Odyssey of Quality and Auspices." *Journal of Social Issues*, 47 (2): 87–104.

Kahn, Alfred J., and Sheila B. Kamerman. 1987. *Child Care: Facing the Hard Choices*. Dover, Mass.: Auburn House.

Kail, Barbara Lynn, and Paula Holzman Kleinman. 1985. "Fear, Crime, Community Organization, and Limitations on Daily Routines." *Urban Affairs Quarterly*, 20, No. 3 (March): 400–408.

Kalmuss, Debra, and Judith A. Seltzer. 1986. "Continuity of Marital Behavior in Remarriage: The Case of Spouse Abuse." *Journal of Marriage and the Family*, 48 (February): 113–120.

Kalmuss, D. S., and M. A. Straus. 1982. "Wife's Marital Dependency and Wife Abuse." *Journal of Marriage and the Family*, 44: 277–286.

Kamerman, Sheila B. 1991. "Child Care Policies and Programs: An International Overview." *Journal of Social Issues*, 47 (2): 179–196.

Kamerman, Sheila B., and Alfred J. Kahn. 1988. *Mothers Alone: Strategies for a Time of Change*. Dover, Mass.: Auburn House.

Kamerman, Sheila B., and Alfred J. Kahn. 1991. *Innovations in European Parenting Policies*. Westport, Conn.: Greenwood.

Kates, Don B., Jr. 1983. "Handgun Prohibition and the Original Meaning of the Second Amendment." *Michigan Law Review*, 82 (November): 204–273.

Katz, Diane, and Richard A. Ryan. 1992. "Symbols of Success, Targets of Rage." *The Detroit News*, May 10: Sec. B, 1.

Keil, Julian E., Susan E. Sutherland, Rebecca G. Knapp, and Herman A. Tyroler. 1992. "Does Equal Socioeconomic Status in Black and White Men Mean Equal Risk of Mortality?" *American Journal of Public Health*, 82 (August): 1133–1136.

Kellam, Susan. 1992. "Parties Hope Job Training Bill Will Spin Political Gold." *Congressional Quarterly*, May 16: 1341–1345.

Kemp, Jack. 1990. "Tackling Poverty: Market-Based Policies to Empower the Poor." *Policy Review* (Winter): 2–5.

Kemper, Peter, and Christopher M. Murtaugh. 1991. "Lifetime Use of Nursing Home Care." *New England Journal of Medicine*, 324 (February 28): 595–600.

Kennedy, Leslie W. 1990. *On the Borders of Crime: Conflict Management and Criminology*. New York: Longman.

Kerschner, Paul A., and Ira S. Hirschfield. 1983. "Public Policy and Aging." In Diana S. Woodruff and James E. Birren (eds.), *Aging: Scientific Perspectives and Social Issues*. 2d ed. Monterey, Calif.: Brooks-Cole.

Kerstein, Robert. 1990. "Stage Models of Gentrification: An Examination." *Urban Affairs Quarterly*, 25 (June): 620–639.

Kessler, Ronald C., James S. House, and J. Blake Turner. 1987. "Unemployment and Health in a

Community Sample." *Journal of Health and Social Behavior,* 28: 51–59.

Kett, J. F. 1977. *Rites of Passage: Adolescents in America, 1970 to the Present.* New York: Basic Books.

Kiecolt-Glaser, J. K., et al. 1987. "Marital Quality, Marital Disruption, and Immune Function." *Psychosomatic Medicine,* 49: 13–34.

Kilborn, Peter T. 1990. "Workers Using Computers Find a Supervisor Inside." *New York Times,* December 23: 1, 13.

Kimmel, Michael S., and Michael A. Messner. 1992. *Men's Lives.* 2d ed. New York: Macmillan.

Kindel, Stephen. 1990. "The Life and Death of Cities." *Financial World,* September 4: 28–30.

King, Nancy R. 1984. "Exploitation and Abuse of Older Family Members: An Overview of the Problem." In J. J. Costa (ed.), *Abuse of the Elderly.* Lexington, Mass.: Lexington Books.

Kinsey, Alfred C., Wardell B. Pomeroy, and Clyde E. Martin. 1948. *Sexual Behavior in the Human Male.* Philadelphia: W. B. Saunders.

Kirk, Stuart A., and Herb Kutchins. 1992. *The Selling of DSM: The Rhetoric of Science in Psychiatry.* New York: Aldine de Gruyter.

Kirsh, Barbara. 1983. "Sex Roles and Language Use: Implications for Mental Health." In Violet Franks and Esther D. Rothblum (eds.), *The Stereotyping of Women: Its Effects on Mental Health.* New York: Springer.

Kitano, Harry H. L. 1976. *Japanese Americans.* 2d ed. Englewood Cliffs, N.J.: Prentice-Hall.

Kleck, Gary. 1991. *Point Blank: Guns and Violence in America.* New York: Aldine de Gruyter.

Kleiman, Dena. 1977. "The Potential for Urban Terror Is Always There." *New York Times,* March 13: Sec. E, 3.

Klein, Carole. 1973. *The Single Parent Experience.* New York: Walker.

Klemesrud, Judy. 1983. "Single Mothers by Choice: Perils and Joys." *New York Times,* May 2: 20.

Kletzer, Lori G. 1991. "Job Displacement, 1979–86: How Blacks Fared Relative to Whites." *Monthly Labor Review,* 114 (July): 17–25.

Kluegel, James R., and Lawrence Bobo. 1991. "Modern American Prejudice: Stereotypes of Blacks, His-panics, and Asians." Paper presented at the annual meeting of the American Sociological Association, Cincinnati, Ohio.

Knopp, Lawrence, M., Jr. 1990. "The Social Consequences of Homosexuality." *Geographical Magazine,* 62 (May): 20–25.

Kolata, Gina. 1991. "Nursing Homes Are Criticized on How They Tie and Drug Some Patients." *New York Times,* January 23: 16.

Korbin, J. E. 1987. "Child Maltreatment in Cross-Cultural Perspective: Vulnerable Children and Circumstances." In R. J. Gelles and J. B. Lancaster (eds.), *Child Abuse and Neglect: Biosocial Dimensions.* New York: Aldine de Gruyter.

Kornhauser, William. 1966. "'Power Elite' or 'Veto Groups.'" In Reinhard Bendix and Seymour M. Lipset (eds.), *Class, Status and Power.* 2d ed. New York: Free Press.

Kosberg, Jordan I. (ed.). 1992. *Family Care of the Elderly: Social and Cultural Changes.* Newbury Park, Calif.: Sage Publications.

Kotelchuck, David (ed.). 1976. *Prognosis Negative: Crisis in the Health Care System.* New York: Vintage Books.

Kotin, Lawrence, and William F. Aikman. 1980. *Legal Foundations of Compulsory School Attendance.* Port Washington, N.Y.: Kennikat Press.

Kozol, Jonathan. 1985. "Illiterate America, Part One: A Third of the Nation Cannot Read These Words." *Public Welfare* (Summer): 11–17.

Kozol, Jonathan. 1991. *Savage Inequalities: Children in America's Schools.* New York: Crown.

Kristof, N. D. 1990. "More in China Willingly Rear Just One Child." *New York Times,* May 9: 1.

Krupnick, Alan A., and Paul R. Portney. 1991. "Controlling Urban Air Pollution: A Benefit-Cost Assessment." *Science,* 252 (April 26): 522–528.

Kupfer, Andrew. 1989. "What to Do About Drugs." *Fortune,* June 20: 39–41.

Kurdek, Lawrence A. 1988. "Correlates of Negative Attitudes Toward Homosexuals in Heterosexual College Students." *Sex Roles,* 18, 11/12: 727–738.

Kurtz, Lester R. 1988. *The Nuclear Cage: A Sociology of the Arms Race.* Englewood Cliffs, N.J.: Prentice-Hall.

Kutchinsky, Berl. 1991. "Pornography and Rape: Theory and Practice?" *International Journal of Law and Psychiatry,* 14: 47–64.

Kutler, Stanley I. 1990. *The Wars of Watergate: The Last Crisis of Richard Nixon.* New York: Knopf.

Kutner, Nancy, and Michael Kutner. 1987. "Ethnic and Residence Differences Among Poor Families." *Journal of Comparative Family Studies,* 18, 3 (Autumn): 463–470.

Lafree, Gary, Kriss A. Drass, and Patrick O'Day. 1992. "Race and Crime in Postwar America: Determinants of African-American and White Rates, 1957–1988." *Criminology,* 30: 157–185.

Langone, John. 1989. "Special Report: Good and Bad News About AIDS—How to Block a Killer's Path." *Time,* January 30: 60–62.

Lantos, Tom. 1992. "The Silence of the Kids: Children at Risk in the Workplace." *Labor Law Journal,* 43 (February): 67–70.

Lappé, Frances Moore, and Joseph Collins. 1988. *World Hunger: Twelve Myths.* San Francisco, Calif.: Institute for Food and Development Policy.

Lasswell, Harold D. 1936. *Politics: Who Gets What, When, and How.* New York: McGraw-Hill.

Lavrakas, P. J., J. Normoyle, W. G. Skogan, E. J. Herz, G. Salem, and D. A. Lewis. 1981. *Factors Related to Citizen Involvement in Personal, Household and Neighborhood Anti-crime Measures.* Washington, D.C.: U.S. Government Printing Office.

Lawson, Roger, and Vic George. 1980. "An Assessment." In Vic George and Roger Lawson (eds.), *Poverty and Inequality in Common Market Countries.* London: Routledge and Kegan Paul.

Leckie, Robert. 1990. *None Died in Vain: The Saga of the American Civil War.* New York: HarperCollins.

Leckie, Robert. 1992. *The Wars of America.* New York: HarperCollins.

Lee, Valerie E., J. Brooks-Gunn, Elizabeth Schnur, and Fong-Ruey Liaw. 1990. "Are Head Start Effects Sustained? A Longitudinal Follow-Up Comparison of Disadvantaged Children Attending Head Start, No Preschool, and Other Preschool Programs." *Child Development,* 61: 495–507.

Le Grand, Julian, and Saul Estrin (eds.). 1989. *Market Socialism.* Oxford: Clarendon Press.

Lemert, E. 1951. *Social Pathology.* New York: McGraw-Hill.

Lempert, Richard. 1983. "The Effect of Executions on Homicides: A New Look in an Old Light." *Crime and Delinquency,* 29: 88–115.

Lenssen, Nicholas. 1992. "Confronting Nuclear Waste." In Lester R. Brown et al. (eds.), *State of the World 1992: A Worldwatch Institute Report on Progress Toward a Sustainable Society.* New York: W. W. Norton.

Leonard, Kenneth E., and Howard T. Blane. 1992. "Alcohol and Marital Aggression in a National Sample of Young Men." *Journal of Interpersonal Violence,* 7 (March): 19–30.

Lerner, William D., and James M. Raczynski. 1988. "The Economic Shaping of Substance Abuse." In Barbara A. Ray (ed.), *Learning Factors in Substance Abuse.* NIDA Research Monograph 84, DHHS Pub. No. (ADM) 88-1576. Rockville, Md.: National Institute on Drug Abuse.

Lettieri, Dan J. 1978. *Drugs and Suicide: When Other Coping Strategies Fail.* Beverly Hills, Calif.: Sage Publications.

Levin, Jack, and William C. Levin. 1982. *The Functions of Discrimination and Prejudice.* New York: HarperCollins.

Levine, Harry Gene. 1983. "Temperance and Prohibition in America." In Griffith Edwards, Awni Arif, and Jerome Jaffe (eds.), *Drug Use and Misuse: Cultural Perspectives.* New York: St. Martin's Press.

Levinger, George, and Oliver C. Moles (eds.). 1979. *Divorce and Separation: Context, Causes, and Consequences.* New York: Basic Books.

Levinson, Robert B. 1988. "Privatization: The Jury Is Still Out." *Corrections Today,* (October): 6.

Levitan, Sar A., and Isaac Shapiro. 1986. "A Weaker Net Under Workers." *New York Times,* September 1: 23.

Levy, Sheldon G. 1969. "A 150-Year Study of Political Violence in the United States." In Hugh Davis Graham and Ted Robert Gurr (eds.), *Violence in America: Historical and Comparative Perspectives.* New York: Bantam Books.

Lewes, Kenneth. 1988. *The Psychoanalytic Theory of Male Homosexuality.* New York: Simon and Schuster.

Lewis, Neil A. 1991. "Guilty Plea Made in Pentagon Case." *New York Times*, March 15: 1.

Lewis, Oscar. 1966. "The Culture of Poverty." *Scientific American*, 2, No. 5 (October): 19–25.

Lewis, Robert A. 1984. "Some Changes in Men's Values, Meanings, Roles and Attitudes Toward Marriage and Family in the U.S.A." In *Social Change and Family Policies*, Part I. Melbourne: Australian Institute of Family Studies.

Liddell, Christine, and Pieter Kruger. 1987. "Activity and Social Behavior in a South African Township Nursery: Some Effects of Crowding." *Merrill-Palmer Quarterly*, 33, 2 (April): 195–211.

Lieberson, Stanley, and Arnold R. Silverman. 1965. "The Precipitants and Underlying Conditions of Race Riots." *American Sociological Review*, 30 (December): 887–898.

Liebschutz, Sarah F., and Alan J. Taddiken. 1986. "The Effects of Reagan Administration Budget Cuts on Human Services in Rochester, New York." In George E. Peterson and Carol W. Lewis (eds.), *Reagan and the Cities*. Washington: Urban Institute Press.

Lifson, Alan R. 1992. "Men Who Have Sex with Men: Continued Challenges for Preventing HIV Infection and AIDS." *American Journal of Public Health*, 82 (February): 166–167.

Light, William J. Haugen. 1986. *Psychodynamics of Alcoholism: A Current Synthesis*. Springfield, Ill.: Charles C Thomas.

Like, Robert, and Stephen J. Zyzanski. 1987. "Patient Satisfaction with the Clinical Encounter: Social Psychological Determinants." *Social Science and Medicine*, 24, No. 4: 351–357.

Lindorff, Dave. 1992. *Marketplace Medicine: The Rise of the For-Profit Hospital Chains*. New York: Bantam Books.

Linz, Daniel, and Edward Donnerstein. 1992. "Research Can Help Us Explain Violence and Pornography." *The Chronicle of Higher Education*, 39 (September 30): B3–B4.

Lippmann, Walter. 1922. *Public Opinion*. New York: Harcourt, Brace.

Lo, Clarence Y. H. 1982. "Theories of the State and Business Opposition to Increased Military Spending." *Social Problems*, 29: 424–438.

Loftin, Colin, David McDowall, Brian Wiersema, and Talbert J. Cottey. 1991. "Effects of Restrictive Licensing of Handguns on Homicide and Suicide in the District of Columbia." *New England Journal of Medicine*, 325 (December 5): 1615–1620.

Logan, Charles H. 1990. *Private Prisons: Cons and Pros*. New York: Oxford University Press.

London, Kathryn A. 1990. "Cohabitation, Marriage, Marital Dissolution, and Remarriage: United States, 1988." *Advance Data from Vital and Health Statistics*. No. 194. Hyattsville, Md.: National Center for Health Statistics.

Longman, Phillip. 1987. *Born to Pay: The New Politics of Aging in America*. Boston: Houghton Mifflin.

Longshore, Douglas, and Jeffrey Prager. 1985. "The Impact of School Desegregation: A Situational Analysis." *Annual Review of Sociology*, 11: 75–91.

Lopata, Helena Z. 1984. "Social Construction of Social Problems Over Time." *Social Problems*, 31: 249–272.

Loscocco, Karyn A., Joyce Robinson, Richard H. Hall, and John K. Allen. 1991. "Gender and Small Business Success: An Inquiry Into Women's Relative Disadvantage." *Social Forces*, 70 (September): 65–85.

Lowman, John. 1992. "Street Prostitution Control: Some Canadian Reflections on the Finsbury Park Experience." *The British Journal of Criminology*, 32 (Winter): 1–16.

Lowy, Martin. 1991a. *High Rollers: Inside the Savings and Loan Debacle*. New York: Praeger.

Lowy, Richard. 1991b. "Yuppie Racism: Race Relations in the 1980s." *Journal of Black Studies*, 21 (June): 445–464.

Lucas, Isidro. 1981. "Bilingualism and Higher Education: An Overview." *Ethnicity*, 8: 305–319.

Luckenbill, David F. 1986. "Deviant Career Mobility: The Case of Male Prostitutes." *Social Problems*, 33: 283–296.

Luckenbill, David F. 1989. "Deviant Career Mobility: The Case of Male Prostitutes." In Delos H. Kelly (ed.), *Deviant Behavior*, 3d ed. New York: St. Martin's Press: 485–503.

Luebke, Barbara F. 1989. "Out of Focus: Images of Women and Men in Newspaper Photographs." *Sex Roles*, 20, 3/4: 121–133.

Luft, Harold S. 1987. *Health Maintenance Organizations: Dimensions of Performance.* New Brunswick, N.J.: Transaction Books.

Lynch, Frederick R., and William R. Beer. 1990. "You Ain't the Right Color, Pal: White Resentment of Affirmative Action." *Policy Review,* 51 (Winter): 64–67.

MacDonald, K., and R. Parke. 1986. "Parent-Child Physical Play: The Effects of Sex and Age of Children and Parents." *Sex Roles,* 15:367–378.

MacKellar, F. L., and D. R. Vining, Jr. 1988. "Research Policy and Review 26: Where Does the United States Stand in the Global Resource Scarcity Debate?" *Environment and Planning Abstracts,* 20: 1567–1573.

Macklin, Eleanor. 1987. "Non-Traditional Family Forms." In Marvin Sussman and Suzanne Steinmetz (eds.), *Handbook of Marriage and the Family.* New York: Plenum.

Maguire, Kathleen, and Timothy J. Flanagan (eds.). 1991. *Sourcebook of Criminal Justice Statistics: 1990.* Washington, D.C.: U.S. Department of Justice, Bureau of Justice Statistics.

Main, Jeremy. 1988. "Here Comes the Big New Cleanup." *Fortune,* November 21: 104–106; 110; 112–114.

Malcolm, Andrew H. 1984. "'Right to Die' Dispute Focuses on Californian." *New York Times,* October 21: 1.

Malone, Thomas F., and Robert Corell. 1989. "Mission to Planet Earth Revisited: An Update on Studies of Global Change." *Environment,* 31, 3 (April): 6–11; 31–35.

Malthus, Thomas Robert. 1960, originally published 1798. *On Population.* Edited by Gertrude Himmelfarb. New York: Modern Library.

Manderscheid, Ronald W., and Mary Anne Sonnenschein. 1990. *Mental Health, United States, 1990.* DHHS Pub. No. (ADM) 90–1708. Washington, D.C.: U.S. Government Printing Office.

Manes, Christopher. 1990. *Green Rage: Radical Environmentalism and the Unmaking of Civilization.* Boston: Little, Brown.

Mansfield, Phyllis Kernoff, Patricia Barthalow Koch, Julie Henderson, Judith R. Vicary, Margaret Cohn, and Elaine W. Young. 1991. "The Job Climate for Women in Traditionally Male Blue-Collar Occupations." *Sex Roles,* 25, Nos. 1–2: 63–79.

Manton, Kenneth G., Clifford H. Patrick, and Katrina W. Johnson. 1987. "Health Differentials Between Blacks and Whites: Recent Trends in Mortality and Morbidity." *Milbank Quarterly,* 65 (Suppl. 1): 129–199.

Marden, Charles F., Gladys Meyer, and Madeline H. Engel. 1992. *Minorities in American Society.* 6th ed. New York: HarperCollins.

Marks, Carole. 1981. "Split-Labor Markets and Black-White Relations, 1865–1920." *Phylon,* 42: 293–308.

Marks, Carole. 1991. "The Urban Underclass." *Annual Review of Sociology,* 17: 445–466.

Markson, E. W., and B. B. Hess. 1980. "Older Women in the City." *Signs: Journal of Women in Culture and Society,* 5 (Spring): 127–141.

Markusen, Ann, and Joel Yudken. 1992. *Dismantling the Cold War Economy.* New York: Basic Books.

"Marriage vs. Single Life." 1982. *ISR Newsletter,* 10: 7.

Marshall, Donald S. 1974. "Too Much Sex in Mangaia." In Erich Goode and Richard Troiden (eds.), *Sexual Deviance and Sexual Deviants.* New York: William Morrow and Co.

Martin, Carol Lynn. 1990. "Attitudes and Expectations About Children with Nontraditional and Traditional Gender Roles." *Sex Roles,* 22, Nos. 3–4: 151–165.

Martin, Don, and Maggie Martin. 1984. "Selected Attitudes Toward Marriage and Family Life Among College Students." *Family Relations,* 33: 293–300.

Martindale, Melanie. 1991. "Sexual Harassment in the Military: 1988." *Sociological Practice Review,* 2 (July): 200–216.

Martinez, Ruben, and Richard L. Dukes. 1991. "Ethnic and Gender Differences in Self Esteem." *Youth and Society,* 22 (March): 318–338.

Marx, Karl. 1964, originally published 1848. *Selected Writings in Sociology and Philosophy.* Edited by T. B. Bottomore and Maximilian Rubel. Baltimore: Penguin.

Marx, Karl. 1967, originally published 1867–1895. *Das Kapital.* New York: International Publishers.

Massey, Douglas S. 1990. "American Apartheid: Segregation and the Making of the Underclass." *American Journal of Sociology,* 96 (September): 329–357.

Massey, Douglas S., Andrew B. Gross, and Mitchell L. Eggers. 1991. "Segregation, the Concentration of Poverty, and the Life Chances of Individuals." *Social Science Research,* 20: 397–420.

Mauldin, W. P. 1975. "Assessment of National Family Planning Programs in Developing Countries." *Studies in Family Planning,* 6: 30–36.

Maume, David J., Jr. 1991. "Child-Care Expenditures and Women's Employment Turnover." *Social Forces,* 70 (December): 495–508.

Mazur, Allan. 1993. "Controlling Technology." In Albert H. Teich (ed.), *Technology and the Future.* 6th ed. New York: St. Martin's Press.

McBroom, William H. 1984. "Changes in Sex-Role Orientations: A Five-Year Longitudinal Comparison." *Sex Roles,* 11, No. 7/8: 583–592.

McCaghy, Charles H. 1985. *Deviant Behavior: Crime, Conflict, and Interest Groups.* 2d ed. New York: Macmillan.

McCall, Robert B. 1988. "Real Men Do Change Diapers." *Parents,* September: 202.

McConnell, Stephen R. 1983. "Retirement and Employment." In Diana S. Woodruff and James E. Birren (eds.), *Aging: Scientific Perspectives and Social Issues.* 2d ed. Monterey, Calif.: Brooks-Cole.

McCoy, Norma L. 1985. "Innate Factors in Sex Differences." In Alice G. Sargent (ed.), *Beyond Sex Roles.* 2d ed. St. Paul, Minn.: West Publishing Company.

McCue, Jack D. 1989. *The Medical Cost-Containment Crisis: Fears, Opinions, and Facts.* Ann Arbor, Mich.: Health Administration Press.

McDonnell, Douglas, Jeanette Irwin, and Marsha Rosenbaum. 1990. "'Hop and Hubbas': A Tough New Mix, A Research Note on Cocaine Use Among Methadone Maintenance Clients." *Contemporary Drug Problems,* 17 (Spring): 145–156.

McKenzie, Richard B. 1984. *Fugitive Industry: The Economics and Politics of Deindustrialization.* Cambridge, Mass.: Ballinger.

McKenzie, Richard B. 1988. *The American Job Machine.* New York: Universe Books.

McKeown, T., R. G. Brown, and R. G. Record. 1972. "An Interpretation of the Modern Rise of Population in Europe." *Population Studies,* 26: 345–382.

McKeown, T., R. G. Brown, and R. D. Turner. 1975. "An Interpretation of the Decline of Mortality in England and Wales During the Twentieth Century." *Population Studies,* 29: 391–422.

McKinlay, John B. 1986. "A Case for Refocusing Upstream: The Political Economy of Illness." In Peter Conrad and Rochelle Kern (eds.), *The Sociology of Health and Illness: Critical Perspectives.* 2d ed. New York: St. Martin's Press.

McKinlay, John B., and Sonja M. McKinlay. 1977. "The Questionable Contribution of Medical Measures to the Decline of Mortality in the United States in the Twentieth Century." *Milbank Memorial Fund Quarterly/Health and Society,* 55: 405–428.

McLanahan, Sara. 1985. "Family Structure and the Reproduction of Poverty." *American Journal of Sociology,* 90: 873–901.

McLanahan, Sara, and Larry Bumpass. 1988. "Intergenerational Consequences of Family Disruption." *American Journal of Sociology,* 94, 1, (July): 130–152.

McLeod, Eileen. 1982. *Women Working: Prostitution Now.* London: Croom Helm.

McPhail, Clark. 1971. "Civil Disorder Participation: A Critical Examination of Recent Research." *American Sociological Review,* 36: 1058–1073.

McPhail, Thomas L. 1987. *Electronic Colonialism: The Future of International Broadcasting and Communication.* 2d ed. Newbury Park, Calif.: Sage Publications.

Meadows, Donella H., Dennis L. Meadows, Jorgen Randers, and William W. Behrens III. 1972. *The Limits to Growth.* New York: New American Library.

Mechanic, David. 1989. *Mental Health and Social Policy.* 3d ed. Englewood Cliffs, N.J.: Prentice-Hall.

Mednick, Sarnoff A., Terrie E. Moffitt, and Susan A. Stack. 1987. *The Causes of Crime: New Biological Approaches.* Cambridge: Cambridge University Press.

Melman, Seymour. 1983. *Profits Without Production.* New York: Alfred A. Knopf.

Merrill, Jeffrey C., and Alan B. Cohen. 1989. "Explicit Rationing of Medical Care: Is It Really Needed?" In Jack D. McCue (ed.), *The Medical Cost-Containment Crisis: Fears, Opinions, and Facts*. Ann Arbor, Mich.: Health Administration Press.

Merton, Robert K. 1949. "Discrimination and the American Creed." In Robert M. MacIver (ed.), *Discrimination and National Welfare*. New York: Harper and Row.

Merton, Robert K. 1968. *Social Theory and Social Structure*. 2d ed. New York: Free Press.

Mesarovic, Mihajlo, and Eduard Pestel. 1974. *Mankind at the Turning Point*. New York: Dutton.

Meyer, Madonna Harrington. 1990. "Family Status and Poverty Among Older Women: The Gendered Distribution of Retirement Income in the United States." *Social Problems*, 37 (November): 551–563.

Michels, Robert. 1966, originally published 1915. *Political Parties*. New York: Free Press.

Michigan Women's Commission. 1974. "Sex Discrimination in an Elementary Reading Program." Lansing, Mich.

Middleton, Russell. 1976. "Regional Differences in Prejudice." *American Sociological Review*, 41: 94–117.

Milby, Jesse B. 1981. *Addictive Behavior and Its Treatment*. New York: Springer.

Miller, Alden D., and Lloyd E. Ohlin. 1985. *Delinquency in the Community: Creating Opportunities and Controls*. Beverly Hills, Calif.: Sage Publications.

Miller, Brent C., and Kristin A. Moore. 1990. "Adolescent Sexual Behavior, Pregnancy, and Parenting: Research Through the 1980s." *Journal of Marriage and the Family*, 52 (November): 1025–1044.

Miller, David L. 1985. *Introduction to Collective Behavior*. Belmont, Calif.: Wadsworth Publishing Company.

Miller, Eleanor M. 1986. *Street Woman*. Philadelphia: Temple University Press.

Miller, N., and M. Brewer. 1984. *Groups in Contact: The Psychology of Desegregation*. Orlando, Fla.: Academic Press.

Miller, Richard Lawrence. 1991. *The Case for Legalizing Drugs*. New York: Praeger.

Miller, Stanton S. 1989. "Energy Efficiency: A Futuristic Goal." *Environmental Scientific Technology*, 23, 2: 149.

Miller, Stuart C. 1969. *The Unwelcome Immigrant*. Berkeley: University of California Press.

Miller, William R. 1984. "Teaching Responsible Drinking Skills." In Peter M. Miller and Ted D. Nirenberg (eds.), *Prevention of Alcohol Abuse*. New York: Plenum.

Millman, Marcia. 1977. *The Unkindest Cut*. New York: Morrow.

Mills, C. Wright. 1956. *The Power Elite*. New York: Oxford University Press.

Mills, C. Wright. 1959. *The Sociological Imagination*. New York: Oxford University Press.

Mincer, Jilian. 1985. "Those Hurt by Drunken Drivers Press Suits Against Drivers' Hosts." *New York Times*, August 9: 1.

Miringoff, Marc L. 1989. *The Index of Social Health, 1989: Measuring the Social Well-Being of the Nation*. Tarrytown, N.Y.: Fordham Institute for Innovation in Social Policy.

Monette, Duane, Thomas Sullivan, and Cornell DeJong. 1990. *Applied Social Research*. 2d ed. Fort Worth, Tex.: Holt, Rinehart and Winston.

Moore, Joan W. 1976. *Mexican Americans*. Englewood Cliffs, N.J.: Prentice-Hall.

Moore, Kristin A., and Thomas M. Stief. 1991. "Changes in Marriage and Fertility Behavior: Behavior Versus Attitudes in Young Adults." *Youth and Society*, 22 (March): 362–386.

Moran, Theodore H. (ed.). 1985. *Multinational Corporations: The Political Economy of Foreign Direct Investment*. Lexington, Mass.: Lexington Books.

Morash, Merry, and Lila Rucker. 1990. "A Critical Look at the Idea of Boot Camp as a Correctional Reform." *Crime and Delinquency*, 36: 204–222.

Morgan, Elaine. 1972. *The Descent of Women*. New York: Stein and Day.

Morris, Aldon D. 1984. *The Origins of the Civil Rights Movement: Black Communities Organizing for Change*. New York: Free Press.

Motley, James B. 1983. *U.S. Strategy to Counter Domestic Political Terrorism*. National Security Affairs

Monograph Series 83-2. Washington, D.C.: National Defense University Press.

Mott, Frank L. 1991. "Developmental Effects of Infant Care: The Mediating Role of Gender and Health." *Journal of Social Issues,* 47 (2): 139–158.

Mumford, Emily. 1983. *Medical Sociology: Patients, Providers, and Policies.* New York: Random House.

Mumford, E., H. J. Schlesinger, and G. V. Glass. 1982. "The Effects of Psychological Intervention on Recovery from Surgery and Heart Attacks: An Analysis of the Literature." *The American Journal of Public Health,* 72: 141–151.

Murdock, George P. 1934. *Our Primitive Contemporaries.* New York: Macmillan.

Murphy, John E. 1988. "Date Abuse and Forced Intercourse Among College Students." In Gerald T. Hotaling, David Finkelhor, John T. Kirkpatrick, and Murray A. Straus (eds.), *Family Abuse and Its Consequences: New Directions in Research.* Newbury Park, Calif.: Sage Publications.

Murray, Charles. 1984. *Losing Ground.* New York: Basic Books.

Mutchler, Jan E., and Jeffrey A. Burr. 1991. "A Longitudinal Analysis of Household and Nonhousehold Living Arrangements in Later Life." *Demography,* 28 (August): 375–390.

Nader, Ralph. 1988. "Run the Government Like the Best American Corporations." *Harvard Business Review,* November/December: 81–86.

Nasar, Sylvia. 1992a. "Cooling the Globe Would Be Nice, But Saving Lives Now May Cost Less." *New York Times,* May 31: Sec. 4, 6.

Nasar, Sylvia. 1992b. "The Rich Get Richer, but the Question Is by How Much." *New York Times,* July 20: Sec. C, 1.

Nathan, Richard P. 1988. *Social Science in Government: Uses and Misuses.* New York: Basic Books.

National Center for Health Statistics. 1984. *Vital Statistics of the United States, 1980.* Vol. II, Sec. 6, Life Tables. DHHS Pub. No. (PHS) 84-1104. Public Health Service. Washington, D.C.: U.S. Government Printing Office.

National Center for Health Statistics. 1991. "Advance Report of Final Marriage Statistics, 1988." *Monthly Vital Statistics Report,* Vol. 40, No. 4, Suppl. Hyattsville, Md.: Public Health Service.

National Center for Health Statistics. 1992. *Health, United States, 1991.* DHHS Pub. No. (PHS) 92-1232. Hyattsville, Md.: Public Health Service.

National Council on Aging. 1975. *The Myth and the Reality of Aging in America.* Washington, D.C.: National Council on the Aging.

National Institute on Alcohol Abuse and Alcoholism. 1988. *Epidemiology of Alcohol-Related Problems in the United States.* DHHS Pub. No. (ADM) 88-1519(A). Washington, D.C.: U.S. Department of Health and Human Services.

National Institute on Drug Abuse. 1991. *National Household Survey on Drug Abuse: Main Findings, 1990.* DHHS Pub. No. (ADM) 91-1788. Washington, D.C.: U.S. Government Printing Office.

Neckerman, Kathryn M., and Joleen Kirschenman. 1991. "Hiring Strategies, Racial Bias, and Inner-City Workers." *Social Problems,* 38 (November): 433–447.

Nelkin, Dorothy. 1984. "Science, Technology, and Political Conflict: Analyzing the Issues." In Dorothy Nelkin (ed.), *Controversy: Politics of Technical Decisions.* 2d ed. Beverly Hills, Calif.: Sage Publications.

Nelson, Richard Y., Jr. 1989. "Inner City 'Truths'." *Journal of Housing* (January/February): 9.

Nero, Anthony V., Jr. 1988. "Controlling Indoor Air Pollution." *Scientific American,* 258, 5 (May): 42–48.

Neugarten, Bernice L. 1982. "Age or Need?" *National Forum: The Phi Kappa Phi Journal,* 62 (Fall): 25–27.

Neugarten, Bernice L., and N. Datan. 1973. "Sociological Perspectives on the Life Cycle." In Paul B. Baltes and K. Warner Schaie (eds.), *Lifespan Development Psychology: Personality and Socialization.* New York: Academic Press.

Newacheck, P. W. 1988. "Access to Ambulatory Care for Poor Persons." *Health Services Research,* 23 (August): 401–419.

Newman, Oscar. 1972. *Defensible Space.* New York: Macmillan.

Newman, Oscar, and Karen A. Franck. 1980. *Factors Influencing Crime and Instability in Urban Housing Developments.* Washington, D.C.: U.S. Department of Justice, National Institute of Justice.

Nimkoff, Meyer F. (ed.). 1965. *Comparative Family Systems.* Boston: Houghton Mifflin.

Noble, Barbara Presley. 1992a. "Legal Victories for Gay Workers." *New York Times,* June 21: Sec. 3, 23.

Noble, Barbara Presley. 1992b. "Testing Employees for Drugs." *New York Times,* April 12: Sec. 3, 27.

Norman, Colin. 1981. *The God That Limps: Science and Technology in the Eighties.* New York: W. W. Norton.

Norton, Arthur J., and Jeanne E. Moorman. 1987. "Current Trends in Marriage and Divorce Among American Women." *Journal of Marriage and the Family,* 49 (February): 3–14.

Novak, Michael. 1978. *The Guns of Lattimer: The True Story of a Massacre and a Trial, August 1897–March 1898.* New York: Basic Books.

Nusberg, Charlotte, with Mary Jo Gibson and Sheila Peace. 1984. *Innovative Aging Program Abroad: Implications for the United States.* Westport, Conn.: Greenwood Press.

O'Brien, Robert, and Sidney Cohen. 1984. *The Encyclopedia of Drug Use.* New York: Facts on File.

O'Connor, James F., and Alan Lizotte. 1978. "The 'Southern Subculture of Violence' Thesis and Patterns of Gun Ownership." *Social Problems,* 25: 420–429.

"Off the Streets, Prostitution Thrives in New York with Little Interference." 1984. *New York Times,* November 14: 16.

Ogburn, William F. 1938. "The Changing Family." *The Family,* 19: 139–143.

Ogburn, William F. 1957. "Cultural Lag as Theory." *Sociology and Social Research,* 41: 167–174.

Ognibene, Peter J. 1980. "Vanishing Farmlands: Selling Out the Soil." *Saturday Review,* May: 29–32.

O'Hare, William, and Jan Larson. 1991. "Women in Business: Where, What, and Why." *American Demographics,* 13 (July): 34–38.

O'Kelly, Charlotte G., and Larry S. Carney. 1986. *Women and Men in Society: Cross Cultural Perspectives in Gender Inequality.* 2d ed. Belmont, Calif.: Wadsworth.

Olinger, John Peter. 1991. "Elder Abuse: The Outlook for Federal Legislation." *Journal of Elder Abuse and Neglect,* 3, No. 1: 43–52.

Organski, A. F. K., Jacek Kugler, J. Timothy Johnson, and Youssef Cohen. 1984. *Births, Deaths, and Taxes: The Demographic and Political Transitions.* Chicago: University of Chicago Press.

Ory, Marcia G. 1978. "The Decision to Parent or Not: Normative and Structural Components." *Journal of Marriage and the Family,* 40: 531–539.

Osanka, Franklin Mark, and Sara Lee Johann. 1989. *Sourcebook on Pornography.* Lexington, Mass.: Lexington Books.

Osborne, David, and Ted Gaebler. 1992. *Reinventing Government: How the Entrepreneurial Spirit Is Transforming the Public Sector.* Reading, Mass.: Addison-Wesley.

Palen, John J. 1987. *The Urban World.* 3d ed. New York: McGraw-Hill.

Pallas, Aaron M., Doris R. Entwisle, Karl L. Alexander, and Peter Weinstein. 1990. "Social Structure and the Development of Self-Esteem in Young Children." *Social Psychology Quarterly,* 53: 302–315.

"Panel Finds No Risk in Tests of Gene-Altered Organisms." 1989. *New York Times,* September 24: 14.

Paradise, Viola I. 1922. *Child Labor and the Work of Mothers in Oyster and Shrimp Canning Communities on the Gulf Coast.* Pub. No. 98, U.S. Children's Bureau, Department of Labor, Washington, D.C.

Parker, Faith Lamb, Chaya S. Piotrkowski, and Lenore Peay. 1987. "Head Start as a Social Support for Mothers: The Psychological Benefits of Involvement." *American Journal of Orthopsychiatry,* 57, 2 (April): 220–225.

Parsons, J. E. 1980. *The Psychobiology of Sex Differences and Sex Roles.* New York: McGraw-Hill.

Parsons, Talcott. 1951. *The Social System.* New York: Free Press.

Parsons, Talcott, and Robert Bales. 1950. *Interaction Process Analysis.* Reading, Mass.: Addison-Wesley.

Paternoster, Raymond, and LeeAnn Iovanni. 1989. "The Labeling Perspective and Delinquency: An Elaboration of the Theory and Assessment of the Evidence." *Justice Quarterly,* 6 (December): 359–394.

Pear, Robert. 1984a. "Health Frauds Said to Prey on Elderly." *New York Times,* May 31: 13.

Pear, Robert. 1984b. "Many Who Lost Aid Work More but Stay Poor, Study Concludes." *New York Times,* March 31: 1.

Pear, Robert. 1988. "Social Security Said to Bridge Gap in Income." *New York Times,* December 28: 1.

Pearson, Jessica, and N. Thoennes. 1982. "Mediation and Divorce: The Benefits Outweigh the Cost." *Family Advocate,* 4, 3: 26, 28–32.

"Peasant's Revolt." 1988. *The Economist,* 306, 7535 (January 30): 27.

Peirce, Neal R. 1992. "The Drug War Is a Rout; Let's Look at Alternatives." *Detroit Free Press,* July 30: 15.

Pelton, Leroy. 1978. "The Myth of Classlessness in Child Abuse Cases." *American Journal of Orthopsychiatry,* 48: 569–579.

Perry, Albert. 1976. *Terrorism from Robespierre to Arafat.* New York: Vanguard Press.

Perry, Joseph B., Jr., and M. D. Pugh. 1989. "Public Support of the Guardian Angels: Vigilante Protection Against Crime, Toledo, Ohio, 1984." *Sociology and Social Research,* 73, 3: 129–130.

Petersen, William. 1966. "Success Story: Japanese American Style." *New York Times Magazine,* January 9: 36.

Petersen, William. 1975. *Population.* 3d ed. New York: Macmillan.

Petersilia, Joan. 1985. "Racial Disparities in the Criminal Justice System: A Summary." *Crime and Delinquency,* 31: 15–34.

Peterson, Iver. 1991a. "Why Older People Are Richer Than Other Americans." *New York Times,* November 3: Sec. 4, 3.

Peterson, James L., and Nicholas Zill. 1986. "Marital Disruption, Parent–Child Relationships, and Behavior Problems in Children." *Journal of Marriage and the Family,* 48 (May): 295–307.

Peterson, Janice. 1990. "The Challenge of Comparable Worth: An Institutionalist View." *Journal of Economic Issues,* 24 (June): 605–612.

Peterson, Paul E. 1991b. "The Urban Underclass and the Poverty Paradox." In Christopher Jencks and Paul E. Peterson (eds.), *The Urban Underclass,* Washington, D.C.: The Brookings Institution.

Peterson, Ruth D., and William C. Bailey. 1991. "Felony Murder and Capital Punishment: An Examination of the Deterrence Questions." *Criminology,* 29: 367–395.

Peterson, Sharyl Bender, and Traci Kroner. 1992. "Gender Biases in Textbooks for Introductory Psychology and Human Development." *Psychology of Women Quarterly,* 16: 17–36.

Peterson, Sharyl Bender, and Mary Alyce Lach. 1990. "Gender Stereotypes in Children's Books: Their Prevalence and Influence on Cognitive and Affective Development." *Gender and Education,* 2, No. 2: 185–197.

Petrocelli, William, and Barbara Kate Repa. 1992. *Sexual Harassment on the Job.* Berkeley, Calif.: Nolo Press.

Pettigrew, T. F. 1988. "Integration and Pluralism." In Phyllis A. Katz and Dalmas A. Taylor (eds.), *Eliminating Racism: Profiles in Controversy.* New York: Plenum.

Phillips, Deborah, Carollee Howes, and Marcy Whitebook. 1991. "Child Care as an Adult Work Environment." *Journal of Social Issues,* 47 (2): 49–70.

Phillips, Ulrich B. 1963. *Life and Labor in the Old South.* Boston: Little, Brown.

Pillemer, Karl, and David Finkelhor. 1988. "The Prevalence of Elder Abuse: A Random Sample Survey." *The Gerontologist,* 28 (1): 51–57.

Pillemer, Karl, and David Finkelhor. 1989. "Causes of Elder Abuse: Caregiver Stress Versus Problem Relatives." *American Journal of Orthopsychiatry,* 59 (April): 179–187.

Pillemer, Karl, and David W. Moore. 1990. "Highlights from a Study of Abuse of Patients in Nursing Homes." *Journal of Elder Abuse and Neglect,* 2: 5–29.

Pinkney, Alphonso. 1972. *The American Way of Violence.* New York: Random House.

Piotrkowski, Chaya, et al. 1987. "Families and Work." In Marvin Sussman and Suzanne Steinmetz (eds.), *Handbook of Marriage and the Family.* New York: Plenum.

Pleck, Joseph H. 1981. *The Myth of Masculinity.* Cambridge, Mass.: MIT Press.

Plissner, Martin. 1978. "Figure It This Way: Figures Can Be Unreliable." *Milwaukee Journal,* March 27: 1.

Pollock, Cynthia. 1987. "Realizing Recycling's Potential." In Lester R. Brown et al. (eds.), *State of the World, 1987: A Worldwatch Institute Report on Progress Toward a Sustainable Society*. New York: W. W. Norton.

Poplin, Dennis E. 1979. *Communities: A Survey of Theories and Methods of Research*. New York: Macmillan.

Porter, Bruce, and Marvin Dunn. 1984. *The Miami Riot of 1980: Crossing the Bounds*. Lexington, Mass.: Lexington Books.

Poskocil, Art. 1977. "Encounters Between Blacks and White Liberals: The Collision of Stereotypes." *Social Forces*, 53: 715–727.

Postel, Sandra. 1986. "Increasing Water Efficiency." In Lester R. Brown et al. (eds.), *State of the World, 1986: A Worldwatch Institute Report on Progress Toward a Sustainable Society*. New York: W. W. Norton.

Postel, Sandra. 1988. "Controlling Toxic Chemicals." In Lester R. Brown et al. (eds.), *State of the World 1988: A Worldwatch Institute Report on Progress Toward a Sustainable Society*. New York: W. W. Norton.

Prucha, Francis Paul. 1985. *The Indians in American Society: From the Revolutionary War to the Present*. Berkeley: University of California Press.

Purcell, Arthur H. 1981. "The World's Trashiest People." *The Futurist*, 15 (February): 51–59.

Purcell, Piper, and Lara Stewart. 1990. "Dick and Jane in 1989." *Sex Roles*, 22, Nos. 3–4: 177–185.

Purdy, Laura M. 1992. *In Their Best Interest? The Case Against Equal Rights for Children*. Ithaca and London: Cornell University Press.

Quindlen, Anna. 1981. "Women's Networks Come of Age." *New York Times Magazine*, November 22: 82ff.

Quinn, R. P., and G. L. Staines. 1977. *The 1977 Quality of Employment Survey*. Ann Arbor: University of Michigan, Institute for Social Research.

Quinney, Richard. 1974. *Critique of Legal Order: Crime Control in Capitalist Society*. Boston: Little, Brown.

Rainwater, Lee. 1977. "A World of Trouble: The Pruitt-Igoe Housing Project." *The Public Interest*, 8: 116–126.

Rankin, Deborah. 1985. "Protecting Your Pension—And Spouse." *New York Times*, March 24: 11.

Rankin, Joseph H. 1983. "The Family Context of Delinquency." *Social Problems*, 30: 466–479.

Rawls, Wendell. 1982. "Women in Prison Sue Kentucky for Sex Bias." *New York Times*, May 12: 1.

Ray, Barbara A. (ed.). 1988. *Learning Factors in Substance Abuse*. NIDA Research Monograph 84, DHHS Pub. No. (ADM) 88-1576. Rockville, Md.: National Institute on Drug Abuse.

Ray, Oakley. 1983. *Drugs, Society, and Human Behavior*. 3d ed. St. Louis: Mosby.

Reiman, Jeffrey H. 1979. *The Rich Get Richer and the Poor Get Prison: Ideology, Class and Criminal Justice*. New York: John Wiley and Sons.

Reiss, Paul J. 1962. "The Extended Kinship System." *Marriage and Family Living*, 22: 263–264.

Relman, Arnold S. 1980. "The New Medical–Industrial Complex." *New England Journal of Medicine*, 303: 963–970.

Reskin, Barbara F., and Patricia A. Roos. 1990. *Job Queues, Gender Queues: Explaining Women's Inroads Into Male Occupations*. Philadelphia: Temple University Press.

Reuter, Peter. 1985. "Eternal Hope: America's Quest for Narcotics Control." *The Public Interest*, 79 (Spring): 79–95.

Reynolds, Helen. 1986. *The Economics of Prostitution*. Springfield, Ill.: Charles C Thomas.

Reynolds, Larry T. 1987. *Interactionism: Exposition and Critique*. Dix Hills, N.Y.: General Hall, Inc.

Rice, Dorothy P., Sander Kelman, and Leonard S. Miller. 1991. "Estimates of Economic Costs of Alcohol and Drug Abuse and Mental Illness, 1985 and 1988." *Public Health Reports*, 106 (May/June): 280–292.

Richardson, Laurel. 1988. *The Dynamics of Sex and Gender: A Sociological Perspective*. 3d ed. New York: Harper and Row.

Richmond-Abbott, Marie. 1992. *Masculine and Feminine: Gender Roles Over the Life Cycle*. 2d ed. New York: McGraw-Hill.

Richter, Maurice N., Jr. 1982. *Technology and Social Complexity*. Albany: State University of New York Press.

Ricketts, Erol R., and Isabel V. Sawhill. 1988. "Defining and Measuring the Underclass." *Journal of Policy Analysis and Management,* 7(2): 316–325.

Ridker, R. 1980. "The No-Birth Bonus Scheme: The Use of Savings Accounts for Family Planning in South India." *Population and Development Review,* 6: 31–46.

Riesman, David. 1961. *The Lonely Crowd.* New Haven, Conn.: Yale University Press.

Rifkin, Jeremy. 1987. "Is Nature Just a Form of Private Property?" *New York Times,* April 26: Sec. 3, 2.

Rifkin, Jeremy. 1991. *Biosphere Politics: A New Consciousness for a New Century.* New York: Crown.

Rio, Linda M. 1991. "Psychological and Sociological Research and the Decriminalization or Legalization of Prostitution." *Archives of Sexual Behavior,* 20: 205–218.

Rist, Ray C. 1979. *Desegregated Schools: Appraisals of an American Experiment.* New York: Academic Press.

Robbins, Jim. 1989. "Saboteurs for a Better Environment." *New York Times,* July 9: Sec. 4, 6.

Robins, L. N., J. E. Helzer, and D. H. Davis. 1975. "Narcotic Use in Southeast Asia and Afterward." *Archives of General Psychiatry,* 32: 955–961.

Robinson, Arthur L. 1980. "Perilous Times for U.S. Microcircuit Makers." *Science,* 208, May 9: 582–586.

Robinson, Bryan E., Patsy Skeen, Carol Flake Hobson, and Margaret Herrman. 1982. "Gay Men's and Women's Perceptions of Early Family Life and Their Relationships with Parents." *Family Relations,* 31 (January): 79–83.

Robinson, David. 1983. "Alcoholics Anonymous: American Origins and the International Diffusion of a Self-Help Group." In Griffith Edwards, Awni Arif, and Jerome Jaffe (eds.), *Drug Use and Misuse: Cultural Perspective.* New York: St. Martin's Press.

Robinson, William S. 1992. *Computers, Minds, and Robots.* Philadelphia: Temple University Press.

Robock, Alan. 1989. "New Models Confirm Nuclear Winter." *Bulletin of the Atomic Scientists,* 45 (September): 32–35.

Robyn, Dorothy L., and Jack Hadley. 1980. "New Health Occupations: Nurse Practitioners and Physicians' Assistants." In Judith Feder, John Holahan, and Theodore Marmor (eds.), *National Health Insurance: Conflicting Goals and Policy Choices.* Washington, D.C.: Urban Institute Press.

Rodgers, Harrell L., Jr. 1990. *Poor Women, Poor Families: The Economic Plight of America's Female-Headed Households.* Armonk, N.Y.: M.E. Sharpe, Inc.

Rogers, Susan M., and Charles F. Turner. 1991. "Male-Male Sexual Contact in the U.S.A.: Findings from Five Sample Surveys, 1970–1990." *The Journal of Sex Research,* 28 (November): 491–519.

Rose, Arnold M. 1967. *The Power Structure: Political Process in American Society.* New York: Oxford University Press.

Rosen, Corey, and Karen M. Youngs (eds.). 1991. *Understanding Employee Ownership.* Ithaca, N.Y.: ILR Press.

Rosenbaum, David E. 1984. "In Four Years, Reagan Changed Bases of the Debate on Domestic Programs." *New York Times,* October 25: 15.

Rosenfeld, Rachel A., and Arne L. Kalleberg. 1991. "Gender Inequality in the Labor Market: A Cross-National Perspective." *Acta Sociologica,* 34: 207–225.

Rosenhan, D. L. 1973. "On Being Sane in Insane Places." *Science,* 179: 250–258.

Ross, Judith W. 1991. "Elder Abuse." *Health and Social Work,* 16 (November): 227–229.

Ross, Michael W., James A. Paulsen, and Olli W. Stalstrom. 1988. "Homosexuality and Mental Health: A Cross-Cultural Review." *Journal of Homosexuality,* 15: 131–152.

Rossell, C. H. 1990. *The Carrot or the Stick for Desegregation Policy.* Philadelphia: Temple University Press.

Rossi, Alice. 1984. "Gender and Parenthood." *American Sociological Review,* 49: 1–19.

Rothfeder, Jeffrey. 1992. *Privacy for Sale: How Computerization Has Made Everyone's Private Life an Open Secret.* New York: Simon and Schuster.

Rounsaville, Bruce J., et al. 1984. "Psychiatric Disorders in Treated Opiate Addicts." In George Serban (ed.), *Social and Medical Aspects of Drug Abuse.* New York: SP Medical and Scientific Books.

Rowe, A. R., and C. R. Tittle. 1977. "Life Cycle Changes and Criminal Propensity." *Sociological Quarterly,* 18: 223–236.

Rubenstein, Richard E. 1987. *Alchemists of Revolution: Terrorism in the Modern World.* New York: Basic Books.

Ruggles, Patricia. 1990. *Drawing the Line: Alternative Poverty Measures and Their Implications for Public Policy.* Washington, D.C.: Urban Institute Press.

Russell, Diana E. H. 1990. *Rape in Marriage.* Bloomington and Indianapolis: Indiana University Press.

Russell, Dick. 1989. "Environmental Tensions: 'We Are All Losing the War.'" *The Nation,* 248 (March 27): 403–408.

Russett, Bruce. 1969. "Who Pays for Defense?" *American Political Science Review,* 63: 412–426.

Ryan, John C. 1992. "Conserving Biological Diversity." In Lester R. Brown et al. (eds.), *State of the World 1992: A Worldwatch Institute Report on Progress Toward a Sustainable Society.* New York: W. W. Norton.

Ryan, William. 1976. *Blaming the Victim.* Rev. and updated ed. New York: Vintage Books.

Sadik, Nafis. 1989. "Discrimination Against Girls." In *State of the World Population Report.* New York: United Nations.

Sadker, Myra, et al. 1986. "Abolishing Misconceptions About Sex Equity in Education." *Theory Into Practice,* 25: 219–226.

Sagan, Carl, and Richard Turco. 1990. *A Path Where No Man Thought: Nuclear Winter and the End of the Arms Race.* New York: Random House.

Salas, Rafael M. 1984. *Reflections on Population.* New York: Pergamon Press.

Sale, Kirkpatrick. 1980. *Human Scale.* New York: Coward, McCann, and Geoghegan.

Sampson, Anthony. 1973. *The Sovereign State of ITT.* Greenwich, Conn.: Fawcett Crest.

Sandefur, Gary D., and Arthur Sakamoto. 1988. "American Indian Household Structure and Income." *Demography,* 25 (February): 71–80.

Sandroff, Lonni. 1988. "Sexual Harassment in the Fortune 500." *Working Woman,* December: 69–71.

Santiago, Anne M., and Margaret G. Wilder. 1991. "Residential Segregation and Links to Minority Poverty: The Case of Latinos in the United States." *Social Problems,* 38 (November): 492–515.

Santino, Umberto. 1988. "The Financial Mafia: The Illegal Accumulation of Wealth and the Financial–Industrial Complex." *Contemporary Crises,* 12: 203–243.

Savin-Williams, Ritch C. 1990. *Gay and Lesbian Youth: Expressions of Identity.* New York: Hemisphere Publishing.

Saxton, Lloyd. 1980. *The Individual, Marriage, and the Family.* 4th ed. Belmont, Calif.: Wadsworth Publishing Company.

Scanlon, Walter F. 1986. *Alcoholism and Drug Abuse in the Workplace.* New York: Praeger.

Schack, S., and R. S. Frank. 1978. "Police Service Delivery to the Elderly." *Annals of the American Academy of Political and Social Science,* 438: 81–95.

Schaefer, Richard T. 1993. *Racial and Ethnic Groups.* 5th ed. New York: Harper and Row.

Schaller, Warren E., and Charles R. Carroll. 1976. *Health, Quackery and the Consumer.* Philadelphia: W. B. Saunders.

Scheff, Thomas J. 1984. *Being Mentally Ill: A Sociological Theory.* 2d ed. New York: Aldine.

Schilling, Robert F., and Alfred L. McAlister. 1990. "Preventing Drug Use in Adolescents Through Media Interventions." *Journal of Consulting and Clinical Psychology,* 58: 416–424.

Schlesinger, Arthur M. Jr. 1986. *The Cycles of American History.* Boston: Houghton Mifflin.

Schnall, Peter L., and Rochelle Kern. 1986. "Hypertension in American Society: An Introduction to Historical Materialist Epidemiology." In Peter Conrad and Rochelle Kern (eds.), *The Sociology of Health and Illness: Critical Perspectives.* 2d ed. New York: St. Martin's Press.

Schneider, Keith. 1992. "Wasting Away." *New York Times Magazine,* August 30: 42–58.

Schneider, William, and I. A. Lewis. 1984. "The Straight Story on Homosexuality and Gay Rights." *Public Opinion,* 7, No. 1 (February/March): 16–20.

Schram, Sanford F. 1991. "Welfare Spending and Poverty: Cutting Back Produces More Poverty, Not Less." *American Journal of Economics and Sociology,* 50 (April): 129–141.

Schuckit, Marc A. 1989. *Drug and Alcohol Abuse.* 3d ed. New York and London: Plenum.

Schuessler, Karl F. 1952. "The Deterrent Effect of the Death Penalty." *Annals of the American Academy of Political and Social Sciences,* 284: 54–63.

Schur, Edwin M. 1965. *Crimes Without Victims.* Englewood Cliffs, N.J.: Prentice-Hall.

Schur, Edwin M. 1988. *The Americanization of Sex.* Philadelphia: Temple University Press.

Schutt, Russell K. 1990. "The Quantity and Quality of Homelessness: Research Results and Policy Implications." *Sociological Practice Review,* 1 (August): 77–87.

Schwartz, Felice N. 1989. "Management Women and the New Facts of Life." *Harvard Business Review,* January/February: 65–76.

Schwartz, Gail Garfield. 1984. *Where's Main Street, U.S.A.?* Westport, Conn.: Eno Foundation for Transportation.

Scott, Wilbur J. 1985. "The Equal Rights Amendment as Status Politics." *Social Forces,* 64, No. 2 (December): 499–506.

Sears, D. O. 1988. "Symbolic Racism." In P. A. Katz and D. A. Taylor (eds.), *Eliminating Racism.* New York: Plenum.

Sears, R. R., E. E. Maccoby, and H. Levin. 1957. *Patterns of Childrearing.* New York: Harper and Row.

Seeman, Melvin, Alice Z. Seeman, and Art Budros. 1988. "Powerlessness, Work, and Community: A Longitudinal Study of Alienation and Alcohol Use." *Journal of Health and Social Behavior,* 29 (September): 185–198.

Segal, Lynne. 1990. "Pornography and Violence: What the 'Experts' Really Say." *Feminist Review,* 36 (Autumn): 29–41.

Segalman, Ralph, and Asoke Basu. 1981. *Poverty in America: The Welfare Dilemma.* Westport, Conn.: Greenwood Press.

Sekaran, Uma. 1986. *Dual-Career Families.* San Francisco: Jossey-Bass.

Sellin, Thorsten. 1959. *The Death Penalty.* Philadelphia: American Law Institute.

Serrin, William. 1989. "The Myth of the 'New Work': A Great American Job Machine?" *The Nation,* 249 (September 18): 269–272.

"Sexual Harassment Cases Still Murky." 1991. *Trial,* 27 (May): 14–15.

Shaiken, Harley. 1987. "A Threat to Dignity? When the Computer Runs the Office." *New York Times,* March 22: Sec. 3, 5.

Shanas, E. 1972. "Adjustment to Retirement: Substitution or Accommodation." In F. Carp (ed.), *Retirement.* New York: Behavioral Publications.

Shea, Cynthia Pollock. 1988. "Shifting to Renewable Energy." In Lester R. Brown et al. (eds.), *State of the World 1988: A Worldwatch Institute Report on Progress Toward a Sustainable Society.* New York: W. W. Norton.

Shefter, Martin. 1985. *Political Crisis/Fiscal Crisis: The Collapse and Revival of New York City.* New York: Basic Books.

Sheley, Joseph F. 1985. *America's "Crime Problem": An Introduction to Criminology.* Belmont, Calif.: Wadsworth Publishing Company.

Sherman, Lawrence W., and Richard A. Berk. 1984. "The Specific Deterrent Effects of Arrest for Domestic Violence." *American Sociological Review,* 49: 261–271.

Shibutani, Tamotsu. 1978. *The Derelicts of Company K.* Berkeley: University of California Press.

Shichman, Shula, and Ellen Cooper. 1984. "Life Satisfaction and Sex-Role Concept." *Sex Roles,* 11, No. 3/4: 227–240.

Shichor, David, and Clemens Bartollas. 1990. "Private and Public Juvenile Placements: Is There a Difference?" *Crime and Delinquency,* 36 (April): 286–299.

Shilts, Randy. 1987. *And the Band Played On: Politics, People, and the AIDS Epidemic.* New York: St. Martin's Press.

Shipp, E. R. 1981. "99 of 100 Arrests in New York City for Felonies Fail to Lead to Prison." *New York Times,* January 4: 1.

Shockley, William B. 1980. "Playboy Interview: William Shockley." *Playboy,* August: 73.

Shulman, Norman. 1975. "Life-Cycle Variations in Patterns of Close Relationships." *Journal of Marriage and the Family,* 37: 813–821.

Sigerist, Henry E. 1977. "The Special Position of the Sick." In David Landy (ed.), *Culture, Disease, and*

Healing: Studies in Medical Anthropology. New York: Macmillan.

Simmons, Jack L. 1969. *Deviants.* Berkeley, Calif.: Glendessary Press.

Simon, Julian L. 1981. *The Ultimate Resource.* Princeton, N.J.: Princeton University Press.

Simons, Ronald L., and Phyllis A. Gray. 1989. "Perceived Blocked Opportunity as an Explanation of Delinquency Among Lower-Class Black Males: A Research Note." *Journal of Research in Crime and Delinquency,* 26, 1 (February): 90–101.

Simons, Ronald L., and Les B. Whitbeck. 1991. "Sexual Abuse as a Precursor to Prostitution and Victimization Among Adolescent and Adult Homeless Women." *Journal of Family Issues,* 12 (September): 361–379.

Simpson, George Eaton, and J. Milton Yinger. 1985. *Racial and Cultural Minorities.* 5th ed. New York: Plenum.

Singer, J. David, and Melvin Small. 1972. *The Wages of War, 1816–1965: A Statistical Handbook.* New York: John Wiley and Sons.

Smith, Douglas A., and Patrick R. Gartin. 1989. "Specifying Specific Deterrence: The Influence of Arrest on Future Criminal Activity." *American Sociological Review,* 54 (February): 94–105.

Smith, Douglas A., and Jody R. Klein. 1984. "Police Control of Interpersonal Disputes." *Social Problems,* 31 (April): 468–481.

Smith, Kevin B., and Lorene H. Stone. 1989. "Rags, Riches, and Bootstraps: Beliefs About the Causes of Wealth and Poverty." *The Sociological Quarterly,* 30, 1: 93–107.

Smith, Neil, and Michele LeFaiure. 1984. "A Class Analysis of Gentrification." In J. John Palen and Bruce London (eds.), *Gentrification, Displacement and Neighborhood Revitalization.* Albany: State University of New York Press.

Smith, Robert B. 1972. "Rebellion and Repression and the Vietnam War." In James F. Short, Jr., and Marvin Wolfgang (eds.), *Collective Violence.* Chicago: Aldine-Atherton.

Smith, Shelley A. 1991. "Sources of Earnings Inequality in the Black and White Female Labor Forces." *The Sociological Quarterly,* 32, No. 1: 117–138.

Smock, Pamela J., and Franklin D. Wilson. 1991. "Desegregation and the Stability of White Enroll-ments: A School-Level Analysis, 1968–84." *Sociology of Education,* 64 (October): 278–292.

Sniderman, Paul M., Thomas Piazza, Philip E. Tetlock, and Ann Kendrick. 1991. "The New Racism." *American Journal of Political Science,* 35 (May): 423–447.

Snipp, C. Matthew. 1989. *American Indians: The First of This Land.* New York: Russell Sage Foundation.

Sobel, L. A. (ed.). 1979. *Pornography, Obscenity and the Law.* New York: Facts on File.

Sommers, Ira. 1988. "The Influence of Environmental Factors on the Community Adjustment of the Mentally Ill." *The Journal of Nervous and Mental Disorders,* 176: 221–226.

Sowell, Thomas. 1981. *Ethnic America: A History.* New York: Basic Books.

Spade, Joan Z., and Carole A. Reese. 1991. "We've Come a Long Way, Maybe: College Students' Plans for Work and Family." *Sex Roles,* 24, Nos. 5–6: 309–321.

Spector, Malcolm, and John I. Kitsuse. 1987. *Constructing Social Problems.* 2d ed. New York: Aldine de Gruyter.

Spilerman, Seymour. 1976. "Structural Characteristics of Cities and the Severity of Racial Disorders." *American Sociological Review,* 41: 771–793.

Spitzer, Kirk. 1992. "Group May Give Women a Fighting Chance at Combat." *Detroit News and Free Press,* July 5: 2.

Spurr, Stephen J. 1990. "Sex Discrimination in the Legal Profession: A Study of Promotion." *Industrial and Labor Relations Review,* 43 (April): 406–417.

Stack, Steven. 1990. "Execution Publicity and Homicide in South Carolina: A Research Note." *Sociological Quarterly,* 31 (Winter): 599–611.

Stahura, John M. 1989–90. "Rapid Black Suburbanization of the 1970s: Some Policy Considerations." *Policy Studies Journal,* 18 (Winter): 279–291.

Stahura, John, C. Ronald Huff, and Brent L. Smith. 1979. "Crime in the Suburbs." *Urban Affairs Quarterly,* 15: 291–316.

Stark, Leonard P. 1991. "Traditional Gender Role Beliefs and Individual Outcomes: An Exploratory Analysis." *Sex Roles,* 24: 639–650.

Steffensmeier, Darrell. 1989. "On the Causes of 'White-Collar' Crime: An Assessment of Hirschi and Gottfredson's Claims." *Criminology*, 27, 2: 345–358.

Steffensmeier, Darrell J., and Emilie Andersen Allan. 1988. "Sex Disparities in Arrests by Residence, Race, and Age: An Assessment of the Gender Convergence/Crime Hypothesis." *Justice Quarterly*, 5, 1 (March): 53–80.

Stegman, Michael A. 1990. "A Bush/Kemp Report Card." *Journal of Housing* (September/October): 237–246.

Stehr-Green, Paul A., and Jeffrey A. Lybarger. 1989. "Exposure to Toxic Waste Sites: An Investigative Approach." *Public Health Reports*, 104, 1 (January/February): 71–74.

Stein, Barry A., and Rosabeth Moss Kanter. 1980. "Building the Parallel Organization: Creating Mechanisms for Permanent Quality of Work Life." *The Journal of Applied Behavioral Science*, 16: 371–386.

Steinberg, Jon. 1985. "Letter from the Editor." *Health/PAC Bulletin*, 16 (March/April): 3.

Steinem, Gloria. 1980. "Erotica and Pornography: A Clear and Present Difference." In L. Lederer (ed.), *Take Back the Night: Women on Pornography*. New York: William Morrow.

Steinmetz, Suzanne K. 1987. "Family Violence." In Marvin B. Sussman and Suzanne K. Steinmetz (eds.), *Handbook of Marriage and the Family*. New York: Plenum.

Stephens, Richard C. 1987. *Mind-Altering Drugs: Use, Abuse, and Treatment*. Beverly Hills, Calif.: Sage Publications.

Sternlieb, George, and James W. Hughes. 1983. "The Uncertain Future of the Central City." *Urban Affairs Quarterly*, 18, No. 4 (June): 455–472.

Stets, Jan E. 1991. "Cohabiting and Marital Aggression: The Role of Social Isolation." *Journal of Marriage and the Family*, 53 (August): 669–680.

Stevens, Robert Warren. 1976. *Vain Hopes, Grim Realities: The Economic Consequences of the Vietnam War*. New York: New Viewpoints.

Stewart, James B. 1991. *Den of Thieves*. New York: Simon and Schuster.

Stitt, B. Grant. 1988. "Victimless Crime: A Definitional Issue." *Journal of Crime and Justice*, 11, No. 2: 87–102.

Stockard, Jean, and Miriam M. Johnson. 1992. *Sex and Gender in Society*, 2d ed. Englewood Cliffs, N.J.: Prentice-Hall.

Stohl, Michael. 1976. *War and Domestic Political Violence: The American Capacity for Repression and Reaction*. Beverly Hills, Calif.: Sage Publications.

Stone, John. 1985. *Racial Conflict in Contemporary Society*. Cambridge, Mass.: Harvard University Press.

Straus, Murray A. 1991. "Physical Violence in American Families: Incidence Rates, Causes, and Trends." In Dean D. Knudsen and JoAnn L. Miller (eds.), *Abused and Battered: Social and Legal Responses to Family Violence*. New York: Aldine de Gruyter.

Straus, Murray, and Richard J. Gelles. 1986. "Societal Change and Change in Family Violence from 1975 to 1985 as Revealed by Two National Surveys." *Journal of Marriage and the Family*, 48 (August): 465–479.

Straus, Murray A., R. J. Gelles, and S. K. Steinmetz. 1980. *Behind Closed Doors: A Study of Family Violence in America*. Garden City, N.Y.: Anchor Press/Doubleday.

Strickland, Daryl. 1986. "Pressure Builds on Retailers to Quit Selling Sex Magazines." *Detroit Free Press*, June 8: Sec. C, 1.

Stroman, Duane F. 1979. *The Quick Knife: Unnecessary Surgery U.S.A.* Port Washington, N.Y.: Kennikat Press.

Strug, David, Eric Wish, Bruce Johnson, Kevin Anderson, Thomas Miller, and Alton Sears. 1984. "The Role of Alcohol in the Crimes of Active Heroin Users." *Crime and Delinquency*, 30, No. 4 (October): 551–567.

Struyk, Raymond J., Douglas B. Page, Sandra Newman, Maria Carroll, Makiko Ueno, Barbara Cohen, and Paul Wright. 1989. *Providing Supportive Services to the Frail Elderly in Federally Assisted Housing*. Washington, D.C.: Urban Institute Press.

"Study Finds Bias in House Hunting." 1991. *New York Times*, September 1: 14.

Sullivan, Thomas J. 1992. *Applied Sociology: Research and Critical Thinking*. New York: Macmillan.

"Superfund, Superflop." 1989. *U.S. News and World Report*, February 6: 47–49.

Suro, Roberto. 1989. "Grass-Roots Groups Show Power Battling Pollution Close to Home." *New York Times,* July 2: 1.

Sutherland, Edwin H. 1925. "Murder and the Death Penalty." *Journal of the American Institute of Criminal Law and Criminology,* 51: 522–529.

Sutherland, Edwin H. 1949. *White Collar Crime.* New York: Dryden.

Sutherland, Edwin H., and Donald R. Cressey. 1978. *Criminology.* 10th ed. Philadelphia: Lippincott.

Suttles, Gerald D. 1968. *The Social Order of the Slum.* Chicago: University of Chicago Press.

Sutton, L. 1983. "The Effects of Alcohol, Marijuana, and Their Combination on Driving Ability." *Journal of Studies on Alcohol,* 44: 438–445.

Swickard, Joe. 1986. "Longer Terms for Repeat Offenders Could Cut Crime Rate, Study Claims." *Detroit Free Press,* September 9: 2.

Switzer, J. Y. 1990. "The Impact of Generic Word Choices: An Empirical Investigation of Age- and Sex-Related Differences." *Sex Roles,* 22: 69–82.

Sykes, Gresham M., and Francis T. Cullen. 1992. *Criminology.* 2d ed. Fort Worth, Tex.: Harcourt Brace Jovanovich.

Syme, S. Leonard, and Lisa F. Berkman. 1979. "Social Class, Susceptibility and Sickness." In Jeannette R. Folta and Edith S. Deck (eds.), *A Sociological Framework for Patient Care.* 2d ed. New York: John Wiley and Sons.

Szasz, Thomas S. 1970. *Ideology and Insanity: Essays on the Psychiatric Dehumanization of Man.* Garden City, N.Y.: Anchor Books.

Szasz, Thomas S. 1987. *Insanity: The Idea and Its Consequences.* New York: John Wiley and Sons.

Szymanski, Albert J. 1976. "Racial Discrimination and White Gain." *American Sociological Review,* 41: 403–414.

Taffel, Selma M., Paul J. Placek, Mary Moien, and Carol L. Kosary. 1991. "1989 U.S. Cesarean Section Rate Steadies—VBAC Rate Rises to Nearly One in Five." *Birth,* 18 (June): 73–77.

Taft, Philip, and Philip Ross. 1969. "American Labor Violence: Its Causes, Character, and Outcome." In Hugh Davis Graham and Ted Robert Gurr (eds.), *Violence in America.* New York: Bantam Books.

Takanishi, Ruby. 1978. "Childhood as a Social Issue: Historical Roots of Contemporary Child Advocacy Movements." *Journal of Social Issues,* 34: 8–28.

Tausky, Curt. 1984. *Work and Society: An Introduction to Industrial Sociology.* Itasca, Ill.: F. E. Peacock Publishers.

Tavris, Carol. 1992. *The Mismeasure of Woman.* New York: Simon and Schuster.

Tavris, Carol, and Carole Wade. 1984. *The Longest War: Sex Differences in Perspective.* 2d ed. San Diego: Harcourt Brace Jovanovich.

Taylor, Ronald B. 1973. *Sweatshops in the Sun: Child Labor on the Farm.* Boston: Beacon Press.

Taylor, Stuart Jr. 1986. "High Court Backs Use of Zoning to Regulate Showing of Sex Films." *New York Times,* February 26: 1.

Teich, Albert H. (ed.). 1986. *Technology and the Future.* 4th ed. New York: St. Martin's Press.

Thio, Alex. 1983. *Deviant Behavior.* 3d ed. Boston: Houghton Mifflin.

Thio, Alex. 1988. *Deviant Behavior.* 4th ed. Boston: Houghton Mifflin.

Thomas, William I., and Dorothy S. Thomas. 1928. *The Child in America.* New York: Alfred A. Knopf.

Thompson, Kenrick S. 1980. "Measuring Beliefs, Perceived Social Pressures, and Decisions About Having Children: A Multi-dimensional Approach." *Journal of Marriage and the Family,* 44: 3–13.

Thompson, Warren S., and David T. Lewis. 1965. *Population Problems.* 5th ed. New York: McGraw-Hill.

Thorkelson, Anne E. 1985. "Women Under the Law: Has Equity Been Achieved?" In Alice G. Sargent (ed.), *Beyond Sex Roles,* 2d ed. St. Paul, Minn.: West Publishing Company.

Thornton, Arland. 1985. "Changing Attitudes Toward Separation and Divorce: Causes and Consequences." *American Journal of Sociology,* 90: 856–872.

Thornton, Robert Y., and Katsuya Endo. 1992. *Preventing Crime in America and Japan: A Comparative Study.* Armonk, N.Y.: M.E. Sharpe.

Thornton, Russell. 1987. *American Indian Holocaust and Survival: A Population History Since 1492.* Norman and London: University of Oklahoma Press.

Thurow, Lester. 1992. *Head to Head: The Coming Economic Battle Among Japan, Europe, and America.* New York: Morrow.

Tienda, M. 1989. "Puerto Ricans and the Underclass Debate." *Annals of the American Academy of Political and Social Science,* 501 (January): 105–119.

Tinbergen, Niko. 1955. "The Curious Behavior of the Stickleback." In *Twentieth Century Bestiary.* New York: Simon and Schuster.

Tittle, Charles R. 1989. "Urbanness and Unconventional Behavior: A Partial Test of Claude Fischer's Subcultural Theory." *Criminology,* 27 (May): 273–306.

Tittle, C., W. Villemez, and D. Smith. 1978. "The Myth of Social Class and Criminality: An Empirical Assessment of the Empirical Evidence." *American Sociological Review,* 43: 643–656.

Tolchin, Martin. 1985a. "As Privately Owned Prisons Increase, So Do Their Critics." *New York Times,* February 11: 2.

Tolchin, Martin. 1985b. "Jails Run by Private Concern Force It to Face Questions of Accountability." *New York Times,* February 19: 9.

Tönnies, Ferdinand. 1963, originally published 1887. *Community and Society.* East Lansing: Michigan State University Press.

Torrey, E. Fuller. 1988. *Nowhere to Go: The Tragic Odyssey of the Homeless Mentally Ill.* New York: Harper and Row.

Totti, Xavier F. 1987. "The Making of a Latino Ethnic Identity." *Dissent,* Fall: 537–543.

Trebach, Arnold S. 1982. *The Heroin Solution.* New Haven, Conn.: Yale University Press.

Triandis, H. C. 1988. "The Future of Pluralism Revisited." In Phyllis A. Katz and Dalmas A. Taylor (eds.), *Eliminating Racism: Profiles in Controversy.* New York: Plenum.

Trice, Harrison M. 1966. *Alcoholism in America.* New York: McGraw-Hill.

Troiden, Richard R. 1989. "The Formation of Homosexual Identities." *Journal of Homosexuality,* 17: 43–73.

Turco, R. P., et al. 1983. "Nuclear Winter: Global Consequences of Multiple Nuclear Explosions." *Science,* 222 (December 23): 1283–1292.

Turco, R. P., and G. S. Golitsyn. 1988. "Global Effects of Nuclear War: A Status Report." *Environment,* 30 (June): 8–16.

Turner, Jonathan, and Alexandra Maryanski. 1979. *Functionalism.* Menlo Park, Calif.: Benjamin/Cummings.

Tyler, Patrick E. 1992. "U.S. Strategy Plan Calls for Insuring No Rivals Develop." *New York Times,* March 8: 1, 4.

Uchitelle, Louis. 1989. "Trade Barriers and Dollar Swings Raise Appeal of Factories Abroad." *New York Times,* March 26: 1, 13.

U.S. Arms Control and Disarmament Agency. 1982. *Arms Control and Disarmament Agreements: Texts and Histories of Negotiations.* Washington, D.C.: U.S. Government Printing Office.

U.S. Bureau of the Census. 1978. *Statistical Abstract of the United States, 1978.* Washington, D.C.: U.S. Government Printing Office.

U.S. Bureau of the Census. 1982. *Statistical Abstract of the United States, 1982–1983.* Washington, D.C.: U.S. Government Printing Office.

U.S. Bureau of the Census. 1984. *Statistical Abstract of the United States, 1985.* Washington, D.C.: U.S. Government Printing Office.

U.S. Bureau of the Census. 1989. *Statistical Abstract of the United States, 1989.* Washington, D.C.: U.S. Government Printing Office.

U.S. Bureau of the Census. 1991. *Statistical Abstract of the United States, 1991.* Washington, D.C.: U.S. Government Printing Office.

U.S. Bureau of the Census. 1991a. *Poverty in the United States, 1990.* Current Population Reports, Series P-60, No. 175. Washington, D.C.: U.S. Government Printing Office.

U.S. Bureau of the Census. 1992. *Statistical Abstract of the United States, 1992.* Washington, D.C.: U.S. Government Printing Office.

U.S. Bureau of the Census. 1992a. *Workers with Low Earnings: 1964 to 1990.* Current Population Reports, Series P-60, No. 178. Washington, D.C.: U.S. Government Printing Office.

U.S. Congress, Office of Technology Assessment. 1989. *New Developments in Biotechnology: Patenting*

Life—Special Report, OTA-BA-370 April, Washington, D.C.: U.S. Government Printing Office.

U.S. Department of Health and Human Services. 1983. *Fifth Special Report to the U.S. Congress on Alcohol and Health.* DHHS Pub. No. (ADM) 84-1291. Washington, D.C.: U.S. Government Printing Office.

U.S. Department of Health and Human Services. 1991. *Aging America: Trends and Projections,* DHHS Pub. No. (FCoA) 91-28001. Washington, D.C.: U.S. Department of Health and Human Services.

U.S. Department of Health, Education, and Welfare. 1969. *Toward a Social Report.* Washington, D.C.: U.S. Government Printing Office.

U.S. Department of Justice. 1992. *Combating Violent Crime: 24 Recommendations to Strengthen Criminal Justice.* Washington, D.C.: U.S. Government Printing Office.

U.S. Department of Labor. 1992. *Employment and Earnings,* 39 (January).

U.S. Department of State. 1991a. *International Narcotics Control Strategy Report.* Department of State Pub. 9853-A. Washington, D.C.: U.S. Government Printing Office.

U.S. Department of State. 1991b. *Patterns of Global Terrorism: 1990.* Department of State Pub. 9862. Washington, D.C.: U.S. Government Printing Office.

U.S. General Accounting Office. 1990. *Methadone Maintenance: Report to the Select Committee on Narcotics Abuse and Control, House of Representatives.* GAO Pub. No. HRD-90-104. Washington, D.C.: U.S. Government Printing Office.

Vallas, Steven Peter. 1988. "New Technology, Job Control, and Worker Alienation: A Test of Two Rival Perspectives." *Work and Occupations,* 15 (May): 148–178.

van de Kaa, Dirk J. 1987. "Europe's Second Demographic Transition." *Population Bulletin,* 42, 1 (March): entire issue.

van der Dennen, J., and V. Falger (eds.). 1990. *Sociobiology and Conflict: Evolutionary Perspectives on Competition, Cooperation, Violence, and Warfare.* London: Chapman and Hall.

Vanderkolk, Barbara Schwarz, and Ardis Armstrong Young. 1991. *The Work and Family Revolution: How Companies Can Keep Employees Happy and Business Profitable.* New York: Facts on File.

Vander Zanden, James W. 1987. *Social Psychology.* 4th ed. New York: Random House.

Van Evra, Judith. 1990. *Television and Child Development.* Hillsdale, N.J.: Lawrence Erlbaum Associates.

Van Horn, Susan Householder. 1988. *Women, Work, and Fertility, 1900–1986.* New York and London: New York University Press.

Vannoy-Hiller, Dana, and William W. Philliber. 1989. *Equal Partners: Successful Women in Marriage.* Newbury Park, Calif.: Sage Publications.

Veatch, R. M., and R. Branson (eds.). 1976. *Ethics and Health Policy.* Cambridge, Mass.: Ballinger.

Verbrugge, Lois. 1979. "Marital Status and Health." *Journal of Marriage and the Family,* 41: 267–285.

Verbrugge, Lois M. 1983. "Multiple Roles and Physical Health of Women and Men." *Journal of Health and Social Behavior,* 24: 16–30.

Vernon-Wortzel, Heidi, and Lawrence H. Wortzel. 1988. "Globalizing Strategies for Multinationals from Developing Countries." *The Columbia Journal of World Business,* 23 (Spring): 27–35.

Veum, Jonathan R., and Philip M. Gleason. 1991. "Child Care: Arrangements and Costs." *Monthly Labor Review,* 114 (October): 10–17.

Vigil, James Diego. 1980. *From Indians to Chicanos: A Sociocultural History.* St. Louis: Mosby.

Vinovskis, Maris A. 1978. "Angels' Heads and Weeping Willows: Death in Early America." In Michael Gordon (ed.), *The American Family in Social-Historical Perspective.* New York: Random House.

Volti, Rudi. 1992. *Society and Technological Change.* 2d ed. New York: St. Martin's Press.

von Hirsch, Andrew. 1985. *Past or Future Crimes: Deservedness and Dangerousness in the Sentencing of Criminals.* New Brunswick, N.J.: Rutgers University Press.

Vroom, P. D., D. Fassett, and R. A. Wakefield. 1981. "Mediation: The Wave of the Future?" *American Family,* 4 (June/July): 8–13.

Waldron, Ingrid. 1986. "Why Do Women Live Longer Than Men?" In Peter Conrad and Rochelle Kern (eds.), *The Sociology of Health and Illness: Critical Perspectives*. 2d ed. New York: St. Martin's Press.

Walker, Nigel, and Mike Hough (eds.). 1988. *Public Attitudes to Sentencing: Surveys from Five Countries*. Aldershot, UK: Gower.

Wallace, Steven P., John B. Williamson, Rita Gaston Lung, and Lawrence A. Powell. 1991. "A Lamb in Wolf's Clothing? The Reality of Senior Power and Social Policy." In Meredith Minkler and Carroll L. Estes (eds.), *Critical Perspectives on Aging: The Political and Moral Economy of Growing Old*. Amityville, N.Y.: Baywood.

Wallerstein, Judith S., and Sandra Blakeslee. 1989. *Second Chances: Men, Women, and Children a Decade After Divorce*. New York: Ticknor and Fields.

Wallerstein, Judith S., and Joan Berlin Kelly. 1980. *Surviving the Breakup: How Children and Parents Cope with Divorce*. New York: Basic Books.

Walther, Robin Jane. 1983. "Economics of Aging." In Diana S. Woodruff and James E. Birren (eds.), *Aging: Scientific Perspectives and Social Issues*. 2d ed. Monterey, Calif.: Brooks-Cole.

Wanner, Richard A., and Lionel S. Lewis. 1978. "The Functional Theory of Stratification: A Test of Some Structural Hypotheses." *The Sociological Quarterly*, 19: 414–428.

"The War Against Pornography." 1985. *Newsweek*, March 18: 58–66.

Ward, Russell A., Mark LaGory, and Susan R. Sherman. 1986. "Fear of Crime Among the Elderly as Person/Environment Interaction." *Sociological Quarterly*, 27: 327–341.

Warner, Sir Frederick. 1988. "The Environmental Effects of Nuclear War: Consensus and Uncertainties." *Environment*, 30 (June): 2–7.

Wasik, Barbara Hanna, Craig T. Ramey, Donna M. Bryant, and Joseph J. Sparling. 1990. "A Longitudinal Study of Two Early Intervention Strategies: Project CARE." *Child Development*, 61: 1682–1696.

Weaver, Warren, Jr. 1981. "Pollster Detects 'Myths' About Problems of Aged." *New York Times*, November 19: 15.

Webb, Susan L. 1991. *Step Forward: Sexual Harassment in the Workplace*. New York: Mastermedia.

Webb, Vincent J., and Ineke Haen Marshall. 1989. "Response to Criminal Victimization by Older Americans." *Criminal Justice and Behavior*, 16 (June): 239–259.

Weber, Jonathan. 1992. "To Trade Wars from Star Wars?" *Los Angeles Times*, July 19: 1, 24.

Weber, Max. 1958, originally published 1919. *From Max Weber: Essays in Sociology*. Trans. and ed. by H. H. Gerth and C. Wright Mills. New York: Oxford University Press.

Weeks, John R. 1986. *Population: An Introduction to Concepts and Issues*. Belmont, Calif.: Wadsworth Publishing Company.

Weinstein, Jerome I. 1990a. "Homesteading: A Solution for the Homeless?" *Journal of Housing* (May/June): 125–164.

Weinstein, Raymond M. 1990b. "Mental Hospitals and the Institutionalization of Patients." *Research in Community and Mental Health*, 6: 273–294.

Weis, Joseph G. 1987. "Social Class and Crime." In Michael R. Gottfredson and Travis Hirschi (eds.), *Positive Criminology*. Newbury Park, Calif.: Sage Publications.

Weisberg, D. Kelly. 1985. *Children of the Night: A Study of Adolescent Prostitution*. Lexington, Mass.: Lexington Books/D.C. Heath.

Weisman, Alan. 1989. "L.A. Fights for Breath." *The New York Times Magazine*, July 30: 14.

Weitzer, Ronald. 1991. "Prostitutes' Rights in the United States: The Failure of a Movement." *Sociological Quarterly*, 32 (Spring): 23–42.

Weitzman, Lenore J. 1985. *The Divorce Revolution: The Unexpected Social and Economic Consequences for Women and Children in America*. New York: Free Press.

Wells, L. Edward, and Joseph H. Rankin. 1991. "Families and Delinquency: A Meta-Analysis of the Impact of Broken Homes." *Social Problems*, 38 (February): 71–93.

Werner, Leslie Maitland. 1985. "84% Repeat Offender Rate Examined." *New York Times*, March 4: 11.

Westermann, William L. 1955. *The Slave Systems of Greek and Roman Antiquity.* Philadelphia: American Philosophical Society.

Westie, F. R. 1964. "Race and Ethnic Relations." In R.E.L. Faris (ed.), *Handbook of Modern Sociology.* Chicago: Rand McNally.

"What Price Day Care?" 1984. *Newsweek,* September 10: 14–21.

Wheaton, Elizabeth. 1987. *Codename GREENKIL: The 1979 Greensboro Killings.* Athens: University of Georgia Press.

Whitam, Frederick L., and Robin M. Mathy. 1985. *Male Homosexuality in Four Societies: Brazil, Guatemala, the Philippines, and the United States.* New York: Praeger.

White, Carmel Parker, and Mark B. White. 1991. "The Adolescent Family Life Act: Content, Findings, and Policy Recommendations for Pregnancy Prevention Programs." *Journal of Clinical Child Psychology,* 20, No. 1: 58–70.

"White House Considers New Population Policy." 1984. *Population Today,* 12, No. 7/8 (July/August): 3.

Williams, J. Allen, Jr., JoEtta A. Vernon, Martha C. Williams, and Karen Malecha. 1987. "Sex Role Socialization in Picture Books: An Update." *Social Science Quarterly,* 68 (March): 148–156.

Willie, Charles V. 1980. *The Caste and Class Controversy.* Bayside, N.Y.: General Hall.

Wilson, Edward O. 1992. *The Diversity of Life.* Cambridge, Mass.: Belknap Press/Harvard University Press.

Wilson, James Q. 1990. "Drugs and Crime." In Michael Tonry and James Q. Wilson (eds.), *Drugs and Crime,* Chicago: University of Chicago Press.

Wilson, James Q., and Richard J. Herrnstein. 1985. *Crime and Human Nature.* New York: Simon and Schuster.

Wilson, William Julius. 1978. *The Declining Significance of Race.* Chicago: University of Chicago Press.

Wilson, William Julius. 1987. *The Truly Disadvantaged: The Inner City, the Underclass, and Public Policy.* Chicago: University of Chicago Press.

Wilson, William Julius. 1991. "Studying Inner-City Social Dislocations: The Challenge of Public Agenda Research." *American Sociological Review,* 56 (February): 1–14.

Winner, L. 1977. *Autonomous Technology: Technics-Out-of-Control as a Theme in Political Thought.* Cambridge, Mass.: MIT Press.

Wirth, Louis. 1938. "Urbanism as a Way of Life." *American Journal of Sociology,* 44: 8–20.

Wisotsky, Steven. 1990. *Beyond the War on Drugs: Overcoming a Failed Public Policy.* Buffalo, N.Y.: Prometheus Books.

Witkin, Gordon. 1991. "The Men Who Created Crack." *U.S. News and World Report,* August 19: 44–53.

Wohl, Stanley. 1989. "The Medical–Industrial Complex: Another View of the Influence of Business on Medical Care." In Jack D. McCue (ed.), *The Medical Cost-Containment Crisis: Fears, Opinions, and Facts.* Ann Arbor, Mich.: Health Administration Press.

Wolfgang, Marvin E., and Franco Ferracuti. 1967. *The Subculture of Violence: Toward an Integrated Theory in Criminology.* London: Tavistock.

Wong, Kenneth K., and Paul E. Peterson. 1986. "Urban Response to Federal Program Flexibility: Politics of Community Development Block Grant." *Urban Affairs Quarterly,* 21: 293–310.

"Work Over Retirement Favored in Harris Poll." 1979. *New York Times,* March 4: 24.

World Bank. 1989. *World Development Report, 1989.* New York: Oxford University Press.

Wright, James D., and Peter H. Rossi. 1986. *Armed and Considered Dangerous: A Survey of Felons and Their Firearms.* Hawthorne, N.Y.: Aldine de Gruyter.

Yancovitz, Stanley R., et al. 1991. "A Randomized Trial of an Interim Methadone Maintenance Clinic." *American Journal of Public Health,* 81 (September): 1185–1191.

Yang, C. K. 1965. *Chinese Communist Society: The Family and the Village.* Cambridge, Mass.: MIT Press.

Young, Robert K., Peggy Gallaher, Julie Belasco, Alicia Barr, and Arthur W. Webber. 1991. "Changes in Fear of AIDS and Homophobia in a University Population." *Journal of Applied Social Psychology,* 21: 1848–1858.

Zald, Mayer N., and John D. McCarthy (eds.). 1987. *Social Movements in Organizational Society: Collected Essays.* New Brunswick, N.J.: Transaction Books.

Zane, J. Peder. 1991. "In Some Cities, Women Still Battle Barriers to Membership in All-Male Clubs." *New York Times,* December 8: 35.

Zaslow, Martha J. 1991. "Variations in Child Care Quality and Its Implications for Children." *Journal of Social Issues,* 47: 125–138.

Zawitz, Marianne W., et al. 1988. *Report to the Nation on Crime and Justice.* 2d ed. Washington, D.C.: U.S. Department of Justice, Bureau of Justice Statistics.

Zebrowitz, Leslie A., Daniel R. Tenenbaum, and Lori H. Goldstein. 1991. "The Impact of Job Applicants' Facial Maturity, Gender, and Academic Achievement on Hiring Recommendations." *Journal of Applied Social Psychology,* 21: 525–548.

Zeitlin, Morris. 1990. *American Cities: A Working Class View.* New York: International Publishers.

Zimbardo, Philip G. 1973. "A Field Experiment in Auto Shaping." In Colin Ward (ed.), *Vandalism.* New York: Van Nostrand Reinhold.

Zippay, Allison. 1991. *From Middle Income to Poor: Downward Mobility Among Displaced Steelworkers.* New York: Praeger.

Zopf, Paul E., Jr. 1984. *Population: An Introduction to Social Demography.* Palo Alto, Calif.: Mayfield.

Zuboff, Shoshana. 1993. "In the Age of the Smart Machine." In Albert H. Teich (ed.), *Technology and the Future.* New York: St. Martin's Press.

Photo Credits

Name Index

Subject Index